THE MOST
TRUSTED NAME
IN **TRAVEL**

Frommer's®

GERMANY

By Rachel Glassberg, Donald Strachan,
Stephen Brewer, Kat Morgenstern,
Andrea Schulte-Peevers, Courtney Tenz
& Caroline Sieg

Published by:

Frommer Media LLC

Copyright © 2017 by Frommer Media LLC. All rights reserved. No part of this publication may be reproduced, stored in a retrieval system, or transmitted in any form or by any means, electronic, mechanical, photocopying, recording, scanning or otherwise, except as permitted under Sections 107 or 108 of the 1976 United States Copyright Act, without the prior written permission of the Publisher. Requests to the Publisher for permission should be addressed to the support@frommermedia.com.

Frommer's is a registered trademark of Arthur Frommer. Frommer Media LLC is not associated with any product or vendor mentioned in this book.

Frommer's Germany, 25th edition
ISBN 978-1-62887-312-2 (paper), 978-1-62887-313-9 (e-book)

Editorial Director: Pauline Frommer
Editor: Holly Hughes
Production Editor: Heather Wilcox
Cartographer: Elizabeth Puhl
Cover Design: Dave Riedy

For information on our other products or services, see www.frommers.com.

Frommer Media LLC also publishes its books in a variety of electronic formats. Some content that appears in print may not be available in electronic formats.

Manufactured in China

5 4 3 2 1

FROMMER'S STAR RATINGS SYSTEM

Every hotel, restaurant and attraction listed in this guide has been ranked for quality and value. Here's what the stars mean:

★ Recommended
★★ Highly Recommended
★★★ A must! Don't miss!

AN IMPORTANT NOTE

The world is a dynamic place. Hotels change ownership, restaurants hike their prices, museums alter their opening hours, and busses and trains change their routings. And all of this can occur in the several months after our authors have visited, inspected, and written about, these hotels, restaurants, museums and transportation services. Though we have made valiant efforts to keep all our information fresh and up-to-date, some few changes can inevitably occur in the periods before a revised edition of this guidebook is published. So please bear with us if a tiny number of the details in this book have changed. Please also note that we have no responsibility or liability for any inaccuracy or errors or omissions, or for inconvenience, loss, damage, or expenses suffered by anyone as a result of assertions in this guide.

CONTENTS

LIST OF MAPS v

1 THE BEST OF GERMANY 1

2 GERMANY IN CONTEXT 15

3 GERMANY ITINERARIES 36

The Regions in Brief 37

The Best of Germany in 1 Week 39

Germany in 2 Weeks 43

The North in 9 Days 47

Romantic Cities & Castles of the South 50

Bavaria & the Black Forest with Kids 53

Prosit! The Rhine, Main & Moselle for Wine Lovers 56

4 BERLIN 59

Essentials 61

City Layout 62

Fast Facts: Berlin 69

Exploring Berlin 70

Where to Stay in Berlin 95

Where to Eat in Berlin 103

Shopping in Berlin 117

Berlin Nightlife 123

Day Trips from Berlin 135

5 SAXONY & THURINGIA 144

Weimar 145

Leipzig 164

Dresden 177

6 NORTHERN BAVARIA & THE GERMAN DANUBE 195

Nürnberg (Nuremberg) 196

Bamberg 215

Bayreuth 222

Regensburg 230

Ulm 237

7 THE ROMANTIC ROAD 244

Würzburg 245

The Upper Romantic Road 261

Rothenburg ob der Tauber 266

The Middle Romantic Road 274

Augsburg 281

Füssen 288

Neuschwanstein & Hohenschwangau 291

The Bavarian Alps 296

8 MUNICH 307

Essentials 309

Fast Facts: Munich 314

Exploring Munich 315

Where to Stay in Munich 338

Where to Eat in Munich 346

Shopping 356

Entertainment & Nightlife 358

Day Trips from Munich 362

9 HEIDELBERG, STUTTGART & THE NECKAR VALLEY 370

Heidelberg 371

Stuttgart 388

Tübingen 403

A Walking Tour of
Tübingen 405

10 THE BLACK FOREST &
BODENSEE 413

Essentials 414

Freiburg im Breisgau 416

Baden-Baden 432

The Black Forest 443

Lake Constance/
Bodensee 466

11 FRANKFURT 488

Essentials 489

Fast Facts: Frankfurt 496

Exploring Frankfurt 496

Where to Stay in
Frankfurt 509

Where to Eat in Frankfurt 512

Frankfurt Shopping 516

Entertainment & Nightlife 519

A Spa Trip to Bad
Homburg 521

12 COLOGNE & THE
RHINELAND 524

Cologne (Köln) 525

Aachen (Aix-La-Chapelle) 543

Düsseldorf 548

Bonn 558

The Rhineland 563

13 THE MOSELLE
VALLEY 588

Essentials 589

Trier 592

Bernkastel-Kues 602

Traben-Trarbach 606

Zell an der Mosel 608

Beilstein 608

Cochem 610

14 THE FAIRY-TALE
ROAD 614

Hanau 616

Steinau an der Strasse 618

Alsfeld 621

Marburg 622

Kassel 627

Hann. Münden 631

Bodenwerder 634

Hameln 636

Bremen 640

15 HAMBURG & THE
NORTH 652

Hamburg 653

Fast Facts: Hamburg 657

Lübeck 689

Sylt 698

16 PLANNING YOUR TRIP
TO GERMANY 702

INDEX 715

LIST OF MAPS

The Best of Germany in 1 & 2
  Weeks   40

Northern Germany in 9 Days   48

Romantic Cities & Castles of the
  South   51

Bavaria & the Black Forest with Kids   54

The Rhine, Main & Moselle for Wine
  Lovers   57

Western Berlin   72

Eastern Berlin   76

Potsdam   136

Saxony & Thuringia   147

Weimar   149

Leipzig   165

Dresden   179

Northern Bavaria   197

Nuremberg   199

Bayreuth   223

The Romantic Road   247

Würzburg   249

Rothenburg ob der Tauber   267

Augsburg   283

Central Munich Attractions   316

Central Munich Hotels &
  Restaurants   340

The Neckar Valley   373

Heidelberg   375

Stuttgart   391

Tübingen Walking Tour   406

The Black Forest   415

Lake Constance   469

Frankfurt   490

The Rhineland   526

Cologne (Köln)   529

Düsseldorf   549

The Moselle Valley   594

The Fairy-Tale Road   617

Bremen   641

Hamburg   654

Around Hamburg   687

Lübeck   691

ABOUT THE AUTHORS

Stephen Brewer has been writing travel guides for three decades. As an editor and writer, he has focused on European coverage for such magazines as *Esquire, Connoisseur,* and *Geo,* and he was a producer of a popular radio travel show for many years. He has written several previous guides for Frommer's, Insight, and other companies, and he authored *Beautiful Small Coastal Towns* for Rizzoli. Stephen divides his time between Manhattan and Italy and travels frequently to Germany, where he is currently tracing his parents' role in postwar rebuilding and refugee resettlement efforts.

Rachel Glassberg moved from Los Angeles to Berlin in 2011 to rediscover her German roots, escape the tyranny of car ownership, and spend less money on rent and pilsner. Within the next year, she found herself deputy editor of the English-language print and online magazine *Exberliner.* In addition to correcting misplaced apostrophes and regulating the use of Berlin clichés like the phrase "poor but sexy," she's reported on Wild West amusement parks, anti-Semitism, German music rights, and food, food, food. In her spare time, she writes songs about the Ampelmann and Sven the Berghain doorman.

Born and raised in Berlin, Germany, **Kat Morgenstern** discovered her passion for travel early on. At the tender age of 18, she left Germany to begin a journey that has taken her halfway around the world and is still in progress today. Professionally, Kat is a grassroots herbalist, ethnobotanist, nature mentor, writer and eco-travel professional. She is the founder and director of Sacred Earth, a network and educational resource for 'plant people' of all species, and of *Sacred Earth Travel*, a dedicated online eco-travel consultancy and the author of several walking guides. Having spent most of her adult life in the UK, the US and France, she currently makes her home between the southwest of England and Germany's southern Black Forest, where she has explored the mountains and vales, mostly on foot.

A native German, **Andrea Schulte-Peevers** has been a professional travel journalist for over 20 years. After spending most of her adulthood in the UK and the USA, she now makes her home back in her beloved Berlin. A Germany content expert, her extensive work portfolio includes guidebooks, articles, online content, photography and consulting about all regions and facets of the country. Her work has been published by Lonely Planet, National Geographic, Michelin, Dorling-Kindersley, *USA Today, Conde Nast Traveler* and many more.

Donald Strachan is a writer and journalist who has written about Europe for publications worldwide, including *National Geographic Traveler*, the *Guardian, Sunday Telegraph, Independent* and others. He resides in London.

Courtney Tenz came to Germany in 2005 as a Fulbright recipient and has lived in Cologne ever since. She is a culture editor at *Deutsche Welle* and writes frequently about German culture and the arts. For this edition, she toured the Mosel Valley and Trier, indulging her love for castles and wine along the way.

A former travel editor at Frommer's, **Caroline Sieg** is a half-Swiss, half-American writer and editor focusing on travel, food, arts, design, and the outdoors. She grew up bilingual (English and German) and has spent most of her life moving back and forth across the Atlantic Ocean, with significant stops in Berlin and Munich. Her favorite things about Germany include the endless cycling paths, convivial outdoor beer gardens, and traditional German breakfasts with heaps of cheese, meat, and homemade jam and freshly baked dark bread.

1

THE BEST OF GERMANY

The word is out and maybe you've heard it: Germany is one of Europe's great travel destinations. Every year, ever more visitors from around the globe are discovering the pleasures of Germany's cities, towns, and countryside. Tourist numbers have risen steadily in the last quarter-century, and show no sign of slowing down.

Germany's appeal is no great mystery. Moody forests, jagged Alpine peaks, and miles of neatly tended vineyards are not just scenic, but also the stuff of legend, places that have inspired fairy tales and where much of Western history has been played out. The Germans more than anyone appreciate the soothing tonic of a hike in the Black Forest or a stroll on North Sea dunes; even seeing these storied lands from a train window can be good for the soul. As for food—well, don't write off the cuisine as just heaping plates of wurst and sauerkraut and schnitzel with noodles. One of the pleasures of traveling in Germany is discovering the subtle differences in regional cuisines, and beyond that, there are the culinary envelope-pushers of Germany's raft of award-winning restaurants, plus a delicious patchwork of ethnic flavors imported through Germany's tolerant immigration policies. You can dine out on the traditions of a vast WHAT.

The pleasures of Germany go way beyond the spectacle of dirndls, lederhosen, Alpine meadows, and half-timbered houses (although the sight of any of these can be a surprisingly potent travel thrill, too).

Ditch the Stereotypes

What about the people? Everyone seems to have an opinion about the "German character" except for the Germans themselves. The militaristic past that continues to haunt Germany has given rise to many stereotypes. But if you connect with just one German person on your trip, chances are that all the stereotypes you've heard will crumble. Germany today is the most pacifist country in Europe, sometimes to the annoyance of its allies. Overall, it has one of the world's highest levels of educational attainment and technological achievement. Germany never got caught up in the real-estate bubble that sent so many countries freefalling into recession, and its unemployment rate is under 5%, the lowest in the European Union. The Germans have their ways of doing things, which sometimes seem stiff and rule-bound, but clearly they're doing something right.

PREVIOUS PAGE: **Narrow lanes lace Bremen's Schnoor district.**

The streets of Berlin, Germany's hip, artsy capital.

Traditional leiderhosen and dirndls still crop up at Oktoberfest in Munich.

Germany is a country where the arts are part of life. The caliber of museums and the collections they hold can be breathtaking. Germany also has a long-established musical tradition (think Bach, Beethoven, and Brahms) and is famed for the excellence of its music performances, with top-notch symphonies and opera companies in many regional cities. A country's cultural heritage is also reflected in its architecture, and Germany is fascinating on that front, too. The visible architectural legacy spans some 1,800 years, from Roman-era walls to Ludwig's 19th-century "fairy-tale castles" in Bavaria to the innovative skyscrapers that define Frankfurt's skyline. Less grandiosely, you'll find half-timbered inns, Bavarian chalets, ruined castles, and an imposing *Rathaus* (town hall) in just about every town or city you visit. While this architectural heritage can also reflect Germany's Nazi past—the remains of Albert Speer's giant Nazi stadium in Nuremberg, the grim prison buildings at Dachau, the ruined Kaiser-Wilhelm Memorial Church in Berlin—after the war the Germans excelled at rebuilding, not just new buildings, but astonishingly exact reproductions of any number of palaces and churches. The Frauenkirche in Dresden is perhaps the greatest of the country's many postwar rebuilding feats.

If you're an active traveler who is interested in hiking, biking, skiing, or swimming, head to the Black Forest, the Bavarian Alps, or the

Bodensee (Lake Constance). Spas and saunas are also a way of life in Germany—dozens of spa towns, or *Kurorte,* are scattered around the country, with thermal bath complexes where you can steam, sweat, swim, and relax. Just keep in mind that many saunas are clothing-optional and co-ed: The Germans are not prudish when it comes to their bodies. This is part of the communal side of German life, like sharing a table at a restaurant—only, of course, you wouldn't do that nude. (Would you?)

GERMANY'S best AUTHENTIC EXPERIENCES

o **Exploring the New Berlin:** The fall of the Berlin Wall in 1989–90 transfixed the world and transformed the divided city into a new world capital. Berlin is still knitting itself together, but it also happens to be the most exciting urban space in Europe. The inexhaustible new Berlin invites exploration on many different fronts, and around the clock. Summer is the ideal time to visit. See chapter 4.

o **Sipping a Beer in a Munich Beer Garden:** There's nothing more enjoyable on a balmy evening than sitting under the trees in one of Munich's leafy beer gardens and trying to lift one of those 1-liter

Germany's cultural legacy resounds in storied venues such as the Dresden Opera House.

steins to your lips. It's a way of life, and a way to meet Germans on their own turf. See chapter 8.

o **Hearing classical music in some of Europe's best venues:** The choice is almost unlimited in this musical country. Germany's capital, **Berlin** (p. 59) is home to seven symphony orchestras, including the famed Berlin Philharmonic, as well as three opera companies. **Hamburg** (p. 652) plays host to the Hamburg State Opera, the Hamburg Ballet, and three highly regarded orchestras. **Cologne** (p. 524) has an amazing array of musical offerings: Major artists appear at Oper Köln (Cologne Opera), the Rhineland's leading opera house, and two fine orchestras—the Gürzenich Kölner Philharmoniker (Cologne Philharmonic) and the Westdeutscher Rundfunk Orchestra (West German Radio Orchestra)—perform in the Kölner Philharmonie concert hall. If your tastes are a little more 21st-century, Berlin, Cologne, and Hamburg all have **techno** music venues that go all night; see "Nightlife" in chapters 4, 12, and 15.

o **Going to a Bundesliga Match:** German soccer (*Fussball*) is on the crest of a wave. Not only is the national men's team reigning world champions, but the country's top league—the Bundesliga—is more popular than ever. With its huge stadiums, fanatical fans, and fair ticket prices, it's the most spectated league in Europe on a weekly basis. You can sample the unique atmosphere for yourself at a **Bayern Munich** (p. 362) or **Eintracht Frankfurt** (p. 508) game.

o **Visiting a Spa:** For a quintessential German experience, visit one of Germany's spa towns—Baden-Baden, Wiesbaden, and Aachen, among others—to bathe, steam, *schvitz*, and swim in one huge complex warmed by thermal waters and dedicated to the goddess *Gesund* (health).

o **Spending Harvest Time in the Vineyards:** Between late August and mid-October, the vineyards on the banks of the Rhine and Moselle rivers turn gold and russet, and workers gather buckets of grapes from terraced rows of vines. This is the perfect time to visit wine towns such as Rüdesheim and Bingen on the Rhine (chapter 10) and Cochem on the Mosel (p. 13). Sip the local vintages and enjoy the scenery.

o **Attending the Bayreuth Festival:** One of the world's premier musical events, the annual Bayreuther Festspiele sees an estimated half-million enthusiasts clamor for only 60,000 tickets. At other times of year you can pay homage to Wagner at the Festspielhaus—the opera venue he created—and his former home, now the Richard-Wagner-Museum. See p. 224.

GERMANY'S best MUSEUMS

o **Alte Pinakothek,** Munich: This gigantic repository of Old-Master paintings could easily fill a day (or two, or three) of your time. Works by major European artists from the 14th to 18th centuries form the basis of the collection, with highlights that include canvases by Dürer, Raphael, Botticelli, Leonardo da Vinci, and Rembrandt. See p. 324.

o **Museum Island,** Berlin: Five museums populate Berlin's Museum Island: Not to be missed are the imposing neoclassical **Altes Museum,** with superlative collections of Greek, Etruscan, and Roman antiquities; and the **Neues Museum,** with its world-class Egyptian antiquities, including the celebrated bust of Queen Nefertiti. See p. 86.

o **Dokumentationszentrum Reichsparteitagsgelände,** Nürnberg: Displays in Hitler's monumental yet incomplete Congress Hall chronicle the Führer's rise to power, celebrated during the Nürnberg rallies when enormous crowds gathered on the adjacent Zeppelinwiese (Zeppelin Field) to listen raptly to the leader's violent denunciations. See p. 203.

o **Museumsufer,** Frankfurt: The Museum Embankment brings top-class culture to a city known more for its financiers. Highlights include Vermeer and the German Expressionists at the **Städel** and sublime sculpture at the **Liebieghaus.** See p. 497.

o **Grünes Gewölbe (Green Vault),** Dresden: There are two Green Vaults, old and new, in Dresden's Residenzschloss; both display a sumptuous assortment of treasures collected by the electors of Saxony from the 16th to the 18th centuries. See p. 182.

o **Lenbachhaus,** Munich: Completely renovated and reopened in 2013, the 19th-century villa of portrait painter Franz von Lenbach houses a stunning collection of late-19th- and early-20th-century paintings

Nürnberg's Dokumentationszentrum Reichsparteitagsgelände chronicles Adolf Hitler's rise to power.

from the Munich-based *Blaue Reiter* (Blue Rider) group, including works by Kandinsky, Paul Klee, Franz Marc, and Gabriele Münter. See p. 329.

o **Kunsthalle,** Hamburg: In Northern Germany's leading art museum, Canalettos, Rembrandts, Holbeins, and other Old Masters share space with modern canvases by Picasso, Warhol, Beuys, Munch, Kandinsky, Klee, and Hockney. See p. 662.

o **Mercedes-Benz Museum & Porsche Museum,** Stuttgart: Germany's well-earned rep for precision engineering and luxury auto travel comes to the fore in these two collections that showcase the output of world-famous hometown auto makers. Whether it's a long, lean Mercedes 500 K convertible or a Porsche 911, the gleaming showpieces turn even nondrivers into car buffs. See p. 393.

GERMANY'S unmissable HISTORIC BUILDINGS

o **Heidelberg Castle,** Heidelberg: This Gothic-Renaissance 16th-century masterpiece was massively expanded as rival rulers competed for control of the Rhineland. The compound never regained its original glory after a 17th-century French attack, and today the ruins brood in dignified severity high above the student revelry and taverns of the folkloric city below. See p. 377.

o **Dom,** Cologne: The largest cathedral in Germany, Cologne's crowning glory took more than 600 years to complete and is now a UNESCO World Heritage Site. The size and stylistic unity of this Gothic marvel will astonish you. See p. 531.

o **Neuschwanstein,** near Füssen: Love it or hate it, this fairy-tale castle is nothing less than phenomenal, the romantic fantasy of "Mad" King Ludwig II. Its fairy-tale allure inspired Walt Disney and attracts mil-

Aachen Cathedral, where Charlemagne once ruled.

lions of visitors; the mountain scenery alone is worth the trip. See p. 294.

o **Residenz,** Würzburg: One of the largest baroque palaces in Germany, built between 1720 and 1744 for the powerful bishops of Würzburg, combines gardens, a gallery of paintings, frescoes by Tiepolo, and enough decoration to satisfy the most demanding appetite for ornamentation. See p. 253.

o **Wartburg Castle,** Eisenach: One of the key moments in German history played out at this medieval castle in Thuringia, where a fugitive Martin Luther translated the New Testament into German. See p. 162.

o **Sanssouci,** Potsdam: Friedrich the Great's retreat was called Sanssouci ("Without Care") because here he could forget the rigors of court life. Germany's most successful blend of landscape and architecture sits among intricate gardens. See p. 137.

o **Dom,** Aachen: Aachen's cathedral encompasses the Octagon, originally part of Emperor Charlemagne's palace, and a Gothic choir where Charlemagne's remains rest in a golden reliquary. From 936 to 1531, emperors of the Holy Roman Empire were crowned here. See p. 545.

o **Schloss Nymphenburg,** Munich: The summer palace of the Wittelsbachs, Bavaria's ruling family, was constructed between 1664 and 1674. While fairly modest as palaces go, it contains some sumptuously decorated rooms. See p. 364.

o **Zwinger,** Dresden: This ornate baroque palace, completed in 1719 for Augustus the Strong (elector of Saxony and king of Poland) still sports some of Augustus's art collections, the most impressive being the Gemäldegalerie Alte Meister (Old Masters Gallery) with paintings by Raphael, Van Dyck, Vermeer, Dürer, Rubens, and Rembrandt. See p. 183.

o **Wieskirche,** outside Füssen: One of the world's most exuberantly decorated buildings sits in a meadow and shimmers with a super-abundance of woodcarvings. See p. 287.

GERMANY'S most romantic LANDSCAPES

o **Bavarian Alps:** In perhaps the most dramatic of all German landscapes, the country's highest mountain, the Zugspitze, towers above the Alpine resort town of Garmisch-Partenkirchen. Ascend to the top via gondola and cog railroad. See p. 296.

Vineyards climb the gentle slopes of the Moselle Valley.

o **Middle Rhine:** Cruises down the scenic midsection of the mighty Rhine, the Mittelrhein, take you past castle-crowned crags and legendary sites, such as Loreley rock, to charming towns in the Rheingau wine region. See chapter 12.

o **Moselle Valley:** The scenic Moselle between Koblenz and Cochem encompasses thousands of acres of terraced vineyards, Roman ruins, medieval castles, and half-timbered riverside towns. See chapter 13.

o **The Romantic Road:** The clue is in the name: The most romantic byway in Germany passes through small medieval towns set within a gorgeous Bavarian landscape of river valley and mountain meadow, before climbing to the Alps and King Ludwig's "fairy-tale castles." See chapter 7.

GERMANY'S best RESTAURANTS

o **Romantik Hotel Zum Ritter St. Georg,** Heidelberg: Lovely old frescoes dining rooms on the ground floor of a landmark hotel set the gold standard for Old-World cooking and service. See p. 383.

o **Tantris,** Munich: When a restaurant receives a Michelin star for something like 25 years, you can safely assume that it's a great place to eat. Tantris's Hans Haas is one of Germany's top chefs, and his restaurant serves the most innovative food in Bavaria. See p. 352.

o **La Soupe Populaire,** Berlin: Berlin's most famous chef—Kreuzberg native Tim Raue—cooks refined but still filling and affordable versions of typical Berlin dishes in a very Berlin location, an industrial mezzanine overlooking an abandoned factory turned exhibition space. It literally does not get any more Berlin than this. See p. 113.

o **Auerbachs Keller,** Leipzig: This ancient and rustic cellar restaurant serves hearty German and Saxon fare. Germany's great writer Goethe used to hang out here, and even set a scene from his play *Faust* in one of the rooms. See p. 173.

The historic Auersbachs Keller restaurant in Leipzig.

o **Schwarzwaldstube,** Baiersbronn: Under the aegis of long-time chef Harald Wohlfahrt, this fine-dining restaurant at the chic Black Forest resort **Hotel Traube Tonbachtal** faces stiff competition from a cluster of Michelin-starred restaurants in one small valley. Unusually for Germany, it offers a full tasting menu for vegetarians.

GERMANY'S best HOTELS

o **The Qvest,** Cologne: The ultimate urban lodgings for design lovers. Revival decorations have been retained from the neo-medieval building's days as the city's archive; a sheen of Scandinavian design sprinkles some 20th-century modernist magic. See p. 538.

o **Taschenbergpalais,** Dresden: Originally a palace built for one of his many mistresses by Augustus the Strong; now faithfully reconstructed as a grand luxurious hotel. See p. 186.

o **Orphée Grosses Haus,** Regensburg: A trio of related accommodations in one of Germany's most beautiful medieval cities combine opulence, style, comfort, and Bavarian hospitality. See p. 234.

o **Wedina,** Hamburg: A good hotel makes its guests feel at home, and these moderately priced accommodations do so in four townhouses on a dignified St. Georg street. See p. 674.

Orphée Grosse Haus in Regensburg offers a smart update on Bavarian hospitality.

- **Mandala,** Berlin: Just off Potsdamer Platz, this quietly elegant luxury hotel wins on many fronts: The central location, calm and comfortable décor, and rooms that are among the largest in Berlin. The on-site bar and restaurant are both noteworthy. See p. 99.

- **Lindenberg,** Frankfurt: This handsome 19th-century townhouse has spacious rooms with a well-judged mix of contemporary and period styling, plus a friendly staff with a can-do ethos. See p. 511.

GERMANY'S best FREE THINGS TO DO

- **Pound the Heidelberg Cobblestones:** This handsome university town on the River Neckar has enchanted everyone from Goethe to Mark Twain, and little wonder: A half-ruined castle perched on a wooded hillside overlooks an unspoiled assemblage of medieval and Renaissance landmarks, while beer flows in the taverns below. See p. 370.

- **Visit Dachau Concentration Camp Memorial Site:** Grim, horrifying, and deeply poignant, Dachau is one of the most important Holocaust memorial sites in Germany. A visit gives you insight into a barbaric chapter of history and puts a human face to its victims. See p. 362.

Cologne's Karneval is Germany's version of Mardi Gras.

- **Take in the Aromas of the Viktualienmarkt:** There are markets and then there are markets like Munich's Viktualienmarkt, a hive of stalls, food stands, and specialty shops that's been around for a couple of hundred years. See p. 319.

- **Walk in the Schwarzwald:** The forest-clad mountains of the Black Forest offers some 24,000 km of delightful hiking trails, lakes, and many scenic lookouts. See chapter 10.

- **Celebrate Karneval in Cologne:** The locals call it *Fasteleer* or *Fastlovend,* but it's Karneval to most Germans, and it's celebrated in Catholic Cologne the way Mardi Gras is celebrated in New Orleans. Parades, floats, balls, parties, and plenty of food and beer characterize this pre-Lenten celebration that natives call their city's "fifth season." See chapter 12.

- **Roam Hamburg's Speicherstadt:** A walk along the quayside reveals one of Germany's most intriguing and hauntingly beautiful districts, where massive warehouses, gabled and turreted, line the canals. A tinge of sea air adds to the pleasure. See chapter 15.

GERMANY'S top SPA TOWNS

o **Aachen:** For more than 2 millennia, the warm mineral waters that flow from thermal springs below Aachen have been used for health and relaxation. Spend a few hours at the Carolus Therme bath complex and you'll be reinvigorated for the rest of your time in Germany. See p. 543.

o **Baden-Baden:** There's no better spa town in Germany, and certainly none more fashionable or famous than this sophisticated retreat in the Black Forest that has hosted royals and commoners alike. Shed your duds at the Friedrichsbad and follow a bathing ritual through temperature-modulated saunas, steam rooms, and pools, finishing up with a cool-down and a relaxing snooze. See p. 432.

GERMANY'S best FOR FAMILIES

o **Seeing the German Emigration Center,** Bremerhaven: Relive the experience of the 7 million Germans who departed for the New World between 1830 and 1974. You can stand on the pier, explore steerage dining rooms and second-class cabins, and even pass through immigration at Ellis Island, New York. See p. 651.

o **Hanging out by the Bodensee:** The shimmering waters of Lake Constance, at Germany's southwestern border, suggest the Mediterranean with resorts, watersports, semitropical gardens, and an almost Italian languor. See chapter 10.

The Black Forest, or Schwarzwald, rewards cyclists as well as hikers.

The Zugspitze in the Bavarian Alps is Germany's highest peak.

o **Scaling the Zugspitze,** Bavaria: The tallest mountain in Germany, soaring 2,960m (9,700 ft.) above sea level, lures view-seekers up its craggy slopes on a thrill ride via cog railway and cable car. Views from the top over the Alps will take your breath away. See p. 298.

o **A Trip to Grimm World,** Kassel: A celebration of the life and work of the Brothers Grimm shows off a first edition of the fairy tales and lets you sit down with the original Seven Dwarves. See p. 628.

o **An Afternoon in the Prenzlauer Berg,** Berlin: The capital's most family-friendly district has parks, playgrounds, and an ice-cream shop on every corner. See p. 66.

o **The Deutsches Museum,** Munich: Start your day at Marienplatz watching the figures spin around on the Glockenspiel (p. 320), then head over to Museums Insel for hands-on fun at this vast museum of science and technology. See p. 331.

2

GERMANY IN CONTEXT

One of Europe's largest, most populous, and wealthiest nations, Germany delivers memorable experiences for every taste, interest, and budget. By all means, do take in the blockbuster sights—Neuschwanstein Castle, Brandenburg Gate, Cologne Cathedral, and the Romantic Road among them. But don't forget to slow down and savor life's little pleasures: a slice of Black Forest cake on the cobbled market square, a scenic drive among wildflower-strewn hills, a crisp Riesling in a candle-lit wine tavern, or a restorative dip in a hot mineral spring.

As you travel around Germany, you'll discover that the past is present wherever you go, from 2000-year-old Roman ruins to grand medieval cathedrals to baroque royal palaces to "ostalgic" relics of the former East Germany. Knowing the history and culture that produced these sights is bound to deepen your appreciation for them. Therefore, the next pages provide you with a crash course in German history, art, architecture, literature, and music, along with other tips to help you get the most out of your trip to this fascinating country.

A BRIEF HISTORY OF GERMANY
Germany Today

Albert Einstein, Martin Luther, Charlemagne, Beethoven, Goethe. Airbags, aspirin, the Christmas tree, MP3, book printing—Germany's contributions to the world are manifold and influential, yet to many Americans its long history remains overshadowed by the horrors of World War II and the Holocaust. How a civilized European nation slipped into the barbaric inhumanity of the Nazi era is a question that continues to haunt survivors, occupy historians, and shadow the Germans themselves. Memorials to the victims of the Holocaust are scattered throughout Germany, including the former concentration camps at Dachau, Buchenwald, and Bergen-Belsen.

The other seminal 20th-century event that affected Germany's contemporary consciousness was the separation of the country into two opposing regimes—capitalist West and communist East—from 1945 to

PREVIOUS PAGE: The haunting Memorial to the Murdered Jews of Europe, in Berlin.

The Berlin Wall's notorious crossing point, Checkpoint Charlie, is maintained as a tourist site.

1989. By the time the Wall came down, East Germany was in many respects a broken country, a corrupt police-state with dwindling resources, decaying infrastructure, and a legacy of environmental pollution. Though most East Germans embraced the democratic changes that came with reunification, there were many who resented what they saw as a wholesale takeover of their country, and who struggled to cope with being thrust into the uncertainties of a free-market economic system.

The cost of reunification was far higher than predicted and took a toll on people's economic and emotional lives. In the east, outdated state-controlled industries that could not compete in a free market economy were scrapped, jobs were lost, and crime—most troublingly, neo-Nazi hate crimes—rose. Yet Germany moved forward.

Today, it's the most prosperous country in Europe and has been for many years. A nation of savers, Germany never gave in to the easy-credit credo, maintained strong regulations and oversight in its banking industry, and therefore weathered the financial crisis of 2008/9 better than most countries.

Politically too, Germany has begun to assert a leadership role within Europe and the world. The effort is led by Angela Merkel, who has served as chancellor since 2005; she even earned the honor of being *Time* magazine's Person of the Year in 2015. Diplomacy, not military might, is her weapon of choice, as she ably demonstrated that year in the Russia-Ukraine conflict and, even more so, during the Greek financial crisis, when she was at the forefront of brokering a bailout deal. But the main reason for *Time*'s accolade was Merkel's decision to throw open the doors for hundreds of thousands of refugees, mostly from the war zones of Syria, Iraq, and Afghanistan. Around a million people arrived in 2015 alone, with another million or more expected in the coming years. "Wir schaffen das!" (We can do it) is Merkel's mantra.

Trier's Porta Nigra gateway, a relic of the Roman Empire era.

Not everyone is quite as optimistic, as the rising popularity of right-wing movements and parties shows. The challenges in integrating such a massive number of newcomers of different and diverse cultural and religious backgrounds will be enormous, even for a country as prosperous and well-organized as Germany.

DATELINE

A.D. 1st century The Roman sphere of influence extends well into the borders of present-day Germany (Germania to the Romans), subduing local Teutonic tribes and planting garrisons at Cologne, Koblenz, Mainz, and Trier.

A.D. 400 The Romans withdraw from Germany; in the next few centuries, the Franks gradually forge an empire, turning a loose conglomeration of German tribes into what eventually will become the Holy Roman Empire.

ca. 800 Charlemagne (Karl der Grosse; 768–814) is responsible for the earliest large-scale attempt to unite the lands of Germany under one ruler.

ca. 900–1500 In 962, the pope names Otto I the first Holy Roman Emperor. Nevertheless, throughout the Middle Ages, power struggles and invasions Ages continually disrupt the unity hammered out by Charlemagne, and Germany remains a collection of small principalities and "Free Imperial Cities" like Hamburg and Lübeck. An

Germany's Architecture

Germany's buildings span some 1,200 years of architectural history and were created in a number of different styles. (The **Porta Nigra,** a 1,800-year-old arched gateway in Trier—see p. 598—is Germany's only remaining Roman-era structure of any significance.) But Germany's rich architectural heritage suffered a devastating blow during World War II, when Allied bombing raids leveled entire cities and left many important buildings and churches in ruins. Some areas escaped damage, such as the medieval towns along the Romantic Road (see chapter 7), but the overall devastation affected nearly the entire country. Many historic buildings you'll see today are actually painstaking postwar reconstructions. Here are examples from around Germany of the major architectural periods.

CAROLINGIAN & OTTONIAN (9TH–11TH C.) The earliest manifestations of a discernibly Germanic architecture date from the period of Charlemagne's rule as king of the Franks (768–814) and Emperor of the West (800–14), called the Carolingian era after Charlemagne. Constructed around 800, **Charlemagne's chapel** in Aachen (p. 545) harkens back to earlier Byzantine models of building. During the next dynasty, founded by Otto I, architecture developed more complex ground plans, with a rational system devised for dividing churches into a series of separate units—a method that would be of consequence in Romanesque design.

ROMANESQUE (11TH–12TH C.) Simple clear forms, thick walls, and rounded arches signal Romanesque architecture, a building style inspired by Roman models. The **cathedral in Mainz** (p. 571) and **Dom St.**

upswing in international commerce from the 11th to 13th centuries leads several trading cities of the northeast to band together as the Hanseatic League.

1500–1700 Social unrest and religious upheaval surge throughout Germany. Martin Luther (1483–1546) battles against the excesses of the Catholic Church and his work has far-reaching implications. As the Protestant Reformation spreads, the Catholic Church launches a Counter-Reformation that culminates in the bloody Thirty Years' War (1618–48), affecting the whole of Europe.

1700–1800 Under Frederick the Great (Friedrich der Grosse; 1740–86), Prussia grows into a European power. German artists, writers, composers, and philosophers usher in the Age of Enlightenment.

Early 1800s After defeating the Austrian and Prussian armies, Napoleon occupies several German cities and causes the collapse of the Holy Roman Empire in 1806. In 1813, Prussian, Austrian, and Russian armies defeat the French emperor in Leipzig, which is followed by the decisive Battle of Waterloo.

continues

Cologne Cathedral represents the pinnacle of Gothic architecture in Germany.

Kilian (p. 251) in Würzburg are two of the largest Romanesque churches in Germany.

GOTHIC (13TH–16TH C.) **Cologne cathedral** (p. 531) is Germany's greatest example of Gothic architecture, a style developed in France and diffused throughout Europe. The Gothic style is characterized by pointed arches, soaring vaults and spires, and flying buttresses.

Mid- to late 1800s Following Napoleon's defeat, Germany's military and political rulers revert to a system of absolute monarchy. Questions of independence and national unity come to a head in the 1848 revolution. When that fails, the Austrian Hapsburg monarchy reimposes sovereignty over Prussia and other parts of Germany. Prussian statesman Otto von Bismarck (1815–98) pushes to consolidate the German people under Prussian leadership. After triumphs in the Franco-Prussian War (1870–71), Bismarck wins over southern German states and, in 1871, becomes first chancellor of the German Empire (Reich).

1914–1918 World War I pits Germany, Austria-Hungary, and Turkey against Britain, France, Italy, and Russia and leaves more 15 million people dead. It ends with Germany's defeat and the abdication of Kaiser Wilhelm II.

1919–1932 The end of the war and the monarchy creates political and social turmoil in Germany. The founding of the Weimar Republic marks Germany's first attempt to establish a democratic and republican government. Stiff war reparations, however, cripple the economy and lead to hyperinflation and hunger until the introduction of a

RENAISSANCE (15TH– EARLY 17TH C.)   Augsburg (p. 281) is one of the best cities in Germany to see Renaissance architecture, a style whose calm precision, orderly repeating lines, and classical decoration harkens back ancient Rome. Renaissance architecture was imported from Italy into southern Germany, while a more highly ornamented Dutch style prevailed in northern Germany, in towns such as **Hameln** (p. 636) or the 17th-century section of **Heidelberg Castle** (p. 377).

BAROQUE (17TH–18TH C.)   The Baroque unites architecture, sculpture and painting into an exuberant style that flourished in Catholic, Counter-Reformation areas in the south of Germany. The **Residenz** (p. 253) in Würzburg, the **Zwinger** palace in Dresden (p. 183), and the palace of **Sanssouci** (p. 137) in Potsdam are important examples. **Munich** (see chapter 8) abounds in the Baroque.

ROCOCO (18TH C.)   Notch up the elements of Baroque and you have Rococo, exemplified by curving walls and staggering amounts of gilded and stucco decoration. A famous example of flamboyant Rococo church architecture is the **Wieskirche** (p. 287) in Bavaria. The style also found expression in theater, such as the **Residenztheater** (p. 359) by François Cuvilliés in Munich.

NEOCLASSICAL (19TH C.)   The stern Neoclassical style was meant to be a rebuke to the excesses of Baroque and Rococo. There are several great examples in **Berlin** (see chapter 4), where the Prussian architect Karl Friedrich Schinkel designed several buildings along the grand avenue Unter den Linden as well as the Altes Museum on Museum Island. His Munich counterpart was Leo von Klenze, who was entrusted with the neoclassical design of **Königsplatz** (p. 327), including the Glyptothek museum and the Propyläen monument.

new currency (Rentenmark). Berlin experiences a cultural heyday during the "Golden Twenties".

1933–1945 The U.S. stock market crash in 1929 plunges Germany into an economic crisis that gives fodder to the Nazi movement. In January 1933 Adolf Hitler (1889-1945) becomes chancellor. As his anti-Semitic agenda becomes apparent, thousands of German Jews flee the country before the outbreak of the Second World War in 1939. Millions of Jews and other "undesirable" minorities throughout Germany and Nazi-occupied

Europe are systematically exterminated in the Holocaust. The war ends on May 8, 1945 with Germany's capitulation.

1948 West German recovery gets underway with U.S. assistance in the form of the Marshall Plan. The Soviet blockade of West Berlin results in the Anglo-American Berlin Airlift, which continues until 1949.

1949–1961 The Cold War intensifies as Germany is split into two states. Bonn becomes the capital of the democratic Federal Republic of Germany, while the communist

continues

Cutting-edge architecture in Germany today: Daniel Libeskind's Jewish Museum in Berlin.

HISTORICISM (LATE 19TH–EARLY 20TH C.) The establishment of the German Empire in 1871 sparked a revival of numerous historic styles, often combining them into a single building. In Dresden, Gottfried Semper, for instance, incorporated Renaissance, Baroque, and neo-classical elements into his addition to the **Zwinger** and the **Semper Operahouse** (p. 192). The most famous building of this era is Ludwig II's **Neuschwanstein** castle (p. 294).

JUGENDSTIL (EARLY 20TH C.) Jugendstil is the German name for Art Nouveau, an early-20th-century European movement that emphasized flowing, asymmetrical, organic shapes. Many Jugendstil villas line the streets of lakeside neighborhoods in **Hamburg** (p. 652).

MODERNISM (1948 ONWARD) A major housing shortage and rebuilding effort in bombed cities in Germany followed the devastation of World War II. Many were rebuilt in a simple, functional style with straight lines and square windows that were more or less identical to Bauhaus. One of the most famous architects of the period was Hans Scharoun, whose

German Democratic Republic (GDR) make East Berlin its capital. The two Germanys develop with highly different political, economic, and social systems.

1961 In order to stop large-scale migration from East Germany to economically flourishing West Germany, the East German government constructs the Berlin Wall and fortifications along the inner German border.

1989 The collapse of the Berlin Wall marks for East Germany the culmination of long-suppressed revolutionary sentiment across central and eastern Europe.

1990 East and West Germany unite under one government with Berlin as its capital.

2005 Angela Merkel, who grew up in the GDR, is elected Germany's first female chancellor.

2013 Angela Merkel is re-elected for a third term as chancellor and is the most powerful leader in Europe.

2015 Germany welcomes a million refugees, mostly from war-torn Syria, Iraq, and Afghanistan. The far-right populist party AfD, which opposes Merkel's open-door policy, gains in strength.

THE bauhaus INFLUENCE

Founded in Weimar in 1919 by Walter Gropius (1883–1969), the Bauhaus School was forced to move to Dessau and finally to Berlin before it was banned by the Nazis in 1933 for being "too modernist." But in its brief and beleaguered 14 years of existence, the Bauhaus managed to revolutionize architecture and design. The ornate historicism that dominated these fields until the end of World War I was replaced with a minimalist aesthetic that focused on the utility and functionality of the object. Everything from houses to factories and cradles to teapots was radically re-imagined, and the Bauhaus creations that emerged have now become icons of modern design. Teachers in the school included artists like Paul Klee and Wassily Kandinsky, and architects like Gropius and Mies van der Rohe. Learn more at the **Bauhaus museums** in Weimar (p. 148) and Berlin (p. 70).

daring **Philharmonie** (p. 124) concert hall in Berlin was completed in 1963.

POSTMODERNISM (1980S ONWARD) Some of the most exciting buildings in Germany have been built since reunification in 1990. Berlin especially is a showcase with Daniel Libeskind's **Jewish Museum** (p. 82) and Helmut Jahn's **Sony Center** (p. 79) being major landmarks. In Cologne, OM Unger's **Wallraf-Richartz-Museum** (p. 535) and the **Porsche Museum** in Stuttgart (p. 394) have made a visual splash.

A Brief History of German Art

Germany abounds in art museums. You can't escape them, nor should you try. The country's rich artistic heritage is on display in even the smallest cities, while metropolises like Berlin and Munich boast world-class collections. The brief chronology below paints the major trends and artists with a broad brushstroke.

CAROLINGIAN & OTTONIAN (9TH–10TH C.) During the Carolingian period mosaics based on earlier Roman and Byzantine models were used to decorate such buildings as Charlemagne's octagonal **Palatine Chapel** (p. 545) in Aachen. Another important art form was elaborately carved ivory book covers. The first outstanding examples of German painting (illuminated manuscripts) and sculpture were created during the Ottonian dynasty. Carved in Cologne in the late 10th century, the Gero cross in **Cologne cathedral** (p. 531) is believed to be the oldest existing large-scale crucifix in the Western world. Fine craftsmanship is apparent in the metalwork of this period as well, with a rare surviving example being the bronze doors at the cathedral of **Augsburg** (p. 282).

ROMANESQUE (11TH–12TH C.)

Romanesque art in Germany was mostly expressed in church building; little remains of fresco painting from this period. A few exceptions are at the **St. Mangkirche** abbey (p. 290) in Füssen and in the **Church of St. Georg** on Reichenau Island (p. 471) in Lake Constance.

GOTHIC (13TH–15TH C.)

As the French Gothic style spread throughout Europe, Germans embraced it with fervor. This was especially true in the field of sculpture, as exemplified by the portals of **Cologne cathedral** (p. 531), and the doors of Augsburg's **Dom St. Maria** (p. 282). The Gothic art collection at the **Wallraf-Richartz Museum** (p. 535) in Cologne is considered one of the best in the world, while the nearby **Schnütgen Museum** (p. 534) has superb examples of medieval stained-glass and sculpture.

Elaborately wrought Gothic decoration on the doors of Augusburg's Dom St. Maria cathedral.

RENAISSANCE (15TH–16TH C.)

German sculpture, particularly carved wooden altarpieces, reached an artistic highpoint in the late 15th century, especially in the expressive works of Peter Vischer, Veit Stoss, and Tilman Riemenschneider. Flemish influence is seen in the paintings of Stephan Lochner, whose "Adoration of the Magi" altarpiece graces **Cologne cathedral** (p. 531). The key artistic figure, however, was Albrecht Dürer, who introduced elements of the Italian Renaissance into his paintings, woodcuts, and engravings; his work's on view in Munich's **Alte Pinakothek** (p. 324), Berlin's **Gemäldegalerie** (p. 71), and Nuremberg's **Germanisches Nationalmuseum** (p. 204). In the 16th century, painting was at its height, with such masters as Hans Holbein the Younger, Matthias Grünewald, Albrecht Altdorfer, Lucas Cranach the Elder, and Hans Baldung, all of whose work can be seen in Munich's **Alte Pinakothek** (p. 324), as well as in other museums around the country.

BAROQUE & ROCOCO (17TH–18TH C.)

Ceiling frescos and swirling, often gilded stuccowork is typical of the exuberant Baroque and Rococo styles, which decorated churches and palaces all over southern Germany. Two notable examples are the **Wieskirche** (p. 287) in Steingaden

The Wieskirche in Steingaden, on the Romantic Road, a masterpiece of rococo decoration.

and the **Asamkirche** (p. 318) in Munich. In **Meissen** (p. 190), production of the first European hard-paste porcelain kicked off in 1708.

ROMANTICISM (19TH C.) The period brought to the fore genre painters such as Moritz von Schwind and Carl Spitzweg. The greatest Romantic artist, though, was Caspar David Friedrich, whose famous "Cross in the Mountains" (1808) hangs in Dresden's **Gemäldegalerie Alte Meister** (p. 184).

EXPRESSIONISM (EARLY 20TH C.) The early 20th century saw the rejection of the traditional styles taught at the art academies and a proliferation of fresh, dynamic and personalized sensibilities. In Germany, Expressionism—with its deliberate distortion of natural forms and emotional intensity—emerged as a key art form. Two artist groups in particular shaped the genre. Founded in Dresden in 1905, **Die Brücke** (The Bridge) included Ernst Ludwig Kirchner, Emil Nolde, and Karl Schmidt-Rottluff; Dresden's **Albertinum** (p. 180) has an especially fine collection of their works. The second group was the Munich-based Der Blaue Reiter (Blue Rider, 1911–1914), which included Franz Marc, Gabriele Münter, Paul Klee, and Wassily Kandinsky; their work can be seen in Munich's **Lenbachhaus** (p. 329). After World War I, **Die Neue Sachlichkeit** (New Objectivity) emerged, with key players being Otto Dix and George Grosz. It was characterized by a more realistic style combined with a cynical, socially critical philosophical stance that was vehemently anti-war. The brilliant, bitter canvases of Dix and Grosz hang in the **Neue Nationalgalerie** (p. 74) in Berlin.

NAZI ERA (1933–45) The Nazi regime, which declared all abstract and expressionist works to be "degenerate," supported only heroic, propagandistic art and led to nothing of artistic significance.

POST–WORLD WAR II (1945–PRESENT) Germany hasn't had one predominant school or movement to define its art since World War II, but it has produced internationally recognized artists such as the iconoclastic sculptor Josef Beuys, painter Anselm Kiefer, painter-sculptor Georg

Baselitz, and the painter and visual artist Gerhard Richter. All four are represented in Stuttgart's **Staatsgalerie** (p. 395) and Cologne's **Museum Ludwig** (p. 533), among others. Richter also created a stunning stained-glass window for the **Cologne cathedral** (p. 531). Anyone interested in contemporary German art should also visit Düsseldorf's **K20** and **K21 museums** (p. 551 and p. 552). In the 25 years since the Wall fell, Berlin has seen an explosion of artistic expression—some 10,000 artists are now living in Berlin. In the 1990s, the nearby city of Leipzig also made a splash in the art scene with the emergence of the New Leipzig School, which is characterized by a return to figurative painting. A leading artist is Neo Rauch, who has his studio in Leipzig's Spinnerei art colony (p. 170); his works can be seen in Leipzig's **Museum der Bildenden Künste** (p. 167).

Germany's Great Musical Tradition

Some of the greatest works of Western music were written by German composers. The roster includes Hildegard of Bingen, Bach, Handel, Beethoven, Brahms, Mendelssohn, Schumann, and Wagner, as well as 20th-century greats Richard Strauss and Kurt Weill. Germany's rich musical history dates back to the medieval *Minnesängers* (troubadours), who held a famous song contest at Wartburg Castle that was later immortalized by Richard Wagner in his opera *Tannhäuser*.

Over the centuries, Germany's musical traditions were fostered in convents, monasteries and churches where composers were hired to write sacred songs, cantatas and oratorios. The most famous among these is Johann Sebastian Bach; two museums chronicle his life and accomplishments—one in his birth town of **Eisenach** (p. 161) and another in **Leipzig** (p. 164)

A statue of Johann Sebastian Bach by St. Thomas's Church in Leipzig, where he served as choirmaster for 27 years.

where he died. The great composer Ludwig Beethoven's birthplace can be visited in **Bonn** (p. 558). **Düsseldorf,** the sometime home of Brahms, Mendelssohn, and Schumann, also has a proud music tradition with an excellent symphony (see p. 548). Fast-forward to the 19th century, and you get the romantic cult of composers such as Richard Wagner and Franz Liszt, both of whose homes are preserved as museums in **Bayreuth** (see p. 222).

Eventually, as opera houses and concert halls became a fixture in German cities, a wider public clamored for musical performances. Today, every major city—and many smaller ones—has its own publicly funded orchestra. Attending a performance at the **Semper Opera** in Dresden (see p. 192), the **Festspielhaus** in Bayreuth (see p. 225), or Berlin's **Philharmonie concert hall** (p. 124) or **Deutsche Oper Berlin** (p. 125) are all seminal experiences for music lovers.

GERMANY IN BOOKS & FILMS
Books
NOVELS

Berlin Noir by Philip Kerr. Bernie Gunther is the dyspeptic Berlin detective in these three thought-provoking crime novels set in Nazi Germany and post-war Berlin and Vienna.

Billiards at Half-Past Nine by Heinrich Böll: A compelling novel by one of Germany's best-known writers about the compromises made by a rich German family during the Hitler years.

The Good German by Joseph Cannon: A war correspondent returns to post-war Berlin in search of a story and a past love.

The Tin Drum by Günter Grass: Perhaps the most famous novel about life in post-World War II Germany, written by a Nobel Prize winner who kept his own Nazi past a secret until 2006.

BIOGRAPHY & HISTORY

Bismarck by Edward Crankshaw: An objective and highly readable life of the first chancellor of the German Empire.

Frederick the Great by Nancy Mitford: Frederick, statesman, scholar, musician, and patron of the arts, sketched with wit and humor.

Germany, 1866–1945 by Gordon Craig: One of the best single accounts of the turbulent political, cultural, and economic life in Germany from the foundation of the German Reich through the end of the Third Reich.

Here I Stand: A Life of Martin Luther by Roland Bainton: A fascinating and meticulously researched account of the Protestant reformer.

Hitler: 1936–1945: Nemesis by Ian Kershaw: Several good biographies about Hitler have been written, including works by Robert Payne, Joachim Fest, and John Toland, but Kershaw's is one of the best.

MEMOIRS

Berlin Diaries, 1940–1945 by Marie Vassilchikov: The secret journals of a young Russian aristocrat who lived and worked in Berlin throughout World War II.

Berlin Journal, 1989–1990 by Robert Darnton: An eyewitness account of the events that led to the opening of the Berlin Wall and the collapse of East Germany's Communist regime.

A Tramp Abroad by Mark Twain: Twain's account of his travels in Germany is as fresh today as when it first was published in 1899.

MISCELLANEOUS

German Family Research Made Simple by J. Konrad: If you're interested in tracing your German roots, this easy-to-follow guide makes the task easier.

When in Germany, Do as the Germans Do by Hyde Flippo: A short, entertaining crash course in German culture, customs, and heritage.

11 Essential Films About Germany

Berlin Alexanderplatz (1980): Rainer Werner Fassbinder's 14-part television adaptation of Alfred Döblin's novel follows a man's involuntary embroilment in the underworld of late-1920s Berlin after being released from prison.

The Blue Angel (1930): The film that made Marlene Dietrich an international star revolves around the doomed love affair of a professor and a nightclub dancer.

Cabaret (1972): A musical based on Christopher Isherwood's *Berlin Stories* and set in Berlin at the brink of World War II.

The Counterfeiters (2007): Oscar-winning film about Operation Bernhard, a Nazi-orchestrated counterfeiting operation carried out in Sachsenhausen concentration camp outside Berlin.

Good Bye, Lenin! (2003): A wry comedy about a young man in East Berlin who tries to keep his bedridden mother, a loyal Communist, from learning that the wall has come down.

The Lives of Others (2006): An Academy Award winner for Best Foreign Language Film, this haunting film reveals how the East German secret police (the Stasi) spied on the country's citizens, destroying and dehumanizing lives.

The Marriage of Maria Braun (1979): Hanna Schygulla stars as a woman married to a soldier in the waning days of World War II.

Metropolis (1927): Fritz Lang's classic of German cinema, in which the Workers plan a revolt against the aloof Thinkers that dominate them in a future dystopia.

Olympia (1938): Leni Riefenstahl's brilliant but creepy documentary about the 1936 Olympics in Berlin.

The Reader (2008): Hollywood adaptation of a novel set in postwar Germany, dealing with the life of an illiterate woman who worked in a concentration camp.

Wings of Desire (1987): An angel roaming the streets of Berlin and recording the angst and joy of ordinary life falls in love with a mortal.

EATING & DRINKING IN GERMANY

Germany may have unified in 1871, and again in 1991, but when it comes to food, all bets are off. Travel to different sections of the country

Bratwurst and sauerkraut, traditional elements of German cuisine.

THE GERMAN FOR BEER IS bier

You don't have to speak German to order a **beer.** It's spelled *Bier* but it's pronounced "beer." And it's such a vital part of German culture that the right to drink a beer with lunch is written into some labor contracts. The traditional *Biergarten* (beer garden), with tables set outdoors under trees or trellises, remains an essential part of German life. A *Bräuhaus* (*broy*-house) serves its own brew along with local food.

Choosing the right beer can seem baffling at first, however, because many German beer styles are not readily found in America. Two of the most recognizable German beer styles are **Pils** and **Weizen,** which exist in North America sometimes as Pilsners or Hefeweizen respectively. Beers brewed in the traditional **Pils** style are often a very clear, pale blonde and have an assertive hoppy bitterness with an alcoholic content ranging between 4.5-5%. **Weizen** beers in Germany are lighter beers, with a yellowish white hue and a mildly hoppy bitterness. These beers are often more heavily carbonated, which results in a tall, white, creamy head.

The traditionally Bavarian **Helles** style is similar to the Pils and Weizen in alcoholic content, but has a full-bodied malty taste, almost no bitterness, and an eye-pleasing strawberry-blonde hue. The **Märzen** style is the beer of choice for many Bavarian beer gardens, an amber-colored brew with a strong hoppy taste and an alcoholic content between 5-6%. It's often associated with Oktoberfest, though you don't have to wait until October for it—it's served from the late spring to mid-autumn.

Schwarzbier ("black beer") gets its name from the dark brown, almost black hue. These beers, with their malty accents, creamy head, and well-balanced taste, are similar to British dark ales and have hints of chocolate, coffee, and vanilla. The slightly rarer **Rauchbiers** ("smoke beers") get their name from a process of drying malts over an open fire, which gives them a smoky flavor. These classic malt-accented brews have an opaque dark amber hue with alcoholic content of 4.8-6.5%.

Regional German ales include the coppery, fruity **Altbier,** a specialty of Düsseldorf, or Cologne's answer, the slightly paler, but otherwise similar, **Kölsch.**

Want something stronger? Ask about **Bocks,** which have an alcoholic content of 6-12%. Three seasonal varieties of Bocks are the golden, hoppy **Maibock** ("May bock"), the malty, smooth **Eisbock** ("ice bock"), and dark malt-accented **Doppelbock,** which traces its history to the "liquid bread" of fasting medieval monks.

and you'll find a wide range of dishes touted as "authentic German" cuisine. The names of kingdoms that ceased to exist well over a century ago—Swabia, Franconia, Schleswig-Holstein—come back into play, as each region claims its own gastronomic turf. Granted, it's generally similar—a meat-centric cuisine that embraces slow cooking, curing, and the silky richness that only animal fats can impart—but travel to more than one region and you may be surprised to see how Germans have resisted culinary homogenization. While the big cosmopolitan cities, notably Berlin and Frankfurt, offer a range of ethnic cuisines, in many towns your dining choices will be mostly traditional food, served in a *gemütlich* environment. Our advice: Go with the flow and always order the most local dishes on the menu, which are probably the ones that the chef learned to cook from his or her *mütter* or *grossmütter*.

As you look at the various regional cuisines, they make sense. Up in the north, where Germany meets the Baltic Sea, fish come more into play, in dishes such as *Aalsuppe* (sweet-and-sour eel soup) or *Rollmops* (pickled herring rolled in sour cream). Bavaria, which shares a long border with Austria, leans toward hearty Danube valley fare in dishes such as *Schweinwurst mit Kraut* (pork sausages with sauerkraut). The northern Rhineland, which shares a border with Belgium and the Netherlands, favors the Low Country sourness of dark bread, potato pancakes, and *Sauerbraten* (beef marinated in wine vinegar and spices). Farther south in the Black Forest, with France and Switzerland across the border, cuisine takes an unexpected gastronomic jump, with a disproportionate number of Michelin-starred restaurants. (Or is it just because the Michelin judges are predisposed toward a French-influenced cuisine?) In the various chapters of this book, we highlight the characteristics of those regional cuisines.

Wine

While beer (see p. 30) is the drink most associated with Germany, wine has in fact a longer tradition in this region, dating back to the Roman times (and who's to argue with a Roman when it comes to viticulture?).

THE BEST OF THE wurst

The German love affair with **Wurst** (sausage) dates from the dawn of history. Every region of Germany has its own specialty, but the overall favorite seems to be *Bratwurst* from Nürnberg, made of seasoned and spiced pork. Germans often take their *Wurst* with a bun and a dab of mustard. **Weisswurst** (white sausage) is a medley of veal, calves' brains, and spleen (nose-to-tail eating at its finest). **Bauernwurst** (farmer's sausage) and **Knockwurst** are variations on the *Frankfurter*, which originated (naturally) in Frankfurt. (Oddly enough, small Frankfurters, which are called wieners or Vienna sausages in the United States and **Wienerwurst** in Germany, are known as *Frankfurters* in Austria.) **Leberwurst** (made from liver) is a specialty of Hesse. **Rinderwurst** and **Blutwurst** (beef sausage and blood sausage) are Westphalian specialties and are often eaten with *Steinhäger* (corn brandy).

In December, traditional Christmas markets come to life on historic market squares throughout Germany.

Germany is best known for the white-wine grapes of the Moselle and Rhine Valleys (see chapters 12 and 13 for information on tours, tastings, and vineyard visits), with varietals such as **Riesling, Weissburgunder,** and **Scheuerebe.** On labels, you'll see the term *Trocken* used to denote dry wines, and *Halbtrocken* for semi-dry.

Under German wine law, there are two categories of quality— *Tafelwein* and *Qualitätswein.* It's the second of these that you want to seek out. Made from ripe, very ripe, or overripe grapes, Qualitätswein (quality wine) is divided into two types: *Qualitätswein mit Prädikat* and *Qualitätswein bestimmter Anbaugebiete* (QbA). If you see **QbA** on the label, it means the wine comes from 1 of the 13 specified winegrowing regions and is made from grapes ripe enough to give the wine the traditional taste of its region. Light, refreshing, and fruity, these everyday wines are meant to be consumed while young. **QmP** includes all the finest wines of Germany. Each carries one of six special attributes on its label: *Kabinet* (lighter and less alcoholic), *Spätlese* (a more intense late harvest wine), *Auslese* (noble wines with an intense bouquet and taste, usually sweet), *Beerenauslese* (rich sweet dessert wines), *Eiswein* (pressed from frozen grapes, to concentrate sweetness and fruity acidity), and *Trockenbeerenauslese* (a rich, sweet, honeylike wine made from overripe grapes).

WHEN TO GO

Peak travel months in Germany are May through October, with another boost in December when the Christmas markets are held and skiers head to the Bavarian Alps. Expect busy roads, lines at attractions and museums, and fewer lodging vacancies, but also long days (the sun sets as late as 9.30pm in June!), lots of festivals, and balmy nights in the beer garden. If travelling in spring, note that there are several holidays between Easter and June (Ascension Day, Labor Day, and Whit/Pentecost Sunday) when Germans like to take mini-vacations and popular places book out quickly.

Weather

Overall, Germany has a predominantly mild, temperate climate. Average summer temperatures range from 20°C–30°C (72°F–80°F). The average winter temperature hovers around 0°C (32°F).

Late spring and early fall can bring the nicest travel days, not too hot and often quite sunny. July and August can get stifling hot and humid, with thunderstorms in the afternoon being no rarity. November to February are the coldest and dullest months with frequent rain, snow, gloom, and sunsets around 4pm. Some museums and attractions curtail their hours or close altogether for the season. On the plus side, there are practically no crowds anywhere except the ski resorts.

Festivals & Special Events

There's more to Germany than Oktoberfest. Germany hums year-round with festivals and special events of all kinds, and these can add an additional sparkle to your trip. Below are some of the most important ones.

JANUARY

New Year's Ski Jump in Garmisch-Partenkirchen (p. 296) is one of Europe's major winter sporting events. www.gapa.de. January 1.

FEBRUARY

Berlin International Film Festival lasts for 10 days and showcases the work of international film directors in addition to the latest German films. www.berlinale.de. Second week in February.

Fasching (Carnival) festivals take place in Catholic cities throughout Germany, reaching their peak on Rose Monday, the Monday before Ash Wednesday. Celebrations in Cologne (see chapter 12)

and Munich (see chapter 8) are particularly famous. A week in February.

MAY

Hamburg Sommer is the umbrella name given to a summer-long series of cultural events in Hamburg (see chapter 15), including concerts, plays, festivals, and special exhibitions. www.hamburg.de/dom. May through July.

Historisches Festspiel "Der Meistertrunk" is a costume festival in Rothenburg ob der Tauber (p. 266) that recreates the story of how a brave citizen saved the town from destruction by drinking a huge tankard of wine (an event called *Der Meistertrunk*). www.meistertrunk.de. On

Whitsuntide (Pentecost), as well as in early September and twice in October.

JUNE

Heidelberg Castle Illumination Heidelberg's romantic castle (p. 377) is illuminated and showered with spectacular fireworks www.schloss-heidelberg.de. One Saturday in early June, mid-July, and early September.

Mozart Festival in Würzburg (p. 245) is a major cultural event in Germany. www.mozartfest.de. Early June to early July.

Gay Pride festivals, featuring parades, performances, and street fairs, take place throughout Germany, with the largest celebrations held in Berlin (see chapter 4), and Cologne (see chapter 12). Berlin: last June weekend; Cologne: first July weekend.

JULY

Schleswig-Holstein Music Festival One of the best music festivals in Europe, classical concerts take place in venues in and around the lovely old city of Lübeck (p. 689). www.shmf.de. July and August.

Bayreuther Festspiele During one of Europe's major opera festivals, the work of Richard Wagner is performed in the opera house in Bayreuth (p. 222) that he himself designed. www.bayreuther-festspiele.de. Late July through late August.

AUGUST

Nürnberger Herbstvolksfest, a big festival in Nuremberg (p. 196), features amusement rides, concerts, and family events. www.volksfest-nuernberg.de. Last week in August to the second week in September.

Alstervergnügen is a popular Hamburg (p. 652) festival with music, dancing, cultural events, food stalls and fireworks set around the Binnenalster Lake. www.hamburg.de/alstervergnuegen Late August or early September.

Stuttgarter Weindorf (Wine Festival) Wine lovers converge on Schillerplatz in Stuttgart (p. 388) to taste a selection of hundreds of Württemberg wines and sample regional food specialties. www.stuttgarter-weindorf.de. Two weeks in late August to early September.

SEPTEMBER

Musikfest Berlin plays host to orchestras, ensembles, conductors, and soloists from around the world. www.berlinerfestspiele.de. Three weeks in September.

Oktoberfest The world's biggest beer festival takes over the Theresienwiese grounds in Munich (see chapter 8) with giant beer tents, oompah bands, parades and amusement rides. www.oktoberfest.de. Mid-September to first Sunday in October.

Cannstatter Volksfest Dating back to 1818, the 16-day beerapalooza in Stuttgart (p. 388) is the second largest in Germany after Munich's Oktoberfest. cannstatter-volksfest.de Late September to early October.

OCTOBER

Frankfurter Buchmesse (Book Fair) The world's largest book fair is a major event in international book publishing. www.buchmesse.de. Mid- or late October.

NOVEMBER

Jazzfest Berlin attracts some of the world's finest jazz artists with concerts staged at various Berlin venues. www.berlinerfestspiele.de. Three days in early November.

Hamburger Dom (also called Winterdom) amusement fair in Hamburg is the biggest public event in northern Germany. www.hamburg.de/dom. November through early December.

DECEMBER

Christmas Markets, sometimes called *Weihnachtsmarkt* (*Weihnachten* means Christmas) or *Christkindlmarkt* (literally, "Christ Child Market"), take place in town squares throughout Germany, most notably Berlin, Cologne, Dresden, Munich, Nuremberg, Rothenburg ob der Tauber. www.germany.travel. Last weekend in November through Christmas.

Holidays

Public holidays are New Year's (January 1), Easter (Good Friday, Easter Sunday, and Easter Monday), Ascension Day (40 days after Easter), Labor Day (May 1), Whit/Pentecost Sunday and Monday (50 days after Easter), Day of German Unity (October 3), Christmas (December 25 and 26). In addition, the following holidays are observed in some German states: Epiphany (January 6), Corpus Christi (10 days after Pentecost), Assumption (August 15), All Saints' Day (November 1) and Reformation Day (October 31).

GERMANY ITINERARIES

3

Wondering where to go in Germany? The best itinerary for you will, of course, depend on what you like to see and do. But here are some ideas: Some show off the highlights, others focus on a few regions, and others cater to special interests, whether that's tasting wine or showing the kids a fine crop of fairy-tale castles.

THE REGIONS IN BRIEF

Germany lies in the heart of Europe, bordered by Switzerland and Austria to the south; France, Luxembourg, Belgium, and the Netherlands to the west; Denmark to the north; and Poland and the Czech Republic to the east. The country encompasses around 357,000 sq. km (137,838 sq. miles) and has a population of about 80 million.

BERLIN Germany's capital draws visitors with glorious museums, diverse cultural offerings, and nightlife that keeps going well into the morning. Southwest of Berlin is **Potsdam,** with a famous palace and elegant gardens.

SAXONY & THURINGIA **Leipzig** is the most important industrial city in the east after Berlin. Once the home of Bach, it is also a cultural treasure, with contemporary art galleries and a famous boys' choir. **Dresden** remains one of the most beautiful cities in Germany, though 80% of its center was destroyed in an infamous 1945 Allied air raid. In the neighboring state of Thuringia, **Weimar** saw its Golden Age as the spiritual capital of the German Enlightenment. Museums and memorials of illustrious residents including Schiller and Goethe are scattered around the historic city center.

FRANCONIA & THE GERMAN DANUBE Some of Germany's greatest medieval and Renaissance treasures came from this region, home of such artists as Albrecht Dürer and Lucas Cranach the Elder. Its historic centers include **Bamberg, Nuremberg,** and **Bayreuth,** where Wagner built his theater and started Festspiele, the famous opera festival. **Regensburg** is one of the best-preserved cities in Germany.

THE ROMANTIC ROAD The *Romantische Strasse* winds south from baroque **Würzburg** to **Füssen** at the foot of the Bavarian Alps. It's a popular route known for its folk traditions, old-world charm, and

FACING PAGE: **Ruined Heidelberg Castle overlooks the historic core of this lively university town.**

Neuschwanstein Castle, a 19th-century Neo-Gothic fantasy in the Bavarian Alps.

unspoiled walled medieval towns, notably **Rothenburg ob der Tauber,** one of Europe's best preserved medieval towns. The road ends at "Mad" King Ludwig's most fantastic creation, **Neuschwanstein Castle.** Nearby, though not officially on the Romantic Road tourist route, are the charming Alpine towns of **Mittenwald** and **Oberammergau,** plus hiking, nature, wildlife, and Alpine ski trails in winter.

MUNICH   As cosmopolitan as Frankfurt or Berlin, with a vast array of museums and palaces, Munich is also kitschy in the best Bavarian tradition. To get into the spirit of Munich life, spend a night at the **Hofbräuhaus** with its huge mugs and oom-pah bands, or stroll through the **Englischer Garten** and sample some Bavarian wine in **Schwabing.**

HEIDELBERG, STUTTGART & THE NECKAR VALLEY   The Neckar Valley's **Burgenstrasse** (Castle Road) has more castles than any comparable stretch along the mighty Rhine, and detours into side valleys to sleepy towns with abundant charm. **Heidelberg** is the apotheosis of romantic Germany, a famous medieval university town with a historic castle. **Stuttgart** is an industrial giant—headquarters of both Mercedes and Porsche—but it's also a city of world-class museums, opera, and ballet.

THE BLACK FOREST & LAKE CONSTANCE   The dense fir landscape of the **Black Forest** actually receives more sunshine than most other places in Germany, making it a great place for spas, hiking, cycling, and cross-country skiing. The classic spa town of **Baden-Baden** and the historic cathedral town of **Freiburg** make good bases for exploring. A little farther south is the northern shore of the Bodensee, as Germans call beautiful **Lake Constance,** which is shared with Austria and Switzerland.

FRANKFURT   Frankfurt is vibrant, dynamic, and flashy—the most Americanized city in Germany. Come here for a thriving, modern, and outward-looking feeling (and food). The world-famous **Städel** is just one among many marquee museums.

COLOGNE & THE RHINELAND   For most visitors, the number-one attraction in Germany is a cruise on this mighty river, flowing for some 1,370km (850 miles) through gorges and past ancient castles and vineyards. Ancient **Cologne** is known for its famous cathedral, the largest in Germany, as well as striking Roman ruins and some of Germany's best modern-art galleries.

THE MOSELLE VALLEY   With its vineyards, castles, and fortresses, the tranquil Moselle Valley is dotted with sleepy towns where you can sample some of the world's greatest white wine vintages. Near the Luxembourg border, ancient **Trier** is practically a theme park of Roman culture and architecture.

THE FAIRY TALE ROAD   If not as architecturally splendid as the Romantic Road (see above), the **Fairy-Tale Road** has treasures for visitors interested in German lore and legend, particularly the tales of the Brothers Grimm, who lived and worked here. It passes through colorful towns with half-timbered buildings and past plenty of castles. Its largest town is easygoing **Bremen,** which offers unique architecture and a fine crop of museums.

HAMBURG & THE NORTH   The port of **Hamburg** is exhilarating. This Hanseatic city along the River Elbe has been beautifully rebuilt into a center of lakes, parks, and tree-lined canals, while being equally famous for its red-light district. In neighboring Schleswig-Holstein, **Lübeck,** the hometown of writer Thomas Mann, has one of the country's best-preserved Altstadts (Old Towns). Nearby is Germany's most cosmopolitan celebrity resort, the island of **Sylt.**

THE BEST OF GERMANY IN 1 WEEK

This 7-day tour begins in **Munich** and ends in **Berlin,** showing off the best of southern and northern Germany. It introduces the country's two greatest cities, two of **King Ludwig II's castles,** and a mighty

The Best of Germany in 1 & 2 Weeks

IN 1 WEEK ●
Days 1 & 2 Munich
Day 3 Füssen
Days 4 & 5 Cologne
Days 6 & 7 Berlin

IN 2 WEEKS ●
Days 1 & 2 Berlin
Day 3 Day Trip to Potsdam
Day 4 Day Trip to Dresden
Day 5 Hamburg

Day 6 Day Trip to Lübeck
Days 7 & 8 Munich
Day 9 Day Trip to Füssen
Day 10 Regensburg
Day 11 Heidelberg

Day 12 Heidelberg &
Baden-Baden
Day 13 Nuremberg
Day 14 Berlin

river—the Rhine—as it flows through the lively city of **Cologne.** Our preferred mode of transport is ICE high-speed train, a comfortable, fast and efficient way to get almost anywhere you want to go in Germany. (For more on traveling around by train, see p. 704.)

DAY 1: Munich ★★★

Head first for **Marienplatz** (p. 320), the city's main square. Here you can watch the **Glockenspiel,** visit the huge **Frauenkirche,** and go up to the top of the **Rathaus** (p. 320) tower for a bird's-eye view. By the **Viktualienmarkt** (p. 319), pick a place for lunch from among dozens of possibilities. Afterward, make your way to **Asam-kirche** (p. 318) for a glimpse of the rococo ornamentation for which southern Germany is famous. In the afternoon, choose a museum: If you're an art lover, the best bet is the priceless collection of Old Masters at the **Alte Pinakothek** (p. 324). Munich is one of Germany's cultural hot spots, so you may want to spend the evening at a concert or the opera.

DAY 2: Munich ★★★

Start your second day in a palace. You need the entire morning to wander through the enormous **Residenz** (p. 321) in central Munich.

Busts and frescoes line the Antiquarium in the Residenz, Munich's former royal palace.

In the afternoon, choose another museum to visit—perhaps the **Neue Pinakothek** (p. 326), a showcase for 19th-century German and European art, or the **Lenbachhaus** (p. 329), with a stunning collection of early German Expressionist art. Fit in a stroll in the bucolic **Englischer Garten,** Munich's oldest, largest, and prettiest park. Relax over a drink or two at the park's famous beer garden.

DAY 3: Füssen ★★

Make your way to **Füssen**—2½ hours away by bus—jumping-off point for Neuschwanstein and Hohenschwangau castles. Try to arrive early, and make **Neuschwanstein Castle** (p. 294) your first stop; Germany's most popular tourist attraction quickly fills as the day wears on. You can easily make the 6.5km (4-mile) trip from Füssen to the castle by bus. Tours of King Ludwig II's fairytale castle take about 1 hour. If you're still in a "royal" mood, visit adjacent **Hohenschwangau Castle,** Ludwig's childhood home (p. 293). Enjoy a stroll in medieval Füssen before settling into a *Weinstube* for dinner.

DAY 4 & 5: Cologne ★★

Hop on the train and make your way to **Cologne** (see chapter 12) on the River Rhine. By fast train, the trip from Füssen takes about 6 to 7 hours. You'll see Cologne's greatest sight—the enormous **Dom** (p. 531)—as soon as you step out of the train station. Enjoy the evening and following day in this lively Rhine-side city by visiting the awe-inspiring cathedral and a couple of its many museums, such as the **Römisch-Germanisches Museum** (p. 534), dedicated to the Romans who made Cologne one of their strategic forts. You can also take a sightseeing **boat ride** (p. 530) along the Rhine. Stay 2 nights in Cologne and have dinner at one of the city's famous beer halls (be sure to sample *Kölsch,* Cologne's delicious beer). The city has a thriving contemporary music scene, too.

DAY 6: Berlin ★★★

In the morning, take one of the sleek, superfast trains to **Berlin** (see chapter 4). The journey takes about 4¼ hours. Huge, sophisticated Berlin has endless things to do (for additional ideas, see "Northern Germany in 1 Week," below). Check into your hotel and then take a sightseeing **bus tour** (p. 89) of the city; otherwise you'll see only a fraction of this enormous metropolis. After your tour, make your way over to the **Brandenburg Gate** (p. 78), the symbol of the city, and the nearby **Reichstag** (p. 83), the country's parliament. Take the elevator up to the modern dome atop the Reichstag for a fabulous view over Berlin (the dome is open late, so come back later if the line is long). From the Reichstag, walk east down **Unter den Linden** to **Museumsinsel (Museum Island),** and stop in at the **Pergamon Museum** (p. 88) to see the massive Pergamon Altar, or visit the **Neues Museum** (p. 88), with its world-class collection of Egyptian antiquities, including the bust of Queen Nefertiti. Berlin is famed for its nightlife, so when darkness falls you have many options (see p. 123).

3

DAY 7: Berlin ★★★

Here's hoping your flight home departs late in the day, so you can go over to the western side of Berlin to stroll

The neoclassical Brandenburg Gate is one of Berlin's most iconic landmarks.

down **Kurfürstendamm,** the renowned boulevard known locally as Ku'Damm, before heading to the airport.

GERMANY IN 2 WEEKS

This itinerary makes a zig-zagging circuit of Germany, from **Berlin** to **Hamburg** in the north, south to **Munich** and its scenic hinterland, and finally west to the university town of **Heidelberg** and the edge of the **Schwarzwald (Black Forest).** See the map on p. 415.

DAY 1: Berlin ★★★

Follow the suggestions for Berlin in our 1-week itinerary (see above) until late afternoon; then, from Museumsinsel, walk to **Friedrichstrasse,** the upscale shopping street of eastern Berlin (p. 117), or visit the **East Side Gallery** (p. 87), the longest preserved section of the Berlin Wall. Or if the day is clear, you might walk over to Alexanderplatz and zoom up to the observation deck of the **Fernsehturm** (p. 80).

DAY 2: Berlin ★★★

Spend your second day on the western side of the city. Head over to the Charlottenburg neighborhood for a tour of **Schloss**

Charlottenburg (p. 75) and a stroll through its gardens. Hit **Kurfürstendamm** (Ku'Damm; p. 63), the most famous boulevard in western Berlin, for lunch or *Kaffee und Kuchen* (coffee and cake). Stop by the **Kaiser-Wilhelm Gedächtniskirche** (p. 71), left as a colossal ruin after the devastation of World War II. Then spend a while strolling in the **Tiergarten,** Berlin's most famous park (p. 92). Have something fun lined up for the evening: Berlin has three opera houses, multiple symphony orchestras, cabarets, variety shows, and countless bars and clubs.

DAY 3: Day Trip to Potsdam ★★

Give yourself 4 to 5 hours for this excursion (via S-Bahn, a 25–40 minute ride), which includes visiting **Schloss Sanssouci** (p. 137), Frederick the Great's rococo palace, and its landscaped grounds. Have lunch in **Potsdam** (p. 136), then return to visit any of Berlin's top museums, such as the **Jüdisches Museum** (p. 82), where Germany's Jewish history is chronicled with art and artifacts.

DAY 4: Day Trip to Dresden ★★★

On the Elbe River about 2 hours south of Berlin by train, Dresden is one of the great art cities of Germany. Focus your attention on the **Albertinum** (p. 180), a vast collection accrued by Saxon rulers; the

Dresden's Zwinger Palace, a baroque masterpiece.

Colorful gabled housefronts line the Trave River in historic Lübeck.

treasury known as the **Grünes Gewölbe** (p. 182) in the Residenzschloss; and the **Zwinger** (p. 183), a restored royal palace containing four museums. This is a long daytrip, but definitely worth the
effort.

DAY 5: Hamburg ★★

From Berlin, head northwest to **Hamburg** (see chapter 15), about
1¾ hours by ICE train. You won't have a lot of time to see this
spread-out metropolis, so we suggest you take two tours: A hop-on,
hop-off bus tour for an overview of the sights, and then a cruise
around the harbor, one of the world's busiest, that has kept Hamburg on the map of commerce for centuries. Where you choose to
spend time depends on your tastes, but top stops are the **Kunsthalle** (p. 662), an outstanding collection of Old Masters and modern works; and **HafenCity** (p. 665), a new waterside quarter. Come
nightfall, you really shouldn't leave Hamburg without a foray to **St.
Pauli** and its famous Reeperbahn, ground zero for salacious
nightlife.

DAY 6: Day Trip to Lübeck ★★

A 45-minute train ride from Hamburg, this port on the Baltic Sea
boasts more buildings from the 13th to the 15th centuries than any

other city in northern Germany—more than just about anywhere else in Europe, for that matter. See p. 689.

DAYS 7 & 8: Munich ★★★

See "The Best of Germany in 1 Week," days 1 and 2, for details on spending these 2 days in Munich. You'll need to trim your itinerary a bit, as the Hamburg–Munich trip is around 5½ hours by train; take an internal flight (see p. 309) to save time.

DAY 9: Day Trip to Füssen ★★

Take a long day trip to **Füssen** (p. 288) to see the most famous tourist attraction in Germany: Ludwig II's **Neuschwanstein Castle** (p. 294). Leave as early as you can, because this fairy-tale castle can get busy. See "The Best of Germany in 1 Week," day 3.

DAY 10: Regensburg ★★

A bit off the beaten path, this is one of Germany's best-preserved medieval cities, the only one unscathed by World War II. Some 1,400 medieval buildings have survived, creating a jumble of steep red-tiled roofs above narrow lanes next to the River Danube. Regensburg is a 1½-hour rail trip from Munich. See p. 230.

DAY 11: Heidelberg ★★

A 4½-hour journey will get you to this ancient university town on the Neckar River by mid-afternoon—just in time for a stroll through the **Altstadt (Old Town),** which looks much as it did a century ago, an architectural mix of styles from Gothic to Neoclassical. Climb up to **Heidelberg Castle** (p. 377), a romantic hilltop ruin overlooking the tiled roofs of the Altstadt.

DAY 12: Heidelberg ★★ & Baden-Baden ★

Begin the day in the **Marktplatz** (p. 374), the Altstadt's main square, dominated by the Gothic **Heiliggeistkirche** (p. 374). Cross the **Alte Brücke** and stroll along Philosophenweg (Philosopher's Way), a 250-year-old promenade with a view of romantic Heidelberg from across the Neckar. Then head 1 hour south to **Baden-Baden** (p. 432), the glamorous spa resort at the edge of the Black Forest, renowned since the Roman era. "Take the waters" at **Friedrichs-bad** (p. 435), a 125-year-old mineral-bath establishment; the experience takes about 3½ hours.

DAY 13: Nuremberg ★★

In about 3 hours, you're in **Nuremberg** (p. 196), where the entire **Altstadt** is a pedestrian zone. Squares with fountains, Gothic churches, and picturesque precincts alongside the Pegnitz river lie below the medieval **Kaiserburg** castle (p. 205). Collections at the **Germanisches Nationalmuseum** (p. 204) include works by

Germany in 2 Weeks

GERMANY ITINERARIES

Renaissance great Albrecht Dürer, whose house is here. The **Doku-mentationszentrum Reichsparteitagsgelände** (Nazi Rally Grounds Documentation Center) (p. 203), housed in the former Nazi Congress Hall, provides an engrossing chronological overview of the rise of Nazism.

DAY 14: Berlin ★★★

Head back to **Berlin** to catch your flight home. The ICE train ride from Nuremberg is about 5 hours. (Alternatively, fly home from **Frankfurt,** a little over 2 hr. from Nuremberg; or from **Munich,** under 2 hr.)

THE NORTH IN 9 DAYS

This weeklong itinerary centers on **Berlin,** one of the most exciting capitals in Europe, and the Hanseatic cities of **Hamburg** and **Lübeck.** We're adding **Dresden,** an art-filled day trip from Berlin. These northern cities are relatively close to one another but worlds apart in terms of culture and atmosphere. To round out the trip, we recommend a 2-day change of pace on the **North Frisian Islands.**

DAYS 1 & 2: Berlin ★★★

When it comes to exploring **Berlin** (see chapter 4), 2 days is hardly enough, but even a short visit will give you a good taste. Besides the

Berlin's East Side Gallery, where urban art covers the former Berlin Wall.

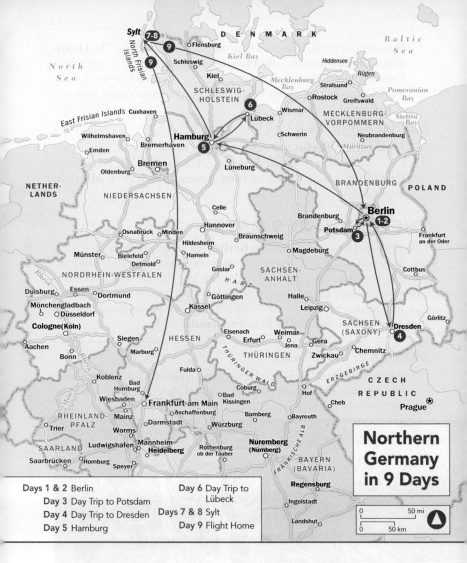

Days 1 & 2 Berlin
Day 3 Day Trip to Potsdam
Day 4 Day Trip to Dresden
Day 5 Hamburg
Day 6 Day Trip to Lübeck
Days 7 & 8 Sylt
Day 9 Flight Home

suggestions in the 1-week and 2-week itineraries above, here are some other options. The longest remaining section of the Berlin Wall is now the **East Side Gallery** (p. 87), an outdoor art exhibit painted by dozens of international artists. A reconstructed stretch is now the **Berlin Wall Memorial/Berliner Mauer Dokumentationszentrum** (p. 87), which documents where the Wall stood and what it looked like. The small **Mauermuseum Haus am Checkpoint Charlie** (p. 83) memorializes a former crossing into East Berlin. Finally, for a glimpse—albeit a somewhat nostalgic one—of what life in the Deutsche Demokratische Republik (DDR) was like, spend an hour or two in the **DDR Museum** (p. 84). Visiting all four of these sites will take up an entire day.

DAY 3: Day Trip to Potsdam ★★

Head here to see **Schloss Sanssouci** (p. 137), Frederick the Great's baroque palace. Give yourself at least 4 hours to tour the palace, stroll through the landscaped grounds, and explore a bit of Potsdam, a 1,000-year-old city and capital of Brandenburg. In the evening, back in Berlin, consider attending a concert or an opera, or just chill out at a bar. There's plenty of choice.

DAY 4: Day Trip to Dresden ★★★

You can get here by train from Berlin in a couple of hours, but be sure to leave early, because there's much to see in Dresden. See "The Best of Germany in Two Weeks," day 2 (p. 43).

DAY 5: Hamburg ★★

Board a train at Berlin's Hauptbahnhof for the 1¾-hour trip to **Hamburg** (see chapter 16). You'll have an afternoon to take in some sights, and to get an idea of what this appealing port city is all about; take a **harbor cruise** (p. 664) to see the wharves that keep Hamburg on the map as Europe's second-largest port (after Rotterdam).

The gardens of Frederick the Great's summer palace, Sanssouci, in Potsdam.

After dark take a walk on the wild side down the **Reeperbahn** (p. 666), the city's famous (or perhaps infamous) red-light district.

DAY 6: Day Trip to Lübeck ★★

See "The Best of Germany in 2 Weeks," day 6 (p. 45).

DAYS 7 & 8: Sylt ★★

Within sight of neighboring Denmark, the windswept resorts of the **North Frisian Islands** attract a mix of fashionable urbanites and solitude seekers from all over Germany. With its watersports, sand dunes, and glorious sunsets, **Sylt** makes the best base. On a second day here, consider the island-hopping options offered by a number of local ferries. See p. 698.

DAY 9: Flight Home

From Sylt, board a train back to Berlin (5½ hr.) or Frankfurt (7½ hr.), the 2 most popular exit airports for intercontinental passengers.

ROMANTIC CITIES & CASTLES OF THE SOUTH

This itinerary highlights a clutch of towns and cities along and close to the **Romantic Road,** a scenic route that rambles through rural **Bavaria,** past meadows and forests to medieval towns and cities, before climbing into the **Alps.** Give yourself an unhurried day and night in each place. You can do this trip by train or rental car.

DAY 1: Würzburg ★★

For many Germans, the south begins at this small, lively city by the River Main. University students add life to its narrow lanes and bright squares. On an easy walk through the Altstadt you can see the **Residenz** (p. 253), one of the most impressive baroque palaces in Germany, and the 10th-century **Dom St. Kilian** (p. 251). The nearly 500-year-old Alte Mainbrücke crosses the Main River to a path up vineyard-covered slopes to the old stronghold **Festung Marienberg** (p. 252), now home to the Mainfränkisches Museum.

The medieval streets of Rothenburg-ob-der-Tauber, a highlight on the Romantic Road.

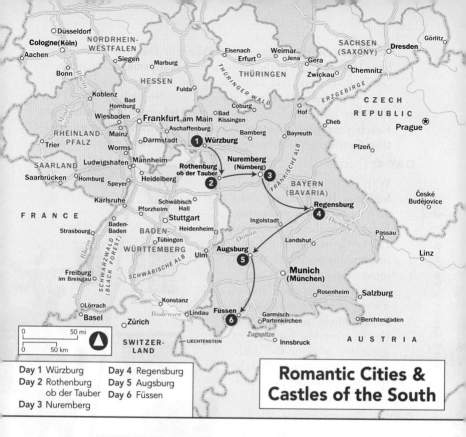

Day 1 Würzburg
Day 2 Rothenburg ob der Tauber
Day 3 Nuremberg
Day 4 Regensburg
Day 5 Augsburg
Day 6 Füssen

Romantic Cities & Castles of the South

DAY 2: Rothenburg-ob-der-Tauber ★★★

For historical panache, no other city in Germany matches **Rothenburg-ob-der-Tauber** (p. 266), a little over an hour from Würzburg by train. For an introduction to this walled medieval city on the River Tauber, walk along the town ramparts from the 16th-century Spitalbastei (a medieval tower-gate) to the Klingentor Tower. At street level you'll find picturesque nooks and crannies, as well as Gothic **St.-Jakobskirche** (p. 271), with a masterful altarpiece by Würzburg sculptor Tilman Riemenschneider.

DAY 3: Nuremberg ★★

This fascinating city of a half-million residents is about 75 minutes by train from Rothenburg. You'll find reminders of Nuremberg's brightest period—the Renaissance, when it bloomed as an artistic powerhouse—and its darkest, when it was the site of Nazi rallies. Looming over the city is the **Kaiserburg,** official residence of German kings and emperors from 1050 to 1571. In the major must-see museum, the **Germanisches Nationalmuseum** (p. 204), you'll find works by Renaissance great Albrecht Dürer, who lived here from 1509 to 1528. In the cobblestoned **Hauptmarkt** square, stalls sell fruit, flowers, and *Lebkuchen,* the delicious honey-and-spice cakes first created here over 500 years ago. Nuremberg's World War II history comes chillingly alive in the **Dokumentationszentrum Reichsparteitagsgelände (Nazi Rally Grounds Documentation Center;** p. 203), housed in the former Nazi Congress Hall.

DAY 4: Regensburg ★★

With some 1,400 medieval buildings, **Regensburg** (about an hour by train from Nuremberg) is the largest medieval city in Germany and the only one to survive World War II intact. Situated at the northernmost point of the Danube, it's a lovely place slightly removed from the restless hustle of modern life. Explorations inevitably lead to the 12th-century **Steinerne Brücke** (p. 231), providing panoramic views of the Altstadt.

DAY 5: Augsburg ★

A stroll through **Augsburg,** 2¼ hours by train from Regensburg, reveals an attractive urban landscape loaded with historic buildings, charming corners, and the lively ambience of a university town. Rathausplatz, the city's main

A wall mural in Regensburg pictures David and Goliath as a medieval allegory.

square, is dominated by the 17th-century **Rathaus** (p. 282) and adjacent **Perlachturm,** capped by a distinctive dome called an "Augsburg onion." The **Fuggerei** (p. 284), the world's first almshouse-complex, was built in 1523 and is still in use today. **Dom St. Maria** (p. 282), Augsburg's cathedral, has paintings by Hans Holbein the Elder.

DAY 6: Füssen ★★

By train you can get from Augsburg to **Füssen** in about 1¾ hours. The town has lovely squares and narrow cobblestone streets, and is the best base for visiting the nearby fairy-tale castle of **Neuschwanstein** (p. 294), built by King Ludwig II. If you have more time, the natural place to extend your trip from here is **Munich;** see "The Best of Germany in 1 Week," above.

BAVARIA & THE BLACK FOREST WITH KIDS

Taking a train, visiting a castle, walking through a market, even riding the U-Bahn—a lot about southern Germany will appeal to the whole family. Many hotels let children stay for free in their parents' room, or for a few euros more; public transportation offers reduced rates for kids; and most attractions have lower entrance fees for children. Just remember to moderate your pace: Less is often more with kids in tow!

DAYS 1 & 2: Munich ★★

The Glockenspiel puts on a daily show in Munich's Marienplatz.

Spend your first days in **Munich** (see chapter 8). The inner city is a car-free zone where you can stroll with ease. There are outdoor cafes around **Marienplatz** (p. 320); while there, catch the **Glockenspiel** show (p. 320) at 11am on the spire of the **Rathaus.** Right next to Marienplatz is the **Viktualienmarkt** (p. 319), the best outdoor market in Germany and a great place to have a casual lunch. Later, you might take a tram or subway to the **Englischer Garten** (p. 333) to wander along its tree-shaded walks, run in the meadows, or sit in the famous beer garden (nonalcoholic refreshments are available). On day 2, make time for the kid-friendly **Deutsches Museum** (p. 331), one of the largest science and technology museums in the world. At the **Spielzeugmuseum** (p. 337) kids can stare open-mouthed at the toys you played with when you were their age.

DAY 3: A Side Trip to Nymphenburg ★

Schloss Nymphenburg (p. 364) is top of your list today. The *Schloss* (palace/castle) is a breeze to get to (it's right in the city on the

Bavaria & the Black Forest with Kids

Days 1 & 2 Munich

Day 3 A Side Trip to Nymphenburg

Days 4 & 5 Garmisch-Partenkirchen & the Alps

Days 6 & 7 Two Fairy-tale Castles

Days 8 & 9 Freiburg

streetcar line), and **Nymphenburg Park** (p. 366) behind the palace is grand and inviting. Its gardens and English-style park have forested paths and some intriguing buildings, including an 18th-century swimming pool and a baroque hunting lodge. Back in the center, the **Deutsches Museum Verkehrszentrum** shows your kids how people got around in the days before the engine, and also what early bicycles and cars looked like.

DAYS 4 & 5: Garmisch-Partenkirchen & the Alps ★★★

Take the train to **Garmisch-Partenkirchen** (1¼ hr.; p. 296) in the Bavarian Alps south of Munich. First order of business: ascend the **Zugspitze** (p. 298), Germany's highest peak (2,960m/9,720 ft.), via a cog railway and a cable car—a thrill for kids. The view from the summit is—what else?—spectacular. If your family enjoys hiking, the area around Garmisch is great hiking country, with all levels of trails. Stay a couple of nights in Garmisch; breathe deep and slow

Cable cars ascend the summit of the Zugspitze for breath-taking views.

down. In winter, there's good skiing and ice-skating in the enormous **Eiszentrum** (p. 297), used for the 1936 Winter Olympics.

DAYS 6 & 7: Two Fairy-Tale Castles ★★

Take the train to **Füssen** (2½ hr.; p. 288) and from there a local bus to **Neuschwanstein** (p. 294), "Mad" Ludwig's fairy-tale castle. Germany's most-visited tourist attraction perches on a rocky spur that requires a good uphill hike to reach. The forested hills all around Neuschwanstein and neighboring **Hohenschwangau Castle** (p. 293)—an outing for your second day here—are full of excellent hiking paths. Stay in Füssen and explore the charming old town on foot.

DAYS 8 & 9: Freiburg ★

Ride the train to **Freiburg** (p. 416), your headquarters in the **Black Forest** (see chapter 11). Consider renting a car for just 1 day: From Freiburg you can make an easy 145km (90-mile) circuit through a scenic part of the Schwarzwald, with stops for short hikes and cable-car rides to the top of the mile-high peak **Belchen,** with spectacular views of the Rhine plain, or the 1,450m (4,750-ft.) summit of a peak called **Seebuck.** You can also stop for a paddle at either of two Black Forest lakes, **Schluchsee** or **Titisee.** Freiburg itself is flat and easy to explore by rented bike with kids of almost any age.

PROSIT! THE RHINE, MAIN & MOSELLE FOR WINE LOVERS

When you raise a glass of wine in Germany, the toast is a simple *"Prosit!"* (pronounced *prohst*). This itinerary takes you to the wine regions of western Germany, beginning and ending in **Frankfurt,** whose airport is the main gateway to North America. On boat rides on the **Rhine** and **Moselle** rivers you will cruise past some of Germany's most famous vineyards. Riesling is the traditional white grape, at its best in the country's west; *Grauburgunder* (pinot gris) and *Weissburgunder* (pinot blanc) thrive in the warmer climes of Germany's southwest. Red *Spätburgunder* (pinot noir) thrives on the volcanic soils of the Kaiserstuhl, northwest of Freiburg.

DAYS 1 & 2: Freiburg ★

From Frankfurt airport, hop on a train for the 2-hour trip to **Freiburg** (p. 416), a lively university town in the Black Forest that just happens to be surrounded by some 1,600 acres of vineyards. Most of the grapes grow on the lower slopes of the nearby **Kaiserstühl (Emperor's Throne),** a volcanic massif (p. 426). Countryside **Straussenwirtschaften** (p. 429) offer uniquely intimate wine and food tastings on the backroads.

The winding Moselle River reflects the lights of Cochem and its castle.

The Rhine, Main & Moselle for Wine Lovers

Map showing region from France, Switzerland, Austria, Czech Republic and Germany with cities including Duisburg, Essen, Dortmund, Göttingen, Mönchengladbach, Düsseldorf, Kassel, Halle, Leipzig, Cologne (Köln), Aachen, Bonn, Siegen, Marburg, Eisenach, Weimar, Erfurt, Jena, Gera, Dresden, Görlitz, Koblenz 3-4, Bad Homburg, Fulda, Coburg, Hof, Cheb, Prague, Wiesbaden 5-6, Frankfurt am Main 7, Aschaffenburg, Bad Kissingen, Bamberg, Bayreuth, Plzeň, Trier, Mainz, Darmstadt, Würzburg, Worms, Nuremberg (Nürnberg), Ludwigshafen, Mannheim, Rothenburg ob der Tauber, Regensburg, České Budějovice, Saarbrücken, Homburg, Heidelberg, Speyer, Schwäbisch Hall, Karlsruhe, Pforzheim, Stuttgart, Heidenheim, Ingolstadt, Landshut, Passau, Baden-Baden, Strasbourg, Tübingen, Ulm, Augsburg, Munich (München), Linz, Freiburg im Breisgau 1-2, Rosenheim, Lörrach, Konstanz, Füssen, Garmisch-Partenkirchen, Basel, Zürich, Lindau, Innsbruck.

Days 1 & 2   Freiburg
Days 3 & 4   Koblenz & the Rheingau
Days 5 & 6   The Moselle Valley
Day 7   Frankfurt

DAYS 3 & 4: Koblenz & the Rheingau ★★★

The train trip to Koblenz takes between 3 and 3½ hours. You can break the journey with a stopover in the **Rheingau** (p. 568), a 36km (22-mile) stretch of the Rhine between **Wiesbaden** and **Assmannshausen,** where wine has been produced since Roman times. Rheingau Rieslings rank among the best white wines in the world. **Koblenz** itself is a genteel town at the confluence of the Moselle and Rhine rivers, and dotted with medieval castles. From Koblenz, you can take a Rhine cruise to **Rüdesheim** or **Bingen** (see p. 568), stopping at either town to sample the local vintage and enjoy traditional Rhineland fare such as *Saumagen* (a haggislike pork or veal dish).

DAYS 5 & 6: The Moselle Valley ★★★

Southwest of Cologne, the **Moselle** (see chapter 13) is another scenic winegrowing region. You can easily make this a day trip from Cologne, but it's better to linger. The scenic valley follows the course of the River Mosel for more than 160km (100 miles) between Koblenz and Trier. Between May and October, cruises depart from Koblenz to **Cochem** (p. 610), a picturesque wine village surrounded by vineyards.

DAY 7: Frankfurt ★

From Cochem return to **Frankfurt** (p. 488), around 2½ hours by train. Wine lovers may need to switch fruits here: The local wine isn't made from grapes but from apples. *Apfelwein* (pronounced *ebb-el-vye* in local dialect) is a dry, alcoholic, 12-proof cider, best enjoyed poured from stoneware jugs at communal tables in the taverns of **Alt-Sachsenhausen,** on the southern bank of the River Main. See "Sachsenhausen & Its Apple-Wine Taverns," p. 518.

If you have a few more days, you can continue a tasting tour of Germany. Wherever you go, look for the local *Weinstube* (wine tavern), a convivial spot to sample Germany's many fine vintages.

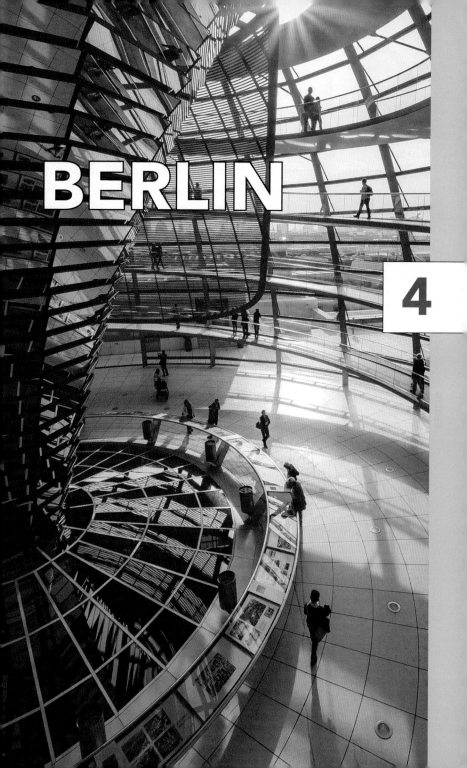

BERLIN

4

Once upon a time, a swampy trading village on the River Spree became the unlikely seat of the Prussian monarchy. Over the next couple of centuries, the capital blossomed into a center of industry, art, science, and thought. By the 1920s, it was poised to become one of the world's greatest cities.

And then: A genocidal dictatorship. A flurry of Allied bombs. And a certain 96-mile concrete behemoth that literally split the city into two.

Now, over a quarter-century since David Hasselhoff yowled "Looking for Freedom" atop a crumbling Berlin Wall, Germany's capital is "catching up" to its former status—at the expense, some say, of what once made it special. That same half-century of war and division that devastated Berlin also turned it into a city where the rules were different, a wild urban frontier of open spaces and cheap rents that attracted and inspired thousands of young, creative dreamers from the rest of Germany and the world. But by this point the investors and corporations have moved in, many of them capitalizing on Berlin's "gritty" image. Prices have skyrocketed. Two of the city's costliest and most contentious post-reunification projects are finally nearing completion: the Berlin-Brandenburg international airport, built to handle an ever-growing influx of visitors; and the Stadtschloss, a gaudy recreation of the Prussian palace that once stood in the city center. Things are changing so fast that a good chunk of the cafés, restaurants, bars, and clubs listed in this book might be gentrified out of existence by the time it's published.

Still here? Good. Because while whining about how "the glory days are over" is a city tradition up there with currywurst and nude swimming, Berlin is and will always be an amazing place to visit. It's home to some of the world's best museums, grandest historical sites, and poignant memorials; its most cutting-edge art and performance; a 24-hour nightlife scene that will spoil you for anywhere else; and restaurants as innovative as they are affordable. Influenced immeasurably by its immigrants and expats, it's nonetheless retained its characteristic "Berliner Schnauze"— that unpretentious, blunt-to-the-point-of-rude attitude you'll find in even the swankiest of locales. And no, that freewheeling, bohemian spirit of the Weimar, West Berlin and post-reunification days hasn't died out

PREVIOUS PAGE: **The ultra-modern dome atop the Reichstag offers sweeping vistas of Berlin.**

just yet. See it all now, while you can... and then come back in a few years to a city that's sure to be different, but no less exciting.

ESSENTIALS
Arriving

BY PLANE   Berlin's two airports, Tegel and Schönefeld, are both set to be phased out after **Berlin-Brandenburg International Airport** (BBI) opens. Supposedly that'll happen in 2017, but given the myriad inspection failures that have marked the past decade of construction, don't bank on it! Check **www.berlin-airport.de** for up-to-date information. In the meantime, you get to experience the joys of **Tegel** (TXL). Located 8km (5 miles) northwest of the city center, the octagonal airport serves European and long-haul destinations and is exceptionally user-friendly: you can get from your plane seat to Alexanderplatz in less than an hour. Buses 128, X9, 109, and express line TXL depart from stops outside the terminal every 10 or 20 minutes from 5am to 11pm. The journey takes between 15 and 40 minutes; tickets cost 2.70€ and can be purchased at the BVG kiosk close to the airport exit or from the ticket machines at the bus station. Validate your ticket by stamping it in the machine on the bus. A taxi ride costs approximately 35€; taxis depart from outside the terminal.

Schönefeld (SFX) airport, 18km (11 miles) southeast of the center, connects with destinations across Europe, Asia, and Africa, and is served by low-cost airlines like easyJet, Ryanair, and Germanwings. Regular S-Bahn trains (S45 and S9) depart from the airport and take about 45 minutes to reach central Berlin. Alternatively, take the Airport Express train (RE7 or RB14), which departs twice an hour from 4:30am to 11pm and takes about 30 minutes to reach Hauptbahnhof, stopping en route at Ostbahnhof, Alexanderplatz, and Friedrichstrasse. Tickets for either cost 3.30€ and can be purchased from the machines on the

The neoclassical Brandenburg Gate, an East Berlin landmark.

platforms. Expect to pay around 40€ for a 45-minute taxi journey into town.

BY TRAIN   You can reach Berlin by train from everywhere in Europe. All long-distance high-speed trains now arrive at and depart from the **Hauptbahnhof** (main train station) at Europa Platz 1 (© **0800-15-07-090** for train schedules; www.hbf-berlin.de). Unless you arrive by a local, regional train, you'll be pulling into this massive new user-friendly terminal. On the main floor there's a BERLIN infostore, one of Berlin's tourist information centers (see "Visitor Information," below). The entrance to the S-Bahn (commuter rail) is on the second floor of the station; the entrance to the U-Bahn (subway or underground train) is on the first floor, and there are buses and trams right outside.

BY CAR   Four Autobahn (freeway) routes enter Berlin from western Germany; three enter from the east. The drive from Frankfurt or Munich takes 6-8 hours, depending on traffic. After you're in Berlin, however, a car is a nuisance: parking is scarce, traffic is killer, and there's barely anywhere you can't go via public transportation.

Visitor Information

At a **BERLIN infostore** you can find information, book a hotel room, buy public transit passes and the money-saving Berlin Welcome Card, and find half-price concert and theater tickets. Berlin has five walk-in infostores: at **Tegel Airport,** Terminal A, Gate 2, open daily 6am to 9pm; **Hauptbahnhof** (main train station), Europaplatz, open daily 8am to 10pm; **Brandenburg Gate,** Pariser Platz, open daily 9:30am to 6pm; **Neues Kranzler Eck,** Kurfürstendamm 21, open Monday through Saturday 9:30am to 8pm, Sunday 10am to 6pm; and **Fernsehturm** (Television Tower), Panoramastrasse 1a, open late May through October daily 10am to 8pm. The **infostores** operate one information line (© **030/25-00-25**), open Monday through Friday 8am to 7pm, weekends 9am to 6pm; it costs a minimum of 0.50€ per minute.

For online info, go to **www.visitberlin.de**; all the information is available in English. You can also download the city's "Going Local" app, available for IOS and Android phones, for more information and tips.

CITY LAYOUT

Sprawling out over some 60 square miles, Berlin is one of those metropolises that doesn't act like a "city" per se. Like New York or Los Angeles, it's a conglomerate of individual neighborhoods, each of which has its own distinctive character and climate.

Though the Wall and the GDR (the East German Democratic Republic; DDR in German) are both long gone, the old political boundaries of

On bustling Friedrichstrasse, the notorious Berlin Wall crossing point Checkpoint Charlie lives on as a tourist site.

East and West still apply to some extent. Thanks to its divided days, Berlin has two major transportation hubs—**Zoologischer Garten** (Bahnhof Zoo) in the west, and **Alexanderplatz** in the east—and two "downtowns," around Charlottenburg's **Kurfürstendamm** and Mitte's **Unter den Linden.** On the other hand, the division wasn't a straight line, and first-time visitors are often surprised to find out that eastern districts like Kreuzberg and Neukölln were actually part of West Berlin.

Western Berlin Neighborhoods

CHARLOTTENBURG Ever since the 1700s, when it was still an independent city built around the royal Schloss Charlottenburg (Charlottenburg Palace; see p. 75), Berlin's far-western borough has oozed old-fashioned affluence. The default commercial center of West Berlin, it lost much luster to Mitte after reunification but remains a premier destination for high-end shopping and entertainment. Its main thoroughfare, the famous **Kurfürstendamm** ("Ku'Damm") has been called Berlin's answer to the Champs-Élysées: a long, wide boulevard lined with hotels, theaters, expensive bars, big-name brands, and department stores.

TIERGARTEN Tiergarten is Berlin's massive central park, surrounded by a business-residential district of the same name. It contains the Berlin

Charlottenburg Palace anchors West Berlin's affluent neighborhood of the same name.

Zoo (p. 93). To its southeast is the **Kulturforum,** a modern-looking arts complex built in 1960s West Berlin to compensate for the disappearance of Museum Island behind the Wall: It houses the Gemäldegalerie art museum (p. 71); and the Neue Nationalgalerie contemporary art museum (p. 74). Right next to that is Potsdamer Platz, a once-bustling square destroyed by WW2 bombs and bisected by the Wall; it was redesigned in the 1990s, to mixed reviews.

GRÜNEWALD/WANNSEE The 38-sq.-km (15-sq.-mile) lake-filled forest Grünewald lies on Berlin's western edge. Rising out of it is the man-made Teufelsberg, (p. 90) one of Berlin's highest hills; to the southwest, there's the popular **Wannsee** (p. 93), home to Europe's longest inland "beach."

SCHÖNEBERG The middle-class neighborhood of Schöneberg has been home to famous Berliners from Albert Einstein to Christopher Isherwood to David Bowie. The otherwise staid suburb is also notable for being the historic center of LGBT Berlin: the world's first gay rights demonstration took place on Nollendorfplatz in 1922, and the area around the station still boasts a high concentration of gay bars and clubs. There's also a burgeoning gallery scene along Potsdamer Strasse.

DAHLEM Once an independent village, this affluent southwestern burg is now the site of Berlin's Free University.

WEDGING AND MOABIT Berlin's perpetually "up-and-coming" north-western boroughs—the former a historically working-class stronghold, the latter an industrial and residential island home to Berlin's largest prison—are where you'll find the "Urberliners" who haven't left their neighborhood for decades, plus immigrants, artists, and students. The **Hauptbahnhof,** Berlin's central train station, is in southeastern Moabit.

Eastern Berlin Neighborhoods

MITTE Like the name (literally, "middle") suggests, Mitte is Berlin's historic center. The Brandenburg Gate, the Reichstag, the TV Tower, and Museum Island are all here, as well as the city's most fashionable boutiques, its buzziest restaurants, its renowned art galleries, and dynamic start-ups. Mitte spent nearly half the 20th century as a bombed-out shadow of its former self; its current renaissance is the product of vast amounts of effort (and money) on the city's part. Stroll down the historic boulevard **Unter den Linden** (see p. 79) from the Brandenburg Gate and see how much construction is still going on. Unter den Linden is intersected by **Friedrichstrasse,** eastern Berlin's preeminent shopping street. Continuing east, you'll hit **Museumsinsel** (Museum Island; see p. 86), a UNESCO World Heritage Site comprising five major art and history institutions, and the grandiose Berliner Dom (Berlin Cathedral). Across from there, yet another construction site marks the future Stadtschloss, Berlin's soon-to-be reconstructed Prussian city palace, and the former location of the Palast der Republik, the GDR's "people's palace," demolished in 2008.

Cross the Spree and you'll be at **Alexanderplatz,** (or simply "Alex"), the always-bustling public square and transit hub, dominated since the 1960s by the 368m (1207ft) Fernsehturm (TV Tower, p. 80). South of there, the Disney-esque Nikolaiviertel (Nicholas Quarter), filled with taverns and riverside restaurants, is a 1987 recreation of the city's oldest neighborhood. Finally, between Alexanderplatz, Torstrasse, and the Spree, Mitte's onetime Jewish quarter is where an international cadre of gallerists, fashionistas, and start-uppers go to shop, work, schmooze, and drink cappuccinos.

KREUZBERG Kreuzberg has been Berlin's alternative heart since the 1960s and 1970s, when the walled-in "island" neighborhood was colonized by punks, squatters, and guest workers from Turkey. Gentrification has smoothed its rough edges—especially on the west side, home to the Jewish Museum (p. 82), the Berlinische Galerie (p. 75), famous Wall crossing Checkpoint Charlie (p. 83), and the shops and restaurants of Bergmannstrasse. In the east, the "Little Istanbul" area around Kottbusser Tor remains an appealingly gritty mishmash of Turkish families, hipsters, and queer radicals, while the streets surrounding marijuana-scented

Görlitzer Park are a treasure trove of independent shops, street art, bars, and cafés.

NEUKÖLLN A poor immigrant neighborhood up until the mid-2000s, this fast-gentrifying southeastern borough is now home to countless international DJs, designers, painters, and professional baristas, who join the original Turkish, Middle Eastern and working-class German residents. The three main thoroughfares—Sonnenallee, Karl-Marx-Strasse, and Hermannstrasse—remain a glut of discount stores, shisha bars, and kebab stands. The adjacent **Tempelhof** neighborhood was formerly Berlin's airport, turned into Berlin's largest public park in 2008.

PRENZLAUER BERG Historically favored by artists, intellectuals, and students, Prenzlauer Berg became a haven for leftist squatters when the Wall came down, and then an ultra-happening nightlife hub around the turn of the millennium. Now its gorgeous pre-war apartments are primarily occupied by wealthy southern Germans and "bourgeois bohemian" types with young children. The cobblestoned streets around **Kollwitzplatz** are lined with charming mid-priced shops, restaurants and cafés.

FRIEDRICHSHAIN Across the Spree from Kreuzberg, bordered by the mural-covered stretch of Berlin Wall known as the East Side Gallery (p. 87), the eastern neighborhood of Friedrichshain is populated by a mix of old punks, young families, and, on weekends, massive crowds of not-exactly-sober students and tourists, thanks to its many cheap bars and rowdy clubs. Bisecting Friedrichshain is the gargantuan socialist-era boulevard **Karl-Marx-Allee** (formerly Stalinallee).

Treptow-Köpenick Berlin's southeast begins with Jonathan Borofsky's famed mid-Spree sculpture *Molecule Man,* flanked on land by riverside bars and leafy Treptow Park. Go there to see the large and imposing Soviet War Memorial. From there it just gets sleepier, ending at the quaint, forest- and lake-filled district of Alt-Köpenick.

LICHTENBERG-MARZAHN If you want an unvarnished, Ostalgia-free idea of life in communist East Berlin, head out to these bleak outlying neighborhoods filled with towering "Plattenbau" (GDR-built prefab social housing). The Stasi Museum (p. 84) is here, as is a substantial northern Vietnamese population. Lately, a few artists and club owners have started to take advantage of the area's still-cheap rents.

Getting Around

BY PUBLIC TRANSPORTATION Berlin's public transit system, the BVG, connects the whole of the city thoroughly and efficiently. The S-Bahn (elevated train), U-Bahn (underground), and bus systems all use the same ticket. Trains run 24 hours on weekends and from 4am to 12:30am

money-saving **TOURIST DEALS**

If you're planning more than two trips on public transportation in Berlin, you'll want a **Tageskarte** (day pass) for 6.90€–7.40€, good for unlimited transportation within the zones you purchase it for. If you're traveling in a group, consider the lesser-known **"small group day ticket,"** which covers up to five people for 16.90€–17.40€. A **weekly pass** is also available for 29.50€.

Planning on marathon sightseeing? Consider the **Berlin WelcomeCard,** good for unlimited public transport in zones AB and discounts on some 200 attractions, among them guided tours, most museums (except Museum Island) and theaters like the Deutsche Oper, Konzerthaus, and Staatsballet. At 19.50€ for 48 hours, 27.50€ for 72 hours, or 35.50€ for 5 days, it's a pretty good deal. The Tageskarte and Berlin WelcomeCard can be purchased at any Berlin Infostore (see p. 62). For more information, visit **www.berlin-welcome card.com**.

A special 72-hour **"Museum Island" pass** grants the above plus free admission to all galleries and museums on Museum Island (p. 86) for 42€. Or, if the free transport isn't as important to you, a **one-day Museum Island pass** for 18€ gives free entry to all five museums. An even better deal may be the three-day **Museum Pass Berlin,** available for 24€ adults, 12€ seniors and students. Available at the central ticket kiosk on Museum Island, it will get you into all Museum Island sites, plus nearly every other museum in Berlin, for free. It's actually a better deal to buy that and three public transit day tickets than it is to get the three-day **Berlin Welcome Card Museumsinsel** (40.50€), which includes transport and Museum Island admission but only grants discounts on the city's other museums.

on weekdays, with night buses covering the interim. Berlin is divided into three tariff zones: AB, BC, and ABC. Barring trips to and from Schönefeld airport or a day out in Potsdam, the only one you're likely to need is AB (2.70€ single fare, valid for 2 hours in one direction). You can buy tickets at a U-Bahn or S-Bahn station and validate them in the station machine before you board. Don't be surprised at the lack of turnstiles; the BVG runs on an honor system, with roving plainclothes controllers checking tickets at random. Riding ticketless, or "Schwarzfahren" as they call it, might seem tempting, but you're in for a 60€ fine if you get caught. For information and routes, call ✆ **030/19-449,** download the free-of-charge "Fahrinfo Plus" app (which can also be used to buy and display mobile tickets!) or visit www.bvg.de.

BY S-BAHN Berlin's above-ground rail system comprises 15 routes, which feed into three main lines going east–west, north–south, and circling around central Berlin. Purchase and validate your ticket at one of the red or yellow machines on the platform before boarding. The S-Bahn operates from 4am to 12:30am on weekdays and 24 hours on weekends.

Entrances are marked with an S on a green background. Some S-Bahn lines intersect with U-Bahn and/or regional train lines, so you can transfer from one to the other. This is the fastest way to get from Charlottenburg in western Berlin to Mitte in eastern Berlin, or to go southwest to Grunewald, Potsdam, and the lakes, or northeast to Oranienburg and Sachsenhausen.

BY U-BAHN   Berlin currently has 10 underground train lines, including the three-station U55 "tourist" route between Hauptbahnhof and the Brandenburg Gate. (An extension to Alexanderplatz, where it'll link up with the U5 line running east, has been in the works for years and will supposedly be completed by 2020). More than 170 stations operate from 4am until midnight on weekdays, 24 hours on weekends. At peak times, trains depart every 3 to 5 minutes. U-Bahn entrances are marked with a U in a blue background. Validate your ticket in one of the validation machines before boarding.

BY TRAM   Berlin's streetcar system is limited almost exclusively to the former East. While the U-Bahn covers Mitte, trams are usually the best way to get around the Prenzlauer Berg and Friedrichshain neighborhoods. Most keep the same hours as the U-Bahn and depart every 10 minutes. You can buy a ticket from a machine once you're inside.

BY BUS   Berlin's buses go everywhere that its trains don't, and run along U-Bahn routes on weekdays from 12:30am to 4am when the trains aren't operating. It's an open secret that public bus routes 100 and 200 double as Berlin's cheapest sightseeing tour—both run from Bahnhof Zoo east to Alexanderplatz, passing countless landmarks along the way. You can buy your ticket from the driver as you get on, but have your money at the ready to avoid dagger stares from locals. Download routes at **www.bvg. de**.

BY TAXI   Taxis wait outside major hotels, stations, and airports round the clock. Most drivers speak some English. There's a minimum charge of 3.90€, plus 2€ per kilometer (1.50€ per km after 7km). If you're going less than 2km (1¼ miles), ask for a "Kurzstrecke" (short-route fare); the driver should switch off the meter and charge a flat 5€. Otherwise, download the MyTaxi app or call ✆ **030/202020.**

BY CAR   Once in central Berlin, there's no need for a car; it's cheaper, quicker, and more carbon friendly to use the excellent public transport network, even for day trips. You can leave your car at one of the free or cheap "Park and Ride" lots around the city's perimeter (see www.carparking.eu/germany/berlin/pr for locations). If you do drive into the inner city, pay-and-display parking costs around 2.50€ per hour from 9am to 6pm or 8pm. Clearly display your ticket on the dash.

BY BICYCLE   Berlin's network of cycling paths and lack of steep hills makes it a paradise for cyclists; when the weather's warm, this is by far the best way to get around like a local. Bike rental shops abound all over the city and tend to charge around 10€ per day; many hotels and hostels also offer free or discounted bike rentals. You'll also see plenty of rental stands operated by the train company Deutsche Bahn. Their red bikes cost 1€ per 30 minutes or 15€ per day plus a one-time registration fee of 3€ per year; to get pedaling, visit callabike-interaktiv.de, download the "Call A Bike" app or call © **0700/05225522.** You'll need to buy an additional reduced fare ticket to take a bike on public transportation.

ON FOOT   You can't expect to cover all of Berlin on foot, but its individual neighborhoods, leafy parks, squares, and riverside and canalside promenades do lend themselves well to leisurely strolling. For information on guided walking tours, see p. 89.

[FastFACTS] BERLIN

ATMs   A surprising number of Berlin's cafes, restaurants, and bars don't take credit cards, so don't get caught without cash. There are plenty of ATMs for withdrawing money 24/7, but make sure you're aware of your bank's foreign transaction fees.

Business Hours   Most banks are open Monday through Friday 9am to 3pm. Most other businesses and stores are open Monday through Friday, 9 or 10am to 6 or 6:30pm and Saturday 9am to 4pm. If you need a midnight snack or drink, "Spätis" ("late shops," essentially convenience stores that sell booze) can be found all over the city, with the highest concentration in Kreuzberg, Friedrichshain, and Neukölln.

Dentists   If you need a dentist, ask your hotel concierge. For a dental emergency, call © **030/89004333.**

Doctors & Hospitals   You'll find a list of Berlin hospitals and English-speaking doctors at www. doctorberlin.de. You can also locate an English-speaking doctor by calling © **01804/22552362.** In case of a medical emergency, call © **030/310031.** To summon an ambulance, dial © **112.**

Emergencies   To call the police, dial © **110.** To summon an ambulance, dial © **112.**

Internet Access   Nearly all hotels and hostels offer Wi-Fi, often (but not always) free. Many bars and cafes also offer free Wi-Fi to customers. The entire Sony Center at Potsdamer Platz is a free Wi-Fi hotspot. For a partial list of other free hotspots, visit **www. hotspot-locations.de.**

Police   The national police emergency number is © **110.** For local police, dial © **030/46644664.**

Newspapers & Magazines   *Exberliner,* an independent magazine available in print or at exberliner.com, is your best source for Berlin news, features and event listings in English (and we'd be saying that even if we didn't work there). You can find it on newsstands, along with the German-language *Zitty, Tip,* and *Berlin-Programm.* For more, check online at www. visitberlin.de.

Pharmacy   Pharmacies (Apotheken) operate during normal business hours; at least one per district operates after hours and on Sundays. The rest of the pharmacies post the nearest 24-hour location on their front door. Two central pharmacies, **Pluspunkt Apotheke** at Friedrichstrasse 60 (© **030/20166173**) and **Apotheke Berlin Hauptbahnhof** (© **030/ 20614190**), are always open 24 hours. Check www. berlin.de for a list of pharmacies by district.

Post Office You'll find post offices scattered throughout Berlin, with large branches at Bahnhof Zoo and Hauptbahnhof (main train station). Most post offices are open Monday through Friday 8am to 6pm and Saturday 8am to 1pm.

Safety Berlin is generally a safe city, but use common sense when you're out and about, especially around tourist party corridors like Warschauer Strasse. Keep an eye on your valuables in crowded places and on public transportation. If you're driving, park your car in a secure lot or garage.

Telephones To make a local call to a land line, dial **030** (the three-digit city prefix in Berlin) followed by the number.

Toilets Clean public toilets are found throughout Berlin, including at all train stations. In most of them you need a .50€ or 1€ coin to get through the turnstile or unlock the stall door. It's customary to tip attendants .50€.

EXPLORING BERLIN

No matter what you want to see or do, Berlin's got it. Of course there are the countless historical sites, monuments, memorials and displays of "Vergangenheitsbewältigung" (coming to terms with the past, something Berlin's had to do quite a bit of since 1945). Then there's culture: 170 museums at last count, housing everything from ancient Egyptian artifacts to Renaissance masters to installations by up-and-coming modern artists. Like nature? As long as it's not winter, you could spend your whole visit wandering around the city's parks, forests and lakes. And if you fancy yourself an urban adventurer, you'll find bunkers, abandoned buildings and street art aplenty. Chances are you'll want some of everything, and that's exactly what you'll find here.

Western Berlin Attractions

Bauhaus-Archiv ★★ MUSEUM   Fans of modern design won't want to miss this small but important museum near Tiergarten, which documents the Bauhaus art and architecture movement of the 1920s. The big names are all here—Walter Gropius, Paul Klee, Vasily Kandinsky—as are the strikingly modern and functional objects, paintings, photos,

---

what's open on **MONDAY?**

Many of Berlin's major museums, galleries and historical sites shut their doors on Mondays, but not all of them. You can still visit the the **Pergamon** (p. 88) and **Neues Museum** (p. 88) on Museum Island, not to mention the **Jewish Museum** (p. 82), the **Berlinische Galerie** (p. 75), the **Bauhaus Archiv** (above), and the **German Historical Museum** (p. 78). The Deutsche Bank Kunsthalle (Unter den Linden 13-15), a smallish space that tends to exhibit important artists, is not only open, but free on Mondays (score one for corporate sponsorship!). As a rule, museums are closed January 1; December 24, 25, and 31; and the Tuesday after Easter—check individual websites if you're not sure.

furniture, and building blueprints they created and inspired. For your own piece of Bauhaus, hit the gift shop (see p. 119).

Klingelhöferstr. 14. www.bauhaus.de. ℂ **030/2540020.** Admission 7€ adults (8€ weekends), 4€ students (5€ weekends), free for children under 18. Weds–Mon 10am–5pm. Bus: Lützowplatz.

Gemäldegalerie (Painting Gallery) ★★★ MUSEUM   The first thing you need to know about the Gemäldegalerie is that it's huge. Seriously: don't come here unless you're ready to spend at least two hours wandering through a breathtaking collection of medieval and Renaissance art spanning six centuries and nearly 2 kilometers. You'll see ancient German triptychs, Dutch masters (including an octagonal room devoted to Rembrandt), and renowned Italian works from Raphael to Caravaggio, among many, many others. Paintings are displayed with minimal info, so get an audio guide (available in English) for the full experience. The **Kupferstichkabinett,** a collection of drawings, sketches, prints, pastels, and other "art on paper" from the likes of Botticelli, Van Gogh, and Warhol, is in the same building. It's worth buying a 16€ Kulturforum combination ticket if you're interested in both and have a half-day to spare.

Matthäikirchplatz 4. www.smb.spk-berlin.de/gg. ℂ **030/266423040.** Admission 10€ adults, 5€ students, children 16 and under free. Tues–Sun 10am–6pm (Thurs until 8pm). U-/S-Bahn: Potsdamer Platz.

Kaiser-Wilhelm Gedächtniskirche (Kaiser Wilhelm Memorial Church) ★★ LANDMARK/MEMORIAL/CHURCH   One of

The modern church beside the ruins of the Kaiser Wilhelm church.

Berlin's most famous landmarks, the Gedächtniskirche (Memorial Church) is a ponderous neo-Romanesque structure from the late 19th century. Built to commemorate the 1871 establishment of the German Empire, the church was blasted by a bomb in World War II, and its ruined shell (dubbed the "hollow tooth" by Berliners) was preserved as a symbol of the ravages of war. You probably won't want to spend more than a few minutes inside. Beside it is its geometric modern counterpart (the "lipstick tube"), designed by Egon Eiermann in 1961. The octagonal church is surprisingly beautiful inside, with gorgeous deep-blue

Western Berlin

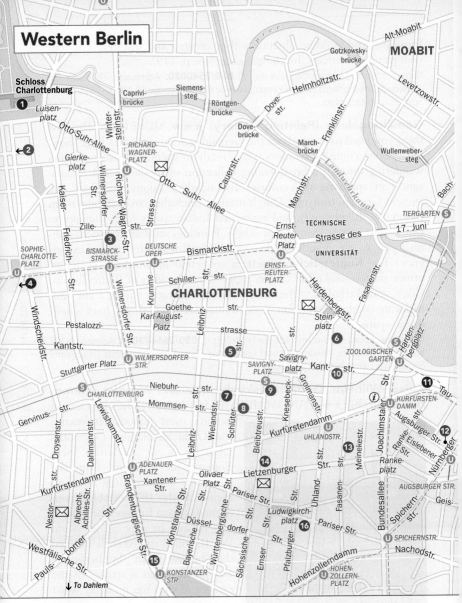

MOABIT

Schloss Charlottenburg

TIERGARTEN

CHARLOTTENBURG

TECHNISCHE UNIVERSITÄT

ZOOLOGISCHER GARTEN

KURFÜRSTENDAMM

AUGSBURGER STR.

↓ To Dahlem

Hamburg

Berlin ★

GERMANY

Frankfurt am Main

Munich

ATTRACTIONS

Bauhaus-Archiv **25**

Berlin Zoo **19**

Gemäldegalerie (Painting Gallery) **26**

Kaiser-Wilhelm-Gedächtniskirche (Kaiser Wilhelm Memorial Church) **11**

Martin-Gropius-Bau **29**

Naturkundemuseum **23**

Neue Nationalgalerie (New National Gallery) **27**

Schloss Charlottenburg (Charlottenburg Palace) **1**

Siegessäule (Victory Column) **21**

Spy Museum **28**

Teufelsberg **4**

Tiergarten **24**

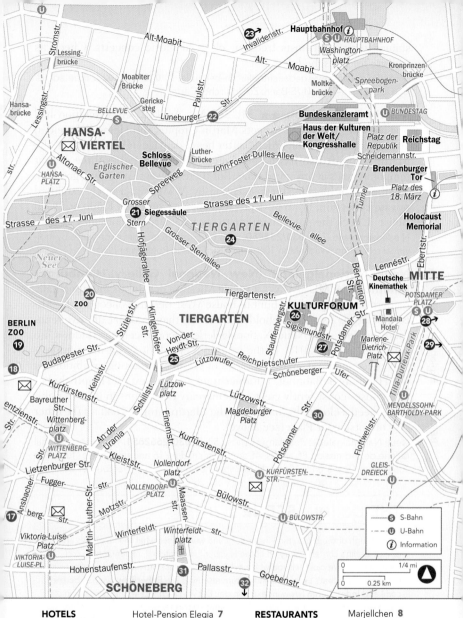

HOTELS

25Hours Bikini
  Berlin **18**
Arco Hotel **17**
Bleibtreu Hotel **14**
Das Stue **20**
Hotel Artemisia **15**
Hotel Domus **16**

Hotel-Pension Elegia **7**
Hotel-Pension Funk **13**
Pension Nürnberger
  Eck **12**

RESTAURANTS

Ana e Bruno **2**
Balicki Ergun **22**
Glass **6**
Ixthys **31**
Lon-Men's
  Noodle House **5**
Lubitsch **9**

Marjellchen **8**
Martha's **32**
Maultaschen
  Manufactur **30**
Paris Bar **10**
Rogacki **3**

stained glass, and hosts frequent classical music concerts. Check its website for the schedule.

Breitscheidplatz. www.gedaechtniskirche-berlin.de. © **030/2185023.** Free admission. Daily 9am–7pm. U-/S-Bahn: Zoologischer Garten.

Martin-Gropius-Bau ★★ MUSEUM   An 1881-era exhibition hall originally designed by architects Martin Gropius and Heino Schmeiden and meticulously reconstructed after heavy damage in World War II, the Martin-Gropius-Bau has no permanent exhibition, rather three or four temporary ones at any given time. But there's always something good on, whether it's a blockbuster installation by Ai Weiwei, a rarely exhibited private collection, or an in-depth retrospective on Frida Kahlo or David Bowie. Check the program online to see what strikes your fancy.

Niederkirchnerstr. 7. © **030/254860.** www.gropiusbau.de. Admission varies by individual exhibition. Weds–Mon 10am–7pm. U-/S-Bahn: Potsdamer Platz.

Neue Nationalgalerie (New National Gallery)/Hamburger Bahnhof ★★ MUSEUM   Ludwig Mies van der Rohe's monumentally modernist glass pavilion, built to house West Berlin's collection of 20th-century art, is a sight to behold in itself. But thanks to an extensive renovation project, the Neue Nationalgalerie's floor-to-ceiling windows are dark until at least 2019. In the meantime, you'll find part of its impressive collection on display in a series of six-month rotating exhibitions at the Hamburger Bahnhof, a former train station next to Hauptbahnhof that houses consistently great contemporary exhibitions in its own right. If you need a closer alternative, try the Martin-Gropius-Bau on the other side of Potsdamer Platz (see above).

Neue Nationalgalerie: Potsdamer Strasse 50. © **030/2662651.** www.neue-national galerie.de. Admission 8€ adults, 4€ students, children 16 and under free. Tues–Sun 10am–6pm (Thurs until 10pm). U-/S-Bahn: Potsdamer Platz. Hamburger Bahnhof:

THE gallery SCENE

Had enough of the big cultural institutions and want to see what the little guys are doing? Berlin's contemporary art scene is young, international, experimental, and always in flux. We can't tell you which exhibitions by which artists in which galleries are hot right now—that's up to arts and culture resources like **Exberliner** (www.exberliner. com) and **Index Berlin** (www.indexberlin.de). But we can direct you to two known gallery and exhibition space hubs: Mitte's **Auguststrasse,** where Eigen & Art, Me Collectors Room, and KW (Kunst Werke) tend to host the must-sees; and **Potsdamer Strasse,** a deceptively drab thoroughfare that's attracted some major gallerists of late. Head down from Potsdamer Platz and try Circle Culture, Guido Baudach, Blain|Southern or any of the other spaces in the former Tagesspiegel newspaper printing press at number 87. With just a few exceptions, Berlin galleries are open Tuesdays through Saturdays from 11am to 6pm.

Invalidenstrasse 50-51. © **030/266424242.** www.smb.museum/en/museums-and-institutions/hamburger-bahnhof. Admission 14€ adults, 7€ students/seniors. Tues–Fri 10am–6pm (Thurs until 8pm); Sat–Sun 11am–6pm. U-/S-Bahn: Hauptbahnhof.

Schloss Charlottenburg (Charlottenburg Palace) ★★ PALACE/CASTLE   One of the grandest reminders of Berlin's Prussian past, Schloss Charlottenburg was inaugurated as a summer retreat for Sophie Charlotte, wife of King Friedrich I, in 1699 and expanded to its present form in 1790. As with so many other Berlin historical sites, what you'll visit is mostly a reconstruction following the palace's near-complete destruction in World War II, but you'll see some of the original furniture and wall décor, as well as a number of magnificent Baroque-era paintings. An exhaustive audio guide helps you explore the former living quarters of Friedrich I and Sophie Charlotte, their porcelain cabinet (replenished floor-to-ceiling with a stunning new collection), and the royal chapel. As of 2014, you can also visit the restored **New Wing,** commissioned by Friedrich II (aka Friedrich the Great) as an ornately rococo precursor to Sanssouci Palace (see p. 137). In the sprawling gardens behind the palace, you can check out the charming **Neuer Pavillon,** an Italianate summer house designed in 1825 by star architect Karl Friedrich Schinkel (not to be confused with the Schinkel Pavillon, an art gallery in Mitte) or see more 1700s-era Berlin porcelain at the former royal teahouse **Schloss Belvedere.** If you're already going to Sanssouci and you're not a Hohenzollern groupie, you may want to skip the palace tour, but the grounds are free to visit and worth a wander no matter what. Luisenplatz. www.spsg.de. © **030/320911.** Admission 12€ adults, 8€ students and ages 13 and under. Tues–Sun 10am–6pm (Nov–Mar until 5pm). U-Bahn: Richard-Wagner-Platz.

> ## Outside the Schloss . . .
>
> Across from the palace on Schlossstrasse, a set of former guard barracks now house a trio of specialist museums well worth stopping in. The **Berggruen** (10€; www.smb.museum) is a treasure trove for fans of Klee and especially late-period Picasso. The **Bröhan** (8€; www.broehan-museum.de) specializes in Art Nouveau and Art Deco. If surrealism is your thing, head for the **Scharf-Gesternberg** collection (10€; www.smb.museum).

Mitte & Eastern Berlin Attractions

Berlinische Galerie ★★★ MUSEUM   The name is misleading: this isn't a gallery, rather a 30-year-old local institution devoted to showcasing Berlin art from past and present. Its permanent collection, on the second level up a crisscrossing staircase, moves chronologically through the city's 20th-century artistic movements, from Expressionism and New Objectivity through West Berlin subculture, with a stopover in Nazi-era neoclassicism. Here's where you'll find important works from Max Beckmann, Otto Dix, and Georg Grosz, among many others. Downstairs is

ATTRACTIONS

Alte Nationalgalerie **28**
Altes Museum **25**
Berlin Wall Memorial **34**
Berlin-Höhenschönhausen
  Memorial **44**
Berlinische Galerie **15**
Bode-Museum **30**
Brandenburger Tor **6**
DDR Museum **26**
Deutsche Kinemathek
  Museum **9**
Deutsches Historisches
  Museum **24**
East Side Gallery **51**
Fernsehturm **47**
Gendarmenmarkt **18**
Jüdisches Museum **14**
Mauermuseum Haus am
  Checkpoint Charlie **17**
Memorial to Homosexuals
  Persecuted Under Nazism **7**
Memorial to the Murdered
  Jews of Europe **8**
Memorial to the Sinti and
  Roma Victims of National
  Socialism **5**
Neues Museum **27**
Neue Synagoge **32**
Neue Wache **23**
Pergamonmuseum **29**
Reichstag (Parliament) **4**
Sammlung Boros **2**
Spreepark **52**
Staatsoper Unter
  den Linden **22**
Tempelhofer Feld **12**
Tierpark **51**
Topography of Terror **11**
Treptower Park **52**

HOTELS

Amano **37**
Arcotel Velvet **33**
Baxpax Downtown Hostel
  Hotel **31**
Circus Hotel **36**
Honigmond Garden Hotel **1**
Hüttenpalast **55**
Lux 11 **40**
Mandala Hotel **10**
Michelberger Hotel **50**
Ostel Hostel **50**

RESTAURANTS

Adana Grillhaus **57**
Azzam **56**
The Bowl **49**
Briefmarken Weine **46**
Crackers/Cookies Cream **21**

Curry 36 **13**
District Mot **38**
Duc Anh **45**
Fischers Fritz **20**
Ganymed **3**
Henne **53**
Horvath **56**
Imbiss 204 **43**
Jolesch **57**
Katz Orange **35**
La Soupe Populaire **42**
Lebensmittel im Mitte **39**
Lucky Leek **41**
Max & Moritz **54**
Nobelhart & Schmutzig **16**
Schiller Burger **56**
Vau **19**
Zur Letzten Instanz **48**

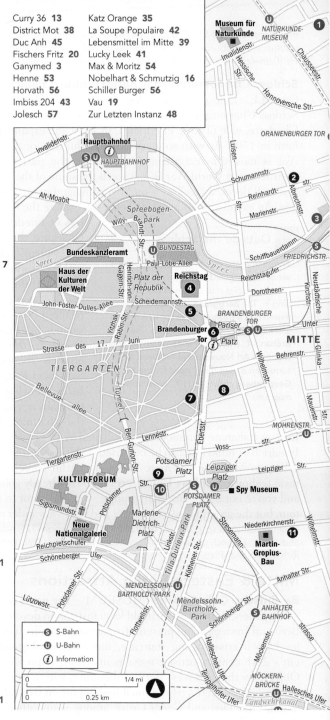

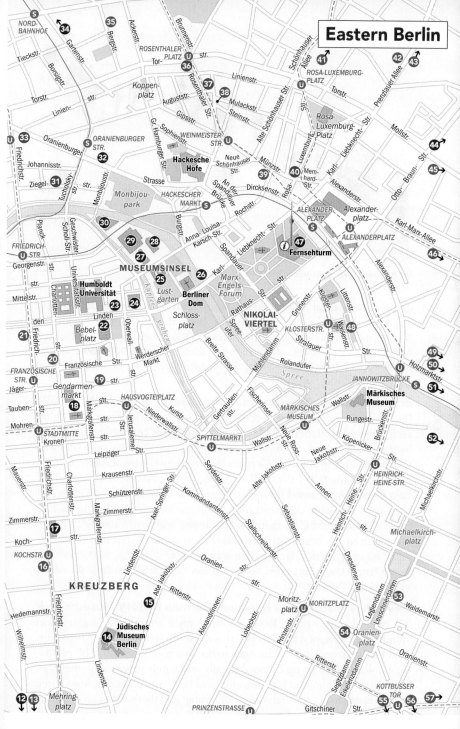

Eastern Berlin

The Berlinishe Galerie showcases Berlin artists, past and present.

devoted to special exhibitions, usually featuring modern-day artists. You'll get reduced admission if you've been to the neighboring Jewish Museum in the past 3 days (and vice versa), so save those ticket stubs. Alte Jakobstrasse 124-128. www.berlinischegalerie.de. ✆ **030/78902600.** Admission 8€ adults, 5€ students, children under 18 free; 4€ every first Monday. Weds–Mon 10am–6pm. U-Bahn: Kochstrasse/Checkpoint Charlie.

Brandenburger Tor (Brandenburg Gate) ★★★ LANDMARK

Berlin's most famous and potent symbol is this neoclassical triumphal arch topped by the famous Quadriga, a four-horse copper chariot drawn by the goddess Victoria. Since its completion in 1791 it's seen many of the major turning points of German history, from the revolutions of 1848 and 1918 to the fall of the Wall in 1989, when hundreds of thousands of East Germans streamed through the gate into West Berlin. Today it's still the site of city-wide demonstrations, celebrations (from New Year's Eve fireworks to World Cup match screenings), and many a selfie. There's not much to see besides the gate itself, but you can step into the interfaith "room of silence" in the right watchtower.
Pariser Platz at Unter den Linden. Free admission. Room of Silence daily 10am–6pm. S-Bahn: Unter den Linden.

Deutsches Historisches Museum (German History Museum) ★★

MUSEUM   Housed in Berlin's former royal armory and a glassed-in spiral annex designed by I.M. Pei, this museum spans 2000 years of German history, from the Middle Ages to the Nazis and beyond. The permanent collection is set up chronologically and barely misses a moment. In fact, there's far too much to see and read here: you'd need at least three or four hours to get through the whole thing, and that's not even counting temporary exhibitions. Our advice? Stick to just one area of interest, be

walking UNTER DEN LINDEN

Laid out in 1647 and extending about 1km (¾ mile) east from the Brandenburg Gate, **Unter den Linden** is one of Berlin's oldest and most famous boulevards. As the name ("under the lindens") hints, the street is famous for its linden trees, planted in 1647 by order of Prussian duke Friedrich Wilhelm I. Today it's lined with both trees and construction, a byproduct of the still-in-progress extension of the U5 subway line—so don't be surprised if you have to navigate a bulldozer or two while strolling past some of Berlin's greatest historical hits.

It begins on the western edge of Tiergarten with the Brandenburg Gate and **Pariser Platz,** an expansive public square and frequent demonstration site lined with embassies and the grand Adlon Hotel. A few blocks later it intersects with Friedrichstrasse, eastern Berlin's biggest shopping street, from which you can make a detour down to the beautiful square **Gendarmenmarkt.**

Just east of Friedrichstrasse stands **Humboldt University,** a renowned seat of learning whose scholars and scientists, including Albert Einstein, have won some 29 Nobel prizes. A 19th-century equestrian statue of Prussian king Frederick the Great looms in front of the university, opposite the square **Bebelplatz** and the currently-under-renovation **Staatsoper Unter den Linden** (see p. 125). Next to the university, Karl Friedrich Schinkel's 1818 **Neue Wache** (New Guardhouse), which originally served as headquarters for the King's Guard, is now dedicated to victims of war and tyranny and contains the Tomb of the Unknown Soldier, the Tomb of the Unknown Resistance Fighter, and the remains of a concentration camp victim. A powerful sculpture called *Grieving Mother* by the great German artist Käthe Kollwitz sits in the center of the otherwise bare room.

The **Zeughaus** (Armory), Berlin's largest baroque building and the first major building to be constructed on Unter den Linden in 1706, houses the exhaustive **Deutsches Historisches Museum** (p. 78). At the eastern end of Unter den Linden squats the neo-baroque **Berliner Dom** cathedral, the city's largest church. Built over the latter half of the 19th century, destroyed in World War II and reconstructed in the 1980s, the grandiose site is only really worth visiting for the Hohenzollern Crypt in the basement, where many members of the former royal family are buried. Just opposite the cathedral is **Museumsinsel** (Museum Island, see p. 86), Berlin's greatest collection of museums.

it the impactful ground-floor exhibit on World War II, where Hitler's old writing desk is displayed, or the second-floor section covering the Napoleonic era, where you'll see the emperor's bicorn hat and sword, discovered by Prussian soldiers after the Battle of Waterloo in 1815.

Unter den Linden 2. www.dhm.de. © **030/203040.** Admission 8€, students 4€, ages 17 and under free. Daily 10am–6pm. U-Bahn: Französische Strasse.

Deutsche Kinemathek Museum für Film und Fernsehen (German Film and Television Museum) ★★ MUSEUM An absolute

must for film and TV buffs, this flashy yet in-depth museum is one of the few highlights of the overbuilt, commercial hell that is the Sony Center Potsdamer Platz. It documents the entire history of German cinema, from *Dr. Caligari* to *Run Lola Run,* in artifacts, costumes, props, and rare film clips. A whole wing is devoted to Berlin and Hollywood legend Marlene Dietrich, including her treasured Chinese doll and a French-language love letter to Jean Gabin excerpted from her diary. Go on a Thursday between 4-8pm, when admission is free—you can spend the money you've saved on a screening at Arsenal, the expertly programmed arthouse theater in the basement.

Sony Center, Potsdamer Strasse 2. www.filmmuseum-berlin.de. ℰ **030/3009030.** Admission 6€ adults; 4.50€ students, seniors, and ages 15 and under. Tues–Sun 10am–6pm (Thurs until 8pm). U-/S-Bahn: Potsdamer Platz.

Fernsehturm (Television Tower) ★★ VIEW/LANDMARK   Built by the Communists back in 1969 to show the technological might of the East German republic, Berlin's iconic TV tower looms at 368m (1,208 ft.). In an effect definitely not intended by the architects, its glittering silver sphere reflects sunlight in the shape of a cross; Berliners, always quick with a nickname, called it "the Pope's revenge." Visible from just about everywhere in the city, the tower is not only a great orientation point for newcomers; it's the prime spot to take in a sweeping 360-degree view of Berlin extending some 40km (25 miles) on a clear day. You take a 40-second high-speed elevator ride up to the mid-sphere observation platform, during which a recorded voice rattles off facts and figures. Sounds like a tourist trap but it's actually rather delightful, if you can stand the lines and the prices. To avoid the former, go very early or very late, reserve a ticket online (19.50€ for peak hours), or make a reservation at the tower's revolving restaurant, which offers a selection of overpriced

Imposing Gendarmenmarkt square, restored to its former baroque glory.

BERLIN'S holocaust MEMORIALS

The most prominent Holocaust memorial in Berlin is unquestionably the **Memorial to the Murdered Jews of Europe,** near the Brandenburg Gate at Cora-Berliner-Strasse 1 (www.holocaust-mahnmal.de). But is it the most effective? American architect Peter Eisenmann's design has attracted its share of criticism since it was unveiled in 2005: it isn't very clear what 2,711 concrete slabs set on uneven ground have to do with the Holocaust. You'll likely see kids playing hide and seek between the stelae (as they're called), or adults, who should know better, taking selfies. The information center beneath it is more somber, paying tribute to the individual lives taken by the Nazi regime.

You'll find smaller, more poignant memorials scattered around the city. On Mitte's **Bebelplatz,** a glass window set on the ground reveals a view of empty bookcases, a reminder of the 20,000 books by Jewish and Communist authors burned by the Nazis on that square in 1933. At **Track 17** at the Grunewald train station, an empty platform and overgrown train tracks pay tribute to the 50,000 Jews deported from Berlin to concentration camps. Little signs around Schöneberg's **Bayerisches Viertel** (Bavarian Quarter) illustrate the 1930s race laws that, among other things, forbade Jews to join choirs, own expensive jewelry, or open veterinary practices. And like other German cities, Berlin is full of **Stolpersteine** ("stumbling stones"), brass sidewalk plaques naming Jewish residents who were deported and killed.

It's also worth remembering that Jews were not the Holocaust's only victims. In Tiergarten, across the street from the Memorial to the Murdered Jews of Europe, is the much smaller **Memorial to Homosexuals Persecuted Under Nazism.** Nearby, next to the Reichstag building, the **Memorial to Sinti and Roma Victims of National Socialism** was opened in 2012.

German basics. For cheapskates, the "Panorama Terrace" of the Park Inn next door offers a similar, though unidirectional, view for 4€.
Panoramastrasse 1A. www.tv-turm.de. ℰ **030/2423333.** Admission 13€ adults, 8€ children under 16. Mar–Oct 9am–midnight; Nov–Feb 10am–midnight. U-/S-Bahn: Alexanderplatz.

Gendarmenmarkt ★★★ PLAZA   Twin churches inspired by Rome's Piazza del Popolo flank this graceful baroque square—the most elegant architectural ensemble in Berlin. Looking at Gendarmenmarkt and the bevy of chic, upscale restaurants and hotels surrounding it today, it's hard to imagine that at the end of World War II, the whole area was a pile of bombed-out, smoldering rubble. It remained in ruins until 1977, when East Berlin finally began its reconstruction. The square was named for the Gens d'Armes regiment, which had its guardhouse and stables here from 1738 to 1782. Its centerpiece is Karl Friedrich Schinkel's imposing neoclassical Schauspielhaus, or theater (now called the **Konzerthaus am Gendarmenmarkt;** see p. 125), completed in 1821. On the north side of the square is the Französicher Dom (French Cathedral), built for the influx of French Huguenots (Protestants) who settled in Berlin after

The poignant Fallen Leaves installation in Berlin's striking Jewish Museum.

being forced to flee Catholic France in 1685, still in use as a Protestant church today. Facing it like a mirror image on the south side is the Deutscher Dom (German Cathedral), which hosts a skippable exhibition on German history.

U-Bahn: Französische Strasse.

Jüdisches Museum (Jewish Museum) ★★★ MUSEUM   Opened in 2001, Berlin's Jewish Museum is as renowned for its striking contemporary architecture as it is for its content. The building's zigzagging shape, the brainchild of American architect Daniel Liebeskind, resembles a lightning bolt or stretched-out Star of David. Inside, it's shot through with deliberately disorienting "voids," "axes," and memorial spaces like the Holocaust Tower, whose heavy iron door gives you a terrifying sense of being trapped inside. The permanent exhibition, a somewhat conventional chronological overview of Jewish history in Germany, seems almost beside the point next to poignant installations like Menashe Kadishman's Shalechet (Fallen Leaves), a triangular void filled with 10,000 screaming iron faces that clank as you cross them. Temporary exhibits tend toward the eyebrow-raising, as in 2012's bizarre *The Whole Truth*, where you could pose queries to a real, live Jewish Berliner sitting in a glass box.

Lindenstrasse 9–14. www.jmberlin.de. ✆ **030/25993300.** Admission 8€, 3€ students, children 6 and under free. Daily 10am–8pm (Mon until 10pm). U-Bahn: Hallesches Tor or Kochstrasse.

Mauermuseum Haus am Checkpoint Charlie (Berlin Wall Museum at Checkpoint Charlie) ★ MUSEUM   Once Berlin's most famous Wall crossing, Checkpoint Charlie has devolved into a beyond-tacky tourist draw where (often inaccurately) costumed guards pose for photos and stamp fake GDR passports. Next to it, this museum documents the Wall's history from its construction in 1961 to its fall in 1989, with an emphasis on East Germans' escape attempts. The layout may be disorganized, and the owner, Alexandra Hildebrandt, a controversial character—as the creator of 2004's Freedom Memorial, a tribute to Wall victims consisting of a field of crosses by Checkpoint Charlie, she was accused of insensitivity and historical inaccuracy. But the photographs, newspaper clippings, and attempted escape devices (chairlifts, false passports, hot-air balloons, even a mini-sub) may give you an idea of how much the Wall continues to mean to some Berliners.

Friedrichstrasse 43–45. www.mauermuseum.de. © **030/2537250.** Admission 13€ adults, 9.50€ students, children 16 and under free. Daily 9am–10pm. U-Bahn: Kochstrasse or Stadtmitte.

Neue Synagogue (New Synagogue) ★ MUSEUM/HISTORICAL SITE   In 1866, an enormous domed synagogue opened on Oranienburger Strasse to accommodate Berlin's then-thriving Jewish community. Less than a century later, that community was gone, and so was the building: damaged during the "Kristallnacht" pogroms of 1938, confiscated by the Nazis in 1940, and bombed into near-complete oblivion by the Allies in 1945. Gradually, both began to make a comeback. The synagogue, originally designed by renowned architect Eduard Knoblauch in eastern Moorish style, was reconstructed in the early 1990s and now holds Conservative-style services for a small congregation. It also hosts an exhibition dedicated to the history of the synagogue and Berlin Jewish life. You'll have to pass armed guards and a security checkpoint to get in, one of many reminders that Germany takes its past mistakes very seriously.

Oranienburger Strasse 28-30. www.centrumjudaicum.de. © **030/88028300.** Museum admission 5€ adults, 4€ students; dome admission 3€ adults, 2.50€ students. Children under 6 free. Apr–Sept Mon–Thurs 10am–6pm, Fri 10am–6pm, Sat 10am–7pm; Oct–Mar Mon–Thurs 10am–6pm, Fri 10am–3pm, Sat 10am–6pm. Dome open Apr–Sept only. U-Bahn: Oranienburger Tor.

Reichstag (Parliament) ★★★ HISTORIC SITE   It's the seat of the German government; it offers a panoramic view of Berlin and it's free of charge to visit: no wonder the Reichstag building is one of the city's most popular attractions. Built in a pompous High Renaissance style between 1884 and 1894, it housed Germany's parliament until 1933, when it was partially destroyed by arson. (It was never proven that the Nazis were

FEELING ostalgic?

Yes, the GDR was a totalitarian surveillance state marked by poverty and paranoia... but hey, wasn't the Trabant a cute car? The longer it's been since the fall of the Wall, the rosier Berliners' view of the old East German regime becomes, a phenomenon called "Ostalgia" (with "Ost" meaning "east"). As a responsible tourist, it's your job to separate the kitsch from the reality.

Case in point: if you believe the (admittedly enjoyable) hands-on exhibits at the **DDR Museum** ★★ (Karl-Lieb-knecht-Strasse 1; www.ddr-museum.de; 𝄢 **030/847123731,** admission 7€ adults, 5€ students), East Germany was nothing but nudism, Spreewald pickles, and camping trips with the Freie Deutsche Jugend socialist youth movement. Opened in 2006, the museum takes you through everyday life in the GDR in 17 themed rooms, laid out like a prefab housing estate. You can answer the phone in the Soviet-era living room, rummage through closets, or rev a Tra-bant's engine. The tone is jokey and ironic throughout, even when it comes to Stasi bugging: put on headphones and listen in on your fellow museumgoers! The museum is open daily 10am to 8pm (U-/S-Bahn: Alexander-Platz).

For a bleaker look at East German existence, you'll have to head further east. First to Lichtenberg, where the old headquarters of East Berlin's state security force have been turned into the **Stasi Museum** ★★ (Ruschestrasse 103; www.stasimuseum.de; 𝄢 **030/5536854,** admission 6€ adults, 4€ students). You'll see the preserved offices of Stasi head Erich Mielke and learn how the GDR government controlled its citizens via force, threats, and comprehensive surveillance. The full impact of their system can be felt at the **Berlin-Höhenschönhausen Memorial** ★★ in the far northeast of the city (Genslerstrasse 66; www.stiftung-hsh.de; admission 6€ adults, 3€ students). A former Stasi prison and interrogation center in use from 1951 until reunification, it's where East German citizens—including many who'd done nothing wrong whatsoever—were subjected to violence, torture, and psychological intimidation. Now it offers tours in English twice a day, at 11:30am and 2:30pm, led by either a historian or a former detainee. Listen to their chilling firsthand account, and then see if you still feel like getting behind the wheel of a "Trabi."

Daily life in the former East Germany is depicted at the DDR Museum.

Ai Weiwei sculpture at the stunning Sammlung Boros.

behind the fire, but it certainly gave them an opportunity to blame the Communists and seize power.) The building received further damage from Allied bombs during World War II and stood vacant until after reunification, when the Parliament moved back to Berlin from Bonn. In the 1990s, it was crowned with a striking new glass dome designed by English architect Sir Norman Foster, and that's where you'll go on your visit. If you don't want to spend hours lining up at the visitor's center, book an appointment online a few days beforehand. After a security and ID check, you'll take an elevator up to the dome. As you walk up its spiraling ramp, a sweeping vista of Berlin opens out before you, optionally narrated by an audio guide. There's also an outdoor observation area and a rooftop café, Käfer's Restaurant Dachgarten (book a table well in advance). History and politics junkies might want to book a 90-minute tour of the whole building, which gives you a closer look at the parliament chambers and hallways lined with graffiti left behind by Soviet soldiers.

Platz der Republik 1. www.bundestag.de. ✆ **030/2270.** Free admission. Tours 11:30 when Parliament is not in session. S-Bahn: Unter den Linden.

Sammlung Boros ★★★ ART COLLECTION   In 2003, art collectors Christian and Karen Boros purchased a gargantuan World War II air-raid shelter in Mitte and turned it into one of the world's most jaw-dropping exhibition spaces, filling its 3000 square meters (over 32,000 square feet) with installations by a who's who of international artists. The second edition of the "Bunker" opened in 2012 and features the likes of Olafur Eliasson, Alicia Kwade, and Ai Weiwei. Even if you don't recognize any of these names, the sheer novelty of seeing contemporary art in such an unusual location should land this place near the top of your Berlin list. Ah, but there's a catch: you can only view the collection on a group tour (in English or German), which you have to book on their website. Last we checked, the closest appointment was about two months out. But plan ahead and you'll be richly rewarded.

Reinhardstrasse 20. www.sammlung-boros.de. ✆ **030/240833300.** Thurs 3pm–8pm, Fri–Sun 10am–8pm. 12€ adults; 6€ students and seniors. U-Bahn: Oranienburger Tor.

The Topgraphy of Terror documents the dark history of the Nazi regime.

Topography of Terror ★★ MEMORIAL Nestled next to a pre-served stretch of Berlin Wall just off Potsdamer Platz lies the old foundation of Hitler's SS and Gestapo headquarters, where the Nazi regime orchestrated the genocide of European Jews, Sinti and Roma, homosexuals, and political opponents. The ruin is now a site of "remembrance and learning," with a concrete and glass information center that documents the history of National Socialism and its crimes against humanity. Niederkirchnerstrasse 8. ℂ **030/254509950.** Free admission. May–Sept daily 10am–8pm; Oct–Apr daily 10am–6pm. U-Bahn: Potsdamer Platz.

Museumsinsel (Museum Island)

Five cultural institutions in the middle of the River Spree form the oldest, most impressive museum complex in Berlin. Built between 1830 and 1930, Museum Island was masterminded by King Friedrich Wilhelm IV both as a public showcase of the royal family's collections and a "sanctuary of art and science." Important note: Since its designation as a UNESCO site in 1999, Museum Island has been undergoing near-constant renovation, and unfortunately, it's the Pergamon Museum's turn right now. Its eponymous altar, arguably the island's star attraction, is closed until 2019.

For multi-museum passes, see "Money-Saving Tourist Deals," p. 67.

Alte Nationalgalerie ★★ MUSEUM Perched high on its base and looking like an ancient Roman temple, Berlin's oldest museum is known for its collection of 19th-century Impressionists, including Pissarro,

REMEMBERING THE berlin wall

It used to be nearly 100 miles long, snaking around the entirety of Allied West Berlin. Now the Berlin Wall has all but vanished. Its longest stretch remains the **East Side Gallery ★★★** (U-Bahn: Warschauer Strasse). Just after reunification in 1990, a 1.3km (0.8-mile) stretch of Wall was painted segment by segment by over 100 international artists including Thierry Noir, Jim Avignon, and Dmitri Vrubel. The latter's depiction of Brezhnev and Honecker passionately kissing has become famous worldwide, but the version you'll see isn't the original: Vrubel repainted it in the late 2000s, during the city's controversial restoration of the gallery's graffiti- and weather-worn sections. Four years later, a real-estate developer removed two sections and began constructing an incongruous luxury apartment building behind the old Wall, sparking protests (and a visit from David Hasselhoff).

While definitely a must-visit, the gallery doesn't give much of an accurate picture of what the Wall was actually like. For that, you've got to see the government's **Berlin Wall Memorial/Berliner Mauer Dokumentationszentrum ★★★** (Bernauer Strasse 111; www.berliner-mauer-dokumentationszentrum.de; Tues–Sat 10am–6pm (Nov–Mar to 5pm); free admission; U-Bahn: Bernauer Strasse). This 230-ft.-long (70m) reconstructed stretch of the Wall stands at Bernauer Strasse and Ackerstrasse, complete with border control towers and "death strip." There's also a documentation center with photos of the area pre-1989 and eyewitness testimonies of what it was like when the Wall stood, and the Chapel of Reconciliation (Kapelle der Versöhnung), a contemporary building on the site of a church that was blown up in 1985 in order to widen the border strip.

Cezanne, Delacroix, Degas, and Van Gogh. Not to mention the Germans: the Romantic, Classical and Modernist movements in 19th-century German art are well represented here, and you'll see works by Adolph von Menzel, Caspar David Friedrich, and many more, plus a few Expressionists to boot.

Bodestrasse 1–3, Museumsinsel. www.smb.museum.de. ✆ **030/20905577.** Admission 10€ adults, 5€ students, children 16 and under free. Tues–Sun 10am–6pm (Thurs until 10pm). S-Bahn: Hackescher Markt.

Altes Museum ★★★ MUSEUM   Renowned Prussian architect Karl Friedrich Schinkel designed this structure, which resembles a Greek Corinthian temple, in 1822. On its main floor is the Antikensammlung (Museum of Antiquities), a vast repository of classical relics including Greek sculptures, jewelry and silverware, and a world-renowned collection of Etruscan and Roman art. The upper floor showcases treasures from late-Hellenistic cremation urns and sarcophagi to mosaics, mummy portraits, and more. A small side gallery is devoted to ancient erotic art and artifacts.

Am Lustgarten, Museumsinsel. www.smb.museum. ✆ **030/20905577.** Admission 10€ adults, 5€ students, children 16 and under free. Daily 10am–6pm (Thurs until 10pm). S-Bahn: Hackescher Markt.

Bode Museum ★★ MUSEUM   The Bode, anchoring the north end of Museum Island, reopened its doors in 2006 after undergoing a massive renovation that turned a rather dark and dull building into a museum showplace. Here you'll find a rich collection of German, French, Dutch, and Italian sculpture (marble, wood, bronze) from the Gothic to the Neoclassical periods. The museum also contains galleries with late-antique and Byzantine works and a major coin collection. The audio guide will help you navigate; give yourself at least a full hour to graze the highlights.

Monbijoubrücke, Bodestrasse 1–3, Museumsinsel. www.smb.museum. © **030/ 20905577.** Admission 12€ adults, 6€ students and children. Tues–Sun 10am–6pm (Thurs until 8pm). U-Bahn: Friedrichstrasse.

Neues Museum ★★★ MUSEUM   There's nothing new about the "New Museum," a Neoclassical building built between 1843 and 1855, except that it's undergone a complete renovation/rebuilding by English architect David Chipperfield and reopened to great acclaim in 2009 after being closed for over 60 years. Most of the building was destroyed in World War II, but portions of its interior survived and were incorporated into Chipperfield's much-praised design. Make a beeline for the glorious Egyptian collection, which includes papyruses, mummy masks, hieroglyphics, and statuary, not to mention Berlin's most famous antiquity, the entrancing and enigmatic bust of Queen Nefertiti (1350 B.C.), who holds crowds spellbound in her own gallery. Meanwhile, the upstairs Museum for Prehistory and Early History holds highlights such as the Neanderthal skull from Le Moustier, Heinrich Schliemann's collection of Trojan antiquities, and the golden mask of Agamemnon.

Bodestrasse, Museumsinsel. www.neues-museum.de. © **030/266424242.** Admission 12€ adults, 6€ students and children. Daily 10am–6pm (Thurs until 8pm). S-Bahn: Hackescher Markt.

Pergamon Museum ★★★ MUSEUM   Scheduled to reopen to the public in 2019, Pergamon's eponymous altar is a glorious, breathtaking sight to behold. Part of the enormous Temple of Zeus and Athena, dating from 180 to 160 B.C., it was discovered in 1876 in western Turkey and is considered one of the Seven Wonders of the Ancient World. Until the altar and its adjoining hall of Greek antiquities reopens, you'll have to settle for the ornate two-storied Market Gate of Miletus, a Roman building facade from the time of Emperor Marcus Aurelius (around A.D. 165) and the Near East Museum in the museum's south wing, which contains one of the world's largest collections of antiquities from ancient Babylonia, Persia, and Assyria. It's a shame the museum hasn't reduced prices after closing off its main draw, but if you have a day pass or Museum Pass anyway, you might as well poke your head in.

Am Kupfergraben 5, Museumsinsel. www.smb.spk-berlin.de. © **030/20905577.** Admission 12€ adults, 6€ students, children 16 and under free. Daily 10am–6pm (Thurs until 8pm). U-Bahn/S-Bahn: Friedrichstrasse.

Organized Tours

WALKING TOURS   For an excellent introduction to Berlin and its history, try one of the themed walking tours offered by **Berlin Walks** (www.berlinwalks.de; ✆ **030/3019194**). "Discover Berlin" is a four-hour introductory tour; "Infamous Third Reich Sites" focuses on former Nazi buildings in central Berlin; "Jewish Life in Berlin" takes you through the prewar Jewish community. Reservations are unnecessary—simply meet the guide at the appointed starting point, listed on the website. Tours (in English) cost 12€ for adults, 10€ for 14- to 25-year-olds. If you're feeling more economical, international guide company **Sandeman's** (www.newberlintours.com; ✆ **030/51050030**) offers a by-donation 2.5-hour distillation of the basics at 10am, 11am and 2pm daily (just look for the red shirts in front of the Brandenburg Gate).

In terms of seeing sights you can't see on your own, a bunker tour from nonprofit historical society **Berliner Unterwelten** ("Berlin Underground"; www.berliner-unterwelten.de) gives you ultimate tourist bragging rights. Knowledgeable, enthusiastic guides grant you both access to some thrilling underground time capsules and fascinating insights into World War II and the Cold War. Tours cost 11€ to 14€, generally leave from the Gesundbrunnen train station and must be booked the same day.

BIKE TOURS   You can cover loads of sightseeing ground on two wheels—as long as you stay out of the way of irate locals who're just trying to bike to work. Your best value among many, many options is the **Fat Tire** company (berlin.fattirebiketours.com; ✆ **030/24047991**), which offers a pretty comprehensive 4.5-hour tour for 26€, including bike rental, starting from the TV Tower at Alexanderplatz.

BUS TOURS   Colorful buses from **BEX Sightseeing**, Kurfürstendamm 216 (www.bex.de; ✆ **030/8804190**), travel along hop-on, hop-off routes through Berlin's tourist arteries, but at 15€-20€ for what's quite an impersonal experience, you're better off just taking a public bus (100 or 200, see p. 68) and reading about the sites you pass, or taking the U-Bahn to places you'd like to explore on foot.

BOAT TOURS   Berlin may be landlocked, but it's full of water nonetheless, and cruising the Spree, the Havel, or the canals opens up a different side of the city. The best-known boat operator is **Stern und Kreisschiffahrt,** stationed at Pushkinallee 15 (www.sternundkreis.de; ✆ **030/5363600**). Try their "Historische Stadtrundfahrt" (Historic City Tour), a 1-hour ride on the Spree, offered daily from March through December. Check their website for departure times and prices. If you feel like doing the paddling yourself, **Kayak Berlin Tours** (www.kajak berlintours.de, ✆ **030/99548018,** stationed at Carl-Herz-Ufer 7) does 2- to 3-hour jaunts through the Spree and Landwehrkanal from April through October.

BERLIN'S abandonment ISSUES

In the unstable post-reunification era, a great number of factories, offices, train stations, and hospitals in Berlin were fenced off and left to rot, especially in the former East. Some were eventually demolished, others were converted into clubs (rule number one of nightlife here: there is no building you can't play techno in), but a few just stayed abandoned, becoming targets for street artists, derelict teens, and adventurous "urban explorers." Over the past few years, higher powers have been taking an interest in these fascinating sites, and now Berlin's most spectacular ruins face an uncertain fate. So uncertain, in fact, that we can't tell you with any confidence whether you'll legally be able to visit Spreepark or Teufelsberg (see below) right now—check online for the latest news, and read Ciaran Fahey's excellent blog *Abandoned Berlin* (www.abandonedberlin.com) for more ideas and updates.

Parks & Outdoor Sites

Spreepark ★★ ABANDONED SITE   A GDR-era amusement park in the southeastern Plänterwald forest, Spreepark is as famous for its look (crumbling roller coasters, overturned dinosaur statues, a creaky Ferris wheel that turns when the wind blows) as for its backstory (unable to sustain the park financially, owner Norbert Witte moved to Peru and eventually turned to drug smuggling). It attracted hundreds of camera-toting trespassers from its abandonment in 2002 until its partial destruction by arson in 2014, which led to higher fences and more security guards. The next year, the park was purchased by government property company Grün Berlin, which plans to open it to the public as early as 2016—but at time of writing, nobody knows whether or not its rusted rides, deemed a safety hazard, will remain.
Kiehnwerderallee 1-3. www.berliner-spreepark.de. S-Bahn: Plänterwald.

Teufelsberg ★★ ABANDONED SITE   You can see it from certain angles in central Berlin: a curious-looking (some might say phallic) three-domed structure perched atop a hill in far-off Grunewald. Make a few inquiries and you'll learn the hill is artificial, made from post-bombing rubble piled up after World War II, and the building is a former NSA listening station, deserted since 1999. Until fairly recently, you could simply slip past a poorly maintained fence to explore the tattered white domes through which Americans once listened in on the Soviet goings-on in East Germany. Now Teufelsberg is in the hands of private investors, who've implemented much heavier security. At the moment, the only way to visit is via a tour, available in German or English. But it's worth the 7€ to 15€ for access to this one-of-a-kind place, which also happens to offer some dazzling specimens of street art and the best panoramic view of Berlin this side of the TV Tower. Budget about 30

Tempelhof airport has been transformed into Berlin's largest public park.

minutes to get here from the Grunewald station, and another hour and a half for walking around.

Teufelsseechaussee 10. Tours at entrance at noon (7€) or bookable through Original Berlin Tours (15€, see www.originalberlintours.com). S-Bahn: Grunewald.

Tempelhofer Feld (Tempelhof Field) ★★★ PARK

When Tempelhof Airport closed in 2008 after 82 years of operation, Berlin did what few other cities would: nothing. The airfield, once the site of the "Operation Vittles" airlift that saved lives during the 1949 Soviet blockade, turned into an enormous public park, complete with grilling areas, allotment gardens, and soccer fields. What seemed like a stopgap turned permanent in 2014, when the city passed a citizen's referendum blocking any development in the entire four-hectare (2-sq.-mile) area. We'll see how long that lasts, but for now, it's evidence that the free-spirited, antiestablishment Berlin of days gone by hasn't quite died out yet. On warm weekends you'll find just about everyone there: athletic types biking, roller skating, skateboarding, skate-surfing, etc., on the disused runways; layabouts carrying beer and picnic necessities from the shops and cafés that line the cobblestoned streets by the Herrfurthstrasse entrance. The kilometer-long terminal building, a relic of Hitler and Albert Speer's plans to turn Berlin into "World Capital Germania," still looms on the outskirts of the field. Variously used for conventions, fashion shows and music festivals, it's currently serving as an emergency shelter for the city's influx of Middle Eastern refugees.

Tempelhofer Feld. Bounded by Neukölln to the east, Kreuzberg to the north, Schöneberg to the west and Tempelhof to the south. Enter at the end of Herrfurthstrasse. U-Bahn: Boddinstrasse.

Tiergarten ★★★ PARK/GARDEN Once a hunting ground for the Prussian royal family, the sprawling Tiergarten is now Berlin's second-largest urban park. While it might lack the square mileage of Tempelhof (see above), it's a sight more pleasant to stroll through, with plentiful trees, canals, and meandering paths laid out by Prussian landscape architect Peter Josef Lenné in the early 19th century. Despite the name (literally, "animal park"), the only animals here worth noting are sequestered away in the Zoologischer Garten **(Berlin Zoo)** in the park's southwestern corner...well, unless you count the trouser snakes in the infamous nude sunbathing area. Above it all glitters *Golden Else,* the angel of victory who tops Berlin's iconic **Sieggessäule** (Victory Column). Erected in 1873 to commemorate Prussia winning the Prussian-Danish War, it was moved to its current spot in the Grosser Stern traffic circle by the Nazis as part of the "World Capital Germania" master plan. Should you feel like indulging your inner Bruno Ganz in *Wings of Desire,* you can ascend to the top of the column via a 290-stair spiral staircase for 3€ (2.50€ students and children). Winded? Head to the perpetually packed beer garden/boathouse **Café am Neuen See,** by the lake in the middle of the park, for a restorative drink and sausage (or curling, in winter).

"Golden Else," the angel atop the Tiergarten's Victory Column.

Tiergarten Park. Bounded on the west by Bahnhof Zoo and the Europa Center, on the east by Berlin-Mitte, the Brandenburg Gate, and Potsdamer Platz. U-Bahn: Zoologischer Garten or Hansaplatz. S-Bahn: Tiergarten or Bellevue.

Treptower Park/Soviet Memorial ★ PARK Granted, Soviet memorials are not known for their subtlety. But this one, built to commemorate the Russians who died in 1945's Battle of Berlin, goes above and beyond. A 12-meter (39-foot) statue of a noble Soviet soldier holds a German child in one arm; with the other, he holds an enormous sword

BERLIN BY water

The **Spree River** runs east-west through the whole of the city, from Jonathan Borofsky's 100-foot *Molecule Man* sculpture in Treptow past the East Side Gallery, Museum Island, and the Reichstag all the way to Schloss Charlottenburg. The stretch between Friedrichshain and Mitte once formed the border between East and West; it's estimated that at least 20 East Berliners drowned trying to cross. Now, the ex-death strip along the northern shore is home to the contentious Mediaspree development, a cluster of media-related corporate HQs including the gigantic Mercedes-Benz Arena, as well as some comparatively scrappy "beach bars" and clubs that elbowed their way in when the area was still a no-man's-land. There's been a much-publicized proposal to create a public swimming area where the river passes Museum Island; we very much doubt that's come to pass by now, but check flussbad-berlin.de for updates.

Parallel to the Spree is the narrow **Landwehr Canal,** an artificial waterway put there in the Prussian days by Tiergarten landscape architect Peter Joseph Lenné. In the west, a memorial on the Lichtensteinbrücke commemorates murdered socialist revolutionary Rosa Luxemburg, whose body was thrown into the canal in January 1919. Towards the east, in Kreuzberg and Neukölln, Berliners flock to the canal's shores to listen to buskers at the Turkish market (see p. 116), people-watch at the pedestrian-only Admiralbrücke bridge, or paddle inflatable rafts.

Berlin is surrounded by countless lakes, and more so than swimming pools, these are the number-one destination when the mercury rises. To the southwest of the city, **Wannsee** is the people's favorite, home to Europe's longest inland beach complete with lounge chairs, beach volleyball courts, and boat rental. Closer to the center, a short walk from the end of the U3 U-Bahn line, **Krumme Lanke** has only a cursory "beach" but boasts clear, deep water...and all the naked Germans you could ever hope to lay eyes on. Beyond that, just about every Berliner has a "secret" lake that they refuse to disclose to tourists for fear of spoiling its pristine water and uncrowded shores—so if it's unbearably hot, try and get a local tipsy enough to let his or her guard down.

crushing a swastika. He towers over a vast field lined with stone reliefs bearing quotes from Stalin. It all serves as a jarring "in your face" both to the Germans and to the USSR's American former allies, and is worth venturing a little off the beaten path for. The rest of Treptower Park, which stretches alongside the Spree River, is pleasant enough for a summer stroll; there's a pond, a rose garden and a few cafés.
Puschkinallee. S-Bahn: Treptower Park.

Especially for Kids

Berlin Zoo/Tierpark ★★ ZOO Berlin's divided days left it with two of everything... including, like Noah's Ark, two of every animal. Of the city's pair of zoos, the Berlin Zoo is the most accessible, nestled right next to Tiergarten and the Zoologischer Garten station. It's also the most exotic, boasting one of the world's widest varieties of animal species, from Asian elephants to capybaras. But a visit to the Tierpark (or "Ost Zoo") in far-off Friedrichsfelde might better assuage your conscience. Built on the site of a royal estate expropriated by the Soviets, it's over 10 times the size of the Zoo in the west but houses less than half as many animals, giving its bears, bison, and manatees room to spread out. Kids (and adults) can navigate its 400 acres with the help of an electric mini-train.

Berlin Zoo: Hardenbergplatz 8. www.zoo-berlin.de. © **030/254010.** Admission 14.50€ adults, 10€ students, 7.50€ children under 16. Daily 9am–5pm. S-/U-Bahn: Zoologischer Garten. Tierpark: Elfriede-Tygör-Strasse 6. www.tierpark-berlin.de. © 030/515310. Apr–Sept daily 9am–6:30pm. Mar and Oct 9am–6pm, Nov–Feb 9am–4:30pm. U-Bahn: Tierpark.

Gemäldegalerie (Painting Gallery) ★★★ MUSEUM
If the wealth of medieval and Renaissance art in Berlin's largest painting gallery doesn't impress your tykes, take them to the "Kinder-Reich," where a series of hands-on activities will help them learn how the Dutch masters created their masterpieces. (See p. 71.)

Naturkundemuseum (Natural History Museum) ★ MUSEUM
After all the Hitler and Stasi talk, sometimes one just wants to go see a good old-fashioned prehistoric lizard. And in fact, Berlin is home to Europe's best-preserved T-Rex skeleton, a behemoth named Tristan discovered in Montana, purchased by a wealthy Dane, and bequeathed to the Natural History Museum in 2015. Tristan's shiny black remains, accompanied by info on how he may have lived and died, are an impressive sight. Less so the rest of the museum, which is of the outdated "taxidermied animals and things in jars" variety.

Invalidenstrasse 43. www.naturkundemuseum.berlin. © **030/20938591.** Admission 8€ adults, 5€ students and children. Tues–Fri 9:30am–6pm, Sat–Sun 10am–6pm. U-Bahn: Naturkundemuseum.

Spy Museum ★ MUSEUM
Capitalizing on Berlin's long history as a "spy capital," this pricey Potsdamer Platz museum presents a sugar-coated, interactive take on the past and future of espionage from Julius Caesar to Julian Assange, with a long stopover in the paranoid Cold War days. Yes, the era's dark side is mostly glossed over in favor of the GDR's most ridiculous spying equipment (bugged bras?) and a whole room of James Bond paraphernalia, but those looking for verisimilitude should go to the Stasi Museum (p. 84). In the meantime, budding Mata Haris or Edward Snowdens can test their mettle by "hacking" Facebook or hurtling through a corridor filled with lasers.

Leipziger Platz 9. www.spymuseumberlin.com. © **030/20620354.** Admission 18€ adults, 14€ students and children. Daily 10am–8pm. S-/U-Bahn: Potsdamer Platz.

WHERE TO STAY IN BERLIN

Finding a hotel room in Berlin is easy: space is plentiful, prices are relatively low, and the city's excellent public transit system means you're not far from the big attractions no matter where you stay. But you'll save precious time and money by booking a hotel online before you arrive. The prices listed in this chapter are undiscounted rack rates; unless a big event is happening in town, you'll likely be able to get a room for less. As of 2014, the bill for your room might also include an added "City Tax" of around five percent. As very few hotels in central Berlin offer free parking, expect to pay about 12€ to 20€ per night to park on site or in an adjacent public lot or garage; you may prefer to park in one of the less expensive lots around the city's perimeter (see p. 68).

If you arrive without a reservation, you can go to the **BERLIN infostore** at Hauptbahnhof, Tegel Airport, or Kranzler Eck (for locations see p. 62), where the staff will help you find a hotel room in your price range. You can also book hotels by calling the Berlin tourist authority at © **030/250025** or by going online at www.visitberlin.de.

Hotels in Western Berlin
EXPENSIVE

Bleibtreu Hotel ★★   For a chic, contemporary place to stay near the Ku'Damm, head to this trend-conscious boutique hotel that emphasizes healthy comfort: no chemicals are used for cleaning, and the natural fabrics used are hypoallergenic. The rooms aren't particularly large, but they're artfully designed and furnished with clear, simple shapes, bright splashes of color, and original artwork. You can customize your room lighting by remote control and adjust the window shades with the touch of a button. One especially nice feature is the free minibar in every room. At the on-site Wellness Center, you can take a pore-cleansing sauna in the herbal steam bath or book a special reflexology, acupuncture, or

---

Rental Apartments

In theory, the city of Berlin is cracking down on vacation rentals, with 2014's formidable-sounding "Zweckentfremdungsverbot" law discouraging short-term subletting. In actuality, that law is nearly impossible to enforce and AirBnBs are plentiful, going for as low as 30€ per night for an entire apartment. For more options, check **oh-berlin.com**, **roomorama.com**, and **9flats.com**, among others. If you're staying for a week or longer, you may be able to find an inexpensive sublet on the longer-term rental site **wg-gesucht.de**. Finally, if you want to stay with a local for free and don't mind a bit of potential squalor, there are plenty of trustworthy Berlin hosts signed up on **couchsurfing.com**.

A penthouse suite at Das Stue.

beauty treatment. There are usually special weekend offers available on the hotel's website.

Bleibtreustrasse 31. www.bleibtreu.com. © **030/884740.** 60 units. 120€–210€ double. Buffet breakfast 19€. **Amenities:** Restaurant; bar; exercise room; room service; sauna; bike rental (10€/day); free Wi-Fi. U-Bahn: Uhlandstrasse.

Das Stue ★★★ Enter the stately former Danish embassy tucked next to the Berlin Zoo, and the first thing you'll see is the gaping mouth of a crocodile head in front of a grand, museum-like staircase. It's that combination of playfulness and elegance that the design hotel Das Stue strives for and—against the odds—totally pulls off. Rooms are modern but not sterile, with impossibly comfortable beds, touch-screen lighting and temperature controls, and clever Scandinavian-style hidden storage. Roam around the building and you'll find a spa with a pool and futuristic Finnish sauna, and sunlit reading nooks equipped with Taschen books on each landing of the staircase. Mediterranean avant-garde restaurant Cinco provides the by-now-requisite Michelin-starred eats; the breakfast buffet also has a Spanish bent, with Iberico ham topping your eggs Benedict. The hotel's a bit removed from public transit and there's not much to see or do in this quiet corner of Tiergarten, but the views over the zoo are lovely—and if you can afford to stay here, you're probably a taxi type of person anyway.

Drakestrasse 1. www.das-stue.com. ☎ **030/3117220.** 78 units. 210€–260€ double. Buffet breakfast 35€. **Amenities:** Restaurants; bar; pool and spa; exercise room; room service; minibar; iMac computers; bike rental; Wi-Fi (free). U-Bahn: Zoologischer Garten.

MODERATE

25Hours Bikini Berlin ★★ Sandwiched between the Zoo and the Kaiser Wilhelm Memorial Church, this new hotel from the 25Hours group is one of several recent attempts to inject some youthful vigor into Berlin's stodgy west side. Thus the trendy "urban jungle" design, the hammocks and iPhone docks in the rooms, and customizable "do not disturb" door hangers with cheeky messages like "Your turn to clean, bro." Trying too hard? Maybe, but the beds and rain shower provide comfort to go with the cool, and free bike rental is a nice touch. The rooftop Monkey Bar and Israeli-influenced Neni restaurant offer decent food and drinks along with excellent views over the city; the latter's where the breakfast buffet, a substantial but overpriced spread, can be accessed for an extra 19€. You can also hang out in the airy third-floor lobby and reception area, which boasts a bakery, bookstore, vinyl record listening nook, and more hammocks.
Budapester Strasse 40. www.25hours-hotels.com/de/bikini. ☎ **030/568373695.** 149 units. 115€–175€ double. Buffet breakfast 19€. **Amenities:** Restaurant; bar; exercise room; room service; sauna; free bike and BMW Mini rental; Wi-Fi (free). S-/U-Bahn: Zoologischer Garten.

Arco Hotel ★ A four-story, turn-of-the-century building on a quiet street near the Ku'Damm houses this comfortable small hotel. Rooms are reasonably large and have high, light-giving windows and modern furniture. The private bathrooms (showers, no tubs) are on the diminutive side, however. One of the nicest features here is the airy breakfast room, which looks out on a courtyard garden (you can eat outside in warm weather). The English-speaking staff, too, is friendly and helpful.
Geisbergstrasse 30. www.arco-hotel.de. ☎ **030/2351480.** 23 units. 67€–117€ double. Breakfast included. **Amenities:** Wi-Fi (free). U-Bahn: Wittenbergplatz.

Hotel Artemisia ★★ Located on the top floors of a large apartment building, Artemisia—a onetime women-only hotel recently gone co-ed—is comfortable and refreshingly free of frou-frou. The rooms are large, light, quiet, and simply furnished but still have a warm ambience heightened by splashes of color. Ten of the 12 rooms have toilets and small showers. You can save money by renting a dorm bed or one of the two rooms that share a toilet and shower. A private rooftop terrace with views over Berlin becomes a gathering spot on warm afternoons and evenings.
Brandenburgische Strasse 18. www.frauenhotel-berlin.de. ☎ **030/8738905.** 12 units. 100€–120€ double. Breakfast included. **Amenities:** Bike rentals (12€/day), Wi-Fi (free). U-Bahn: Konstanzer Strasse.

INEXPENSIVE

Hotel Domus ★★   Set in an unusually pretty section of Wilmersdorf, down the street from St. Ludwig's Church and within walking distance of the Ku'Damm, this modern, frill-free, and newly renovated hotel has a calm, appealing simplicity. The rooms, which face an inner courtyard or the street, are comfortable and quiet (thanks to soundproof windows) and tastefully decorated with contemporary furniture, while the bathrooms are unusually large and have either a shower or a tub.

Uhlandstrasse 49. www.hotel-domus-berlin.de. ℂ **030/318797270.** 73 units. 58€–88€ double. Breakfast included. **Amenities:** Bar; Wi-Fi (free, in lobby only). U-Bahn: Hohenzollernplatz or Spichernstrasse.

Hotel-Pension Elegia ★   This modest, well-run pension in Charlottenburg is one of the best deals in western Berlin, and its location couldn't be more convenient to the cafe-restaurant-shopping streets around Savignyplatz and the Ku'Damm. The 12 rooms, all on the second floor of a turn-of-the-century apartment building (no elevator), are simple and clean with contemporary furniture, wooden floors and stucco ceilings. Three street-facing rooms have balconies; the rooms facing the courtyard can be a bit dark, but they're very quiet. There's also a two-bedroom apartment. Share a bathroom and you'll save even more. Breakfast is not offered here, but there are lots of cafes and bakeries in the area.

Niebuhrstrasse 74. www.hotel-pension-elegia.de. ℂ **030/49807220.** 12 units. 39€–59€ double. S-Bahn: Savignyplatz. **Amenities:** Free Wi-Fi.

Hotel-Pension Funk ★   The former home of silent-movie star Asta Nielsen doesn't seem to have changed much in the past 90 years or so. Its rooms and public spaces are old-fashioned and comfortable, replete with original Art Nouveau windows, plasterwork ceilings, and the kind of sturdy, made-to-last furnishings that once defined German comfort and elegance. It also boasts a top location off Ku'Damm. Save money by booking a room with shared bathroom.

Fasanenstrasse 69. www.hotel-pensionfunk.de. ℂ **030/8827193.** 14 units. 52€–129€ double. Breakfast included. U-Bahn: Kurfürstendamm or Uhlandstrasse.

Pension Nürnberger Eck ★   An atmospheric B&B on the second floor of a building near the Europa Center, the Nürnberger Eck features high-ceilinged rooms with heavy doors that open off a long, dark hallway. Although the eight rooms are stylistically something of a mishmash—with patterned wallpaper, Oriental rugs, and big pieces of furniture—the pension does convey an Old Berlin charm. The lower rates are for rooms with shared bathrooms.

Nürnberger Strasse 24A. www.nuernberger-eck.de. ℂ **030/2351780.** 8 units, 5 with bathroom. 70€–92€ double. Breakfast included. U-Bahn: Augsburgerstrasse.

Hotels in Mitte & Eastern Berlin

EXPENSIVE

Honigmond Garden Hotel ★★ Yes, there's a garden here and romantics will fall in love with its creeping vines, potted plants, and trees. This 19th-century hotel's gracious, high-ceilinged rooms are also period pieces of pleasure, with hardwood floors, stucco walls, antiques, and even some canopied four-poster beds. All in all, there's a warm, welcoming, old-fashioned charm and atmosphere here that's lacking in many of the area's glossier hotels.

Invalidenstrasse 122. www.honigmond-berlin.de. © **030/284455077.** 44 units. 125€–230€ double. Breakfast included. **Amenities:** Restaurant; bar; room service, Wi-Fi (free). U-Bahn: Naturkundenmuseum.

Lux 11 ★★ This Mitte design hotel strives to be casual and hip at the same time, with comfy, low-to-the-floor sofas and coffee tables, room dividers with flat-screen TVs, and wonderfully comfortable beds with gleaming white linens offset by bright pink-and-fuchsia spreads. Perhaps the hallway lighting's just a bit too artfully dim, but Lux gets points for its suites with small kitchens, the open bathrooms equipped with rain showers, and large closets. Some of the rooms are more like apartments, making them perfect for longer stays. At street level you'll find an Aveda spa, a café and designer boutique, and the trendy shops and cafés of the Scheunenviertel. You can easily walk to Hackescher Markt or Museum Island from here, or go anywhere in the city from the Alexanderplatz train station.

Rosa-Luxemburg-Strasse 9–13. www.lux-eleven.com. © **030/9362800.** 72 units. 149€–229€ double. Buffet breakfast 18€. **Amenities:** Restaurant; bar, Wi-Fi (free). S-Bahn: Alexanderplatz.

The Mandala Hotel ★★★ Potsdamer Platz may be the antithesis of zen, but this understated yet luxe hotel, opened in 1999, succeeds in being a calm oasis amid the commercial chaos. You can chill out with a cocktail at the chic Qui lounge, dine on-site at the glass-walled, Michelin-starred Facil restaurant, or enjoy a sauna or spa treatment at the top-floor Ono spa. The large rooms and suites have a quiet, soothing, contemporary decor with natural finishes of wood and stone and large bathrooms that feature high-quality toiletries and bathrobes. The ambience is both understated and very luxe. Room options range from simple doubles to executive suites with balconies to a fabulous penthouse. An opulent breakfast buffet is served in the lovely Facil, surrounded by bamboo and greenery.

Potsdamer Strasse 3. www.themandala.de. © **030/590050000.** 167 units. 180€–800€ double. Buffet breakfast 30€. **Amenities:** Restaurant; bar; exercise room; room service; spa; Wi-Fi (free). U-Bahn: Potsdamer Platz.

MODERATE

Arcotel Velvet ★★ Close to all the Mitte nightlife, the Arcotel Velvet is modern, exciting, and inviting—and you can find some terrific deals here. The building's glass façade affords floor-to-ceiling and wall-to-wall windows in the rooms, creating a sense of openness and light—and, just as importantly, making you feel like you're part of the city just outside. The views over the rooftops of Berlin from the suites and junior suites on the upper floors are romantic and memorable. Throughout the hotel you'll encounter original pieces of art from local artists. Breakfast costs an addition 17€, but there are lots of cafes around where you can eat for less.

Oranienburger Strasse 52. www.arcotel.at. ✆ **030/2787530.** 85 units. 89€–230€ double. Breakfast 17€. **Amenities:** Restaurant; bar; bikes; room service; Wi-Fi (free). S-Bahn: Oranienburger Strasse.

Michelberger Hotel ★ Within spitting distance of the East Side Gallery and all the Kreuzberg and Friedrichshain bars and clubs, this boutique hotel (which also boasts a locavore restaurant and its own coconut water) is geared toward touring indie bands, designers, and other members of the rarified creative class. Its casual lobby bar has become a hangout for locals and tourists alike, and its rooms resemble Brooklyn lofts with plenty of unfinished wood and quirky industrial touches. A fun place to stay, but also representative of a certain brand of Berlin snobbiness: their press rep actually told us they'd rather not host guidebook readers, preferring "independent travelers." Bu.t hey, if you think you can hang with the cool kids, go. Or better yet, walk up in a full sweatsuit and fanny pack, look the receptionist straight in the eye and ask what time the Brandenburg Gate opens. Tell 'em Frommer's sent you.

Warschauer Strasse 39. www.michelbergerhotel.com ✆ **030/29778590.** 100 units. 90€–100€ double. Buffet breakfast 16€. **Amenities:** Restaurant; bar; room service; sauna; bike rental; Wi-Fi (free). S-/U-Bahn: Warschauer Strasse.

INEXPENSIVE

Amano ★ Berliner Ariel Schiff's growing local hotel franchise tries to split the difference between boutique and budget, and while the sleek, black-white-mirrored rooms in each of the four-and-counting locations might fall a bit more on the cheap than chic side of the equation, they'll still give you a clean and comfortable night's sleep. That is, if you want to sleep: Amano's bars, from the namesake one in central Mitte to the sophisticated Apartment atop Amano Grand Central by Hauptbahnhof, make some of the best cocktails in town, so you'll have the advantage of being able to begin or end your night out right where you're staying.

Auguststrasse 43 (Amano), Torstrasse 136 (Mani), Heidestrasse 62 (Grand Central), Große Präsidentenstrasse 7 (Zoe). www.amanogroup.de. ✆ **030/8094150.** 70€–100€ double. Buffet breakfast 15€. **Amenities:** Bar, restaurant, Wi-Fi (free).

Baxpax Downtown Hostel Hotel ★ Nothing fancy here, but if your goal is a really inexpensive place to stay in Berlin, this clean, friendly hostel/hotel in Mitte should do. The rooms have been simply designed and furnished and there's a cafe and a roof terrace for relaxing and meeting fellow backpackers and explorers. You can stay in an eight-bed dorm room, a more private double room with a shower and toilet, or a small studio with a bathroom. Baxpax has two other hostels in eastern Berlin: one in Kreuzberg at Skalitzer Strasse 104 (✆ **030/69518322**; S-Bahn: Schlesisches Tor), and another in Mitte at Chauseestrasse 102 (✆ **030/ 28390935**; U-Bahn: Oranienburger Tor), all sharing the same website. Ziegelstrasse 28. www.baxpax.de. ✆ **030/27874880.** 17€–28€ dorm bed w/o bathroom; 35€–60€ double w/shower and toilet. Breakfast 5.50€. **Amenities:** Cafe, Wi-Fi (free). S-Bahn: Oranienburgerstrasse.

Circus Hotel ★ For a virtuous, "green" stay, head to this modestly priced, youth-oriented boutique hotel. Everything possible here is recycled, most of the lamps have energy-saving bulbs, and there's no A/C (but there is heat in the winter). Local artists have put up installations in some of the common areas. As for the rooms, they're far more style-savvy than one usually gets in this price bracket, mixing cheerily colorful walls (think orange, aqua, or deep red, off-set by white), 1960s-esque furniture created by the hotel's designer (Sandra Ernst), and homey bric-a-brac. Rain showers in the bathrooms are another unexpected luxury. The on-site restaurant emphasizes local produce (there's a generous breakfast buffet); guests gather there and in the lovely garden courtyard. Circus also operates a hostel right across the street from the hotel at Weinbergsweg 1A (✆ **030/20003939**) with 16 simple bedrooms, costing 29€ to 31€ for a dorm bed, 29€ to 43€ for a double. A step up from the usual grungy hostel bars, their pub Katz & Maus brews its own beer and serves its party-worn guests breakfast till 1pm (5€). Rosenthaler Strasse 1. www.circus-berlin.de. ✆ **030/20003939.** 60 units. 89€–99€ double. Buffet breakfast 9€. **Amenities:** Restaurant; bar; bike rentals, Wi-Fi (free). U-Bahn: Rosenthaler Platz.

Hüttenpalast ★★ There may be no more disgusting word in the English language than "glamping," but if you're looking for the most unique place to stay in the hipster heart of Neukölln, you'll find it in this budget "glam camping" retreat. On the ground floor of an old factory, the owners have set up 12 repurposed trailers and wooden cabins that sleep anywhere from one to four people. It's all whimsical as hell: there's an original 1930s "Dübener Egg" trailer perched atop a flight of stairs; while the white 1970s-era "Little Sister" has a skylight that projects stars, triangles and musical notes. The interiors might be a bit cramped, but you're meant to hang out with your fellow glampers in the chairs in front

Hipster "glamping" at the Hüttenpalast.

of your dwelling, or in the lush courtyard garden while enjoying your complimentary morning coffee and croissant. The bathrooms are shared, just like at a real campground. Not into roughing it? There are six "normal" rooms available, but that'd be defeating the point of staying here. Hobrechtstrasse 65. www.huettenpalast.de. © **030/37305806.** 18 units. 69€–74€ double w/ shared bath. Continental breakfast included. **Amenities:** Café, Wi-Fi (free). U-Bahn: Hermannplatz.

Ostel Hostel ★ If you're curious about life in the now-defunct GDR (that is, former Communist East Berlin), here's your chance to indulge in what Berliners call Ostalgia, a kind of kitschy nostalgia for Soviet culture (without the Stasi spying on you, and with better food). Near the Ostbahnhof train station, the East Side Gallery, and techno temple Berghain, this tower-block hotel wafts you back to the recent yesteryears of Russian bad taste. A picture of a beaming East German official adorns the reception, where clocks show the time in Commie Moscow, Havana, and Beijing. You can snooze in a prefab apartment decorated with Soviet-era furnishings and portraits of vanished politicians, check into the Stasi suite complete with (inoperable) bugging devices, or bed down in the budget pioneer dorm like a good little apparatchik. Except for bed linens and towels, don't expect the luxuries of the decadent West. But you will probably have a good time and a decent night's sleep, and wake up glad that the Wall fell. Plus, the staff members here are nicer than anyone ever was during the GDR days.

Wriezener Karree 5. www.ostel.eu. ⓒ **030/5768660.** 32€–37€ double, some w/ shared bath. Buffet breakfast 7.50€. **Amenities:** Wi-Fi (free). S-Bahn: Ostbahnhof.

WHERE TO EAT IN BERLIN

If you were to go back to Berlin at the turn of the millennium and tell your average resident that the German capital would someday become a foodie destination, they'd laugh so hard they'd choke on their schnitzel. But where the reigning culinary philosophy used to be "Hauptsache satt" ("the main thing is to get full"), today's worldly, eco-conscious Berliners are suddenly paying attention to what's on their plate. They're vegetarian, vegan, gluten-free, paleo, or whatever the latest dietary craze is by the time you read this. They favor kimchi over sauerkraut, quinoa over pota-toes, and American-style gourmet burgers over their grandma's Buletten.

Which isn't to say local tradition has completely died out. At wood-paneled Kneipen (pubs) and street-side Imbisses (fast food stands), a silent majority hunkers down over blood sausage, pickled herring, and the notorious Berlin specialty Eisbein: cured pork knuckle, braised until quiv-ering and gelatinous. Meanwhile, a new generation of young and creative chefs are reinventing and updating their parents' old favorites, with the help of meat and produce sourced from small farms in the surrounding Brandenburg countryside. And gourmands outside the country are taking notice: at last count, Berlin had 20 Michelin-starred restaurants.

Though prices have been creeping up, dining out remains ultra-affordable, especially compared to the rest of Germany. Just be aware that many restaurants don't take credit cards, and you're still expected to tip on sit-down meals. Around 10% is the norm, unless your restaurant bill already says "Bedienung" (service charge).

michelin **FOR LUNCH**

Going upscale for your midday repast has two major benefits: a) it's a chance to sam-ple some of Berlin's best cooking at relatively bargain prices, and b) these restaurants are often the most edible option in the big fat culinary dead zones around the city's major tourist attractions. Some of the best lunch deals in town include the one-star **Vau** by Gendarmenmarkt (see p. 115; 32€/2 courses; 45€/3 courses); the modern, two-star **Facil** in Potsdamer Platz's Mandala Hotel (p. 99; 36€/2 courses; 48€/3 courses); the trendy, one-star **Pauly Saal** in a made-over Jewish girl's school on Mitte's gallery row (Auguststrasse 11-13; www.paulysaal.com; 36€–56€/2–4 courses); and German-Asian fusion at **Tim Raue**'s two-star namesake by Checkpoint Charlie (Rudi-Dutschke-Strasse 26, www.tim-raue.com; 48€–78€/3–6 courses).

Restaurants in Western Berlin

Ana e Bruno ★★★ ITALIAN   It may seem counter-intuitive to come to Berlin for an Italian meal, but this charming bistro by Schloss Charlottenburg is worth the trip. For over 25 years, chef Bruno Pellegrini, who hails from Lake Como, has been putting a modern spin on Italian classics. Ingredients are absolutely fresh and authentic. The menu changes seasonally and always features fish, meat and game. You can also go vegetarian: the linguine with shaved truffle is divine, but then again, so are all the pastas. If you're feeling indecisive, choose one of the chef's tasting menus and sample a bit of everything.

Sophie-Charlotten-Strasse 101. www.a-et-b.de. ℂ **030/3257110.** Main courses 19€–34€; fixed-price menus 65€–95€. Daily 5–10:30pm. S-Bahn: Sophie-Charlotte-Platz.

Balikci Ergun ★ TURKISH/FISH   We're of two minds about recommending this place. It's a pain to get to and the food is satisfying, but not mind-blowing. But then again, this is the type of restaurant that "off the beaten path" eaters live for, a cozy decades-old Turkish tavern hidden under the S-Bahn tracks that transports you from Berlin to a harbor somewhere in Istanbul. Handwritten messages from happy customers, penned in Turkish, German, and English, line the walls and tables and even dangle from the ceiling. On the menu: Fish, fish, and more fish (well, and calamari), cooked simply and served with a bit of lemon and some grilled bread. Eat it with a luscious green salad and a glass of wine, raki, or Turkish beer, have a chat with the jovial owner, and see if you feel like adding your own love note to the pile. Go on a weekend and you might catch some live music or belly dancing.

Lüneburger Strasse 383. ℂ **030/3975737.** Main courses 7€–16€. Daily 3pm–midnight. S-Bahn: Bellevue.

Glass ★★ MODERN   This is the kind of restaurant you wouldn't think you'd find on Berlin's stuffy west side till recently: ultra-modern, vegetarian- and even vegan-friendly, run by a young Israeli. Count yourself lucky that the times are a-changing. The stripped-down, decoration-free interior gives the place an informal vibe, but chef Gaal Ben Moshe's food is anything but. Delicate, impressionistically plated dishes—like vibrantly colored vegetables arranged on a bed of edible "dirt," or the already-famous "candy box" dessert, a tabletop explosion of sweet stuff amid literal smoke and mirrors—recall molecular gastronomy temples like Chicago's Alinea (where Ben Moshe once worked) in every way but price.

Uhlandstrasse 195. ℂ **030/54710861.** www.glassberlin.de. Reservations required. Vegetarian, non-vegetarian, or vegan fixed-price menu 75€–95€. Tues–Sat 6–11pm. S-Bahn: Savignyplatz.

Ixthys ★ KOREAN   Locals call it the "Jesus Imbiss," and within a split second of walking in, you'll realize why. Every inch of this little Korean joint is covered in German-language scripture: the walls, yes, but also the menu. That it's survived over 15 years in godless Berlin is testament to its excellent bibimbap (rice bowls), bulgogi (marinated beef), and noodle soup, cooked up by friendly ladies as intent on filling your belly as they are on saving your soul.

Pallasstrasse 21. ℃ **030/81474769.** Main courses 6€–10€. Mon–Sat noon–10pm. U-Bahn: Winterfeldtplatz.

Lon Men's Noodle House ★ TAIWANESE   Looking for a quick, affordable, and delicious bite near Ku'damm? Your best bet might be to head north to the stretch of Kantstrasse between Savignyplatz and Stuttgarter Platz, which, although undeserving of the "Chinatown" sobriquet it's been getting lately, is indeed home to the city's highest concentration of Asian restaurants. In particular, this humble family-owned stall has been in operation since the 1990s and is a great place to grab a warming bowl of beef noodle soup, wontons in chili oil, or steamed buns filled with crispy duck.

Kantstrasse 33. ℃ **030/31519678.** Main courses 5€–10€. Daily noon–11pm. S-Bahn: Savignyplatz.

Lubitsch ★ CONTINENTAL   Named for Ernst Lubitsch, the German film director of the 1920s, this elegantly minimalist café and restaurant (paneled walls, white tablecloths, fresh-cut flowers) opposite the FK66 movie theater is popular with Berlin's television and film folk as well as locals and tourists. You can drop in for just a coffee and pastry, or order a well-prepared Wiener schnitzel, homemade blood sausage, or the house burger. Dinner runs a bit high, but lunch here is a bargain at just 10€ for 2 courses.

Bleibtreustrasse 47. www.restaurant-lubitsch.de. ℃ **030/8823756.** Main courses 12€–24€, 2-course lunch menu 10€. Mon–Sat 10am–midnight; Sun 6pm–1am. U-Bahn: Kurfürstendamm.

Marjellchen ★★★ EAST PRUSSIAN   Around since the 1980s, this Prussian throwback (complete with oil lamps and vested waiters) isn't the kind of place foodies flock to. But the cooking is honest, reliable, and authentic in a way that's quite satisfying—if you're a meat eater, at least. For an appetizer, try homemade aspic, smoked Pomeranian goose, or fried chicken legs. Main courses are something of an adventure: stewed pickled beef with green dumplings and cabbage, smoked ham in cream sauce, pork kidneys, or roast elk with chanterelle mushrooms. The less adventurous will still enjoy the Königsburger Klöpse (Prussian-style veal meatballs), which come with parsley potatoes and beetroot.

Mommsenstrasse 9. www.marjellchen-berlin.de. ℃ **030/8832676.** Main courses 11€–24€. Daily 5pm–midnight. Closed Dec 23, 24, and 31. U-Bahn: Adenauerplatz or Uhlandstrasse.

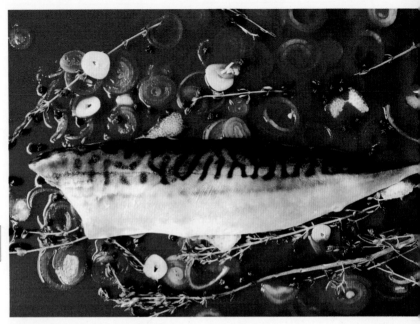

An innovative mackerel dish at Martha's.

Martha's ★ GERMAN/INTERNATIONAL Coined in 2007, the term *neue deutsche Küche* ("new German cuisine") is actually a bit out-moded by now. But there's nothing outmoded about young chef Manuel Schmuck's innovative Asian- and Mediterranean-influenced, German-inspired dishes. One of Berlin's best bread baskets (try the blood sausage roll!) sets the stage for well-executed, gorgeously presented entrees like cod tempura with nori remoulade, or calf sweetbreads with truffle and ponzu sauce. The atmosphere's more chaotic than the sedate Schöneberg surroundings would suggest, more so after 11pm when the restaurant becomes a cocktail bar.

Grunewaldstrasse 81. www.marthas.berlin. © **030/78006665.** Reservations recommended. Main courses 17€–30€. Tues–Sun 6pm–2am (kitchen closes 10:30pm). U-Bahn: Eisenacher Strasse.

Maultaschen Manufaktur ★ GERMAN/SWABIAN Ask your aver-age Berliner about Swabians and you'll hear two kinds of remarks: complaints about how those wealthy southwest Germans have ruined Berlin by buying all of the apartments, and a grudging appreciation of Maultauschen, a kind of ravioli traditionally filled with minced meat, herbs, spinach, and breadcrumbs. In this no-frills specialty restaurant, it's freshly prepared and dunked in broth, browned in butter, baked with cheese, or smothered in sauce. Vegetarians are well catered for with sun-dried-tomato-feta and spinach-mozzarella versions.

Lützowstrasse 22. www.maultaschen-manufaktur.de. ✆ **0176/41140435.** Main courses 8€–12€. Mon–Sat 6pm–midnight. U-Bahn: Kurfürstenstrasse.

Paris Bar ★ FRENCH Once a rowdy celebrity and artist haunt, this Charlottenburg bistro's star has faded somewhat. But the none-too-tasteful paintings adorning the walls, from the private collection of the late art-world legend Martin Kippenberger, are as colorful as ever—as are the handful of aging regulars you'll likely see at the bar. The menu's a mix of French standards and German and Mediterranean crowd-pleasers, all of it more expensive than you'd expect. But it's worth stopping by if you're craving a peek into the 1970s Charlottenburg of yore along with your steak-frites.

Kantstrasse 152. ✆ **030/3138052.** Main courses 13€–32€. Daily noon–2am. U-Bahn: Uhlandstrasse.

Rogacki ★★★ GERMAN Beneath the green awnings and fish sign lies the best deli in Berlin, a nearly 90-year-old institution where greying society ladies, overalled blue-collar types, and overwhelmed-looking tourists lunch side by side. Whether you're looking for smoked eel, pickled herring, translucent headcheese, or a dizzying variety of potato salads, you'll find it here, purveyed by no-nonsense aproned employees. You can order delicacies a la carte from the various counters; fill a plate with fried cod and potato salad at the cafeteria station in back; or head to the bar in the center for oysters and a glass of wine. No matter what, you'll probably have to eat standing up, which is part of the charm.

Wilmersdorfer Str. 145. www.rogacki.de. ✆ **030/3438250.** Main courses 5€–10€. Mon–Weds 9am–6pm, Thurs 9am–7pm, Fri 8am–7pm, Sat 8am–4pm. U-Bahn: Bismarckstrasse.

Restaurants in Mitte & Eastern Berlin

Adana Grillhaus ★★ TURKISH You might've had a döner sandwich or two, but you haven't had a real Turkish kebab in Berlin until you've been to one of Kreuzberg or Neukölln's *Ocakbasi,* charcoal-perfumed grill houses that make up in flavor what they lack in mood lighting. This 20-year-old family-owned joint is among the best of the lot, and certainly beats the overrated tourist trap Hasir down the road. Order anything with lamb and you won't leave disappointed: the ground Adana Kebab, the chops, and the ribs are all juicy, smoky, and perfectly seasoned. Eat them with grilled bread and a plate or two of *Meze* (starters), like the addictive eggplant and red pepper salad. If you want to fit in with the

STREET eats

Let's talk **currywurst.** Berlin's signature street snack, the legend goes, was invented after World War II when an enterprising bratwurst seller poured British-obtained ketchup and curry powder over her grilled sausages. Now you can find it on nearly every street corner, bought by tourists, construction workers, and drunks. Don't expect it to reach any level of culinary sophistication, but the ketchup-drenched sausage bits, which you eat with a wooden pick alongside fries or a bread roll, can be good in a primal sort of way.

If you must, join the hordes at the famous **Curry36** in Kreuzberg (36 Mehringdamm; U-Bahn Mehringdamm) or its eastern counterpart **Konnopke's** under the Eberswalder Straße U-Bahn station in Prenzlauer Berg. Both serve a passable version and have fast-moving lines—to avoid holding them up, remember to specify "mit Darm" or "ohne Darm" (with or without casing) when you order. At **Witty's,** next to KaDeWe in Schöneberg ((Wittenbergplatz 5, U-Bahn Wittenbergplatz), the sausage is organic and the sauce actually has a little kick to it. For a LOT of kick, **Curry & Chili,** a snack bar in the middle of the Wedding (at the intersection of Osloer Strasse and Prinzenallee) sauces their 'wurst at 10 different spice gradients, from 11,000 to over 7 million Scoville units; eat them all and you'll get your picture on the wall! (You may also have to go to the hospital.)

If there's one street food everyone in Berlin eats, it's the **döner kebab.**

Invented here by Turkish guest workers in the early 1970s, it combines spit-roasted meat, fresh vegetables, and flavorful sauces in crisp toasted flatbread… when it's good. When it's not it's basically grease-soaked cardboard, so choose your stand wisely. Look for a place with distinct striation in its rotating meat cone, rather than a grainy mystery mass, and don't pay less than 2.50€. **Mustafa's** (next to Curry36 on Mehringdamm), with chicken, roasted vegetables, and goat cheese, is the most popular kebab in Berlin for a reason, but the sandwich, while delicious, doesn't justify what can be an hour-long wait. Go right at opening time (10:30am), or hit up **Imren** (Boppstrasse 10, U-Bahn Schönleinstrasse) for a juicy veal version that won't disappoint. Or go for a döner crawl around Kottbusser Tor in Kreuzberg's "Little Istanbul" neighborhood, featuring **Doyum** (Admiralstrasse 36) and **Tadim** (Adalbertstrasse 98).

locals, wash down your meal with a glass or two of raki (a pastis-like liquor) and finish with *Künefe,* a syrup-soaked cheesy pastry. Manteuffelstrasse 86. www.adanagrillhaus.de. ☏ **030/6127790.** Main courses 10€–18€. Daily 5pm–midnight. U-Bahn: Görlitzer Bahnhof.

Azzam ★ LEBANESE   Along Neukölln's still-gentrifying Sonnenallee lies "Little Beirut," a colorful stretch of Arabic restaurants, bakeries, shisha bars, and grocery stores interrupted by the odd organic supermarket and third-wave coffee shop. In the middle of it is this always-packed hole-in-the-wall, where just a few euros will get you a feast of spit-roasted schwarma, freshly fried falafel, halloumi cheese, and/or grilled vegetables. The must-order is *musabaha,* a chunky mortar-pounded version of hummus that's so good that neighborhood Israelis come to the

Palestinian-owned spot to eat it. Like everything else, it's served with pickles, fresh herbs, and pita bread; come with an appetite or be prepared for leftovers.

Sonnenallee 54. ✆ **030/30131541.** Main courses 3.50€–6€. Daily 8am–midnight. U-Bahn: Rathaus Neukölln.

The Bowl ★ VEGAN   If you're in the mood for a virtuous, restorative breakfast or lunch after a night hitting the clubs or a morning strolling the East Side Gallery, you could do a whole lot worse than this California-style organic "clean eating" restaurant, appropriately located above a vegan grocery store in Friedrichshain. Free of animal products, gluten, or refined sugar, the namesake bowls contain a jumble of ingredients like lemon quinoa, curried pumpkin, sesame-coated avocado, and teriyaki hibiscus sauce, to surprisingly tasty and filling effect. For breakfast, there's porridge or chia pudding; to drink, homemade kombucha or organic beer. The service is, shall we say, "relaxed," but the view over Warschauer Brücke is worth lingering over.

Warschauer Strasse 33. www.thebowl-berlin.com. ✆ **030/89654973.** Main courses 10€–14€. Tues–Sun 11am–11:30pm, Mon noon–11:30pm. U-/S-Bahn: Warschauer Strasse.

Briefmarken Weine ★ ITALIAN   It may not be German, but an Italian restaurant and wine bar in a former stamp collecting shop on a Stalinist boulevard is as Berlin as it gets. An excellent wine list complements a small but delicious menu of pasta and antipasti with ingredients brought over from the owner's native Campania, to be savored in a charming, candlelit atmosphere.

Karl-Marx-Allee 99. www.briefmarkenweine.de. ✆ **030/42025292.** Reservations recommended. Main courses 10€–15€. Mon–Sat 7pm–midnight. U-Bahn: Weberwiese.

Crackers/Cookies Cream ★ INTERNATIONAL / VEGETARIAN "Food is the new clubbing," or so the refrain goes in Berlin nowadays. For better or worse, the city's onetime nightlife magnates have started serving up beets instead of beats. Take Heinz "Cookie" Gindullis, who in 2007 opened a refined all-vegetarian restaurant, Cookies Cream, above his legendary hotspot Cookies. Thanks to chef Stephan Hentschel's cooking, the venture proved so successful it outlived the club, which shut down in 2015. Gindullis and Hentschel covered its dance floor with tables and opened Crackers, a French-leaning eatery that serves free-range beef entrecote and wild-caught monkfish fillet to assorted mon-eyed creative types. With DJs soundtracking your meal, either one is a good option if you're feeling too old to party hearty but too young to go to bed early.

Cookies Cream: Behrenstrasse 55. www.cookiescream.com. ✆ **030/27492940.** Reservations recommended. Fixed-price dinner menus 45€–55€. Tues–Sat from 6pm. **Crackers:** Friedrichstrasse 148. www.crackersberlin.com. ✆ **030/680730488.** Mains 16€–35€. Daily from 6pm. S-/U-Bahn: Friedrichstrasse.

District Mot ★ VIETNAMESE   Despite Berlin's 40,000-strong population of migrants from both northern and southern Vietnam, most Vietnamese food here fell short of the mark until very recently. Thank the Germans, for whom anything more exotic than sweet-and-sour chicken was once a frightening specter. This riotously colorful and immensely popular Mitte hangout is proof that attitudes have changed. Decorated to resemble a Saigon street corner, it serves a wide selection of beyond-authentic small plates and main courses from pho noodle soup to fried silkworms. Then again, if there's one thing that surpasses young Berliners' hunger for authenticity, it's their hunger for fusion hamburgers, and so it's the banh bao burger, which comes topped with mango on a rice flour bun, that's become District Mot's most-sought-after offering.
Rosenthaler Strasse 62. www.districtmot.com. © **030/20089284.** Main courses 8€–19€, lunch specials 6.50€. Mon–Thurs, Sun noon–1am, Fri–Sat noon–2am. U-Bahn: Rosenthaler Platz.

Duc Anh ★ VIETNAMESE   District Mot (see above) not authentic enough for you? Head way out east to the Dong Xuan Center, a massive wholesale warehouse complex in Lichtenberg that's a shopping, business, and meeting point for eastern Berlin's community of migrants from northern and central Vietnam. Some came here in the GDR years on "guest worker" contracts; others came in the 1990s after a disastrous series of Pacific typhoons. All come to eat at Duc Anh, a noisy, crowded food hall that serves delicious *bun cha* (grilled pork with rice noodles and herbs) among a maze of menu offerings listed in both German and Vietnamese.
Dong Xuan Center Halle 3, Herzbergstrasse 128. © **030/55152038.** Main courses 6€–15€. Wed–Mon 9am–9pm. Tram: Herzbergstrasse/Industriegebiet.

Fischers Fritz ★★★ FRENCH/SEAFOOD   At this elegant palace of haute cuisine in the tony Regent Hotel, the creative cooking of chef de cuisine Christian Lohse has earned two Michelin stars every year since 2008. Dining here is a gourmet adventure featuring the freshest produce and products of land and sea—but the sea predominates. Start with carpaccio of halibut and fennel salad, and then savor Icelandic sea trout with pea emulsion, or steamed fillet of sea bass. The dessert menu ranges from classic (fresh white chocolate mousse) to downright exotic (bittersweet artichoke ice cream, anyone?). The wine cellar is outstanding, and the service is deft. There's a smart-casual dress code, so leave your running shoes at the hotel.
Charlottenstrasse 49. www.fischersfritzberlin.com. © **030/20336363.** Reservations required. Main courses 30€–75€; fixed-price dinner 130€–170€. Daily 6:30–10:30pm. U-Bahn: Französische Strasse.

Ganymed ★★ FRENCH   If this cozy riverside brasserie seems old-fashioned, it's for a reason: Ganymed has been around since 1929, surviving World War II and even the GDR days, when dining out was rare.

Fischer's Fritz, a tony temple of haute cuisine.

You won't find any surprises on the menu, just hearty French classics like escargots, Beaujolais-braised lamb knuckle, or whole grilled sea bream with fennel. Playwright Bertolt Brecht was said to have eaten here, so stop by before or after a play at his Berliner Ensemble (p. 126) and pretend you're "dancing on the volcano" in the twilight of the Weimar era. Schiffbauerdamm 5. www.ganymed-brasserie.de. ✆ **030/28599046.** Main courses 12€–28€; 3-course fixed-price dinner 33€. Daily noon–midnight. U-Bahn: Friedrichstrasse.

Henne ★ GERMAN   True to its name, "Hen" serves chicken. Crispy corn-fed chicken, to be exact, fried to order and served with nothing but a slice of bread. (Coleslaw and potato salad are available as sides.) Over a century old, the pub was once patronized by JFK, and a photo of the honorary "Berliner" still hangs over the bar. Come here without a reservation and you may be out of (c)luck, but not far away and equally chickeny is Middle Eastern rotisserie **Hühnerhaus 36** (Skalitzer Strasse 95a; U-Bahn Görlitzer Bahnhof). Leuschnerdamm 25. www.henne-berlin.de. ✆ **030/6147730.** Reservations recommended. Half chicken 8.30€. Tues–Sat 6–11pm, Sun 5–11pm. U-Bahn: Moritzplatz.

Horvath ★★★ GERMAN/AUSTRIAN   Since chef Sebastian Frank took it over in 2010, the casually elegant wood-paneled restaurant by Kreuzberg's Landwehrkanal has skyrocketed to prominence, earning its first Michelin star in 2011 and its second in 2015. Have one taste and you'll understand the accolades. These are exquisitely plated yet unpretentious dishes that nod to Frank's Austrian homeland while elevating local and seasonal ingredients like turnips, chanterelle mushrooms, and pumpkin to delectable heights. That said, vegetarians may want to save their money, as meat, and especially wild game, is where Horvath really shines.

Paul-Linke-Ufer 44a. www.restaurant-horvath.de. ✆ **030/61289992.** Reservations required. 5- to 9-course fixed-price dinner 80€–120€. Wed–Sun 6:30–10:30pm. U-Bahn: Kottbusser Tor.

Imbiss 204 ★★ GERMAN/BERLINER   Stake out a table in this itty-bitty, unromantic storefront in Prenzlauer Berg for a taste of the kind of working-class German food time forgot, cooked by a pair of chefs who put just that little extra amount of care into each dish. Gigantic portions of freshly cooked Buletten (meat patties), Käsespätzle (the southern German version of mac 'n' cheese), and schnitzel, served with homemade sauces and heaps of vegetables on the side, are both delicious and immensely filling. You can even enjoy your meal with a glass of Riesling, though the fast-food ambience means you won't want to linger too long. Check the chalkboard for specials like Sauerbraten (roast beef with gravy) or asparagus when in season.

Prenzlauer Allee 204. www.imbiss204.de. ✆ **030/24038543.** Main courses 7€–14€. Mon–Fri noon–10pm. Tram: Prenzlauer Allee/Danziger Strasse.

Horvath's unpretentious entrance belies its gourmet prominence.

Jolesch ★ AUSTRIAN   This stylish, dimly lit Kreuzberg restaurant has two menus, one devoted to traditional Austrian dishes and one to modern twists on them. Our advice? Skip the curried trout tartare and stick with the irresistibly crispy Wiener schnitzel—it's one of Berlin's best. An only slightly inferior pork version can be found on the 3-course lunch menu, a steal at 11.50€.

Muskauer Strasse 11. www.jolesch.de. ⓒ **030/6123581.** Main courses 15€–29€, lunch 9.50€ (2 courses) or 11.50€ (3 courses). Sun–Fri 11:30am–midnight, Sat 5pm– midnight. U-Bahn: Görlitzer Bahnhof.

Katz Orange ★★★ INTERNATIONAL   Located in the courtyard of a gorgeous brick brewery building, this five-year-old celebrity and foodie favorite set the standard for many zeitgeisty "slow food" Berlin restaurants to come: organic ingredients, responsibly raised meat, and plentiful vegetarian and vegan options. The menu is small, the dishes creative and satisfying, the cocktail bar worth lingering at after-hours. For a more accessible and affordable taste of Katz, including their famous pulled pork, have a sandwich at lunch-only offshoot **Contemporary Food Lab Canteen** (Lindenstrasse 20; www.cfl-canteen.com) in Kreuzberg.

Bergstrasse 22. www.katzorange.com. ⓒ **030/983208430.** Reservations required. Main courses 15€–26€. Mon–Sat 6pm–3am. U-Bahn: Oranienburger Strasse.

La Soupe Populaire ★★★ MODERN BERLINER   Tim Raue is Berlin's local boy made good, a Kreuzberg gang member turned celebrity chef who owns five restaurants at last count. The eponymous restaurant Tim Raue by Checkpoint Charlie is the most celebrated, with two Michelin stars and ultra-refined, Asian-influenced cuisine. But La Soupe Populaire, intended as a nod to the chef's working-class roots, is by far the most "Berlin." It starts with the location, a skylit metal mezzanine deep within the cavernous ruin of a former brewery, and continues with the food, a series of playful, sophisticated takes on Raue's favorite childhood dishes. Most in demand are the classic Königsberger Klopse, breadcrumb-sprinkled veal meatballs in a rich Riesling sauce with a silky potato puree and apple-beet salad. Yes, you might feel a little silly paying 12€ for an upscale version of "Hawaii Toast" (ham, cheese, and pineapple baked on bread, traditionally enjoyed by German kids and drunk students, augmented here with green pepper and a cherry reduction). But you'll enjoy every bite—and the baroque-industrial mise-en-scene that goes with it.

Prenzlauer Allee 242. www.lasoupepopulaire.de. ⓒ **030/44319680.** Dinner reservations required. Main courses 14€–18€. Thurs–Sat noon–2:30pm and 5:30–10:30pm. Tram: Prenzlauer Allee/Metzer Strasse.

Lebensmittel im Mitte ★ GERMAN   That telltale odor in German public toilets between April and June can only mean one thing:

Spargelzeit! Berliners are very serious about their "asparagus time," but not all restaurants give due reverence to those succulent white stalks (the chlorophyll-deprived kind is the default here in Germany). At this rustic southern German nook in Mitte, they're shipped in from nearby asparagus capital Beelitz and cooked just right, al dente yet tender. Eat them with clarified butter and new potatoes alongside ham, smoked salmon, or schnitzel. If it's not Spargelzeit, check the chalkboard for the daily specials, which are likely to be equally seasonal and well prepared. Rochstrasse 2. © **030/27596130.** Main courses 8€–21€. Mon–Fri noon–11pm, Sat 1–11pm. S-Bahn: Hackescher Markt.

Lucky Leek ★★ VEGETARIAN   When *Saveur* magazine named Berlin the "new vegetarian capital" in 2015, this was the restaurant they pointed to. In fact, even carnivores will want to give this airy Prenzlauer Berg eatery a shot. Chef Josita Hartanto creates elegantly composed, complexly flavored dishes that just happen to be meatless, like truffled chestnut ravioli in a basil-mushroom broth or black coconut risotto with teriyaki seitan. The menu changes often; check the website for current offers and be aware that you can only order courses a la carte on Wednesday, Thursday, or Sunday. Kollwitzstrasse 54. www.lucky-leek.de. © **030/66408710.** Main courses 15€–20€, fixed-price menu 33€–55€. Weds–Sun 6–10pm. U-Bahn: Senefelderplatz.

Max und Moritz ★ GERMAN/BERLINER   A Kreuzberg neighborhood favorite since 1902, this simple tavern has withstood war, gentrification, and Berlin's onslaught of veganism. Nothing fancy here, just hearty pub grub like potato soup, herring with onions, the traditional Berliner Eisbein (pork knuckle, listed on the English menu as "pickled pork foot"), and of course sausage, to be washed down with copious amounts of beer in an appealingly old-timey atmosphere. The "Schlachteplatte" (literally "slaughter plate") gets you a bit of everything, with cabbage, mustard, potatoes, and salad on the side. A ballroom in the back hosts concerts and regular tango classes. Oranienstrasse 162. www.maxundmoritz berlin.de. © **030/69515911.** Main courses 9€–17€. Daily 5pm–1am. U-Bahn: Moritzplatz.

Lucky Leek raises the bar for vegetarian cuisine.

Nobelhart & Schmutzig ★★★ MODERN GERMAN "Brutally local" is the catchphrase at what's currently Berlin's hottest reservation, opened in 2015 and already anointed with a Michelin star. Owner/sommelier Billy Wagner and chef Micha Schäfer limit the nightly 10-course menu to ingredients from within about a 250-kilometer (155-mile) radius of Berlin. This means no pepper, citrus fruit, olive oil, or chocolate—but plenty of fruits, vegetables and preparations you won't taste anywhere else, like pickled dandelion buds, ground ivy, and grapeseed oil cream. Take a seat around the massive open kitchen, choose meat or vegetarian, and prepare your palate for a challenge, especially in winter, when pickles, brassicas, and sour and bitter flavors rule. It may not always be delicious or especially filling, but it's one of the most memorable dinners to be had in Berlin—especially if you leave the drinks to the ultra-charismatic Wagner, whose course-by-course pairing is a near-theatrical experience. Book this one a few months in advance.

Friedrichstrasse 218. www.nobelhartundschmutzig.com. © **030/25940610.** Reservations required. Fixed-price dinner 80€. Tues–Sat 6:30pm–10pm. U-Bahn: Kochstrasse/Checkpoint Charlie.

Schiller Burger ★ HAMBURGERS Berlin does hamburgers better than most US cities these days, and certainly better than Hamburg. Who here does it best is an entirely subjective matter, but our personal favorite is this narrow fast-foodery by Tempelhofer Feld in Neukölln. With juicy, medium-rare beef (or a veggie patty), fresh toppings, and the best homemade buns we've eaten anywhere, it makes for a satisfying stop on your way into or out of the park. Or elsewhere: Schiller's burgers have become so in demand that it's now a growing mini-franchise.

Herrfurthstrasse 7. www.schillerburger.com. © **030/55871716.** Burgers 5€–7€. Sun–Thurs noon–11pm, Fri–Sat noon–1am. U-Bahn: Herrfurthstrasse.

Vau ★★★ INTERNATIONAL In 1997, chef, musician, and TV personality Kolja Kleeberg broke new ground by opening a modern gourmet restaurant in post-reunification East Berlin. He's been awarded with a Michelin star every year since then. His menus (split between "composition" and "improvisation") emphasize classic French cuisine such as lobster consommé with tarragon or veal breast confit, but stretch culinary boundaries to include modern German cooking and seasonal specialties. Dishes are deftly prepared and can be surprisingly unfussy. You might find pork with bok choi, artichokes, and onion ketchup; pastrami with baked onions and mustard; and various fish choices. It's a good choice for a memorable meal, especially if Kleeberg himself is in the kitchen.

Jägerstrasse 54–55 (near Gendarmenmarkt). www.vau-berlin.de. © **030/2029730.** Dinner reservations required. Fixed-price menus 32€–45€ (lunch), 120€–160€ (dinner). Mon–Sat noon–2:30pm and 7–10:30pm. U-Bahn: Hausvogteiplatz.

BERLIN'S food markets

The first stop any food aficionado in Berlin ought to make is the sixth floor of famed department store **KaDeWe ★★★** (p. 119), with 7,000 square meters (75,000 square feet) devoted to the world's finest delicacies. You could spend hours just wandering around gaping at the German sausages, French pastries, Asian tropical fruit, and prohibitively priced American breakfast cereals. But at some point you will get hungry, and that's where the many eat-in counters come into play. Make a bee-line for the oyster bar to slurp fresh shellfish next to moneyed West Berliners taking a break from their weekly shopping (U-Bahn: Wittenbergplatz.)

For an up-to-the-minute snapshot of today's Berlin food scene, go to Kreuzberg, where a revamped 19th-century market hall has become ground central for all things local-seasonal-artisanal. On Tuesday, Friday, and Saturday afternoons (Tues, Fri noon-8pm, Sat 10am-6pm) **Markthalle IX ★★** (Eisenbahnstrasse 42-43; U-Bahn Görlitzer Bahnhof) fills with hungry hipsters ogling a carefully curated selection of cheese, produce, meat and fish from small, ethical farms. There's plenty of prepared food, too; try an American-style barbecue sandwich from **Big Stuff BBQ** with a glass of Heidenpeter's ale, brewed right there in the basement. Or visit on a Thursday night (5pm-10pm), when Berlin's trend-conscious gourmet street food vendors gather to ply everything from vegan bratwurst to Korean tacos.

If you prefer to do your grazing out-of-doors, head to Schöneberg's **Winterfeldplatz ★** on a Saturday (10am-4pm; U-Bahn: Nollendorfplatz). It's home to Berlin's biggest farmer's market, where local fruit and veggies are sold alongside handmade sauerkraut, French crepes, and Thai dumplings. Speaking of Thai: on warm weekend days, a dedicated and talented group of home cooks from southeast Asia congregate in Wilmersdorf's **Preussenpark** (U-Bahn: Fehrbelliner Platz) to sell noodle soup, spring rolls, blisteringly spicy papaya salad, and more, a phenomenon that the locals simply call **"Thai Park" ★**.

Finally, if you're in Berlin on a Tuesday or a Friday, you've got no excuse to miss the **Turkish Market ★★★** on the southern bank of Neukölln's Landwehrkanal (11am-630pm; U-Bahn Schönleinstrasse), where a long row of vendors hawk produce, meat, fish, spices, olives, bread, and spreads. Shopping here is loud, chaotic and lots of fun; just don't get too caught up in the excitement ("Ein Kilo, ein Euro!") or you'll wind up with five crates of mushy avocados. When in doubt, a goat cheese-arugula flatbread wrap, a cup of fresh-squeezed pomegranate juice, and a couple pieces of baklava will more than suffice.

Zur Letzten Instanz ★ GERMAN   Fair warning: any place billed as the "oldest restaurant in Berlin" and touted by Anthony Bourdain isn't *not* going to be full of tourists. But this much-restored two-story guesthouse, opened as a courthouse-adjacent pub in 1621, does manage to have some local regulars—and waitstaff with the appropriate amount of "Berliner Schnauze" attitude. The food is average, about on a par with many similar taverns in the nearby Nikolaiviertel. But if you want to eat by the same tiled stove where Napoleon was rumored to have warmed his feet, order a hunk of pork knuckle (amusingly called *Einstweilige Verfügung,* or "Interim Disposal," on the legalese-themed menu) and go to town. Reservations essential.

Waisenstrasse 14–16 (nr Alexanderplatz). www.zurletzteninstanz.de. ✆ **030/2425528.** Reservations recommended. Main courses 12€–20€. Mon–Sat noon–1am. U-Bahn: Klosterstrasse.

SHOPPING IN BERLIN

Berlin's trademark creativity, inventiveness, and resourcefulness extends not only to its culture, but also to its stuff. So before you pick up that generic Fernsehturm keychain or Buddy Bear snow globe, consider supporting one of the many hard-working, independent designers who call the German capital home. Chances are you'll wind up with a more meaningful, longer-lasting reminder of your time here.

Likewise, there's no need to spend too much time or money on Berlin's pair of shopping "high streets": the glitzy **Ku'damm** (Kurfürstendamm) in the west and the revitalized **Friedrichstrasse** in the east. Both are teeming with all the major brands you'd expect, and the Russians who love them. If you're American, you'll find better prices on this stuff back home.

More unique boutiques can be found off Ku'damm's main drag, on **Bleibtreustrasse, Fasanenstrasse,** or the area around **Breitscheidplatz,** although for impossibly chic homegrown design, you've really got to head to Mitte's **Hackescher Markt** area. Despite encroachment by big names and Scandinavians, you'll still find a bevy of locally owned shops in the **Hackesche Höfe** courtyard complex and on **Alte Schönhauser Strasse** and its side streets, especially **Mulackstrasse.** Some of the designers based around there, like sunglasses specialist Mykita, also have outposts in the newish **Bikini Berlin** mall by Bahnhof Zoo, a trendy, "curated" mix of local and international brands.

If your style tends toward the lower-fi, take a stroll down Kreuzberg's **Oranienstrasse** between Görlitzer Bahnhof and Moritzplatz, starting at punk stronghold Core Tex Records, ending at art supply mecca Modulor Materials, and hitting myriad indie vintage, streetwear and book shops in between.

Finally, some of Berlin's best treasures are to be found at its **markets,** be they food (see p. 116), flea (see p. 120) or art and design (check www.berlin.de/special/shopping/designmaerkte for dates). And if you're here in late November or December, you won't be able to avoid the ubiquitous **Christmas markets**—just follow the scent of spiced mulled wine and look for wooden huts selling toys, woodcarvings, and gingerbread.

Candy & Confections

Bonbonmacherei ★   You can't help but love an old-fashioned candy store like this one in Mitte, where the sweets (bonbons, in German) are still made by hand in small batches. Pick up a bag of sour limes, malt-flavored cubes, or the famous leaf-shaped Berliner Maiblätter (candies shaped like tiny leaves and flavored with woodruff). Heckmannhöfe, Oranienburger Strasse 32. *©* **030/44055243.** No credit cards. S-Bahn: Oranienburger Strasse.

Rausch ★★   Sure, the Brandenburg Gate's fine as it is... but what if it was made of solid chocolate? Find out at Berlin's most famous chocolatier (formerly Fassbender & Rausch), located off the Gendarmenmarkt. The Rausch family has been in the game for around a century, and now makes their milk and dark bars, truffles and edible Prussian landmarks from ethical, direct-trade beans. Charlottenstrasse 10. www.rausch.de. *©* **0800/0301918.** U-Bahn: Französische Strasse.

Wald Königsberger Marzipan ★   At this family-run store in Charlottenburg, Germany's beloved almond paste is handmade according to an 80-year-old recipe and browned or "flamed" on the surface in true Königsberg tradition. Pestalozzistrasse 54a. *©* **030/323-82-54.** U-Bahn: Wilmersdorfer Strasse.

China & Porcelain

KPM (Königliche Porzellan-Manufaktur) ★★★   For 250 years, KPM has been producing some of the finest "white gold" in the world.

Shopping for hand-painted porcelain at the KPM flagship store.

The "kingly" name comes from its patron Frederick the Great, and many of its current pieces are hand-painted and hand-decorated with patterns based on traditional 18th- and 19th-century designs. There are sales outlets throughout Berlin, including the KaDeWe department store (see below), Friedrichstrasse 158 in Mitte, and Kurfürstendamm 27 (in the Kempinski Hotel Bristol). But the best selection is at the KPM flagship store and manufactory, where you can also take a guided tour (12€; Sat 3pm) and see the craftspeople at work. Wegelystrasse 1. www.kpm.de. ✆ **030/39009215.** U-Bahn: Tiergarten.

Department Stores

Galeries Lafayette ★★ Opened in 1996, this outpost of the famed Parisian emporium was key to the rejuvenation of Friedrichstrasse. Five floors showcase fashion from French and German designers, as well as accessories and beauty products; the basement food emporium is where French expats and Francophiles go for baguettes, pate, and cheese. Französische Strasse 23. www.galeries-lafayette.de. ✆ **030/209480.** U-Bahn: Französische Strasse.

Kaufhaus des Westens (KaDeWe) ★★★ The "Shopping House of the West" is the biggest department store in continental Europe, a century-old grand dame with sumptuous window displays and five floors of upscale merchandise, including men's and women's fashion, accessories, linens, and housewares. Even if you're shopping-averse, you'll want to make a beeline for the drool-inducing sixth-floor food hall (see p. 116). Tauentzienstrasse 21. www.kadewe.de. ✆ **030/21210.** U-Bahn: Wittenbergplatz.

Design

Bauhaus Shop ★★★ Not to be confused with the home improvement store of the same name, the shop at the Bauhaus Archive Museum of Design (see p. 70) offers home and office decor designed and inspired by artists from the movement. Pick up an eye-catching yet practical ashtray or eggcup, or a 1924 optical top that will turn your toddler into a modern design snob before he or she is old enough to say "Ludwig Hirschfeld-Mack." Klingelhöferstrasse 14. www.bauhaus.de. ✆ **030/2540020.** U-Bahn: Nollendorfplatz.

Modulor ★★ A two-floor creative mecca anchoring Kreuzberg's Aufbauhaus complex, Modulor is where Berlin's myriad artists and artsy wannabes go to buy their paints, canvases, 3D printing supplies, and Styrofoam heads. Even if you've never picked up a paintbrush in your life, chances are something here will inspire you. There's also a decent selection of coffee-table books about Berlin art, design, and architecture. Prinzenstrasse 85. www.modulor.de. ✆ **030/690360.** U-Bahn: Moritzplatz.

BERLIN sunday flea markets

If you're in Berlin on a non-rainy Sunday, a visit to a flea market is imperative. But with over 50 spread across the city, you've got to figure out what you're looking for. For pure vibes, join the hungover hordes at **Mauerpark,** close to the Berlin Wall Memorial (Bernauer Strasse 63-64; U-Bahn Bernauer Strasse), between 8am to 6pm. You might not find bargains on the clothes, records, and GDR memorabilia, but you can nibble on street snacks, listen to buskers, and even belt karaoke in a packed amphitheater. For a more genteel atmosphere and less picked-over wares, check the nearby **Flohmarkt am Arkonaplatz** (Arkonaplatz; U-Bahn Bernauer Strasse), open from 10am to 6pm and conveniently surrounded by cafés. For a casual neighborhood shop-and-stroll, the funkier **Flohmarkt Boxhagener Platz** (Boxhagen Platz; S-Bahn Frankfurter Tor), open 10am to 6pm, offers abundant kitsch, sort-of antiques, and used clothing. On the west side, the **Original Berliner Trödelmarkt** (Strasse des 17. Juni 110-114; S-Bahn Tiergarten; 10am-5pm) is where you'll find the real (and commensurately priced) antiques, like silver and KPM porcelain, although WWII completists searching for that original copy of *Mein Kampf* will probably leave disappointed. Personally, we most often find ourselves at the **Kunst- und Trödelmarkt am Fehrbelliner Platz** in Wilmersdorf (U-Bahn Fehrbelliner Platz, 10am-4pm). Not only does it have manageable crowds and a reliably decent selection of vintage clothes and knick-knacks, it also happens to border "Thai Park" (see p. 116), the authentic street food market run by enterprising southeast Asians on warm weekends. For other Berlin flea markets (including some on Saturdays!), go to **www.visitberlin.de**.

Flea-market shopping at Boxhagen Platz.

Stilwerk ★★ This temple of design in Charlottenburg is spread out over four floors and carries high-end brands like Bang & Olufsen, Mösch, and Niessing. Whether you're looking for understated jewelry or ultra-sleek home furnishings, this is the place. Kantstrasse 17. www.stilwerk.de. ✆ **030/315150.** S-Bahn: Savignyplatz.

Fashion

Andreas Murkudis ★   Alongside all the contemporary galleries in the ex-Tagesspiegel building on Potsdamer Strasse, this immense, blindingly white concept store by local design magnate Murkudis fits right in. Clothes, housewares, and cosmetics are displayed like modern art pieces and priced similarly. Potsdamer Strasse 81e. www.andreasmurkudis. com. ℂ **030/28093070.** U-Bahn: Rosa-Luxemburg-Platz.

Claudia Skoda ★★   From chunky sweaters to snug-fitting dresses, Skoda's colorful knitwear is elegant, feminine, and modern. Browse through the Berlin fashion icon's latest collection at her chic boutique in Mitte. Alte Mulackstrasse 8. www.claudiaskoda.com. ℂ **030/40041884.** U-Bahn: Weinmeisterstrasse.

Darklands ★   If you're willing to spend four figures to ensure your entry into any club in the city, buy a get-up at this hard-to-find warehouse near Hauptbahnhof, which specializes in the wearable equivalent of Berlin techno. Expect leather, mesh, and avant-garde cuts, all of it black, of course. Heidestrasse 46-52, Building 7. www.darklandsberlin.com. No phone. S-Bahn: Hauptbahnhof.

Hut Up ★   Wanna get "felt" up? Check out the selection of one-of-a-kind hats, bags, dresses, and baby booties made from raw wool by designer and felter Christine Birkle. Auguststrasse 49. www.hutup.de. ℂ **030/28386105.** S-Bahn: Oranienburger Strasse.

Jünemann's Pantoffel-Eck ★★★   You can't get any more German than the humble Hausschuh ("house shoe"). Whether you're afflicted with Ostalgia or just cold feet, you'll appreciate this GDR-era institution's affordable low- or high-cut slippers (from 15€), made by hand by the founder's great-grandson. Torstrasse 39. www.pantoffeleck.de. ℂ **030/4425337.** U-Bahn: Rosa-Luxemburg-Platz.

Koko von Knebel ★   He won't trim your dog's fur, but in-demand celebrity hairdresser Udo Walz shills gem-encrusted collars, raincoats, and lingerie for pampered pooches at the campy fashion boutique next to his salon. Uhlandstrasse 181. www.kokovonknebel.com. ℂ **043/19970868.** U-Bahn: Uhlandstrasse.

Mykita ★★   Is it ironic that some of the world's best sunglasses are made in Berlin, where the very word "sun" leaves residents' vocabularies entirely for nine months a year? Maybe, but these are some gorgeous frames, light, sleek, and hand-assembled, and Mykita will do regular prescription specs too. Rosa-Luxemburg-Strasse 6. www.mykita.com. ℂ **030/ 67308715.** U-Bahn: Rosa-Luxemburg-Platz.

Souvenirs & Specialties

Ampelmann ★   When the traffic lights in the GDR turned green, the be-hatted Ampelmann was the "walk" figure you saw. Nowadays his beloved silhouette appears not only on lights in the West, but on retro lamps, T-shirts, umbrellas, keychains, bottle openers, and much, much more at six shops across the city. Hackesche Höfe, Potsdamer Platz, Karl-Liebnicht-Strasse, Gendarmenmarkt, Unter den Linden, Kranzler Eck; more info at www.ampelmann.de.

Erzgebirgshaus ★ For those who never want Christmas to end, this traditional store offers a year-round selection of hand-carved wooden decorations from the Erzgebirge, a region in Saxony. Pick up nutcrackers, incense-smoking carved figures, and candelabras. Friedrichstrasse 194–199. www.erzgebirgshaus.de. ℂ **030/20450977.** U-Bahn: Stadtmitte.

Frau Tonis ★★ With its smokers, drinkers and inattentive dog owners, Berlin is hardly a nice-smelling city, but at Stefanie Hanssen's modern perfumery, it makes scents. (Sorry!) Customize your own blend or go with locally produced classics like the intoxicating violet-tinged "Veilchen," modeled after Marlene Dietrich's favorite fragrance. Zimmerstrasse 13. www.frau-tonis-parfum.com. ℂ **030/20215310.** U-Bahn: Kochstrasse/Checkpoint Charlie.

Neurotitan ★ Next to the more commercial Hackesche Höfe lies Haus Schwarzenberg, an unrenovated artist-owned courtyard space covered in punky murals. Up a screamingly colorful staircase in its back building, this cult shop and gallery sells edgy comics, graphic novels, prints, and zines, mostly by Berliners. Come here if you're looking to please the art lover or rebellious teenager in your life. Rosenthaler Strasse 39. www.neurotitan.de. ℂ **030/30872576.** U-Bahn: Weinmeisterstrasse.

Ostpaket ★★★ Longing to scratch that Ostalgia itch in souvenir form? Head straight to this make-believe GDR Kaufhaus. It's got a few historical inaccuracies—no lines, for one, and everything's in stock—but the products, like the chalky "Schlager-Süsstafel" chocolate bar and cult Novum-brand soap, are so on point that the owner estimates 60% of her customers are onetime East Berliners looking for a taste of childhood. Spandauer Strasse 2. www.ostpaket.de. ℂ **030/28884518.** S-Bahn: Hackescher Markt.

Space Hall ★ Berlin's got oodles of record sellers, but crate digging is often a disappointing experience, thanks to an army of DJs who snap up all the decent finds. Show up early enough at this low-lit, electronica-focused Kreuzberg shop and you might just beat them to it. Zossener Strasse 33. www.spacehall.de. ℂ **030/6947664.** U-Bahn: Gneisenaustrasse.

Vintage Fashion

Glanzstücke ★ This glittery boutique in Mitte's Hackesche Höfe specializes in fashion from the 1920s-1960s and carries vintage costume jewelry, evening bags, feather boas, and more. Hackesche Höfe. www.glanzstuecke-berlin.de. ℂ **030/2082676.** S-Bahn: Hackescher Markt.

BUYING the wall

Cold War Berlin's most formidable symbol is today its most sought-after souvenir. In gift shops across the city, you'll see little fragments of concrete encased in plastic bubbles or embedded in Plexiglas, sold alongside certificates claiming their authenticity. So, are they for real? Short answer: Probably! Though the individual vendors pushing dubious unlabeled rocks near the East Side Gallery and Checkpoint Charlie are mostly selling fakes, the majority of fragments sold through official venues can be traced to one man: Volker Pawlowski, an enterprising Berliner who bought a 300-meter stretch of Berlin Wall back in 1991. But while that concrete chunk might be the genuine article, the paint on it probably isn't. Pawlowski has admitted to spray-painting his Wall pieces himself to make them more appealing to authenticity-craving tourists.

Made in Berlin ★   The secondhand clothes, shoes, and accessories at thse Mitte shops may not all be made in Berlin, but they're high-quality and in line with current trends (think 1960s sunglasses the size of computer screens). Shop during Wednesday's Happy Hour from 10am to 3pm and you'll get a 20% discount. Friedrichstrasse 114a and Neue Schönhauser 19. ✆ **030/24048900.** U-Bahn: Friedrichstrasse or S-Bahn Hackescher Markt.

Mimi ★★   Step way, way back in time at this Schöneberg gem featuring elegant evening gowns, lacy blouses, and ornate accessories from 1850 on, so authentic that they've been rented out for Berlin-shot period films like *The Grand Budapest Hotel* and *The Reader*. Goltzstr. 5. www.mimi-berlin.de. ✆ **030/23638438.** U-Bahn: Eisenacher Strasse.

Waahnsinn ★   Come here to search out new and secondhand fashion, and kitschy gifts like miniature Fernsehturms, beaded ball gowns, retro lamps, and authentic lederhosen—what else would you expect in a store whose name means "nonsense"? Rosenthaler Strasse 17. www.waahnsinn-berlin.de. ✆ **030/2820029.** U-Bahn: Rosenthaler Platz.

BERLIN NIGHTLIFE

All the rumors you've heard about nightlife in Berlin are true. No, really. A plethora of inventively repurposed spaces, a surplus of creative, international residents who don't tend to have day jobs, and an exceptionally relaxed attitude towards alcohol and other substances make for a bar and club scene that literally does not stop. Add to that the city's legendary opera, classical, and theater institutions, which continue to be both relevant and affordable, and it's no wonder locals here find themselves muttering things like "Why did I go to that recital for voice, 18th-century lute, and sewing machine when I could've been dancing to techno in the dog biscuit factory?" on a regular basis. Whether you're looking to go loud, soft, upmarket, downtempo, traditional, bleeding-edge avant-garde, or anywhere in between, you will find something to do—this we promise. Avoiding that first-world affliction known as FOMO ("fear of missing out") may be trickier.

First, you'll want to find out what's going on. For a well-balanced overview, look to the event listings in the English-language print and online magazine *Exberliner* (www.exberliner.com). More comprehensive but less curated listings can be found in the German-language *Zitty* (www.zitty.de) and the *Berlin Programm* (www.berlin-programm.de), while the Berlin section of *Resident Advisor* (www.residentadvisor.net) is the most reliable club guide.

If you want to see a popular opera, a ballet, or the Philharmonic, you'd be advised to book well in advance. If you're not as picky, discount tickets for same-day performances are available at **Hekticket** (www.hekticket.de, © **030/2309930**), with outlets in the Deutsche Bank foyer by Bahnhof Zoo (Hardenbergstrasse 29; U-Bahn: Zoologischer Garten, Mon-Sat noon-8pm, Sun 2pm-6pm) and on Alexanderplatz (Alexanderstr. 1, U-/S-Bahn: Alexanderplatz, Mon-Fri noon-7pm). For rock and jazz concerts, buy tickets through **KonzertKasse36,** either online (www.koka36.de, © **030/61101313**) or at its kiosk in Kreuzberg (Oranienstrasse 29, U-Bahn: Kottbusser Tor, Mon–Fri 9am–7pm, Sat 10am–4pm).

A few extra pointers: Like restaurants, many Berlin bars don't take credit cards, so bring cash on your night out. Tipping is not strictly necessary but appreciated; when in doubt, round up to the nearest euro. With a few exceptions, the club scene here is generally more "dressed-down" than in other cities—you're there to dance, so leave the high heels at home. Live classical, rock, and jazz concerts start more or less when they're advertised, but don't even think about showing up at a club before midnight.

> ### Discounted Tickets
>
> Unsold day-of-performance tickets for music, dance, and theater are available for up to 50% off at **Hekticket** (see below) and the **BERLIN** infostores (see p. 62). A **Berlin Welcome Card** (see p. 67) allows you to buy reduced-price tickets (usually 25% off) at over 30 major venues, including the ballet and opera houses. If you're a student or senior, you might be entitled to a steep discount or very inexpensive rush tickets depending on the venue.

The Performing Arts

CLASSICAL MUSIC

Berliner Philharmoniker (Berlin Philharmonic) ★★★ One of the world's best orchestras, the Berlin Philharmonic performs under the baton of Sir Simon Rattle (to be succeeded by Kirill Petrenko in 2019) in the acoustically superb Philharmonie in the Kulturforum. Tickets are pricy and sell out fast, but cheapskates and procrastinators can still get a taste at the free "lunchtime" chamber music concerts held Tuesdays at 1pm in the foyer. Herbert-von-Karajan-Strasse 1. www.berlin-philharmonic.com. © **030/25488999.** U-Bahn: Potsdamer Platz.

A modern-dress production of *Don Giovanni* at the esteemed Desutsche Oper Berlin.

Deutsche Oper Berlin ★★★ This opera company performs in Charlottenburg in a splendid modern post-war opera house, presenting a full repertoire of classic and contemporary operas, recitals, and ballet with a focus on living composers. Bismarckstrasse 35. www.deutscheoper berlin.de. ✆ **030/34384343.** U-Bahn: Deutsche Oper. S-Bahn: Charlottenburg.

Komische Oper Berlin ★★★ The "Comic Opera" has become one of the most highly regarded ensembles in Europe with Barrie Kosky's innovative, contemporary productions of operas, operettas, ballets, and musicals. Behrenstrasse 55–57. www.komische-oper-berlin.de. ✆ **030/202600.** U-Bahn: Französische Strasse. S-Bahn: Friedrichstrasse or Unter den Linden.

Konzerthaus Berlin ★★★ Schinkel's splendid neoclassical building on Gendarmenmarkt hosts regular performances by the Berlin Symphony Orchestra and Deutsches Sinfonie Orchestra in its glittering, pitch-perfect main hall, plus chamber music and musical theatre performances in the two smaller halls above the foyer. Gendarmenmarkt. www.konzerthaus.de. ✆ **030/203092101.** U-Bahn: Französische Strasse.

Staatsoper ★★★ Under musical director Daniel Barenboim, Berlin's oldest opera company provides a stage for opera, chamber concerts, recitals, and ballet of remarkable quality; they also have a focus on new music. Their historic house on Unter den Linden is scheduled to reopen in 2017 after extensive renovations; in the meantime, performances take place at the Schiller Theater on Bismarckstrasse. Unter den Linden 7. www.staatsoper-berlin.org. ✆ **030/20354555.** U-Bahn: Französische Strasse.

DANCE
Uferstudios ★ Berlin's forward-thinking contemporary dance scene needs no translation, and at this world-renowned dance school and

performance space housed in an ex-BVG depot in Wedding, you can experience it right at the source. The complex is also home to Piano Salon Christophori, an antique piano repair workshop that hosts intimate classical concerts. Uferstrasse 8. www.uferstudios.com. ✆ **030/46060887.** U-Bahn: Nauener Platz.

THEATER

Berliner Ensemble ★ If you're a fan of legendary director Bertolt Brecht, make a pilgrimage to his historic theater company, now performing in Mitte's ornate Theater am Schiffbauerdamm. They run works by the master (his *Three-Penny Opera* sells out regularly) alongside contemporary German playwrights, all auf Deutsch. Bertolt-Brecht-Platz 1. www.berliner-ensemble.de. ✆ **030/28408155.** S/U-Bahn Friedrichstrasse.

Hebbel am Ufer (HAU) ★★ Whether an adaptation of *Infinite Jest* or a jukebox musical by expat provocateur Peaches, this trio of venues near Kreuzberg's Landwehrkanal is the place to go for edgy, irreverent, pop-culture-savvy contemporary dance and theater performances, as well as the occasional concert. Stresemennstrasse 29 (HAU1), Hallesches Ufer 32 (HAU2), Tempelhofer Ufer 10 (HAU3). www.hebbel-am-ufer.de. ✆ **030/2590040.** U-Bahn: Hallesches Tor.

Maxim Gorki Theater ★★★ Devoted to Soviet Realism in the GDR era, this rejuvenated Mitte mainstay now produces pointed, relevant "post-migrant" theater that addresses race and immigration in modern-day Berlin, performed by a talented, diverse ensemble. All productions are shown with English surtitles after their premieres. Am Festungsgraben 2. www.gorki.de. ✆ **030/202210.** S/U-Bahn: Friedrichstrasse.

Volksbühne ★★ Under the venerable Frank Castorf, the East Berlin "People's Theater" whose grand edifice dominates Rosa-Luxemburg-Platz became known for epic post-modern endurance-fests, impenetrable even to German speakers. As of 2017, he's been replaced by Chris Dercon of London's Tate Modern, so expect greater user-friendliness and English accessibility. Rosa-Luxemburg-Platz. www.volksbuehne-berlin.de. ✆ **030/24065777.** U-Bahn: Rosa-Luxemburg-Platz.

VARIETY SHOWS, CABARET & COMEDY

Comedy Café Berlin ★ A few years ago, it would've been ludicrous to recommend English-language comedy in Berlin. And, okay, the genre is still finding its feet, with an overabundance of bitter expats telling "How 'bout those Germans?" jokes. But you can catch the best stand-ups and improvisers on the fast-growing scene (and a sprinkling of touring alternative comedians) in this new international comedy venue. Roseggerstrasse 19. www.comedycafeberlin.com. ✆ **01521/4660257.** U-Bahn: Karl-Marx-Strasse.

Friedrichstadt Palast ★ Enter the massive historic theater on Friedrichstrasse and experience Berlin's cheesy, often bewildering version of a Las Vegas-style revue: dancers, acrobats, dazzling lighting, loads of costume changes, and songs with lyrics seemingly pulled from Google Translate. Friedrichstrasse 107. www.friedrichstadtpalast.de. ℭ **030/23262326.** U-/S-Bahn: Friedrichstrasse.

Prinzipal ★ This closet-sized Kreuzberg speakeasy is intended as a nod to the decadent Berlin cabarets of the 1920s, as immortalized in *Cabaret,* but owes just as much to the American neo-burlesque movement, as immortalized by Dita von Teese in your hastily closed browser window. Racy, uninhibited performances take place over expensive cocktails every Saturday night. Oranienstrasse 178. www.prinzipal-kreuzberg.com. ℭ **030/61627326.** U-Bahn: Kottbusser Tor.

Wintergarten Varieté ★★ The largest and most nostalgic Berlin variety theater, the Wintergarten offers an extravagant nightly variety show featuring magicians, clowns, jugglers, acrobats, and live music. Potsdamer Strasse 96. www.wintergarten-variete.de. ℭ **030/588433.** U-Bahn: Kurfürstenstrasse.

The Club Scene

JAZZ

A Trane ★★ This small and smoky Charlottenburg jazz house features top-name musicians from all over the world, plus high-caliber late-night jam sessions on Saturdays. If you don't like the line-up on a given night, try the equally venerated Quasimodo a few blocks away. Pestalozzistrasse 105. www.a-trane.de. ℭ **030/3132550.** S-Bahn: Savignyplatz.

Sowieso ★★ The established big names might play out west in A-Trane and Quasimodo, but this living-room-sized nook in Neukölln is where jazz connoisseurs go for an affordable breath of fresh musical air. Depending on the night, you might catch a microtonal synth performance from players in Berlin's experimental "echtzeitmusik" scene, an hour of improvisation from a touring Japanese combo, or a trombone set by East German free-jazz legend Conny Bauer. Weisestrasse 24. www. sowieso-neukoelln.de. ℭ **01577/2879965.** U-Bahn: Boddinstrasse.

ROCK & INDIE CLUBS

ACUD ★★ A 1990s-era arts collective in Mitte comprising a theater, art gallery, cinema, bar, and venue, ACUD was a decrepit, druggy shadow of its former self by the time a group of wealthier artists bought it out in 2014. Now it's back on the scene with an indie-leaning concert program, club nights, films, open mics, and great Moscow Mules. Veteranenstrasse 21. www.acudmachtneu.de. ℭ **030/44359497.** U-Bahn: Rosenthaler Platz.

Silent Green ★   Are crematoriums the new swimming pools? In 2015, Stattbad Wedding, a repurposed bathing hall turned club, venue, and exhibition space, was unexpectedly forced to close. Taking its place as "quirky cultural space that's worth the trip to Wedding," Silent Green is a stunning chimneyed complex with a morbid past that puts on rock and electronic concerts, art exhibitions, and DJ nights. It's worth checking the website to see what's going on. Gerichtstrasse 35. www.silent-green. net. ✆ **030/46067324.** S-/U-Bahn: Wedding.

SO36 ★★★   Back in the 1970s, Esso was to Berlin what CBGB was to New York, a punk rock and New Wave haven frequented by Iggy Pop, David Bowie, and a generation of disaffected young West Berliners. Now its two large rooms offer a varied program of live bands and DJ nights, from punk to Asian house, techno to funk. The club is also famous for its monthly Gayhane parties, where Berlin's small but lively gay and lesbian Turkish community comes to mingle over Oriental beats. Oranienstrasse 190. www.so36.de. ✆ **030/61401306.** U-Bahn: Kottbusser Tor.

DANCE CLUBS

Clärchens Ballhaus ★★★   A landmark in old East Berlin, this dance hall opened in 1913 and has reemerged as a fabulously retro place for all-ages ballroom dancing in an atmosphere complete with bow-tied waiters and silver tinsel. There's salsa, swing, waltz, or tango every night

Retro ballroom dancing at the Clärchens Ballhaus.

and you can brush up your footwork at one of the regular free-of-charge dance classes. Auguststrasse 24. www.ballhaus.de. ℰ **030/2829295.** S-Bahn: Oranienburger Strasse.

Dean ★ Contrary to reports, Mitte nightlife didn't die when derelict dive Delicious Donuts was replaced by this sleek, black-banquetted club owned by the neighboring Amano Hotel. It did transform into something a bit more moneyed and mature, but if you can foot the bill, you'll have a genuinely decent time getting down to funk, R'n'B, and hip hop on Dean's pocket-sized LED-illuminated dance floor. Rosenthaler Strasse 9. www.amanogroup.de/eat-drink/dean. ℰ **030/8094150.** U-Bahn: Rosenthaler Platz.

Kaffee Burger ★ One of the final holdovers from the anything-goes Torstrasse club scene of yesteryear, this trashy-but-fun venue was popularized as a meeting point for artists, musicians and actors in the 1970s GDR, and then again as the site of writer Wladimir Kaminer's wild Russendisko parties in the 2000s. These days it hosts concerts, readings, and dance nights, turning into a somewhat icky pick-up spot after 1am. Torstrasse 60. www.kaffeeburger.de. ℰ **030/28046495.** U-Bahn: Rosa-Luxemburg-Platz.

TECHNO CLUBS

Berghain ★★★ If you've ever heard anyone wax poetic about Berlin's techno scene, this is the club they meant. A towering former power station fitted with one of the world's best sound systems, it attracts big-name DJs, in-the-know celebrities, and never-ending lines for hedonistic parties that start late on Saturday and end sometime Monday morning. Much ink has been spilled on how to ace the door policy, which is more selective than most Ivy League schools: go on a Sunday afternoon, wear lots of black, don't talk in line, memorize the DJ lineup... to which we can only add, make sure you have a backup plan (like Tresor, p. 130). If you do get in, you'll find pounding minimal techno in the main Berghain hall and house music in the upstairs Panorama Bar, spun to enthusiastic, often-shirtless crowds. Prudes, take heed: Berghain's past as a gay fetish bar lives on in downstairs male only sex club Lab.Oratory and in the main club's hidden "darkrooms" (in which, it is safe to say, no photos are developed). Am Wriezener Bahnhof. www.berghain.de. ℰ **030/29360210.** S-Bahn: Ostbahnhof.

Club der Visionäre ★★ Relaxed and effortlessly cool, this canal-side shack at the nexus of Kreuzberg and Treptow is the place to be on balmy summer evenings. When the weather's warm, young clubbers laze on the deck, gulp cold beer, and drift away to minimal chill-out music. Am Flutgraben 1. www.clubdervisionaere.com. ℰ **030/69518944.** U-Bahn: Schlesisches Tor.

4

BERLIN'S adult playgrounds

Some of the city's best hotspots aren't single venues, but miniature villages that offer something for partiers of every persuasion.

On summer weekends, the spot where the Landwehrkanal meets the Spree River (U-Bahn: Schlesisches Tor) swarms with young revelers 24/7. The big draw is floating pool **Badeschiff ★★★** which offers swimming, drinks, and DJs for a modest entry fee. American-style burger restaurant **White Trash Fast Food** abuts the popular canal-side watering hole **Club der Visionäre** (p. 129). Across the canal is **Chalet,** a techno club with a welcoming beer garden (and not-so-welcoming door policy).

Also along the Spree lies **Holzmarkt ★★** (Holzmarktstrasse 25, S-Bahn Jannowitzbrücke), the still-growing reincarnation of the late lamented techno-hippie compound Bar25. They'll gladly let you drop 50€-plus on dinner at their high-end restaurant **Fame,** and you're welcome to visit the theater, gallery, urban garden, or beach bar... but speak English in line at club **Kater Blau** and you may be given das Boot.

Then there's Friedrichshain's crumbling train repair depot **R.A.W. Gelände ★★** (Revaler Strasse 99; U-Bahn Warschauer Strasses), home of two clubs (techno bunker **Suicide Circus** and reggae/punk-leaning **Cassiopeia**), two live venues (jazz/Balkan/hip-hop hangout **Badehaus Szimpla** and the larger **Astra Kulturhaus**), a clubby swimming pool **(Haubentaucher),** and an indie art gallery/venue/beer garden **(Urban Spree).** There's also rock climbing, an outdoor movie theater, a skate park, street food stands—and lots of drug dealers, which can add an aggressive vibe. Afternoons and early evenings are more relaxed, and the graffiti-strewn grounds offer prime photo ops.

Tresor ★   Didn't make it into Berghain? The door policy in this massive labyrinthine power plant is much more relaxed, the DJ lineups are quite similar, and you'll be dancing in the descendant of one of Berlin's oldest and most influential clubs: Owner Dmitri Hegemann effectively kicked off the entire techno scene when he opened the original Tresor by Potsdamer Platz in 1991. The more adventurous should check out the smaller **OHM** next door, where Goth-tinged experimental beats echo off tiled walls. Köpenicker Strasse 70. www.tresorberlin.com. ☎ **030/69537721.** U-Bahn: Heinrich-Heine-Strasse.

Watergate ★★   Berlin's second-most-famous club opened in 2002, back in eastern Kreuzberg's pre-gentrification days; co-owner and ex-punk Steffen "Stoffel" Hack recalls having to persuade passersby to come inside. Now the entire area has become one of Berlin's major party corridors, and an extremely un-punk crowd swarms at Watergate's gates every weekend. Times may have changed, but the DJs here remain ahead-of-the-curve, the flashing LED ceiling remains entertaining, and the riverside terrace is still one of the best places in town to watch the sun rise at the end of a long night. Falkensteinstrasse 49. www.water-gate.de. ℡ **030/61280394.** U-Bahn: Schlesisches Tor.

Bars, Beer Gardens & Cafes

Closing hours for bars can be are tricky, since they are not required by law to stop serving alcohol at any set time. Many stay open "until the last customer leaves," which can vary wildly.

BEER GARDENS & BREWERIES

Eschenbräu ★ Why go all the way to a back courtyard in the hinterlands of Wedding for a beer? Because it's damn good beer, made right on the premises since before "craft beer" was a thing here, and you'll be drinking it in a lively outdoor garden or intimate cellar bar with nary a fellow tourist in sight. Try a glass of toasty Dunkel or see which seasonal specialties brewmaster Martin Eschenbrenner has on tap. Triftstrasse 67. www.eschenbraeu.de. ℡ **0162/4931915.** Daily from 5pm-1am (3pm-1am May-Sept). U-Bahn: Leopoldplatz.

Golgatha ★★★ In the heart of Kreuzberg's Viktoriapark, this leafy beer garden becomes an open-air club after 10pm, with DJs spinning electro, rock, and pop. You can come to dance or just have some drinks on the terrace. German brews including Kreuzberg Monastery dark beer (which actually comes from another Kreuzberg, some 400km away from Berlin's) go well with snacks from the charcoal grill. Dudenstrasse 40. www.golgatha-berlin.de. ℡ **030/7852453.** Apr–Sept daily 9am-midnight; closed Oct–Mar. U-Bahn: Platz der Luftbrücke.

Hopfenreich ★★ After decades of mass-produced pilsner, the craft beer movement has taken hold of Berlin, with an ever-increasing number of local brewers producing hoppy American-style ales and even reviving forgotten German styles. Sample the best of the scene and beyond at this clean, smoke-free craft pub, featuring a vast, ever-changing selection of microbrews and knowledgeable, English-speaking bartenders who'll be happy to lob over a recommendation. Sorauer Str. 31. www.hopfenreich.de. ℡ **030/88061080.** Daily 4pm-2am. U-Bahn: Schlesisches Tor.

Prater Garten ★★★ This 600-seat beer garden in Prenzlauer Berg is the city's oldest, dating from 1837, and attracts a wonderfully diverse crowd of locals and tourists. Here's the place to try the traditional Berliner Weisse, a sour low-alcohol brew flavored with brightly colored syrup and sipped through a straw. (Like currywurst, you only need to have it once.) Order snacks from the outdoor grill or eat a heartier meal inside. Kastanienallee 7–9. www.pratergarten.de. ℡ **030/4485688.** Apr–Sept daily noon-10pm; closed Oct-Mar. U-Bahn: Eberswalder Strasse.

Südblock ★★★ This neighborhood hangout—a chill, welcoming space where Kreuzberg's queer, leftist and Turkish communities converge over beer, coffee and Flammkuchen—opened in 2010, but feels like it's been around for much longer. The expansive patio is packed on warm days; go inside the glass-walled building itself and you may encounter anything from a debate on gentrification to a karaoke drag show. Admiralstrasse 1-2. www.suedblock.org. ✆ **030/60941853.** Daily from 10am (closing time depends upon events). U-Bahn: Kottbusser Tor.

BARS/CAFES

Ä ★★ Wander around Neukölln's Weserstrasse and its environs, and you'll find countless near-identical Wohnzimmerkneipen ("living room bars") with mismatched second-hand furniture, stripped walls, and young, international drinkers. As the original, Ä has remained pleasantly unpretentious: the beer's still cheap, the bartenders still speak German and there's a separate non-smoking section (a rarity for the area). Go on a Wednesday evening for acoustic concerts in the candlelit back room. Weserstrasse 40. www.ae-neukölln.de. ✆ **0177/4063837.** Daily 5pm–1am or later. U-Bahn: Rathaus Neukölln.

Ankerklause ★★ On the banks of Kreuzberg's Landwehrkanal, this nautical-themed canalside shack offers cheap drinks, late breakfasts, and a nice waterside terrace. The crowd is young, tattooed, and rowdy, especially on weekends when the sun goes down and the jukebox selections get turned up. Kottbusser Damm 104. www.ankerklause.de. ✆ **030/6935649.** Tues–Sun 10am–4am, Mon 4pm–4am. U-Bahn: Schönleinstrasse.

Café Einstein ★★★ This legendary Viennese-style cafe in an atmospheric old townhouse (reputed to have once been the home of Goebbels' mistress) serves mellow house-roasted Kaffee and freshly made Kuchen (cake) as well as breakfast, lunch, and dinner. There's another branch at Unter den Linden 42 and a Starbucks-like chain of the same name, but this one's the real thing. If you're more in a drinking mode, go upstairs to cocktail bar **Lebensstern,** which you'll recognize from the pub scene in Tarantino's *Inglourious Basterds.* Kurfürstenstrasse 58. www. cafeeinstein.com. ✆ **030/2615096.** Daily 9am–1am. U-Bahn: Wittenbergplatz.

Café Wintergarten im Literaturhaus ★★ If you're looking for a serene and sophisticated respite from the garish Ku'damm, you'll find it in this 19th-century villa surrounded by a leafy garden. A prime spot for afternoon coffee and cake, or perhaps a heartier breakfast or lunch, among well-heeled ur-Charlottenburgers. Alone? Bring a book; you'll fit right in. The Literaturhaus itself hosts regular German-language readings and literary exhibitions. Fasanenstrasse 23. www.literaturhaus-berlin.de. ✆ **030/8825414.** Daily 9am–midnight. U-Bahn: Uhlandstrasse.

Klungerkranich's outdoor terrace.

Dr. Pong ★★ Berlin loves ping pong like no other European city, and at this smoky Prenzlauer Berg dive, you can witness that love affair in action every night. Players of all skill and sobriety levels run around the table batting balls in the round-robin version of the game that Germans inexplicably call "Chinese." Hardcore regulars bring their own paddles, but you can rent one from the bar. Eberswalder Strasse 21. www.drpong.net. No phone. Mon–Sat 8pm–3am or later, Sun from 6pm (Oct–Apr) or 7pm (May–Sept). U-Bahn: Eberswalder Strasse.

Edelweiss ★ Locals either love or hate Kreuzberg's Görlitzer Park, that big grassy area that's become a Berlin synonym for grass of a different kind. In the middle of all the dreadlocks, drum circles, and dogs, an old train station provides the ideal platform for people-watching over an afternoon tea, coffee or beer. On Tuesday nights, head to the smoky upstairs room for one of Berlin's best jazz jam sessions. Görlitzer Strasse 1-3. www.edelweiss36.com. ✆ **030/61074858.** Mon–Sat 10am–3am. U-Bahn: Görlitzer Bahnhof.

Klunkerkranich ★★★ Incongruously perched on a mall parking garage, this outdoor hipster hangout offers a lovely 360-degree view of southeastern Berlin to be savored over coffee, beers, and/or snacks served out of wooden huts. Evenings bring DJs, live music, and epic sunsets, but also entrance fees and long lines. To avoid aggravation, go right at opening time or in late fall, when they heat the huts (and the wine) for a cozy ski-lodge feel. Karl-Marx-Strasse 86 (take mall elevator to 5th floor). www.klunkerkranich.de. No phone. Mar–Dec Thurs–Fri 4pm–1:30am, Sat–Sun noon–1:30am. U-Bahn: Rathaus Neukölln.

St. Oberholz ★★ The throbbing heart of Berlin's hyped start-up scene (aka "Silicon Allee") is a two-floor café and co-working space on Rosenthaler Platz that hums at all hours with the whine of espresso machines, the clack of fingers on MacBook keyboards, and conversations about pivots and venture capital. If you've got some emails to send, bring your laptop here and join the fray. Rosenthaler Strasse 72a. www.sanktoberholz.de. ℂ **030/24085586.** Mon–Thurs 8am–midnight, Fri 8am–3am, Sat 9am–3am, Sun 9am–midnight. U-Bahn: Rosenthaler Platz.

Schwarzes Café ★★ Whether you need a late-night pick-me-up, an early-morning breakfast, or the other way around, look for the neon parrot sign on Kantstrasse. A welcome spot of anarchy in buttoned-up Charlottenburg, this two-story relic from the 1970s serves a motley crowd 24 hours a day, (nearly) every day. Prices are a bit high for what you get, but you won't find the atmosphere anywhere else in the West. Kantstrasse 148. www.schwarzescafe-berlin.de. ℂ **030/3138038.** Daily 24 hours, closed Tuesdays 3am–10am. S-Bahn: Savignyplatz.

Solar ★★ One of the best views of Berlin by night is to be had from this sleek, glassed-in lounge on the 17th floor of a nondescript high-rise in Mitte. Kick back with an overpriced drink and a dressed-up crowd as the city's landmarks twinkle below. There's a fancy fusion restaurant as well, if you want a meal with your view. Stresemannstrasse 76. www.solarberlin.com. ℂ **0163/765225700.** Daily 6pm–2am or later. S-Bahn: Anhalter Bahnhof.

COCKTAIL BARS

Le Croco Bleu ★ End your meal at Tim Raue's La Soupe Populaire (see p. 113) with a cocktail at this fancifully decorated bar, where industrial chic meets fairytale whimsy. Drinks are expertly mixed and unfailingly inventive (like the Fairy Floss, topped with absinthe cotton candy), with commensurate prices. Prenzlauer Allee 242. www.lecrocobleu.com. ℂ **0151/58247804.** Thurs–Sat 6pm–midnight or later. U-Bahn: Senefelderplatz

Victoria Bar ★★ Aside from its gay cruising spots, the neighborhood of Schöneberg is home to a handful of grown-up, sophisticated cocktail bars that hit a pleasing middle ground between the greying tourist haunts of Charlottenburg and the fedora'd mixology of Neukölln. This one's the oldest and most old-school, eschewing fancy infusions in favor of well-crafted Sidecars, Aviations, and whiskey sours. Regulars order the off-menu "Hildegard Knef Gedächtnis Gedeck": an ice-cold shot of vodka and champagne chaser served on a silver platter. Potsdamer Strasse 102. www.victoriabar.de. ✆ **030/25759977.** Sun–Thurs 6:30pm–3am, Fri–Sat 6:30pm–4am. U-Bahn: Kurfürstenstrasse.

Gay & Lesbian Bars

Kumpelnest 3000 ★★ Gay or straight, you're welcome here; all that's asked is that you enjoy a good time in what used to be a brothel. This crowded and chaotic place is really mostly a bar, but don't be surprised if you end up dancing to disco classics. Lützowstrasse 23. www.kumpelnest 3000.com. ✆ **030/2616918.** Daily 7pm–6am. U-Bahn: Kurfürstenstrasse.

Prinzknecht ★ The gay bars around Schöneberg's Nollendorfplatz are rather infamous for being meat markets; if you're looking for something classier, this one's brick-lined, subtly lit, and mobbed with ordinary guys who just happen to like guys. It's also got a darkroom, lest you forget what part of town you're in. Fuggerstrasse 33. www.prinzknecht.de. ✆ **030/ 23627444.** Daily 3pm–3am. U-Bahn: Viktoria-Luise-Platz.

SchwuZ ★★★ While Schöneberg's gay scene tends to be older, male, and sex-focused, Kreuzberg and Neukölln's is young, mixed, and more politicized, usually preferring "queer" over "gay." Its epicenter is this 40-year-old Berlin institution, which recently relocated from a small basement to a huge former Kindl brewery with a great sound system. An inclusive—dare we say straight-friendly?—crowd parties to house, disco, and pop across three dance floors. Rollbergstrasse 26. www.schwuz.de. ✆ **030/57702270.** Check website for events. U-Bahn: Rathaus Neukölln.

Möbel-Olfe ★ Squeeze into this tiny, smoky spot off Kottbusser Tor to drink a beer among punks, drag queens, and exuberantly dressed regulars. You won't be able to sit down, but you might make new friends. Tuesdays are "Mädchendisko," ladies' night. Reichenberger Str. 177. www. moebel-olfe.de. ✆ **030/23274690.** Tues–Sun 6pm–4am.

DAY TRIPS FROM BERLIN

Ach, Brandenburg! Since the days of Frederick the Great, Berliners have headed out to the mostly-rural region to relax, take in some nature, and get away from the stresses of the big city. Their number-one destination? Potsdam, Brandenburg's capital and the site of Frederick's grandiose Sanssouci Palace. Since reunification, however, more and more of the area's other treasures have been opening up to international visitors. So, yes, start with Potsdam, but if you've got a little more time to spare, consider a former concentration camp, an overgrown abandoned hospital, a wetland nature reserve...

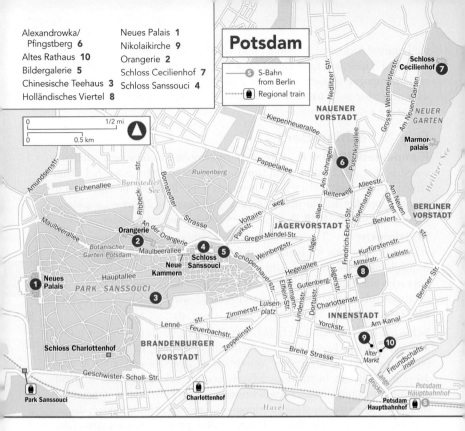

Potsdam & Sanssouci Palace ★★★

24km (15 miles) SW of Berlin

The baroque town of Potsdam on the Havel River is justly famous for Frederick the Great's **Schloss Sanssouci** (Sanssouci Palace), often called "Germany's Versailles" and the architectural signature of one of the country's most dominating personalities. Allow yourself at least half a day to visit this remarkable palace and its beautiful grounds. Potsdam, a former garrison town and now the capital of the state of Brandenburg, celebrated its 1,000th anniversary in 1993 and has historic sites of its own, but Sanssouci should be your top priority. Either before or after touring the palace, spend some time wandering through **Sanssouci Park,** a spread of magnificently landscaped gardens with a bevy of historic buildings, all of which are well-signposted within the park and share the same information number and website as the palace. Each charges a separate admission; buy a **Sanssouci+** combination ticket (19€) if you'd like to see more than just the palace and Bildergalerie.

GETTING THERE   From Berlin, **S-Bahn** line S7 stops at the Potsdam Hauptbahnhof (train station). Hop on bus no. 695 in front of the station and ride nine stops to the Schloss Sanssouci stop. Cross the road, turn left, and you'll almost immediately come to a flight of stairs leading up to the palace. If you don't want to hassle with transportation, the **Bex** sightseeing bus company (see p. 89) offers Potsdam-Sanssouci tours; the cost is generally about 45€ for a half-day.

GETTING AROUND   If you don't have a Berlin Welcome Card with Potsdam included (zones ABC), you can buy a day ticket for the city's bus system at the Potsdam Information center, which can also help you with walking, boat, and tram tours.

VISITOR INFORMATION   **Potsdam-Information,** Babelsberger Strasse 16, next to platform 6 in the train station (www.potsdam-tourism.com; *℃* **0331/27558899**), is open Monday through Saturday 9:30am to 6pm and Sundays from 10am to 4pm.

Royal Potsdam

Schloss Sanssouci ★★★ PALACE   One of the greatest and most beautiful examples of European rococo, Sanssouci was built between 1745 and 1747 as Frederick's summerhouse, a place where he could let his wig down, discuss weighty matters with French philosopher Voltaire,

Sanssouci Palace, a rococo gem.

and make music with composer Carl Philip Emanuel Bach. In short, Sanssouci ("without cares") was a sort of summer resort for an enlightened monarch. The king loved it so much that he requested to be buried there—and in fact, that's his grave right in front of the palace. (Why are there potatoes on it instead of flowers? Fred's supposedly the one who introduced Germans to the humble spud, arguably his most long-lasting accomplishment.) Atop a gorgeous terraced vineyard, the long, one-story building is crowned by a dome and flanked by two round pavilions. On a 45-minute audio tour (available in English), you'll be able to wander through its restored halls, from the elliptical white-and-gold Marble Hall to the ornately rococo Music Room to the Voltaire Room, where the philosopher slept surrounded by fanciful bird and flower decorations. Amazingly, the palace survived both World War II bombing and the GDR unscathed. The East German government, normally disdainful of anything Hohernzollern, even lobbied for it to become a UNESCO world heritage site. (It did, in 1990.) Fred the Great created the original design for the grounds, and his planning still is evident in the restored vineyard terraces and the area immediately around the palace.

Park Sanssouci. www.spsg.de. © **0331/9694200.** Admission 12€ adults, 8€ seniors/students. Apr–Oct Tues–Sun 10am–6pm (Nov–Mar to 5pm).

Bildergalerie (Picture Gallery) ★★ MUSEUM   Set on the eastern side of the palace grounds, this building was completed in 1763 and displays Frederick the Great's collection of works from the Italian Renaissance and baroque eras. Its unassuming facade hides a sumptuous marble and gold interior with paintings by Peter Paul Rubens (1577–1640), Caravaggio (1571–1610), and Anthony van Dyck (1599–1641). Pick up a flyer in English detailing the most important works and give yourself at least 30 to 45 minutes to see the highlights.

Park Sanssouci. Admission 6€ adults, 5€ seniors/students. May–Oct Tues–Sun 10am–6pm.

Chinesische Teehaus (Chinese Teahouse) ★ ARCHITECTURAL SITE   This little gem of a rococo building in Sanssouci park resembles a Chinese pagoda. Ornamental "Oriental" buildings like this were all the rage in 18th-century Europe. The privileged classes would retire here to drink a new beverage called "tea." The inside of the building is not open to the public, but the statues on the outside are worth a gander.

Neues Palais (New Palace) ★ PALACE   On the far-western end of Sanssouci park lies its biggest and, as the name might suggest, newest building, completed in 1769 and used by the Hohenzollern family as a place to welcome foreign dignitaries and hold special events. Inside you can see luxurious rococo rooms filled with paintings and antiques, although the two grandest attractions—the marble hall and palace theater—are undergoing renovations and not available to the public.

Park Sanssouci. Admission 8€ for guided tour. Sat–Thurs 9am–5pm (Nov–Mar until 4pm).

Schloss Cecilienhof, site of the Potsdam Conference in 1945.

Orangerie ★ GALLERY   The mid-19th-century Orangerie, west of the palace, contains copies of paintings by Raphael and features ornately decorated salons.

Park Sanssouci. Admission 3€. Mid-May to mid-Oct Fri–Wed 10am–5pm.

Schloss Cecilienhof (Cecilienhof Palace) ★★ PALACE   Located a few miles northeast of Sanssouci, this palace was completed in 1917 during the Prussian era's death throes. Today the manor-style building is less famous as a royal residence (its inhabitants, Crown Prince Wilhelm and Duchess Cecelie, only lived there for a year before the 1918 revolution stripped the Hohernzollerns of their power) than as the site of 1945's Potsdam Conference. Here the heads of the Allied powers, including U.S. President Harry Truman, British prime minister Winston Churchill, and Russian dictator Joseph Stalin, met to negotiate the aftermath of World War II. Parts of the palace are now used as a hotel, but you can still tour the rooms where the conference happened with an English audio guide.

Am Neuer Garten 8. Admission 6€ for tour. Tues–Sun 9am–5pm (Nov–Mar until 4pm).

More of Potsdam

Although your priority when visiting Potsdam will probably be Sanssouci, the city itself has many charming streets and historic areas to explore before or after your visit to the palace and gardens. You won't want to spend much time wandering around the generic "downtown" area, but budget a couple hours for one or more of the following.

Alexandrowka/Pfingstberg ★★ NEIGHBORHOOD   This one-time Russian colony looks as if it were transported into Potsdam from a Slavic fairy tale: rows of beautifully molded wooden cottages, surrounded by gardens and fruit orchards. In fact, the houses, located about a 10-minute walk north of downtown, were originally built for a group of Russian singers around 1826 by King Friedrich III, as an ode to his friendship with the late Czar Alexander I. Skip the museum, but you may want to have tea in the charming Gartencafé or wander up the hill just behind Alexandrowka to the Russian Orthodox church built there. From that point, it won't take long to hike up the Pfingstberg, Potsdam's highest hill. It's crowned by the Belvedere, an Italian Renaissance-style building commissioned by Friedrich IV in the 1840s, and the Temple of Pomona, a little pavilion and lookout point designed in 1800 by a young Karl Friedrich Schinkel (1781–1841) before he became Germany's most ubiquitous royal architect.

Nikolaikirche ★★ CHURCH   Rising above Potsdam's cobblestoned marketplace square, this mighty neoclassical church, completed in 1837 and inspired by Santa Maria Maggiore in Rome, is yet another of Karl Friedrich Schinkel's handiworks. Damaged in World War II and finally reopened to the public in 1981, it now holds occasional concerts—check website for details.
Am Alten Markt. www.nikolai-potsdam.de *(C)* **0331/2708602.** Admission free to church, tower 5€. Daily 9am–5pm.

Altes Rathaus (Old Town Hall) ★ MUSEUM   The Greco-Roman-inspired town hall beside the Nikolaikirche dates from the mid–18th century and has a noteworthy Corinthian colonnade. Perched on top of the cupola is the Greek Titan Atlas, bent under the weight of the earth. The Altes Rathaus underwent a complete transformation and reopened in 2013 as the Forum for Art and History, with a permanent exhibit that walks visitors through Potsdam's 1,000-year history.
Am Alten Markt 9. www.potsdam.de *(C)* **0331/2896868.** Admission 5€ adult, children under 18 free. Tues–Fri 10am–5pm; Sat–Sun 10am–6pm.

Holländisches Viertel (Dutch Quarter) ★★ NEIGHBORHOOD   Centered around Am Bassin and Benkerstrasse, the picturesque Dutch Quarter is named after the Dutch craftsmen who came to Potsdam in the mid–18th century at the invitation of "Soldier King" Frederick Wilhelm I. As you wander the cobbled lanes past gabled houses, look for Am Bassin 10, where Mozart lived in 1789, and the Italianate belfry of nearby St. Peter und Paul Kirche (1870). Antiques shops, boutiques, and galleries line Benkerstrasse. A bit farther to the northwest, the neo-Gothic Nauener Tor (1755) is one of Potsdam's last remaining city gates.

WHERE TO EAT

Der Butt ★★ GERMAN/FISH   Stopped giggling yet? Let's eat. This Dutch Quarter restaurant—which gets its admittedly hilarious name from the nickname of Friedrich Wilhelm IV—serves fresh, well-cooked, reasonably priced fish dishes to in-the-know Potsdamers. Try a dish of eel, trout, or perch fished from the Havel river, pan-fried and served with potatoes and cucumber salad. To drink, there's beer from local brewery Potsdamer Braumanufaktur.

Gutenbergstrasse 25. www.der-butt.de ✆ **0331/2006066.** Main courses 14€–20€. Daily noon–midnight.

La Maison du Chocolat ★ DESSERTS   On warm days, the terrace here is the best place to enjoy the Holländisches Viertel's Dutch-style ambiance. The old-world cafe is famed for its thick, smooth homemade hot chocolate and fruit tarts.

Benkertstrasse 20. www.schokoladenhaus-potsdam.de. ✆ **0331/2370730.** Desserts and snacks 5€–8€.

Sachsenhausen ★★

35km (22 miles) NE of Berlin

Sachsenhausen, the closest concentration camp to Berlin, doesn't make for the most cheery of afternoon jaunts, but it's one of the most important sites you can visit if you're looking to learn how exactly Germany's horrific Konzentrationslager system came into being. The camp is at Straase der Nationen 22 (www.stiftung-bg.de; ✆ **03301/200200**) and is open daily 8:30am to 6pm from mid-March to mid-October; the rest of the year, it's open Tuesday to Sunday 8:30am to 4:30pm.

Over 200,000 people were imprisoned in the triangular compound during the Nazi era: first political prisoners, then Jews, Sinti and Roma, homosexuals, and others deemed "inferior." But Sachsenhausen was more than just a camp. This was the administrative nerve center of the Nazis' entire concentration camp network. From here, the SS carefully and methodically planned out the extermination of millions of people, and the meticulous documentation of their efforts, displayed in the on-site museum, is just as chilling as the remains of the gas chambers, barracks, and execution trench. Like all of Germany's camps, this one was liberated in 1945, but as Berliners well know, the end of World War II didn't necessarily mean a reprieve from brutality. A separate museum on the grounds is devoted to Sachsenhausen's five-year afterlife as a Soviet internment camp for former Nazi supporters, during which at least 12,500 inmates died of starvation. You'll need a few hours to see everything and let it all sink in. A guided tour (15€ per group, available in English) is very worth it. There's not much else worth seeing in surrounding Oranienburg, so pack a lunch and make this a one-and-back.

To get there, take the S1 **train** to Oranienburg station, the last stop. Take bus line 804 or 821 from there to the Sachsenhausen memorial, labeled "Gedenkstätte."

Beelitz-Heilstätten ★

46km (29 miles) SW of Berlin

It feels like the premise for a horror movie: a sprawling, crumbling, overgrown 200-year-old hospital clinic in the middle of the Brandenburg woods. Built in 1898 in response to Berlin's increasing number of consumption cases, this clinic also treated soldiers wounded in World War I—including one Adolf Hitler. Since its abandonment in 1995, it has slowly turned from an insider tip among intrepid explorers to a family-friendly tourist attraction, complete with a treetop walkway, the **Baumkronenpfad,** that lets you look down on the ruins of the women's clinic (9.50€). To actually walk around on the grounds, you need to go on a tour (4€ in German; see **potsdamurlaub.de** for details); to legally enter a select few buildings, you'll have to book a "photo tour" with company **Go2Know** (40€-70€). The rest of the complex is off-limits...officially, at least. If you're coming here between April and June, it's worth taking the bus or driving into the town of Beelitz itself to sample northern Germany's best Spargel (white asparagus) right at its source.

To get there, take the **RE7 train** directly to the Beelitz-Heilstätten stop; you can go on to Beelitz proper on bus number 643 (get off at Am Lustgarten). To return to Berlin from the Beelitz Stadt train station, take the **RB33 train** north to Wannsee and switch to the S-Bahn 5 or 7 from there.

Spreewald ★★

100km (62 miles) SE of Berlin

An hour's train ride from Berlin, accessible from the town of **Lübbenau,** Spreewald is a lush forest interspersed with narrow, meandering waterways. Provided the weather cooperates, the UNESCO-designated biosphere is a pleasure to explore, either by foot or, preferably, on a boat. The traditional thing to do is get on a Kahnfahrt, a guided tour through the canals on a gondola-like contraption propelled via a man with a pole. These move very, very slowly and make lots of stops—the fastest version still takes about two hours. The easily bored will want to set their own pace by renting a canoe or kayak. You can do either in English at the **Grosser Spreewald Hafen** (Dammstrasse 77a, Lübbenau, www.grosser-kahnhafen.de; ✆ **035/422225**).

Alternately, take a walk through the woods from Lübbenau to **Lehde,** a tiny fishing village where the mail is still delivered by boat. Here you'll find the last traces of the Sorbs, Germany's vanishing Slavic ethnic minority, as well as a handful of waterside restaurants and cafés serving freshly smoked fish and myriad permutations of the famous Spreewaldgurken (Spreewald pickled cucumbers).

Lest you think it's all too quaint, we're obliged to warn you that the Spreewald also attracts a very particular kind of German holidaymaker, the type who likes to get absolutely wasted off beer and schnapps and listen to Schlager music in wholesome, UNESCO-protected surroundings.

To get there, take the RE2 **train** from Berlin-Ostbahnhof to the Lübbenau (Spreewald) station. A straight 20-minute walk up Poststrasse (directly opposite the station) will take you to the **tourist office** at Ehm-Welk-Strasse 15; a bit past there you'll find the major boat rental stands.

SAXONY & THURINGIA

5

Back in the days when these regions were part of East Germany, their famous cities were difficult to visit. Since reunification, however, they've been beautifully revived, and are refreshingly less touristy than their counterparts in southern Germany. There's Dresden, its baroque splendor at least partly restored; Leipzig, where Johann Sebastian Bach spent most of his musical life as cantor (choirmaster) of St. Thomas Church; and Meissen, famous for its exquisite porcelain. In the neighboring state of Thuringia, Weimar maintains its aura as an 18th-century cultural and philosophical hotbed, which two hundred years later gave birth to the Bauhaus movement.

The region also allows you to walk in the footsteps of Protestant reformer Martin Luther, who studied and became a monk in **Erfurt,** translated the New Testament while in hiding in **Eisenach**'s Wartburg castle, and preached in **Lutherstadt Wittenberg.** He is buried in the castle church onto whose door he nailed his 95 Theses 500 years ago in 1517.

Outside Dresden or Leipzig, you can find some of Germany's most unspoiled countryside and untouched villages, where rural traditions still linger. Since reunification, the tourist infrastructure has caught up and is now on par with other parts of the country. Hotels have been built, tourist facilities have been developed, and getting around is easier than ever thanks to an excellent network of trains and roads.

WEIMAR ★★

260km (162 miles) SW of Berlin, 24km (15 miles) E of Erfurt

Weimar, a beautiful 1,100-year-old town on the edge of the Thuringian Forest, retains much of its historic flavor: Many of its important historical monuments were spared bombing in World War II. Its atmospheric, narrow, winding streets, lined with houses from various periods, give the town its old-world character. A 19th-century writer called Weimar "one of the most walkable towns of Europe," and it still fits into that category.

Weimar's history as a cultural center is centuries old. Famed Renaissance painter Lucas Cranach the Elder worked here in the 16th century.

From 1708 to 1717, Bach was court organist. In 1775, Johann Wolfgang von Goethe settled in Weimar at the invitation of the court of "Dowager Duchess" Anna Amalia and her son, Duke Karl August, whose family ruled the duchy of Saxe-Weimar-Eisenach from 1741 until 1918. Goethe, in turn, drew other notables such as Herder and Schiller. Later in the 19th century, Franz Liszt was musical director of the National Theater; under his auspices, Wagner's *Lohengrin* premiered here in 1850. Richard Strauss picked up Liszt's baton in 1889. It was also in Weimar that the German national assembly met in February 1919, in the aftermath of World War I, to draw up the constitution for what was to be called the Weimar Republic, Germany's ill-fated first experiment with democracy.

Essentials

ARRIVING

BY TRAIN Weimar has regular direct links to Eisenach (trip time: 1 hour) and Erfurt (15 minutes). Connections to major cities such as Leipzig, Dresden, or Berlin require a change in Erfurt.

BY CAR Weimar is served by the A4 Autobahn. It's about a 2-hour drive from Dresden, 3 hours from Berlin.

VISITOR INFORMATION

Head for **Tourist-Information Weimar,** Markt 10 (www.weimar.de; © **03643/7450**). From April to October the office is open Monday to Saturday from 9:30am to 7pm and Sunday from 9:30am to 3pm. It closes one hour earlier between November and March.

Exploring Weimar

Weimar enjoys a scenic location on the Ilm River, set against the back-drop of the Ettersberg and Vogtland hills. The city has many popular sights, but perhaps the best thing to do here is simply wander about on foot. A walk at night through the old streets that once felt the footsteps of Goethe, Bach, Wagner, and Schiller can be richly rewarding.

The town's main square, the **Marktplatz,** or market square,

Goethe Garden House, in Park an der Ilm.

Saxony & Thuringia

retains the old flavor of the city. Painter Lucas Cranach the Elder lived here during his last year, from 1552 to 1553. Look for the **Lucas Cranach the Elder House,** richly decorated outside and bearing a coat of arms of the Cranach family. Today it houses a small theater that specializes in Goethe and his contemporaries.

For a picnic or stroll, we suggest a visit to **Park an der Ilm** flanking the little river for about 1km (2/3 miles). It was landscaped during the time of Goethe, whose first Weimar residence (today's **Goethe Garden House;** see below) stands right in the park; **Liszt-Haus** (p. 150) is on the western edge of the park at Marienstrasse 17. Or, if you've had a little too much Schiller and Goethe, flee the inner city and escape to the **Bauhaus Universität** (Bauhaus University) on Marienstrasse.

Bauhaus-Museum ★ MUSEUM   With the founding of the Staatliches Bauhaus art and design school by Walter Gropius in 1919, Weimar became the birthplace of the most influential aesthetic movement of the 20th century. Its modernist approach did not please the city's conservative government, however, and the school moved to Dessau in 1925. A shiny new museum is set to be completed by 2019, in time for the Bauhaus centennial, but until then this small museum opposite the German National Theater has exhibits about the school's curriculum, its famous professors such as Paul Klee and Wassily Kandinsky, and its approaches to fine art, design, and architecture. While here, you might as well snap a selfie with the famous statue of Goethe and Schiller in front of the theater.

Theaterplatz 1. www.klassik-stiftung.de. ✆ **03643/545400.** Admission 4€ adults, 3€ students and seniors. Apr–Oct Sun–Mon 10am–6pm; Nov–Mar Sun–Mon 10am–4pm.

Goethe Gartenhaus (Goethe's Garden House) ★ HISTORIC HOUSE   Avid Goethe fans will also want to make the pilgrimage to this modest cottage where he and his family first lived after moving to Weimar in 1776. It's in a lovely location right in the middle of a romantic park running along on the Ilm River. The tour takes in the living quarters with their original furnishings as well as drawings produced by Goethe while living here.

Park an der Ilm. www.klassik-stiftung.de. ✆ **03643/545400.** Admission 6€ adults, 4.50€ students and seniors, children 16 and under free. Apr–Oct Tues–Sun 10am–6pm; Nov–Mar Tues–Sun 10am–4pm.

Goethe Nationalmuseum ★★★ MUSEUM & HISTORIC HOUSE This museum is a monument to Johann Wolfgang von Goethe (1749-1832), Germany's literary lion and author of such famous works as *The Sorrows of Young Werther* and the epic drama *Faust.* The modern museum incorporates the baroque manor where he lived with his family from 1782 until his death; feel the spirit of the great man as you stroll through

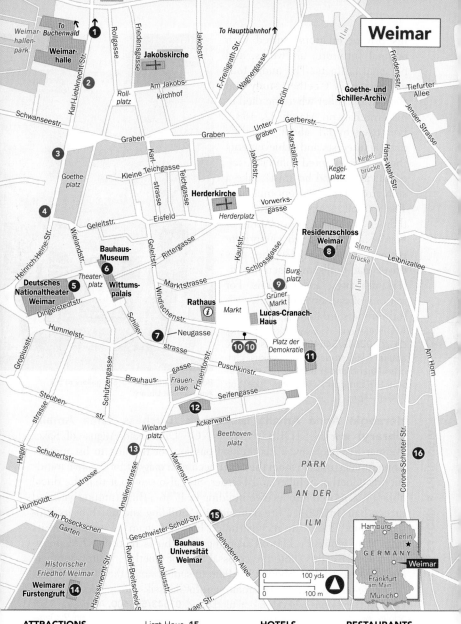

Weimar

ATTRACTIONS

Bauhaus-Museum **6**
Deutsches Nationaltheater **5**
Goethes Gartenhaus **16**
Goethe-Nationalmuseum **12**
Herzogin Anna Amalia
  Bibliothek **11**

Liszt-Haus **15**
Neues Museum Weimar **1**
Schillers Wohnhaus **7**
Schlossmuseum **8**
Weimarer Fürstengruft **14**

HOTELS

Amalienhof Hotel
  Weimar **13**
Grand Hotel
  Russischer Hof **4**
Hotel Elephant **10**
Labyrinth Hostel **3**

RESTAURANTS

Anna Amalia **10**
Lava Soul Kitchen **2**
Residenz Café &
  Restaurant **9**

his private quarters stuffed with original furniture, art works, and personal artifacts. The audio tour culminates in Goethe's study and the tiny chamber where he died in his armchair on March 22, 1832. For background about Goethe's diverse interests and achievements (he was also a noted politician, scientist, artist, and botanist), take a spin around the adjacent museum. The exhibit is divided into such themes as Genius, Love, World, or Nature and is peppered with private mementos, including Goethe's grey travel coat, quills, manuscripts, letters, drawings, and minerals. For reasons of conservation, daily visitor numbers are limited.

Am Frauenplan 1. www.klassik-stiftung. de. ℂ **03643/545400.** Admission 12€ adults, 8.50€ students and seniors, children 16 and under free. Apr–Oct Tues– Sun 9:30am–6pm; Nov–Mar Tues–Sun 9:30am–4pm.

Bookshelves line the rococo gallery of the Anna Amalia Library.

Herzogin Anna Amalia Bibliothek (Duchess Anna Amalia Library) ★★ HISTORIC BUILDING

Duke Karl August of Saxe-Weimar-Eisenach owed his lifelong passion for the arts to his mother Anna Amalia, under whom the court became a magnet for creative minds such as Goethe, Schiller and Herder. She also saw to it that the ducal library was moved into its own building in 1766—this stunning galleried rococo hall. In 2004, a fire damaged the building and much of its contents. Since 2007, the reconstructed hall can again be admired in its frilly glory alongside famous paintings and busts featuring Enlightenment heavyweights (note the colossal bust of Goethe). Visitor numbers are highly restricted. Show up at 9am to score one of the 70 day tickets or secure one in advance by emailing info@klassik-stiftung.de.

Platz der Demokratie. www.klassik-stiftung.de. ℂ **03643/545400.** Admission 7.50€ adults, 6€ students and seniors, children 16 and under free. Tues–Sun 9:30am–2:30pm.

Liszt-Haus ★ HISTORIC HOUSE

The Hungarian composer and pianist Franz Liszt spent summers between 1869 and his death in 1886 in this house on the western edge of the Park on the Ilm River. Some of thte furnishings are still original, as are numerous personal mementos, letters, composition sheets, and Liszts's Bechstein grand piano. An exhibit on the ground floor gives background on his life and lets you listen to some of his works.

Marienstrasse 17. www.klassik-stiftung.de. ✆ **03643/545400.** Admission 4€ adults, 3€ students and seniors, children 16 and under free. Apr–Oct Wed–Mon 10am–6pm; Nov–Mar Wed–Mon 10am–4pm.

Neues Museum (New Museum) ★ MUSEUM   This imposing neo-Renaissance building entered the cultural field in 1869 as the Grand Ducal Museum; it was renamed New Museum at its reopening in 1999. It presents changing exhibits of modern art. Always on view above the central staircase is the monumental sculpture *Goethe and Psyche,* created in 1851 by Karl Steinhäuser.

Weimarplatz 5. www.klassik-stiftung.de. ✆ **03643/545401.** Admission 5.50€ adults, 3.50€ students, children 16 and under free. Apr–Oct Tues–Sun 10am–6pm, Nov–Mar Tues–Sun 10am–4pm.

Schillers Wohnhaus (Schiller's Residence) ★★ HISTORIC HOUSE Goethe and Schiller are often named in the same breath and for good reason: they were contemporaries, friends, and arguably the greatest poets ever to come out of Germany. (They were even buried side by side—see p. 152). Schiller, who only lived to be 45 years old, is perhaps best known for his play *Wilhelm Tell,* which he wrote while living at this house. The most authentic and interesting room is his study, which looks as if he had just left. He took his last breath in 1805 in the bed next to the desk.

Schillerstrasse 12. www.klassik-stiftung.de. ✆ **03643/545400.** Admission 7.50€ adults, 6€ students and seniors, children 16 and under free. Apr–Oct Tues–Sun 10am–6pm; Nov–Mar Tues–Sun 10am–4pm.

Schlossmuseum (Castle Museum) ★ MUSEUM   The art collection amassed by the dukes of Saxe-Weimar-Eisenach can now be admired in three wings of the Stadtschloss (city castle), the one-time ducal palace. There are some extraordinary works here from the Middle Ages until around 1900. The exhibit starts off with a bang on the ground floor with the Cranach Gallery, lined with paintings by Lucas Cranach the Elder, including the famous portrait of Martin Luther disguised as "Squire George" while in hiding at Wartburg Castle (p. 162). On the floor above, the focus is on paintings, sculptures, and handicrafts of the Classical and Biedermeier periods (18th and early 19th centuries) while the top floor showcases modern German and French paintings and sculptures. There's original period furniture throughout as well as four rooms dedicated to Goethe, Schiller, the poet Christoph Martin Wieland, and the philosopher Johann Gottfried Herder.

Burgplatz 4. www.klassik-stiftung.de. ✆ **03643/545400.** Admission 7.50€ adults, 6€ students and seniors, children 16 and under free. Apr–Oct Tues–Sun 9:30am–6pm; Nov–Mar Tues–Sun 9:30am–4pm.

Weimarer Fürstengruft (Ducal Vault) ★ MEMORIAL   Karl August of Saxe-Weimar-Eisenach and other ducal family members are buried alongside the remains of Goethe and Schiller in this idyllic cemetery just south of the old town. While paying your respects to these great minds, don't forget to study the lovely architecture of the two-storied neoclassical mausoleum. Behind its curtain of columns, a star-spangled dome dominates the foyer, from which steps lead down to the crypt where caskets are chronologically arranged by date of death.

Historischer Friedhof, Am Poseckschen Garten. www.klassik-stiftung.de. © **03643/ 545400.** Admission 4€ adults, 3€ students and seniors, children 16 and under free. Apr–Oct Tues–Sun 10am–6pm; Nov–Mar Tues–Sun 10am–2pm.

Outside Weimar

Buchenwald Concentration Camp & Memorial Site ★★   The
contrast between Weimar's lofty, intellectual vibe and this achingly desolate site on a hillside not far from the town, could not be greater. About 250,000 people were imprisoned in Buchenwald concentration camp between 1937 and 1945—Jews, Slavs, Gypsies, homosexuals, political opponents, prisoners of war, Jehovah's Witnesses, social misfits, criminals, and other "undesirables." Some 56,000 perished here and in 136 subcamps, before the U.S. Army liberated Buchenwald in 1945. Among the prisoners was famed author and Nobel Peace Prize winner Elie Wiesel. (For more about his experiences at Buchenwald, read his best-selling book, *Night*.)

Today, the prisoners' fate is commemorated by the **Gedenkstätte Buchenwald** (© **03643/430200;** www.buchenwald.de). It's a haunting

A grim motto in wrought iron at the Buchenwald Concentration Camp.

place indeed. As you approach the camp gate, you'll notice a clock set to 3.15—the time U.S. troops arrived. In the left wing are detention cells where prisoners were held, tortured, and murdered. Past the gate— cynically inscribed with the words "Jedem das Seine" (To each his own)—a wide, windy field opens up where the barracks and other buildings once stood. Most were destroyed in the 1950s, but eerie black rocks mark their outline. Among the remaining buildings is the crematorium, where you can still see the row of incineration ovens. The large building down the sloped grounds is the depot, where inmates' clothing and personal effects were stored. It now houses the main exhibit on the history of the concentration camp. Exhibits illustrate the unspeakable atrocities practiced in Buchenwald, from medical experiments on inmates to extermination transports of children and sick prisoners. Also addressed is Buchenwald's post-WWII role as the Soviet-run Special Camp No. 2, an internment camp for Nazis. Between 1945 and 1950, one in four of the roughly 28,000 people held here died.

In 1958 the East German government built a massive **memorial** about 1km (⅔ mile) outside the camp. Incorporating three mass graves, it consists of a stele path, sculptures, and a bell tower.

Admission to the Gedenkstätte Buchenwald is free. The grounds are open until sunset but museum hours are only between 10am and 6pm (to 4pm November to March). On Mondays, only the crematorium and the detention cells in the gate building are open for visitors between 10am and 3pm. Last admission is 30 minutes before closing. Budget at least 90 minutes to do the place justice. It's well worth investing in the multimedia guide (3€), watching the free 30-minute subtitled documentary in the visitor center, or, if you understand German well enough, joining a guided tour.

The memorial is about 11km northwest of Weimar. Bus No. 6 makes the 20-minute trip from Goetheplatz or Hauptbahnhof almost hourly. (For bus information, go to **www.sw-weimar.de**.) Drivers can follow the brown "Gedenkstätte Buchenwald" signs from central Weimar.

Where to Stay in Weimar

Amalienhof Hotel Weimar ★   This private villa was built in 1826 when Goethe still lived just down the street. Run with panache and a personal touch, it still exudes the flair of the period with elegant furnishings in classical Biedermeier style. Rates include a generous breakfast buffet, which is served on the rooftop terrace in summer. Views of Weimar and the surrounding area are spectacular from up here. Rooms don't accommodate a ton of luggage, so if you need more space, consider booking one of the vacation apartments (three-night minimum stay), where you can even prepare small meals in the kitchenette.

Amalienstrasse 2. www.amalienhof-weimar.de. ✆ **03643/5490.** 23 units. 80€–105€ double. 59€–79€ apartment. Buffet breakfast included. Free parking. **Amenities:** Room service; free Wi-Fi.

The Hotel Elephant, Weimar's most famous hotel.

Grand Hotel Russischer Hof ★   This palatial abode began life in 1805 as the guesthouse for Russian aristocrats visiting Weimar and has welcomed Goethe, Tolstoy, Wagner, and other luminaries. Today it's still a fine place to hang your hat during your stay in Weimar. From the lavish lobby all the way to the top, this place oozes old-world charm. The air-conditioned rooms come in various sizes, with those in the historic wing facing Goetheplatz sporting more flair and character. Still, the décor is sophisticated throughout, especially in the suites. The fancy Czar Suite even comes with its own private whirlpool bath. Even if you're not an overnight guest, consider a visit to the hotel's fine dining restaurant **Anastasia.**

Goetheplatz 2. www.russischerhof-weimar.de. ✆ **03643/7740.** 126 units. 90€–200€ double. Breakfast 19.50€. Parking 19.50€. **Amenities:** Bar; gym; restaurant; room service; sauna; free Wi-Fi.

Hotel Elephant ★★   Goethe, Schiller, Putin, Obama, and countless other famous names have slept, caroused, or at least eaten at this venerable hotel in a prime position overlooking the scenic Markt. Even Adolf Hitler kept an apartment here—in fact, in 1937 he ordered the original hotel (opened in 1696) to be torn down and replaced with what you see today. After WWII, the Elephant languished for a decade, only to be reopened at the behest of Nobel Prize-winning writer Thomas Mann, who had immortalized the hotel in his 1939 novel *Lotte in Weimar* (published in English as *The Beloved Returns*). Today, the Elephant is still Weimar's most famous hotel. A classy art deco makeover and a small museum's worth of original art by such 20th century heavyweights as Otto Dix and Georg Baselitz beautifully soften the 1930s architecture. Rooms are comfortable, although not as well outfitted as might be expected (no air-conditioning, for example). It's worth spending a little extra for a room with a view of the Markt. And don't miss the sumptuous breakfast buffet!

Markt 19. www.hotelelephantweimar.com. © **03643/8020.** 99 units. 115€–270€ double; 220€–600€ suite. Breakfast 20€. Parking 15€. **Amenities:** Bar; 2 restaurants; room service; Wi-Fi 6€, free in lobby.

Labyrinth Hostel ★ Don't worry, you won't get lost checking into this labyrinth, Weimar's delightful indie hostel in a super-central location right in the old town. There are single, double, and dorm rooms, each creatively designed by a local artist. Most are drenched in bold colors and sport murals, chandeliers, and handmade furniture. Some have a private bathroom. One dorm is set aside for women and comes with a big mirror and a dressing table. Free tea and coffee let you keep your buzz on all day long, and there's also a well-equipped communal kitchen for whipping up some pasta and making new friends.

Goetheplatz 6. www.weimar-hostel.com. © **03643/811822.** 21 units. 42€–54€ double; 14€–21€ dorm Breakfast 4€. **Amenities:** Wi-Fi (free).

Where to Eat in Weimar

Anna Amalia ★★ GERMAN/ITALIAN One of only two restaurants in Thuringia to have a coveted Michelin star, the Anna Amalia at the Hotel Elephant will treat you to a dinner of culinary fireworks. This is due to the expertise and imagination of Marcello Fabbri, who has presided over the kitchen for over 20 years. He digs deep into his repertoire to produce such Italian-influenced gourmet morsels as foie gras with quince spumoni or stockfish cannelloni with steamed artichokes. The dining room is fairly formal with a panoramic window front overlooking a small garden with a terrace. Service is impeccable.

Am Markt 19. www.restaurant-anna-amalia.com. © **03643/8020.** 3-course dinner 72€, 10€ for each additional course. Tues–Sat 6:30pm–11:30pm. Closed Jan & Feb.

Lava Soul Kitchen ★ GERMAN/INTERNATIONAL This next-gen eatery provides a welcome antidote to Weimar's many traditional restaurants. The affable owners Sven and Juliane have harnessed their considerable gastro experience to create a modern, upbeat German kitchen with international influences. Only top ingredients find their way into such dishes as pulled pork burger with coleslaw or honey-coriander grilled duck with red cabbage. All main courses are accompanied by your choice of homemade potato wedges, a salad, grilled sweet potatoes, or almond dumplings. Reservations are recommended at dinnertime and essential for brunch on the first and last Sunday of the month.

Karl-Liebknecht-Strasse 10a. www.lava-weimar.de. *℃* **03643/4790080.** Main courses 10.50€–34.50€. Tues–Fri 11:30am–2:30pm and 6–10pm, Sat 6–10pm; 1st and last Sun of month 10:30am–2:30pm.

Residenz Café & Restaurant ★★ INTERNATIONAL   Locally known as Resi, this buzzy venue next to the ducal palace was founded in 1839 by the court confectioner; it's the oldest coffeehouse in Weimar. Marlene Dietrich reportedly loved hanging out for ice cream while studying music in town around 1920. Today, Resi is still a great place no matter where the hands of the clock might be. Be it for breakfast, a nightcap, or anything in between, its cozy rooms are always packed with people from all walks of life. The extensive menu features classic café fare, from soups and pasta to grilled meats and Thuringian specialties, including plenty of meat-free options.

Grüner Markt 4. www.residenz-cafe.de. *℃* **03643/59408.** Main courses 7€–22€. Daily 8am–midnight.

Nightlife & Entertainment

Weimar is home to one of the oldest theatres in Germany, the **Deutsches Nationaltheater** ★, Theaterplatz 2 (www.nationaltheater-weimar.de; *℃* **03643/7550**), founded as a court theatre by none other than Goethe himself back in the 18th century. Today, its ensemble presents a

Weimar's oldest coffeehouse, the Residenz Café.

THE THURINGIAN FOREST: GERMANY'S green HEART

"There is indeed no forest on all the earth as beautiful as the Thuringian," wrote the Danish novelist Martin Anderson Nexö. Hikers and nature lovers have long extolled the scenic beauties of the **Thüringer Wald ★★**, often called "the green heart of Germany"; it was once the stomping grounds of such philosophers and artists as Goethe, Schiller, Martin Luther, and Bach. The scenic, 150km (100-mile), northwest-to-southeast ramble known as the **Thuringian High Road** was one of the most popular destinations for East German schoolchildren and campers before reunification. You can take a lowland driving version by following Route 88 between **Eisenach** and **Ilmenau,** a city that Goethe loved.

Just as attractive as the region's scenic beauty are the many unspoiled, charming medieval villages that pepper the landscape. **Dornburg** has a series of three palaces, perched high above the Saale River. **Altenburg,** directly south of Leipzig, is the home of a hilltop castle. Just outside Erfurt, **Arnstadt,** founded in 704, is the oldest town in the Thuringian Forest, with medieval walkways and buildings that are now being restored to their former glory.

progressive repertoire of classical and modern plays and opera, not only in the original space but in three other venues, including a repurposed power station called E-Werk. Franz Liszt directed the affiliated symphony orchestra, even conducting the world premiere of Richard Wagner's opera *Lohengrin* in 1850. Tickets cost 14€ to 75€ And can be booked online, by email, or via the tourist office.

Weimar is not exactly a party town but if you're looking for a fun ambience, head to **C-Keller & Galerie Markt 21 ★**, Markt 21 (www.c-keller.de; ✆ **03643/502755**), which combines an art gallery with a café that serves beer, wine, tea, and light meals after 6pm. After 9pm, the cellar bar draws a youthful crowd for drinking, concerts, and dancing.

Day Trips from Weimar

ERFURT ★★

One of the most visited cities of eastern Germany, the Thuringian state capital Erfurt still exudes the spirit of a medieval market town. About 15 miles (24 kilometers) west of Weimar, this charming town—first mentioned in 742—brims with historic houses, medieval bridges, winding cobblestone alleys, and sky-piercing church spires amid ornamented Renaissance and baroque facades. Erfurt emerged from World War II relatively unscathed and remains one of the best places to see what

Erfurt's picturesque Krämerbrücke bridge.

yesterday's Germany looked like. Nearly everything of interest is concentrated in the Altstadt (Old Town) area.

ESSENTIALS Erfurt is about a 15-minute train ride from Weimar; there are several connections hourly. The towns are linked by Hwy B7 and the A4 Autobahn. The **Erfurt Tourist-Information** is at Benediktsplatz 1 (✆ **0361/66400;** www.erfurt-tourismus.de). It's open Monday to Saturday 10am to 6pm and Sunday 10am to 3pm. Staff rent the iGuide, a handheld mini-computer that provides a self-guided tour of Erfurt, also in English. It costs 7.50€ for four hours or 10€ all day.

Exploring Erfurt

The historic center of Erfurt is like a 3-D architectural textbook, its streets and lanes lined with a pleasing mix of half-timbered homes, Gothic churches, and stately Renaissance mansions. One of the town's curiosities is the **Krämerbrücke ★★★ (Merchants Bridge;** www.kraemer bruecke.de), which is the oldest bridge north of the Alps that's still completely lined with inhabited buildings, 62 in all. Built in 1325, today it's home to several dozen teensy stores. A foundation sees to it that only artists or artisans live or work here, so no tacky souvenir shops! In fact, many shop owners live above their stores. Lest you think "how romantic," drop by the **Haus der Stiftung ★**, Krämerbrücke 31 (✆**0361/6548381**) to discover how cramped quarters actually are. It's open daily from 10am to 6pm; admission is free.

Erfurt's ecclesiastical center is the **Domberg,** where two adjacent Gothic churches linked by a 70-step open staircase form an impressive architectural ensemble. (It's a spectacular backdrop for the annual **Domstufen-Festspiele** (www.domstufen.de), one of Germany's finest open-air summer music festivals.) To the left looms the **Dom St. Marien ★★** (Cathedral; www.dom-erfurt.de; *©* **0361/6461265**), which is entered via a triangular portal decorated with sculptures of the Apostles. Inside, take a moment to appreciate the lofty dimensions before turning your attention to the luminous medieval stained-glass windows above the lavish baroque high altar and intricately carved choir stalls. The oldest works are a bronze candelabrum in the shape of a man (called "Wolfram") and a Romanesque Madonna, both from 1160. Another key attraction is the Gloriosa, the world's largest medieval free-swinging bell, which weighs a hefty 11.5 tons. It can only be seen on guided tours offered from Thursday to Sunday between April and October.

The Dom's neighbor is the **Church of St. Severi ★** (*©* **0361/ 6461265**), a Gothic hall church with five naves. Its most important feature is the monumental sarcophagus (ca. 1365) that holds the remains of the 4th-century saint Severus of Ravenna (look for it in the back of the southernmost aisle). Another eye-catcher is the baptismal font, which is lidded by a masterfully carved 15-meter-high (45-feet-high) canopy.

Both the Dom and St. Severi are open Monday to Saturday 9:30am to 6pm and Sunday from 1pm to 6pm on Sunday. Between November and April, they close at 5pm. Admission is free.

The life of the reformer Martin Luther is also closely entwined with Erfurt. As the legend goes, in 1505, while a student at the local university (one of the oldest in Germany), Luther got caught in a thunderstorm and, frightened to death, vowed to become a monk should he survive the tempest. He did, entered the Augustinian monastery, and was ordained to the priesthood in 1507 at the Dom. Guided tours of the **Augustinerkloster ★**, Augustinerstrasse 10 (in German, *©* **0361/576600**), the monastery where he lived until 1511, include a stop in his humble cell. Tours cost 7.50€ for adults and 4€ for students, and take place Monday to Saturday at 11am, noon, 1pm, and 3pm as well as Sunday at 11am.

Erfurt's Jewish history is powerfully commemorated in the **Old Synagogue ★**, Waagegasse 8 (*©* **0361/6551520;** www.alte-synagoge. erfurt.de), which has origins around 1100, making it one of the oldest synagogues in Europe. After the pogroms of 1349, it was used as a storehouse and then became a dance hall and restaurant in the 19th century, which remained open until 1993. Remnants from this period are still visible on the upper floor. The rest of the building contains an exhibit on the history and culture of Erfurt's Jewish community. In the basement, you'll squint at the shiny Erfurt Treasure, a hoard of 28kg (62 pounds) of gold and silver objects found by accident in 1998 during nearby excavations. Its star attraction is a golden Jewish wedding ring. Admission is 8€ for adults, 6€ students and seniors. It's open Tuesday to Sunday 10am to 6pm.

Where to Stay in Erfurt

Hotel Zumnorde ★★   This family-owned boutique hotel exudes traditional classiness in both public areas and the tranquil rooms. The shiny wooden furniture (extra-long beds!) goes well with the heavy drapes and carpeted flooring. Be sure to treat yourself to the exceptional breakfast buffet featuring top quality cheeses, regional cold cuts, smoked salmon, homemade salads, and even sparkling wine. At day's end consider unwinding in the petite rooftop sauna before tucking into inspired Thuringian fare in the supercozy **Weinstube,** a wine restaurant with wood-burning fireplace, dark furniture, and a long bar with art deco elements. The roast duck carved at the table is the signature dish. This is the kind of unstuffy hotel restaurant that's also on the radar of locals, especially weekdays at lunchtime when the business brigade invades for the daily specials. In summer, a quiet beer garden beckons.

Weitergasse 26. www.hotel-zumnorde.de. ✆ **0361/56800.** 47 units. 119€–160€ double; 169€–210€ suite. Breakfast buffet included. Parking 13€. **Amenities:** Bar; restaurant; room service; sauna; free Wi-Fi. Closed December 23–27.

Pension Sackpfeifenmühle ★   With only three doubles, this is one of the smaller lodging places in Erfurt, but what it lacks in size, it makes up for in charm and character. Landscape designer and mother of three Marlen Wiedenstritt has created a personal retreat where exposed wooden beams hint at the building's pedigree as a medieval mill first mentioned in 1248. Rooms 1 and 2 have a view of the little Walkstrom stream, while fresh flowers in the breakfast room, an honor bar, and pleasant art by family friends add to the affable ambience.

Lange Brücke 53. www.sackpfeifenmuehle.de. ✆ **0361/34329268.** 3 units. 69€–74€ double. Buffet breakfast included. Parking 6€. **Amenities:** Wi-Fi (free).

Where to Eat in Erfurt

Faust Food ★ GERMAN   Thuringia's most famous culinary ambassador is a humble roast sausage subtly spiced with marjoram and garlic, called Thüringer Wurst. You'll come across it throughout the region, but to bite into one of Erfurt's best, report to this easy-going self-service eatery ensconced in a medieval barn. The menu is a carnivore's dream with not only sausages but also spare ribs, burgers, and lamb kebabs getting the sizzle treatment on the indoor charcoal grill.

Waagegasse 1. www.faustfood.de. ✆ **0361/64436300.** Reservations recommended. Main courses 2€–10€. Mon–Sat 11am–11pm, Sun 11am–7pm.

Kromers ★★ GERMAN   Candle-lit and cozy, this restaurant with its romantic vaulted cellar is the most convivial spot in town to sample the Thuringian approach to slow food. Regionally sourced, seasonal ingredients star in such dishes as tender pork cheeks, honey-glazed duck, or rabbit ragout, preferably paired with crispy-fried potatoes or fluffy Thuringian dumplings. When ordering wine, don't bother with anything but the white Hauswein (house wine)—a full-bodied, slightly fruity blend of two typically German grape varietals: Riesling and Müller-Thurgau. Insiders finish up a grand meal with a fruit or herb schnapps from the nearby Fahner distillery.

Kleine Arche 4. www.kromers-restaurant.de. *©* **0361/64477211.** Reservations necessary. Main courses 14€–17€. Tues–Thurs 5pm–10pm, Fri–Sun 11:30am–10pm.

Pier 37 ★ GERMAN   This modern and upbeat restaurant's setting in a historical mill next to a sprightly rivulet makes for a most enchanting dining spot in fine weather. But even if the sun's not out, it's well worth snagging a table or booth amid the exposed brick walls and picking a favorite from the menu that teeters between tradition and innovation. Translation: expect both a classic rump steak and such unusual flavor combinations as vanilla-infused cod with Hokkaido pumpkin and coconut.

Lange Brücke 37a. www.pier37.de. *©* **0361/6027600.** Main courses 9€–25€. Daily 11am–11pm.

Shopping

Artisanal stores are scattered throughout the Altstadt. One find is **Blaudruckwerkstatt im Dürerhaus,** Schlösserstrasse 38 (www.blaudruck-erfurt.de, (*©* **0361/6421393**), which makes tablecloths, aprons, and other textiles from fabric blue-dyed by hand with indigo extracted from the woad plant, a regional tradition dating to the 13th century. The material is then printed (also by hand) with pretty paisley or floral patterns. Mustard aficionados should swing by **Born Senf-Laden,** Wenigemarkt 11 (www.born-feinkost.de, *©* **0361/740340**), where you can taste (and buy, of course, at very reasonable prices) such exotic blends as tomato-olive mustard or curry mustard. It's at the foot of the Krämerbrücke, only steps from **Goldhelm Schokoladen Manufaktur,** Krämerbrücke 12-14 (*©* **0361/6609851**), where Alex Kühn fashions irresistible truffles, exotic pralines (try the matcha-yuzu) and chocolate bars, all by hand, in a workshop behind the pint-sized store.

EISENACH ★★

Eisenach lies on the northwestern edge of the Thuringian Forest, 50km (30 miles) west of Erfurt. Its headlining attractions are the Wartburg, one of Germany's finest castles, as well as sights associated with Martin

Luther and Johann Sebastian Bach (who was born here). The compact old city center centers on a market square ringed by half-timbered houses.

ESSENTIALS   Eisenach is 30 minutes by train west of Erfurt and 1 hour west of Weimar; there are several connections hourly. Access by car is via the A4 Autobahn. For tourist information, contact **Eisenach Tourist-Info,** Markt 24 (www.eisenach-info; ✆ **03691/79230**), open Monday to Friday 10am to 6pm, Saturday and Sunday 10am to 5pm.

Exploring Eisenach

Straddling a crag just south of town, the imposing **Wartburg ★★★**, Auf der Wartburg (www.wartburg-eisenach.de; ✆ **03691/2500**) is one of the most famous sights in Thuringia. More than 1,000 years old, it is one of the best preserved castles in Germany. Past its massive gate, you'll first reach the *Vorburg* (outer bailey), flanked by half-timbered buildings. Beyond lies the Romanesque *Palas* (residential wing), which along with the south tower, forms the oldest part of the compound. It's well worth climbing the tower for head-spinning views of Eisenach and the Thuringian Forest. The 45-minute guided tours take you inside the Palas, where highlights include the richly muraled Sängersaal (Singers' Hall), site of the legendary 13th-century minstrel's contest that was later immortalized by Wagner's opera *Tannhäuser.* The Wartburg's most famous resident was Martin Luther, who hid here after being excommunicated by

Massive Wartburg Castle rises on a crag above the Thuringian Forest.

GERMAN men of ideas: **MARTIN LUTHER (1483–1546)**

"I am more afraid of my own heart than of the pope and all his cardinals. I have within me the great pope, Self."

Field of Study: Priest, monk, theologian, reformer.

Revolutionary Insight: His *95 Theses* questioned the culture of church indulgences (donating money to guarantee salvation). It evolved into a critique of Catholic corruption and a rejection of papal infallibility, sparking the Protestant Reformation. Luther's views spread quickly, thanks in part to the recent invention of the printing press.

Controversy Quotient (0 to 5): (5+) Excommunicated by Pope Leo X and declared heretic/ outlaw by Holy Roman Emperor Charles V in 1521; ordained as a monk in 1507, but married in 1525; late in life spouted virulent anti-Semitic views.

Little-Known Fact: Met his wife, Katherina von Bora, while abetting her escape from a Cistercian convent; smuggled her (and other nuns) out in a wagon filled with herring barrels.

the pope, following his refusal to recant his critical views of the church at the Diet of Worms in 1521. (Luther used his 10-month protective stay wisely, by translating the New Testament from ancient Greek to German—thereby incidentally laying the foundation for a modern, unified version of the language.) A visit to Luther's study is the final stop on the tour. Along the way, you'll also get a chance to peruse the treasures of the museum, including paintings of Luther by Lucas Cranach the Elder, wall hangings and an ornately paneled armoire.

Admission to the castle grounds is free; tours cost 9€ for adults, 5€ for students (children 6 and under are free). The grounds are open daily 8:30am to 8pm, with the last tour at 5pm (from November to February, the last tour is 3:30pm and gates close at 5pm). The 1:30pm tour is in English. Bus No. 10 runs hourly from Eisenach train station up to the Wartburg, a 20-minute ride; from the bus stop, it's a steep 10- to 15-minute walk up to the castle.

The city's most famous son, Johann Sebastian Bach (1685–1750), is celebrated at **Bachhaus Eisenach,** Frauenplan 21 (www.bachhaus.de; ℂ **03691/79340**). Rooms in the half-timbered house are furnished in period style and illustrate his life and career through 250 original mementos. A special treat is the 20-minute concert played hourly on baroque instruments. A highlight in the modern annex: a room with "bubble-chairs" where you can sit and listen to Bach's music. Admission costs 9€ for adults, 5€ for students, children 6 and under enter free. It's open daily 10am to 6pm.

Luther fans should swing by the **Lutherhaus,** Lutherplatz 8 (www.lutherhaus-eisenach.de; ✆ **03691/29830**), a charming half-timbered beauty where the reformer reportedly stayed as schoolboy. A new permanent exhibition explores Luther's historic translation of the New Testament and the impact it had on German language, literature, and music. Admission is 8€ for adults, 6€ students and seniors. It's open daily 10am to 5pm (closed Mondays Nov–Mar).

Where to Eat & Stay in Eisenach

Hotel Kaiserhof ★   This august hotel has certainly seen ups and downs during its 120-year history, but it's now sitting pretty in a prime location just outside the sole surviving medieval city gate. Rooms are spacious by German standards, decorated in floral Laura Ashley style, and outfitted with numerous mod-cons. A new wing with shops, a sauna, and beauty salon was recently added. The Turmschänke restaurant (main courses 15€–26€) in a romantic tower serves regionally inspired international cuisine.

Wartburgallee 2. www.kaiserhof-eisenach.de. ✆ **03691/88890.** 64 units. 106€–136€ double. Buffet breakfast included. Parking 5€. **Amenities:** Bar; restaurant; room service; sauna; Wi-Fi (free).

LEIPZIG ★★

164km (102 miles) SW of Berlin, 111km (69 miles) NW of Dresden, 126km (78 miles) NE of Erfurt

One of eastern Germany's most charismatic cities, Leipzig owes its moniker "City of Heroes" to its leading role in the downfall of the Berlin Wall in 1989. Since then, it has resumed its historic role as one of Germany's economic, cultural, and artistic powerhouses. A visit here can be absolutely invigorating. Glassy skyscrapers and vibrant nightlife add a cosmopolitan flavor you don't encounter in much of the rest of the region. The approximately 29,000 students who study in the area (as Nietzsche, Goethe, and Angela Merkel once did) help add a spark.

Leipzig is also famous for its musical legacy, being not only the birthplace of Richard Wagner and the creative stomping ground of Felix Mendelssohn-Bartholdy, but also the city where Johann Sebastian Bach worked as choirmaster for 27 years. For contemporary sounds, hit the bars and clubs in the Südvorstadt district, near the main university campus, or in the western suburb of Plagwitz.

Essentials

ARRIVING

BY PLANE   The **Leipzig-Halle Airport** lies 11km (7 miles) northwest of the city center and has connections to 50 destinations in 16 countries, mostly within Europe. For **airport information,** call ✆ **0341/2241155**

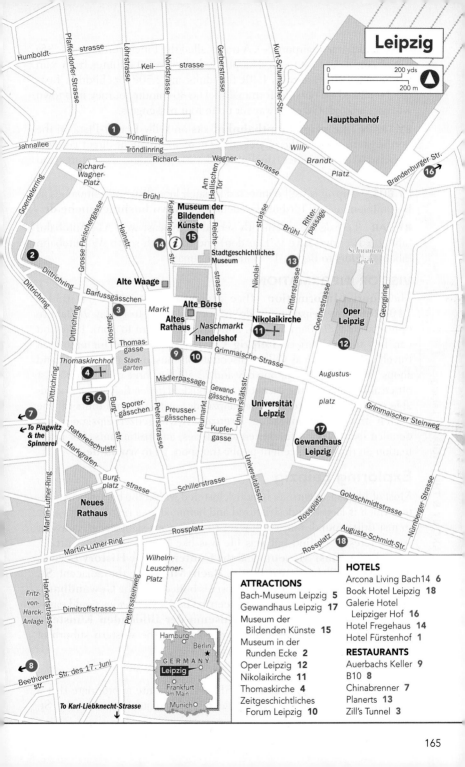

Leipzig

0 — 200 yds
0 — 200 m

Hauptbahnhof

Humboldt-strasse
Pfaffendorfer Strasse
Löhrstrasse
Keil-strasse
Nordstrasse
Gerberstrasse
Kurt-Schumacher-Str.

Jahnallee
Tröndlinring
Tröndlinring
Willy-Brandt-Platz
Brandenburger Str.

Richard-Wagner-Platz
Richard-
Wagner-
Strasse
Am Hallischen Tor

Goerdelerring
Brühl
Brühl
Ritter-passage

Grosse Fleischergasse
Katharinenstr.
Museum der Bildenden Künste
Reichsstrasse
Nikolaistrasse
Ritterstrasse
Schwanen-teich

Dittrichring
Hainstr.
Stadtgeschichtliches Museum
Georgiring

Dittrichring
Barfussgässchen
Alte Waage
Oper Leipzig
Goethestrasse

Klosterg.
Markt
Alte Börse
Nikolaikirche

Thomas-gasse
Altes Rathaus
Naschmarkt
Handelshof

Thomaskirchhof
Stadtgarten
Mädlerpassage
Grimmaische Strasse

Thomaskirchhof
Gewandgässchen
Augustus-platz

Burg-gässchen
Sporergässchen
Preusser-gässchen
Neumarkt
Universitätsstr.
Universität Leipzig

To Plagwitz & the Spinnerei
Ratsfreischulstr.
Peterstrasse
Kupfer-gasse
Gewandhaus Leipzig

Markgrafen
Burg-platz strasse
Schillerstrasse
Universitätsstr.

Martin-Luther-Ring
Neues Rathaus
Rossplatz
Grimmaischer Steinweg

Martin-Luther-Ring
Rossplatz
Goldschmidtstrasse
Nürnberger Strasse

Fritz-von-Harck-Anlage
Dimitroffstrasse
Peterssteinweg
Wilhelm-Leuschner-Platz
Rossplatz
Auguste-Schmidt-Str.

Beethoven-str.
Str. des 17. Juni

To Karl-Liebknecht-Strasse

Hamburg
Berlin
GERMANY
Leipzig
Frankfurt am Main
Munich

ATTRACTIONS
Bach-Museum Leipzig **5**
Gewandhaus Leipzig **17**
Museum der Bildenden Künste **15**
Museum in der Runden Ecke **2**
Oper Leipzig **12**
Nikolaikirche **11**
Thomaskirche **4**
Zeitgeschichtliches Forum Leipzig **10**

HOTELS
Arcona Living Bach14 **6**
Book Hotel Leipzig **18**
Galerie Hotel Leipziger Hof **16**
Hotel Fregehaus **14**
Hotel Fürstenhof **1**

RESTAURANTS
Auerbachs Keller **9**
B10 **8**
Chinabrenner **7**
Planerts **13**
Zill's Tunnel **3**

(www.leipzig-halle-airport.de). A train called the Flughafen Express (S5) runs from the airport to the Hauptbahnhof every 30 minutes from 5am to midnight. The fare costs 4.40€ for adults and 2.50€ for children. Taxis can be picked up outside Terminal B. The 30-minute journey into town will cost around 35€ each way for up to four passengers.

BY TRAIN **Leipzig Hauptbahnhof** sits on Willy-Brandt-Platz on the northeastern edge of the city center. There are frequent direct connections to German cities, including Berlin, Dresden, Frankfurt, and Munich.

BY BUS Leipzig is well connected by such long-distance companies as Berlinlinienbus and Flixbus. For details, see **www.busliniensuche.de**.

BY CAR Leipzig is conveniently served by the east-west A14 Autobahn (about a 1½ hour drive to Dresden) and the north-south A9 Autobahn (about 2 hours to Berlin, 1½ hours to Weimar).

VISITOR INFORMATION

The **Tourist-Information** office at Katharinenstrasse 8 (© **0341/ 7104260;** www.leipzig.travel.de) is open Monday to Friday 9:30am to 6pm, Saturday 9:30am to 4pm, and Sunday 9:30am to 3pm. Here you can buy the well-priced **Leipzig Card,** which is good for unlimited travel within Leipzig as well as discounts on museums, restaurants, and shops. It costs 11.50€ for one day and 22.50€ for three days. The tourist office also publishes the excellent free booklet *Hidden Leipzig* (also available on-line at www.verborgenes-leipzig.de), with tips and tours off the beaten track. The magazine *Kreuzer* (www.kreuzer-leipzig.de) has detailed listings of cultural events, galleries, and restaurants. For information on the city's excellent public transport, go to **www.l.de**.

Exploring Leipzig

Most of Leipzig's sights are handily clustered within the historic city center, which is largely pedestrianized and hemmed by a ring road. It's a joy to just drift around, but if you want to focus your sightseeing, consider your interests. To find out was life was like behind the Iron Curtain, swing by the **Stasi Museum** and the **Contemporary History Forum.** Music fans will be drawn by the **Bach Museum,** the adjacent **St. Thomas Church** where the composer is buried, and the **Gewandhaus,** one of Germany's top classical concert halls. Art-ficionados could easily spend a couple of hours at the **Museum der Bildenden Künste** or exploring the offbeat **Spinnerei** art colony in the western suburb of Plagwitz.

CITY CENTER

Bach Museum Leipzig ★ MUSEUM   It's quite appropriate that a museum dedicated to Bach should be located just opposite the St.

Interactive displays at Bach Museum Leipzig.

Thomas Church where he worked as a cantor for 27 years. Learn all about the private and professional life of the great composer in a dozen themed rooms with exhibits and interactive stations. Highlights include an organ console that Bach played in 1743, an ornate oak chest that once belonged to the Bach family, original compositions, and letters, as well as a famous portrait by Elias Gottlob Haussmann (donated in 2015 by American philanthropist William H. Scheide).

Thomaskirchhof 15/16. www.bachmuseumleipzig.de. © **0341/9137202.** Admission 8€ adults, 6€ students and seniors, children 16 and under free. Tues–Sun 10am–6pm. S-Bahn 1, 2, 3, 4, and 5 or bus 89 to Markt.

Museum der Bildenden Künste (Museum of Fine Arts) ★★

MUSEUM   The civic engagement of Leipzig art collectors and their donations laid the groundwork for this impressive art collection in the 19th century; in 2004 it found a new home in a striking postmodernist building of glass, concrete, limestone, and oak. At once monumental and intimate, it's a perfect setting for the paintings, sculpture, videos, and installation spanning 600 years of mostly European art. The collection of Old Masters includes 18 works by Lucas Cranach the Elder, while rooms dedicated to Max Beckmann and Max Klinger constitute highlights among the New Masters. (Look for Klinger's epic sculpture *Beethoven*, wrought from bronze, various types of marble, glass, ivory, and gemstones.) Older works are often juxtaposed with edgy creations by members of the New Leipzig School (Neo Rauch, Thilo Baumgärtner), a seminal movement in the 1990s and early 2000s. Art created in the GDR is another focus with a major work being *Behind the Seven Mountains* (1973) by Wolfgang Mattheuer.

Katharinenstrasse 10. www.mdbk.de. ℂ **0341/216990.** Admission 5€ adults, 3.50€ students and seniors. Tues & Thu–Sun 10am–6pm; Wed noon–8pm. S-Bahn 1, 2, 3, 4, and 5 or bus 89 to Markt.

Museum in der Runden Ecke (Stasi Museum) MUSEUM   Back during the Cold War, this building housed the Leipzig headquarters of the Stasi, the East German Ministry for State Security. Today, its sinister function is revealed in a permanent exhibit called *Stasi—Power and Banality* that explores the history, structure, and methods of the GDR's much-feared secret police. For 40 years, it systematically infiltrated society to eradicate any tendril of opposition. Methods used included spying, telephone surveillance, checking letters, and observation. Those targeted by the Stasi often ended up in horrible prisons; a faithful reconstruction of a prison cell is also part of the exhibit. Rooms have been pretty much left in their original state, down to the grey linoleum floors, surveillance cameras, and barred windows. The exhibition also traces the steps local people took to throw off the Communist regime and end Stasi terror.

Dittrichring 24. www.runde-ecke-leipzig.de. ℂ **0341/9612443.** Free admission. Daily 10am–6pm. Bus 89 or Tram 9 to Thomaskirche, or tram 1, 3, 4, 7, 12, 14, and 15 to Goerdelerring.

Nikolaikirche (Church of St. Nicholas) ★★ CHURCH   Leipzig's oldest church, founded in 1165, was originally built in Romanesque style

Exuberant plasterwork at the Church of St. Nicholas.

SINGING THROUGH THE CENTURIES: THE ST. THOMAS boys choir

Leipzig's Thomanerchor (St. Thomas Boys' Choir, www.thomanerchor.de) is one of the most famous boys' choirs in the world and—having been founded in 1212—certainly one of the oldest. From 1723 until 1750, the choir was directed by Johann Sebastian Bach. The boys sing on such occasions as services, baptisms, weddings, funerals, and public events, and also entertain foreign audiences with their angelic voices on international concert tours. The choir has about 100 members between the ages of 9 and 18, who live in a boarding school. Each newcomer is assigned a "mentor" from among the trusted older members of the choir, and all members are required to eat, sleep, study, and rehearse according to a semimonastic regimen. When not touring, the boys can be heard at the **St. Thomas Church** during Sunday services at 9:30am and 6pm (free) and during one-hour concerts Fridays at 6pm and Saturdays at 3pm (2€). Concerts are hugely popular, so arrive early to snag a spot in the pews.

but repeatedly altered over the centuries—its striking neoclassical interior and exuberant pastel color scheme dates to the late 18th century. Most eye-catching are the rose-hued columns that culminate in light green capitals shaped like palm trees. The church is equally famous for hosting peace prayers every Monday throughout the 1980s, thereby contributing to the Peaceful Revolution that brought down the GDR in 1989.

Nikolaikirchhof 3. www.nikolaikirche.de. ✆ **0341/1245380.** Free admission. Mon–Sat 10am–6pm, 10am–4pm Sun. S-Bahn 1, 2, 3, 4, and 5 or bus 89 to Markt.

Thomaskirche (Church of St. Thomas) ★ CHURCH Leipzig's most famous resident, Johann Sebastian Bach (1685–1750), was cantor at this mighty church from 1723 until his death. He's buried just in front of the altar and his likeness also peers down from a bright stained-glass window in the south aisle. Both Mozart and Mendelssohn performed in the Thomaskirche as well, and Wagner was baptized in the marble-and-alabaster font in 1813. For a superb view of Leipzig, it's well worth climbing up the tower. Tours go up Saturdays at 1pm, 2pm, and 4:30pm and Sundays at 2pm and 3pm. Tickets cost 2€. The church is also where you can hear the world-famous St. Thomas Boys' Choir sing (see above).

Thomaskirchhof 18. www.thomaskirche.org. ✆ **0341/222240.** Free admission. Daily 9am–6pm. Bus 89 or tram 9 to Thomaskirche.

Zeitgeschichtliches Forum Leipzig (Leipzig Forum of Contemporary History) ★ MUSEUM Despite the unwieldy name, this is really one of the better GDR museums in the country. Documents, photographs, videos, and objects explain what led to the division of

Stella Hamberg sculptures on display at the Spinnerei's Eigen+Art gallery.

Germany, shed light on daily life under socialism, discuss the opposition movement, trace events that led to the Peaceful Revolution and reunification in 1990, and examine the contemporary challenges in rejoining east and west. Note that a planned revamp may keep the exhibit closed for several months in 2016 or 2017.

Grimmaische Strasse 6. www.hdg.de/leipzig. ℰ **0341/22200.** Free admission. Tues–Fri 9am–6pm, Sat–Sun 10am–6pm. S-Bahn 1, 2, 3, 4, and 5 or bus 89 to Markt.

BEYOND THE CITY CENTER

If you're the type of traveler that likes to explore beyond the obvious, an easy 20-minute S-Bahn ride out to Leipzig's western suburb of **Plagwitz** may be in order. Together with neighboring **Lindenau,** to which it is linked by the idyllic Karl-Heine-Kanal (canal), this once industrial area is becoming increasingly hip, creative and trendy. Its heart is the **Spinnerei,** Spinnereistrasse 7 (www.spinnerei.de; ℰ **0341/4980222**), a vast 19th-century cotton mill that remained in operation until 1992 and has since morphed into Germany's hottest artist colony, and the birthplace of the New Leipzig School art movement. Its main protagonists, Neo Rauch and Thilo Baumgärtner, are among the 120 artists, designers, and other creatives who maintain their studios in this labyrinth of red-brick halls. Over a dozen galleries, including the prestigious Eigen + Art, Galerie Kleindienst, and Maerzgalerie, present the work of resident and other artists. A schedule of current shows can be found at **www.spinnerei galerien.de**. Hours vary but most galleries are open Tuesday to Saturday noon to 6pm. You're free to walk around on your own (pick up a map in the "archive massiv" building just past the entrance). Guided tours of select galleries run on the hours Fridays noon to 4pm, Saturdays 11am to 4pm, and cost 11€, or 8€ students and seniors.

The nearby **Karl-Heine-Strasse** is Plagwitz's main artery, where a growing number of cafés, shops, bars, clubs, and restaurants have opened, including Chinabrenner (p. 174), Täubchenthal (p. 175), Elipamanoke (p. 175) and the **Schaubühne Lindenfels,** Karl-Heine-Strasse 50 (www.schaubuehne.com; ✆ **0341/484620**), a theater-cinema-bar combo ensconced in a grand old ballroom building.

S-Bahn No. 1 makes the trip from Markt to the Plagwitz station in 15 minutes. For the Spinnerei, go left upon exiting the station and left again into Spinnereistrasse; the entrance will be about 100m (300 ft.) on your left. For Karl-Heine-Strasse, turn right from the station and continue straight across the intersection.

Where to Stay in Leipzig

Arcona Living Bach14 ★★ This stylish apartment hotel has a lot more going for it than a superb location next to the Bach Museum and opposite the St. Thomas Church. The feel-good vibe starts in the light-flooded lobby with its small reception area and candy-colored wing chairs. Bold colors—dove blue, raspberry red, olive green, and lilac—also add a cheerful touch to the airy und uncluttered apartments whose design picks up on the music theme. Sheet music from a Bach cantata, for instance, doubles as wall paper, and there are chic hanging lamps reminiscent of organ pipes. Apartments come in five configurations and spread across the historic front house and a modern addition. Those in the "Partita" category face the garden, making them the quietest. The onsite restaurant serves regional dishes and has a good wine selection. Breakfast, also served in the restaurant, features a live egg-cooking station and such neat extras as honey served straight from a honeycomb. Thomaskirchhof 13/14. www.bach14.arcona.de. ✆ **0341/496140.** 52 units. 90€–200€ apartment. Breakfast 17€. **Amenities:** Bar; restaurant; gym; sauna; Wi-Fi (free). S-Bahn: 1, 2, 3, 4, 5, bus: 89 to Markt.

Book Hotel Leipzig ★ A wall-sized photograph of an historic print shop leaves no doubt that the name is the game in this hotel in a quiet street just a five-minute walk from Augustusplatz. Not surprisingly, there are books throughout, from the shelf built into the reception desks to the nightstands in the rooms; even the room numbers are designed to look like the back of a book's spine. The rooms themselves come in four categories. The smallest ("comfort") is pretty snug, so you may want to spend a little extra for more space. The "superior," for instance, comes with a bright yellow sofa bed, while the "deluxe" has a balcony. In all of them, plenty of light falls through floor-length windows onto furnishings in soothing natural colors.

Auguste-Schmidt-Strasse 6. www.book-hotel-leipzig.de. © **0341/5500950.** 43 units. 99€–130€ double. Continental breakfast included. Parking 8€. **Amenities:** Wi-Fi (free). Closed over Christmas. Tram: 4, 7, 8, 10, 11, 12, 15 to Augustusplatz.

Galerie Hotel Leipziger Hof ★★ If you love modern art, and especially the works of the New Leipzig School, consider booking into this darling privately owned hotel whose public areas and rooms are splashed with hundreds of original works by regional painters. Furnishings may not be of the latest vintage but all is clean and comfortable and most bathrooms are spacious and fully tiled in bright white. There's even one suite sporting nostalgic GDR decor. A rich buffet breakfast provides a great start to a day, while the restaurant offers freshly prepared, seasonal dishes in the evenings. There is also an on-site art gallery. It's less than a mile's walk (or a short tram ride) from the central train station.

Hedwigstrasse 1–3. www.leipziger-hof.de. © **0341/69740.** 73 units. 87€–195€ double; 165€ junior suite. Buffet breakfast included. Parking 7€. **Amenities:** Sauna (10€); Wi-Fi (free). Tram: 1, 3, or 8 to Hermann-Liebmann-Strasse./ Eisenbahnstrasse.

Hotel Fregehaus ★★ This darling boutique hotel is the brainchild of Sabine Fuchshuber, who deftly drew upon her career as an architect in turning one of Leipzig's oldest building into a stylish oasis of tranquility. Built around 1706, the Fregehaus once belonged to a banker who counted Goethe among his clients. Rooms are tucked into the back of an enchanting courtyard shared by an antique store and a flower shop. All sport creaky wooden floors, comfortable beds, and an eclectic mix of fixtures and furniture, acquired at flea markets, auctions, design, and antique stores. No two rooms look alike: one might have a Murano chandelier, another an ornate gold-framed mirror or an Eames rocking chair. Some have original art created by friends of the family. The larger doubles face the courtyard and have more light. Amenities are basic: there's a TV and free Wi-Fi, but no spa or minibar (although wine, soft drinks, and water are available for purchase at the reception). Days start with a breakfast buffet set up in the sunny lounge lined by high-backed fire-engine-red sofas.

Katharinenstrasse 11. www.hotel-fregehaus.de/en. © **0341/26393157.** 20 units. 76€–136€ double. Breakfast 11€. **Amenities:** Wi-Fi (free). Closed over Christmas. S-Bahn: 1, 2, 3, 4, and 5 bus: 89 to Markt.

Hotel Fürstenhof ★★ An aura of timeless elegance pervades this boutique grand hotel in a neoclassical 1770 building, which has hosted such celebs as Bill Clinton and the Dalai Lama. As you enter, your view will be drawn to the central Wintergarten bar, which is lidded by an ornate glass dome and serves not only classic drinks but also a value-priced business lunch (12.50€). In the evening, the stylish Villiers fine dining restaurant welcomes patrons with high ceilings, crystal chandeliers, and an excellent selection of wines. Wine is also the focus of the less formal bistro-style Vinothek 1770, which pours 69 of them by the glass. The air-conditioned rooms are outfitted in a modern interpretation of neoclassical style and come in a variety of sizes, color schemes, and amenity levels.

Tröndlinring 8. www.hotelfuerstenhofleipzig.com. © **0341/1400.** 90 units. 165€–425€ double; 285€–2250€ suite. Breakfast 28€. Parking 28€. **Amenities:** 2 bars; 2 restaurants; gym; indoor pool; room service; sauna; Wi-Fi 16€, free in lobby. Tram: 1, 3, 4, 7, 9 and 12 to Goerdelerring.

Where to Eat in Leipzig

Auerbachs Keller ★★ SAXON/INTERNATIONAL   Right by the entrance of Leipzig's famous Mädlerpassage shopping arcade, a bronze group of characters from *Faust*, sculpted in 1913, beckons you down a stone staircase into this perennially popular cellar restaurant. This is indeed the tavern where Goethe came to drink as a student, which later inspired the scene in *Faust* where Mephisto and Faust meet a band of drunken students. The restaurant is divided into two sections. The rustic Grosser Keller (Big Cellar) has a jovial beer hall–type ambiance and specializes in rib-sticking Saxon soul food. The Historische Weinstuben (Historical Wine Tavern) serves upscale German food in four fancifully decorated rooms. No credit cards are accepted.

Mädlerpassage, www.auerbachs-keller-leipzig.de. Grimmaische Strasse 2–4. © **0341/216100.** Historische Weinstube courses 30€–36€, fixed-price menus 54€–91€; Grosser Keller main courses 15€–27€. Historische Weinstube Mon–Sat 6pm–midnight. Grosser Keller daily noon–midnight. S-Bahn 1, 2, 3, 4 and 5 or bus 89 to Markt.

B10 ★★ INTERNATIONAL   One of Leipzig's hippest restaurants is helmed by Paul Berry, an Australian chef who sailed the high seas for 15 years, cooking for such celebs as Lenny Kravitz and Hillary Clinton. Having settled down in Leipzig, he now woos discerning diners with healthy, eclectic, and delicious fare inspired by the cuisines of the world, especially from Asia and the Mediterranean. The menu is small but always in flux. Berry is a genius at juxtaposing seemingly incompatible ingredients to create surprising flavors and textures. Since he believes that good food must be paired with a good wine, he's put together a hand-picked selection of fine bottles, many available by the glass. The decor is spacious, angular, and cosmopolitan and beautifully matches the food. Also a good spot to drop by just for a nightcap. It's a small place, so book ahead.

Beethovenstrasse 10. www.the-b10.com. © **0341/64086440.** Main courses 17€–28€. Mon–Fri 11:30am–1am, Sat 4pm–1am, no lunch Jan–Feb. Bus: 89 to Mozartstrasse.

Chinabrenner ★ CHINESE   The name translates as "China burner" and indeed, if you're not careful what you order, you'll risk setting your tastebuds on fire. This hot restaurant in a converted metal foundry near the Spinnerei art complex is well worth the pilgrimage for its excellent and authentic Chinese food. Strangely, it is helmed not by an immigrant from Sichuan but by Thomas Wrobel, a local wood artist, self-taught chef, and passionate Sinophile. The menu consists of elevated street food favorites like grilled meat skewers, green-tea-smoked duck, and sweet-and-sour meatballs. If you can stand the heat, order the hilariously named "pockmarked old lady's tofu," aka ma po tofu. Bring a crowd so you can share several dishes. No credit cards are accepted.
Giesserstrasse18. www.chinabrenner.de. ✆ **0341/2409102.** Main courses 7€–23€. Mon noon–3pm, Tues–Sat noon–11pm. S-Bahn: 1 to S-Bahnhof Plagwitz; bus: 60 to Antonienstrasse/Giesserstrasse, tram: 14 to Karl-Heine-Strasse/Giesserstrasse.

Planerts ★★ ASIAN FUSION   At Planerts' the concept of casual fine dining is borne out both in the upbeat décor and on the plate. Patrons are welcomed to a large, high-ceilinged dining room with spaciously arranged tables and original art hung on charcoal grey walls. Exposed pipes create urban flair that culminates in the open kitchen, where a small army of chefs fusses over such palate-pleasers as halibut with king prawn, beetroot, and wasabi, or a ridiculously fragrant green coconut curry. One constant on the menu is the dim sum, an artfully presented trio of tender dumplings whose fillings reflect whatever's in season. Budget gourmets should swing by at lunchtime for the *Tagesgericht* (daily special) priced at under 10€.
Ritterstrasse 23. www.planerts.com. ✆ **0341/99999975.** Main courses 18€–28€. Mon–Sat noon–3pm and 6pm–midnight. Tram: 4, 7, 8, 10, 11, 12, 15 to Augustusplatz.

Zill's Tunnel ★ SAXON   With its heavy wooden furniture, wainscoting, and murals with historical scenes, this traditional restaurant oozes German *Gemütlichkeit* (coziness). Although it's at the end of a pub-packed party drag, it offers quality food and drink, an authentic ambience, and warm Saxon hospitality—and has done so since 1841. Back then, the original beamed ceiling was replaced with a vaulted one. Since the proprietor's name was Zill, it was only natural to call the place Zill's Tunnel. The upstairs dining room is a more formal wine restaurant,

> ### Shopping in Leipzig's Passagen
>
> Leipzig can look back on a particularly long history as a trading town, having held its first trade fair in 1165. Today, its center is still laced by a unique network of historic shopping arcades and courtyards—known as "Passagen"—filled with charming boutiques and specialty stores. Many of these Passagen are architectural masterpieces in their own right, such as the famous Mädlerpassage. The tourist office has an entire pamphlet with a map showing the locations of all 31 Passagen.

with open fireplace and antique furniture. The food offerings favor carnivores with such waist-expanding dishes as boiled pork knuckle with
dumpling or venison in juniper-red wine sauce. Be sure to try a glass of
the local brew Leipziger Gose, a top-fermented beer with slightly sweet
and salty notes.

Barfussgässchen 9. www.zillstunnel.de. © **0341/9602078.** Main courses 10€–15€.
Daily 11:30am–midnight. S-Bahn 1, 2, 3, 4, and 5 or bus 89 to Markt.

Nightlife & Entertainment

Leipzig's active nightlife offers something for everyone. In the city center,
the tiny **Barfussgässchen** (nicknamed "Drallewatsch") off the Markt is
jam-packed with cafés and bars and busy all day and into the night. The
main party strip, albeit with a more alternative flavor, is in the Südstadt
district along **Karl-Liebknecht-Strasse** ("Karli") just south of the center. An up-and-coming nightlife zone is **Karl-Heine-Strasse** in the
industrial-arty western suburb of Plagwitz.

THE PERFORMING ARTS   Given its great musical legacy, it's no surprise
that Leipzig is home base of one of Germany's finest orchestras, the
Gewandhausorchester ★★★. For the 2017/18 season, the Lithuanian
conductor Andris Nelsons will become its music director, thereby following in the footsteps of Felix Mendelssohn-Bartholdy who held the post
from 1835 to 1847. The orchestra performs in the **Gewandhaus,** Augustusplatz (www.gewandhaus.de; © **0341/1270280;** tram: 4, 7, or 15), a
modern hall built in 1981. It faces the acclaimed **Oper Leipzig,** Augustusplatz 12 (www.oper-leipzig.de; © **0341/1261275**), which presents
not only opera but also musicals and ballet.

CLUBS   As in Berlin, electronic sounds dominate Leipzig's club scene.
One of the oldest dance venues in town is **Distillery,** Kurt-Eisner-
Strasse 108A (known as "Tille"; www.distillery.de), where top DJs like
Andre Galuzzi or Tama Sumo often helm the decks on Fridays and Saturday. It's within walking distance of the partly crowdfunded **Institut
für Zukunft,** An den Tierkliniken 38-40 (www.ifz.me), which hosts readings, concerts, parties, and workshops Thursday to Saturday. In Plagwitz,
Täubchenthal, Wachsmuthstrasse 1 (www.taeubchenthal.com) spins
hip hop, soul, and electro and also hosts concerts several times a week in
a cleverly converted old wool mill. While in Plagwitz, also check out **Elipamanoke,** Markranstädter Strasse 4 (www.elipamanoke.de), the self-
titled "sound lab for electronic music" in a gritty industrial space; it's open
Friday and Saturday from 11pm to 8am. The only remaining section of
the old town fortifications, **Moritzbastei,** Universitätsstrasse 9 (www.
moritzbastei.de; © **0341/702590**) has been a student-flavored cultural
center since 1982 (yes, Angela Merkel's day). In a vaulted warren of
rooms, it presents an eclectic non-mainstream program of concerts,

theater, film screening, art exhibits, dance parties and other events. A café serves coffee and light meals from 10am (Saturday from noon, closed Sunday), while at night a cocktail bar and a wine bar welcome relaxed crowds.

Day Trips from Leipzig

LUTHERSTADT WITTENBERG ★

It's hard to imagine that a revolution originated in this quiet little town on the Elbe River, yet it did, in 1517, when a local priest named Martin Luther nailed his critique of corrupt church practices to the door of the Castle Church, launching the Protestant Reformation. Five hundred years later, the attractively restored town attracts Luther pilgrims from around the world.

ESSENTIALS Wittenberg lies about 70km (43 miles) north of Leipzig and 110km (68 miles) southwest of Berlin. Access by car is via the A9 Autobahn and Hwy. 2. Trains from Berlin and Leipzig stop in Wittenberg at least once hourly. **Lutherstadt Wittenberg Tourist-Information,** Schlossplatz 2 (www.lutherstadt-wittenberg.de; ✆ **03491/498610**) is open 9am to 8pm Monday to Friday and 10am to 4pm Saturday and Sunday from April to October; the rest of the year, hours are 10am to 4pm Monday to Friday and 10am to 2pm Saturday and Sunday.

Exploring Wittenberg

Martin Luther is buried in the **Schlosskirche (Castle Church) ★★**, Friedrichstrasse 1A (www.schlosskirche-wittenberg.de;✆**03491/402585**) alongside his friend and fellow reformer Philipp Melanchton. The original wooden doors where Luther nailed his theses burned in a 1760 fire and were replaced in 1858 by today's bronze doors. The church is closed for restoration until 2017.

The former Augustinian monastery where Luther lived for 35 years, first as a monk and then, after its dissolution, with his family, is today the **Lutherhaus Wittenberg ★★**, Collegienstrasse 54 (www.martinluther. de; ✆ **03491/42030**), the world's largest museum on the Reformation. Aside from detailing milestones in Luther's life and his impact on history, it also displays such artifacts as his monk's robe, a Luther bible, manuscripts, and medals. Hours are April to October daily 9am to 6pm, November to March Tuesday to Sunday 10am to 5pm. Admission is 6€ for adults, 4€ students and seniors.

Another key Luther site is the **Stadtkirche (Parish Church) ★**, Judenstrasse 35 (www.stadtkirchengemeinde-wittenberg.de; ✆ **03491/ 403201**), where Luther did most of his preaching. It is considered the "Mother Church of the Reformation" because the first mass in German (rather than Latin) and the first communal holy communion were held here. Note the main altar by Lucas Cranach the Elder and the elaborate

Martin Luther's home, a former Augustinian monastery in Wittenberg.

baptismal font by Hermann Vischer. The church is open Monday to Saturday 10am to 6pm and Sunday 11:30am to 6pm (from November to Easter, it closes at 4pm daily). Admission is free. There's a weekly English-language service on Saturday at 5pm.

Where to Eat & Stay in Wittenberg

Brauhaus Wittenberg ★ No two rooms are alike in this charming hotel—one has a four-poster bed and red velvet drapes, another comes with a vaulted ceiling and wooden floors, and then there's the one with the animal print carpet and tiger painting. Since the place is smack dab in the center of town and attached to a brewery with a restaurant, there may be some ambient noise—bring earplugs if you're a light sleeper! Follow up a tour of the brewery (daily at 4pm, 13€) with a mug of the house brew, perhaps while tucking into a schnitzel or roast pork knuckle. In summer, the beer garden is a lovely place to sit and relax.

Markt 6. www.brauhaus-wittenberg.de. ✆ **03491/433130.** 40 units. 84€–89€ double. Buffet breakfast included. Free parking. **Amenities:** restaurant; Wi-Fi (free).

DRESDEN ★★★

198km (123 miles) S of Berlin, 111km (69 miles) SE of Leipzig

Dresden, once known as "Florence on the Elbe," was celebrated throughout Europe for its architecture and art treasures. Then came the night of February 13, 1945, when Allied bombers rained down phosphorus and high-explosive bombs on the city. By morning, the Dresden of legend was but a memory. No one knows for sure how many died, but the number is certainly in the tens of thousands. If you're interested in the subject, you might want to read Kurt Vonnegut's novel *Slaughterhouse Five*.

Since reunification in 1990 Dresden has undergone a rapid and dramatic restoration and is once again a major sightseeing destination. Its churches, palaces, cultural institutions, and museums rank among the finest in all of Germany.

Essentials

ARRIVING

BY PLANE   The small **Dresden International Airport** (www.dresden-airport.de, © **0351/8813360**) lies 10km (6 miles) north of the city center and has direct flights to and from a dozen German and European cities. The S-Bahn No. 2 makes the 20-minute trip into town every half hour. A taxi in town costs about 20€.

BY TRAIN   Dresden has two main rail stations, the **Hauptbahnhof,** on Wiener Platz, and the **Dresden-Neustadt,** at Schlesischer Platz. S-Bahn trains nos. S1 and S2 and tram no. 3 connects the two. There are frequent connections between Dresden and major and regional cities, including direct bi-hourly service to/from Berlin (trip time: 2 hr.) and Frankfurt (trip time: 4½ hr.) as well as twice-hourly connections to Leipzig (trip time: 1-1½ hr.).

BY BUS   Dresden is well connected by such long-distance companies as Berlinlinienbus and Flixbus. For details, see **www.busliniensuche.de**.

BY CAR   Dresden is on the east-west A4 Autobahn. The A13 comes in from Berlin, a 2-hour drive. Leipzig is about an 80-minute drive away via the A14.

VISITOR INFORMATION

Dresden Tourist Information (www.dresden.de; © **0351/501 501**) operates two branches: one at the Hauptbahnhof (daily 8am to 8pm) and another next to the Frauenkirche in the QF-Passage at Neumarkt 2 (Monday to Friday 10am to 7pm, Saturday 10am to 6pm, and Sunday 10am to 3pm).

GETTING AROUND

BY PUBLIC TRANSPORTATION   Dresden's historic core is best seen on foot, but to explore further afield, bus and tram lines are a good alternative. Single trips within the entire city cost 2.30€ and day passes (*Tageskarte*) are 6€. Tickets are sold from vending machines at most stops and inside trams. The S-Bahn extends into nearby towns, including Meissen.

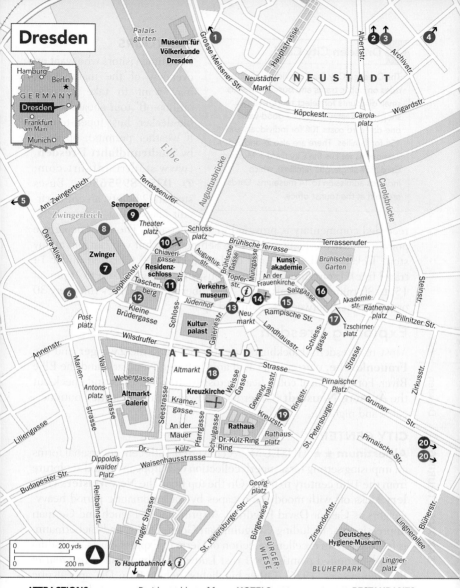

Dresden

Museum für Völkerkunde Dresden

Palais-garten

Neustädter Markt

NEUSTADT

Köpckestr.

Carola-platz

Wigardstr.

Elbe

Terrassenufer

Am Zwingerteich

Zwingerteich

Semperoper

Theater-platz

Schloss-platz

Brühlsche Terrasse

Terrassenufer

Ostra-Allee

Zwinger

Chiaveri-gasse

Kathedrale

Residenz-schloss

Augustus-str.

Brühlsche Gasse

Münzgasse

Kunst-akademie

Brühlscher Garten

Steinstr.

Carlsbrücke

Taschen-berg

Topfer-str.

An der Frauenkirche

Salzgasse

Akademie-str.

Rathenau-platz

Pillnitzer Str.

Sophienstr.

Kleine Brüdergasse

Schloss-str.

Verkehrs-museum

Jüdenhof

Neu-markt

Rampische Str.

Schiess-gasse

Tzschirner-platz

Post-platz

Galeriestr.

Kultur-palast

Landhausstr.

ALTSTADT

Wilsdruffer

Strasse

Pirnaischer Platz

Grunaer Str.

Zirkusstr.

Annenstr.

Marien-strasse

Wall-strasse

Webergasse

Altmarkt

Weisse Gasse

Gewand-hausstr.

Kreuzstr.

Ringstr.

St. Petersburger Str.

Antons-platz

Seestrasse

Altmarkt-Galerie

Kreuzkiche

Kramer-gasse

Rathaus

Rathaus-platz

Pirnaische Str.

Lingnerallee

Lilliengasse

An der Mauer

Pfarrgasse

Schulgasse

Dr.-Külz-Ring

Blüherstr.

Dr.-Külz-Ring

Waisenhausstrasse

Dippoldis-walder Platz

Budapester Str.

Prager Strasse

Reitbahnstr.

St. Petersburger Str.

Georg-platz

Bürgerwiese

Zinnendorfstr.

Deutsches Hygiene-Museum

Lingner-platz

BÜRGER-WIESE

BLÜHERPARK

0 — 200 yds
0 — 200 m

To Hauptbahnhof & (i)

ATTRACTIONS

Albertinum **16**
Frauenkirche **14**
Gemäldegalerie
  Alter Meister **7**
Gläserne Manufaktur **20**
Grünes Gewölbe **11**
Kathedrale St. Trinitas **10**
Militärhistorisches
  Museum **2**
Residenzschloss **11**
Semperoper **9**
Zwinger **7**

HOTELS

Gewandhaus Dresden **19**
Hotel Suitess **15**
Kempinski Hotel
  Taschenbergpalais **12**
Pension Raskolnikoff **4**
QF Hotel **13**
Star Inn Hotel Premium
  Dresden am Haus
  Altmarkt **18**

RESTAURANTS

Alte Meister **8**
Brauhaus Watzke **1**
BrennNessel **5**
Kastenmeiers **17**
Lesage **20**
Lila Sosse **3**
William **6**

BUS TOURS

First-time visitors who want an overview of the main sights may want to take a "hop-on-hop-off" tour aboard a double-decker bus (open-topped if weather permits), operated by **Stadtrundfahrt Dresden,** (www.stadtrundfahrt.com; ✆ **0351/8995650**). Buses stop at 22 points; an entire circuit takes about 2 hours. Prerecorded commentary is provided in 18 languages. The main departure point is on Theaterplatz next to the Semperoper, but you can join at any stop. Tickets, sold online and on board, cost 20€ (children under 14 travel free). From April to October buses run daily 9:30am to 10pm, at 15- to 30-minute intervals; from November to March, they run every 30 or 60 minutes, between 9:30am and 8pm.

Exploring Dresden

Most of Dresden's blockbuster sights, including the **Zwinger** and the **Frauenkirche,** cluster in a small area between Neumarkt and the Elbe River. For more local color, head across to the other bank and check out the **Äussere Neustadt** (Outer New Town) with its eclectic boutiques, cafés and nightlife.

CITY CENTER

Albertinum ★★ MUSEUM   A converted 16th-century arsenal forms an imposing setting for a superb collection of European art and sculpture from the 19th century to today. On the top floor, the **New Masters Gallery** kicks off with moody landscapes by such Romantic period heavyweights as Caspar David Friedrich. A sprinkling of French and German impressionists, including Gauguin, Van Gogh, Degas, and Liebermann, is followed by an excellent selection of German Expressionists, including a newly acquired painting by Ernst Ludwig Kirchner called *In Front of the Hairdresser's* (1926). Other highlights include Otto Dix' apocalyptic war vision *Der Krieg* (War, 1929) and the *Auschwitz Cycle* by Gerhard Richter (2014), a viscerally abstract work based on four photographs taken in 1944 by an anonymous prisoner. The **Sculpture Collection,** housed in the baronial second-floor rooms, presents works from 5 millennia, but is especially strong when it comes to 19th-century German artists such as Christian Daniel Rauch and Max Klinger.

Brühlsche Terrasse or Georg-Treu-Platz. www.skd.museum. ✆ **0351/49142000.** Admission 10€ adults, 7.50€ students and seniors, children 17 and under free. Tues–Sun 10am–6pm. Tram: 1, 2, or 4 to Pirnaischer Platz.

Frauenkirche (Church of Our Lady) ★★★ CHURCH Crowned by a dazzling dome, this grand church is Dresden's most famous landmark. Built between 1726 and 1743, it was destroyed by Allied planes in February 1945, and throughout the Cold War, the pile of blackened stones was conserved as an evocative war memorial. After reunification in 1990, however, a citizens' group revived efforts to reconstruct the church. Support poured in from around the world—in the U.S., German-born American Günter Blobel founded the nonprofit organization Friends of Dresden, and in Britain, the Duke of Kent became royal patron of the Dresden Trust. Reconstruction of the baroque beauty was completed in 2005 at a cost of about $220 million. About 3,500 original stones, easily recognizable by their charred surface, were incorporated into the elegant building with its elaborate altar. A free organ concert and guided tour (in German) takes place between noon and 1pm. Concerts and services are also held regularly. The dome can be climbed for 8€ (students and seniors 5€).

Destroyed in 1945, the reconstructed Frauenkirche once more presides over Dresden's historic core.

Neumarkt. www.frauenkirche-dresden.org. ✆ **0351/65606701.** Admission free. Daily 10am–noon and 1–6pm. Tram: 1, 2, or 4 to Altmarkt.

Soaring above the City

A nostalgic way to travel is aboard Dresden's two historic *Bergbahnen* (mountain railways) that ascend steeply above the Elbe River in the scenic suburb of Loschwitz. The **Standseilbahn** (funicular) has linked Loschwitz with the villa-studded Weisser Hirsch district since 1895. Nearby, the world's oldest **Schwebebahn** (suspension railway, 1901) links Loschwitz with a viewing platform at Loschwitzhöhe. Both railways operate daily year-round. Roundtrip fares on either are 5€ for adults and 3€ for children. For details and operating hours, see **www.dresdner-bergbahnen.de**. The nearest bus station is Körnerplatz (take tram no. 10 to Pohlandplatz and then bus 61 to Körnerplatz, or take a taxi, which will cost about 17€).

Kathedrale St. Trinitas (Dresden Cathedral) ★ CHURCH   Saxony's largest house of worship was originally built from 1739 to 1751 as the royal court church. Its façade is crowned with 78 sculptures of saints, while the crypt holds the elaborate sarcophagi of the Saxon rulers and a box said to contain the heart of August the Strong. In the main church, note the stone pulpit by baroque star sculptor Balthasar Permoser and the 18th-century Silbermann organ (concerts 11:30am Wednesday and Saturday).

Schlossplatz. www.kathedrale-dresden.de. (℃ **0351/4844712.** Admission free. Mon–Thurs 9am–5pm, Fri 1–5pm, Sat 10am–5pm, Sun noon–4pm. Tram: 4, 8, or 9 to Theaterplatz.

Grünes Gewölbe (Green Vault) ★★★ MUSEUM   Saxon ruler August the Strong, who ruled from 1694 to 1733, was a passionate admirer of the arts who amassed a dazzling collection of handcrafted treasures, wrought of gold, silver, enamel, and ivory and adorned with gemstones and mother-of-pearl. The collection is so vast that it is displayed in two separate museums, both in the Residenzschloss (see below). The intimate **Historical Green Vault** consists of a series of sumptuously decorated baroque-style rooms where 2,500 works of art are displayed on shelves or on ornate tables, just as they were during August's time. Highlights include the Hall of Precious Objects (note the goblets fashioned from gilded ostrich eggs) and the Jewel Room. Admission here is by timed ticket, which can—and should—be booked online in advance since there's a strict lid on daily visitor numbers. However, there's no need to be disappointed if you can't get in, because the **New Green Vault** holds perhaps even more extravagant objets d'art, including a cherry pit engraved with 185 faces and a frigate with paper-thin ivory sails. It's all presented in a modern setting and admission is included in the general ticket to the Residenzschloss.

Schlossplatz. www.skd.museum. ℃ **0351/49142000.** Admission 12€, students and seniors 9€, children under 17 free. Combination ticket with Residenzschloss 21€. Wed–Mon 10am–6pm. Tram: 4, 8, or 9 to Theaterplatz.

Residenzschloss ★★★ PALACE   This hulking edifice served as the residence of the Saxon rulers from 1485 to 1918. Despite various alterations and modernizations, it never lost its distinctive High Renaissance architectural character. Reconstruction of the building, which was leveled in 1945, began in 1986 and is still ongoing. Today it houses some of Dresden's most important collections of art. Aside from the stunning **Grünes Gewölbe** (Green Vault, see above), you can admire magnificent weapons and armor in the **Rüstkammer** (Armoury) ★★; a collection of prints and drawings in the **Kupferstich-Kabinett** ★, coins in the **Münzkabinett** ★ and Ottoman art in the **Türckische Kammer** (Turkish Chamber) ★★. The **Hausmannsturm** ★ (Hausmann Tower; Mar–Oct

The baroque Zwinger complex contains three museums.

Wed–Mon 10am–6pm) can be climbed for a panoramic vista over Dresden and the Elbe.

Schlossplatz. www.skd.museum. ℰ **0351/49142000.** Admission including Neues Historisches Gewölbe 12€, students and seniors 9€, children under 17 free. Combination ticket with Historisches Grünes Gewölbe 21€. Wed–Mon 10am–6pm. Tram: 4, 8 or 9 to Theaterplatz.

Zwinger ★★★ MUSEUM August the Strong, elector of Saxony (also king of Poland), commissioned the architect M.D. Pöppelmann and the sculptor Balthasar Perlmoser to build this baroque masterpiece. Completed in 1719, it served primarily as a venue for courtly festivities. Today, the vast square complex holds a trio of museums, including the superb **Old Masters Gallery,** the **Porcelain Collection** with fragile masterpieces from Meissen, Japan, and China, and the **Mathematisch-Physikalischer Salon** with its prized collection of historic scientific instruments and clocks.

   Pöppelmann initially conceived the Zwinger as the forecourt of a new (never realized) palace to be built towards the Elbe River. The harmonious blend of architecture, sculpture, and gardens is best appreciated on a stroll around its central courtyard. The most splendid entrance is the **Kronentor** (Crown's Gate) from the west side (Ostra-Allee). Straight ahead is the Semper Wing, which was added by Gottfried

Cruising to Saxon Switzerland

About 30km southeast of Dresden, the small national park called **Saxon Switzerland** is one of Germany's most enchanting landscapes, a mosaic of fantastically shaped rock formations, rugged pinnacles, table-top mountains, deep gorges, and sheer sandstone cliffs. It's a paradise for hikers, rock climbers, and cyclists. Best of all: Admission is free! The loveliest way to get to Saxon Switzerland from Dresden is aboard a cruise boat operated by **Sächsische Dampfschiffahrt** (© **0351/866090;**

www.saechsische-dampfschiffahrt.de). From May to mid-October, three boats daily depart up the Elbe from the landing docks below Brühlsche Terrasse for the four-hour trip to Rathen (one departure the rest of the year).Tickets cost 15€ one way and 20€ round-trip. Most people opt to go one way by boat and come back by train (S-Bahn No.1), which runs hourly, takes 33 minutes, and costs 6.20€. En route you'll pass several beautiful castles and the famous "Blaues Wunder" (Blue Wonder) bridge from 1883.

Semper in 1855 and today houses the Old Masters Gallery. To your left, the famous **Wall Pavilion** features ornate sculpture, curved galleries, and sweeping staircases, one of which leads to the **Nymphs' Bath,** a graceful grotto-style fountain studded with mythological figures. On the opposite end, a porcelain carillon adorning the façade, the **Glockenspiel Pavilion,** chimes classical tunes up to four times daily (except from January to Easter).

The most important museum in the Zwinger is the **Gemäldegalerie Alte Meister** (Old Masters Gallery), which counts among its showpieces Raphael's *Sistine Madonna,* Giorgione's *Sleeping Venus,* Correggio's *Holy Night,* and Vermeer's *Girl Reading a Letter.* You can feast your eyes on Flemish, Dutch, and German paintings by Van Dyck, Dürer, and Rembrandt, among others. The Rubens collection includes his spectacular *Neptune,* full of rearing horses, and an exquisite *St. Jerome.* After WWII, many works were whisked to Moscow as war booty but returned in 1955/56.

Theaterplatz 1. www.skd.museum. © **0351/49142000.** Courtyard admission free, museums 10€ adults, 7.50€ students and seniors, children 17 and under free. Museums open Tues–Sun 10am–6pm. Tram: 4, 8, or 9 to Theaterplatz.

OUTSIDE THE CITY CENTER

Gläserne Manufaktur (Transparent Factory) ★ This architecturally striking glass building on the edge of the huge Grosser Garten (Big Garden) city park opened in 2002 as the futuristic assembly plant of Volkswagen's Phaeton luxury sedan. Production ceased in March 2015 but will resume with another model, most likely an electric vehicle, in 2017. Meantime, 75-minute tours of the facility, which centers on a 49m-high (150ft) atrium, will continue to be offered, albeit with a focus on the future of automobiles, including e-cars and digital cars. You'll also learn about the architecture, about the outdoor speaker system that emulates bird language to keep birds from flying into the façade, and other fascinating tidbits. Call ahead to make sure that it's not closed for a private event. The gourmet restaurant Lesage (p. 189) is here as well.

Lennéstrasse. www.glaesernemanufaktur.de. ℂ **0351/4204411.** Tours 7€. Mon–Fri 8:30am–7pm, Sat–Sun 9am–6pm. Tram: 1, 2, 4, 10, 12, and 13 to Strassburger Platz.

Militärhistorisches Museum ★ MUSEUM   Don't expect a glorification of German military might in this intriguing museum housed in a 19th-century arsenal and a modern wedge-shaped extension by Daniel Libeskind. Although it does chronicle German military conflicts from the Middle Ages to the present, the exhibit also examines the causes and social corollaries of war by zeroing in on such topics as the exploitation of animals in war or the economy of armed conflict. It's a bit outside the city center, but easily reached by tram.

Olbrichtplatz 2. www.mhmbundeswehr.de. ℂ **0351/8232803.** Admission 5€ adults, 3€ students and seniors. Mon 10am–9pm, Tues–Sun 10am–6pm. Tram: 4, 7, 8, and 9 to Stauffenbergallee.

Where to Stay in Dresden

Lodging options in Dresden cover the entire price spectrum from charming hostels to five-star luxury properties. If you're in town for a short time, opt for a place in the Altstadt or Neustadt.

Gewandhaus Dresden ★★★
One of only two hotels in Germany that are part of Marriott's prestigious Autograph Collection, the Gewandhaus occupies the restored premises of what originated in 1768 as a cloth-makers' trading house. Thoroughly updated in 2015, its design smoothly blends the baroque `sauna, steam room, and gym. Rooms, which encircle a glass-covered atrium with ornate wrought-iron balconies, are good-sized and feature custom-designed

The atrium of the Gewandhaus hotel, converted from an 18th-century trading house.

furniture (love those silvery steamer-trunk-style armoires!). The city's best steakhouse, called **(m)eatery,** and the café **Kuchengalerie** with its divine cakes, provide sustenance.

Ringstrasse 1. www.gewandhaus-hotel.de. © **0351/49490.** 97 units. 125€–265€ double. Breakfast 22€. Parking 15€. **Amenities:** restaurant; bar; gym; pool; room service; sauna; Wi-Fi (free). Tram: 1, 2, 3, 4, 7, 8, 9, or 12 to Pirnaischer Platz.

Hotel Suitess ★★ This boutique charmer packs all the comforts and amenities of a grand hotel into one compact package. Rooms feature gracious Biedermeier touches, including dark furniture, heavy drapes, and wing chairs. A small 24-hour spa beckons with a whirlpool, sauna, steam room, and a terrace with an Instagram-worthy view of the Frauenkirche dome. The same perspective presents itself from the fine-dining restaurant **Moritz.** Gin lovers will likely be drawn to the flamboyant **Dresden Gin House** on the ground floor (smoking allowed).

An der Frauenkirche 13. www.suitess-hotel.com. © **0351/417270.** 25 units. 145€–230€ double. Breakfast 23€.Parking 20€. **Amenities:** restaurant; bar; gym, pool, sauna; room service; Wi-Fi (free). Tram: 1, 2, 3, 4, 7, 8, 9 or 12 to Pirnaischer Platz.

Kempinski Hotel Taschenbergpalais ★★★ Luxury is taken very seriously at this faithful replica of the 18th-century baroque palace built by August the Strong for his favorite mistress, the Countess Cosel. Only a massive marble staircase survived the WWII bombing, but that didn't stop a real estate developer from resurrecting the landmark as a hotel in 1995. Although it may lack the gravitas of the original, the Taschenberg still has old-world splendor galore. A uniformed doorman escorts guests via the forecourt to the lofty lobby which segues to restaurants, a bar, and a café. All flank a large central courtyard that turns into an ice rink in winter. The high-ceilinged rooms come in various sizes and configurations, but all sport fine furniture, classic décor, and sumptuous sheets in regal red, blue, and white. The nicest rooms overlook the Zwinger or the Opera. A separate elevator leads to the lovely pool area with co-ed sauna and massage services. An indulgent breakfast buffet includes eggs cooked to order, honey served from a honeycomb, and all-you-can-drink sparkling wine.

Taschenberg 3. www.kempinski-dresden.de. © **0351/49120.** 214 units. 140€–300€ double; from 325€ suite. Breakfast 31€. Parking 25€. **Amenities:** 2 restaurants; bar; gym; indoor pool; room service; sauna; Wi-Fi (free). Tram: 4, 8 or 9 to Theaterplatz.

Pension Raskolnikoff ★ Don't be put off by the exterior: behind the drab façade lies a beloved gastropub with attached guesthouse that both exude alternative charm. In the 1980s, this 18th-century building in the Äussere Neustadt (Outer New Town) became an artists' squat and still attracts a sizeable share of creative minds. At these rates, you know you're not getting the Ritz, but the interior has been nicely restored indeed. Rooms are comfortable enough and come with tiny bathrooms with showers. The coziest are in the attic, reached via a steep wooden staircase. There's also a small communal kitchen, in case you're not tempted by the hearty seasonal fare dished up in the living-room-style pub with open kitchen below.

Böhmische Strasse 34. www.raskolnikoff.de. ✆ **0351/8045706.** 8 units. 47€ single, 64€ double. **Amenities:** restaurant; bar; Wi-Fi (free).

QF Hotel ★★★   Dostoyevsky and Chopin stayed in the earlier incarnation of this chic lifestyle hotel in a dreamy location next to the Frauenkirche. Today it's once again popular with artists and creative types who appreciate the sleek, contemporary design by Lorenzo Bellini. It's well worth spending a little extra money on a superior unit, which comes with views of the historic Neumarkt, a separate tub and shower, as well as top quality hand-filtered coffee and Japanese tea-making facilities. The breakfast buffet far exceeds the norm with such thoughtful extras as freshly made smoothies, regional cheeses and cold cuts, and scrumptious breads and pastries baked in-house. There's no restaurant, but the Bellini Bar beckons with snacks, afternoon tea, and a full drinks menu.

Neumarkt 1. www.qf-hotel.de. ✆ **0351/5633090.** 95 units. 90€–135€ double. Breakfast 23€. Parking 22€. **Amenities:** Bar; Wi-Fi (free). Tram: 1, 2, or 4 to Altmarkt.

Star Inn Hotel Premium Dresden am Haus Altmarkt ★   Older Dresdeners still have fond memories of the traditional dance café that flourished in this historic building during GDR times. The three-star Star Inn that opened its doors in early 2015 still channels some of the pre-reunification nostalgia in the chandeliers, the patterned wall fabrics, and the tray-shaped plates in the breakfast room (the former dance hall). Stop by the coffee house to study its historic photographs, then proceed upstairs to the reception desk via a grand black marble staircase (elevator available). Rooms and suites vary widely in terms of size and layout, but are all nicely decked out in light, natural colors; bathrooms boast rain showers and are divided from bedrooms by a glass wall. Small groups and families favor the family rooms with two queen-size beds. The nicest units overlook the historic Altmarkt square.

Altmarkt 4. www.starinnhotels.com. ✆ **0351/307110.** 123 units. 79€–159€ double. Breakfast 13€. Parking 15€. **Amenities:** Cafe; Wi-Fi (free). Tram: 1, 2, or 4.

Where to Eat in Dresden

Alte Meister ★ INTERNATIONAL   When it became time to restore the Zwinger after WWII, the job of directing the artistic process fell to German sculptor Albert Braun. He set up his studio in a lofty pavilion wedged between the Gallery of Old Masters and the Semper Opera. In

1991, the stylish Alte Meister café and restaurant took over the space, with its high pillars, barrel-vaulted ceiling, and panoramic windows. Come here for a coffee break between museums, a leisurely lunch, or a refined dinner. In summer, it's lovely to sit on the balcony or in the courtyard behind a sculpture of the composer Karl Maria Weber. The kitchen creates culinary alchemy with such ambitious dishes as peanut-encrusted veal filet drizzled with rosemary jus and paired with mashed turnip.

Theaterplatz 1A. www.altemeister.net. © **0351/4810426.** Main courses 7.50€–25€. Daily 11am–midnight. Tram: 4, 8, or 9 to Theaterplatz.

Brauhaus Watzke ★★ GERMAN A 19th-century ballroom has taken on new life as a bustling brewpub. Always on tap are the unfiltered Watzke Pils, a tart pilsner, and the smooth and slightly sweet Altpieschner Spezial, but it's also well worthwhile trying the seasonal beer of the month. All cost 3.40€ per half liter. The ambience is boisterous, whether you sit in the enchanting beer garden with sweeping Elbe views or make new friends inside at long wooden tables next to the shiny copper brew kettles. The menu of earthy German soul food goes well with the beer. Choose from snacks like sausages or potato wedges or go the whole hog with Saxon specialties such as marinated pot roast or crispy pork knuckle. There are even a few fish and vegetarian options thrown in for good measure.

Kötzschenbroder Strasse 1. www.watzke.de. © **0351/852920.** Main courses 8€–19€. Daily 11am–midnight. Tram: 4, 9 or 13 to Altpieschen.

BrennNessel ★★ VEGETARIAN Vegetarians or vegans should point the compass to this cute 350-year-old "hobbit house" that survived the WWII bombing raids. Be sure to book ahead—empty tables are a rare sight in the wood-beamed dining room with its cheerful cornflower-blue chairs or in the vine-framed courtyard. The menu leans toward casseroles, noodle dishes, stews, and sautés, largely made to order and inextricably tied to the region and the seasons. A recent winter menu star, for instance, was a wicked gnocchi-kale casserole laced with mushrooms, apples, dried tomatoes, walnuts, and smoked cheese. The regular menu also includes one or two meat dishes—handy in case you're accompanied by a hardcore carnivore. Vegans should ask for the separate menu.

Schützengasse 18. www.brennnessel-dresden.de. © **0351/4943319.** Main dishes 9€–15€. Daily 11am–midnight. Tram: 4, 11, or 20 to Am Zwingerteich.

Kastenmeiers ★★ FISH This vibrant seafood restaurant in the Kurländer Palais, a rebuilt rococo palace, is always packed to the gills—and for good reason. The first thing you spot upon entering is the well-stocked bar, but soon all eyes are on the open kitchen where Gerd Kastenmeier and a small army of chefs perform their culinary wizardry. Kastenmeier swears on using only the finest and freshest ingredients, which includes the lobster and trout still swimming in two tanks suspended above the kitchen. Compositions may look deceptively simple but are actually built on a foundation of creativity and old-school technique to coax maximum flavor out of each ingredient. The two high-ceilinged dining rooms get ample charm from exposed red brick walls, which double as a gallery space. In summer, the action moves to the romantic courtyard.

Tzschirnerplatz 3-5. www.kastenmeiers.de. ⓒ **0351/48484801.** Business lunch Mon–Fri 11€–21€, main courses 20€–80€. Mon–Fri noon–11pm, Sat–Sun 5–11pm. Tram: 3, 7, 8 or 9 to Synagoge.

Lesage ★★ INTERNATIONAL   Before becoming head chef of Lesage, Thorsten Bubolz cooked up a storm at the venerable Taschenbergpalais (p. 186). Amid the relentlessly purist décor of the Volkswagen's high-tech Gläserne Manufaktur (p. 184), he lets his imagination run wild in composing progressive plates from market-fresh ingredients. A typical meal might start with dainty baked chicken pralines, move on to robust red-wine tagliatelle with braised rabbit, and wrap up with a sinful crème brûlée teamed with orange ragout and yogurt ice cream. The daytime bistro menu brings breakfast, burgers, and bagels as well as the "VW Currywurst" signature dish: a smoked and boiled sausage that's slivered and doused with tangy ketchup and curry powder. Clued-in foodies also invade for Sunday brunch (11am to 3pm, 35€), which includes a tour of the factory.

Lennéstrasse 1. www.lesage.de. ⓒ **0351/4204250.** Dinner & brunch reservations required. Main courses 16€–30€. Bistro menu 4.50€–9€. Sun–Wed 9am–6pm, Thurs–Sat 9am–10pm. Tram: 1, 2, 4, 10, 12, or 13 to Strassburger Platz.

Lila Sosse ★ GERMAN   Modern German dishes served in glass preserve jars are the distinctive feature of this bustling restaurant in the whimsically decorated courtyard complex called Kunsthofpassage (www.kunsthof-dresden.de) in the Outer Neustadt. Largely local and seasonal ingredients steer the menu, which may include such mouthwatering selections as cheese spaetzle with fried-onion-sauce, or oxtail ragout with root vegetables. Two or three dishes should fill most tummies, especially if you order a side of the delicious crusty bread with parsley-almond pesto. And don't miss the tangy homemade lemonade, especially in summer when tables spill out into the artsy courtyard.

Alaunstrasse 70. www.lilasosse.de. ⓒ **0351/8036723.** Reservations advised. Tapas 4€–10€. Mon–Fri 4–11pm, Sat–Sun noon–11pm. Tram: 13 to Alaunplatz.

STATE-OF-THE-ART china: MEISSEN PORCELAIN

In 2010, Meissen celebrated its 300th anniversary as a center for the manufacture of quality porcelain. Since 1710, the Elbe River town has been the home of Meissen porcelain—so-called Dresden china. (Meissen is just 24km (15 miles) downriver from Dresden, and the name of the larger city, which was the capital of Saxony's royal house, has attached itself indelibly to Meissen's pride and joy.) The early makers of this "white gold" were virtually held prisoner here because the princes who ruled both Dresden and Meissen carefully guarded the secret to its production.

Meissen porcelain got its start when the Saxon ruler Augustus the Strong, a patron of the arts and a fanatical porcelain collector (he owned almost 15,000 pieces) commissioned the alchemist Johann Friedrich Böttger to transmute gold from base metals. That project went nowhere, naturally, but with the aid of scientist Ehrenfried Walther von Tschirnhaus, Böttger successfully produced Chinese-style porcelain instead. That was enough to keep Augustus happy, since expensive Chinese porcelain had long bedazzled Europe, and until Böttger and von Tschirnhaus got to work, had resisted the best efforts of European craftsmen to re-create it.

The new homegrown china was made inside Meissen's medieval Albrechtsburg castle until 1865, when production shifted to the current site a bit outside the town center. Most of the iconic tableware patterns sold today, such as the Swan and the cobalt-enhanced Blue Onion motifs, have been in production since the 1700s at the Staatliche Porzellan-Manufaktur Meissen (Meissen State Porcelain Manufactory). To this day, all the ornate painting, decoration, and other effects are still done by hand. This makes Meissen porcelain pricey, but each piece is a unique product, made by highly skilled craftsmen. The delicacy of the brush stroke, the richness of color, or the sheen of the glazes make the items highly prized.

William ★ GERMAN The William in question is Shakespeare, of course, which is apropos given that this smart restaurant occupies a prime spot inside the Dresden theater. Walk through a transparent rope curtain into the high-ceilinged dining room where Art Nouveau ornamentation, dark furniture, a long bar, and a gold-and-red color scheme set the stage. Under the guidance of Michelin-starred chef Stefan Herrmann, time-honored German classics are given the progressive treatment, which translates into such dishes as corn poulard with parsnip, or brook trout with beluga lentils and kohlrabi. The menu changes frequently, drawing on whatever seasonal bounty is available. Special events range from Champagne Day to Sunday brunch and wine evenings. The bar is a nice spot for early evening drinks.

Theaterstrasse 2. www.restaurant-william.de. © **0351/65298220.** Main courses 15€–24€. Mon–Fri 11am–11pm, Sat–Sun 10am–11pm. Tram: 4, 8, or 9 to Theaterplatz.

Art and Technique Despite its fragile nature, Meissen porcelain is technically a "hard" or "hard-paste" porcelain, made from the feldspar (ore-free) clay kaolin, also known as china clay, that's mined at a quarry in Mehren, 5km (3 miles) west of Meissen. The ingredients are mixed in a proprietary recipe and fired in a kiln at around 1,200°C (2,192°F) to produce the famous translucent white china.

Form and Content Among the products that have emerged from the Meissen workshop are dinner services and other tableware, human and animal figurines, clocks, candlesticks, snuffboxes, and classic Chinese and Japanese scenes and motifs. Art Nouveau and Art Deco works were produced between the late 19th and early 20th centuries. Some of the most exquisite antique pieces depict classical Greek and Roman myths and legends.

Red Porcelain Production of Meissen porcelain was one of socialist East Germany's few profitable industries. Indeed, the Staatliche Porzellan-Manufaktur Meissen was of great importance to the country's economy because it brought in coveted foreign currency. Purchasers from the capitalist West snapped up the china, causing demand to outstrip supply. Ownership of the factory reverted to the state of Saxony after Germany's reunification in 1990.

Real or Fake? To be tolerably sure that you're looking at a real piece of Meissen porcelain (though it's not an absolute guarantee), look on the bottom for the distinctive cobalt-blue crossed-swords logo, derived from Augustus the Strong's coat of arms, an official hallmark granted in 1724.

A Porcelain Feast In addition to the Meissen porcelain in the **Erlebniswelt** museum (p. 194), the world's largest single collection is in Dresden's **Zwinger Palace** (p. 183). There's even a full-size glockenspiel of Meissen porcelain bells in the palace's gate tower.

—George McDona

Shopping

Department stores and high-street chains line the pedestrianized **Prager Strasse,** which links the main train station with the Altstadt. The **Altstadt** itself brims with high-end boutiques, some of which cluster in the elegant **QF-Passage ★** next to the Frauenkirche. Aside from a branch of the luxury watchmaker A. Lange & Söhne, you'll find fine Italian shoes at Prisco, and local sweets and cakes at Emil Reimann. The tourist office is here as well as the upscale hair and make-up salon **Brockmann & Knoedler ★** (www.brockmannundknoedler.de; ✆ **0351/48433840**), where you can get an "organic haircut" that keeps you looking good twice as long as a regular one. In December, the Altstadt turns into a winter wonderland during the celebrated **Weihnachtsmarkt ★★★**, one of the oldest Christmas market in Germany (since 1434). Any time of year, you can buy handmade Christmas ornaments and figurines at **Weihnachtsland am Zwinger** ★, Kleine Brüdergasse 5 (www.weihnachtsland-dresden.com; ✆ **0351/2153888**).

Across the Elbe River via Augustusbrücke, the **Barockviertel** (Baroque Quarter) brims with antiques stores and local designer boutiques. A standout among the latter is **Dorothea Michalk** ★ Rähnitzgasse 18 (www.dorothea-michalk.de; ✆ **0351/8106101**) who specializes in impeccably tailored, customized dresses, tops, and coats with a flattering feminine edge. A short walk further south, in the Outer Neustadt, you'll find the **Kunsthofpassage** ★★, Alaunstrasse 70 (www.kunsthof-dresden.de; ✆ **0351/8106617**), a whimsically decorated courtyard ensemble with about 20 indie boutiques, galleries and cafés.

Nightlife & Entertainment

THE PERFORMING ARTS The **Semperoper (Semper Opera House)** ★★★, Theaterplatz 2 (www.semperoper.de; ✆ **0351/4911705**) ranks among the top opera houses in the world. Both Wagner and Weber conducted here. Gottfried Semper, who also mapped out the picture gallery in the Zwinger, designed the Renaissance-style two-tiered building, which was completely restored after World War II and has supreme acoustics. Good seats can be had for 31€ to 210€. Book as far ahead as possible. No performances mid-July to mid-August.

Until the restoration of its permanent home, the Kulturpalast, is completed, the **Dresden Philharmonie** (www.dresdnerphilharmonie.de; ✆ **0361/4866866**) performs at such venues as the Albertinum, the Frauenkirche and the Schauspielhaus. Tickets cost 20€ to 32€.

PUBS & BARS On Theaterplatz, an extensive whisky selection stars at the oak-paneled **Karl May Bar** ★ (✆ **0351/4912720**) at the Taschenbergpalais (p. 186), which pays homage to 19th-century adventure writer Karl May, born in nearby Radebeul. It's also well worth trying one of the cocktails created by the award-winning bar chef Niko Pavlidis.

Two other special places are out in Outer Neustadt. Belly up to the long custom-made wooden bar at the delightful wine bar **Weinzentrale** ★★, Hoyerswerder Strasse 26, (www.weinzentrale.com; ✆ **0351/89966747**), presided over top sommelier Jens Pietzonka, who curates a weekly selection of 10 by-the-glass offerings (from 3.50€) as well as a listing of 500 bottles from around the world, offered in a cork-bound menu. The convivial gastropub **Zapfanstalt** ★, Sebnitzer Strasse 15 (www.zapfanstalt.com; ✆ **0351/21996354**) has made it its mission to serve only the very best brews. That translates into 20 beers on tap plus over 100 bottled varieties from around the world, matched by a menu of German comfort food.

Albrechtsburg castle, birthplace of German porcelain.

Day Trips from Dresden

MEISSEN ★

Only 25km (16 miles) northwest of Dresden, Meissen flanks both banks of the Elbe and makes for an easy day trip. It is the birthplace of European porcelain making (the Chinese had figured out the formula some 2,000 years earlier), which was first manufactured here in 1710 in the towering Albrechtburg castle. Today, a modern factory still churns out the precious fragile tableware which is, of course, for sale throughout the charming town with its crooked lanes and historic houses.

ESSENTIALS   Meissen is served by the S-Bahn No. 1 from Dresden-Hauptbahnhof every half-hour. Tickets cost 6.20€ and the trip time is 30 minutes. Driving via Hwy B6 takes about 45 minutes. For a more leisurely excursion, boats operated by **Sächsische Dampfschiffahrt** (www.saechsische-dampfschiffahrt.de, ℗ **0351/866090**) leave daily between May and mid-October at 9:45am from Dresden's Brühl Terrace. Trips cost 10€ and take 3 hours. **Tourist-Information Meissen,** Markt 3 (www.touristinfo-meissen.de, ℗ **03521/41940**) is open April to

October Monday to Friday 10am to 6pm, Saturday and Sunday 10am to 4pm; from November to March, hours are Monday to Friday 10am to 5pm and Saturday 10am to 3pm (closed Saturdays in January).

Exploring Meissen

Meissen's impressive silhouette is defined by two landmarks set grandly atop the Burgberg hill. The compact Gothic cathedral **Dom zu Meissen ★**, Domplatz 7 (www.dom-zu-meissen-de, ℂ **03521/452490**) was built between 1260 and 1450 and became the burial place of the Saxon rulers in 1428. Major works of art include an altar painting by Lucas Cranach the Elder and rare Meissen porcelain. Admission costs 4€, or 6€ with a 30-minute German-language guided tour. Hours are April daily 10am to 6pm; May to October Monday to Friday 9am to 6pm and Saturday 9am to 5pm; and November to March daily 10am to 4pm. Rubbing up again the Dom, the red-roofed late Gothic **Albrechtsburg ★**, Domplatz 1 (www.albrechtsburg-meissen.de, ℂ **03521/47070**) is the castle where Meissen porcelain production began in 1710. An excellent, partly interactive exhibit explains how this happened and explores the history of the Wettiner, the powerful dynasty that ruled Saxony from the Middle Ages until 1918. The castle is open March to October daily 10am to 6pm, November to February daily 10am to 5pm. Admission is 8€ for adults, 4€ students and seniors.

But the prime attraction in town is the **Erlebniswelt Haus Meissen ★**, Talstrasse 9 (www.meissen.com, ℂ **03521/468208**), which is fun even if you're not a fan of fancy porcelain. Visits start with audio-guided tour of the Schauwerkstätten (workshops), where artisans demonstrate the complex and highly skilled processes of turning, embossing, underglazing, and painting porcelain. This is followed by the **Porcelain Museum,** which showcases exemplary pieces from 300 years of Meissen. The exhibit is open May to October daily 9am to 6pm, and November to April daily 9am to 5pm.

Where to Eat in Meissen

Restaurant Vincenz Richter ★ GERMAN/SAXON Despite its heavy beamed ceiling, décor of guns and armor, and framed old paintings, the kitsch factor is kept pleasantly in check at this hugely popular restaurant in a vine-sheathed 1523 building just uphill from the market. The kitchen whips up sophisticated Saxon and German dishes, such as local brook trout with saffron foam or braised ox cheeks. The wine offering is exemplary. Reservations recommended.

An der Frauenkirche 12. www.vincenz-richter.de. ℂ **03521/453285.** Main courses 13€–19€; fixed-price menus 17€–39€. Tues–Fri noon–2pm and 5pm–10pm; Sat noon–11pm, Sun noon–3pm.

NORTHERN BAVARIA & THE GERMAN DANUBE

Northern Bavaria might not hit quite the same Alpine high notes as Neuschwanstein Castle or exude the oom-pah-pah exuberance of Munich, but Bavarians who occupy these landscapes would not have it any other way. Here, tucked into vineyard-clad hills and low forested mountains, are medieval and Renaissance cities that happen to be some of the most treasure-filled places in Germany. While plenty of castles and half-timbered houses satisfy a yearning for a typically picturesque German experience, the off-the-beaten track beauty of much of this region also plunges you into the real Germany.

There's Nürnberg, which delivers centuries worth of art and architecture plus the legacy of World War II and Germany's postwar rebuilding. Bamberg not only has a remarkably unspoiled Altstadt, it outdoes even Munich when it comes to making and consuming beer. Bayreuth, of course, is ground zero for musical devotees of Richard Wagner. To the southwest, along Germany's stretch of the Danube, Regensburg displays one of Europe's largest swaths of medieval architecture, and prosperous Ulm shows off its magnificent medieval Munster. All these places are connected by quick rail links and good roads, making it easy to get from one to another. What's more, this region—traditionally called Franconia—boasts its own highly touted wine, its own food (think bratwurst grilled over a beech-wood fire), and a thriving beer culture.

NÜRNBERG (NUREMBERG) ★★★

109km (68 miles) SE of Würzburg

Few cities in the world conjure such disparate images of beauty and horror. During the 15th and 16th centuries, Nürnberg enjoyed a cultural flowering that made it the center of the German Renaissance, a northern Florence. The great Albrecht Dürer is one of many artists who produced masterpieces in the city's studios. Koberger set up his printing press here, and Regiomontanus built an astronomical observatory. Workshops

Previous Page: The soaring spires of Ulm's cathedral.

See Chapter 7 for the Romantic Road

turned out gingerbread, handmade toys, and the world's first pocket watches, the so-called Nürnberg eggs.

Yet the art and architecture that elevated Nürnberg turned out to be the city's Achilles heel. Adolf Hitler was completely enamored with the Nürnberg's huge swaths of half-timbered houses, steeped and gabled rooftops, and cobbled lanes and squares; he considered it to be the most German of German cities and therefore chose to stage his massive Nazi rallies here. Think of the "Heil Hitler-ing" masses and goose-stepping soldiers in Leni Riefenstahl's film *Triumph des Willens (Triumph of the Will)*, which also includes footage of the Führer's plane flying low over Nürnberg's medieval lanes and stone towers.

Attached to the city, too, were the infamous Nürnberg laws, the 1935 legislation that stripped Jews

Medieval Kaiserberg castle overlooks Nürnberg's historic core.

and other non-Aryans of their German citizenship and basic rights and set the stage for the Holocaust. Nürnberg became known as the ideological center of the Third Reich, and therefore the city was a choice target for Allied bombers. On January 2, 1945, some 525 British Lancasters rained fire and destruction on Nürnberg. The bombings left most of the historic center and surroundings a smoldering ruin and killed 60,000 Nürnbergers. Another reckoning came in 1946, when Nürnberg's Justice Palace hosted the War Crimes Tribunal that tried 23 leading Nazi war criminals for conspiracy and crimes against world peace, the rules of warfare, and humanity.

Yet in the years since then, Nürnberg has regained its vitality, prosperity, and much of its handsome pre-war appearance, as what's new blends in with the reconstructed houses of the old city. In the Altstadt, surrounded by medieval ramparts, Gothic churches and sway-backed medieval houses rise above lively squares and line the banks of the Pegnitz River.

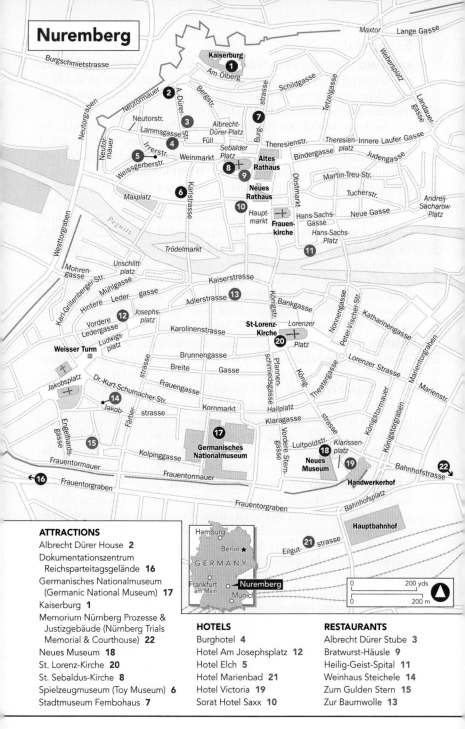

Nuremberg

ATTRACTIONS

Albrecht Dürer House **2**

Dokumentationszentrum
Reichsparteitagsgelände **16**

Germanisches Nationalmuseum
(Germanic National Museum) **17**

Kaiserburg **1**

Memorium Nürnberg Prozesse &
Justizgebäude (Nürnberg Trials
Memorial & Courthouse) **22**

Neues Museum **18**

St. Lorenz-Kirche **20**

St. Sebaldus-Kirche **8**

Spielzeugmuseum (Toy Museum) **6**

Stadtmuseum Fembohaus **7**

HOTELS

Burghotel **4**

Hotel Am Josephsplatz **12**

Hotel Elch **5**

Hotel Marienbad **21**

Hotel Victoria **19**

Sorat Hotel Saxx **10**

RESTAURANTS

Albrecht Dürer Stube **3**

Bratwurst-Häusle **9**

Heilig-Geist-Spital **11**

Weinhaus Steichele **14**

Zum Gulden Stern **15**

Zur Baumwolle **13**

Essentials

ARRIVING   Nürnberg Flughafen **airport,** 6km (4 miles) north of the city center, is served by a dozen or so airlines, with flights to and from many European cities. For information and schedules, visit www.airport-nuernberg.de or call ✆ **0911/93700.**

For **train travel,** the Nürnberg Hauptbahnhof lies on several major German rail lines. Travel time to Frankfurt is 2 hours; to Würzburg, 1 hour; to Berlin, 5 hours; and to Munich, 1 hour. For information and schedules, visit www.bahn.de or call ✆ **01805/996633.** The station is right at the edge of the Altstadt, connected by the Königstrasse to the old city.

Regional **bus** service to neighboring towns within Franconia is offered by OVF Omnibusverkehr Franken GmbH, Nelson Mandela Platz 18 in Nürnberg (www.ovf.de; ✆ **0911/430570**). The main Nürnberg bus terminal is just outside the east entrance of the Hauptbahnhof.

By **car** from Munich, take the A9 Autobahn (driving time, about 1 hour and 40 minutes); from Frankfurt, head southeast along the A3 Autobahn (a little over 2 hours); from Würzburg, follow the A3 southeast (1 hour); from Berlin, take the A9 Autobahn south (4 hours).

VISITOR INFORMATION   Nürnberg's tourist office, at Hauptmarkt 18 (tourismus.nuernberg.de; ✆ **0911/23360**), is open Monday to Saturday 9am to 6pm. From May to October, it is also open Sunday 10am to 4pm.

A **Nürnberg card** (23€), available at the tourist office, gives you admission to ten museums and free public transportation for 2 days, but it may not be worth the cost unless you plan to visit all ten museums and to use a lot of public transport (see below). Here's a better scheme: at most city museums, if you add 2.50€ to your admission, you get a Day Ticket for free entry to other museums for the rest of the day.

GETTING AROUND   Nürnberg has a **subway** system (U-Bahn) and all lines stop at the Hauptbahnhof (main railway station), meaning you can get just about anywhere in the city from there. Some of the world's first driverless trains operate on the route, so you can position yourself in the front car and have a Walter Mitty fantasy while navigating underground Nürnberg. Most **buses** and trams also stop at the Hauptbahnhof; bus no. 36 handily cuts through the heart of the old town. One-way fares within the city cost 2.60€. A Day Ticket Solo, valid for the entire transportation network from midnight to midnight, costs 5.10€. You can purchase tickets from machines next to major stops. For more information, visit **www.vag.de** or call ✆ **0911/2834646.**

You can get just anywhere within the old city by **walking.** Venturing farther afield, you'll need to take a bus to the Dokumentationszentrum (p. 203) and the U-bahn to Memorium Nürnberg (p. 205). For a **taxi,**

Christmas Starts Here

In late November and December, Nürnberg stages what's claimed to be one of the world's largest, most famous, and oldest Christmas markets, with stalls selling food, crafts, and other wares filling the Hauptmarkt and adjoining lanes. This huge **Christmasmarkt** possibly dates to 1610, when the practice of giving children gifts at Christmas was still new (a practice said to have originated when Martin Luther began giving his own children Christmas presents). It opens every year with Christkind, an angelic figure in white robes, giving an address from the balcony of the 14th-century **Frauenkirche** church on the Hauptmarkt square. Christkind is a young woman between the ages of 16 and 19, chosen by a jury from a long list of competitors. She must be at least 5 feet 2 inches tall and have a head for heights, as she makes the much-attended address while lashed to a high, narrow balcony with ropes. Christmasmarkt begins the Friday before the first Sunday in Advent, and runs through December 24.

call ✆ **0911/19410.** The base fare and first kilometer cost 2.70€ each, while each additional kilometer adds on 1.35€.

GUIDED TOURS **Walking tours** in English depart from the tourist office on the Hauptmarkt daily at 1pm, from April through December; the fee is 8€. The enthusiastic guides are usually bursting with information and will fill your head with fascinating tidbits, such as why the large blocks of sandstone on facades are so often riddled with holes. (Answer: in medieval times, when the stones were put in place, the only way to lift them was to insert hooks and hoist them with ropes.)

A tour of the city's **Historic Rock Cut Cellars** will let you explore subterranean Nürnberg, which is riddled with passageways and vaults, dug out to store beer in the Middle Ages. Tours begin with a beer tasting at the Altstadthof brewpub, Bergstrasse 19 (www.historichefeisen-gaenge.de; ✆ **0911/236–02731**). Most tours are in German (Monday to Friday at 11am and 1, 3, and 5pm, weekends hourly from 11am to 5pm), but there's an English-language tour on Sunday at 11:30am. Tours last 75 minutes and cost 6.50€. The brewery is also the starting point for a **Casements and Water Supply Conduits** tour exploring tunnels dug deep within the castle walls to carry water in the Middle Ages (they were used well into the 20th century). Tours (in German) are led daily at 3:15pm, with additional tours on weekends at 4:15pm, and cost 6€. If you do join one of the German tours, guides and your fellow tourists will usually translate the essentials.

Exploring Nürnberg

From the Hauptbahnhof (train station), you can walk through the underground **Königstor-passage** to the top of **Königstrasse,** the main street

Frauenkirche, the centerpiece of Nürnberg's Hauptmarkt square.

that cuts through the old city. **Königstor,** the round tower on the left as you enter the old city, is a remnant of one of five gates in the old city walls. Originally there were 3 miles of walls; about 2½ miles still stand, in many places still protected by a dry moat. Within Königstor and other round towers are earlier square towers—the curved fortifications were a 16th-century innovation designed to deflect cannon balls. Just down Königstrasse, the impressive **Nassauhaus** (closed to the public), is one of the last remaining tower residences that nobility built high and mighty, proof of their wealth and power. As Königstrasse continues past the church of **St. Lorenz** (p. 206), wander east off Lorenzerplatz to see a relic of the World War II bombings: The haunting shell of **Katharinenkirche** (St. Catherine's Church), left just as it was when the fires died out in 1945. Today it serves as a setting for summertime concerts. For a brief time after the war, city officials considered leaving all of Nürnberg in similar ruin as a reminder of the horrors of war.

Königstrasse becomes the heart of the central shopping precinct (in many parts closed to cars) and crosses the river. Just to the west you'll notice a romantic-looking covered bridge. The upper level, however, was actually the residence of the town hangman—reason enough for residents to avoid that part of the riverside. Pretty little **Pegnitz Island** below the bridge is these days lined with quaint cottages but was the medieval pig market, and likewise off limits to anyone with notions of social standing.

Hauptmarkt, the central market square, is just north of the river. From the adjoining **Rathausplatz** steep streets lead to the foot of **Kaiserburg** (p. 205), the city's medieval castle. A walk through the old city, from the Hauptbahnhof to the castle, will take you about 30 minutes.

Albrecht Dürer House ★ HISTORIC HOME   One of Nürnberg's few surviving 15th-century sandstone half-timbered burgher's houses also happens to have been the home of one of its most illustrious native sons, Albrecht Dürer (1471–1528). The artist lived and worked here from 1509 to 1528, and many of his etchings and woodcuts hang in rooms filled with furnishings of the period. An English-language audio tour, supposedly narrated by Dürer's wife Agnes, introduces you to the artist: the son of a prosperous goldsmith, he achieved considerable fame and fortune when he was still in his twenties, and even in his own time was widely known as one of the great artists of the Northern Renaissance. (In the words of Goethe: "In truth and nobility, and even in beauty and grace, Dürer, if one really knows him with heart and mind, is equaled by only the very greatest Italian masters.") His effect on printmaking for the past 500 years has been profound. As you'll see in the many reproductions of his self-portraits scattered around the five floors, the artist was a commanding and handsome presence. The house is still a hive of creativity, as artists in the top-floor studio turn out reproductions of the master's works, using the same methods.

Am Tiergartnertor, Albrecht-Dürer-Strasse 39. www.museen.nuernberg.de. ℂ **0911/2312568.** Admission 5€ adults, 3€ students and children 6–18; children 5 and under free. Tues–Fri 10am–5pm; Thurs 10am–8pm; Sat–Sun 10am–6pm; July–Sept also open Mon 10am–5pm.Tram: 4. Bus: 36.

Dokumentationszentrum Reichsparteitagsgelände ★★ HISTORIC SITE   Adolf Hitler made Nürnberg the locale for his massive Nazi rallies, commissioning his architect, Albert Speer, to design a congress hall and assembly grounds in the grandiose, neoclassical style the Führer favored. The war prevented either from being completed, but the unfinished congress hall now houses bunker-like concrete and brick galleries filled with photographs documenting the rise and fall of Nazi Germany. Displays (texts are in German but translated in English-language audiotapes) chronicle Hitler's rise to power. You'll see images of the Nürnberg rallies, when hundreds of thousands of civilians and soldiers gathered on the adjacent Zeppelinwiese (Zeppelin Field) to listen to Hitler rant. Mixed in are coverage of the Nürnberg laws, which stripped non-Aryans of their rights, and the ensuing Holocaust. The focus is on the role of propaganda in elevating Hitler to a mythic character, but it begs the question of how a civilized nation let itself descend to such horror. At least the center raises the issues, and it's encouraging to see the exhibits so well attended by young people for whom the war is part of a distant past.

Bayernstrasse 110. www.museen.nuernberg.de. © **0911/2315666.** Admission 5€ adults, 3€ students and children, 5.50€ one adult and up to three children, 10.50€ two adults and up to three children. Mon–Fri 9am–6pm; Sat–Sun 10am–6pm. S-Bahn: 2 to Dutzendteich. Bus: 36 from the city center Is the easiest way to reach the center.

Germanisches Nationalmuseum (Germanic National Museum) ★★★

MUSEUM   Germany's largest art and culture museum spans the millennia to show off painting, sculpture, crafts, arms and armor—if something's part of Germany's national heritage, it's here, making this former

Ernst Ludwig Kirchner's Self Portrait as Drunkard at the Germanic National Museum.

Carthusian monastery (plus modern annexes) the equivalent of the Smithsonian Institution or the British Museum. A tour begins before you even get inside the door, with the Way of Human Rights: 29 columns inscribed, in different languages, with the Universal Declaration of Human Rights, adopted by the U.N. General Assembly in 1948. (An oak tree represents all others whose languages aren't on the pillars.) The effect is especially haunting in a city that once laid such waste to human rights.

An excellent audio guide (in English) hits the museum's highlights; focusing on just these could easily take half a day. There's a crude stone hand axe from 100,000 years ago, one of the world's first-known tools; a medieval bone-crushing torture device called the Spanish Boot; and a Bauhaus-era kitchen from Stuttgart, the latest in pre-World War II German home design. In a touching glimpse of antiquity, you'll see Roman roof tiles imprinted with the paw marks of dogs who wandered onto a work site while the terracotta was still wet. There's a Dr. Seuss-like tall gold conical hat imprinted with astrological symbols, worn by cult priests 3,000 years ago. (A bricklayer found its fragments in a field in the 1950s.) The Erdapfel (Earth Apple) is the first-known globe, created by geographer Martin Behaim in Nürnberg between 1491 and 1493, just before news of Columbus' discovery of the New World spread across Europe (note how the Americas are missing). In the Old Master galleries is Albrecht Dürer's tender portrait of his aging mother, possibly painted as a keepsake to take on his extensive travels in Italy and the Netherlands. (A companion piece of his father is in Florence's Uffizi Gallery.) Less touching is Lucas Cranach's cynical *Ill-Matched Couple*, in which a scrawny elderly man grabs the breast of a lascivious-looking younger woman, as she dips her hand into his purse. The work of early 20th-century Expressionists, on the top floor of the north wing, includes Ernst Ludwig Kirchner's *Self-Portrait as Drunkard*, scorned as degenerate by the Nazis, which you can compare to nearby works by their officially "preferred" artists: look for an especially fatuous picnic scene of a risibly Aryan-looking blond man and his dirndl-clad wife.

Kartäusergasse 1. www.gnm.de ✆ **0911/13310.** Admission 8€ adults, 5€ children, 10€ families. Tues and Thurs–Sun 10am–6pm; Wed 10am–9pm. U-Bahn: Opernhaus.

Kaiserburg ★ CASTLE For 500 years, beginning in 1050, German kings and emperors ruled from this vast hilltop fortress looming above the city from the northern edge of the Altstadt. The Knights' Hall and Imperial Hall, with heavy oak beams and frescoed ceilings, evoke all the medieval regal splendor you'd expect from chambers where Frederick Barbarossa relaxed between campaigns to subdue the Italian peninsula. Most telling of the era's social hierarchy is the Imperial Chapel—actually two chapels, one above the other, so an emperor and his court could worship in the airy, bright upper chapel, while lesser members of his retinue prayed in the dark, dank chamber below. Don't miss the Deep Well, a 50m-long (165-ft) shaft, dug in the 13th-century when the bastions were built; a camera lowered into the well's depths dramatizes its invaluable role in providing fresh water during a siege. For an extra euro you can tour the **Imperial Castle Museum,** filled with shields, armor, and weaponry. (You have to feel sorry for the poor fellows who had to lug such heavy equipment for days across an often hostile countryside.) The castle gardens' views across the city rooftops might have you agreeing with Martin Luther, who opined that "Nürnberg shines throughout Germany like a sun among the moon and stars."

Burgstrasse 13. www.schloesser.bayern.de. ✆ **0911/2446590.** Admission 6€ adults, 4€ students, children 16 and under free; combined ticket with Imperial Castle Museum, 7€ and 6€. Apr–Sept daily 9am–6pm; Oct–Mar daily 10am–4pm. Bus: 36. Tram: 4.

Memorium Nürnberg Prozesse & Justizgebäude (Nürnberg Trials Memorial & Courthouse) ★★★ HISTORIC BUILDING In the famous war trials that began on November 20, 1945, Courtroom 600 saw 23 leading Nazi war criminals tried before the Allied International Military Tribunal for conspiracy and crimes against world peace, the rules of warfare, and humanity. Among them were Albert Speer,

Hermann Göring, Rudolf Hess, and some of Hitler's other closest associates. Afterward, 10 were hanged. The trials became a milestone in judicial history: For the first time, sentences were pronounced according to the principle of the personal responsibility of the individual. The room is still a functioning courtroom, so entrance is not guaranteed—ask the guard at the door. A third-floor gallery tells the story of the trial in great detail with text, photographs, and recordings. Displays are in German but accompanied by an excellent English-language audio guide. Allow about 2 hours to experience the exhibition thoroughly, and be prepared for wrenching footage from the liberation of the concentration camps, shown as evidence at the trials. Plans are in the works to decommission the courtroom, leaving it available for visits at all times during Memorium visiting hours, and to open a portion of the attached prison where the accused were held during the trials.

Bärenschanzstrasse 72. www.memorium-nuremberg.de. © **0911/32179372.** Admission 5€ adults, 3€ students and children. Wed–Mon 10am–6pm. U-Bahn: Bärenschanze.

Neuesmuseum ★ ART MUSEUM   One of the city's most stunning architectural statements, with a bold glass front that reveals labyrinthine spiral staircases within, isn't entirely out of place in the Altstadt. From most angles, the curving façade reflects the medieval walls, melding the old and the new quite effectively. Many of its large stark-white gallery spaces are usually filled with special exhibitions of contemporary art. The permanent collection also changes, with rotating displays from Die Neue Sammlung-International Design Museum Munich, which could be anything from 1950s household furnishings to late 20th-century office equipment. Paintings on view usually include colorful abstract paintings by Gerhard Richter, a pillar of the contemporary German art scene, as well as installation pieces by such international artists as British sculptor Phyllida Barlow.

Klarissenplatz. www.nmn.de. © **0911/240206.** Admission 6€ (1€ on Sun). Tues and Thurs–Sun 10am–6pm, Wed 10am–8pm. U-Bahn: Hauptbahnhof.

St. Lorenz-Kirche (Church of St. Lorenz) ★★★ RELIGIOUS SITE   In Nürnberg's largest and most majestic church, every element seems to soar heavenward—which, of course, is exactly what the architects of this Gothic edifice, begun in 1270, intended. Rows of pillars disappear into the vaulting above the nave, with *The Angelic Salutation* (1519) suspended high above mere mortals below. Bavarian master sculptor Veit Stoss (1450–1533) carved this colorful piece in linden wood, depicting the emotional moment when the Angel Gabriel tells the Virgin Mary that she will be the mother of Christ. The carving is so delicate that you can almost see the wind rustling through the Virgin's gown.

(You might also notice a few fractures in the wood: In the 17th century, cash-strapped church administrators sold the valuable chain on which the piece hung and replaced it with a rope, which eventually broke, sending the glorious sculpture crashing to the floor. It took a team of craftsmen many months to piece its fragments back together.) Similarly uplifting is a **tabernacle** by stone sculptor Adam Kraft, whose lacy tracery in the form of a Gothic tower rises 19m (62 ft.) into the vaulting. (Look for Kraft's eerily lifelike self-portrait, crouching in one of the monument's supports.) Among the many saints portrayed there is the church's namesake, St. Lorenz, holding an iron grill. When Roman

The Angelic Salutation in the Church of St. Lorenz.

authorities demanded that Lorenz (Lawrence), an early church deacon, turn over ecclesiastic treasures, he brought them the poor, saying "Behold in these poor persons the treasures which I promised to show you." As punishment he was tied to a spit and burned over a roaring fire. After roasting for a time, he allegedly said, "I'm well done, turn me over"—a wisecrack that has earned him a place as patron of chefs and cooks. Aside from these monuments, look for a curious set of high-backed wooden chairs with attached trays—so-called craftsmen chairs, dating to the Middle Ages when trade guilds were responsible for collecting donations for the church. Each guild had a chair, and members took turns sitting in them and glaring at the penny-pinching faithful until they deposited their *pfennigs* in a pail attached to the tray in front. Another intriguing bit of stone carving is on the parapet of the narrow stone staircase next to the south entrance: A fat rat with a sausage in his mouth. The story goes that church fathers once shut up a disobedient monk inside the church walls. His brothers secretly brought him so much food that the church rats grew fat on his leftovers, thus betraying the monk's ruse.

Lorenzer Platz 10. www.lorenzkirche.de. © **0911/2446990.** Free admission. Mon–Sat 9am–5pm; Sun 1–4pm. U-Bahn: Lorenzkirche.

St. Sebaldus-Kirche ★ RELIGIOUS SITE Nürnberg's oldest church, consecrated in 1273, houses the shrine of its namesake saint, the city patron. Legend has it that Sebald was the son of a Danish king who, after marrying a beautiful French princess, abandoned his bride on their wedding night to answer the call. Sebald came to live as a hermit in the forests around Nürnberg, where his knack for turning icicles into fuel made him a big hit with poor peasants who couldn't afford wood. Despite Sebald's life of self-imposed poverty, his tomb is a splendid brass monument by Nürnberg's own Peter Vischer (1455–1529), who with the aid of his five sons labored on his finest work for 11 years. The canopy and pillars are lavishly crowded with snails, dolphins, foliage, and even an image of Visher himself, a stout bearded figure wielding the tools of his trade. When this church adopted the principles of the Reformation around 1525, it was quite a coup for Martin Luther, who rightly observed that Nürnberg was "Germany's eye and ear"—a reference to the 21 Nürnberg printing presses that soon began spreading Lutheran doctrines around Germany.

Albrecht-Dürer-Platz 1. www.sebalduskirche.de. ℅ **0911/2142500.** Free admission. Jan–Mar daily 9:30am–4pm; Apr–May and Oct–Dec daily 9:30am–6pm; June–Sept daily 9:30am–8pm. Sun services 8:30 and 10am. U-Bahn: Lorenzkirche.

Spielzeugmuseum (Toy Museum) ★ MUSEUM   Nürnberg was famous for its "Dockenmacher" (doll makers) in the Middle Ages, and by the 19th century was turning out popular tin toys. The city still hosts a much-attended annual toy fair. So, it's only fitting that one the world's most renowned and largest toy collections is displayed in a rebuilt burgher's house in the old town, with just a fraction of its massive holdings shown in rotating displays on four floors behind a Renaissance façade. Kids might even be lured away from their video games and MP3 players (you'll learn these were invented in Nürnberg, too) to admire model trains chugging through Alpine landscapes and utterly charming doll houses furnished with stunning Biedermeier miniatures. There are also circuses and Noah's Arks, carved out of wood from the Orr Mountains near Dresden.

Karlstrasse 13–15. museen.nuernberg.de/spielzeugmuseum. ℅ **0911/231–3164.** Admission 5€ adults, 3€ students and children. Tues–Fri 10am–5pm, Sat–Sun 10am–6pm. U-Bahn: Lorenzkirche.

Stadtmuseum Fembohaus ★ MUSEUM   Step into this medieval merchant's palace to see how the other half lived 500 years ago. Lavish rooms behind a stone façade include a warmly paneled Family Hall; rooms in the rear open off a traditional Dockengalerie, a wooden gallery surrounding an inner court. "Docken" refers to the parapet's wooden spindles, each fashioned from a single piece of wood—a Nürnberg specialty (also used to make wooden dolls in the nearby **Spielzeugmuseum,** above). The real treasure is tucked away in an attic: a scale replica of the prewar city, carved from linden wood in the early 1930s. A

A number of lesser monuments are worth looking for as you walk through Nürnberg. On the corner of the **neo-Gothic bank building** just north of St. Lorenz-Kirche on Konigstrasse, a niche hold an anonymous statue of a saint, a local building tradition. But when the bank was competed in the 1920s, German currency was so devalued that it took a wheelbarrow full of notes to purchase a loaf of bread—therefore earning the figure the nickname "Saint Inflatious." The **Schöner Brunnen (Beautiful Fountain)** on the Hauptmarkt is a stone pyramid, 18m (60 ft.) high, from 1396, adorned with 40 figures arranged in four tiers. They represent philosophy, the liberal arts, local princes, prophets, and church fathers—that is, just about everything an enlightened medieval townsperson would want to know about. It's said that if you turn the brass ring on the railing any noble wish you might have will come true. Another Hauptmarkt attraction is the **Männleinlaufen clock,** set into the façade of the 14th-century Frauenkirche; seven electors of the Holy Roman Empire glide out of the clockworks at noon and prance around Emperor Charles IV, who destroyed a synagogue on the site in 1355 to build the church for the christening of his son Wenzel. Near the Albrecht Dürer house in the medieval Tiergartnerplatz, *The Hare* is a rather perplexing 1984 sculptural reference to Dürer's *Junger Feldchase (Young Hare).*

Dürer's original watercolor is an almost photographic rendering; here the animal is depicted quite grotesquely in bronze. West of the Altstadt, at the foot of the White Tower on Brükenstrasse, look for the **Marriage Carousel Fountain,** artist Jurgen Faber's cynical take on marriage (to be fair, he was going through a divorce when he created this in the 1980s). Sculpted scenes evolve from a sensual nude couple while her spurned, skeletal spouse looks on from the sidelines.

The Schöner Brunnen fountain in the Hauptmarkt.

ten-minute audio presentation (available in English) points out major landmarks and gives a brief city history. This masterful rendering—invaluable when it came time to reconstruct Nürnberg after World War II—had only survived because curators hid it, along with other art treasures, in the beer cellars that run deep beneath the city. Now called the **World War II Art Bunker** (entrance around the corner at Obere Schmiedgasse 52), that hiding place can be visited on guided tours

(German only) daily at 2:30pm, as well as Friday and Saturday at 5:30pm; cost is 6€.

Burgstrasse 15. museen.nuernberg.de/fembohaus. ⓒ **0911/231–2595.** Admission 5€, 3€ students and children. Tues–Fri 10am–5pm, Sat–Sun 10am–6pm. U-Bahn: Lorenzkirche.

Where to Stay in Nürnberg

EXPENSIVE

Hotel Am Josephsplatz ★★★ In this historic center, this tall house from 1675 has been thoughtfully brought up to date without losing its homey ambiance. Most of the nicely sized bedrooms are equipped with pine armoires and other comfortable, traditional furnishings; a few are more contemporary, and a few others are quite grand, with high frescoed ceilings and canopied beds. All have use of a sauna, exercise room, and roof terrace. Buffet breakfast is served in paneled rooms off the reception area, a ground-floor lounge faces a garden, and all floors are connected by an elevator.

Josephsplatz 30–32. www.hotel-am-josephsplatz.de. ⓒ **0911/214470.** 36 units. 108€–120€ double. Buffet breakfast included. Parking nearby 8€–15€. **Amenities:** Gym; sauna; Wi-Fi (free). U-Bahn: Weisser Turm.

Sorat Hotel Saxx ★★ Contemporary floor coverings evoke old tapestries and floor-to-ceiling Durer reproductions make a nod to this hotel's historic Hauptmarkt surroundings, but the ambiance in the compact, white-and-beige guest rooms (with just a hint of color here and there) is strictly and crisply contemporary. Low-slung beds and built-in wood fixtures are smartly utilitarian, offsetting views from many windows across the medieval cobblestone expanses. Even a Scrooge could get into the holiday spirit when the Christmas Market is in full swing just outside the double-pane windows. A ground-floor café, breakfast room, and coffee lounge open to sidewalk terraces in good weather, making this chic spot seem all the more a part of its historic surroundings.

Hauptmarkt 17. www.sorat-hotels.com. ⓒ **0911/242700.** 103 units. 115€–140€ double. Rates include Continental breakfast; buffet breakfast 10€. Parking in in-house garage, 16€. **Amenities:** Restaurant; bar; Wi-Fi (free). Tram: 6 or 9. Bus: 36 or 46.

MODERATE

Burghotel ★ The pool and sauna in the cellar make this Old Town choice a standout, and the location near the castle just off the Hauptmarkt is especially handy for seeing the sights. Best of the accommodations are the large, so-called comfort rooms on the upper floors, furnished in pleasant contemporary style and with views over the old town. Smaller "standard" rooms on lower floors are a bit dated but comfortable, with built-in wooden table and chair sets in some that add a touch of traditional coziness. If you find your room view looks out at the wall of the house next door, head up to the rooftop terrace for a good view over the town.

Lammesgasse 3. www.burghotel-nuernberg.de. © **0911/238896.** 55 units. 87€–217€ double. Rates include buffet breakfast. Parking nearby, 6€. **Amenities:** Restaurant; pool; sauna; exercise room; Wi-Fi (free). Tram: 6 or 9. Bus: 36 or 46.

Hotel Victoria ★★ Ever since this neo-Gothic inn opened in 1898, the Königstrasse address has been one of the most convenient places to sleep in town, close to the train station but just inside the walls near all the Old Town sights. Broad staircases, a quiet reading room tucked away on a mezzanine, and a grand, high-ceilinged breakfast room are flourishes from that age of more-gracious travel. Guest quarters are a little more utilitarian, but many look down into the next-door Handwerkerhof for a bit of medieval ambiance; all have high ceilings and large windows, offset with contemporary wood built-in cabinets and headboards. Late-night rabble-rousers from surrounding bars can be noisy, so ask for a room off the street.

Königstrasse 80. www.hotelvictoria.de. © **0911/24050.** 12 units. 89€–99€ double. Buffet breakfast included. **Amenities:** Bar; Wi-Fi (free). U-Bahn: Hauptbahnhof.

INEXPENSIVE

Hotel Elch ★★ A half-timbered house just below the castle is the atmospheric setting for bright rooms enlivened with simple contemporary furnishings, wooden floors, modern art, and colorful glass chandeliers. The occasional *elch* (elk) head and antlers also make an appearance, as do enough old beams and rough-hewn walls to remind you that this place has been an inn since 1357. A hearty buffet breakfast is served in the cozy ground-floor Schnitzelria, which serves the eponymous specialty at other meals. This place fills up quickly, especially on weekends, so reserve well in advance.

Irrestrasse 9. www.hotel-elch.com. © **0911/2492980.** 12 units. 69€–99 € double. Buffet breakfast included. **Amenities:** Restaurant; bar; Wi-Fi (free). Tram: 6 or 9. Bus: 36 or 46

Hotel Marienbad ★ It's not all about convenience at this pleasant and welcoming stop just outside the train station's west entrance. A member of the Haag family is usually on hand, as they have been for the past 50 years, making the Marienbad a cherished institution on the Nürnberg hospitality scene. No-frills contemporary-styled rooms have excellent beds and soundproofed windows to ensure a good night's sleep, along with small luxuries like deep soaking tubs in some of the updated bathrooms. The blocks around the station can be a bit lifeless, but it's easy to slip into the Old Town via the underground Königstor-Passage.

Eilgutstrasse 5. www.nuernberg-hotel-marienbad.de. © **0911/203147.** 12 units. 72€–89€ double. Buffet breakfast included. **Amenities:** Wi-Fi (free). U-Bahn: Hauptbahnhof.

Where to Eat in Nürnberg

Nürnbergers are good café sitters: Even in cold weather they huddle on café terraces in the pedestrian zones. An especially friendly atmosphere prevails at arty **Treibhaus,** Karl-Grillenberger-Strasse 28 (www.cafe treibhaus.de, ✆ **0911/223041**), which serves breakfast, sandwiches, and salads throughout the day, and cocktails and light dinners at night. Consider washing down your meals with RotBier, a red beer brewed in the city since the 14th century. **Hausbrauerei Altstadthof,** Bergstrasse 19 (Hausbrauerei-Altstadthof.de; ✆ **0911/244-9859**) still makes the beer according to old methods and serves it in a cozy pub; the brewery also holds tastings.

EXPENSIVE

Albrecht Dürer Stube ★★★ FRANCONIAN   In this intimate, low-ceilinged room hung with old prints you expect the old master himself to stride in and give his long locks a shake before tucking into a big platter of "Schäufele," shoulder of pork with dumplings, or another local favorite. The warm wood, crisp linens, and ceramic-tile stove are especially well suited to a winter meal, as is the heavy, meat-leaning menu, but the half-timbered house draws a big crowd any time of year. Evening reservations are essential if you don't want to wait for a table—though the square out front is a pleasant place to do so.

Albrecht-Durer Strasse 6. www.albrecht-duerer-stube.com. ✆ **0911/227209.** Main courses 16€–23€. Mon–Thurs 6pm–midnight, Fri–Sat 11:30am–2:30pm and 6pm–midnight. U-Bahn: Lorenzkirche.

MODERATE

Heilig-Geist-Spital ★ FRANCONIAN   Perched above the river, this former poorhouse, hospital, and wine warehouse has been in business for 650 years, serving sustenance in one form or another. Lepers were once allowed into the city for just three days a year at Easter to be tended here, and poor families were given room and board in exchange for spending murderously long hours at huge spinning wheels. These days candlelight and dark paneling create a romantic mood, and you won't have to spin for the pork knuckle and other hearty Franconian fare, accompanied by more than 100 wines. A fountain provides soothing sounds for summertime dining on the terrace. Winter specialties include a lot of game, though the stags' heads and other beasts mounted on the walls might make you reconsider.

Spitalgasse 16. www.heilig-geist-spital.de. ✆ **0911/221761.** Main courses 10€–18€. Daily 11am–11pm. Bus: 46 or 47.

Weinhaus Steichele ★ FRANCONIAN/BAVARIAN   This former bakery is an old-time favorite with Nürnbergers, serving straightforward fare in atmospheric, wood paneled, antiques-filled surroundings. Its unabashedly traditional fare includes such dishes as pork roast with finger dumplings and delectable little Nürnberg sausages cooked over an open fire and served with sauerkraut. Attentive service and a good selection of Franconian wines and local beers add even more punch to a meal. The family also runs a 56-room inn upstairs and in a modern annex.

Knorrstrasse 2. www.steichele.de. ✆ **0911/202280.** Main courses 8€–20€. Mon–Sat 11am–midnight; Oct–May also Sun 11am–3pm. U-Bahn: Weisser Turm.

Zur Baumwolle ★★ FRANCONIAN   Old Nürnberg inns don't get cozier or more welcoming than this one, and that's saying a lot. Pork roast with dumplings and sauerkraut and other rustic favorites keep a loyal crowd of locals happy; you'll share tables with them in a lamp-lit, wood-beamed, low-ceilinged room, and probably be encouraged to linger over an after-dinner beer or schnapps. The staff does an admirable job of helping outsiders work their way through choices that include several daily specials.

Alderstrasse 18–20. www.zurbaumwolle.de. ✆ **0911/227003.** Main courses 8€–15€. Mon–Fri 11:30am–3pm and 5:30–11pm, Sat 11:30am–11pm. U-Bahn: Weisser Turm.

INEXPENSIVE

Bratwurst-Häusle ★★ FRANCONIAN   It's hard to walk through the Hauptmarkt without making a stop at this friendly and authentic würsthaus that's as appealing inside as it is out. You can choose between a table outside on the warm-weather terrace or in the timbered, rustically furnished room inside, but wherever you sit, you'll enjoy Nürnberg's best. Sausages are made in-house, precisely following a 1348 edict that mandates that sausages be 7 to 9cm (2.7 to 3.5 inches) long, 22 millimeters (.8 inches) thick, and contain 20 to 25 grams (.7 to .9 ounces) of choice pork. The house turns out some 10,000 finger-sized sausages a day, served smoked, grilled, and best of all, as *Sauer Zipfel,* boiled in white wine with onions and juniper. They're served with fresh horseradish from local gardens and the best *kartoffelsalat* (potato salad) in town.

Rathausplatz 1. www.die-nuernberger-bratwurst.de. ✆ **0911/227695.** Main courses 6.50€–12€. Mon–Sat 10am–10pm. U-Bahn: Lorenzkirche.

Zum Gulden Stern ★★ FRANCONIAN   Settle into the cozy timbered room of the oldest eating house in Nürnberg, from 1419, for a taste of local perfection: sausages grilled according to an age-old method on a beechwood fire in front of you. Accompaniments are just as authentic: Sauerkraut produced by a local farm family and enhanced with melted pork lard; potato salad prepared fresh daily with potatoes from a market-farming area just outside the city; and cream horseradish made according to a 150-year-old recipe. The Franconian wines are chosen with same care.

Zirkelschmiedsgasse 26. www.bratwurstkueche.de. ✆ **0911/2059288.** Main courses 6€–10€. Daily 11am–10pm. U-Bahn: Weisser Turm.

Sausages on the grill at Zum Gulden Stern.

Shopping

Just outside the city wall across from the train station, **Handwerkerhof** (Am Königstor; www.handwerkerhof.de; ✆ **0911/98833**), a walled precinct of faux-medieval cottages, is unabashedly touristic, but still worth a visit. Artisans create the products for which Nürnberg has been known since the Middle Ages: glassware, pewter (often in the form of beer mugs), intricate woodcarvings, and toys. The adjoining Historische Bratwurst-Glöcklein, an authentic-seeming beer hall, serves traditional Nürnberg-style bratwurst with sauerkraut and boiled potatoes. Handerwerkerhof was created in 1972 as part of the 500th anniversary of Albrecht Dürer's birth and was such a hit that the city decided to keep it in place. It's open Monday through Saturday from Mid-March through Dececember, 10am to 10pm.

Rose Weihreter, Puppendoktor (Unten Kramergasse 16; ✆ **0911/209597**), herself a puppeteer, runs the sort of shop you could only find in medieval lanes beneath a castle: A small room stuffed to the rafters with antique dolls, puppets, marionettes, and doll accessories. Rose is also one of the few craftspeople for miles around who still mends broken dolls and puppets. The shop is open 3 days a week, on a changing basis; if it's closed, a sign on the door will tell you when to come back.

Artisans at **Neef** (Winklestrasse 29; www.confisserie-neef.de; ✆ **0911/223384**) make what most Nürnbergers consider the best pastries in town, along with fanciful marzipan creations almost too artful to eat. You can sample them in the adjoining café, open Monday through Saturday 10am to 6pm (until 5pm on Sat). Nürnberg claims to have invented Lebkuchen, a honey cake similar to gingerbread (though Ulm, p. 237, also makes that claim); at any rate, Lebkuchen has been all the rage in Nürnberg since a 1487 celebration when Holy Roman Emperor Friedrich III handed out pieces of the sweet cake emblazoned with his portrait to some 4,000 delighted youngsters. These days, the recipe for Nürnberger Lebkuchen is protected by European law; one official producer is **Lebkuchen Schmidt,** Plobenhofstrasse 6, (www.lebkuchen-schmidt.com; © **0911/225568**). Try the variation with chocolate icing and almonds—it's almost irresistible.

BAMBERG ★★

61km (38 miles) NW of Nürnberg

You'll come to this charming little city, set in the rolling Franconian hills where the Regnitz River flows into the Main, to walk up and down the narrow cobblestone streets of a remarkably unspoiled Altstadt. Along the lanes and squares stand proud old houses, dignified palaces, and lofty churches, with styles ranging from Romanesque to Gothic, Renaissance

Bamberg's Altes Rathaus, perched on its own island.

to baroque, up to the eclecticism of the 19th century. At one point the meandering waters rush past the ornate frescoed Rathaus, marooned on its own terribly picturesque little point of land.

You'll also come to Bamberg to drink beer. Bamberg and beer go together like barley and hops. The town has been called "a beer drinker's Eden" (there are more breweries here than in Munich, with nine in the old town alone) and the average Bamberger drinks 190 liters of beer a year, making the rest of the Germans look like teetotalers by comparison. The beverage of choice in Bamberg is *Rauchbier,* a smoked beer first brewed in 1536.

Throughout the Middle Ages Bamberg was the seat of powerful prince-bishops, church authorities with lots of secular clout. For a time from the 11th century the city was the center of the Holy Roman Empire, the church-controlled lands of Central Europe. Some zealous town promoters, hoping to strengthen ties to Rome, detected seven hills among the many rises on Bamberg's landscape, like the seven hills of Rome; for this reason Bamberg became known as the Franconian Rome. (Bambergers refer to the Italian capital as the "Italian Bamberg.") The imposing Kaiserdom, or Imperial Cathedral, still commands the high point above the old town.

Essentials

ARRIVING   You can get to the **Bamberg Bahnhof** from Nürnberg in just 1 hour on trains that run about every half hour. Between Bamberg and Bayreuth, direct trains run about every hour; the trip takes about 1hour and 15 minutes. For information and schedules, visit www.bahn. de or call © **01805/996633.** By **car** you can reach Bamberg from Nürnberg on the A73.

VISITOR INFORMATION   The Bamberg tourist office is in the city center on Geyerswörthstrasse 5 (www.bamberg.info; © **0951/2976200**). It's open Monday to Friday 9:30am to 6pm, weekends 9:30am to 2:30pm (from January to March it's closed Sundays).

Exploring Bamberg

It's an easy 25-minute walk from the train station to the **Domplatz,** where Bamberg's major sights are set; you can also take bus 910 (fare 1.80€) from the front of the station. If you're walking, you'll cross the city center, traversing several river channels and canals; Haupwachstrasse leads through Maximillianplatz, the commercial heart of the town, then the marketplace, Grünermarkt. The oldest part of town crowds the riverbanks around the **Altes Rathaus** (Old Town Hall), set on its own island. From there, narrow cobblestone lanes lead up to Domplatz and the cathedral.

Altes Rathaus ★★ LANDMARK   In the Middle Ages, Bamberg was two towns divided by the Regnitz River: the powerful ecclesiastical town of the prince-bishopric and the secular town of the burghers. Determined not to play favorites, the town authorities built this castle-like Gothic structure at the end of an island in the middle of the river, halfway between the two factions—a true middle-of-the-road (or river) political stand. By claiming the marshy land as their own, the *burgermeisters* let the church know they didn't intend to cede the town to ecclesiastical interests; as merchants who prospered from lucrative trade routes on the Regnitz and Main Rivers they held sway, too. The town council met in the well-preserved and highly polished **Rococo Room;** other old salons in the Rathaus gleam today with the **Ludwig Collection** of china and porcelain. Among the finery is a porcelain monkey orchestra, in which dandified chimps play a variety of 18th-century instruments, and a huge soup tureen in the shape of a turkey. (For more on German porcelain, see p. 190.) From the island, you get a camera-worthy view of so-called Little Venice, where the river once washed right against the half-timbered cottages along the banks, allowing fisherfolk to moor their boats right outside their front doors. These days the houses are fronted with pretty waterside gardens.

Obere Brücke 1. www.museum.bamberg.de. © **0951/871871.** Admission 4.50€. Tues–Sun 9:30am–4:30pm.

Kaiserdom (Imperial Cathedral) ★★ CATHEDRAL   The four towers of this 13th-century hillside edifice dominate the skyline and steer you to a treasure that is reason enough to come to Bamberg. Sculptor Tilman Riemenschneider (you'll meet him in Würzburg, see p. 252) labored for 14 years over the **tombs** of Heinrich II, King of Germany and Holy Roman Emperor, and his wife, the Empress Cunigunde. A bit of storytelling in stone depicts five episodes from the life of the couple, who built the cathedral and many other religious institutions across Germany. In one, Cunigunde walks across fiery hot plowshares to prove to Heinrich that she had been faithful to him during a long absence. She had more than her husband's peace of mind at stake: The couple was childless, so word spread that Cunigunde was virginal, putting her in a league with the Virgin Mary; she later became a nun and was canonized. Her miracles included one depicted here, a gift for extinguishing flames by making the sign of the cross. Another scene depicts Heinrich on his deathbed, as a tiny lion—a symbol of strength, now diminished—seems to slink away from the dying king. The king and queen lie together in stone effigy on the top of the tomb: note that Cunigunde lies on the left, the spot usually reserved for royal males in such imagery, while Heinrich is on the right, a position symbolizing undying loyalty. You can look down upon this scene from stairs that ascend from the tomb to one of the church's two altars, one at each end of the nave. Veit Stoss, whose beautiful carving of the Annunciation hangs above the nave of St. Lorenz-kirche in Nürnberg (see p. 206), carved the **nativity altar** in the south transept when he was close to 80. He made the altar for a church in Nürnberg at the request of his son, a prior, but when his son refused to accept Protestant doctrine the altar was rejected and moved here to Bamberg (the elder Stoss was never paid). Also note a mysterious 13th-century equestrian statue, the **Bamberger Reiter.** The identity of this crowned but weaponless horseman has been debated for centuries; Nazi propaganda claimed it was an idealized Christian king pointing the way to eastern lands they were meant to conquer. Current thought identifies him as Stephen, an 11th-century Hungarian king. The cathedral also houses the only papal tomb

Tilman Riemenschneider tombs in Bamberg's Kaiserdom.

north of the Alps, that of Pope Clement II; a bishop of Bamberg, Clement served less than a year before dying, possibly from poisoning, in 1047 while traveling to Rome.

Domplatz. www.bamberger-dom.de. © **0951/502330.** Free admission. May–Oct Mon–Fri 9:30am–6pm, Sat 9:30–11:30am and 12:45–6pm, Sun 12:30–1:45pm and 2:45–6pm. Nov–Apr Mon–Sat 9:30am–5pm, Sun 12:30–1:45pm and 2:45–5pm. Church treasury (Diözesanmuseum) 3€ adults, 2€ students and children 8–14, children 7 and under free.

Gärtnerstadt (Market Gardener's Quarter) ★ NEIGHBORHOOD

Bambergers have been ardent vegetable growers since the Middle Ages, and this district on and around Mittelstrasse (a few blocks southeast of the Hauptbahnhof) grew up to accommodate the enthusiasts, who counted 540 master market gardeners among their numbers by the middle of the 19th century. Many plots still flourish in view behind low stone walls, and much of the produce is sold in the city's central marketplace, the Grünermarkt. The neighborhood houses are distinctive: They're entered through a large covered gateway, wide and high enough to accommodate a horse and wagon, that leads to a courtyard, with stables and storage sheds. Living quarters open off the gateway, which doubled as a threshing floor. You can enter one of the dwellings, the **Gärtner- und Häckermuseum** (Market Gardeners' and Wine-Growers' Museum) at Mittelstrasse 34. Authentically furnished rooms show off the cozy comfort in which a 19th-century market-gardener family lived; in season, visitors can taste the licorice that's still cultivated in the adjacent garden.

Gärtner- und Häckermuseum, Dr. Hubertus Habel. Mittelstrasse 34. www.ghm-bamberg.de. ✆ **0951/3017–9455.** Admission 3€. May–Oct Wed–Sun 11am–5pm.

Neue Residenz (New Residence) ★ PALACE   This 17th-century palace of the prince-bishops of Bamberg became notorious in 1815 when a corpse found beneath the windows of the palace turned out to be Marshal Louis-Alexandre Berthier, Napoleon's former chief of staff. (Having married the Bavarian Duchess Maria Elisabeth, he retired to Bamberg after Napoleon was exiled to Elba.) Otherwise the palace is known for having Europe's most famous rose gardens, in which more than 4,500 roses of 48 species are laid out along gravel paths shaded by linden trees. If you wish to step inside the palace, you can join a guided tour (in German only) that shows off Gobelin tapestries, parquet floors, baroque furnishings, and other rich possessions of these clerics with decidedly secular tastes. Upstairs, a branch of the Bayerische Staatsgalerie (Bavarian State Gallery) houses a few of the masterpieces collected by Mad King Ludwig; among them is Lucas Cranach's almost surrealistic depiction of Abraham slaying his son Isaac on God's command, set against a German backdrop complete with medieval peasants. The romantic-looking half-timbered Gothic structure next to the palace is the **Alte Hofhaltung,** the residence of the prince-bishops until the Neue Residence replaced it.

Domplatz 8. www.schloesser.bayern.de. ✆ **0951/519390.** Admission 4.50€ adults, 3.50€ children. Apr–Sept daily 9am–6pm; Oct–Mar daily 10am–4pm.

Where to Stay in Bamberg

Brauerei Speziale ★★   If you've ever dreamt of sleeping in a brewery—maybe indulging in the house brews and then crawling upstairs to a good bed covered with a fluffy eiderdown—well, here's your chance. The brewery operation downstairs dates to 1536 and has been in the hands of the Merz family since 1892. Upstairs they offer two floors of cozy, simply-but-nicely furnished guest rooms with big casement windows, high ceilings, and polished wood floors; those on the top floor are tucked under the eaves. Some family rooms that sleep three or four are

Bamberg's Romantic Hero

One of many colorful characters who took up residence in Bamberg over the centuries, writer, composer, and artist E.T.A. Hoffmann came to Bamberg in 1808 and struggled almost constantly, losing his job as theater manager and forced to work as a stagehand and music teacher. His love affair with a young student became a scandal, and in 1813 he left town for Dresden. Hoffmann's imaginative works of fantasy inspired Jacques Offenbach's opera *Tales of Hoffmann* and Tchaikovsky's ballet *The Nutcracker*. This romantic genius died in Berlin of syphilis at the age of 47 and is honored in Bamberg with the E.T.A. Hoffmann Theatre.

close to being cavernous. Warning, though: If you're booked into one of the few rooms that share the immaculate hallway bathrooms, you might want to limit your intake downstairs. Wherever you lay your head, you can drop into the paneled Stube in the morning and start the day with a hearty buffet breakfast and—what else?—a beer.

Obere Königstrasse 10. www.brauerei-spezial.de. © **0951/24304.** 14 units (some with shared bath). 60€–85€ double. Buffet breakfast included. **Amenities:** Restaurant; bar; Wi-Fi (free).

Hotel Brudermuehle ★★   A perch on the riverbank ensures that the sound of the rushing water fills every nook and cranny of this charming old mill house. A table window in the lower level of the dining room puts you at eye level with passing boats, while upper-floor guest rooms look over the water. Others open onto the tidy streets of the old town. All are done in pleasing contemporary style in soothing pastels, with a few old-world touches such as fluffy eiderdowns and the occasional old beam jutting across a wall or ceiling.

Schranne 1. www.brudermuehle.de. © **0951/95522.** 20 units. 120€–130€ double. Buffet breakfast included. **Amenities:** Restaurant; bar; Wi-Fi (free).

Hotel National ★   Behind the wonderfully ornate baroque façade with its curved corners and elaborate ironwork, everything is sleek and contemporary—at least in many of the guest rooms, where low-slung beds sit on polished wood floors and built-in tables double as desks. Other rooms and suites are a bit more traditional, with the heavy armoires and plump armchairs you'd expect to find in this 19th-century station hotel. It still provides a handy place to stay near the station, with the center and historic sights a pleasant 10-minute walk away in the other direction.

Luitpoldstrasse 37. www.hotel-national-bamberg.de. © **0951/509980.** 41 units. 79€–110€ double. Buffet breakfast included. Parking 7€. **Amenities:** Restaurant; bar; room service; Wi-Fi (free).

Where to Eat in Bamberg

Brauerei Speziale ★★   These wood-paneled pub rooms smell of beechwood smoke, as the operation famously makes two kinds of smoked beer, a Lager Rauchbier, with 40% smoked malt (the other 60% is from traditionally dried Bavarian barley malt) and a Märzen Rauchbier, with 70% smoke malt and quite a bit darker. Both are good accompaniments to a house specialty, *Shäuffle*, pork shoulder roasted with onions and beer and served with *Klösse* (potato dumplings).

Obere Königstrasse 10. www.brauerei-spezial.de. *©* **0951/24304.** Main course 6€–12€. Sun–Fri 9am–11pm, Sat 9am–2pm.

Historischer Brauereiausschank Schlenkerla ★ FRANCONIAN
This genuinely *gemütlich* (cozy) 600-year-old beer hall filled with long tables beneath a frescoed ceiling is sacred ground in Bamberg, source of the house's own hearty malt, dispensed from oak barrels. The brewery's name comes from *Schlenkern,* or dangle, probably a reference to the hobbling gait of the 18th-century brewer who appears on the bottle. He helped perfect the process of drying malt over the open flames of beechwood fires to impart just the right hint of smokiness, producing the Rauchbier (smoked beer) for which Bamberg is famous. The house also shows off its smoking techniques in the kitchen, turning out such favorites as *Bierbrauervesper* (Brewmaster's Break, with smoked meat and sour-milk cheese) and *Rauchschinken* (smoked ham).

Dominikanerstrasse 6. www.schlenkerla.de. *©* **0951/56060.** Main courses 7€–12€. Daily 9:30am–11:30pm.

Zum Sternia ★ FRANCONIAN   Bamberg's oldest inn is this wursthaus from 1380, where you can settle onto a well-burnished bench and tuck into liver dumplings and sauerkraut or a big platter of sausages. Daily offerings are listed on a blackboard in a script that might test anyone's reading knowledge of German, but the friendly staff can translate. Yellow-stucco pub rooms are hung with old farm implements; there's also a small beer garden. Several Bamberg beers, including those from large local brewer Maisel, are available on tap and in bottles.

Langestrasse 46. sternla.de. *©* **0951/28750.** Main courses 6€–15€. Daily 10am–11pm.

Shopping

For a taste of Bamberg, stop by the town market, when vendors in the central marketplace, **Grüner Markt,** do a brisk business Monday through Saturday, from 8am to 5pm or so. Stalls are piled high with carrots, onions, potatoes, apples, and other produce from gardens in the Market Gardener's Quarter (see p. 218).

Bamberg is known for its antiques shops, many of which are clustered in the old quarter on a hillside beneath the cathedral. Few are as renowned as **Senger,** Karolinenstrasse 8 (www.senger-bamberg.de; © **0951/54030**), a specialist in religious statuary. If you want to leave town with a piece by Veit Stoss or Tilman Riemenschneider under your arm, this is the place to pick one up. Otherwise, you can just take a look at the museum-quality pieces on display in the cavern-like cellars, a perfectly Gothic setting for the stone and wood carvings on view.

BAYREUTH ★★

64km (40 miles) E of Bamberg, 92km (57 miles) NE of Nürnberg

Nearly everything you'll want to see in this little city is somehow related to two extraordinary past residents, Richard Wagner and Margravine Wilhelmine. The legacy of Wagner (1813–1883) includes an annual opera festival in the **Festspielhaus,** the concert hall he built. While Wagner put Bayreuth on the map of the classical music world, he was not always kind to his adaptive town. He once allegedly commented, "A doctor here will never prescribe a bath or ban a beer since he has no knowledge of the former and is all too fond of the latter."

Even without the Wagner connection, Bayreuth would stand out on the Bavarian landscape, thanks to Margravine Wilhelmine (1709–1758). This personable and talented woman was sister of Prussian king Frederick the Great, a granddaughter of Britain's King George I, and an out sized personality who shaped the city's cultural and architectural legacy. Herself a gifted artist, writer, composer, and decorator, Wilhelmine did her best to turn Bayreuth into a German Versailles.

Another presence in town is the ghost of a Nazi past. Hitler was an ardent fan of Wagnerian music and close friend of Winifred Wagner, the English-born wife of Richard Wagner's son, Siegfried. She took over directorship of the town's Wagner Festival after Siegfried's death in 1930, often welcoming the Führer and other party officials to concerts and her home. Bayreuth was not only a center of Nazi ideology but also housed a concentration camp where work was conducted on the V-2, the long-range rocket Germany was developing to destroy cities in Russia and England.

Little wonder Bayreuth became a prime target for Allied bombers, who destroyed much of the city in 1945 raids. Much of the baroque architecture remains, however, as do the Altstadt (Old Town), museums, palaces, and Wagner shrines. You can top off a visit with some grandiose Wagnerian music (you can hear recordings of every piece the master ever wrote at the Richard Wagner Museum) and a beer or two from some 200 breweries in the surrounding Franconian hills.

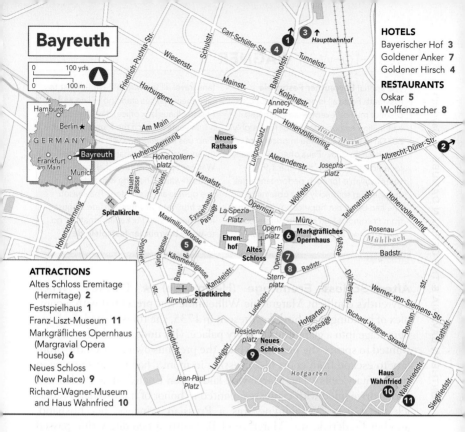

Bayreuth

0 ———— 100 yds
0 ———— 100 m

HOTELS
Bayerischer Hof **3**
Goldener Anker **7**
Goldener Hirsch **4**

RESTAURANTS
Oskar **5**
Wolffenzacher **8**

ATTRACTIONS
Altes Schloss Eremitage
  (Hermitage) **2**
Festspielhaus **1**
Franz-Liszt-Museum **11**
Markgräfliches Opernhaus
  (Margravial Opera
  House) **6**
Neues Schloss
  (New Palace) **9**
Richard-Wagner-Museum
  and Haus Wahnfried **10**

Essentials

ARRIVING   Express trains arrive from Nürnberg every hour; the trip takes about 1 hour. Direct trains between Bayreuth and Bamberg run about every hour; the trip takes 1 hour and 15 minutes. For information and schedules, call ✆ **01805/996633** or visit www.bahn.de. Access by car from Nürnberg is via the A9 Autobahn. If you're coming from Bamberg, it's 75 km (44 mi) on the A73, about a 50-minute drive.

VISITOR INFORMATION   Bayreuth's tourist office is near the unattractive new Rathaus, at Opernstrasse 22 (www.tourismus.bayreuth.de; ✆ **0921/88588**). It's open Monday to Saturday 9am to 6pm. From May to October, it is also open Sunday 10am to 2pm.

Exploring Bayreuth

Much of the inner city is closed to cars. The Altstadt, where most of the main sights are located, is small enough so that you can see almost everything on foot. From the train station, you can take bus no. 305 (fare 1.60€) to the Festspielhaus, bus no. 302 to reach Schloss Eremitage, or bus no. 314 to the Neues Schloss.

wall-to-wall **WAGNER**

The annual **Bayreuther Festspiele** (Bayreuth Festival) is one of the world's premier musical events—an estimated half-million enthusiasts clamor for roughly 60,000 tickets that range in price from about 40€ to 320€. Fans often wait years for a ticket, and even then the 1,900 seats available for each performance get snapped up so quickly that obtaining one can be all but hopeless. A few tickets from "no shows" go on sale before each performance; some die-hard Wagner fans travel all the way to Bayreuth just to take their chances standing in line at the Festspielhaus box office, day after day.

In years in which the four-opera *Der Ring des Nibelungen* cycle is presented (every five to seven years), three other Wagner operas are staged as well; in years in which *The Ring* is not staged, five operas are presented. The season runs from late July through late August; for schedules and ticket information, go to **www.bayreuther-festspiele.de**.

Altes Schloss Eremitage (Hermitage) ★ PALACE When Bayreuth's ebullient Margravine Wilhelmine was presented with a complex of buildings as a birthday present in 1735, she transformed the faux-hermitage into a glamorous country palace. (It's understandable why she wanted to spruce the place up a bit—the previous owners used the property to escape from court life, dressing in monks' habits and sleeping in rudimentary cells.) The Margravine laid out an English-style garden and a long drive lined with cypresses planted in honor of her brother, Frederick the Great. (Wilhelmine was a Prussian princess; her husband, another Frederick, was Margrave of Bayreuth, a hereditary title passed down from the Middle Ages.) Wilhelmine gathered her salon of artists and intellectuals here (Voltaire was a visitor to Bayreuth) and she wrote her memoirs in the elaborately decorated **Chinesisches Spiegelkabinett (Chinese Mirror Chamber);** its shattered mirrors today are said to have been her response to aging and vanity. Within the gardens are fountains, cascades, a grotto inhabited by raucous nymphs, and the so-called Ruined Theater, a faux-ancient fantasy. Her *Memoires de Ma Vie (Memories of My Life)* are not terribly relevant today but are an intricate portrayal of court life of the time; while at the Eremitage she also wrote an opera and several pieces of chamber music. The Eremitage continued to host famous guests long after the Margravine's death: King Ludwig II of Bavaria stayed here when he attended the first Wagner Festspiele in the new Festspielhaus in 1876. He arrived in secrecy in the dead of night, allowing only Wagner to greet him, and saw no one but the composer during his stay.

On Rte. 22, 5km (3 miles) northeast of Bayreuth. www.schloesser.bayern.de. © **0921/759690.** Gardens free; palace 4.50€ adults, children 17 and under free. Gardens open 24 hr. Palace Apr–Sept daily 9am–6pm; Oct 1–15 10am–4pm. Closed Oct 16–Mar.

Festspielhaus ★★★ OPERA HOUSE

The operas of Wagner are dispensed like a musical Eucharist to Wagnerian pilgrims at the Festspielhaus, the opera house he built with the backing of King Ludwig II of Bavaria. Tickets to the Richard Wagner opera festival held in this huge hall, one of the largest opera houses in Europe, are almost impossible to obtain; there's an 8-year waiting list (see p. 224). You may, however, visit the theater on guided tours (in German) and see the huge stage and all sorts of other theatrical innovations. Wagner promised his fans, upon laying the cornerstone in 1872, the "unveiling and clear presentation of onstage images that will seem to rise up before you from an ideal world of

A bust of composer Richard Wagner outside the Festspielhaus, specifically built to stage his operas.

dreams and reveal to you the whole reality of a noble art's most meaningful illusion." The orchestra is out of sight, so that the music rises up "spectrally from the 'mystic abyss'…[and] transports [the audience] to that inspired state of clairvoyance." It was all part of Wagner's ideal of *Gesamtkunstwerk,* synthesizing music, drama, and visual artistry for total artistic effect. (Not everyone, of course, is transported; some agree with Lady Henry in Oscar Wilde's *Picture of Dorian Gray,* who likes Wagner's music because, "It is so loud that one can talk the whole time, without people hearing what one says.") The wooden hall has no heating or air-conditioning, and all seats are hard wood, the idea being that creature comforts shouldn't interfere with the creative endeavors onstage. These days, all sorts of computer-assisted stage mechanics ensure smooth productions, but sitting through an hours-long opera in a stiff wooden seat in the hot, stuffy hall can seem like trial by fire for even the most ardent fan. Productions have been a family affair almost ever since the epic 15-hour *Ring* cycle was first presented here in 1876: When the composer died in Venice, his wife, Cosima Liszt, took over, and his grandsons, Wolfgang and Wieland, have produced the operas in the post-World War II years. Katharina Wagner, the great-granddaughter of Richard Wagner and great-great granddaughter of Franz Liszt, is the current director of the Bayreuther Festspiele, which runs from late July to late August.

Am Festspielhügel 1–2. www.bayreuther-festspiele.de. ✆ **0921/78780.** Guided tour 5€. Tours in German only; English leaflets available. Sept–May Tues–Sun at 10 and 2pm. No tours during rehearsals or at festival time.

Franz-Liszt-Museum ★ MUSEUM Wagner's wife, Cosima (1837–1930), was the daughter of Franz Liszt (1811–86), the great Hungarian-born composer and piano virtuoso. Cosima's first husband was the composer and conductor Hans von Bülow, a pupil of her father; she left him soon after meeting Wagner, her father's contemporary and 23 years her senior. Liszt is overshadowed by his son-in-law in Bayreuth, and the museum's text is in German only, yet you'll see enough among the portraits, first editions of scores, and other memorabilia to sense the appeal of this remarkably gifted and energetic man. His stage presence was so mesmerizing that Europe was gripped by "Listzomania"; the pianist would throw his handkerchiefs and gloves to hysterical fans, like a rock star of today. One critic described him as "all sunshine and dazzling splendor." Looking at the portraits, sketches, and photographs of this handsome man, you can see why he became involved in countless love affairs. (He had a preference for wealthy countesses; Cosima was the daughter of one of them.) Touring Europe constantly as a concert pianist, Liszt came to know most of the great musicians and composers of the 19th century, and it was he who first introduced Wagner's operas to audiences in Weimar and elsewhere in Germany. The two larger-than-life egos often clashed, yet Liszt lived here, next door to the Wagners (see p. 228), for many years, and is buried in the local cemetery. The museum includes a shrine-like room where the composer died, three years after Wagner's death; he had just seen productions of *Parsifal* and *Tristan and Isolde,* staged by Cosima. A plaster cast immortalizes those hands that could bring music out of a keyboard like few others have since.

Wahnfriedstrasse 9. © **0921/5166488.** Admission 2€. Sept–June daily 10am–noon and 2–5pm; July–Aug daily 10am–5pm. Bus: 302 or 307 to Villa Wahnfried.

Markgräfliches Opernhaus (Margravial Opera House) ★ OPERA HOUSE Behind the wooden doors of the finest and best-preserved baroque theater in the world is an ornate interior constructed entirely of wood, glowing with vivid reds and greens and festooned with gilded stuccowork and chandeliers. Reopening in 2017 after a four-year restoration, the opera house was built under the auspices of the Margravine Wilhelmine, with an interior designed by the great theater architect Giuseppe Galii Bibiena. It was formally opened by the Margravine's brother, Frederich the Great, in 1748, to celebrate the marriage of the Margravine's daughter, Elisabeth Fredericka Sophie, whom Casanova once described as "the most beautiful princess in German." Her ill-fated marriage was not a success, but the theater fared well under the patronage of the Margravine, an actor, director, and composer herself. The house went dark and the doors were locked after her death in 1758, saving this treasure from subsequent renovations and leaving the interior perfectly intact. Wagner considered staging his operas here but found the stage too small and the 520 seats inadequate. Even so, Bayreuth's

The stunningly preserved baroque interior of the Margräfliches Opernhaus.

other festival, the Musica Bayreuth, is held here late in May, and concerts are also given during the summer. The theater is included on the UNESCO World Heritage List.

Opernstrasse. www.schloesser.bayern.de. © **0921/7596922.** Guided tours (in German only). Admission 5.50€ adults, children 5 and under free. Apr–Sept daily 9am–6pm; Oct–Mar daily 10am–4pm.

Neues Schloss (New Palace) ★★ PALACE   Margravine Wilhelmine's love of the airy, flowered Rococo style shows through in this three-story horseshoe-shaped structure completed in 1754, shortly after the Margravine and her husband came into his inheritance. The decor created by the Italian stucco-master Pedrozzi is particularly evident in the Mirror Room, the Japanese Room, and the Music Room. The creative freedom the Margravine enjoyed in Bayreuth may well have made up for a miserable childhood at the hands of distant royal parents and a sadistic governess who came close to crippling her. She was married off to the Margrave of Bayreuth against her wishes, and his, as he was in love with her sister. His infidelities caused her no small amount of embarrassment in the court of Bayreuth, though she accepted them with the same good nature with which she chose to ignore his lisp. Despite their differences, the couple shared a general bonhomie. Lucky guests enjoyed their company in the salon, with its rich walnut paneling and carved palm trees that seem to sway on the walls. The Margravine, her husband, and their daughter are buried in the nearby **Schlosskirche** (Castle Church), a lovely single-aisled church painted rose-pink and decorated with stuccowork.

Ludwigstrasse. www.schloss.bayern.de. ✆ **0921/759690.** Guided tours (in German; English leaflets available) 5.50€ adults, children 17 and under free. Tours given Apr–Sept daily 9am–6pm; Oct–Mar Tues–Sun 10am–4pm.

Richard-Wagner-Museum and Haus Wahnfried ★★ HISTORIC HOUSE   King Ludwig II of Bavaria gave Wagner the funds to build a comfortable little manor, and Wagner lived in Wahnfried House from 1874 until his death in Venice of a heart attack in 1883. His much-younger wife, Cosima, remained in the house for 47 more years, becoming known as the "mistress of Bayreuth." The few pieces of furniture that remain (much of it was lost in World War II bombings) evoke family life in the grandiose, double-height reception hall; pieces that are not original to Wagner's residence are covered in white cloth, as if the couple and their large household were merely away on a trip. With a little imagination it's easy to imagine Wagner playing the piano as Cosima and the couple's five children gather round (three of their own, two from Cosima's firsr marriage). For all his musical bluster, Wagner was a bit of a homebody, or so his diaries suggest. "What a joy to us our children," he enthuses in one entry, and in another, "a fat capon soon lifts the spirits." Former dressing rooms are filled with the couple's clothing and other personal effects, including Cosima's stylish gowns and one of the maestro's well-cut overcoats. A lower level and adjacent glass pavilion by Berlin architect Volker Staab display original scores, stage sets, and costumes. Lounges are set up with leather chairs and headphones for listening to the complete recordings. Some of these can be enjoyed via the Interactive Score, an ingenious bit of technological gadgetry that looks like a huge book, with various interpretations highlighted note by note on illuminated pages. The **Siegfried Wagner House,** next to Haus Wahnfried, was built for Wagner's son, whose widow, Winifred, lived here until 1980. The almost homey spaces show off an airy 1930s design, with a rusticated fireplace room, a dining room filled with a sturdy table and chairs, and a sun-filled garden room. Hitler stayed here on several occasions, and appropriately enough, displays address the uncomfortable relationship between Wagnerian music, the festival, and National Socialism. Wagner and Cosima are buried in front of a small rotunda at the end of the garden, surrounded by many of their beloved hounds.

Richard-Wagner-Strasse 48. www.wagnermuseum.de. ✆ **0921/757280.** Admission 8€. Apr–Oct daily 9am–5pm (Tues and Thurs 8pm); Nov–Mar daily 10am–5pm.

Where to Stay in Bayreuth

Bayerischer Hof ★★★   The location next to the train station might seems a bit workaday, but beyond the big doors is a world of Bavarian luxury. Above an over-upholstered salon are big, beautifully appointed guest rooms, each decorated differently—you may sink into plush carpeting or be tempted to waltz on a shiny parquet floor. All are done with soothing pastel shades, comfortable armchairs and couches, and a tasteful mix of European antiques and modern design pieces. This is a popular hotel with performers and Wagner fans, who can practically step off the train into the lobby then make the short trip by tax or bus up the street to the Festspielhaus. A garden, sun terrace, and small spa are perfect for a break between performances.

Bahnhofstrasse 14. www.bayerischer-hof.de. ⓒ **0921/78600.** 50 units. 85€–130€ double. Buffet breakfast 14€. Parking 11€. **Amenities:** Restaurant; bar; sauna; Wi-Fi (free).

Goldener Anker ★★   When you step into a hotel and encounter a fellow behind the desk in a frilly blouse and long waistcoat, you know you're in for a bit of time travel. The Graf family has been running this inn in the center of town next to the Markgräfliches Opernhaus for the past 250 years. They richly evoke their inn's colorful past with more antiques and glimmering knickknacks than you'd see in a historic *schloss,* thick Persian carpets, and framed photographs of Richard Strauss, Arturo Toscanini, and a chorus of other illustrious guests. Stylish and comfortable rooms have canopied beds and acres of rich fabric. As American novelist Norman Mailer once gushed, "It seems as if the walls whisper recent and ancient history."

Opernstrasse 6. www.anker-bayreuth.de. ⓒ **0921/7877740.** 35 units. 138€–168€ double. Buffet breakfast included. Parking 10€. **Amenities:** Restaurant; babysitting; room service; Wi-Fi (free).

Goldener Hirsch ★   Front window boxes loaded with flame-red geraniums cue you in to the hominess to expect from these pleasant guest rooms above a restaurant, halfway between the train station and the Old Town. The unpretentious décor is reminiscent of an American roadside motel that's been spruced up with pine armoires and fluffy down comforters. A few of the doubles are enormous, while the tidy little singles with a day bed and fold-down berth are the essence of economy and efficiency.

Bahnhofstrasse 13. www.bayreuth-goldener-hirsch.de. ⓒ **0921/1504-4000.** 42 units. 85€–125€ double. Buffet breakfast. Parking 5€. **Amenities:** Bar; restaurant; Wi-Fi (free).

Where to Eat in Bayreuth

Wine shop **Lunas,** at number 17 on pedestrian shopping street Maximilanstrasse (www.lunas-delikatessen.de; ✆ **0921/530-4633**), serves wine by the glass and antipasto platters and other light fare at the end of a courtyard.

Oskar ★ FRANCONIAN/INTERNATIONAL A large central dining room, designed like a greenhouse and flooded with light even on a gray winter day, and a trio of smaller, cozier, wood-paneled *Stuben* are bustling all day into the early-morning hours. The busy kitchen sends out lots of old-fashioned Franconian favorites, such as loin of beef with horseradish sauce and Bayreuther-style *Klos* (potato dumplings), as well as big platters of sausages, hearty breakfasts, salads, snacks—the menu is large and the service is friendly.

Maximilianstrasse 33. www.oskar-bayreuth.de. ✆ **0921/5160553.** Main courses 6€–14€. Mon–Sat 8am–1am; Sun 9am–1pm.

Wolffenzacher ★★ FRANCONIAN A popular gathering spot since the 16th century, Wolffenzacher encourages diners to settle in with friends among its paneled walls, or, in good weather, in the sunny beer garden out front. The house has been a bakery, a brewery, and an inn for wayfarers; these days it's a local favorite for such hearty Franconian dishes as beef brisket in horseradish gravy or braised beef cheek in a pepper-red wine sauce, along with some lighter fish dishes and seasonal vegetarian choices.

Badstrasse 1. www.wolffenzacher.de. ✆ **0921/64552.** Main courses 9€–16€. Daily 11am–10pm.

REGENSBURG ★★★

100km (62 miles) SE of Nürnberg, 122km (76 miles) NE of Munich

You have some compelling reasons to get off the beaten track and come to Regensburg, one of Germany's best-preserved medieval cities and one of very few to remain completely unscathed by World War II bombings. The Rathaus, market hall, and some 1,400 medieval buildings have survived and create a jumble of steep, red-tiled roofs above narrow lanes and lively squares. Strategically poised on the northernmost reaches of the Danube River, Regensburg was a Celtic settlement, then a Roman outpost known as Castra Regina, and the center from which, beginning in the 7th century, Christianity spread throughout Germany and even into central Europe via the river. Regensburg was also a major hub for trade, and by the 12th century the town was pouring its wealth into churches, towers, and some genuinely lovely houses and public buildings. Some of

Regensburg's more famous contemporary residents have been Oskar Schindler, Pope Benedict, and the princely Thum und Taxis family, whose palace you can visit.

Essentials

ARRIVING Regensburg's **Hauptbahnhof** is on major rail lines, including Passau-Regensburg-Nürnberg and Munich-Landshut-Regensburg, with frequent connections in all directions. From Munich, it's a 1½ hour trip; from Nürnberg, 1 hour and 15 minutes; and from Frankfurt, 3 hours. For rail information and schedules, visit www.bahn.de or call © **01805/996633.** Access by **car** is via the A3 Autobahn from east and west and the A93 from north and south.

GETTING AROUND Nearly all places of interest to visitors are in **Regensberg's Altstadt (Old Town),** an easy 10-minute stroll from the Hauptbahnhof; almost the entire area is closed to car traffic. Bright yellow Altstadt buses line up along Maximilianstrasse, next to the station. One-way fare is 1€, and a day ticket valid for up to five people costs 2€ (purchase on the bus). Note: there's no service on Saturday and Sunday.

VISITOR INFORMATION The tourist office is at Rathausplatz 3 (www.tourismus.regensburg.de; © **0941/5074410**). Hours are Monday to Friday 9am to 6pm, Saturday 9am to 4pm, Sunday 9:30am to 4pm (November to March, it closes Sundays at 2:30pm).

Exploring Regensburg

Start your explorations with a panoramic view of the roofs and spires of the Altstadt (Old Town) from the 12th-century **Steinerne Brücke** (Stone Bridge). This lovely span built between 1135 and 1146 crosses the Danube on 16 arches. A major engineering feat in its day, the bridge opened up land routes between northern Europe and Venice, making Regensburg a major trading center. For a quick trip back to the Middle Ages, stroll down Hinter der Grieb, an alleyway lined with high-towered 15th-century houses.

Dom St. Peter's ★ CATHEDRAL The town's most majestic edifice has towered over the Domplatz since the 13th century, though its formidable presence is deceiving—constructed with easily eroded limestone and green sandstone, this French Gothic cathedral is continually deteriorating and constantly in need of shoring up. Even the massive spires are 1950s makeovers, fortified with more durable materials. Two little stone gremlins in niches on either side of the main entrance are known as *The Devil* and *The Devil's Grandmother,* suggesting that evil in any guise is to be left at the door. In this cathedral, salvation takes on a refreshingly humane aspect. Soaring vaulting suggests a protective canopy under which all are welcome, and acres of sumptuous stained glass seem to embrace the faithful in light and color. The most famous panel is of the church's namesake St. Peter, holding his symbolic key to the kingdom; more than 100 images of St. Peter appear in the nave and chapels. The most popular figure, though, is the Archangel Gabriel, a happy-looking fellow affixed to a pillar near the altar. The cathedral is home to the world's oldest boys' choir, the 1,000-year-old Chor Dompatzen, which performs every Sunday at 10am mass, open to all. Within the mossy **cloisters** are some of the church's earliest remnants: the frescoed 11th century Aller Heiligenkapelle (All Saints' Chapel) and

Gothic St. Peter's cathedral at night.

Sankt Stephan Kirche (St. Stephen's Church), where the altar is a hollowed-out limestone rock with a passageway into early Christian tombs. Domplatz. www.regensburger-dom.de. © **0941/5865500.** Free admission. Mon–Sat 8–5, Sun noon–4.

Domschatzmuseum and Diözesanmuseum St. Ulrich ★ MUSEUM Scattered around the cathedral precincts you'll find a wealth of other ecclesiastical treasures. Among them are the richly embroidered garments in the Domschatzmuseum, testimony to Regensburg's role as a textile center. Statuary from the 11th century and a trove of gold chalices and goblets are shown off in the St. Ulrich church, an appropriately early Gothic building to one side of the cathedral. Domplatz 2. www.regensburger-dom.de. © **0941/51688.** Admission 2€ adults to either, 3€ to both.

Historisches Museum (History Museum) ★ MUSEUM Long ago, the Romans established a garrison town, Castra Regina, that became their power base on the upper Danube. Though the encampment covered an area of almost 25 hectares (62 acres), not much remains. (The ancient **Porta Praetoria,** behind the cathedral, is the most impressive reminder. Through the grille beside its eastern tower you can see the original level of the Roman street, nearly 3m (10 ft.) below—which is why you often have to step down into the churches of Regensburg.) Roman artifacts are showcased in this former monastery, including a stone tablet noting the establishment of the garrison, an altar to the god Mercury, and several Christian tombstones from the late Roman period. You'll also see the colorful canvases of Albrecht Altdorfer (1480–1538), a Regensburg master of the so-called Danube School; look closely at his biblical scenes and you'll notice Bavarian landscapes and Germanic medieval towns in the backgrounds.

Dachauplatz 2–4. www.regensburg.de/museumsportal. © **0941/5072448.** Admission 2.20€ adults; 1.10€ students, seniors, and children 8–18; 4.40€ families; children 7 and under free. Tues–Sun 10am–4pm (until 8pm on Thurs).

Schloss Thum und Taxis ★★ PALACE   It's not unusual to bump into royalty walking around Regensburg, since the town is home to one of Germany's wealthiest and most distinguished aristocratic clans. In 1812, the monastic holdings of St. Emmeram's Abbey, founded in the 8th century, were granted to the princes of Thum und Taxis, who had made a fortune establishing Europe's first postal system. The family has since converted their property into a 500-room palace so extravagant that, according to current doyenne Gloria, Princess von Thurn und Taxis, it "makes Buckingham Palace look like a hut." The presence of this former international party girl, once known as Princess TNT, is part of the allure of a visit to the palace (by guided tour only, some in English). The staterooms, rococo staircase, conservatory, chapels and former cloisters, even a royal bedroom or two are certainly grand. Things seem more sedate at the palace now, compared to the days when the princess threw multi-day, celebrity-studded bashes. The vast courtyard is still the setting for a lively Christmas market and summertime concerts.

Emmeramplatz. www.thurnundtaxis.de. © **0941/50480.** Admission 13.50€ for 90 min. tour, 10€ for 1 hr. tour. Mid-Mar to Oct daily, tours hourly 10:30am–4:30pm; Nov to mid-Mar weekends, tours hourly 10:30am–3:30pm.

Where to Stay in Regensburg

Bischofshof am Dom ★   A former ecclesiastical academy established by the bishops of Regensburg provides lodgings that are traditional yet surprisingly informal, even a bit quirky. Many face a sunny inner garden behind the cathedral, and all are individually decorated—some in English country-house style, others in contemporary urbanity. An atmospheric *Weinstube* (wine bar) downstairs spills into a beer garden.

Krauterermarkt 3. www.hotel-bischofshof.de. © **0941/58460.** 55 units. 138€–148€ double. Buffet breakfast included. Parking 12€. Bus: Altstadt bus or 1. **Amenities:** Restaurant; bar; Wi-Fi (free).

Orphée Grosses Haus ★★★ Any one of this trio of sister hotels would be a top choice for a stay in Regensburg. For sheer opulence it's hard to resist the **Grand Hotel Orphée** (Grosses Haus, in German), a baroque house at Untere Bachgasse 8, where ornate ceilings and elaborate furnishings will make you feel like German nobility; many of the huge rooms are suitable for families, with day beds for extra guests and plenty of parquet expanses. The **Petit Hotel Orphée** (Kleines Haus, in German) at Wahlenstrasse 1 occupies the former home of a prosperous merchant clan and offers individually furnished rooms with antique washstands and bedsteads, rich fabrics, and welcoming couches and armchairs (there's no reception; you'll get the key from the Grand Hotel Orphée around the corner). **Country Manor Orphée,** Andreasstrasse 26, across the Steinerne Brücke (Stone Bridge) from the Altstadt, spreads across an upper floor of a 16th-century salt warehouse; six of the ten tile-floored, casually chic apartments (all with kitchenettes) open to patios overlooking the Danube.

Grand Hotel Orphée (Untere Bachgasse 8); Petit Hotel Orphée (Wahlenstrasse 1); Country Manor Orphée (Andreasstrasse 26). www.hotel-orphee.de.© **0941/596020** for Grand Hotel and Petit Hotel; © **0941/59602300** for Country Manor. Grand Hotel: 25 units, 125€–195€. Petit Hotel: 15 units, 75€–175€. Country Manor: 10 units, 135€–155€. Buffet breakfast included. Parking 6€ at Grand Hotel and Petit Hotel. **Amenities:** Restaurant; bar; Wi-Fi (free).

Where to Eat in Regensburg

Historiche Wurstkuchl ★★ BAVARIAN The Historic Sausage Kitchen opened 900 years ago to feed crews building the adjacent Steinerne Brücke (Stone Bridge) and ever since has been serving the delectable little bratwursts, cooked over beechwood fires in the small kitchen. These days the place dispenses more than 6,000 sausages a day, serving six, eight, or ten to a platter, accompanied by house-made grainy mustard, sauerkraut or potato salad, and bread, all washed down with the house beer. In decent weather you can sit outdoors at one of the picnic tables beneath the bridge. Only floodwaters put a dent in business here—they frequently close the place down, as watermarks on the walls testify.

Thundorferstrasse 3. www.wurstkuchl.de. Platters 7.50€–12€. Daily 8–7 (Nov–Mar closes at 3pm on Sun).

Haus Heuport ★ BAVARIAN/INTERNATIONAL You'll be smitten with the views of the magnificent façade of the cathedral, but the meal, service, and surroundings—a heavy-beamed Gothic hall or sunny cobbled terrace—will also win you over. Opt for the traditional pork roast or duck breast, or venture into some of the kitchen's more creative ventures, such as salmon with Tyrolean bacon or a lasagna with pike and spinach. This is also a popular spot for breakfast and Sunday brunch.

Domplatz 7. www.heuport.de. © **0941/5999297.** Main courses 7€–25€. 9am–11pm.

Restaurant Orphée ★★ FRENCH   Tired of German cooking and Hofbrauhaus-like environs? Take a quick trip to Paris in this delightful dining room that pronounces itself the most authentic French bistro east of the Rhine. Wainscoting, watercolors, wicker chairs, and the rest of the 1890s décor make good the claim, as does a big selection of homey bistro classics—from crepes to quiche to cote d'agneau, accompanied by French wines and service that is a lot more warmly Bavarian than snooty Parisian. This hospitable place, on the ground floor of the Grand Hotel Orphée, is open just about all the time, welcoming guests for coffee, wine, snacks, or any meal of the day.

Unterre Bachgasse 8. www.hotel-orphee.de. ✆ **0941/596020.** Main courses 12€–30€. Mon–Sat 8am–1am.

A Side Trip to Passau ★

117km (73 miles) SE of Regensburg

This small city tucked into a far corner of Germany near the Austrian border has a quaint Altstadt, a proud twin-towered cathedral, and a medieval fortress, the Veste Oberhaus, high above town. But what will draw you here are the glittering waters of the mighty Danube. As the river flows through Passau on its way from the Black Forest to the Black Sea, it is joined by two tributaries, the Ilz and Inn. The trio of rivers creates a spectacular landscape viewed from miles of waterside walkways.

ESSENTIALS

Hourly **train service** from Nürnberg takes 2 hours, from Regensburg, 1¼ hours (www.bahn.de, ✆ **01805/996633**) Access by **car** is by the A3 Autobahn. See also "Cruising the Danube," below. The **tourist office** at Rathausplatz 3 (✆ **0851/955980**) is open daily.

EXPLORING PASSAU

The **Altstadt,** an easy walk east from the Hauptbahnhof along Ludwigstrasse, clings to an ever-narrowing rocky spur above the confluence of

---

Cruising the Danube

Topping the list of things to do in Passau is taking a boat tour along the Danube and its tributaries, the Inn and the Ilz. Trips around local waters and upstream to Regensburg take from 45 minutes to half a day, cost 8.40€ and up, and depart from Passau's Fritz-Schäffer Promenade. Among the operators are **Wurm and Köck** (www.donauschiffahrt.de).

You may also board one of the passenger ferries run (Apr–Oct only) practically every day from Passau downstream to the Austrian city of **Linz.** These trips take 5 hours downstream and 6 hours upstream, cost 23€ per person, and depart from the city's riverfront piers at 9am and noon. For information contact the **Donau-Schiffahrt Line** (www.donauschiffahrt.de).

The River Danube flows past Passau's quaint Altstadt.

the Inn and the Danube. The little lanes converge at a point of land that resembles the prow of a ship, overlooking the confluence, with the Ilz flowing in from the north. Rising high above the Old Town's gabled houses are the twin towers of the grand baroque **Dom (St. Stephen's Cathedral),** Domplatz 9 (✆ **0851/39241**), with a gaudily decorated interior. It boasts the world's largest organ, with 17,974 pipes; rousing 30-minute concerts are given May to October, Monday to Saturday, at noon; there's a second performance on Thursday at 7:30pm. Concerts cost 4€ for adults, 2€ for students and children 13 and under. (Thursday evening tickets run 5€ to 8€ for adults, based on your seat, and 5€ for children.) The Dom is open Monday to Saturday 8 to 11am and 12:30 to 6pm. Admission is free.

On the banks of the Danube below, the 13th-century **Rathaus** is decorated with painted murals that provide a quick visual lesson in town history. There's a Glockenspiel in the tower from which characters emerge to musical accompaniment at 10:30am, 2, and 7:25pm; on Saturday there's an additional appearance at 3pm.

WHERE TO EAT IN PASSAU

Löwen Brauhaus ★   FRANCONIAN/GERMAN   The 13th-century Rathaus, like most town halls in Germany, is equipped with a Rathskeller.

This one has a contemporary décor that still suggests woodsy, dark-paneled coziness. Alcoves and a riverside terrace provide settings for a quick snack of wursts or hearty meals of *Leberknödel* (liver-dumpling) soup and pork shank, slow-cooked for hours, served with dumplings and *Sauerkraut*. These and other local favorites are served with beer from brewers within the town limits.

Rathausplatz 2. www.loewen-brauhaus.de © **0851/3793-2057.** Main courses 7€–15€. Daily 10am–midnight.

ULM ★

97km (60 miles) SE of Stuttgart, 138km (86 miles) W of Munich

You'll know you're getting closer to Ulm when the city's telltale beacon appears on the horizon—the soaring steeple of Ulm Minster, the tallest in Christendom. The city has been a major stop on shipping routes since the Middle Ages, known for the linen and hides that its merchants dispatched along the Danube toward Genoa, Venice, Amsterdam, and London in return for iron, wood, and wine. At one time, the coins the city minted were so widely distributed that it was said "Ulm money rules the world."

Honored Citizens

The Nobel Prize–winning theoretical physicist Albert Einstein was born in Ulm in 1879. Although his family moved to Munich when he was one, he did occasionally visit in the years before fleeing Nazi Germany in 1933, and Ulm is proud to claim him as one of their own. Einstein, best known for his theory of relativity, was also a peace activist who deeply regretted his role in developing the atom bomb—he later said, "If only I had known, I should have become a watchmaker." In 1952, Einstein was offered the post of president of Israel. He declined, saying, "I lack both the natural aptitude and the experience to deal properly with people." He is commemorated with a stained-glass window in Ulm Minster and with an abstract sculpture near his birthplace at Bahnhofstrasse 20.

Brother and sister Hans and Sophie Scholl were also born in Ulm, Hans in 1918 and Sophie in 1921. They were executed in Munich in February 1943, having been caught distributing leaflets published by the White Rose resistance group. Amid the darkness of the Nazi terror, the group printed such prescient statements as "Nothing degrades a civilized nation of culture more than allowing itself to be ruled without resistance by an irresponsible, despotic clique, driven and obsessed by dark desires and irrational urges." On news of the murder of Polish Jews they wrote, "Here we see the most monstrous crime against mankind, an atrocity that is rivaled by no other in the history of mankind." Hans and Sophie are honored with a memorial in front of the site of their childhood home (now the Deutsche Bank) on one side of Münsterplatz and with bronze busts in the Stadthaus, also on Münsterplatz.

Declining fortunes, plagues, and World War II bombings have lain waste to a lot of Ulm's onetime splendor, though this prosperous modern city retains some of its old ambiance, especially in the riverside Fishermen's and Tanners' Quarter. Just across the Danube is the city's twin, Neu-Ulm, and more than a ribbon of water divides them: Ulm is in the state of Baden-Würtemberg, while Neu-Ulm is in Bavaria. Both are the subject of a popular German tongue twister, the equivalent of the English "Peter Piper picked a peck of pickled peppers": *In Ulm, um Ulm und um Ulm herum* ("In Ulm, around Ulm, and all around Ulm").

Essentials

ARRIVING   The Ulm **Hauptbahnhof** is on several major and regional rail lines, with frequent connections in all directions. Trains from Munich take 1 hour and 25 minutes; from Stuttgart, 70 minutes; from Cologne, 3 hours and 15 minutes. For rail information and schedules, visit www.bahn.de or call © **01805/996633.** Access by **car** is via the A8 Autobahn east and west or the A7 north and south. It takes about 1½ hours to drive to Ulm from Munich and about 3 hours to drive from Frankfurt.

VISITOR INFORMATION   Ulm's tourist office at Marktplatz 1 (www.tourismus.ulm.de, © **0731/1612830**) is open Monday to Friday 9am to 6pm and Saturday 9am to 4pm. From April to December, it's also open Sunday 11am to 3pm.

SPECIAL EVENTS   The city's big summer bash is **Schwörwoche** (Oath Week), in mid-July. The serious part of the proceedings is a speech by the mayor and his or her pledge to uphold the town's 1397 constitution. The rest is pretty much all about frivolity, with a fun fair, the Lichtserenade (Light Serenade), when lanterns float down the Danube, and the Nabada, a parade of gaily decorated boats. During the Fischerstechen (Fishermen's Jousting) event, costumed contenders try to knock each other off shallow-bottomed fishing boats.

A memorial to Albert Einstein, who was born in Ulm.

Frescoes decorate the exterior of Ulm's medieval Rathaus.

Exploring Ulm

It's easy to find your way in Ulm—simply set your sights on the cathedral spire, rising high above Münsterplatz. If it's foggy, which it often is in Ulm in winter, just follow Bahnhofstrasse and its continuation, Hirschstrasse, from the train station. Then *voila,* looming in front of you will be the massive Gothic **Ulm Münster** (p. 241). It's symbolic of the new and old natures of this city that the other great presence on Münsterplatz is the sleek, contemporary, glass and white-granite **Stadthaus,** a sort of public gathering spot and art gallery designed by New York-based architect Richard Meier. Just to the south is Marktplatz, surrounded by the medieval Rathaus and the strikingly new **Weishaupt Gallery** (see p. 242). Beyond, the lanes of the **Fishermen's and Tanners' Quarter** (see p. 238) meander south to the banks of the Danube.

Rathaus ★★ HISTORIC BUILDING   One of Ulm's finest medieval showplaces has been used as a warehouse, prison, and a butcher's marketplace, but city fathers appropriated the fine structure as a town hall in 1419. Ornate frescoes emblazon the façade, depicting valor, bravery, obedience, justice, and other qualities expected of stalwart citizens of an important and prosperous town. A pulpit on the east side was used to deliver proclamations on civic matters and one on the west was used, a bit too frequently, to proclaim death sentences. The astronomical clock, a 16th-century addition below a large gable, beautifully and intricately indicates lunar phases, the position of the sun and the moon, and the zodiac. Hanging over the main staircase inside is a flying machine constructed by A. L. Berblinger, an Ulm tailor. On a blustery May day in 1811, in the presence of several dukes and princes of Bavaria, Berblinger attempted to catch an updraft and take flight from a riverside cliff.

Instead, he plunged into the cold waters of the Danube and had to be hauled out by fishermen.

Marktplatz 1. www.ulm.de. ✆ **0731/1610.** Free admission. Mon–Fri 9am–6pm (Thurs until 8pm), Sun 11am–6pm. Closed Sat.

Ulmer Museum ★ MUSEUM   Handsome galleries show off some noteworthy, if minor, works by Klee and Kandinsky, as well as graceful Gothic sculpture by Hans Multscher, a master craftsman who came to Ulm to work on the cathedral. The star of the show, however, is the *Löwenmensch* (Lion Man, or Lion Person, sometimes known as *Löwenfrau,* or Lion Woman). This 40,000-year-old ivory representation of a human body with a lion's head stands less than a foot tall and is the world's first-known zoomorphic, or animal-shaped, sculpture. Discovered in fragments in a nearby cave in 1939, pieces were tucked away in a storeroom during World War II and forgotten for almost 30 years. Even then, the head was not discovered until 1998, when the elegant little statuette was fully assembled and restored.

Marktplatz 9. www.museum.ulm.de. ✆ **0731/1614300.** Admission 3.50€ adults, 2.50€ students, children 14 and under free; free for all Fri. Tues–Sun 11am–5pm (Thurs until 8pm).

down by the **RIVER**

Ulm's most colorful neighborhood is a warren of half-timbered houses that crowd little lanes on a slope descending from the Marktplatz to the banks of the Danube. Donkeys once plodded up the incline, bearing goods from riverside docks for storage in the Weinhof, or Wine Court, the largest of the city's medieval warehouses. Adding to the picturesque charm of the place is the Blau River, whose babbling waters dart beneath windows and under little bridges before meeting the Danube.

The rushing waters once propelled mills; the oldest, Isaac's Mill, is at Fischergasse 17. The river also supplied tanneries with the great volumes of water the tanning process requires, and flushed away the waste created when tanners boiled cattle flesh to separate fat from the hides. You'll still see wooden shingles on the tanner's houses, placed there to protect the facades from the acidic liquid that dripped from hides hanging to dry.

Many other residents made their living fishing or as sailors; they proudly called themselves *Räsen,* or rough. An especially attractive sailor's house, known as the Schönes Haus, or Beautiful House, is at Fischergasse 40.

A long section of the city wall still fronts the Danube; it's topped these days with a view-filled walkway. One of the little lanes that gives access from the quarter to the riverside is known as Vaterunsergase, or Lord's Prayer Lane. Locals give two different explanations for the name: Either because one can say the Lord's Prayer in the time it takes to walk this short lane, or because—in less savory times—residents uttered that prayer as they dumped cadavers into the river.

Ulm Münster ★★★ CATHEDRAL   A sculpted sparrow is perched high atop the roof of this massive edifice, a masterpiece of the German Gothic style. It says something about the good nature of Ulm's citizens that they chose this modest little bird as their symbol, rather than a heraldic eagle or menacing hawk. As the story goes, when the cathedral was under construction in the 14th century, builders could not fit the beams they laid crosswise on their carts through the narrow city gates. They were about to destroy the gates to make room for the beams when they saw a sparrow building a nest and noticed how it placed a piece of straw lengthwise into its beak to maneuver it into place. They repositioned the beams into the carts lengthwise and saved the gates. In the end, the cathedral they erected was nothing short of ingenious. The vast interior could accommodate 20,000 souls, twice the medieval population of the town, and was the largest church in the land at the time, with 51 altars (even now, among German churches only the cathedral in Cologne is larger). A carving on one cornerstone shows the mayor and his wife placing the church on the shoulders of the master builder, whose talents included marshaling townspeople to carry stones from their demolished church outside the town walls to the worksite. They did not complete, however, the two planned towers, as the main one began to collapse before it was completed—"the people fled from the church as they thought the minster was going to fall down." Before the job could be resumed, the town was out of money, and it was not until 1890 that the single steeple was topped off at 162m (531-ft.), the tallest of any cathedral tower in the world. Among those who were not drawn to the beacon were Allied bombers during World War II, who spared the church while laying waste to much of the rest of the city.

A plaque on the vestibule floor marks the center of the steeple, a vertigo-inducing climb of 768 steps above. Far ahead, at the end of the five-aisle nave, supported by soaring columns and sweeping arches, you'll see a splash of light-infused red. It's the cloak of Christ ascending, portrayed in a medieval stained-glass window, yet from most of the massive space, the red shape looks more like an inviting heart, beckoning the faithful closer. Midway down the nave are the choir stalls, carved with hundreds of figures in the workshops of local craftsman Jorg Syrlin between 1468 and 1474. Biblical figures appear on one side, classical philosophers and writers on the other, a secular show of humanism that befits such an architectural triumph.

Münsterplatz 1. www.ulmer-muenster.de. ✆ **0731/9675023.** Münster free; tower 4€ adults, 2.50€ children (buy tickets 1 hr. ahead). Open daily, July–Aug 8am–7:45pm; Apr–June and Sept 8am–6:45pm; Mar and Oct 9am–5:45pm; Nov–Feb 9am–4:45pm.

Weishaupt Gallery ★ MUSEUM   Over the past five decades Sieg-fried and Jutta Weishaupt have amassed a fuel-technology fortune and also become Germany's leading collectors of modern art. They show off their works by Roy Lichtenstein, Andy Warhol, Mark Rothko, Willem de Kooning, Keith Haring, Karl Gerstner, and many others on a rotating basis in galleries behind a bold glass facade designed by Berlin architect Wolfram Wöhr. A bridge connects the gallery with the Ulmer Museum. Marktplatz 9. www.museum.ulm.de. ✆ **0731/1614300.** Admission 3.50€ adults, 2.50€ students, children 14 and under free; free for all Fri. Tues–Sun 11am–5pm (Thurs until 8pm).

Where to Stay in Ulm

Hotel am Rathaus & Reblaus ★★★   Antiques and old paintings fill these two tastefully decorated houses in the Old Town; the photogenic rooftops, towers, and the Rathaus (Town Hall) just outside the windows seem like decorative pieces themselves. Inside, some rooms in the main hotel and the equally charming half-timbered annex are nicely furnished with folksy painted cupboards and other period pieces, while others are stylishly contemporary, with dark walls, soothing white furnishings, and soaking tubs hidden behind frosted glass partitions. All rooms are equipped with fine linens, excellent lighting, and other welcome touches. Kronengasse 8–10. www.rathausulm.de. ✆ **0731/968490.** 34 units. 88€–120€ double. Buffet breakfast included. Free parking. Closed late Dec to mid-Jan. **Amenities:** Wi-Fi (free).

Hotel Bäulme ★   This 600-year-old house offers no-frills accommodation and lots of quaint charm in simply furnished rooms that don't have much more than beds and plain wood desks. These homey quarters look out on medieval lanes or across yards in back to the Munster and its tower; the sound of bells tolling is a perfect touch in the otherwise quiet, car-free neighborhood. Downstairs, a buffet breakfast starts the day in a delightful, paneled *stube* warmed by an ornate tile stove. Kohlgasse 6. www.hotel-baeumle.de. ✆ **0731/62287.** 13 units. 98€–112€ double. Buffet breakfast included. **Amenities:** Wi-Fi (free).

Hotel Schiefes Haus ★★   The so-called Crooked House is probably the most watched-over structure in town: Neighbors have been waiting for this decidedly lopsided, half-timbered structure to slip into the Blau River ever since 1443, when it began to sink perceptibly into the gravel riverbed. The house was already a century old by then, and a convenient base for fishermen who could pass their catch up through a hatch into a riverside room. That's now an enclosed terrace, where you can recline in a lounger and watch the river rushing beneath you. It's hard not to feel woozy in the cozy bedrooms upstairs, where floors slope and old beams and stone walls seem to tilt in helter-skelter fashion—but that's half the fun. Levels attached to the bed frames assure guests they're sleeping at a straight angle, and the ever-present sound of rushing water is enough to lull even a die-hard insomniac to sleep.

Schwörhausgasse 6. www.hotelschiefeshausulm.de. © **0731/96730.** 11 units. 119€–148€ double. Buffet breakfast included. **Amenities:** Wi-Fi (free).

Where to Eat in Ulm

Zunfthaus der Schiffleute ★★ BAVARIAN/SEAFOOD   This former guild headquarters and pub for local fishermen was built some six centuries ago on a little harbor on the Danube, with the Blau River racing past the back door. Water was channeled into troughs where fish were kept fresh for the market, and fishermen and their families took up residence on the upper floors; a restaurant eventually opened in the old guildhall below. Fish was the specialty, of course. In days before dams prevented the Danube from flooding regularly, fish would even swim right up the kitchen door. Fresh fish is still the specialty, while it would be quite forgivable to order meat-heavy Franconian specialties instead.

Fischergasse 31. www.zunfthaus-ulm.de. © **0731/64411.** Main courses 9€–19€. Daily 11am–midnight.

Zur Forelle ★ SWABIAN/SEAFOOD   Innkeeper Jakob Schwenk got a permit to serve local fishermen here in 1626, and this institution also known as Häusle (Little House) has been doing a brisk business ever since. Behind the geranium-bedecked half-timbered façade are several paneled dining rooms where the namesake *forelle* (trout), plucked from freshwater basins in the river out front, is served grilled, baked, and sauteed in preparations that have delighted such distinguished guests as Albert Einstein. Ulm-style herb-and-salmon soup is a start for meals that also venture into the meaty side of things. In summer, a riverside terrace is the most romantic place in town for a meal.

Fischergasse 25. www.zurforelle.com. © **0731/63924.** Reservations recommended. Main courses 10€–22€. Daily 11am–3pm and 5pm–midnight.

Zur Lochmühle ★ SWABIAN/GERMAN   One of old Ulm's most photo-worthy sights, a riverside mill where the waterwheel began spinning in 1356, is also a popular spot for a casual meal. Though it seems rushing waters could sweep the warmly paneled rooms and waterside beer garden away at any moment, the kitchen seems to take its inspiration from the nearby Saurmarkt (Sow's Market), with favorites like Schweinebraten topping a long menu of other hearty Swabian classics.

Gebergasse 6. www.lochmuehle-ulm.de. © **0731/67305.** Main courses 8€–16€. Daily 11am–11pm.

THE ROMANTIC ROAD

F

or many travelers, Germany hits its scenic high notes along the so-called Romantische Strasse, or Romantic Road, a route that rambles through southern Bavaria (and a tiny portion of adjoining Baden-Württemberg). The 350km (220 miles) of specially marked lanes and secondary roads wind south from the vineyard-clad hills surrounding Würzburg through an unfolding panorama of mostly rural landscapes, eventually rising into mountain pastures backed by craggy Alpine peaks near Füssen. Along the way are fields and woodlands, half-timbered villages, and fantasy castles built by the legendary King Ludwig II. The route dishes up plenty of storybook scenes of old Germany, not to mention great art and architecture, bustling town life, and country walks.

Officially, the route the German government drew up after World War II takes in 28 towns and villages. You could easily hit the high points in and around Würzburg, Rothernburg ob der Tauber, and Füssen by car, bus, or train in three or four days, but we recommend taking a little more time. Give yourself room to explore—to bike or hike through the Tauber Valley, visit the beautiful Herrgottskirche in little Creglingen, ascend a mountaintop, or bend your elbow in a historic tavern or two. Fans of mountain scenery may also want to wander off the Romantic Road at its southern terminus to take in a section of the Bavarian Alps around Garmisch-Partenkirchen—these peaks may not be part of the official "romantic" route, but they most definitely fit the description.

WÜRZBURG ★★

280km (174 miles) NW of Munich, 119km (74 miles) SE of Frankfurt, 109km (68 miles) NW of Nürnberg

Würzburg, at the northern end of the Romantic Road, is a cosmopolitan place, with 125,000 residents, of whom 30,000 are students. That student population, needless to say, brings a lot of vivacity to the city's narrow lanes and bright squares. Due in large part to the youthful presence, it's said that Würzburgers drink like priests on holiday—an image supported by the fact that Wurzburg has 64 churches and 400 wine taverns, or roughly, a church for every Sunday and a tavern for every day.

FACING PAGE: Tiny Mittenwald is known for its hand-crafted violins.

> ### Doing the Romantic Road on Two Feet or Two Wheels
>
> A well-marked, 460-km (275-mile) cycle route follows the Romantic Road, as does the 500-km (300-mile) Long Distance Walking Trail. The cycle trail is geared to leisure riders and follows side roads and specially laid paths along the Romantic Road car route; grades are fairly level except for some stretches in the foothills around Füssen. Hikers wander a little farther off the beaten path, into some national parklands and along protected river valleys. Cyclists and hikers have the option of hopping onto the Romantic Road Coach for stretches, or, with advance arrangement, using the buses to transport luggage to designated towns. For more information, go to www.romantischestrasse.de.

Würzburg's preference for wine over beer becomes clear as soon as you notice the town is swathed in vineyards that climb the surrounding hillsides above its gabled rooftops. The most prominent is the Würzburger Stein—at 85 hectares (210 acres) it's the largest vineyard in Germany, and, planted in 779, it's also purportedly the oldest. The town proudly claims that one of the best customers for the local wine was the poet Goethe, who had a standing order for 400 bottles a year. You'll also soon notice that wine merchants here sell *Bocksbeutels,* the green, narrow-necked wine bottles designed so monks could tuck them under their robes.

On the night of March 16, 1945, Würzburg was leveled by a bombing raid. A plan to leave the city in ruin as a testimony to the horrors of war was scrapped and nearly every major structure has been restored. The modern city blends in harmoniously with medieval remains and reconstructions. Würzburg isn't picture-book pretty, the way Rothenburg and some other towns you'll come to on the Romantic Road are, but that doesn't distract from its appeal, and there's plenty to see in a day.

Essentials

ARRIVING

BY TRAIN The **Würzburg Hauptbahnhof** lies on several major and regional rail lines, with frequent connections to all major German cities. From Frankfurt, 30 trains arrive per day (trip time: 1 hr., 10 min.); from Munich, 20 trains (2 hr., 10 min.); from Nürnberg, 30 trains (1 hr.); and 12 trains from Stuttgart (2 hr., 15 min.). For rail information and schedules, call © **01805/996633** or visit www.bahn.com.

BY BUS See "Romantic Road Info & Bus Tours," p. 248.

BY CAR Access is via the A7 Autobahn from north and south or the A3 Autobahn from east and west. The A81 Autobahn has links from the southwest.

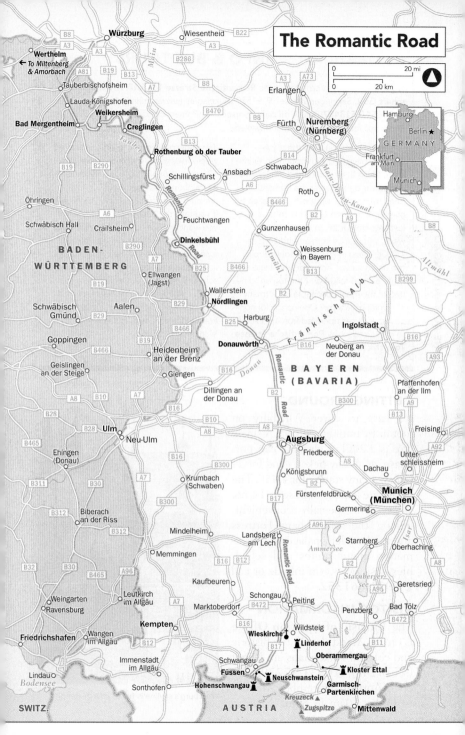

romantic road INFO & BUS TOURS

A good source of information is the **Romantische Strasse Touristik Arbeitsgemein-schaft GbR,** Segringer Strasse 19, 91550 Dinkelsbühl (www.romantischestrasse.de; ✆ **09851/5513487**), which officially oversees the Romantic Road and offers brochures and maps for drivers, cyclists, and walkers.

Several bus tours ply the route—you'll be besieged with options in Würzburg, Munich, Frankfurt, and other cities and towns on and near the Romantic Road. Most offer transport, guides, and overnight accommodations on trips that last anywhere from an overnight to a week, with prices from around 250€ to 1,200€. If you're game for doing a road trip on your own, however, you'll find the route easy to follow and the region to be one of the most hospitable in Germany.

Don't have a car? One option for non-drivers is buses operated from mid-April to mid-October by **Romantische Strasse Touristik** (www.romanticroadcoach.de)

that allow passengers to hop on and off where they want. The entire route takes 12 hours, though you won't see much on a straight run, as "rest stops" in towns are brief. The scheme is only worthwhile if you take the time to get off wherever you want and spend a night or two. Riding these buses is certainly easier than trying to navigate the often sparse public-transport options, and it may save you some money, too. A 6-month pass cost 122€, and Eurail pass holders receive a 20% discount. Daily departures are from Frankfurt and Füssen at 8am and from Munich at 10:30am.

GETTING AROUND

It's easy to cover Würzburg on foot or by tram (streetcar). A single fare is 2.20€, or else you can purchase an all-day ticket, good for 24 hours, at any station for 4.45€. The same fare applies to buses. The no. 9 bus is especially convenient, linking the Marienberg Fortress and the Residenz palace. For information about routes and schedules, visit www.vvm-info.de or call ✆ **0931/361352.**

VISITOR INFORMATION

The **Tourist Information Office** is on the Marktplatz in the historic and colorful Falkenhaus am Markt (see p. 249); ✆ **0931/372398.** It's open April to December Monday to Friday 10am to 6pm, Saturday

Würzburg's skyline is full of church steeples.

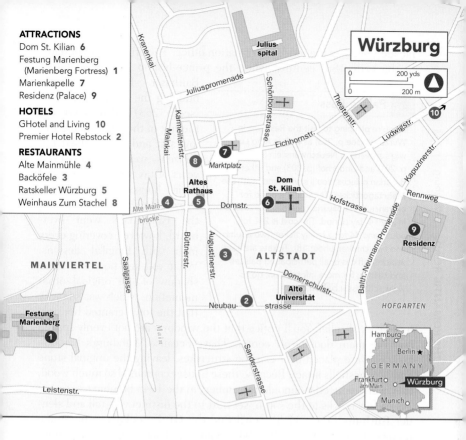

Würzburg

ATTRACTIONS
Dom St. Kilian **6**
Festung Marienberg
  (Marienberg Fortress) **1**
Marienkapelle **7**
Residenz (Palace) **9**

HOTELS
GHotel and Living **10**
Premier Hotel Rebstock **2**

RESTAURANTS
Alte Mainmühle **4**
Backöfele **3**
Ratskeller Würzburg **5**
Weinhaus Zum Stachel **8**

10am to 2pm (from May to October it's also open on Sundays from 10am to 2pm); hours from January to March are Monday to Friday 10am to 4pm, Saturday 10am to 1pm. In the adjacent public library you can avail yourself of restroom facilities, a café, and free Wi-Fi.

SPECIAL EVENTS   The annual **Mozart Festival,** www.mozartfest-wuerzburg.de, is staged over the entire month of June. The venue for most of the concerts is the baroque Residenz palace (see p. 253).

Exploring Würzburg

The town center is the **Marktplatz** (marketplace), where vendors sell produce and sausages from stalls in the shadow of lovely red-and-white **Marienkapelle** (**St. Mary's Chapel;** see p. 253). A gilded statue of Mary high atop the steeple is literally two-faced, built to rotate in the wind so she always looks upon the town with one of two benign countenances. Another presence on the square is the **Falkenhaus,** or House of the Falcon (a statuary falcon perches on the highest pinnacle of the façade), housing the tourist information office. The ornate exterior dates to the early 18th century, when the prince-bishop and his architect Balthasar Neumann were building the palatial Residenz (see p. 253) and decided that the rest of the town should follow suit and spruce itself up. Citizens were offered seven years of tax relief if they redid their houses with elegant stucco facades. The owner of the Falkenhaus went overboard, however, covering every inch with fanciful designs. What you see now is a mere shadow of the original ornamentation, which was so tacky that the town granted her only four years of relief. You'll notice that the windows are not evenly spaced and the main door is off center. That's because Wurzburg's baroque facades were placed over existing structures, leaving the original stone and timber shells intact. Because these houses contained so much wood, they were reduced to smoldering embers in the 1945 bombing.

> ### Palace Pass
>
> If you're planning to visit the Residenz in Wurzburg (see p. 253) as well as King Ludwig's spreads at Neuschwanstein (see p. 294) and Linderhof (p. 303) and other Bavarian palaces, you'll save money with the **Mehrtagesticket.** The ticket is good for entrance to 40 Bavarian palaces and castles in any 14-day period. The cost is 24€ for adults and 44 for a family ticket (two adults and two children under 18). Tickets are sold at ticket offices of all participating palaces and castles; for more information, go to www.schloesser.bayern.de.

A few blocks to the south, set next to the distinctively tall and slender **Rathaus** (Town Hall), you'll find the **Grafeneckart,** a one-room memorial to that March 16, 1945, bombing. That evening, in 17 minutes, 225 British Lancasters dropped 1,000 tons of explosives to reduce 90% of the city to a smoldering ruin, killing 5,000 civilians. Photos (with English captions) and a model of the ruined town testify to the destruction and the 20-year-long reconstruction, much of it by so-called Trümmerfrauen (rubble women). From here, follow Domstrasse east to the cathedral, **Dom St. Kilian** (p. 251) and then Hofstrasse further east to the impressive 18th-century **Residenz** (see p. 253), the prince-bishops' palace. **Franconia,** a statue-rich fountain in the square facing the palace's courtyard entrance, was erected in 1814, when the kings of Bavaria usurped the power of the prince-bishops. The fountain celebrates this historic region's artistic accomplishments in the form of Würzburg woodcarver and sculptor Tilman Riemenschneider and the great Renaissance painter Matthias Grünewald (at one time it was erroneously believed he had been born in Würzburg).

A short walk west of the Rathaus you'll find the **Alte Mainbrücke (Old Main Bridge),** completed in 1543, which crosses the Main River with a flourish, adorned with twelve enormous baroque saints and prince-bishops sculpted out of sandstone. In good weather, the bridge is a popular place to enjoy a glass of wine, sold at two small stalls that are allowed to each dispense only 200 glasses at a time. From the end of the bridge a well-marked footpath climbs up the vineyard-clad hillside to the **Marienberg Fortress** (see p. 252). If the uphill climb looks too much for you, you can also ride up there aboard the number 9 bus.

Dom St. Kilian ★ CHURCH Würzburg's prince-bishops worshipped and were laid to rest in this 11th-century Romanesque church, where a large menorah near the entrance pays tribute to Christianity's roots in Judaism. What you see here today is the result of a massive restoration effort that raised the church from ruin in the aftermath of World War II. Many of the prince-bishops' funerary monuments line the elegantly simple nave; others reside for eternity in the Schönborn Chapel, designed by Balthasar Neumann, architect of the Residenz (see p. 253). The finest monuments are by Würzburg sculptor Tilman Riemenschneider (see box on p. 252). One of the best things about visiting churches here in Würzburg and elsewhere along the Romantic Road is seeing Riemenschneider's work. His great genius lay in his ability to capture human empathy in wood, stone, or whatever medium he worked in. On the left side of the nave, for example, he commemorated prince bishop Rudolf von Scherenberg, portraying him in advanced age. The wily old bishop was voted into power at the age of 65, largely because the highly political body thought he would soon expire and leave the post open again; he outwitted and outlived many of his opponents, expiring at the age of 95. The scissors in his coat of arms are a visual cue to his name, which translates as "Scissor Man." Next to him is prince bishop Lorenz von Bibra, looking robust and prideful. The beaver in his coat of arms is a clue to his real name, von Bieber, which von Bibra found to be too common. (May we assume his followers were known as von Beliebers?) The Dom is dedicated to St. Kilian, an Irish missionary who came to Würzburg in 686 and soon converted ruling Duke Gozbert and many of his subjects to Christianity. Kilian, however, ran afoul of the duke's wife, Geilana, when he tried to convince the duke that the couple's marriage was invalid, since Geilana was the widow of his brother. The irate duchess had Kilian and his two companions, Colman and Totnam, beheaded. Their skulls rest in a crypt beneath the altar and are paraded through the streets on St. Kilian's Day, July 9. Their other bones are in the baroque Neumünster across the courtyard, a compromise that has allowed both churches to benefit from the largess of pilgrims over the years.

Domstrasse (at the end of Schönbornstrasse). ✆ **0931/3211830.** Free admission. Easter–Oct Mon–Sat 10am–5pm, Sun 1–6pm; Nov to Easter Mon–Sat 10am–noon and 2–4:30pm, Sun 12:30–1:30pm and 2:30–6pm.

WÜRZBURG'S master CARVER

Tilman Riemenschneider (1460–1531) lived and worked in Würzburg for 48 years, serving as both a councilor and mayor while gaining considerable fame for his sculptures and carvings. He married four times, oversaw a household of nine children and stepchildren, and owned several houses as well as vineyards. During the Peasants' Revolt of 1525, this master woodcarver sided with the rebels and incurred the wrath of the prince-bishops. As a result of his political views, Riemenschneider was imprisoned and tortured, and his hands were broken, ending his artistic career. He died shortly after being released from prison, leaving behind scores of incredibly expressive wood sculptures that adorn churches and museums in Würzburg, Rothenburg, and elsewhere along the Romantic Road.

Festung Marienberg (Marienberg Fortress) ★ HISTORIC SITE
It's a 30-minute trek along a well-marked footpath through hillside vineyards up to this mighty fortress, affording views of the city and surrounding vineyards (bus no. 9 also climbs the hill). From 1253 to 1720 the hilltop fortress/palace, surrounded by massive bastions, was home to the powerful prince-bishops who, beginning in 743, ruled this part of Franconia on behalf of the Holy Roman Empire. As becomes clear in the **Fürstenbaumuseum,** the tapestry-and-painting-filled residential wing of the massive complex, the prince-bishops enjoyed a lavish lifestyle that was far from modest. In adjacent galleries, town models show medieval Würzburg, along with a horrifying glimpse of the town after bombings in 1945. Another wing houses the **Mainfränkisches Museum (Main-Franconian Museum),** where the prized possessions are 81 wood-carved sculptures by Tilman Riemenschneider (see box above), the so-called master of Würzburg and one of the greatest northern sculptors of the Middle Ages. Also within the walls of the massive complex is the **Marienkirche (St. Mary's Church),** in the inner courtyard, founded in the 8th century and rebuilt in the 11th century, making it the oldest church in Germany. The modest church was traditionally the final resting place of the entrails of the prince bishops (the rest of their bodies were interred in the Dom St. Kilian cathedral in the town below—see p. 251). The **Fürstengarten (Prince's Garden)** offers a great viewpoint of the Alte Mainbrücke, the cathedral, and the historic town center.

Festung Marienberg. www.mainfraenkisches-museum.de. © **0931/205940.** Admission to Mainfränkisches Museum 4€ adults, 2€ students, children under 14 free. Apr–Oct Tues–Sun 10am–5pm; Nov–Mar Tues–Sun 10am–4pm. Fürstenbaumuseum 4.50€ adults, 3.50€ students, children under 18 free. Apr–Oct Tues–Sun 9am–6pm. Tours of the fortress (in English and German) 3.50€ adults, 2.50€ students. Apr–Oct Tues–Sun 10am–4pm.

Marienkapelle ★ CHURCH

The Mariencapelle, built by Würzburg merchants in defiance of the prince-bishops.

Built by merchants in the 14th and 15th centuries, this red-and-white church on Marktplatz is dedicated to the city's patron saint. Interestingly, a synagogue stood here until 1349, when plague decimated the city and the blame fell on members of the sizeable Jewish community, who were killed or expelled. From the beginning the church that replaced it was a statement of rebellion, built by merchants for citizens, without the backing of the city's powerful prince-bishops and Rome. Instead, the church supported itself by the little shops huddled against its walls; structures like these are known in Germany as "swallow shops," as they resemble swallows' nests tucked against the side of a house. You'll get an idea of the merchants' attitude toward church hierarchy and aristocrats in a carving of the Last Judgment over the West Portal, where finely robed clergy and their elite supporters are among those condemned to hell. Flanking the south portal are touchingly humane sculptures of Adam and Eve, by Würzburg sculptor Tilman Riemenschneider (see box p. 252). Note that these are replicas, as are the sculptor's loving depictions of the 12 apostles in the interior; the originals are in the Mainfränkisches Museum in the Marienberg Fortress (see p. 252). An exuberant, glittering silver statue of "Madonna in Her Glory" is on the wall that once enclosed the chimney of the mikvah, the ritual baths beneath the long-gone synagogue.

Marktplatz. Daily 9am–7pm. Free admission.

Residenz (Palace) ★★ PALACE

Prince-Bishop Johann Philipp Franz von Schönborn had a passion for elegance and splendor that the staid, musty salons of the Marienberg Fortress could not satisfy. So in 1720 he commissioned what over the next 50 years was to become one of Germany's grandest and most elaborate baroque palaces. It's best to see the palace on a guided tour, as the gilded, mirrored, and frescoed interiors are rich in detail you might otherwise miss on your own. Architect Balthasar Neumann (1687–1753), whose talents included a rare

Balthasar Neumann designed Würzburg's stately baroque Residenz.

combination of technical skill and an eye for beauty and harmony, over-saw the design of the 350-room palace, and his masterpiece shows a unity of purpose and design unusual in structures of such size. Von Schönborn's successor, Prince-Bishop Carl Phillip von Greiffenclau, had the foresight to hire the Venetian painter Tiepolo to fresco the *Treppenhaus* (staircase), where in the largest fresco ever painted, Apollo is surrounded by other gods and women representing the four corners of the world, rendering a climb to the upper hall into a theatrical event. A keen-eyed observer might note that the fierce, naked maiden representing America is being served hot chocolate, then an exotic elixir, as she sits astride a crocodile among cannibals. Tiepolo worked some specific portraits into the Europa section, where he depicts himself as well as his son Giovanni, who accompanied him from Venice. Tiepolo also painted the frescoes in the **chapel** and the **Imperial Hall,** where he portrays, among other themes, the 1156 marriage in Würzburg of emperor Frederick Barbarossa to Beatrice of Burgundy. Among some spectacular visual tricks in the Imperial Hall is the dog who seems to perch on a pillar in front of a scene depicting the investiture of Franconian duke Herold; as you walk around the room, the dog transforms from a sleek pup into a plump, grizzled hound. As you walk down the hallways, notice a number of doors that are only about four feet tall—they were built to accommodate a staff of dwarves, who scrambled through tight passages within the walls to tend to the ceramic tile stoves that warm the salons.

An interesting historical sidenote: Much of the Residenz's splendor would have been lost had it not been for an American art historian and soldier, John Davis Skilton, one of the so-called Monuments Men. When he came to Würzburg after the 1945 bombing, he found the palace a burned-out ruin, with the Tiepolo frescoes intact but exposed to the elements, so he constructed a makeshift roof to preserve them. He's honored in a Memorial Room that chronicles the destruction of the palace and Würzburg and the restoration efforts.

Residenzplatz 2, Tor B. www.residenz-wuerzburg.de. © **0931/355170.** Admission 7.50€ adults; 6.50€ students, children, and seniors. Apr–Oct daily 9am–6pm; Nov–Mar daily 10am–4pm. Guided tours in English (included in admission) 11am and 3pm, also 4:30pm Apr–Oct.

Where to Stay in Würzburg

GHotel and Living ★★ Staying in one of these bright, good-sized rooms in a glass tower just outside the center puts a contemporary slant on Wurzburg, as you gaze out through floor-to-ceiling windows upon the town spreading beneath your feet. Lots of in-room work space, a fitness center, and a buzzy lobby bar cater to the trimly suited millennials who favor this base while in town for business, though the proximity to the Residenz, other sights, and train station make this a good choice for sightseers, too. An excellent buffet breakfast is included in the extremely reasonable room rates.

Schweinfurter Strasse 1-3. www3.ghotel.de. © **0931/359-620.** 204 units. 55€–110€ double. Buffet breakfast included. Parking 8.50€. **Amenities:** Restaurant, bar; fitness room; sauna; Wi-Fi (free).

Premier Hotel Rebstock ★★ A 5-minute walk from the cathedral, behind a rococo facade dating from at least 1408 is a surprisingly

---

FIGHTING THE PROTESTANT menace

Würzburg remained faithful to the Roman Catholic Church throughout the Reformation, partly through the efforts of Julius Echter von Mespelbrunn, a 17th-century prince-bishop (you'll see an elaborate tapestry tracing his family line in the Fürstenbaumuseum in the Marienberg Fortress). Von Mespelbrunn staunchly defended Würzburg against Protestant incursions by banishing Lutheran preachers and demanding that public officials be Catholic. Würzburg still has a large Catholic population and is known as "the town of Madonnas" because of the more than 100 statues of its patron saint that adorn the house fronts. The best known is the baroque "Patrona Franconiae," the so-called Weeping Madonna, standing among other Franconian saints along the buttresses of the 15th-century Alte Mainbrücke.

contemporary interior that breaks out of any cookie-cutter notion of the hotel's Best Western affiliation. Some noteworthy design touches appear in the skylit rotunda downstairs, set up as a café/winter garden, and in guest quarters of all sorts of sizes and styles upstairs. Most accommodations lean toward crisp, clean lines and a businesslike look, though some veer off into odd shapes and more traditional and more posh decor.

Neubaustrasse 7. www.rebstock.com. ℂ **0931/30930.** 72 units. 140€–160€ double. Parking 10€. Buffet breakfast 16€. **Amenities:** Restaurant; bar; room service; Wi-Fi (free).

Where to Eat in Würzburg

Local Würzburg specialties include *Zwiebelkuchen,* similar to a quiche Lorraine, and *Frankische Mostsuppe,* a light wine soup. White Franconian wine seems to go well with just about anything that shows up on a Würzburg table.

Alte Mainmühle ★★ FRANCONIAN   It's a challenge to cross the Alte Mainbrücke (Old Main Bridge) without stepping into this timbered, two-story tavern perched romantically off one side of the bridge over the rushing current. In fact, you don't even have to step inside—a window near the entrance dispenses wine by the glass, to be sipped alongside the bridge's railings. A seat on the summertime terrace comes with nice views of river traffic, the town, and the fortress, but for sheer coziness it's hard to beat the woody, fire-warmed interior. The menu ranges through a full complement of grilled meats, fish (of course), sausage and dumplings, and other local specialties that taste all the better because you're sitting midstream in a river.

Alte Mainbrücke. ℂ **16777.** Main courses 8€–23€. Tues–Sat 10am–midnight.

Backöfele ★ FRANCONIAN/GERMAN   Even the locals don't really know whether to call this place a beer hall, a wine cellar, or a restaurant, but everyone loves the old-world, stone-floored ambiance, located just a couple of streets south of the Rathaus. Well-prepared traditional schnitzels, sausages, and other standards are served here in huge quantities. A Würzburg favorite, pikeperch with noodles and a salad, is usually on the list of specials. Reservations are recommended.

Ursulinergasse 2. www.backoefele.de. ℂ **0931/59059.** Main courses 7€–29€. Mon–Sat noon–11pm; Sun noon–10pm.

Ratskeller Würzburg ★★ FRANCONIAN/INTERNATIONAL   At this 500-year-old tavern with wood floors and frescoed walls tucked into the cellars of the Rathaus, some of the nooks and crannies are dark, paneled, and traditional, while other corners of the sprawling space are chicly urbane. The menu includes a lot of tasty Franconian fare—schnitzel stuffed with liverwurst and schäufele, pork shoulder with cabbage and potato dumplings—but also fans out to pastas and other international selections. Beverages stay close to home: Würzburger beer and lots of Franconian white wines. Get reservations for weekend meals.

Langgasse 1 (near the Alte Mainbrücke). www.wuerzburger-ratskeller.de. ② **0931/ 13021.** Main courses 8€–26€. Daily 11:30am–10:30pm.

Weinhaus Zum Stachel ★★ FRANCONIAN/INTERNATIONAL
No other wine house in Würzburg is as old as this one, dating from 1413, and none has a bloodier past. Some of the leaders of the Peasant War of 1524–25 stayed here, just off the Marktplatz, and their preferred weapon, the stachel (spike ball), gives the place its name and hangs out front. Some of the fearsome-looking spikes also hang over tables in the vine-draped outdoor courtyard, adding a bit of derring-do to sipping wines from the restaurant's own vineyards while tucking into generous portions of hearty classics like rump steak with onions and freshwater fish prepared according to old family recipes.

Gressengasse 1. www.weinhaus-stachel.de. ② **0931/52770.** Main courses 12€–23€. Tues–Sat 11am–midnight.

Side Trip from Würzburg

The Celts named the River Main some 3,000 years ago, using their word for "snake" to describe the meandering stream. West of Würzburg the river flows through lush farmland and vineyards. Along the banks are the once important port of Miltenberg and, in the hills above, the picturesque village of the Amorbach, surrounding a splendid abbey. While it's easy to see these two historic towns on a day trip from Würzburg, a couple of hotels here warrant an overnight stay.

GETTING THERE By **car** from Würzburg, take the A3 west and then B469 into Miltenberg and on to Amorbach (another 11km/7 miles south). There's at least one **train** connection per hour from Würzburg to Miltenberg (trip time: 90 minutes); frequent trains make the 12-minute trip from Miltenberg to Amorbach. For railway information, visit www. bahn.de or call ② **01805/996633.**

VISITOR INFORMATION Miltenberg's tourist office is in the Town Hall, Engelplatz 69 (www.miltenberg.info; ② **09371/404119**). From April through October it's open Monday to Friday 9am to 6pm and Saturday 10am to 4pm; from November through March, Monday to Friday 9am to 5pm. In Amorbach, the tourist information office is at Marktplatz 1 (www.amorbach.de; ② **09373/20940**) and is open from late March to November, Friday to Sunday 11:30am to 3:30pm.

MILTENBERG ★★

71km (44 miles) W of Würzburg

Half-timbered Miltenberg stretches for 2km (1 ½ miles) or so along the Main, tucked between the riverbanks and steep slopes of surrounding hillsides. In the town's 14th- and 15th-century heyday, the port boomed with river trade. Boats traveled along the Rhine into the Main, and were often off-loaded at Miltenberg for an overland trip toward Nürnberg, or vice versa. **Mainzertor** (Mainz Gate) at the west side of town and **Würzburg-tor** (Würzburg Gate) at the east end collected hefty tolls from traders, while the 500-year-old *weinhaus* on the town's market place and other warehouses filled up with valuable goods. Miltenberg also had a valuable export of its own, red sandstone, quarried in the surrounding hills and brought down to the riverbanks to be shipped throughout Europe. As you walk around, you'll notice that many of the town's finer residences are built of red sandstone.

Picturesque Miltenberg on the River Main.

The center of all this activity was the marketplace, or **Schnatterloch.** The narrow lanes around it comprise what's known as the **Schwarzviertel** (Black Quarter), since its beautiful, tall houses with high gables lie in the shadow of the hills and get little sunlight during the winter. This is the chilliest part of town, too, and on summer evenings a cool scented breeze almost always wafts in from the surrounding woodlands, bringing a little extra frisson to enjoying a beer or glass of wine at one of the cafes on the square. On the north side of the market square, you'll see the rococo residence that was the birthplace of composer Joseph Martin Kraus (1756–1792), often called the "Swedish Mozart" because he became a musical director in the royal court in Stockholm. Not only was Kraus' chamber music similar to Mozart's, he also died in his prime of tuberculosis. From the marketplace, with a red sandstone fountain to one side, the **Hauptstrasse** leads through the medieval town, passing many half-timbered houses in which the beams are laid out in the form of a St. Andrew's cross.

Museum Stadt Miltenberg/Museum Burg Miltenberg ★

MUSEUM   Miltenberg shows off its treasures on the marketplace (in

Museum Stadt Miltenberg) and in the castle above the town (in Museum Burg Miltenberg). On the marketplace, a former vicarage, a grammar school, and two Renaissance residences have been combined into a city museum, featuring such objects as a bronze statuette of the god Mars and other Roman artifacts, along with a 14th-century canoe and other relics from everyday life in the town over two millennia. The best testament to life in former centuries are the old rooms themselves, including a medieval kitchen and a latrine. In those days, chimneys extended only as high as the attics, where smoke gathered before seeping out through loose roof tiles, no doubt rendering life in the rooms below an odiferous and hazy business. A few galleries show off paintings by artists who have long been drawn to the picturesque town, as well as some glass paintings—religious scenes painted on reflective surfaces that were once popular with the faithful who, while believing that looking into a mirror was a sinful act of vanity, could catch a glimpse of themselves in a righteous way. An uphill path off the marketplace leads to the museum's other site, the white-walled, steep-roofed Schloss Miltenberg, surrounding a grassy courtyard backed by gardens. The old Knight's Hall and chambers are not a repository for the usual standard-issue tapestries and suits of armor, but instead are hung with 20th- and 21st-century paintings that compete with sweeping views over the town and river into the surrounding forests. Windows in the second-floor men's room might offer the best vistas in Germany.

Hauptstrasse 169–175. www.museen-miltenberg.de. ✆ **09371/668504.** Admission 4€ each museum, 6€ both. Museum Stadt Miltenberg: Apr–Oct, Tues–Sun 10am–5:30pm; Nov–Jan, Wed–Sun 11am–4pm. Museum Burg Miltenberg: Apr–Oct Tues–Fri 1pm–5:30pm, Sat–Sun 11am to 5:30pm; closed Nov–Mar.

AMORBACH ★

11km (7 miles) S of Miltenberg

At first glance, little Amorbach seems like just another quaint German town, a collection of half-timbered houses, some of them a bit artfully askew, adorned with flower boxes. Despite the humble appearance, however, Amorbach was once the seat of a rich and powerful Benedictine abbey, and the abbey church and some grand halls still stand here, attesting to its onetime importance. Helping finance such a display of wealth was the Tithe Barn (on Kellereigasse in the town center), built in 1488 to accommodate the so-called "Zenth," or "Tenth." That was the portion of the harvest and other holdings that peasants were required to pay to the church, and the crops, farm animals, and other goods were stored in this sturdy structure.

Abteikirche St. Maria ★★ RELIGIOUS SITE   An abbey was founded in Amorbach in 743, and over the centuries the holdings grew to include vast tracts of farmland and forest. The abbey and church were refurbished in the mid-18th century in a great show of wealth and power, with twin pepper-pot steeples and a grand stone staircase leading into the church to suggest the riches within. The humble faithful were made to feel their lowly station behind an ornate wrought iron grill that separated commoners from the monks and their aristocratic visitors. All could enjoy the sonorous output of what at the time was the world's largest organ, with 5,116 pipes. The ornate baroque stuccowork embellished with colorful frescoes is entirely original (this is unusual, as such work has usually been restored many times), and the plaster still bears the fingerprints and tool marks of the artisans. These workers obviously had a sense of fun and created many optical illusions, such as a saint's leg that seems to come right out of the ceiling. A fresco of scenes from the life of St. Benedict includes portraits of the master mason as well as the monk who kept the keys to the wine cellar, a bit of flattery intended to keep the fellow favorably disposed to the artists. High above the nave are the openings to two rooms, one on each side, both warmed by stoves—in the otherwise unheated church, one was reserved for the abbot and opened to his private apartments, and another more modest chamber was reserved for sick monks.

Kirchplatz. www.fuerst-leiningen.de. ✆ **09373/971545.** Admission 2.50. Mon–Fri 10am–4pm, Sat–Sun 11:30am–4pm.

Kloster Amorbach ★ PALACE   The abbey adjoining the church is actually a palace, with a double-height reception hall where the abbot received important visitors. Columns are painted with a rope motif, suggesting that faith binds us all together, but this room is really about worldly opulence, decorated with rich stuccowork and glittering with mirrors. A gallery could accommodate a 17-piece orchestra that provided musical accompaniment to banquets. In the library, doorways and staircases are concealed behind false bookcases, creating harmony and symmetry. Ceiling frescoes provide a look at world geography as it was known in the late 18th century, and also depict a strange-looking gadget consisting of glass spheres that could generate electricity; the device was the pride of the monastery, purchased for an astronomical sum. The abbey was dissolved in 1803 and became the palace of the princes of Leiningen, whose portraits line the hallways. Among them is a nephew of Queen Victoria. The royals still live in Amorbach, in a homier palace down the street.

Schlossplatz. www.fuerst-leiningen.de. ✆ **09373/971545.** Guided tour, conducted in German, 4.50€. Daily noon and 3pm.

WHERE TO STAY IN AMORBACH & MILTENBERG

Der Schafhof Amorbach ★★★   Benedictine monks settled onto this hillside around 1450, and little has changed since then, except that their quarters were converted to a country manor in 1721, which now is one of the region's finest hotels. Sheep still graze the meadows, and most of the produce and even the fish served in two excellent restaurants come from the property. Guest quarters are spread between the main house and a converted barn, showing off old stone work and heavy cross beams, with soothing views over the idyllic countryside. Many of the units are set up for families or can be combined, and some open to terraces. The extensive grounds are laced with walking paths that lead to a lake for summer swims.

Otterbachtal, Amorbach. (From Amorbach, follow N47, Nibelungenstrasse, west for 5km/3 mi). www.schafhof.de. © **09373/97330**. 24 units. 105€–180€ double. Continental breakfast included. **Amenities:** 2 restaurants; room service; sauna; Wi-Fi (free).

Schmuckkästchen Hotel ★★ One of the finest houses in Miltenberg, with a tall gable rising high above the marketplace, was built by a businessman in 1508 and over the years has been featured in photographs, travel posters, and a 1950s film classic, *The Spessart Inn*. Today its beautifully refurbished, crisply decorated guest rooms are prime perches for watching the comings and goings in the square below, and with the fine beds and comfortable armchairs, you will be tempted to stay put and do just that—when you do venture out, a path outside the front door leads up to the castle and the town museum is just across the square. Breakfast is served in the welcoming, richly paneled ground-floor café.

Marktplatz 185, Miltenberg. www.hotel-schmuckkaestchen.de. © **09371/5500**. 11 units. Double 115€. Buffet breakfast included. **Amenities:** Café; Wi-Fi (free).

WHERE TO EAT IN AMORBACH

Gasthaus zum Riesen ★★ GERMAN One of the region's old-time favorites has been serving since the 12th century, welcoming Emperor Frederick Barbarossa and many other esteemed personages throughout the centuries. No one's standing on ceremony, though, and the sprawling, dark paneled dining room hosts a mix of welcoming townsfolk who enjoy, often to noisy excess, the output of the local brewery, Brauhaus Faust. The kitchen accompanies the tasty brews with liver dumpling soup, platters piled high with pork filets and sausages, and other classics.

Hauptstrasse 99, Miltenberg. www.riesen-miltenberg.de. © **09371/989948**. Main courses 8€–19€. Mon–Wed 11am–midnight; Thurs–Sat 11am–1am.

THE UPPER ROMANTIC ROAD

Just outside Würzburg, the Romantic Road soon passes southwest through quietly beautiful, rolling farmland. The rural scenery is some of the prettiest on the route, and nestled among the gentle hills are two especially attractive villages, Weikersheim and Creglingen. These landscapes are part of the state of Baden-Württemberg. You'll cross back into Bavaria as you follow the Romantic Road southeast from Creglingen toward Rothenburg.

GETTING THERE From Würzburg, the Romantic Road follows Route 2310 to Wertheim, then Route 506 winding along the River Tauber to Tauberbischofsheim. From there, take Route 290 to Bad Mergentheim, then the L2251 along the Tauber to Weikersheim and Creglingen. Or you can drive directly from Würzburg to Bad Mergentheim via Route 19 to pick up this section of the road. Direct trains pull into Weikersheim from Würzburg every 2 hours throughout the day (trip time: 90 min.). For information about railway schedules, visit www.bahn.de or call © **01805/996633.**

VISITOR INFORMATION The tourist office in Weikersheim is at Marktplatz 7 (www.weikersheim.de; © **07934/10255**) and is open Monday, Wednesday, and Thursday 8am to 5; Tuesday 8am to 6pm; and Friday 8am to 1pm. The office in Creglingen is at Bad Mergentheimer Strasse 14 (www.creglingen.de; © **07933/631**) and is open Monday to Thursday 8am to noon and 2 to 6pm, and Friday 8am to 12:30pm and 2 to 4pm.

Weikersheim

40km (25 miles) S of Würzburg

A lovely little town alongside the River Tauber, Weikersheim offers a fancy-looking town hall and many half-timbered houses surrounding a broad marketplace. Pleasing as these village scenes are, however, they're overshadowed by one of the region's great showplaces, the magnificent Schloss Weikersheim and its beautiful gardens, overlooking the town just west of the Marktplatz.

Schloss Weikersheim ★★★ PALACE   In 1586, Count Wolfgang II of Hohenhofe reestablished Weikersheim as his family's main residence and ordered that its old moated castle be replaced with a new Renaissance palace. Though the count was a minor player in European politics, he had illusions of grandeur, creating a harmonious, three-winged assemblage that includes a **Rittersaal** (Knights' Hall) that is one of the most magnificent rooms in Germany. A frescoed bestiary on the ceiling frieze suggests the game that could be bagged in the surrounding woodlands, though the inclusion of lions, elephants, and some utterly fantastical creatures, all with stucco antlers, trunks, and horns protruding into the room, is a bit of over-promise. Representations of Ludwig and his wife,

Pull Over for a Soak

Bad Mergentheim would not really warrant a stop (except for a quick glance at its castle, a 16th-century stronghold of Teutonic knights) were it not for a shepherd named Franz Gehring. In 1826 Gehring stumbled upon a mineral spring that ever since has put the town on the map for spa goers, who swear by the soothing effects of its sodium sulfate-rich waters. Today the place to soak in the waters is **Solymar Therme**, Erienbachweg 3 (www.solymar-therme.de; © **07931/481-300**), a hedonistic thermal establishment on a hillside just outside town. Many of the mineral rich pools are indoor-outdoor, offering the chance to defy the weather from heated waters year-round, while whirlpools, saunas, steam rooms, fireside lounges, and extensive terraces turn a swim into an indulgence that would satisfy a Roman emperor. A swim is 4.50€, but it's worth splashing out for access to the saunas and other spalike facilities for 20€. Bad Mergentheim is 50km (30 miles) southwest of Würzburg and 12km (8 miles) north of Weikersheim.

Bad Mergentheim's main attractions are its mineral springs and spas.

Magdalena, recline like Roman nobles on either side of the entrance to their private chambers. Ludwig's bedroom is equipped with a toilet cabinet, making it one of the world's first en suite bathrooms, while Magdalena's room is frescoed with a scene of Cleopatra's suicide, with a fearsome-looking viper that must have inspired nightmares. Pictured among the ancients in the frescoes is the artisan who created the scenes, his spectacles covered in plaster dust. Count Carl Ludwig laid out the formal gardens in the 18th century, with paths and formal plantings stretching toward an orangerie. Taking their place among statues of gods and goddesses are the Weikersheimer Zerge (Weikersheim Dwarves), some rather unflattering representations of Ludwig's court.

Marktplatz 11. www.schloss-weikersheim.de *©* **07934/992950.** Admission 5.50€ adults, 2.80€ children, 14€ families. Apr–Oct, daily 9am–6pm; Nov–Mar, daily 10am–noon and 1–5pm.

Creglingen

16km (10 miles) E of Weikersheim

At first glance, Creglingen seems like another pretty, half-timbered backwater, and even if you're just embarking on a Romantic Road trip, you've already seen a few. (Little Röttingen, between Weikersheim and Creglingen, is more of a beauty, even with just a roadside glance at its acres of half-timbering, peaked roofs, and swaths of medieval wall.) But there was a time when pilgrims came to Creglingen from throughout Germany to pay homage at the Herrgottskirche (Chapel of Our Lord). Today's pilgrims are more likely to be art lovers, flocking here to gaze upon the chapel's extraordinary altar and other interior decorations. And once you're here, there are a couple of other quirky museums worth a stop.

Fingerhutmuseum (Thimble Museum) ★ MUSEUM   Just up the road from the Herrgottskirche is the largest collection of thimbles in Europe. Suppress a cynical yawn long enough to appreciate some genuinely enticing small works of art, including a thimble fashioned from bone 30,000 years ago, examples that the Romans made from metal, and others made of brass that was smelted in Creglingen during the Middle Ages. Victorian times were the heydays of thimble-making, with some elaborate items fashioned as richly plumed peacocks and others that did double duty as miniature chess sets. While signage is in German, a few key phrases are in English and the folks behind the counter are usually pleased to point out the top thimbles, admired by collectors around the world.

Kohlesmühle 6, Creglingen. www.fingerhutmuseum.de. *©* **07933/370.** Admission 2€. Apr–Oct, Tues–Sun 10am–12:30pm and 2–5pm; Nov, Dec, and Mar, Tues–Sun 1–4pm. Closed Jan.

Herrgottskirche (Chapel of Our Lord) ★★★ CHURCH   Back in 1384, a farmer plowing his fields claimed to have unearthed a sacred host, and the discovery was accompanied by the appearance of Jesus with a phalanx of angels. A church was built on the spot, Creglingen became a place of pilgrimage, and between 1505 and 1510 famed carver Tilman Riemenschneider (see box p. 252) was commissioned to create an altar. The work is one of his most exquisite creations, with figures representing the Assumption of the Blessed Virgin into heaven, framed by scenes from her life. The expressive figures catch the light in such a way that they seem animated, and the sculpture changes in appearance throughout the day with the shifting sun. On August 15, the feast of the Assumption, sunlight illuminates Mary's face in a heavenly glow. Beside the entrance of the church are figures that now seem innocent but at one time instilled fear in all who entered: two hens pecking at one another—a notice that any thoughts conflicting with church dogma were to be set aside—and a man thinking, a warning that no thought-challenging doctrines were allowed. Protruding from the right side exterior wall of the church is the so-called Tetzelkanzel (Tetzel pulpit), where Dominican friar Jacob Tetzel (1465–1519) preached to pilgrims assembled in the surrounding fields. Tetzel was essentially a snake-oil salesman who traded in indulgences, extracting fees from the faithful in exchange for the forgiveness of their sins. His mercenary practices led to a scandal that prompted Martin Luther's break with the church.

1km S of Creglingen on L1005. www.herrgottskirche.de. © **07933/338.** Admission 2€. Apr–Oct daily 9:15am–6pm; Nov–Mar Tues–Sun 1–4pm.

Lindleinturm ★ MUSEUM   Margarete Bottiger, who earned her living as a housemaid, lived in this tower from 1927 until her death in 1993, and the rooms—one to a floor, connected by ladderlike stairways—are just as she left them, filled with worn furniture, knickknacks, old appliances, and household products from long-ago decades. Ms. Bottiger shared her quarters with an unhealthful number of cats, who had access to the top-floor kitchen via a ladder from the adjacent town wall.

Stadtgraben 12, Crelingen. © **07933/451.** Admission free. Easter–Oct Fri 10am–noon, Sat–Sun 10am–noon and 2–5pm. Closed Nov–Easter.

Where to Stay & Eat on the Upper Romantic Road

Gasthaus Herrgottstal ★   Markus and Martina Hagenmüller operate this bright, airy guest house on a hillside overlooking Creglingen. The hosts make sure their home is as welcoming as everything else about this pleasant village, and their large well-equipped rooms, all with up-to-date bathrooms, share a pleasant downstairs terrace where drinks and meals from the in-house café are served in good weather. The guesthouse is popular with cyclists, who are offered free bike storage.

Herrgottstal 13, Creglingen. www.gaestehaus-herrgottstal.de. © **07933/528.** 9 units. From 60€ double. Breakfast included. Free parking. **Amenities:** Restaurant; Wi-Fi (free).

Hotel Laurentius ★★   It only seems right that Weikersheim should offer a place to stay that's as stylish as its beautiful palace—stylish in an entirely different way from the palace's frescoed salons, that is. These quarters are chic and spare, with lots of comfortable, contemporary flair that perfectly complements the beautiful marketplace and green hills just outside the large windows. All these attractive accommodations are different, though all are accented with beams, sloping ceilings, and other features of the centuries-old house; a few have terraces. Downstairs is a welcoming bar and bistro, an intimate gourmet restaurant, and a market that sells local wines and produce.

Marktplatz 5, Weikersheim. www.hotel-laurentius.de. © **07934/91080.** 13 units. From 95€ double. Buffet breakfast included. Free parking. **Amenities:** 2 restaurants; bar; room service; sauna; Wi-Fi (free).

ROTHENBURG OB DER TAUBER ★★★

51km (32 miles) SE of Würzburg, 20km (12 miles) SE of Creglingen

One of Europe's best-preserved medieval towns serves up a heady dose of romantic, fairytale Germany, with tall timbered houses that lean over cobbled lanes enclosed within ramparts and towers. Rothenburg thrived as a market town, specializing in wool and textiles, well into the 17th century. Then the Thirty Years War and the Black Death decimated the population and left the town impoverished and off the beaten path—a blessing in disguise, as it turned out. Without the money to spruce itself up or expand, Rothenburg's medieval town remained unchanged, as it if it had fallen into a deep slumber for the past 500 years or so.

Almost excessively picturesque, this little town has been sketched, painted, and photographed so many times that it often seems familiar even to visitors who never stepped through the gates before. Rothenburg inspired the village setting of Walt Disney's film *Pinocchio,* the Nazis cherished Rothenburg as the quintessential German village, and in World War II the American army, aware of the town's renowned beauty, negotiated a surrender to spare it from bombardment. Not

Rothenburg ob der Tauber's perfectly preserved medieval walls.

Rothenburg ob der Tauber

HOTELS
Altfränkische
  Weinstube **11**
Burg Hotel **7**
Gasthof Goldener
  Greifen **2**
Hotel Reichs-
  küchenmeister **9**

RESTAURANTS
Ratsstube **3**
Restaurant
  Meistertrunk **6**
Zum Pulverer **5**

ATTRACTIONS
Kriminalmuseum
  (Criminal Museum) **1**
Rathaus (Town Hall) **4**
Reichsstadtmuseum
  (Imperial City Museum) **10**
St-Jakobskirche
  (Church of St. James) **8**

surprisingly, almost everyone who comes to southern Germany follows the well-beaten path to Rothenburg, but that doesn't mean you shouldn't join their ranks. If you can, however, come off-season, between September and May, or simply linger in the evening after the day trippers leave, when life in this enchanting place resumes its normal pace.

Essentials

GETTING THERE   Access by car is the A7 from Würzburg. By train, Rothenburg is connected with hourly rail service to the junction of

Steinach, which has frequent connections to Würzburg (total trip time: 1 hr.) The trip to Munich takes 3 hours, 2½ hours to Frankfurt. **Note:** When trying to reach this gem of a town, some travelers have suddenly discovered themselves at a Rothenburg somewhere else in Germany. To avoid the confusion, make sure to ask for a ticket to "Rothenburg ob der Tauber." For train information, visit www.bahn.com or call *C* **01805/99663.**

VISITOR INFORMATION **Rothenburg Tourismus Service,** on the Marktplatz (www.rothenburg.de; *C* **09861/404800**), is open May to October, Monday to Friday 9am to 6pm, and Saturday and Sunday 10am to 5pm; from November to April, it's open Monday to Friday 9am to 5pm, and Saturday 10am to 1pm. Among other services, the tourist office can give you a map that shows the bike path along the Tauber River, so you can explore the surrounding countryside and some of the old mills surrounding Rothenburg. You can rent a bike at **Rad und Tat,** Bensenstrasse 17 (www.radtat.de; *C* **09861/87984**), for about 12€ per day.

WALKING TOUR Prime evening entertainment in Rothenburg is the **Night Watchman's Tour,** when a costumed guide is an escort for a walk along cobbled lanes and the ramparts for some wittily narrated time travel back to the Middle Ages (www.nightwatchman.de). From March to December, tours are conducted nightly in English, departing from the Marktplatz at 8pm. The cost is 7€ adults, 4€ kids 12 to 18, free for kids under 12.

Exploring Rothenburg ob der Tauber

Rothenburg is enchantingly contained within its old walls. If you're coming from Würzburg and Creglingen, you'll probably enter from the north, into Schrannenplatz; from the south and the train station, the entrance is Rodertor. **Marktplatz** is the center of the old town, presided over by the historic **Rathaus** (see p. 270). Streets around the Rathaus are lined with former warehouses, where grain and corn were stored to feed the town, along with wool and other goods. Just to the north of Marktplatz you'll find **St-Jakobskirche** (p. 271) and the **Reichsstadtmuseum** (p. 270) just to the north. To the south is the **Kriminalmuseum** (p. 269).

If you follow Schmiedgasse south through town, you walk right into the most iconic Rothenburg scene of all: The Plonleintor stands at a fork in the road, fronted by a high-gabled, half-timbered house, creating an irresistibly photogenic cityscape. From there, Spitalgasse leads into the most bucolic part of the old Rothenburg, a narrow appendage at the far southern end of town where the walls were extended to enclose the medieval hospital (now housing offices, with the Gothic chapel still in use) and a long-vanished castle. The grounds are now parkland, with views into the valley of the Tauber River.

For an overview of the town, take a walk on its ancient **ramparts,** on a covered walkway most of the way. The route runs between the massive 16th-century **Spitaltor** tower, at the south end of the Spitalgasse, to the **Klingentor,** at the northwest edge of the old town (this tower once housed the city's water tank). It should take about 45 minutes to walk its length. Along the way, you can climb the five-story-high **Rödertor** to a small exhibition describing an air raid in 1945 that leveled a large part of the eastern end of town; entry is 1.50€ for adults, 1€ for children.

Kriminalmuseum (Criminal Museum) ★ HISTORIC SITE   It paid to stay on the right side of the law in the Middle Ages, as these four floors devoted to medieval style law and order prove. Chastity belts, shame masks, terrifying torture devices, a beer barrel-shaped stockade for drunks, a cage for bakers whose bread was too small or too light—sadists with a historical bent will be in seventh heaven. The less bloodthirsty might enjoy some of the documents pertaining to historic court proceedings and commerce in Rothenburg, though the executioners' cloaks and masks suggest that medieval law might not have followed an "innocent until proven guilty" mantra. It seems that even a minor infraction could earn you a collar with inward-pointing spikes around your neck, a mouth

Rothenburg offers street after street of photo ops.

pear (a rough-hewn iron object) inserted in your mouth to punish lying and slander, or an outfit of chicken feathers, a mark of promiscuity. The 1395 hospital that houses the museum was redone in 1718, giving Rothenburg its only Baroque facade.

Burggasse 3–5. www.kriminalmuseum.rothenburg.de. © **09861/5359.** Admission 4€ adults, 2.80€ students, 2.40€ children 6–17. Open daily, Apr 11am–5pm; May–Oct 10am–6pm; Mar and Dec 1–4pm; Jan–Feb and Nov 2–4pm.

Rathaus (Town Hall) ★ LANDMARK

Part Gothic, from 1240, and part Renaissance, from 1572, Rothenburg's town hall is decorated with intricate friezes and a large stone portico opening onto the main market square. A climb to the top of the 60m (200-ft.) tower provides a view that sweeps across town and far into the Tauber Valley. You'll be standing where sentries once kept an eye out for fires, ringing the bell every quarter-hour to prove that they were awake and on the job. Today a clock atop the adjoining Councilor's Hall keeps time for the town, putting on a show at the top of the hour between 10am and 10pm. As far as glockenspiel shows in Germany go, this one is a bit lackluster but lends a charming bit of local color: two doors in the gable flip open, chimes sound, and out come *Bürgermeister* Nusch and the Catholic general who challenged him to consume a huge tankard of beer in order to save the town during the Thirty Years War (you'll learn the full story at the Reichsstadtmuseum, p. 270). In the halls below, councilors once conducted the business of the prosperous city state, one of Europe's great centers of commerce by 1400; their private quarters included their own tavern (now housing the tourist office, see p. 268). Notice the iron bars on the side of the Rathaus: These originally served as measuring tools, marking off els (the length between the elbow and fingertips, roughly a yard) and rods (the equivalent of four meters). These were used to measure goods brought into town so that tolls and taxes could be assessed.

Marktplatz. © **09861/40492.** Admission: Rathaus free; tower 1.50€ adults, 1€ children. Rathaus open Mon–Fri 8am–6pm. Tower hours: Apr–Oct daily 9:30am–12:30pm and 1–5pm; Dec daily noon–3pm; Nov and Jan–Mar Sat–Sun and holidays noon–3pm.

Reichsstadtmuseum (Imperial City Museum) ★ HISTORIC SITE

In 1631, during the Thirty Years' War, the Protestant city of Rothenburg was captured by General Tilly, commander of the armies of the Catholic League. He promised to spare the town from destruction if one of the town burghers could drink down a huge tankard full of beer in one draft. *Bürgermeister* Nusch accepted the challenge and succeeded, thus saving Rothenburg. The tankard—with a capacity of 3.5 liters, more than 7 pints—is part of the historical collection of Rothenburg, housed in this 13th-century Dominican nunnery. Impressive as the vessel is, the story,

raise a toast **TO THE *BÜRGERMEISTER***

Rothenburg's famous 17th-century drinking binge, in which the *Bürgermeister* (mayor) downed a tankard of beer to save the town, is re-enacted in a play, "Die Meistertrunk" ("The Master Draught"), first performed in 1881. These days it's part of a festival that takes place every September/October. Hundreds of citizens dress up in period costumes and, of course, drink beer.

like many juicy historical accounts, is apocryphal—Rothenburg actually simply paid off the invading troops to spare the town. Historians do, however, verify the past purpose of the barrel out front, where the nuns left bread for the poor and women left unwanted babies. The convent cloisters are especially well preserved, as is the medieval kitchen, said to be the oldest in Germany. Take time to study the 12-panel, 1494 "Rothenburg Passion," by local painter Martinus Schwartz, which depicts scenes from the suffering of Christ; soldiers and bystanders are dressed in medieval garb, while some of the backdrops are scenes of old Rothenburg. Paintings by Englishman Arthur Wasse (1854–1930) show off Rothenburg as picture perfect and romantic as today's postcards do. Wasse studied art in Munich and became so enamored of Rothenburg that he spent most of the rest of his life here. His paintings and reproductions were extremely popular in England, and by the late 19th century had inspired multitudes of travelers to visit Rothenburg.

Klosterhof 5. www.reichsstadtmuseum.rothenburg.de. ℗ **09861/939043.** Admission 4€ adults, 3€ students and children 6–18, 8€ family ticket. Apr–Oct daily 10am–5pm; Nov–Mar daily 1–4pm.

St-Jakobskirche (Church of St. James) ★ CHURCH   Rothenburg lies on the pilgrim trail to Santiago de Compostela in Spain, site of the remains of St. James (Jakob). The town's main church, infused with mellow light from its original stained glass, has long been a stop on the route, completed in 1471 with soaring spires and a high vaulted ceiling that draws the eye up toward heaven. At the apex of the ceiling of the choir, notice a deliberate imperfection in the stones, which was done as a symbol of faith—the last stone veers slightly to the left, just as the head of Christ leaned toward the left as he hung on the cross. Color-saturated medieval stained glass depicts biblical scenes, including one with a local twist—on the right side of the choir is a scene of the Israelites in the desert, with angels throwing them not manna but pretzels. Throughout the Middle Ages, the church's big draw was the Reliquary of the Holy Blood (1270), a rock-crystal capsule said to contain three drops of the blood of Jesus Christ. Würzburg sculptor Tilman Riemenschneider (see box p. 252) crafted the Altar of the Holy Blood in intricately carved wood to house the shrine. The center panel depicts the Last Supper, with Christ and the disciples set against background arches that mimic the windows of this church. The figures are touchingly human, right down to the veined feet. You'll notice Riemenschneider adds a twist: Judas, not Christ, sits at the center of the table, suggesting that God is willing to shed his grace even on sinners. It's easy to miss the apostle John, as he rests beneath the rest of the grouping, asleep with his head in the lap of Christ, the great giver of comfort. The so-called Twelve Apostles Altar also depicts the disciples, among many scenes on its colorful panels, but most riveting is a scenario of the body of St. James being carried into Rothenberg, with the Rathaus in the background—the oldest known rendering of the city.

Klostergasse 15. ℰ **09861/700620.** Admission 2€ adults, .50€ children. Apr–Oct Mon–Sat 9am–5:30pm, Sun 11am–5:30pm; Dec daily 10am–5pm; Nov and Jan–Mar daily 10am–noon and 2–4pm.

Where to Stay in Rothenburg ob der Tauber

Altfränkische Weinstube ★★   Six rooms in a 650-year-old house on a quiet back street exude charm and comfort, with heavy beams, polished armoires, oil paintings, and spruce bathrooms with deep tubs. A generous breakfast next to a blue ceramic stove nicely starts off a day. For other meals step into the *weinstub* (wine tavern) downstairs, where Franconian specialties are served next to an open fire in winter and on a romantic terrace in the summer. If you're feeling homesick, stick around on a Wednesday evening when the local English club meets at the hotel.

Kloisterhof 7. www.altfraenkische.de. ℰ **09861/6404.** 6 units. 75€–82€ double. Buffet breakfast included. Free parking. **Amenities:** Restaurant; Wi-Fi (free).

Burg Hotel ★★   Parts of this ancient stone house tucked into the walls date to the 9th century. The views over the valley of the River Tauber probably haven't changed much since then, and they take center stage in the bright, aerie-like breakfast room, a small terrace, and many of the guest rooms, including a multi-floor suite. Others look over the adjoining monastery garden, and all are thoughtfully furnished to provide a lot of traditional luxury. Just across the street are the beautiful gardens and excellent restaurant of the Burg Gartenpalais, another excellent hotel owned and operated by the same people.

Klostergasse 1–3. www.burghotel.eu. ℰ **09861/94890.** 15 units. 110€–180€ double. Buffet breakfast included. Free parking. **Amenities:** Sauna; spa; Wi-Fi (free).

Gasthof Goldener Greifen ★   A medieval mayor of Rothenburg is your host, in spirit at least, in these no-frills but comfortable accommodations in his former home. Some of the rooms in a wing extending into the garden are small and pretty basic, and priced accordingly, while those in the main house are high-ceilinged, rather grandly proportioned, and geared to families (some sleep five). All have attractive and sensible furnishings, and many are enlivened with wooden ceilings and other character-supplying features. Most atmospheric is the 650-year-old common room and the breakfast room, fitted out of the mayor's office (note the toasty closet designed to keep his parchments dry). The in-house restaurant specializes in Franconian fare with tasty dishes like marinated beef, and moist roast goose leg soaked in a savory gravy, and a side of red kraut and potato dumplings. Try it with the bold Taubertäler red wine.

Obere Schmiedgasse 5 (off Marktplatz). www.gasthof-greifen-rothenburg.de. © **09861/228.** 14 units. 65€–98€ double. Buffet breakfast included. Free parking. Closed Dec 22–Jan 3. **Amenities:** Restaurant; Wi-Fi (free).

Hotel Reichsküchenmeister ★ Deep armchairs, lots of blond wood, and firm beds topped with fluffy duvets makes these traditional, bright rooms extremely comfortable without being stuffy or overfurnished. They're all different, vary considerably in size, and occupy a centuries-old merchant's house and a slightly less desirable (and less expensive) house across the street. A sauna, steam room, and whirlpool are welcome tonics after a day pounding the cobblestones. The excellent in-house restaurant spreads into a beautiful beer garden in warm weather.

Kirchplatz 8 (near St. Jakobskirche). www.reichskuechenmeister.com. © **09861/9700.** 45 units. 150€–240€ double. Buffet breakfast. Parking 5€ in the lot; 8€ in the garage. **Amenities:** Restaurant; bar; bikes; Jacuzzi; sauna; Wi-Fi (free).

Where to Eat in Rothenburg

Many bakeries in town sell the local pastry called *Schneeballen* (snowballs), a tasteless blob of pastry coated in sugar and cinnamon. Save your euros and spend your calories otherwise, maybe for a beer.

Ratsstube ★ FRANCONIAN Dark wood, vaulted ceilings, lots of copper, and more antlers than you'd find in a zoo's deer house provide a true tavern atmosphere in this character-filled old place. A center-of-town location across the square from the Rathaus keeps the kitchen busy throughout the day, and the *Sauerbraten,* game, and other local favorites on the long menu board are very well done.

Marktplatz 6. www.ratsstuberothenburg.de. © **09861/5511.** Main courses 10€–15€. Mon–Sat 9am–10pm; Sun 9am–6pm.

Restaurant Meistertrunk ★ FRANCONIAN A wood-paneled stube on the ground floor of an elegant hotel specializes in local cooking, along the lines of *Shäuffle,* pork shoulder roasted with onions and beer, and *Maultaschensuppe* (stuffed pasta in broth). These homey offerings taste all the better in warm weather, when meals are served in a beautiful rose garden that seems like country retreat.

Herngasse 26. www.burggartenpalais.de. © **09861/874-7430.** Main courses 9€–18€. Daily noon–2pm and 6–9pm.

Zum Pulverer ★ FRANCONIAN   The polished, woody interior of this restaurant, dating from 1902, is not really that old by Rothenburg standards, but the chairs with hand-carved backs depicting the town's medieval councilors and other idiosyncratic touches evoke a long-gone era. The straightforward menu sticks to bratwurst and other basic fare; the kitchen outdoes itself with cakes and pastries, all made in-house.
Herrngasse 31. www.zumpulverer.de. ✆ **09861/976162.** Main courses 8€–12€. Mon and Wed–Fri 5–10:45pm and Sat–Sun noon–11:30pm.

Shopping

Every day is Christmas in Rothenberg, or so you'll think when you step into Käthe Wohlfahrt's **Weihnachtswerkstatt (Christmas Workshop),** Herrngasse 1 (www.wohlfahrt.com; ✆ **098614090**), or into its across-the-street annex. Wohlfahrt is a national institution, with cozy emporia in towns around Germany and stalls at Christmas markets. Here in Rothenberg the shops are ablaze with glittering trees and carols that even in summer inspire hordes of shoppers in shorts and T-shirts to fill their baskets with ornaments, many exquisitely handcrafted, along with everything from coy clothing to cuckoo clocks. If you wish to turn a shopping spree into an educational experience, climb the stairs to the **Deutsches Weihnachtsmuseum** (German Christmas Museum; www.weihnachts museum.de; ✆ **09861/409–365**) for a serious look at how Christmas became such a big blowout—from the first documented tree trimming, in Strasbourg in 1605, to the development of cheap candle wax in 1818 that allowed the middle classes to illuminate trees the same way aristocrats did. By the late 19th century, you'll learn, it was believed in all good German households that "Trees must shine, glitter, sparkle, and dazzle so that you must shade your eyes"—a belief the Wohlfahrt folks obviously still take to heart. The museum is open April to Christmas, daily 10am to 5pm; from January to March, it's open Monday to Saturday 10am to 4pm, and Sunday 10:30am to 4pm. Admission is 4€ adults, 2€ children 6 to 11, 7€ families, with 2 adults.

For another dose of cuteness, head down the street to **Teddyland,** Herrngasse 10 (www.teddyland.de; ✆ **09861/8904**), with more than 5,000 stuffed bears, the largest teddy bear population in Germany. Bear images are also printed on everything from T-shirts to bags and watches.

THE MIDDLE ROMANTIC ROAD

South of Rothenburg, the Romantic Road crosses gentle countryside to three historic towns. Two of them, Dinkelsbühl and Nördlingen, share with Rothenburg the distinction of being the only towns in Germany to be entirely surrounded by their walls; they supply enough half-timbered charm to supply the most voracious appetite for medieval ambiance.

Donauwörth has been less fortunate in retaining its historic architecture, but what remains is lovely, and the town is beautifully situated at the confluence of the Wörnitz and Danube Rivers.

GETTING THERE   If you're driving, follow the "Romantische Strasse" signs south from Rothenburg ob der Tauber. Nördlingen and Donauwörth lie on main train routes; Nördlingen is 1 hour from Augsburg, while Donauwörth is 35-45 minutes from Augsburg. For Dinkelsbühl, the nearest train station is in Dombühl; a local bus from Dombühl to Dinkelsbühl takes about 30 minutes. Visit www.bahn.de or call ℂ **01805/996633** for schedules.

VISITOR INFORMATION   In **Dinkelsbühl,** the tourist office shares quarters with the town museum in the Altrathaus on Altrahausplatz (www.dinkelsbuehl.de; ℂ **09851/902440**); it's open daily, 10am to 5pm. In **Nördlingen,** the office is at Marktplatz 2 (www.noerdlingen. de; ℂ **09081/84116**); it's open daily 9am to 6pm. The tourist office in **Donauwörth** is at Rathausgasse 1 (www.donauwoerth.de; ℂ **0906/ 789151**) and is open May to September, weekdays 9am to noon and 1 to 6pm, weekends 3 to 5pm; from October to April, hours are Monday to Thursday 9am to noon and 1 to 5pm, and Friday 9am to 1pm.

Dinkelsbühl ★

105km (65 miles) SE of Würzburg, 45km (27 miles) S of Rothenburg

Like nearby Rothenburg, smaller Dinkelsbühl is beautifully preserved in its medieval glory, but it's not nearly as popular—which makes a walk along its cobblestone streets, past half-timbered houses painted in pastel colors, even more like stepping into an authentic slice of old Germany.

A complete ring of **medieval fortifications** surrounds the town, with 18 towers offering views of the sea of sienna-tiled roofs with storks roosting on top. One compelling reason to stay here overnight is so that you can make the rounds with the night watchman, who, from April to October, begins his duties at 9pm in front of the münster church on Marktplatz (from November through March, the watchman only works on Saturday evenings; there's no charge for joining him).

The huge late-Gothic **Münster St. Georg ★**, completed at the very end of the 15th century, seems out of proportion for such a small town, reflecting the enormous wealth that once poured in from trade— Dinkelsbühl was on the lucrative route between Frankfurt and Wurzburg and the south. Tradesmen and guilds donated the funds, convinced that doing so would help ensure eternal salvation. You'll see signs of various crafts throughout the church, including a stained-glass window in the rear that's decorated with pretzels, a gift of bakers. A memorial near the entrance commemorates Christoph von Schmidt (1768–1854), a

Horse-drawn "tourist wagons" carry sightseers around picturesque Dinkelsbühl.

popular children's book author who also wrote the words to the Christmas carol "O Come all Ye Faithful."

Dinkelsbuhl was popular with late-19th and early 20th-century painters, whose works hang among exhibits on the Reformation and the Thirty Years' War in the **Haus der Geschichte Dinkelsbühl ★**, Altrathausplatz 14 (www.hausdergeschichte-dinkelsbühl.de; **℗ 09851 902 440**). Especially appealing are the canvases by Joseph Kühn Jr., who moved to Dinkelsbühl in 1901. He bequeathed his personal collection, including a work that would be the pride of any big-city museum— the expressionist masterpiece *Bäuerlinsturm* (1938) by Karl Schmidt-Rotluff, one of the founders of the Brücke art movement.

Dinkelsbühl has long had a soft spot for the little ones, especially since the Thirty Years War, when a contingent of children successfully pleaded with a Swedish general about to lay siege to spare their town. Dinkelsbühl re-enacts the event for 10 days in July during the **Kinderzeche** (Children's Festival; www.kinderzeche.de).

Nördlingen ★
30km (19 miles) S of Dinkelsbühl

Still surrounded by its original walls, Nördlingen looks like another charming relic from the Middle Ages. Even so, the town's big day came earlier . . . quite a bit earlier, as in 15 million years ago. That's when a meteorite at least half a mile in diameter crashed to Earth at more than 72,500kmph (45,000 mph). The impact sent debris flying as far as the present-day Czech Republic and created a crater three miles deep, called the Ries. The impact site soon filled with water and sludge, but as you approach Nördlingen along the Romantic Road you can still see how the town lies at the center of a vast depression, surrounded by fields laid out in a vaguely circular pattern. The Ries is the most researched meteorite-impact site on earth; its scientific importance is explored in the **Rieskrater-Museum ★**, Eugene-Shoemaker-Platz 1 (www.rieskratermuseum. de; ✆ **09081/84710**). Among displays documenting the gee-whiz aspects of the event (the meteorite hit the earth with 200,000 times the force of the atomic bomb dropped on Hiroshima) are photos of Buzz Aldrin and Neil Armstrong in the countryside outside town, training for the *Apollo 11* lunar mission. The geology around Nördlingen resembles that of the moon, which is much more prone to meteorite impacts than Earth is. The museum is open Tuesday to Sunday from 10am to 4:30pm (from November to April it closes between noon and 1:30pm). Admission is 4€ for adults, 1.50€ for students and children ages 6 through 11, and free for children 5 and under.

More meteor trivia in Nördlingen: **St. Georgskirche ★**, on the southern side of the Marktplatz, is the largest building in the world to be built from suevite, a rock found in meteorite craters. Scientists were clued in to the town's remarkable geological history when they found coesite, a gas that can only be formed by a meteorite impact, in the church's building stones. The baptismal font is from 1492, a significant date in Nördlingen's fortunes, since the founding of trade routes to the New World eventually caused a decline in Nördlingen's prominence as a trading center, a decline hastened by war and disease. It's free to visit the church, which is open Easter to October, Monday to Friday 9:30am to 12:30pm and 2 to 5pm, and Saturday and Sunday 9:30am to 5pm.

Until the late 15th century, Nördlingen was such a significant trading center that it hosted a famous trade fair, the *Pfingstmesse,* for ten days every spring, bringing merchants and buyers from throughout Germany and the rest of Europe. Streets and squares were so packed that a temporary bridge was constructed between the Rathaus and the so-called Bread and Dance House (part banquet hall and part marketplace/warehouse)— the span's disastrous collapse during one fair is well documented. Throughout the old town you can still see the massive warehouses once used to store corn and other goods. Especially impressive is the **Klösterle,** just north of the Marktplatz, a Franciscan monastery that after the Reformation became a granary. The façade is brightly painted, so effectively that it takes some time to realize that some of the windows

The cunningly painted façade of the Klösterle, a former monastery and now a hotel in Nördlingen.

are mere decoration. The mason who undertook a medieval renovation is pictured, too, giving instructions to his carpenters.

Rising high above town is the 90m (300-ft.) **Daniel tower ★★**. At night, every half hour between 10pm and midnight, the town watchman calls out from the steeple, *"So G'sell so"* (roughly, "So that's how it is"). The phrase comes from an incident in 1440, when a woman came out at night to look for her pigs and found them rubbing against the open town gates. As it turns out, guards had left the gates open to give access to would-be invaders. Her cry roused the townsfolk, the guards were executed, and ever since the phrase has been a reassuring anthem that someone is keeping an eye out for trouble. You can climb the tower via steep stone steps and seemingly endless wooden staircases, passing a medieval winch used to hoist up building materials. At the top are panoramic views that nicely show off rooftops, the town walls, and the shape of the surrounding Ries. You'll probably meet Wildenstein, a charming tomcat who prowls the heights. You can climb the tower daily from April to October, 9am to 5pm (later in summer); admission is 3€ for adults and 2€ for students and children.

You can also get a nice look at Nördlingen from the covered parapet on top of the perfectly preserved **walls;** they would have been demolished had it not been for an 1826 edict from the Bavarian king Ludwig I, an ardent medievalist. Along the way, you'll pass 11 towers, five fortified gates, and get bird's-eye views of tidy cottage gardens.

Donauwörth

40km (25 miles) S of Nördlingen

This prosperous and appealing little city at the confluence of the Danube and Wörnitz Rivers had the misfortune to become a center of weapons manufacture during World War II, creating a prime target for Allied bombings that destroyed most of the now-reconstructed historic center. While Donauwörth does not have the same authentic medieval ambience of other stops along the Romantic Road, the town offers up enough historical flavor and riverside scenery, along with a few landmarks, to fill a couple of hours.

Actually, as quiet and affable as Donauwörth seems, this onetime river port on trade routes between Nürnberg and Munich has a surprisingly bloody past. In 1606, a Lutheran mob here attacked a Catholic procession, helping to foment the Thirty Years War, the religious conflict that more or less devastated central Europe. In another major European conflict, the early 18th-century War of Spanish Secession, more than 5,000 French troops drowned at Donauwörth while trying to swim across the Danube to escape the British.

As befits its position on the Romantic Road, Donauwörth is also the setting for a famous tale of love gone awry. As legend has it, around 1260, Maria Brabant was sequestered in a castle on Mongold Rock near what remains of the town walls (a plaque marks the spot), while her husband, Duke Louis II of Bavaria, traveled his realm. It seems Maria wrote two letters, one to her husband and one to a platonic male friend. A messenger mixed up the letters and the duke, getting the wrong impression, did what any red-blooded male of the time would do: he killed the messenger, rushed home, threw a maid off the battlements, and had his wife beheaded. To his credit, he later repented and founded a monastery near Munich.

Today, Donauwörth lays on plenty of charm, with the remains of its oldest quarter, the Ried, tucked onto a little island reached through the **Riederstor.** On the mainland, the **Reichsstrasse** is lined with proud medieval burgher houses, most of which are reconstructions—you can tell which ones are authentically old because their facades tip and lean a bit. At the top of the old town is **Klosteranlage Heilig Kreuz ★**, or Monastery of the Holy Cross, founded in 1030 when the town's Count Mangold I came back from the Crusades with what was purportedly a sliver of the cross upon which Christ died. (Such fragments were wildly popular across Europe and inspired a real whopper of a medieval yarn, *The Legend of the True Cross,* that included such characters as the Queen of Sheba and King Solomon and imbued the wooden shards with all sorts of mystical powers.) The present church is itself a bit of lavish embellishment, dating from 1720, with every surface covered in elaborate stucco decoration and gilt statuary. The church is open daily from 9am to 6pm and admission is free.

Donauwörth is also home to the **Käthe-Kruse-Puppen-Museum** ★, Pflegstrasse 21a (© **0906/789170**), a showplace for one of the world's most prestigious doll companies. Käthe Kruse set up production around 1910, after getting her start making dolls for her nine children; she moved operations to Donauwörth from East Germany in the 1950s. Dolls are still made by hand (artisans must train for three years before being allowed to paint the eyes) and today's products don't vary greatly from the prized pieces you'll see in the displays. Signage is in German, but the charming specimens speak for themselves. From April to October, the museum is open Tuesday to Sunday 2 to 5pm; November to March it is open Wednesday, Saturday, and Sunday 2 to 5pm. Entrance costs 2.50€ for adults, 1.50€ for children and students. A little shop on the premises sells a small selection of dolls.

Where to Stay & Eat Along the Middle Romantic Road

Hotel Goldene Rose ★★ This character-filled old inn on the marketplace in Dinkelsbühl has been receiving guests since 1450 and over the years has hosted King Ludwig I of Bavaria, Queen Victoria, and many other luminaries. These days the ambiance is a little less regal, though sleeping in one of the oldest hotels in Germany certainly imparts a provenance to the homey old rooms, many overlooking the main square and münster. The best are the grand, high-ceilinged second-floor rooms in front of the house. Downstairs is a pleasant restaurant and the Braustuberl, where beams are carved with images of craftsmen and carp is served three ways (best with horseradish and apples).
Marktplatz 4, Dinkelsbühl. www.hotel-goldene-rose.de. © **09851/57750.** 34 units. 85€–150€ double. Buffet breakfast included. Free parking. **Amenities:** 2 restaurants; bar; Wi-Fi (free).

Hotel Weiss Rose ★★ Stay at this old inn long enough and you might be inspired to pick up a paint brush—the artists who turned Dinkelsbühl into a summer art colony a century ago boarded here, and some left their work behind in the dark-paneled dining room as payment. Terms these days are more in keeping with modern times, as are the bright, crisply decorated rooms where plain furniture and beds topped with fluffy duvets sit on shiny wood floors. Art students still stay here in the summer, when a beer or meal can be the occasion for a friendly gathering of kindred spirits.
Steingasse 12, Dinkelsbühl. www.deutsches-haus-dkb.de. © **09851/579890.** 12 units. 100€ double. Rates include buffet breakfast. **Amenities:** Restaurant; Wi-Fi (free).

NH Klösterle Nördlingen ★ This hotel's origins as a 13th-century monastery are all but lost amid its modern wings and efficient atmosphere, though views onto Nördlingen's gabled houses and steep red roofs will keep you in a medieval frame of mind. Rooms are spacious but big-chain business hotel in style, with all the typical comforts. A big warm-weather terrace and the proximity of the town's attractions will lure you outside.

Beim Klösterle 1, Nördlingen. www.nh-hotels.de. ✆ **09081/87080.** 98 units. 80€– 145€ double. Buffet breakfast included. Parking 10€. **Amenities:** 2 restaurants; bar; bikes; exercise room; indoor pool; room service; sauna; Wi-Fi (free).

Weib's Brauhaus ★★ Female brewmasters put this popular spot on the map, where house-made beers emerge from copper vats tucked beneath the old beams. The big friendly room is as popular with diners as it is with drinkers, and a few dishes, including the popular Weib's Töpfle ("woman's pot") uses the house brew as a major ingredient, in this case as the base of a sauce that tops tender *Schwein Rückensteak* (pork loin).

Unter Schmiedgasse 13, Dinkelsbühl. www.weibsbrauhaus.de. ✆ **09851/579490.** Main courses 8€–12€. Thurs–Mon 11am–1am, Wed 6pm–1am.

Wirtshaus Meyers-Keller ★ CONTINENTAL Despite the homey sounding "wirsthaus" label, Nördlingen's best address for dining (in an old inn 2km/1¼ miles outside the walls) is all about refined taste and restrained modern style that highlights the inspired creations of chef Joachim Kaiser. Ingredients are seasonal and for the most part local, with an emphasis on organic meat and wild seafood, served a la carte or on several creative tasting menus.

Marienhöhe 8, Nördlingen. www.meyerskeller.de. ✆ **09081/4493.** Reservations required. Main courses 16€–24€; fixed-price menus 75€–140€. Wed–Sun 11:30am– 2pm; Tues–Sun 5:30–10pm.

AUGSBURG ★

63km (38 miles) S of Donauwörth, 177km (106 miles) S of Rothenburg, 68km (42 miles) NW of Munich

The only big city along the Romantic Road, with a population of about 260,000, Augsburg was founded some 2,000 years ago by the Roman emperor Augustus and hit its cultural heyday during the Renaissance. If you're on the trail of half-timbered quaintness, you may not be tempted to linger for too long in Augsburg, but don't discount it too quickly— there's plenty to see along its lively, cosmopolitan streets.

Essentials

GETTING THERE From Donauwörth, take Rte. 2 south to Augsburg. Access from Munich and Frankfurt is via the east-west A8 autobahn.

About 90 InterCity trains arrive here daily from all major German cities, including 60 a day from Munich (trip time: 30–50 min.) and 35 from Frankfurt (3–4½ hr.). For train information, visit www.bahn.com or call © **01805/996633.**

VISITOR INFORMATION   The tourist information office is at Rathausplatz 1 (www.augsburg-tourismus.de; © **0821/502070**). From April to mid-October, it's open Monday to Friday 9am to 6pm, Saturday 10am to 5pm, and Sunday 10am to 3pm. From mid-October to March, it's open Monday to Friday 9am to 5pm, Saturday 10am to 5pm, and Sunday 10am to 3pm.

Exploring Augsburg

Most of the sights in Augsburg are on or near **Rathausplatz,** where the **Rathaus** is a formidable presence—eight stories high and commanding one end of the vast space, it must have seemed like a skyscraper when it was first built in 1620, and it's still astonishing. The visual grandeur doesn't diminish in the main town meeting hall, the Goldener Saal (Golden Chamber), with a gold-leaf coffered "floating" ceiling (it hung from iron chains) and huge wall frescoes. Adjacent to the Rathaus, the **Perlachturm** is a soaring spire capped by a distinctive dome called an "Augsburg onion." A climb to the top rewards you with a marvelous view of the old town center. Admission is 2€ adults, 1€ children 7–14, free for children 6 and under. The tower is open daily from 10am to 6pm.

Leading south off Marktplatz, the town's main street, **Maximilianstrasse,** is known as the Imperial Mile and graced with old burghers' houses and three fountains by the Renaissance Dutch sculptor Adrien de Vries. The **Fugger-Stadtpalais (Fugger City Palace),** with the main entrance at Maximilianstrasse 36, was the one-time home of the town's wealthiest Renaissance family (see box p. 286). Its many rooms are built around courtyards, and you can step into one of them, the Damenhof, or Ladies' Court. Given the family's connections with the Medicis, it's perhaps not by accident that this courtyard evokes the garden of a lavish Florentine palazzo.

Dom St. Maria ★ CHURCH   A five-minute walk north of the Marktplatz, the cathedral of Augsburg has the distinction of containing some of the oldest stained-glass windows in the world. Dating from the 12th century, these severe but colorful panels in the south transept depict Old Testament prophets. Old as they are, they are younger than the cathedral itself, which was begun in 944, was partially rebuilt in Gothic style in the 14th century, and later redone in the Baroque style. A 19th-century remodeling introduced neo-Gothic elements, when many of the cathedral's artworks, including an altarpiece by Hans Holbein the Elder, were acquired to augment the Gothic ambiance. The original 11th-century

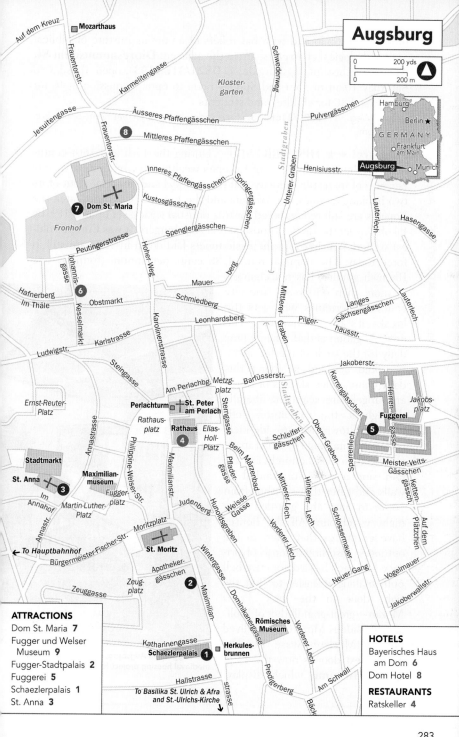

Augsburg

Auf dem Kreuz
Mozarthaus
Frauentorstr.
Karmelitengasse
Jesuitengasse
Äusseres Pfaffengässchen
Kloster-garten
Schwedenweg
Pulvergässchen
Mittleres Pfaffengässchen **8**
Frauentorstr.
Inneres Pfaffengässchen
Kustosgässchen
Springergässchen
Henisiusstr.
Stadtgraben
Unterer Graben
Lauterlech
Hasengasse
7 Dom St. Maria
Fronhof
Peutingerstrasse
Spenglergässchen
Spenglergässchen
Johannis-gasse
Hoher Weg
Mauer-berg
Langes Sachsengässchen
Lauterlech
Hafnerberg
Im Thäle
6
Kesselmarkt
Obstmarkt
Schmiedberg
Leonhardsberg
Mittlerer Graben
Pilger-hausstr.
Ludwigstr.
Karlstrasse
Karolinenstrasse
Steingasse
Am Perlachbg.
Metzg-platz
Barfüsserstr.
Jakoberstr.
Stadtgraben
Karrengässchen
Herren-gasse
Jakobs-platz
Ernst-Reuter-Platz
Annastrasse
Philippine-Welser-Str.
Perlachturm
Rathaus-platz
St. Peter am Perlach
Rathaus **4**
Elias-Holl-Platz
Stengasse
Pfladergasse
Beim Märzenbad
Schleifer-gässchen
Oberer Graben
Fuggerei **5**
Sparrenlech
Meister-Veits-Gässchen
Stadtmarkt
Maximilian-museum
Fugger-platz
Maximilianstr.
Judenberg
Weisse Gasse
Hunoldsgraben
Mittlerer Lech
Hinterer Lech
Schlossermauer
Ketten-gässch.
Auf dem Plätzchen
St. Anna **3**
Im Annahof
Annastr.
Martin-Luther-Platz
Moritzplatz
Bürgermeister-Fischer-Str.
St. Moritz
Wintergasse
Maximilianstr.
Vorderer Lech
Neuer Gang
Vogelmauer
Jakoberwallstr.
To Hauptbahnhof
Zeuggasse
Zeug-platz
Apotheker-gässchen
2
Dominikanergasse
Römisches Museum
Neuer Gang
Am Schwall
Bäck-
Katharinengasse
Schaezlerpalais **1**
Herkules-brunnen
Predigerberg
Hallstrasse
To Basilika St. Ulrich & Afra and St.-Ulrichs-Kirche

GERMANY
Hamburg
Berlin ★
Frankfurt am Main
Augsburg
Munich

| 0 | 200 yds |
| 0 | 200 m |

ATTRACTIONS
Dom St. Maria **7**
Fugger und Welser Museum **9**
Fugger-Stadtpalais **2**
Fuggerei **5**
Schaezlerpalais **1**
St. Anna **3**

HOTELS
Bayerisches Haus am Dom **6**
Dom Hotel **8**

RESTAURANTS
Ratskeller **4**

bronze doors, adorned with bas-reliefs of a curious mixture of biblical and mythological characters, are in the adjacent **Diözesanmuseum St. Afra** (www.bistum-augsburg.de; ℭ **0821/3166333**), open Tuesday to Saturday 10am to 5pm and Sunday noon to 6pm. Admission is 4€ for adults, and 3€ for children and students.

Hoher Weg. ℭ **0821/3166353.** Free admission. Mon–Sat 7am–5pm; Sun noon–5pm.

Fuggerei ★★ HISTORIC SITE   During the 15th and 16th centuries, Augsburg became one of Europe's wealthiest communities, mainly because of its textile industry and the political and financial clout of its two banking families, the Welsers and the Fuggers. Centuries later, the Fuggers are still remembered for this unusual legacy, set up in 1519, by Jakob Fugger the Rich, to house poorer Augsburgers. It was Europe's oldest welfare housing, and the basic tenets laid down in 1521 are still in force today. The nominal rent of 88 cents per annum (formerly one Rhenish guilder) has not changed in more than 450 years (the city council determines who gets the break—it's based on need). The only obligation is that tenants pray daily for the souls of the founders. It would be hard to forget this daily chore, since statues of saints and angels are scattered liberally throughout the miniature, self-contained town, with 67 identical cottages containing 147 small apartments, as well as a church, a fountain, and a park, surrounded by walls and gates that are shut from 10pm to 5am and guarded by a night watchman. All the houses have entrances that open to the outdoors, instilling a sense of privacy, and each has a distinctive bell pull, making it easier to find the right door in the dark. Franz Mozart—great-grandfather of Wolfgang Amadeus Mozart—once lived here at Mittlere Gasse 14. The house next door is now the **Fuggerei Museum,** which displays

The Fuggerei in Augsburg, an enlightened medieval housing project for the poor.

rough-hewn furniture, wood-paneled ceilings and walls, a cast-iron stove, and the bric-a-brac of everyday 16th- and 17th-century life. Also on show is an updated apartment equipped with modern fittings; both quarters suggest that life in an almshouse needn't be without material comforts.

At the end of Vorderer Lech. www.fuggerei.de. *©* **0821/3198810.** Museum 4€ adults, 3€ students and children. Museum Apr–Sept daily 8am–8pm; Oct–Mar daily 9am–6pm. Tram: 1.

St.-Anna-Kirche (St. Anne's Church) ★ CHURCH   Martin Luther
stayed in this former Carmelite monastery in 1518 when he was called to Augsburg to recant his revolutionary 95 Theses before a papal emissary. Even without this historic provenance, the church is a treasure, containing paintings by Lucas Cranach, who was a friend of Luther and spent time in Augsburg. Cranach's delightful *Christ Blessing the Children,* in the chancel, is an anachronistic scene of well-dressed medieval matrons crowding around Christ with their plump babes in arms; the image was wildly popular in the 16th century, and Cranach's workshop cranked out dozens of copies. A side chapel built for Augsburg's beneficent Fugger family is the final resting place of Jakob, the clan's richest and most powerful member, whose eternal surroundings are fairly modest considering that by some accounts he was the richest man who ever lived. In the Goldschmiedekapelle (Goldsmith's Chapel), the eponymous donors are buried beneath frescoes depicting Herod ordering his high priests to find Christ. Augsburg's city market is next to the church.

Im Annahof 2. www.st-anna-augsburg.de. *©* **0821/450175100.** Free admission. Daily 9am–5pm. Free 1-hr. tours (in German) daily at 3pm.

Schaezlerpalais ★ MUSEUM   This 60-room mansion built between
1765 and 1770 houses the **Deutsche Barockgalerie** (German Baroque Gallery), showcasing 17th- and 18th-century paintings by artists active in Augsburg and its surrounding vicinity. You probably won't recognize many of the names, but there are a couple of works by Hans Holbein the Elder as well as Veronese and Tiepolo. Albrecht Dürer's portrait of Jakob Fugger the Rich does justice to the Augsburg moneyman who monopolized 16th-century German banking, not unlike the Medicis in Florence. Don't miss the mansion's Festsaal, an enormous banqueting hall lavishly decorated with Rococo frescoes, stuccowork, mirrors, and wall paneling. Historical records show that on April 28, 1770, Marie Antoinette danced away the night here.

Maximilianstrasse 46 (facing the Hercules Fountain). www.kunstsammlungen-museen.augsburg.de. *©* **0821/3244102.** Admission 7€ adults, 5.50€ for students, children 9 and under free. Tues 10am–8pm; Wed–Sun 10am–5pm.

MEET THE fuggers

By the late 1400s Augsburg had become a center of banking and finance thanks to the efforts of the Fuggers, an incredibly wealthy local family. The aptly named Jakob Fugger the Rich (1459–1529) served as the Holy Roman Empire's banker and was the financier behind the Hapsburgs, who were in debt to him to the tune of some four million ducats (very roughly, that's about $20 million, an unthinkable sum in Renaissance Europe). Jakob was so rich and so powerful that during an exchange with Charles I he had the temerity to say, "It is well known that without my help, Your Majesty would no longer wear the crown of the Holy Roman Empire." It was this same Jakob who founded the Fuggerei, the world's first almshouses (see p. 284), in exchange for the daily prayers of its impoverished residents. The power and influence of the Fuggers, as well as their banking colleagues the Welsers, comes to light in the **Fugger und Welser Museum,** in a Renaissance house near the cathedral at 23 Ausseres Pfaffengässhen (www.fugger-und-welser-museum.de; 𝄐 **0821-502-070**); it's open Tuesday to Sunday, 10am to 5pm, and admission is 5€, 4€ for school children.

Where to Stay & Eat in Augsburg

Rathausplatz is lined with cafes and coffee houses, and stands sell Weisswurst, a veal and pork sausage that's a local favorite.

Bayerisches Haus au Dom ★ BAVARIAN   Follow up a visit to the cathedral with a meal at one of the elbow-burnished maple tables in this

The Wieskirche, the baroque masterwork of the Zimmermann brothers.

not your ordinary **COUNTRY CHAPEL**

An hour's drive south of Augsburg, and half an hour from Füssen, the tiny **Wieskirche** ★★ in the village of Wies isn't directly on the Romantic Road, but it's a detour you should not miss. It's one of the world's most exuberantly decorated buildings, a true Rococo masterpiece.

How did such a gem come to be built in this out-of-the-way spot? Sometime in the 1730s, it was noticed that in a remote mountain meadow, a rough-hewn statue of Christ being scourged before his crucifixion was crying. Over the next decade, pilgrims began flocking to the site, and eventually the great Dominikus Zimmermann (1685–1766), a Bavarian architect and stuccoist, and his brother, Johann Baptist Zimmerman (1680–1758), a renowned frescoist, were commissioned to create a proper shrine. They worked on the church from 1746 to 1754; Dominikus was so enchanted with his creation that he built a small home in the vicinity and spent the last decade of his life here.

The rather sober façade of the little white church gives no hint of what lies within: A light-flooded interior with an enormous cupola, shimmering with a superabundance of woodcarvings, gilded stucco, columns, statues, and bright frescoes. The overall effect is to make the supernatural seem present, as indeed seems to be the case for those who claim to have been cured of various ailments while praying in front of the statue.

If you're driving, follow B17 to Steingaden; signs from there indicate the way 3km (2 miles) south to Wies. A bus heading for the church leaves Füssen six times per day Monday to Friday (once per day on the weekend); check the timetable at the station for bus information or ask at the Füssen tourist office (see p. 293). The church is open daily, except during services and guided tours, from 8am to 8pm in summer and 8am to 5pm in winter (www.wieskirche.de; ☏ **08862/501**).

cozy, wood-paneled tavern from 1270. You can go the traditional route with schnitzel or sausages (or the delicious pork cutlets coated in pretzel crumbs and mustard), or eat lightly on a selection of salads, cold cuts, and cheese. A lot of regulars take a seat on the benches to nurse a beer or two, served in a shady beer garden in good weather.

Johannesstrasse 4. www.bayerischeshaus.de. ☏ **0821/3497990**. Main courses 6€–15€. Mon–Fri 11am–midnight; Sat 10am–midnight; Sun 10am–11pm.

Dom Hotel ★   A choice spot across from the cathedral is not coincidental—the rather nondescript surroundings were at one time an ecclesiastical guest house, with a roster of guests who included Martin Luther. You won't find a lot of historic ambiance in the pleasantly functional rooms, though those on the top floor are tucked under rafters and many are cozily beamed. In warm weather, breakfast is served in a garden beside the town's medieval fortifications.

Frauentorstrasse 8. www.domhotel-augsburg.de. ☏ **0821/343930**. 52 units. 92€–135€ double. Buffet breakfast included. Free parking in lot; 6€ in garage. **Amenities:** Exercise room; indoor heated pool; sauna; Wi-Fi (free).

Ratskeller ★ BAVARIAN   True to its name, Augsburg's 400-year-old community-oriented eatery is tucked deep below the towering Rathaus, flowing across high, brick-vaulted rooms that are cozy in winter and cool in summer. The menu offers up pretty standard Bavarian sausage-and-schnitzel-variety fare to a big crowd of business folks and shoppers, but veers away from the beer-only tradition with sophisticated cocktails during an evening-long happy hour. It also caters to a late-night crowd with a menu of pizzas and salads.

Rathausplatz 2. www.ratskeller-augsburg.de. ✆ **0821/31988238.** Main courses 8€–18€. Sun–Thurs 11am–1pm and Fri–Sat 11am–2pm.

FÜSSEN ★★

92km (57 miles) S of Augsburg, 119km (74 miles) SW of Munich

This little town at the southern terminus of the Romantic Road in the foothills of the Bavarian Alps is a workhorse compared to the show ponies down the road, the castles at Neuschwanstein and Hohenschwangau. But Füssen is more than just a jumping-off point and makes an attractive showing on its own, with a cluster of gabled houses sheltering on medieval lanes beneath the Hohes Schloss, a fine Gothic castle. If you're arriving by train, you'll be traveling in good historic company: Richard Wagner used to take the train down here to visit his patron, King Ludwig II. And should you need reminding that this is an old town, the main shopping street, Reichenstrasse, follows the main street of a Roman garrison, Via Claudia, the route that once connected Venice and Augsburg.

Essentials

GETTING THERE   Access by car is via the A7 autobahn from the north. If you're following the official Romantic Road route, you'll reach Füssen via the B17 from Augsburg. Trains from Munich and Augsburg arrive frequently throughout the day. Train time from Munich is 2 hours, or 1 hour 45 minutes from Augsburg. For information, visit www.bahn.de or call ✆ **01805/996633.**

VISITOR INFORMATION   The tourist office is at Kaiser-Maximilian-Platz 1 (www.fuessen.de; ✆ **08362/93850**). Hours vary but in summer are usually Monday to Friday 8:30am to 6:30pm, Saturday 9am to 2:30pm, and Sunday 10am to noon; in winter hours are Monday to Friday 9am to 5pm and Saturday 10am to noon.

Exploring Füssen

On a nice day, when everyone in town takes a seat in an outdoor cafe along **Reichstrasse,** the main street, Füssen seems to be wholeheartedly committed to the good life, but this was once a workaday

A footbridge crosses the Lechfall just outside of Füssen.

trading post. A walk over to the banks of the Lech River, on the south side of town, shows off the swift-moving currents that kept Füssen in business, in the days when river rafts took goods that had been portaged across the Alps and transported them downstream to Augsburg. Riverside mills (some of the smokestacks still stand) turned out textiles. A well-marked trail leads to the **Lechfall,** a waterfall less than a kilometer (½ mile) south of town. A pedestrian footbridge spans the falls, located where the Lech River squeezes through a rocky gorge and over a high ledge.

Hohes Schloss ★ CASTLE   The aptly named "High Castle," surrounded by formidable white walls and reached from the parish church below by a steep lane, was once the summer residence of the prince-bishops of Augsburg. While the coffered Rittersaal (Knight's Hall) suggests pomp and ceremony, the courtyard frescoes, providing the illusion of many more gables and windows than are actually there, add a refreshingly light touch to the otherwise somber surroundings. The princely chambers house paintings and sculptures by 15th- and 16th-century Bavarian masters, including the Sippen Altar panels from 1510, showing eight chilling scenes of plague and war.

Magnusplatz. © **08362/903146.** Museum 6€. Apr–Oct Tues–Sun 11am–4pm, Oct–Mar, Fri–Sun 1–4pm.

St. Mangkirche ★ CHURCH   Magnus, an 8th-century Irish mission-ary, founded this abbey on the site of his wilderness cell, and he's buried here—or was, as his bones went missing sometime in those dark ages (all that remains is a tiny sliver of clavicle that hangs above the altar). Some of the former monks' cells and some rather grand frescoed halls house the **Heimatmuseum,** one of the world's stellar collections of lutes and violins. Europe's first lute-makers' guild was founded in Füssen in the 16th century, and for the next three centuries the town was also renowned for its violin makers, whose equipment is on show as well. The **Chapel of St. Anne** is frescoed with a macabre *Totentanz* or "dance of death," a popular medieval European allegorical theme in which corpses succumb to a violin-playing specter, thus proving—less the faithful ever forget it—that death comes to us all.

Town center. Abbey: ✆ **08362/6190.** Admission by free tours (in German) on Tues and Thurs at 4pm and Sat at 10am (hours vary greatly throughout year; check with the tourist office). Heimatmuseum: ✆ **08362/903146.** Admission 3€. Apr–Oct Tues–Sun 10am–5pm, Nov–Mar Tues–Sun 1–4pm. Chapel of St. Anne: Free admission. Apr–Oct Tues–Sun 10am–5pm, Nov–Mar Tues–Sun 1–4pm.

Where to Eat & Stay in Füssen

Altstadt-Hotel zum Hechten ★   The same family has run this spotless guesthouse just below the castle for generations, and their notion of old-fashioned Bavarian hospitality goes well beyond flower-boxes at the windows. Rooms are smartly streamlined and almost con-temporary in design, with sleek low-lying furnishings interspersed with some traditional pieces. Some have balconies, and all have use of a sauna and solarium. The inviting stube-style restaurant adheres to the mantra that if it's not from the region, it's not worth serving—or as they say it here, "everything that comes into our pots, come from our waters, fields, and meadows."

Ritterstrasse 6. www.hotel-hechten.com. ✆ **08362/91600.** 35 units. 94€–100€ dou-ble. Buffet breakfast included. **Amenities:** Restaurant; sauna; Wi-Fi (free).

Hotel Hirsch ★★ BAVARIAN   *Hirsch* in German means stag, although here the name has more to do with the game-in-season menu than any attempt at hunting-lodge décor. Instead, the grand salons have a digni-fied look with acres of polished blond surfaces that are just as spruce now as they were a century ago when this gracious old hotel began win-ing and dining tourists to the nearby Ludwig castles. Ever-changing menus in the *bierstube* and more formal dining room often include some memorable standouts like wild duck and trout from local rivers. Upper floors house bright, comfortably appointed and traditionally furnished bedrooms.

Kaiser-Maximilian-Platz 7. www.hotelhirsch.de. ✆ **08362/93980.** Main courses 10€–18€. Daily 11:30am–2pm and 6–9:30pm.

Hotel Sonne ★★ The famous castles are out of sight down the road, but in this old gabled house with modern extensions at the edge of the old town, the spirit of high-living royalty is a playful presence. The rooms here are smartly decorated and supremely comfortable, and the public areas are attractive. The image of King Ludwig stares from huge wall murals, costumed mannequins line the hallways, and paintings and photos of Bavarian woods and brooks soothe the nerves—as does the top floor sauna and sun room. A sunny terrace bar is a prime gathering spot. Prinzregenteplatz 1. www.hotel-fuessen.de. © **08362/9080.** 50 units. 110€–135€ double. Buffet breakfast included. **Amenities:** 2 restaurants; bar; sauna; Wi-Fi (free).

Madame Plüsch ★★ BAVARIAN There's not an antler, hunting horn, or cowbell in sight in this plush, urbane outpost of intimate dining that calls itself a "nostalgia restaurant." On the lower floor of a house from the 16th century, velvet furnishings, lamps, china, and knickknacks are mostly from the 1920s, though the décor makes allowance for any piece that's a bit quirky and fits into the parlor-like atmosphere of these low-ceilinged dining rooms. Deftly prepared meals are not nearly as dainty as the décor, however—as if to satisfy appetites whetted by the mountain air, the menu focuses on roast beef and grilled steaks. If you're intent on throwing any concern about cholesterol to the wind, try the Das Pfandlt, with sausage, roasted meats, and cheese dumplings. Drehergasse 48. www.madame-pluesch.de. © **08362/930-0949.** Main courses 10€–24€. Daily 11am–11pm.

Zum Schwanen ★ BAVARIAN At this traditional inn, a flavorful blend of Swabian and Bavarian cuisine ranges farther afield into Eastern Europe. So, along with homemade sausage and roast pork, the kitchen also prepares goulash, paprika rice, and some other hearty, non-local dishes that nonetheless seem well suited to the mountain environs. Service is attentive, and portions are generous. Brotmarkt 4. www.schwanan-fuessen.de. © **08362/6174.** Main courses 7€–18€. Tues–Sat 11:30am–2pm and 6:30–10pm.

NEUSCHWANSTEIN ★★★ & HOHENSCHWANGAU ★

7km (4 miles) E of Füssen

Füssen would be just another quaint alpine town if it weren't for the two blockbuster attractions lying just to the east: the "Royal Castles" of Hohenschwangau and Neuschwanstein. Maximilian II built Hohenschwangau atop a medieval ruin in 1836; his son, King Ludwig II, began the extravagantly romantic Neuschwanstein on an adjoining hilltop in the 1860s. These two royal castles combine fantasy and beautiful settings amid Alpine peaks and valleys and will probably be your most memorable stop along the Romantic Road.

The more fanciful of the two is multi-turreted Neuschwanstein, the ultimate fantasy creation of Ludwig, the strange, self-obsessed monarch who has become one of the legendary figures in Bavarian history. Neuschawanstein was only one of Ludwig's many excesses, which eventually threatened to bankrupt the kingdom; in 1886, at age 41 and before his castle was completed, Ludwig was declared insane. Three days later, he was found drowned in Lake Starnberg on the outskirts of Munich, along with the physician who had declared him unfit. It has never been determined if Ludwig was murdered or committed suicide. While he has been the subject of biographies, films, plays, and even a musical, his most lasting legacy may be this dream castle, which has drawn millions of visitors to this part of Bavaria over the years.

Essentials

GETTING THERE   Nineteen buses a day arrive from Füssen (www.rvo-bus.de). From the train station, take bus 73 in the direction of Steingaden / Garmisch-Partenkirchen or bus 78 in the direction to Schwangau; the stop for the castles is Hohenschwangau / Alpseestrasse. By car, head east from Füssen along the B17.

Neuschwanstein, the most famous of "mad" King Ludwig's fantasy castles.

Information about the region and the castles is available at the tourist office in Füssen, Kaiser-Maximilian-Platz 1, Füssen (www.fuessen.de; ✆ **08362/93850**).

SPECIAL EVENTS In September, Wagnerian concerts and other music are performed in the Singer's Hall at Neuschwanstein. For information and reservations, contact the tourist office, **Verkehrsamt,** at the Rathaus in Schwangau (✆ **08362/938523**). Tickets go on sale in early June and sell out rather quickly.

Visiting the Royal Castles

The royal castles of Hohenschwangau and Neuschwanstein are the most popular tourist attractions in Germany, receiving nearly a million visitors a year. In any season, especially during the summer crush, you're well advised to reserve tickets for both castles in advance online at www. hohenschwangau.de, up to two days before your visit. You'll be asked to select a desired time slot for the visit and by return email you'll be instructed when to pick up your tickets at the office near the parking lot of the castles, where you'll pay. You can show up without a reservation but be prepared for long waits to enter, provided tickets are not sold out.

You can see the castles only on guided tours, which last about 35 minutes each and are cursory at best, designed to herd visitors through as quickly and efficiently as possible. Tours in English are available throughout the day. A tour number and entry time are printed on your ticket. Once you reach the castles, a digital sign informs you when your tour is ready. When the time comes, feed your ticket into the turnstile in front of the respective castle and you will be ushered to the meeting point with your guide. *Note:* It is imperative to arrive by the time indicated on your ticket; otherwise, you will have to go back to the kiosk at the base and pick up a new ticket and start all over again.

From the ticket office, it's an easy amble over to Hohenschwangau. There are three ways to reach Neuschwanstein from here. You can make the steep half-mile climb from the Hohenschwangau parking lot, or you may take a bus from outside the ticket office (fare is 1.80€ for the ride up and 1€ to return). However, the traditional way to reach Neuschwanstein is by horse-drawn carriage, also leaving from in front of the ticket office; the cost for this is 6€ for the ascent and 3€ for the descent. *Note:* Lines to crowd into one of the carriages can be long, and there is no guarantee of arrival time at the castle entrance—if you miss your timed entry, you're out of luck. It's best to forgo the ride unless you have plenty of time to wait in line to board a carriage and make the ascent before your timed entry into the castle.

Hohenschwangau ★ CASTLE Ludwig II's father, Crown Prince Maximilian (later Maximilian II) purchased the 12th-century castle of

7

THE ROMANTIC ROAD

Neuschwanstein & Hohenschwangau

The Perfect Shot

The best views of Neuschwanstein are from Marienbrücke, a bridge that crosses over the Pöllat Gorge at a height of 90m (300 ft.) and is reached on a steep path from the castle and the road leading up to it. From that vantage point, you, like Ludwig, can stand and meditate on the glories of the castle and its panoramic surroundings. If you want to photograph the castle, do it from here instead of at the top of the hill, where you'll be too close for a good shot.

the knights of Schwangau in 1832 and had it completely restored in faux medieval style. This decorative scheme comes to the fore in the Hall of the Swan Knight, named for the wall paintings depicting the saga of Lohengrin (a Germanic hero associated with the swan; the name of the castle literally translates as High Swan County Palace). Ludwig II spent much of his joyless childhood at Hohenschwangau with his strait-laced father and his mother, Queen Maria of Prussia. As a young man he received Richard Wagner in its chambers; the music room on the second floor contains copies of letters between Ludwig II and the composer, and the grand piano on which the two played duets. Although Hohenschwangau has the comfortable air of a home, the heavily Gothic halls and chambers recall knights' castles of the Middle Ages. Maximillian's restorations were part of a 19th-century European craze for re-creating medieval settings—a concept that his son would later take to new extremes with Neuschwanstein.

Alpseestrasse www.hohenschwangau.de. ✆ **08362/930830.** Admission 12€ adults, children 18 and under free. Combined ticket with Neuschwanstein: 23€ adults, children 18 and under free. Apr–Sept daily 8am–5:30pm, Oct–Mar daily 9am–3:30pm.

Neuschwanstein ★★★ CASTLE   Floating in the clouds atop a rugged hilltop above little villages and mountain lakes, King Ludwig II's folly was conceived as a romantic homage to the Middle Ages and to the Germanic mythology evoked in the music of Richard Wagner. As Ludwig wrote to the composer, "It will also remind you of 'Tannhäuser' (Singers' Hall with a view of the castle in the background), 'Lohengrin' (castle courtyard, open corridor, path to the chapel). . . ." He began work on the castle in 1868, shortly after the death of his grandfather, Ludwig I, left him with a considerable private fortune. Construction of this dream palace continued for 17 years; for years, Ludwig watched the progress through a telescope from neighboring Hohenschwangau. Between 1884 and 1886, the king lived in the partly-completed Neuschwanstein on and off for a total of 170 days. He was at Neuschwanstein when he received news of his dethronement, on the basis of mental instability. Three days later he was found dead. All work on the castle stopped immediately, leaving a part of the interior uncompleted.

Just as Ludwig built Neuschwanstein to recreate legend, his ersatz version of a distant past has become the iconic European

Murals in Neuschwanstein reflect the king's passion for medieval legends.

castle—appropriated most famously by Walt Disney as Cinderella's Castle at Disneyland. It's no accident that one of Ludwig's designers was the Wagnerian set designer Christian Janck, who ensured that almost every room suggests legend and saga. The king's **study** is decorated with painted scenes from the medieval legend of Tannhäuser. Murals in the king's **bedroom** portray the doomed lovers Tristan and Isolde (a mood reinforced by scenery—through the balcony window you can see a waterfall in the Pöllat Gorge, with the mountains in the distance). The **Sängerhalle** (Singer's Hall) takes up almost the entire fourth floor and is modeled after Wartburg castle in Eisenach, the site of the Meistersinger's song contests in the Middle Ages; frescoes depict the life of Parsifal, a mythical medieval knight. Ludwig's illusions of grandeur come quite forcibly to the fore in the unfinished **Throne Rome,** designed to resemble a Romanesque basilica, with columns of red porphyry, a mosaic floor, and frescoes of Christ looking down on the Twelve Apostles and six canonized kings of Europe.

After you leave the guided tour, you can make your way down to the enormous kitchens of the castle. Here you'll be reminded that this castle was built in the 19th century, not in the Middle Ages: The automatic grills and huge stoves are indicative of technological innovations used throughout the castle, which include running water, flush toilets, central heating, electric buzzers to summon servants, even telephones. Neuschwanstein Strasse. www.hohenschwangau.de. © **08362/930830.** Admission 12€ adults, children 18 and under free. Combined ticket with Hohenschwangau 23€ adults, children 18 and under free. Apr–Sept 8am–5pm, Oct–Mar 9am–3pm.

THE BAVARIAN ALPS ★★

The Romantic Road might end in Füssen, but that certainly doesn't mean the romance wanes. Just to the east the Bavarian Alps begin to pierce the sky in earnest, with a surfeit of scenery, miles of ski runs and hiking trails, and plenty of Alpine coziness in Garmisch-Partenkirchen and other mountain villages. Even King Ludwig found the mountain air in these parts inspiring; in a remote glen he created **Schloss Linderhof,** another exuberant fantasy that many consider even more beautiful than its more famous sibling to the west.

ARRIVING Access to Garmisch-Partenkirchen and other towns in the region by car is via the A95 autobahn. The scenic drive from Garmisch-Partenkirchen to Füssen is via the B23 and the B17 and takes about an hour. For train travel, Garmisch-Partenkirchen and Mittenwald lie on the major Munich-to-Innsbruck rail line, with frequent connections in all directions. You can also reach Garmisch-Partenkirchen in about 2 hours by train from Augsburg, with a change in Weilheim. Trains run between Garmisch-Partenkirchen and Füssen every 90 minutes; the trip takes just under 2 hours. For information and schedules, visit www.bahn.com or call © **01805/996633.**

VISITOR INFORMATION **Garmisch-Partenkirchen**'s tourist office is at Richard-Strauss-Platz 2 (www.garmisch-partenkirchen.de; © **08821/180700**). It's open Monday to Saturday 8am to 6pm, and Sunday and holidays 10am to noon. **Tourist-Information Mittenwald,** at Dammkarstrasse 3 (www.mittenwald.de; © **08823/33981**), is open Monday to Saturday. The **Oberammergau** tourist office is at Eugen-Papst-Strasse 9A (www.oberammergau.de; © **08822/92274**); it's open Monday to Friday, 9am to 6pm, and Saturday, 9am to 1pm.

Garmisch-Partenkirchen ★★

97km (60 miles) SW of Munich, 117km (73 miles) SE of Augsburg, 66km (40 miles) E of Füssen

These two side-by-side villages make up Germany's top Alpine resort, where you might come to ski, to hike, to climb, or simply to gaze at some spectacular mountain scenery. A lot of Europeans come here just to see and be seen, because making a wintertime appearance is Garmisch is still de rigueur in some social circles. Unless you plan on strapping on a pair of skis to test your mettle on a high-altitude run, the biggest thrill you're likely to have is ascending the Zugspitze, Germany's highest

Alpine hiking trails beckon in the Bavarian Alps.

mountain, via cog railway and cable car. For that matter, seeing country folk in traditional dress, mountain chalets bedecked with window boxes, or cattle plodding through village lanes can be a bit of a thrill, too. Garmisch-Partenkirchen makes a nice way station on your travels between the Romantic Road towns to the north and Ludwig's castles, just to the west of here.

EXPLORING THE RESORT AREA

The 1936 Winter Olympics put Garmisch-Partenkirchen on the map, with a lot of Nazi fanfare stealing the show from the athletes. The most famous competitor to emerge from the games was Norwegian figure skater Sonja Heine, whose twirls on the ice at the **Olympic Ice Stadium** earned her three gold medals, launched a Hollywood career, and made her a favorite of gossip columnists (her affairs with boxer Joe Louis and actors Tyrone Power and Van Johnson, along with her vile temper and Nazi sympathies, supplied plenty of juicy material). You can take a spin yourself on the three public rinks (Adlerstrasse 25, © **08821/ 753291;** 4.20€ adults, 2.40€ kids 6–15; public skating daily July to mid-May 11am–4pm). The **Ski Stadium,** with two ski jumps and a slalom course, is on the slopes at the edge of town. In 1936, more than 100,000 people watched the events in this stadium, and the World Cup Ski Jump is held here every New Year's Day.

Both towns are geared to strolling and café sitting, with enticing lanes backed by Alpine peaks and lined with wooden-shuttered chalets, many with colorful religious scenes painted on their facades. Garmisch

FOOTLOOSE ON THE hohenwege

Alpine hiking is a major summertime attraction in Garmisch-Partenkirchen. People come from around the world to roam the mountain paths (called Hohenwege, or "high ways"), to enjoy nature and watch animals in the forest. A network of funiculars and cable cars ascend to various points in the mountains where you can hike and admire the panoramic views.

An easily accessible destination is the 1,240m (4,070-ft.) **Eckbauer peak**, which lies on the southern fringe of Partenkirchen. You can take a chairlift to the top, have a drink at a Berggasthof (a guesthouse or cafe, usually in a high-altitude and rural location) and in less than an hour make the descent on relatively easy trails through a forest. The cable car departs year-round from the **Eckbauerbahn** (www.eckbauerbahn.com; *☏* **08821/3469**), adjacent to the ski stadium in Garmisch. A round-trip fare costs 12€ for adults, 7€ for children ages 6 to 16, and free for children 5 and under.

The rugged **Alpspitz region** begins about 1.6km (1 mile) southwest of Garmisch. The Kreuzeckbahn lift carries you up and across a rugged landscape to the lowest station of the Hochalm cable car, which then takes you up to a 1,050m-high (6,500-ft.) summit called Osterfelderkopf. Here, hiking trails skirt areas of wildflowers, unusual geologic features, and lush alpine meadows. Return to Garmisch on the Alpspitzbahn, a scenic 10-minute descent above gorges, cliffs, and grassy meadows. Cable cars run year-round approximately every half-hour 8:30am–4:30pm (Mar–June until 5pm, July–Aug until 5:30pm). Round-trip fare is 21€ adults, 16€ kids 6–15.

Another hearty hike is through the **Partnachklam,** a gorge with a roaring stream at the bottom and sheer cliff walls rising on either side of the trail. The bottom of the gorge is less than 1km (½ mile) south of Garmisch's ski stadium. The tourist office supplies maps and info on these and other routes.

is the larger, more fashionable, and livelier of the two, though Partenkirchen's cobblestoned, flower-bedecked main street, Ludiwgstrasse, is especially picturesque. (It's historic, too, as the street is said to trace the Via Claudia, the Roman road route between Venice and Augsburg.) An pleasant in-town excursion is to walk along the pine-scented Philosopher's Walk at the edge of Partenkirchen, with views to the peaks that form a backdrop to the 18th-century Chapel of St. Anton.

TO THE TOP OF THE ZUGSPITZE ★★★

The tallest mountain in Germany, soaring 2,960m (9,700 ft.) above sea level, lures view seekers up its craggy slopes on a tremendously popular thrill ride. The only challenge is deciding how to make the ascent, but whichever way you go, you'll be treated to phenomenal mountain views all the way up, at the top, and on the way down—provided, of course, it's not snowing or the mountain is otherwise enshrouded in cloud cover, in which case the trip is pointless. One way begins on the **Zugspitzbahn** (cog railway), which departs from its own depot behind Garmisch-Partenkirchen's main railway station. The train travels uphill, past boulder-strewn meadows and rushing streams, to the Zugspitzplatte, a high plateau with sweeping views, where you transfer to a cable car, the Gletscherbahn, for a 4-minute ride up to the summit. The second way is to take the Zugspitzbahn for a shorter trip, disembarking at the **Eibsee Sielbahn** (Eibsee Cable Car), which carries you the rest of the way to the top. Round-trip tickets allow you to ascend one way and descend the other, in order to enjoy the widest range of spectacular views. When you reach the top, you can linger on a sunny cafe terrace before making the descent. Round-trip fares are 42€ for adults, 32€ for ages 16 to 18, and 23€ for ages 6 to 15; fares increase by about 10€ in the popular summer season. For more information, contact the **Bayerische Zugspitzbahn,** Olympiastrasse 27, Garmisch-Partenkirchen (www.zugspitze.de; © **08821/7970**).

A HIKE TO KONIGSHAUS AM SCHACHEN ★

Perhaps with Wagner's music ringing in your ears—or, okay, "The Sound of Music"—you can hike through Alpine meadows up to the remote mountainside lodge that in 1872 King Ludwig II had built in a style that crosses a Swiss chalet with a Greek temple. The ground-floor rooms resemble those of a simple mountain dwelling, but upstairs is the Türkische Saal (Turkish Hall), a Moorish fantasy out of "The Arabian Nights" where low divans surround a fountain. Ludwig would sit here in Eastern attire in the company of his hookah-smoking retinue. The effect is all the more extravagant considering that teams of workers had to cart all the building materials up the mountainside. More than 1,000 species of Alpine flora grow in an adjacent botanical garden. The only way to reach the lodge is by a well-marked trail that makes a fairly easy, 10km (6-mile) ascent up the mountain. Once up there, admission is by guided tour (in German only, but guides will usually explain things in English if you ask), at 11am, 1pm, 2pm, and 3pm. Tours cost 4.50€ adults, 3.50€ children, kids under 14 free; For more information, go to **www.schloesser.bayern.de**. Allow at least half a day for the hike and your time at the lodge.

Mittenwald ★

18km (11 miles) SE of Garmisch-Partenkirchen

Wedged in a pass of the Karwendel Range just before the Austrian border, Mittenwald is an idyllic mountain resort. Alpine architecture is everywhere here, from frescoed facades to wooden balconies and over-hanging eaves. On the square stands a monument to Matthias Klotz, who introduced violin making to Mittenwald in 1684 and sparked a local industry of this highly specialized craft that continues today.

EXPLORING MITTENWALD

Mittenwald's chief attraction is the town itself, its most notable feature being the **painted houses ★★** that line the main street. The village can be explored in about an hour and a half. In winter it's a picture postcard of snow-laden charm, and in summer a mass of flowering facades with pots of geraniums, clinging to houses with their richly decorated gables.

The town's museum, which contains a workshop, has exhibits that trace the history of violins and other stringed instruments from their invention through various stages of their evolution. The **Geigenbau und Heimatmuseum ★**, Ballenhausgasse 3 (www.geigenbaumuseum-mittenwald.de, ✆ **08823/2511**), is open Tuesday to Sunday 10am to 5pm in the high season, and 11am to 4pm in the low season. Admission is 4.50€ for adults, 3.50€ for students, and 2€ for children. The museum is closed November 5 to December 10.

Statue of Matthias Klotz, master violin-maker, in Mittenwald.

In the surrounding country-side, the scenery of the Wetter-stein and Karwendel ranges offers constantly changing panoramas. Some 130km (80 miles) of hiking paths wind up and down the mountains around the village. You can hike through the hills on your own, take part in mountain-climbing expeditions, or take horse-and-carriage trips and motorcoach tours to nearby villages. The **Karwendelbahn Mittenwald** (www.karwendelbahn.de, ✆ **08823/8480**) cable car, which operates year-round, climbs to a height of 2,244m (7,360 ft.), where numerous ski trails become hiking trails in summer. In winter, the 7km-long (4-mile) Dammkar downhill slope offers some of the best skiing and snowboarding around. A ride on the cable car costs 22€ round-trip; it runs daily 9am to 4:30pm, and until 7:30pm in summer.

SHOPPING

Professional musicians have sought out the classical stringed instruments crafted here for centuries. Prices may be steep, but a visit to **Geigenbau Leonhardt,** Mühlenweg 53A (www.violin-leonhardt.de, ©08823/8010), is educational—even if you're just browsing the array of instruments.

Oberammergau ★

20km (12 miles) N of Garmisch-Partenkirchen

No one could ever accuse the residents of this pretty town set in a wide mountain valley of sitting around doing nothing. They put on a world-famous passion play every 10 years and in the meantime make intricate wood carvings and paint the fronts of their houses with utterly charming frescoes. You can stroll through this beehive of activity in about an hour, but you'll want to spend most of your time here just outside of town at **Schloss Linderhof ★★★**, the most aesthetically pleasing of King Ludwig's castles.

EXPLORING OBERAMMERGAU

The citizens of Oberammergau have a long tradition of painting frescoes on their houses, an ages-old approach to curb appeal known as *Lüftmalerei.* Some are based on scenes from "Hansel and Gretel," "Little Red Riding Hood" (at Ettaler Strasse 48 and 41, respectively) and other fairy tales,

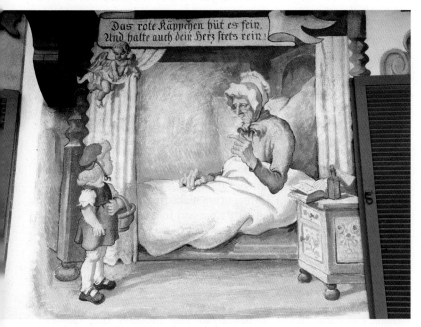

Das rote Käppchen hüt es fein,
Und halte auch dein Herz stets rein!

Fairy-tale frescoes adorn the housefronts of Oberammergau.

SHOPPING FOR woodcarvings

Oberammergau is world-famous for its woodcarving, but before you buy you should keep in mind that even some of the most expensive "handmade" pieces may have been roughed in by machine prior to being finished off by hand. If you're a serious shopper, make your first stop the village woodcarver's school, the **Pilatushaus,** Ludwig-Thoma-Strasse 10 (© **08822/949511**), to learn the hallmarks of quality you should be looking for. You can watch local carvers, painters, and sculptors as they work from June to October, Tuesday to Sunday 3 to 5pm. Two reliable shops with a wide range of carvings are **Holzschnitzerei Franz Barthels,** Schnitzlergasse 4 (© **08822/4271**), and **Toni Baur,** Dorfstrasse 27 (© **08822/821**), both with a sophisticated inventory of woodcarvings crafted from maple, pine, and linden.

while others depict beer hall joviality and other typical snippets from Bavarian life. The most famous, though, is a reverential rendering of Jesus being judged by Pontius Pilate in the frescoes on Pilatushaus, at Ludwig-Thoma-Strasse 10 (the headquarters of a carvers' and artisans' workshop).

For alpine experiences and great views, whisk up **Berg Laber,** the mountain that rises to the east of the town, or **Berg Kolben,** to the west. The 10-minute ascent up Berg Laber via an enclosed cable-gondola costs 17€ per person (www.laber-bergbahn.com; © **08822/4770**) for a single trip, but if you're outdoorsy, you might prefer the open-air ride up Berg Kolben via chairlift (www.kolbensesselbahn.com; © **08822/4760**) for 9.50€ round trip. The Berg Laber cable car runs from December through October.

Kloster Ettal ★ RELIGIOUS SITE   Just south of Oberammergau, the vast Benedictine monastery of Ettal sits at the heart of the same-named village in a high, narrow alpine valley. It's a surprisingly grandiose church to be standing in such a relatively isolated spot. Founded in 1330 by Emperor Ludwig IV of Bavaria, it became an immensely popular place of pilgrimage, a magnet for the faithful who hiked through the valley to honor the Virgin Mary, the patroness of heavily Catholic Bavaria. The elaborate facade and dome of the Lady Chapel that you see today were part of an exuberant 18th-century makeover by Enrico Zucalli, an 18th-century Swiss architect with a passion for the Italian Baroque. A statue of the Virgin is by the sculptor Giovanni Pisano (1250–c. 1315), whose works grace so many churches throughout Tuscany. Early visitors were shown hospitality with the cloister's much-loved liqueur and beer, both named Ettaler for a nearby peak, and you may have some, too, in the adjoining Braustuberl.

Ettal, 3km (2 miles) south of Oberammergau (on the road to Garmisch-Partenkirchen). www.kloster-ettal.de. © **08822/740.** Free admission. Daily 7am–8pm. Hourly buses run from Oberammergau's Rathaus and Bahnhof in daytime.

Passiontheater (Passion Theater) ★ THE PERFORMING ARTS

Oberammergau put on its first *Passionspiele* (Passion Play) in 1634 to give thanks for being spared from the plague, and the townsfolk have been staging the same 16-act drama, depicting Christ's journey to the Cross, almost ever since. The whole town participates, with a cast of 2,000 (actors must be natives or have lived in the town for at least 20 years). Non-actors work behind the scenes to build sets and sew costumes—one thing they don't do is make wigs or beards, since appearance-altering props are not allowed in this realistic portrayal. In extreme adherence of the age-old theatrical ploy to always leave the audience wanting more, they stage the 5½-hour epic only once every decade (in years that end in 0) in a much-anticipated season that runs from mid-May to early October. In the years between Passion Play performances, however, the theater does not remain dark; it's a much-attended venue for other drama, film, and music. Meanwhile, behind-the-scenes tours show off stage mechanics and the costumes and sets used for the big show. Tickets for the guided tours (some in English) include admission to the Pilatushaus workshops (see p. 302) and the sophisticated little **Oberammergau Museum,** where exhibits show off the town's woodcarving and also include rotating exhibits, often of contemporary German artists working in various media.

Passionswiese 1. © **08822/92310.** Admission 8€ adults, 3€ children. Daily 9:30am–5:30pm.

Schloss (Castle) Linderhof ★★★ CASTLE

In 1869, King Ludwig II transformed a former royal hunting lodge into a small, dazzling-white château meant to resemble the Petit Trianon at Versailles. The ornate exterior is restrained when compared to the interior, which is a riot of Neo-Rococo flashiness, glittering with gold leaf, mirrors, and crystal and ivory chandeliers. On prominent display in the Music Room is the king's piano-harmonium; his long suffering teacher sniped into his diary, "Today I had my last lesson with the king. What a blessed day!" Among some ingenuous contrivances are a dining table that rose from the kitchens at mealtimes so that the king would not have to deal with servants, thus allowing him to carry on, undisturbed, conversations with his imaginary dinner companions Louis XV and Marie Antoinette. Ludwig was nocturnal and spent his nights lounging and reading in the Hall of Mirrors, where the candlelight seemed to be reflected endlessly, clouding the lines between reality and unreality, not unlike the king's state of mind. The park, with its formal French gardens, is more appealing than the overwrought interiors and fascinatingly playful. Here, as in Neuschwanstein down the road (p. 294), you're left to wonder if Ludwig was a dreamer or just plain mad. He would retreat to the Moorish Kiosk to indulge his Arabian Nights fantasies (also played out at Konigshaus Am Schachen, above Garmisch-Patrenkirchen; see p. 299) by smoking a

King Ludwig II's Versailles-inspired Linderhof Castle.

chibouk (a Turkish tobacco pipe) and having his retinue treat him as an Asian prince. In the Grotte (Grotto), an artificial cave with stalagmites and stalactites designed to re-create stage sets for Richard Wagner's opera *Tannhäuser,* he would be rowed over a waterfall-fed lake in a swan-shaped boat; his pet swans glided beside him and special lighting effects simulated the illumination in the Blue Grotto on Capri.

Bus line 9622 runs from Oberammergau's railway station to Schloss Linderhof six times per day, beginning at 10:25am; the last bus leaves Linderhof at 6:56pm. Round-trip fare is 13€. For bus information, call **RVO Bus Company** (www.rvo-bus.de; ✆ **08821/948274**). If you're driving, follow signs from Oberammergau to Ettal, go another 5km (3 miles) to Draswang; from there follow the signs to Schloss Linderhof. Linderhof 12. www.schlosslinderhof.de. ✆ **08822/92030.** Admission to palace (by guided tour only, some in English) and park buildings, 8.50€ adults (1€ less in winter). Parking 2€. Apr–Oct 15 daily 9am–6pm; Oct 16–Mar 10am–4pm. Closed Nov 1; Dec 24, 25, 31; Jan 1; park buildings closed Oct 16–Mar.

Where to Stay in the Bavarian Alps

A lot of townsfolk in these alpine towns and villages have gone into the *Gästehäus* (guesthouse) business, offering rooms in their homes, usually for 30€ to 50€ per person with breakfast. Tourist offices provide lists.

Gasthof Fraundorfer ★   You can't miss the frescoed facade depicting a family feast right in the middle of Partenkirchen. The subjects might be the Fraundorfers themselves, who've been welcoming guests into their cozy rooms and restaurant for more than 150 years. Furnishings are playfully Bavarian, with four-poster beds and polished wooden tables in some and sleigh beds (with colorful luges used as footboards) and fanciful log furniture in others. Some of the larger units can accommodate up five guests.

Ludwigstrasse 24, Garmisch-Patrenkirchen. www.gasthof-fraundorfer.de. ✆ **08821/9270.** 31 units. 86€–98€ double; 115€–192€ family room. Buffet breakfast included. Free parking. **Amenities:** Restaurant; room service; sauna; Wi-Fi (free).

Hotel Rheinischerhof ★★★ BAVARIAN   You'll feel right at home the moment you plop down in a comfy arm chair or on an eiderdown-covered bed in this big chalet at the western end of Garmisch. Hand-crafted woodworking and balconies enliven the large, bright, and very comfortable guest rooms spread over a couple of houses, and the hospitality is as warm as the décor. Among many amenities are a spa area with saunas and steam rooms, a garden with a small pool, and a wood-paneled restaurant that's a fine alternative to in-town choices, a short walk or bus ride away (free tickets courtesy of the hotel).

Zugspitstrasse 76, Garmisch-Patrenkirchen. www.rheinischerhof-garmisch.de. ✆ **08821/9120.** 38 units. From 100€–120€ double. Breakfast included. Free parking. **Amenities:** Restaurant; bar; pool; sauna; Wi-Fi (free).

Hotel Zugspitze ★★   Balconies, geraniums, and even a few turrets lend a lot of old-fashioned charm to this Garmisch city-center hotel that also passes muster as a gracious mountain resort. Alpine accents abound in the fire-warmed lounges and paneled dining room, while comfy pine-furnished bedrooms look over the charming townscape and peaks through French doors and big windows. Downstairs is a large, well-heated pool and attached saunas/steam rooms, opening to pretty gardens.

Klammstrasse 19, Garmisch-Partenkirchen. www.hotel-zugspitze.de. ✆**08823/9010.** 45 units. 100€–1400€ double. Buffet breakfast included. Free parking. **Amenities:** Restaurant, bar, indoor pool, room service, sauna, Wi-Fi (free).

Where to Eat in the Bavarian Alps

Braustuberl ★ BAVARIAN   A 350-year-old brew pub lays on the alpine charm in cozy rooms filled with well burnished rustic furnishings and covered in frescoes. There's a pretty, good-weather beer garden out back. The kitchen lives up to its end of the deal with simple, well-prepared local specialties of the schnitzel-with-noodles variety.

Fürstenstrasse 23, Garmisch-Patrenkirchen. www.braeustueberl-garmisch.de. ✆ **08821/2312.** Main courses 8€–16€. Daily noon–11pm.

Die Alpenrose ★ BAVARIAN   The ornately decorated façade with bursting window boxes has been a beacon since the days when stage-coaches journeying across the Bavarian Alps stopped in Mittenwald to let passengers give their jolted bones a rest. Even before then, the 14th-century house was part of a monastery The downstairs Josefikeller, with handmade chairs, flagstone floors, hand-painted ceiling, and a square-tiled stove in the center, is still a welcoming stop for anyone wandering through town, offering pork roasts, hearty soups, stews, and other mountaineer-worthy fare. Upstairs are 19 similarly cozy rooms

Obermarkt 1, Mittenwald. www.hotel-alpenrose-mittenwald.de. © **08823/92700.** Main courses 8€–14€ per person. Daily noon–9pm.

Koch's ★★ BAVARIAN/INTERNATIONAL   Everything that appears on the table in this small intimate room in the heart of Garmisch is freshly sourced. Farm produce, local game and fish, and house-made pastas find their way into dishes that vary from schnitzel and noodles to some such straightforward yet refreshing choices as tender fillet of beef with rosemary potatoes, pike-perch on creamed sauerkraut, and duck breast with Krautfleckerl (thick noodles). Ice cream and other desserts are also made in-house

Bankgasse 16, Garmisch-Patrenkirchen. www.kochs-garmisch.de.© **08821/969899.** Main courses 10€–18€. Wed–Mon 5:30–10pm.

Zum Wildscühtz ★★ BAVARIAN   Leave your vegan cravings at the door of this lair for carnivores, where a woody interior as cozy as huntsman's forest lodge is the setting for seasonal game, or just about any other foodstuff derived from four-legged creatures. Pork knuckle, schnitzels, and other classics are many cuts above standard-issue Bavarian fare, and the venison sausage and other house-cured meats are works of art. An appreciative local following makes evening reservations mandatory.

Bankgasse 9, Garmisch-Patrenkirchen. © **08821/3290.** Main courses 9€–21€. Daily 11:30am–10pm.

MUNICH

8

Munich (München, pronounced *Mewn*-shin, in German) is a town that likes to party. Walk through the Altstadt (Old City) on a sunny day or a balmy evening and you'll see people sitting outside in every square, drinking, eating, and enjoying life. And there is a lot of life to enjoy in Bavaria's attractive capital, which seems to epitomize a certain beer-drinking, oom-pah-pah image many people still have of Germany (an image, by the way, that makes most Germans laugh or cringe). The beer and oom-pah-pah is definitely here—you'll find it at the famous Hofbräuhaus and other beer halls—but suds and songs sung in swaying unison are only one part of Munich. The other part is rich, cultured, and sophisticated, with a kind of proud, purring prosperity that supports the arts on a grand scale and appreciates the finer things in life (such as the BMWs that are produced here). In addition to having several world-class museums, it can lay claim to having the richest cultural, gastronomic and retail life in southern Germany. It's softer and less gritty than Berlin or Hamburg, particularly in its lovely and lively inner core, where church bells chime and the streets are paved for people, not cars.

Historically Catholic, and associated with the Italian Counter-Reformation, Munich's (and Bavaria's) architectural legacy includes exuberantly decorated baroque and rococo churches and palaces of a kind rarely seen in northern Germany (one notable exception being Sanssouci palace outside Berlin); and grand neoclassical monuments and buildings from the time of Ludwig I (1786–1868), who wanted to make his capital city a "new Athens." (Much of the city had to be rebuilt after World War II bombing, however.) Munich's wholehearted embrace of traditional feasts and festivities is also aligned to its Catholic heritage, and these seasonal events still bring Münchners together and make visitors feel welcome. The kingdom of Bavaria, created by Napoleon in 1806, lasted until 1918, and a sense of that privileged royal past still lingers in Munich. But this

PREVIOUS PAGE: **Sidewalk café across from the Altes Rathaus.**

is also a city where it's a tradition to share a communal table in a beer hall and enjoy the company of complete strangers.

Think of Munich as the capital of *Gemütlichkeit,* that not-quite-translatable adjective that means something between cozy and good-natured. Once you visit, you'll understand why it's long been called Germany's "secret capital"—the place where most Germans would live if they could.

ESSENTIALS

As one of Germany's major cities, Munich has no lack of transportation options. Like Frankfurt, Munich has an international airport, so you can fly there directly from many destinations including North America, Great Britain and Asia, and it is easily accessible from anywhere within Germany or Europe.

Arriving

BY PLANE   airport.com; © **089/9752-1313**) is located 29km (18 miles) northeast of the city center. Opened in 1992, the airport is among the most modern and efficient in the world. The S-8 **S-Bahn light-rail train** (© **089/4142-4344**) connects the airport with the **Hauptbahnhof** (main train station) in downtown Munich. Trains leave from the S-Bahn platform beneath the airport every 20-25 minutes daily between about 4am and 10:45pm, less frequently through the night. The fare for the 40-minute trip is 10.80€ adults. (If you are going to be using public transportation once in the city, you'll save money by buying an **All-Zone Tageskarte/Day Ticket** for 12.40€ and using it to get into the city. Note that the "day ticket" is valid until 6am the following day—in other words, NOT 24 hours.) The **Lufthansa Airport Bus** (www.airportbus-muenchen.de; © **0180/583-8426**) runs between the airport and the main train station in Munich every 20 minutes from about 6:30am to 10:30pm. The trip takes about 40 minutes and costs 10.50€ one-way or 17€ round-trip. A **taxi** to the city center costs about 75€ and can take more than an hour if traffic is heavy.

BY TRAIN   You can easily reach Munich by train from any city in Germany or Europe. Daily trains arrive from Frankfurt (trip time: 3¾ hr.) and Berlin (trip time: 6 hr.). Munich's **Hauptbahnhof,** on Bahnhofplatz near the city center, is one of Europe's largest train stations, with a hotel, restaurants, shopping, and banking facilities. A train information office on the mezzanine level is open daily from 7am to 8pm; you can also call **Deutsche Bahn** (www.bahn.de; © **11861** for train information and schedules). Connected to the rail station are the city's extensive **S-Bahn** rapid-transit system and the **U-Bahn** (subway) system (see p. 313).

HOW TO "do" OKTOBERFEST

The world's greatest beer festival starts in September and runs to the first Sunday in October. All the *trinken und essen* (drinking and eating) at this giant 2½-week party takes place at the traditional **Theresienwiese** ("Wiesn" for short) festival grounds, where different beers are sold in 14 different tents, each with its own atmosphere and food (sausage and sauerkraut prevail). If you've got kids with you (they'll love the rides), the **Augustiner tent** is considered to be the most family-friendly tent. The best food is found at **Käfer's Wiesn'n-Schanke.**

Oktoberfest beer is delicious but strong, with a 5% to 7% alcohol level, and it's served in 1-liter portions. Translation: Pace your beer drinking and drink plenty of water, or you may find yourself on the floor instead of at the table. The

Wiesn welcomes millions of visitors, but only has seating for about 100,000, so if you want to sit, especially on busy weekend evenings, it's imperative to arrive early—the gates open at 10am—and claim your space.

BY CAR   Think twice about driving to or in Munich. Most of downtown is a pedestrian-only area—wonderful if you're a walker, a nightmare if you're a driver. Traffic jams are frequent, and parking spaces are elusive and costly. If you plan on making excursions into the countryside, renting a car in the city center instead of trekking out to the airport is more convenient. Car-rental companies with windows at the main train station include **Avis** (www.avis.com; ✆ **089/1260-000**), **Hertz** (www.hertz. com; ✆ **089/1295-001**), and **Sixt Autovermietung** (www.sixt.com; ✆ **089/550-2447**).

Visitor Information

Munich's tourist office, **Fremdenverkehrsamt München** (www. muenchen.de; ✆ **089/233-96500**), operates two tourist information centers where you can pick up a map of Munich and get information on cultural events. The one located in the **Hauptbahnhof** (main train station) at Bahnhofplatz 2 is open Monday through Saturday 9am to 8pm and Sunday from 10am to 6pm; this office offers a hotel-booking service. A second branch of the tourist office is located in the city center at Marienplatz in the **Neues Rathaus (New Town Hall);** hours are Monday through Friday 9am to 7pm, Saturday 9am to 4pm, and Sunday 10am to 2pm.

City Layout

Munich sprawls in all directions outward from the city center, or Innenstadt, which lies west of the Isar River. This is the area of most interest to visitors. Within the Innenstadt, the city's historic medieval core, or

The Virgin Mary tops a column in Marienplatz, Munich's historic heart.

Altstadt, is now a pedestrian-only district. At its heart is the famous **Marienplatz** square (see p. 320). From Marienplatz, a pedestrianized shopping corridor—Kaufingerstrasse and then Neuhauserstrasse—leads west to **Karlsplatz,** nicknamed "Stachus," where one of the ancient city gates once stood, and continues via Schützenstrasse to the **Hauptbahnhof,** the main train station.

North of Marienplatz, Dienerstrasse leads to the former royal palace, the **Residenz** (see p. 322), with a sprawling complex that fronts onto two major squares, **Max-Joseph-Platz** and **Odeonsplatz.** Radiating out from here are four major boulevards, built in the 19th century by the Bavarian kings to create a "new" Munich north of the medieval core. From Max-Joseph-Platz, the fashionable dining and shopping street **Maximilianstrasse** runs east to the River Insel; parallel to it, **Prinzregentenstrasse** begins just north of the palace gardens (the Hofgarten) and also runs east to the Insel. From Odeonsplatz, **Briennerstrasse** rolls grandly west to **Königsplatz** and the Museum Quarter (see p. 324); it eventually turns into **Nymphenburger Strasse,** which continues west to the Bavarian royals' summer palace, Schloss Nymphenburg (see p. 364). Leading north from Odeonsplatz, **Ludwigstrasse** passes through the university area and the once-Bohemian district **Schwabing,** which is bordered on the east by an extensive public park, the Englischer Garten.

South and west of Marienplatz, **Sendlinger Tor** and **Gärtnerplatz** are major intersections in the district known as **Glockenbachviertel,** a popular area for dining and nightlife. **Theresienwiese,** where Oktoberfest is held, is located southwest of the Altstadt.

The Neighborhoods in Brief
ALTSTADT (OLD CITY)
The oval-shaped **Altstadt (Old City)** centers around **Marienplatz,** a large paved public square dominated by the **Altes Rathaus** and **Neues**

Rathaus, with its picturesque Glockenspiel. Several major churches are also in the vicinity. **Kaufingerstrasse,** a pedestrian-only shopping street, starts at the west end of Marienplatz, and **Tal,** a retail and restaurant street, begins at the east side of the square. Just to the south of Marienplatz is the **Viktualienmarkt,** a wonderfully lively outdoor market. East of Marienplatz lies the **Platzl** quarter, famed for its nightlife, restaurants, and the landmark **Hofbräuhaus,** the most famous beer hall in the world. **Odeonsplatz,** to the north of Marienplatz, is one of Munich's most beautiful squares, site of the **Residenz** (former royal palace) and the giant **National Theatre,** home of the Bavarian State Opera.

KÖNIGSPLATZ & THE MUSEUM DISTRICT

Running west from Odeonsplatz is Briennerstrasse, a wide shopping avenue that leads to **Königsplatz (King's Square).** Flanking this large square are three neoclassical buildings constructed by Ludwig I and housing Munich's antiquities: the **Propyläen,** the **Glyptothek,** and the **Antikensammlungen.** Another trio of world-famous art museums— the **Alte Pinakothek (Old Masters Gallery),** the **Neue Pinakothek (New Masters Gallery),** and the **Pinakothek Moderne Kunst (Gallery of Modern Art)**—are located just northeast of Königsplatz.

SCHWABING

Ludwigstrasse connects the Altstadt with Schwabing, a former artists' quarter located north of the Altstadt and known for its cafes, restaurants, and nightlife. This northern section of the city, with **Leopoldstrasse** as its artery, had a Bohemian heyday before World War I and has become a restaurant and entertainment area popular with students and tourists. The **Englischer Garten** spreads out along its eastern border, while **Olympiapark** and Josephsplatz mark its western border.

GÄRTNERPLATZVIERTEL & GLOCKENBACHVIERTEL

South of the Inner City and straddling the Isar River are the **Gärtnerplatzviertel** and **Glockenbackviertel.** The former is named after the roundabout of the same name that sits in its center; both are home to concentration of independent boutiques, hip coffee shops, trendy restaurants, and a buzzing bar scene.

OLYMPIAPARK

Northwest of the city center, the site of the 1972 Olympics is now a multipurpose complex hosting concerts, sporting events, fairs and more. **BMW Welt,** the car maker's showroom, museum and factory, is located here.

NYMPHENBURG

Nymphenburg, about a 20-minute tram ride northwest of the city center, is of interest to tourists primarily because of **Schloss Nymphemburg,** the summer palace of Munich's long-ruling family, the Wittelsbachs. The ornately decorated palace with its adjacent museums and beautifully landscaped grounds make a trip here worthwhile.

BOGENHAUSEN & HAIDHAUSEN

East of the Isar River, outside the city center, lie **Bogenhausen** and **Haidhausen,** leafy and upmarket residential neighborhoods where you find many hotels and restaurants.

Getting Around

Munich is a large city, only slightly smaller than Berlin or Hamburg. The best way to explore is by walking and using the excellent public-transportation system. In the Altstadt, you can walk to all the attractions—in fact, you have to, because the Altstadt is a car-free zone.

BY PUBLIC TRANSPORTATION   An extensive network of **U-Bahn** (subway), **S-Bahn** (light-rail), **Strassenbahn** (trams), and **buses** makes getting anywhere in the city relatively easy. You'll probably use the underground U-Bahn and the aboveground **Strassenbahn** systems most frequently. The same ticket entitles you to ride U-Bahn, S-Bahn, trams, and buses. Purchase tickets from vending machines in U-Bahn and S-Bahn stations; the machines display instructions in English. You also can buy tickets in the tram or from a bus driver. Tickets must then be **validated** in the machines found on U-Bahn and S-Bahn platforms and in buses and trams; stick your ticket into the machine, which stamps it with the date and time. A validated ticket is valid for 2 hours. You can transfer as often as you like to any public transportation as long as you travel in the same direction.

Munich has **four concentric fare zones.** Most, if not all, of your sightseeing will take place in Zone 1, which includes the city center. A **single ticket** *(Einzelfahrkarte)* in Zone 1 costs 2.70€ if you pay cash and 2.60€ if you pay with a card; short trips (up to 4 stops) cost 1.40€ if you pay cash and 1.30€ if you pay with a card. For information, call the public-transportation authority, **MVV,** at ✆ **089/41424344,** or visit it online at www.mvv-muenchen.de.

Saving Money on Transportation

A **Tageskarte** (day ticket) good for a day of public transportation travel within the inner city costs 6.40€ for one adult; a **Partner Tageskarte** costs 12.29€ and is good for up to 5 people traveling together. A **3-Tageskarte** (3-day ticket) costs 16€; the **partner 3-tageskarte,** good for up to 5 people traveling together, costs 28.20€. You can buy these cards from U-Bahn and S-Bahn platform ticket vending machines or at station ticket windows.

BY TAXI   Taxis are cream-colored, plentiful, and expensive. You can get a taxi at one of the stands located all across the city, or you can hail a cab on the street if its rooftop light is illuminated. Taxi fares begin at 3.40€ and rise by 1.60€ per kilometer; there's an additional 1.30€ charge to order a taxi by phone. Call **Taxizentrale** at 🕿 **089/21610** for a radio-dispatched taxi. The **Über** ride-hailing service is also active in Munich, with many vehicles in the city limits.

BY BICYCLE   Munich is a bike-friendly city. One of the most convenient places to rent a bike is **Radius Bikes** (www.radiustours.com; 🕿 **089/5434877740**), at the far end of the Hauptbahnhof at Arnulfstrasse 2. The charge is 4 to 5€ per hour (2-hour minimum), or 15€ to 20€ per day. A deposit of 50€ or a credit card number is required; students receive a 10% discount. E-bikes are also available for daily rentals (38€). Radius Bikes is open mid-March through October daily 8:30am to 7pm; between May and August hours extend to 8pm.

[FastFACTS] MUNICH

8

Business Hours Most banks in the center city are open Monday to Friday 9am to 4 or 5pm; several also have Saturday hours. Most businesses and stores are open Monday to Saturday 9am to 6pm, although some close in the early afternoon on Saturday.

Dentists For an English-speaking dentist, go to the **Klinik und Poliklinik für Kieferchirurgie der Universität München,** Lindwurmstrasse 2A (🕿 **089/51600;** U-Bahn: Goetheplatz), the dental clinic for the university. It deals with emergency cases and is always open.

Doctors For 24-hour medical service, go to **Schwabing Hospital,** Kölner Platz 1 (🕿 **089/30680;** U-Bahn: Scheidplatz).

Emergencies For emergency medical aid or the police, phone 🕿 **110.** Call the fire department at 🕿 **112.**

Internet Access Chances are, Wi-Fi will be available either free or for a nominal charge at your hotel. WiFi is free at any **Starbucks** as well as at many restaurants and cafes.

Pharmacy/ Drugstores For an international drugstore where English is spoken, go to **Bahnhof Apotheke,** Bahnhofplatz 2 (🕿 **089/594119;** www.hauptbahnhof apo.de; U-Bahn/S-Bahn: Hauptbahnhof), open Monday to Friday 8am to 6:30pm and Saturday 8am to 2pm. If you need a prescription filled during off hours, call 🕿 **089/557661**

for locations of open pharmacies. The information is recorded and in German only, so you may need to get someone from your hotel staff to assist you.

Post Offices The most central post office is the **Postbank** at Bahnhofplatz, opposite the main train station exit; it's open Monday to Friday 8am to 7pm, and Saturday 9am to 3pm.

Safety Munich, like all big cities, has its share of crime, especially pickpocketing and purse and camera snatching, but it is generally a safe city. Most robberies occur in the much-frequented tourist areas, such as Marienplatz and the Hauptbahnhof, which can be particularly dangerous at night if you are traveling alone. Use caution and common sense.

MUNICH'S other FESTIVALS

EXPLORING MUNICH

Munich is one of the great sightseeing cities in Germany, bursting with first-rate museums, fascinating architecture, historic palaces, and beautiful parks. Enjoying Munich is easy, but if your time is limited, you'll have to make some difficult decisions because there is so much to see.

Asamkirche, a dazzling example of Bavarian rococo.

The Altstadt

Munich's historic center is at the top of almost every first-time visitor's itinerary, beginning with a stop at the wonderfully photo-op-worthy **Marienplatz** square (see p. 320)—timed just right, of course, to watch the **Glockenspiel** (see p. 320) put on its twice-daily show. Many other sights are packed into this compact area as well. The ramparts that once surrounded the medieval city were dismantled in the 19th century, but traces of them remain in the stout stone towers and arches of three Gothic city gates—**Isartor,** which dates from 1337, to the east of Marienplatz, the older **Sendlingertor** to the southwest, and the crenellated 16th-century **Karlstor** to the west at Karlsplatz. (Locals, by the way,

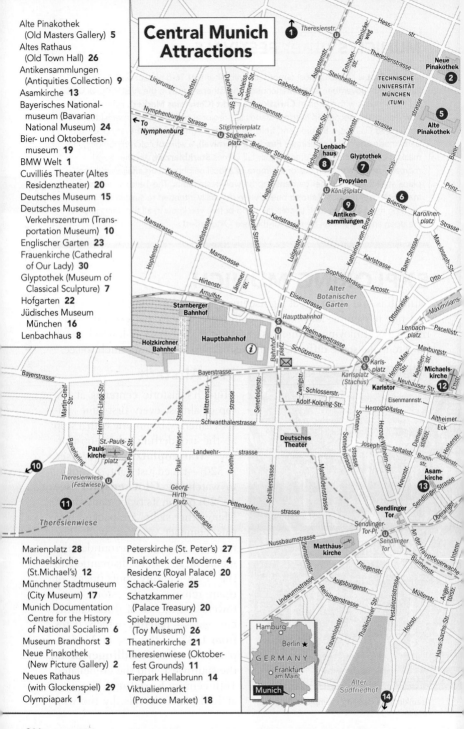

Alte Pinakothek
(Old Masters Gallery) **5**
Altes Rathaus
(Old Town Hall) **26**
Antikensammlungen
(Antiquities Collection) **9**
Asamkirche **13**
Bayerisches National-
museum (Bavarian
National Museum) **24**
Bier- und Oktoberfest-
museum **19**
BMW Welt **1**
Cuvilliés Theater (Altes
Residenztheater) **20**
Deutsches Museum **15**
Deutsches Museum
Verkehrszentrum (Trans-
portation Museum) **10**
Englischer Garten **23**
Frauenkirche (Cathedral
of Our Lady) **30**
Glyptothek (Museum of
Classical Sculpture) **7**
Hofgarten **22**
Jüdisches Museum
München **16**
Lenbachhaus **8**

Central Munich Attractions

Marienplatz **28**
Michaelskirche
(St.Michael's) **12**
Münchner Stadtmuseum
(City Museum) **17**
Munich Documentation
Centre for the History
of National Socialism **6**
Neue Pinakothek
(New Picture Gallery) **2**
Neues Rathaus
(with Glockenspiel) **29**
Olympiapark **1**

Peterskirche (St. Peter's) **27**
Pinakothek der Moderne **4**
Residenz (Royal Palace) **20**
Schack-Galerie **25**
Schatzkammer
(Palace Treasury) **20**
Spielzeugmuseum
(Toy Museum) **26**
Theatinerkirche **21**
Theresienwiese (Oktober-
fest Grounds) **11**
Tierpark Hellabrunn **14**
Viktualienmarkt
(Produce Market) **18**

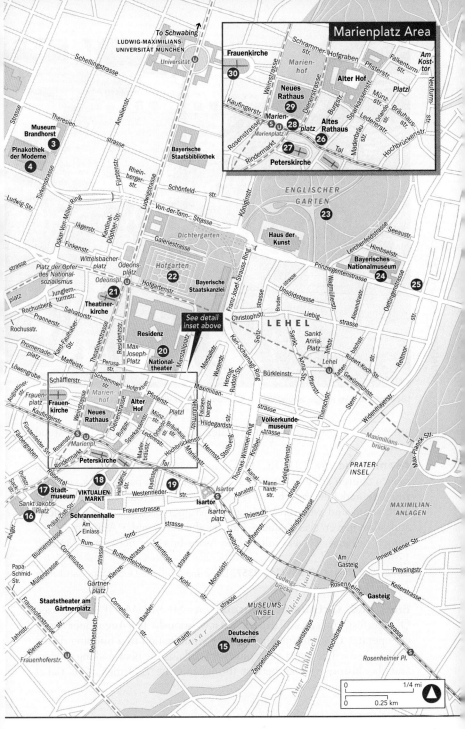

Marienplatz Area

To Schwabing

LUDWIG-MAXIMILIANS-
UNIVERSITÄT MÜNCHEN

Universität

Frauenkirche

30

Neues
Rathaus

29

Marien-
platz

28

Altes
Rathaus

26

Peterskirche

27

Alter Hof

Am
Kostor

Platzl

Schellingstrasse

Theresien-
strasse

**Museum
Brandhorst** **3**

**Pinakothek
der Moderne** **4**

Bayerische
Staatsbibliothek

Schönfeld-str.

ENGLISCHER
GARTEN

23

Haus der
Kunst

Bayerisches
Nationalmuseum **24**

25

Hofgarten

22

Bayerische
Staatskanzlei

LEHEL

Theatiner-
kirche

21

Residenz

Max-
Joseph-
Platz

National-
theater **20**

See detail
inset above

Sankt-
Anna-
Platz

Lehel

Frauen-
platz

**Frauen-
kirche**

Marien-
hof

Neues
Rathaus

Alter
Hof

Platzl

Völkerkunde-
museum

Maximilians-
brücke

Peterskirche

Marienpl.

18

**Stadt-
museum** **17**

VIKTUALIEN-
MARKT

Westenrieder-
str.

19

Isartor **5**

Isartor-
platz

PRATER-
INSEL

MAXIMILIAN-
ANLAGEN

16

Sankt-Jakobs-
Platz

Schrannenhalle

Am
Einlass

Am
Gasteig

Preysingstr.

**Staatstheater am
Gärtnerplatz**

Gärtner-
platz

MUSEUMS-
INSEL

Gasteig

**Deutsches
Museum** **15**

Rosenheimer Pl. **5**

0   1/4 mi

0   0.25 km

Locals and tourists mingle around the open-air food stalls of Viktualienmarkt.

always call Karlsplatz "Stachus," after a popular pub that once stood here.)

Asamkirche ★★ CHURCH   For a dizzying hit of Italianate Bavarian rococo church architecture at its most flamboyant, pay a quick visit this small, remarkable church that is a bit off the main tourist circuit, a short walk south and west of Marienplatz. Multicolored marbles, gold leaf, and silver cover every square inch of the rectangular Asamkirche, so named because it was built by the Asam brothers between 1733 and 1746.

Sendlinger Strasse. © **089/260-9357.** Daily 8am–5:30pm. U-/S-Bahn: Sendlinger Tor.

Bier- und Oktoberfestmuseum ★ MUSEUM   If you missed Oktoberfest, you can still experience it vicariously. The Augustiner Brewery operates this cultural and culinary combination in a building dating back to 1327. The multi-story museum explains the beer-making process and the history of Oktoberfest throughout the centuries. Your ticket includes a voucher for a glass of beer and a traditional snack such as the Bavarian cheese *Obatzda* with *Leberwurst* (liver sausage) or *Schmalz* (chicken fat spread over freshly baked rye bread. After 6pm you can return to the restaurant for regional Bavarian fare such as beer-infused goulash and noodles, sausage salads and *Schnitzels.*

Sterneckstrasse 2. www.bier-und-oktoberfestmuseum.de. ✆ **089/24243941.** Admission 4€. Tues–Sat 1–6pm; beer hall Tues–Sat 6pm–midnight. U-/S-Bahn: Isartor.

Frauenkirche (Cathedral of Our Lady) ★ CATHEDRAL   Munich's largest church, completed in the late 15th century, was a pile of smoldering rubble at the end of World War II, with only its landmark twin onion-domed towers from 1525 remained standing. The painstakingly rebuilt Gothic church is strikingly simple and dignified, and the view from the tower is spectacular.

Frauenplatz (near the Rathaus) 1. www.muenchner-dom.de. ✆ **089/2900820.** Free admission to church; tower 3€ adults, 1.50€ children. Church daily 7am–8:30pm; tower Apr–Oct daily 10am–5pm. U-/S-Bahn: Marienplatz.

Jüdisches Museum München (Jewish Museum) MUSEUM   From the original suggestion of the idea in 1928, the creation of a Jewish museum in Munich took more than 75 years to become a reality. This striking modern building, constructed along with the adjacent synagogue and community center, opened in 2007 and displays a variety of exhibits about Jewish culture. The history of Munich as it concerns the Jews is explored on all three floors; other exhibits give background on the

VISITING THE viktualienmarkt (PRODUCE MARKET)

Located on the square of the same name, close to Marienplatz, the Viktualienmarkt has been serving Munich residents for nearly 200 years and is a wonderful place to stroll and sniff and take in the local scene. On a sunny Saturday it might seem like the entire poulation of Munich is here, not just enjoying the lively atmosphere but actually food shopping. In an area the size of a city block, you find butcher shops, cheese sellers, a coffee roaster, a juice bar, fish sellers, wine merchants, dozens of produce stalls, a whole section of bakeries stocked with dozens of different kinds of Bavarian breads and rolls, and a popular beer garden where on any given day you are likely to see locals in lederhosen and feather hats, proudly strutting their stuff. Most of the permanent stands open at 6am and stay open until 6pm on weekdays, or until 1pm on Saturday. You can buy food at the market stalls and eat it in the beer garden if you buy a beer, a soda, water, or other beverage at the beer-garden drink stand. You can easily find the market from Marienplatz; it's bounded by Prälat-Zistl-Strasse on the west, Frauen Strasse to the south, Heiliggeiststrasse on the east, and Tal on the north.

Diaspora and illuminate Jewish traditions, religious holidays, and rites of passage, from circumcision to bar mitzvahs and funerals.

St.-Jakobs-Platz 16. www.juedisches-museum-muenchen.de. ℂ **089/23396096.** Admission 6€ adults, 3€ students and seniors, free for children 5 and under, 9€ family ticket (2 adults and up to 4 children). Tues–Sun 10am–6pm. U-Bahn or S-Bahn: Marienplatz.

Marienplatz ★★★ PLAZA   The traditional heart of Munich is this large pedestrian-only square named in honor of the Virgin Mary, a gilded version of whom gazes benevolently down from the tall stone column in the middle of the square. On the north side is the **Neues Rathaus (New City Hall),** bristling with spires in full-on 19th-century Gothic Revival style, and famous for its **Glockenspiel** (see box below). Like hiking? Huff-and-puff your way up the 55 steps of the tower (you can also hop on an elevator) and take in the city panorama (tower admission 1.50€; open Monday to Friday 9am–7pm and Saturday to Sunday 10am–7pm). To the right of the Neues Rathaus stands the building it replaced, the 15th-century **Altes Rathaus (Old City Hall),** with its much more plain but authentically Gothic tower.

Michaelskirche (St. Michael's Church) ★ CHURCH   A single-nave church with a soaring barrel-vaulted ceiling completed in 1597, St. Michael's is the largest Renaissance church north of the Alps. Bronze statues of Bavarian kings decorate the Baroque façade, while the elaborate stucco-work of the interior represents episodes from the life of Jesus.

Neuhauserstrasse 52. ℂ **089/231-7060.** Free admission. Mon–Sat 8:30am–7pm; Sun 6:45am–10pm. U-/S-Bahn: Marienplatz.

Münchner Stadtmuseum (City Museum) ★   Housed in a 15th-century armory, this museum chronicles Munich's history and the everyday lives of its residents. The one must-see exhibit is the *Moriskentanzer* **(Moorish dancers),** featuring ten carved and brightly painted 15th-century wooden figures. The second-floor photo museum traces the early history of the camera back to 1839. On the third-floor there's a

---

WATCHING THE glockenspiel

The best show on Marienplatz takes place at 11am and 9pm daily (also at noon and 5pm during the holiday seasons) when the 43-bell Glockenspiel on the 280-foot central spire of the Neues Rathaus goes through its paces. Brightly painted mechanical figures reenact two famous events from Munich's history: the knights' tournament during the 1586 wedding feast of Wilhelm V and Renate of Lorraine, and, one level below, the *Schäfflertanz* (Coopers' Dance), first performed in 1683 to express gratitude for the end of the plague.

historic collection of marionettes and hand puppets and a gallery of fairground art, which includes the oldest-known carousel horses, dating from 1820. A cafeteria in the museum's main courtyard is open daily 10am to midnight.

St. Jacobs-Platz 1. www.stadtmuseum-online.de. © **089/23322370.** Admission 7€ adults, 3.50€ students. Tues–Sun 10am–6pm. U-/S-Bahn: Marienplatz.

Peterskirche (St. Peter's Church) ★ The bell tower of this 13th-century Gothic church, remodeled during the baroque era, is known locally as "Altes Peter" (Old Pete). You get a splendid view from the top, but you have to climb (and climb and climb) 306 steps to see it. The interior of the church contains baroque-era sculptures and some glorious ceiling frescoes by Johann Baptist Zimmermann, the genius behind the Wieskirche pilgrimage church in southern Bavaria (see p. 287). Don't miss the bizarre relic in the second chapel (on the left): the gem-studded skeleton of St. Mundita, who stares at you with two false eyes in her skull.

Rindermarkt 1 (near the Rathaus). © **089/2604828.** Church free; tower 1.50€ adults, 1 € children. Mon–Sat 9am–6pm (Nov–Mar until 5pm). U-/S-Bahn: Marienplatz.

Theatinerkirche ★ CHURCH Named for the Theatines, a group of Roman Catholic clergy, this church is Munich's finest example of Italian baroque architecture. The church was begun by Italian architects in 1663 and was completed by German court architects about a century later. Fluted columns lining the center aisle support the arched ceiling of the nave. Every surface appears to be loaded with dollops of fanciful white stuccowork. The dome above the transept is decorated with an ornate gallery of large statues. Dark wooden pews and a canopied pulpit provide the only color in the all-white interior.

Theatinerstrasse 22. © **089/2106960.** Free admission. Mon–Fri 10am–1pm and 1:30–4:30pm; Sat 10am–3pm. U-Bahn: Odeonsplatz.

The Residenz (Royal Palace Complex)

Before building castles in the countryside became à la mode, the Bavarian royal family, the Wittelsbachs, resided here, a short walk north of the Marienplatz. Underground portions remain from the original 1358 castle called the Neuveste, but most of what you see in this immense palace dates from the 16th century or later. The whole is a hodgepodge of styles: a Palladian facade facing the Hofgarten, Renaissance sections along Residenzstrasse, a Florentine front overlooking Max-Joseph-Platz. Its role as a royal dwelling expired with the kingdom itself in 1918, and the bombs of the subsequent World War took their toll. Yet, just like the Frauenkirche, the Münchners rebuilt the prized palace piece by piece, a fact that makes a visit here well worth it. A combined ticket gives you entry

The ornate Imperial Hall in the Residenz, designed to impress.

to all three parts of the complex, but there's so much to see here, you'll have to pick and choose. The **Residenz Museum** will take over two hours to visit if you let it; if you are strapped for time, the one must-see is the engrossing **Schatzkammer.** Then there's the unique **Cuvilliés Theater,** which some may delight in while others shrug at. Also part of the complex are the **Hofgarten** (see p. 322) formal gardens, the **Bavarian State Theater** (p. 359), and the **Nationaltheater** (see p. 359).

Residenz (Royal Palace) ★ PALACE Tour maps of the Residenz, which has more than 120 rooms, lead through countless corridors and galleries, built in different eras for different Wittelsbach rulers, and it can be somewhat difficult to keep them all straight. Some rooms are worth lingering in, however. When it was completed by 1571, the long **Antiquarium** was the first addition to the original Neuveste. Although it was first intended as a gallery to house Albrecht V's sculpture collection, the 66m-long (216-ft.) hall was soon converted into a banquet room and it was definitely designed to impress. Sixteen ceiling paintings by Peter Candid (c. 1548-1628) portray fame and virtue, while depictions of 102 Bavarian towns by Hans Donau the Elder (c. 1521-1596) blanket the rest of the high vaulted ceiling. Admire the marble table in front of the chimney as well as the two credenzas by Friedrich Sustris containing rare majolica porcelain. The **Grotto Courtyard,** the royalty's secret little piece of Italy, links the Antiquarium with the **Ancestral Gallery,** an over-the-top celebration of gilded stucco and portraits that was intended to boast the Wittelsbach family's claim to the throne (note the towering family tree midway down the gallery). The neighboring **Porcelain Cabinet** is an early Rococo gem, showcasing fine ceramic pieces in a mirrored room with gilded stucco by Johann Baptist Zimmermann (see the Wieskirche, p. 287). Maximilian I's own private **Ornate Chapel,** with its dazzling blue-and-gold ceiling, was painstakingly reconstructed to its original design. The magnificent **Imperial Hall and Staircase** boast a riot of Baroque decoration, clearly intended to wow guests as they arrived to the court. François de Cuvilliés's **Green Gallery,** elegantly wallpapered in green silk damask, also arouses the imagination, given the lavish soirees that once occurred here.

Max-Joseph-Platz 3. www.residenz-muenchen.de. ℰ **089/290671.** Combination ticket for Residenzmuseum, Schatzkammer, Theater 13€ adults, 11€ seniors, free for students and children. Free audio guides available in English. Daily Apr–Sept 9am–6pm; Oct–Mar 10am–5pm, last entry one hour before closing. U-Bahn: Odeonsplatz.

Cuvilliés Theater ★★ ARCHITECTURAL SITE

Located in the Brunnenhof section of the palace complex, the Cuvilliés Theater is a highlight for fans of Rococo, for it's one of the few theaters constructed in the style, and it's been marvelously well-preserved. The royal family sat in its box at the back of the theater rather than next to the stage. Notice how rarely any motifs are repeated in the decoration, from the red draperies lining the balconies, to the faux curtains on either side of the stage, to each telemon and caryatid in between each box. Mozart's premiere of *Idomeneo* took place here in 1781, a sellout needless to say. Today the theater is still in use for performances by the Bavarian State Opera and the Bayerischestaatshaupiel (see p. 359).

Residenzstrasse 1. www.residenz-muenchen.de. ℰ **089/290671.** Combination ticket for Residenzmuseum, Schatzkammer, Theater 13€ adults, 11€ seniors, free for students and children. Free audio guides available in English. Daily Apr–Sept 9am–6pm; Oct–Mar 10am–5pm, last entry one hour before closing. U-Bahn: Odeonsplatz.

Schatzkammer (Treasury) ★★ PALACE

The Residenz's palace treasury rivals its counterparts in Dresden and Vienna and is one of the most important treasuries in Europe. Arranged chronologically, the first three rooms feature rare and priceless pieces, including an English queen's crown. Cast in Paris around 1375 and bequeathed to the Wittelbachs when Blanche of England married into the family, this is the oldest English crown in existence (since when Oliver Cromwell had

Weekends are definitely a great time to visit Munich's top art museums, with special pricing that encourages locals to spend their free time looking at great art. On Saturday, you can enjoy the treasures in all three Pinakotheks (Alte, Neue, der Moderne), Museum Brandhorst, and Schack-Galerie for 1€. On Sunday, the Glyptothek, Antikensammlungen, and the Bayerisches Nationalmuseum reduce their prices to 1€.

most of the other English crown jewels melted down in 1649). The equally impressive 16th-century Renaissance statue of *St. George Slaying the Dragon* was likely given as a gift for Wilhelm V, whose face looked a lot like the knight's.

Max-Joseph-Platz 3. www.residenz-muenchen.de. ℂ **089/290671.** Combination ticket for Residenzmuseum, Schatzkammer, Theater 13€ adults, 11€ seniors, free for students and children. Free audio guides available in English. Daily Apr–Sept 9am–6pm; Oct–Mar 10am–5pm, last entry one hour before closing. U-Bahn: Odeonsplatz.

Museumsviertel (Museum Quarter)

You could spend days exploring the four art museums that make up the Museum Quarter, also called the Kunstareal. All four are worth visiting, but the enormous **Alte Pinakothek,** with its world-class collection of Old Masters, is a must-see. The smaller **Neue Pinakothek,** featuring gems from the 19th century, and the **Pinakothek der Moderne** and **Museum Brandhorst,** both in new buildings and dedicated to 20th-century art, round out this rather amazing collection of museums.

Alte Pinakothek (Old Masters Gallery) ★★★ ART MUSEUM Pinakothek means "painting gallery," and the nearly 800 paintings on display in this enormous building represent the greatest European artists of the 14th through 18th centuries. It was opened in 1836, and built specifically to display one of the gems of the royal family's collection, Peter Paul Rubens's massive *The Last Judgment.* (The Wittelsbachs were particularly fond of the Dutch masters, and assembled quite an impressive collection of their work.) The museum is so immense that you can easily spend several days exploring the two floors of exhibits. To make the most of your time here, pick up a museum guide at the information desk, decide which paintings you particularly want to see, and then spend at least 2 to 3 hours. A free audio tour in English is available in the lobby. Important highlights include ten paintings by **Albrecht Dürer,** including the haunting *Self-Portrait with Fur-Trimmed Robe,* painted in 1500 when he was 29; it's the first self-portrait ever painted by an artist. The Italian school is well represented with canvases by **Raphael, Leonardo da Vinci** and **Botticelli.** The red-walled **Rubenssaal** displays 17

Old Masters hang in the Alte Pinakothek.

large-scale canvases by Rubens, with more by the great Dutch painter in an adjoining salon. **Rembrandt** is also well represented; take a look at his *Self-Portrait,* painted in 1629 when he was 23. **Francois Boucher**'s loving portrait of Madame de Pompadour (1756) is a highlight from the French school. **Pieter Bruegel the Elder**'s Bosch-like *Land of Cockaigne* (1567) and *Harbor Scene with Christ Preaching* (1598) are also worth seeking out. *Note:* Until 2018, various sections of the museum will be closed for renovations. Inquire online for the most up-to-date status of what is open and closed during your visit.

Barer Strasse 27. www.pinakothek.de. © **089/23805216.** Admission 7€ adults, 5€ students and seniors; Sat 1€; during renovations 2€ adults, 2€ students and seniors. Tues–Sun 10am–5pm (Tues until 8pm). U-Bahn: Theresienstrasse. Tram: 27. Bus: 100.

Museum Brandhorst ★ ART MUSEUM   Paintings, sculpture, works on paper, and art installations from the mid– to late 20th century are showcased in this striking museum which opened in 2009. Udo and Anette Brandhorst donated their collection of contemporary art, assembled over a lifetime, to this museum. Constructed with sustainable "green" features, the building is the most avant-garde museum in the city, with an intriguing façade clad in multi-colored ceramic rods. On display are works by American artists including a large collection of works by Cy Twombly, the American artist celebrated for his calligraphic-style graffiti paintings. Other artists featured include Andy Warhol, Jean-Michel Basquiat, and Alex Katz; the controversial British artist Damien Hirst, famous for his series of dead animals preserved in formaldehyde; the German painter Sigmar Polke; and an unusual collection of books illustrated by Picasso.

Kunstareal, Theresienstrasse 35A. www.museum-brandhorst.de. ℰ 089/238052286. Admission 7€ adults, 5€ children 5–16; Sat 1€. Tues–Sun 10am–6pm (Thurs until 8pm). U-Bahn: Königsplatz or Theresienstrasse. Bus: 100 or 154.

Neue Pinakothek (New Picture Gallery) ★★★ ART MUSEUM

After its original neoclassical building was destroyed in World War II, this museum—a world-class showcase for 19th-century German and European art—was re-housed in this postmodern stone building built in 1981. Not quite as daunting as the nearby Alte, the Neue still contains a wealth of major artworks. The museum focuses primarily on two collections. The first is German, with an emphasis on Romantic works and those associated with Ludwig I, the king of Bavaria from 1825 to 1848, who was a great patron of the arts and an ardent collector. Sublime landscapes by the German artist Casper David Friedrich (1174-1840), including *Summer* (1807) and *Riesengebirge with Rising Fog* (1819), illuminate the Romantic style of painting. The second collection highlights European Impressionism, starting with Edouard Manet and continuing with canvases by Van Gogh (one of his *Sunflowers* from 1888), Monet, Goya, Munch, Degas, Renoir, and Klimt. English artists whose works are on view include Thomas Gainsborough, Joshua Reynolds, and William Turner. A tour of the highlights takes a couple of hours; an audio tour in English is free with your admission.

Barerstrasse 27 (across Theresienstrasse from the Alte Pinakothek). www.pinakothek. de. ℰ 089/23805195. Admission 7€ adults, 5€ students and seniors; Sat 1€. Wed–Mon 10am–6pm (Wed until 8pm). U-Bahn: Theresienstrasse. Tram: 27. Bus: 100.

Pinakothek der Moderne ★★ ART MUSEUM

Munich's modern art museum contains four collections, all housed in a pristine white box of a building, designed by Stefan Braunfels and opened in 2002. The most important is the **Staatsgalerie moderner Kunst (Gallery of Modern Art),** displaying major 20th-century classics by internationally known artists including Matisse, Picasso, Gris, Ernst, Giacometti, and others. Alongside you'll find a wealth of excellent German modern art, represented by *Die Brücke* artists like Kirchner and Schmidt-Rotluff, and the *Blaue Reiter* group with Kandinsky, Franz Marc, and Auguste Macke. Sculpture, photography, and video are also part of this collection. The other museum holdings include the **Neue Sammlung (Craft and Design Collection),** the **Museum of Architecture** (architectural drawings, photographs, and models), and the **Graphische Sammlung**

The Pinakothek de Moderne, a pristine setting for modern art.

(Graphics Collection), which is not open to the general public except by request.

Barerstrasse 40. www.pinakothek.de. © **089/23805360.** Admission 10€ adults, 7€ students and seniors; Sat 1€. Tues–Sun 10am–6pm (Thurs until 8pm). U-Bahn: Odeonsplatz.

Königsplatz

Ludwig I (king of Bavaria from 1825 to 1848) set out to make Munich a second Athens, an endeavor best embodied in the classically inspired architecture of Königsplatz, 2 blocks south of the Museumsviertel. Here, flanking the templelike **Propyläen** monument, stand the **Antikensammlungen** and **Glyptothek,** twin museums with stately columned entrances, which were built to house the king's collections of Greek and Roman artifacts. If antiquities don't interest you, the nearby **Lenbachhaus** with its outstanding collection of late 19th- and early 20th-century German art is definitely worth the trip.

Antikensammlungen (Antiquities Collections) ★ ART MUSEUM
An essential stop for anyone interested in ancient art, this museum's five main-floor halls house a world-class collection of more than 650 Greek vases, from a pre-Mycenaean version carved in 3000 B.C. from a mussel

shell to large Greek and Etruscan vases. If you like antiquities but ancient vases ain't your thing, opt for the more interesting Glyptothek across the square.

Königsplatz 1. www.antike-am-koenigsplatz.mwn.de. © **089/59988830.** Admission 3.50€ adults, 2.50€ students and seniors; Sun 1€. Tues–Sun 10am–5pm (Thurs until 8pm). U-Bahn: Königsplatz.

Glyptothek (Museum of Sculpture) ★★ART MUSEUM   Located directly across from the Antikensammlung, the Glyptothek exhibits Germany's largest collection of ancient Greek and Roman sculpture, exhibited in light-flooded galleries on pedestals which allow you to view the statues from all angles. A major highlight of the collection is marble statues from the pediments of a temple from the island of Aegina, a priceless relic which ranks up there with the Pergamon Altar in Berlin or the still-disputed Acropolis marbles in London's British Museum. Also check out the 6th-century-B.C. *kouroi* (statues of youths), the colossal *Sleeping Satyr* from the Hellenistic period, a sublime bust of Caesar Augustus, and a haunting collection of Roman portraits.

Königsplatz 3. www.antike-am-koenigsplatz.mwn.de. © **089/286100.** Admission 3.50€ adults, 2.50€ students and seniors; Sun 1€. Tues–Sun 10am–5pm (Thurs until 8pm). U-Bahn: Königsplatz.

The Glyptothek displays Germany's premier collection of classical sculpture.

Lenbachhaus ★★★ ART MUSEUM   Centered around an Italianate villa built by the painter Franz von Lenbach between 1887 and 1891 to serve as his residence and atelier, this museum today displays a dazzling collection of late-19th and early-20th-century German Impressionist and Expressionist art. The museum, which reopened in 2013 after a complete refurbishment that added a new wing, is especially known for its outstanding collection of works by the *Blaue Reiter* (Blue Rider) school of artists working in Munich before World War I. Bold colors and abstract forms characterize the work of the artists represented, including Wasily Kandinsky, Paul Klee, Franz Marc, and Gabriele Münter. The treasure-trove of art here also includes painters from von Lenbach himself to modernists such as Joseph Beuys, Ellsworth Kelly, and Sol LeWitt. Exhibitions or contemporary work are held in the new wing and in the adjacent Kunstbau.

Luisenstrasse 33. www.lenbachhaus.de ℂ **089/2333200.** Admission 10€ adults, 5€ students. Tues–Sun 10am–6pm (Tues until 9pm). U-Bahn: Königsplatz.

Munich Documentation Centre for the History of National Socialism ★ MUSEUM   Often called the Nazi museum in the press, this museum dedicated to tracing the history of fascism and socialism in Germany opened its doors in 2015. The museum sits on the former site of the Nazi headquarters, where the birth of the party took place. Through the use of audiovisual clips and detailed documents, including original swastika flags and SS (Nazi) uniforms, the museum does an excellent job of explaining the origins of Adolf Hitler's beliefs, why Munich became the cradle of the party, how the fascist movement grew, and how Hitler's party eventually took over the country with its ideology.

Briennerstrasse 34. www.ns-dokuzentrum-muenchen.de ℂ **089/23367000.** Admission 5€ adults, 2.50€ children 5–16. Tues–Sun 10am–7pm. U-Bahn: Königsplatz or Odeonsplatz.

Prinzregentenstrasse

At the southern end of Munich's most famous public park, the sprawling Englischer Garten (see p. 333), stately Prinzregentenstrasse was the last-built of the "new" Munich's four monumental boulevards. (See City Layout, p. 310). Today it is dominated by museums—principally the immense **Bayerisches Nationalmuseum** (see below), but also the **Haus der Kunst,** a venue for rotating contemporary art exhibitions, and the delightful if quirky **Schack-Gallerie** (see p. 330).

Bayerisches Nationalmuseum (Bavarian National Museum) ★★ MUSEUM   In 1855, King Maximilian II inaugurated this shrine to the arts in Bavaria, with a collection so big that it had to location-hop until it found its home in this ornate building by Gabriel von Seidl, architect of the Lenbachhaus (p. 329) and parts of the Deutsches Museum (p. 331). The vast collection includes sculpture, painting, folk art, ceramics, furniture, and textiles in addition to clocks and scientific instruments. It can be overwhelming if you try to see everything, so linger over items that interest you and stroll past the rest. The museum's collection of early and medieval **church art** is particularly worthwhile—look for the Romanesque sculptures from Wessobrunn monastery, the original 1490 Gothic altar that once stood in Peterskirche (see p. 321), and an entire room of wood sculptures by the great German mastercarver **Tilman Riemenschneider Room** (1460–1531, see box on p. 252). The museum also contains a famous collection of **Christmas Nativity cribs** from Bavaria, Tyrol, and southern Italy. Some other highlights to search out: a collection of Bavarian beer steins *(Humpen)*; **Jakob Sandtner's models** of Bavarian cities; a Renaissance **ceremonial hammer** used by the Pope to open the doors of St. Peter's, given in 1550 to the Augsburg cardinal; **King Othon's coronation garb** (1835), which was made for the Bavarian-born King of Greece but never worn; and a fascinating **astronomical floor clock** with a hilarious ensemble of cherubs and animals of the zodiac (look for the baby being pinched by Cancer's claw).

Prinzregentenstrasse 3. www.bayerisches-nationalmuseum.de. ✆ **089/2112401.** Admission 7€ adults, 6€ students and seniors, free for children 14 and under; Sun admission for all 1€. Tues–Sun 10am–5pm (Thurs until 8pm). U-Bahn: Lehel. Tram: 17. Bus: 100.

Schack-Galerie ★ MUSEUM   To appreciate this florid and romantic overdose of sentimental German paintings of the 19th century, you've got to enjoy fauns and elves at play in picturesque, even magical, landscapes. Such art has its devotees. Obviously, if you're a Picasso cubist, you'd be better off going elsewhere. But this once-private collection adheres to the Baroque tastes of Count Adolf Friedrich von Schack of Schwerin (1815–94), who spent a rich life acquiring works by the likes of Spitzweg, Schwind, Fuerbach, and others, many others—some of whom frankly should have been assigned to the dustbin of art history. Still, in all, we find a visit here fun, at least on a rainy, gray day. It's like wandering back to a lost world.

Prinzregentenstrasse 9. www.pinakothek.de. ✆**089/23805224.** Admission 4€ adults, 3€ children; Sat 1€. Wed–Sun 10am–6pm, first and third Wed of each month until 8pm. U-Bahn: Lehel Bus: 100.

Outside Central Munich

BMW Welt ★★ ARCHITECTURAL SITE/MUSEUM/FACTORY TOUR   If you have any interest in the luxury brand BMW (Bavarian Motor Works), take the short trip out to Olympiapark to see the BMW Welt showroom. Architecturally, this new-car showroom is a boldly

BMW Welt combines an auto showroom, factory tour, and museum.

dramatic structure with soaring lines and a glass-enclosed hourglass-shaped spiral ramp, which leads up to a skybridge to the museum and factory buildings, all part of the BMW Welt complex. The interior of the showroom is sinuous and sexy, showing off all the latest models like perfectly lit celebrities. This is BMW's delivery center in Germany, and there's a gallery where you can watch emotional owners picking up the keys to their new BMWs. Have a look around (it's free), and if you're a car buff, buy your ticket for the 2-hour tour of the **BMW Munich Plant** where you'll see the cars assembled. The company's superb collection of vintage vehicles is housed in the fascinating but overpriced **BMW Museum.** Organized into categories (history, technology, racing, design), it includes motorcycles and automobiles from the company's beginning in 1929 to a hydrogen-powered roadster of the future.

Am Olympiapark 1. www.bmw-welt.com. ✆ **0180/1118822.** Museum admission 10€ adults, 7€ seniors and children; factory tour 6€ adults, 3€ seniors and children. Showroom daily 7:30am–midnight; museum daily 9am–6pm; factory tours Mon–Fri 8:30am–10pm. U-Bahn: Olympiazentrum.

Deutsches Museum ★★ MUSEUM   Located on the Museumsinsel, an island in the Isar River, this is the largest science and technology museum in the world and one of the most popular attractions in Germany. It's at least a 15- or 20-minute walk from the sights around

Marienplatz, so you'll probably want to block out at least half a day to visit here—you'll need it, because this huge collection includes some 15,000 exhibits in 50 department. True, most of the important inventions highlighted here are German-made, but that's because Germans were at the forefront of so many scientific developments in the 19th century and onward—such as the first electric dynamo (built by Siemens in 1866), the first diesel engine (Rudolf Diesel, 1897), and the laboratory bench at which the atom was first split (Otto Hahn, Lise Meitner, and Fritz Strassmann, 1938). Some exhibits are interactive, and there are regular demonstrations of glass blowing, papermaking, and how steam engines, pumps, and historical musical instruments work. You'll see historic items from the ancient (a full-scale replica of the famous cave full of Stone Age paintings found in Altamira, Spain) to the dawn of the modern era (a Model A biplane flown by the Wright brothers at Tempelhof airport in 1908) to the future (labs where you can study DNA). The astronomy exhibit is the largest in Europe, complete with a planetarium and a two-domed observatory with a solar telescope. Unless you have a keen interest in science and technology, however, this enormous museum can be a bit mind-numbing, because many of its historic objects are displayed as relics without much dynamic presentation. The **Verkehrszentrum,** the museum's spin-off transportation museum (see below), is far more intriguing. **Note:** The Deutsches Museum is currently undergoing an modernization program that will run through 2019; while the museum will remain open, various sections will be closed for renovation, so check on-line to see which areas are affected at the time of your visit.

Museumsinsel 1. www.deutsches-museum.de. © **089/21791.** Admission 11€ adults, 7€ seniors, 4.50€ students. Daily 9am–5pm. U-Bahn: Schwanthalerhöhe.

Deutsches Museum Verkehrszentrum (Transportation Museum) ★★ MUSEUM

How have people transported themselves for the last 200 years? You'll find out at this intriguing museum, a spin-off of the **Deutsches Museum** (see above) that focuses on mobility technology, travel, and urban transport. Here you can see "Puffing Billy," an early steam-engine locomotive from 1814, step into a passenger train from the late 19th century, and peer inside a modern high-speed ICE train. There's a wonderful collection of horse-drawn carriages, and some of the bicycles on display are 150 years old. And then there's the superlative collection of historic automobiles, including Daimlers, Opels, Mercedes, Tatas, Citroens and Bugattis. All these vehicles are exhibited in three historic exhibition halls dating from 1908, which have been restored to their original appearance.

Theresienhohe 14a. www.deutsches-museum.de/verkehrszentrum. © **089/500806762.** Admission 6€ adults, 4€children. Daily 9am–5pm. U-Bahn: Schwanthalerhöhe.

Transportation of all modes is the theme of the Deutsches Museum Verkerhszentrum.

Parks & Gardens

Englischer Garten (English Garden) ★★★ PARK Munich's famous city park is one of the largest (922 acres) and most beautiful city parks in Europe. Established in 1789, the Englischer Garten also is the oldest public park in the world. Its name comes from the fact that it was not only designed by an Englishman, Sir Benjamin Thompson, but was laid out in the informal English style of landscape architecture, meant to replicate natural countryside. You can wander for hours along its miles of tree-shaded walks. Special features include a **Japanese teahouse** on a small island at the park's south end; a large lake, **Kleinhesseloher See,** which you can paddle around on pedal boats; and the round, hilltop temple called the **Monopteros,** constructed in the 19th century, which offers great views of Munich's Altstadt. A giant beer garden (open Apr–Oct) occupies the plaza near the picturesque **Chinesischer Turm (Chinese Pagoda),** a postwar reconstruction of a park folly first built in 1790. The banks of the **Eisbach,** the stream that runs through the park, are popular nude-sunbathing spots; on a section of the stream at the park's southern end, surfers and kayakers can even ride manmade waves.
Bounded on the south by Von-der-Tann Strasse and Prinzregentenstrasse, on the west by Königstrasse, on the east by Lerchenfeldstrasse. Free admission. U-Bahn: Odeonsplatz.

Swimmers and sunbathers in the Englischer Garten.

Hofgarten ★ PARK   Laid out in formal Italianate style, this former royal garden on the north side of the Residenz (see p. 322) is now a city park, open to all. Flanked by neoclassical buildings, it's a pleasant spot of green in the center city, with gravel paths, geometrical pruned hedges, low flower beds, and neat shade trees. A round arcade in the center, called Diana's Temple, is topped by a vaguely god-like figure of a hunter meant to represent Bavaria.

Bounded on the west by Odeaonsplatz and on the north by Galeriestrasse. Free admission. U-Bahn: Odeonsplatz.

Olympia Park ★ PARK   Although the Olympic flame has long since moved on, the Olympic Grounds, built for the 1972 summer games held in Munich, remain a pleasant green area for picnics, walks, and sporting activities. The hall and stadium still host periodic events and concerts, and rising above it all is the **Olympischer Berg (Olympic Mountain),** erected on a pile of World War II rubble, which offers sweeping views of the city. Vistas from the top of the **Olympiaturm (Olympia Tower; ℂ 089/30672750)** are even better; the tower also contains the fine dining spot **Restaurant 181 (ℂ 089/350948181;** www.restaurant181. com). For those who remember the horrific Black September attack on the Israeli team during the 1972 Olympics—a tragedy in which 11 Israeli athletes, a German police officer, and five Palestinian terrorists perished—there is a **memorial marble** listing the names of the 11 Israelis. The memorial can be found just west of the U-Bahn station Olympiazentrum; the building where the hostage standoff began still stands at Connolystrasse 31.

www.olympiapark.de. ✆ **089/54818181.** Tower access 7€ adults, 4.50€ students. Tower: daily 9am–midnight. U-Bahn: Olympiazentrum.

Tierpark Hellabrunn ★ ZOO   Tierpark Hellabrunn, located on the Isar River about 6km (4 miles) south of the city center, is home to the Munich Zoo, one of the largest zoos in the world. Thousands of animals—many of them rare or endangered species—roam free in large enclosures, designed to replicate their natural habitats. Opened in 1911, Hellabrunn was one of the world's first "geo-zoos," which display animals in groups according to their geographical origins. A walk through the attractive park is recommended even if you're not a zoo buff. There's a big children's zoo, as well as a large aviary.

Tierparkstrasse 30. ✆ **089/625080.** www.zoo-munich.de. 9am–6pm (in winter, 9am–5pm); 14€ adults, 5€ children 4 to 14, and free for children 3 and under. U-Bahn: Thalkirchen.

Olympia Tower, rising above Olympia Park, offers great views from the top.

Organized Tours

BY BUS

CitySightseeing (www.citysightseeing-munich.com) offers a 1-hour **Stadtrundfahrt (City Tour)** on double-decker open-top buses, with hop-on, hop-off service at 13 different stops. Tours depart daily (10am–5pm) about every 20 minutes from Bahnhofsplatz in front of the main train station; cost is 20€ adults, 9€ children. Buy your ticket onboard or get a discounted price online. To go farther afield and visit major attractions in Munich's environs (such as Neuschwanstein, Ludwig II's famous castle), contact **Sightseeing Gray Line,** Schützenstrasse 9 (www.grayline.com; ℂ **089/54907560**). All tours have miltilingual commentary.

BY BIKE

For a more active experience, tour Munich by bicycle with the English-speaking ex-pats at **Mike's Bike Tours** (www.mikesbiketours.com; ℂ **089/2554-3988**). The 4-hour tour (31€ adults, 16€ children) spins around the sights of central Munich, including an hour in a beer garden (lunch not included). Tour depart daily from March through mid-November at

11:15am; from mid-April through August there's also a tour at 4pm. All tours meet 15 minutes before setting off, under the tower of the Altes Rathaus on Marienplatz. No need to reserve, just show up. Tour price includes bike rental and helmet. In the winter, tours are held only on Saturdays at noon, and you must reserve in advance.

ON FOOT

Munich Walk Tours (www.munichwalktours.de; ✆ **0171/274-0204**), conducted in English, include a daily 10:45am City Walk tour (also at 2:45pm in high season), or a 2½-hour Hitler's Munich tour (Nov–Mar daily at 10:15am) for 12€ adults, 10€ under 26, free for kids under 14. Additional offerings include a Beer and Brewery tour as well as a food walk exploring Bavarian cuisine. All walks meet at Tourist Information on Marienplatz. No need to reserve; you pay the guide (identifiable by a yellow sign).

Especially for Kids

The place to start for families is the same place everybody else starts: on the Altstadt's picturesque **Marienplatz** (p. 320), where you can catch a performance of the **Glockenspiel**'s mechanical jousting knights (see p. 320). Inside the nearby Altes Rathaus you'll also find the **Spielzeug-museum,** a historical toy collection (✆ **089/294-001;** 4€ adults, 1€ children; daily 10am–5:30pm).

Among Munich's major museums, the one that appeals most to kids is the **Deutsches Museum** (p. 331), especially with the hands-on activities of the **Kids Kingdom** section, designed for children ages 3 to 8. Even kids who aren't particularly science-minded can enjoy the galleries displaying historical toys, musical instruments, and clocks (the Sundial Garden is a fun place to hang out, literally watching the time pass as the sun moves in the sky). A smaller branch of the Deutsches Museum, the **Deutsches Museum Verkehrszentrum** (p. 332), is even more kid-friendly, with three soaring halls full of cars, trains, bikes, and motor-bikes. The **Münchner Stadtmuseum** (p. 320) also has lots of appeal for youngsters, with its exhibits of marionettes, hand puppets, and carousel horses.

When it's time to let the young ones blow off some steam outdoors, head for the huge **Englischer Garten** (p. 333), where you can rent a pedal boat to go out on the lake; there's also a vintage carousel near the Chinesischer Turm. And if the weather's good, a trip out to **Tierpark Hellabrunn** (p. 335) zoo is definitely in order to watch polar bears, giraffes, Siberian tigers, and silvery gibbons sport themselves in their native environments.

WHERE TO STAY IN MUNICH

Hotels in Munich are more expensive than elsewhere in Germany, and rooms are scarce (and prices higher) during Oktoberfest and when trade fairs are in town. It's a good idea to book your Munich hotel room in advance. The highest prices in this section are for rooms during Oktoberfest and trade fairs.

Take note that breakfast is no longer routinely included in the price of every hotel room, especially at luxury hotels; if breakfast is offered, but for an additional charge, you can opt instead to have your morning repast at one of Munich's many cafes or bakeries. Also note that, while most hotels offers some kind of parking arrangement, it can be pricey. If you are beginning a driving tour around Germany with a stop in Munich, our advice is to use Munich's excellent public transportation system to get around the city, and wait until you leave the city to pick up your rental car.

If you arrive in the city without a room, the **Fremdenverkehrsamt** (tourist office) in the main train station can book a room for you; the service is free, but the tourist office collects a 10% deposit of the total value of the room; the hotel then deducts this amount from your bill.

In the Altstadt

Bayerischer Hof ★★★ This is a grand hotel, in all senses of the word. It offers every amenity and service you could possibly want in a large, centrally located Altstadt hotel, including a pool, sauna, spa, cinema and a famous nightclub. The largest and oldest hotel in Munich (it celebrated its 175th anniversary in 2014), the Bayerischer Hof is for those who want the best of traditional service and comfort—and who don't mind or even welcome the relative anonymity that comes with staying in such an enormous labyrinth (it has five inner courtyards). The double rooms here are fairly spacious, with gleaming marble bathrooms and a decor that manages to be both timeless and up-to-date. This is the kind of hotel that offers many room and suite options, some of which are spectacular (from 3,700€ a night, they should be). There are several dining options, too, including a Ratskeller in the vaults below the hotel, where Munich's salt was once stored. The breakfast room (always check to see whether you can get breakfast included in your room rate) is a glass-walled eyrie on the sixth floor with an outdoor terrace.
Promenadeplatz 2–6. www.bayerischerhof.de. ✆ **800/223-6800** in the U.S. or 089/21200. 340 units. 270€–380€ double. Breakfast not included in all rates. Parking 34€. **Amenities:** 2 restaurants, 2 bar-lounges, nightclub, pool, sauna, fitness center, cinema, WiFi (free). U-/S-Bahn: Marienplatz.

Centro Hotel Mondial ★ Located near the Asamkirche and Viktualenmarkt, this efficient, modern hotel is a little south of the historic

The Blue Spa, one of many luxe amenities at the Bayerischer Hof hotel.

center, but it's just a hop and a skip from the well-connected Sendlinger Tor U-Bahn stop, and it's also quite a good value, cost-wise. The rooms are fairly small, with simple, comfortable furnishings—in most cases, a wood-trimmed bed, desk, and chair in a functional if uninspiring decor. But they have nice little balconies and are kept spotlessly clean. Bathrooms are compact and have showers. For a quieter room, request one that faces the courtyard.

Pettenkoferstrasse 2. www.centro-hotels.de. © **089/5434-8880.** 57 units. 92€–189€ double. Breakfast 9€. Parking 13€. **Amenities:** Wi-Fi (free). U-Bahn: Sendlinger Tor.

Cortiina ★ Located a stone's throw from Marienplatz, this boutique hotel is a pleasant and super-convenient spot to park your bags in Munich's Altstadt. In fact, its that location that's the deciding factor for most guests. But there are other perks here, including suites with kitchenettes and little balconies in a building adjacent to the hotel (these are the Cortiina's most homelike accommodations). The standard double rooms are a bit on the drab side for a so-called "design hotel," but they're comfortable nonetheless, with swank, oversized bathrooms (with eco-friendly REN bath products and, in many, soothing soaking tubs). The hotel caters to many longer-stay business travelers, who appreciate the kitchenette units. The Café/Bar (a modern, minimalist café during the day

HOTELS

Anna Hotel **13**
Bayerischer Hof &
  Palais Montgelas **20**
Centro Hotel Mondial **16**
Cortiina **27**
Creatif Hotel Elephant **8**
Eden-Hotel-Wolff **9**
Gästehaus Englischer
  Garten **6**
Hotel Jedermann **11**
Hotel Schlicker **31**
Hotel Torbräu **38**
Hotel Uhland **15**
La Maison **4**
Louis Hotel **30**
Mandarin Oriental **26**
Pension Westfalia **17**
Wombat's City Hostel
  Munich **12**

RESTAURANTS

Alois Dallmayr **24**
Andechser am Dom **23**
Augustiner Gross-
  gaststätte **14**
Beim Sedlmayr **33**
Biergarten Chinesischer
  Turm **7**
Café Ignaz **1**
Das Maria **19**
Gandl **39**
Gaststätte zum
  Flaucher **35**
Georgenhof **3**
Glockenbach **18**
Hofbräuhaus
  am Platzl **25**
Kochspielhaus **34**
La Fabbrica **10**
Matsuhisa **26**
Nürnberger Bratwurst
  Glöckl am Dom **22**
Paulaner am
  Nockherberg **36**
Prinz Myshkin **29**
Riva **37**
Rue des Halles **40**
Schelling-Salon **2**
Seehaus **7**
Spatenhaus **21**
Tantris **5**
Zum Alten Markt **32**
Zum Dürnbräu **28**

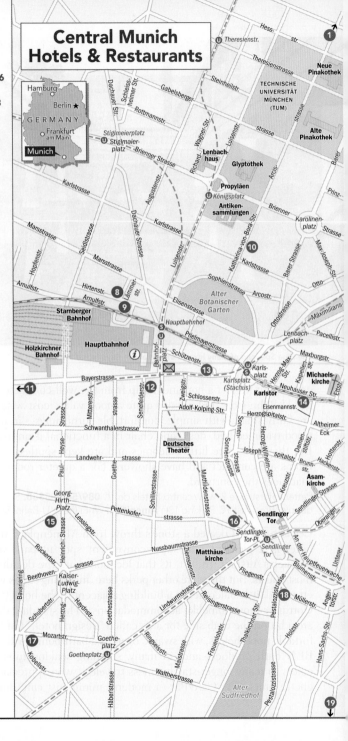

Central Munich
Hotels & Restaurants

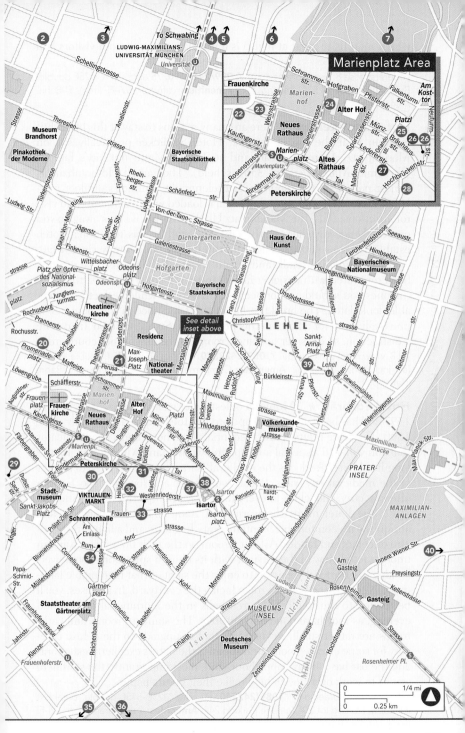

Marienplatz Area

To Schwabing

LUDWIG-MAXIMILIANS-
UNIVERSITÄT MÜNCHEN

Universität

Schellingstrasse

Theresienstrasse

Museum
Brandhorst

Pinakothek
der Moderne

Bayerische
Staatsbibliothek

Türkenstrasse

Ludwig-Str.

Amalienstr.

Fürstenstr.

Rhein-
berger-
str.

Schönfeld-   str.

Von-der-Tann- Strasse

Oskar-von-Miller-Ring

Jägerstr.

Kardinal-
Döpfner-Str.

Finkenstr.

Galeriestrasse

Dichtergarten

Haus der
Kunst

Wittelsbacher-
platz

Platz der Opfer
des National-
sozialismus

Odeons-
platz

Hofgarten

Bayerische
Staatskanzlei

Lerchenfeldstrasse   Seeaustr.

Himbselstr.

Bayerisches
Nationalmuseum

Prinzregentenstrasse

Wagmüllerstr.

Oettingenstrasse

Alexandrastr.

Rochusberg

Rochusstr.

Prannerstr.

Salvatorstr.

Jungfern-
turmstr.

Odeonspl.

Hofgartenstr.

Christophstr.

Unsöldstrasse

Bruder-
strasse

Liebig-
strasse

LEHEL

Sankt-
Anna-
Platz

Sankt-
Anna-
str.

Robert-Koch-Str.

Tiftstr.

Reitmor-
str.

Promenade-
platz

Maffeistr.

Löwengrube

Theatiner-
kirche

Residenz

See detail
inset above

Karl-Scharnagl-Ring

Seitz-
strasse

Pfarrstr.

Lehel

Widenmayerstr.

Theatinerstrasse

Karl-Faulhaber-Str.

Residenzstr.

Max-
Joseph-
Platz

National-
theater

Marstallplatz

Bürkleinstr.

Adelgundenstr.

Anna-Str.

Thierschstr.

Maximilians-
brücke

Max-Planck-Str.

Schäfflerstr.

Schrammer-
str.

Marien-
hof

Pfisterstr.

Platzl

Maximilian-
strasse

Herzog-
Rudolf-Str.

Frauen-
platz

Frauen-
kirche

Weinstr.

Neues
Rathaus

Alter
Hof

Dienerstrasse

Münz-
str.

Falcken-
bergstr.

Völkerkunde-
museum

Augustiner-
str.

Kaufingerstr.

Marienpl.

Burgstr.

Sparkassenstr.

Bräuhaus-
str.

Neuturmstr.

Hildegardstr.

Herrnstr.

Thomas-Wimmer-Ring

Kanal-
str.

PRATER-
INSEL

Fürstenfelder Str.

Färbergraben

Rosenstr.

Rindermarkt

Peterskirche

Mader-
bräustr.

Ledererstr.

Hochbrückenstr.

Tal

Mariengrundstr.

Radlsteig

Knöbel-
str.

MAXIMILIAN-
ANLAGEN

Dultstr.

Sack-
str.

Stadt-
museum

Heiligegeiststr.

Westenriederstr.

Isartor

Isartor-
platz

Steinsdorfstrasse

Mann-
hardt-
str.

Sankt-Jakobs-
Platz

VIKTUALIEN-
MARKT

Prälat-Zistl-Str.

Frauen-
strasse

Schrannenhalle

Am
Einlass

Rum-
ford-
strasse

Aventinstr.

Isartor-
platz

Thiersch-
strasse

Liebherrstr.

Zweibrückenstr.

Am
Gasteig

Innere Wiener Str.

Preysingstr.

Kellerstrasse

Gasteig

Anger

Blumenstrasse

Corneliusstr.

Buttermelcherstr.

Klenze-

Kohl-
str.

Morassistr.

strasse

Ludwigs-
brücke

Kleine

Rosenheimer Str.

Papa-
Schmid-
Str.

Müllerstrasse

Gärtner-
platz

Cornelius-

Baader-

Reichenbach-

str.

Erhardt-

Isar

MUSEUMS-
INSEL

Lilienstrasse

Zeppelinstrasse

Hochstrasse

Staatstheater am
Gärtnerplatz

Fraunhoferstrasse

Klenze-
str.

Jahnstr.

Frauenhoferstr.

Deutsches
Museum

Isar

Auer Mühlbach

Rosenheimer Pl.

0 ——————— 1/4 mi
0 ——————— 0.25 km

341

which morphs to a bar at night) is a popular spot with both visitors and locals.

Ledererstrasse 8. www.cortiina.com. ℭ **089/2422490.** 75 units. 149€–575€ double. Buffet breakfast 24.50€. Parking 22€. **Amenities:** café/bar; Wi-Fi (free). U-Bahn: Marienplatz.

Hotel Schlicker ★★ There are many reasons to stay at this hotel, but location is at the top of the list. Hotel Schlicker practically sits on Marienplatz, Munich's heart and soul (and where the city's famous Christmas Market, see p. 356, is held). The famed Hofbräuhaus is almost next door, the fabulous Viktuelenmarkt, Munich's outdoor market, is around the corner, and the area is loaded with restaurants and visitor attrctions. Plus, the Marienplatz U-Bahn station is steps away, so you can easily get anywhere in the city. The staff at this traditional hotel, established over 400 years ago and run by the same family since 1890, are extraordinarily friendly and helpful. Some of the rooms have recently been renovated with designer fabrics in muted color schemes; these are the ones you should ask for because the others, while perfectly serviceable, look dated. The breakfast buffet that's included in the room rate is unusually good for a hotel in this price range. Street noise on Tal can be a distraction, so consider booking a room on the quiet inner courtyard.

Tal 8. www.hotel-schlicker.de. ℭ **089/2428870.** 68 units. 165€–225 € double. Breakfast included. Parking 15€. **Amenities:** Complimentary bikes, Wi-Fi (free). U-Bahn: Marienplatz.

Hotel Torbräu ★ Munich's oldest hotel welcomed its first guest in 1497 and has been owned and operated by the Kirchlechner family since 1890. These are pretty sound credentials for a hotel and a good indicator that you will find a special atmosphere within…and without, too, for the long-lived hotel overlooks the medieval Isartor (gate) that used to be part of the medieval city walls. Because of its age and location, the Torbräu offers a cozy and close-to-everything stay. Completely refurbished in 2012, the hotel mixes the warmth of traditional wood paneling and antiques with comfortable, contemporary furniture and a light, fresh palette of colors and fabrics. Ask for a room on the fifth floor if you want an unobstructed view of the Altstadt with its church spires, or a room overlooking the Isartor if you want to enjoy the sight of that memorable landmark. Need quiet? Ask for a room facing the courtyard. In all cases, you'll be treated to the sound of church bells in the morning, afternoon and evening, as they have done for centuries. The standard rooms and bathrooms are rather small, so you may want to upgrade to the deluxe category for some extra legroom. **Schapeau** is the hotel's excellent restaurant, and the bar has a lively happy hour. And, most importantly, the staff here seems to work overtime to help make their guests happy.

Tal 41. www.torbraeu.de. ℭ **089/242340.** 90 units. 225€–515€ double. Breakfast included. Parking lot 20€, garage parking 24€. **Amenities:** 2 restaurants; bar; Wi-Fi (free). U-Bahn: Isartor.

Louis Hotel ★★★ This chic Altstadt hideaway is the only hotel in Munich that has rooms overlooking the lively Viktualienmarkt. But despite this marquee location it truly is a hideaway, because the hotel entrance is so unobtrusive that you pass right by and never know it's there. While it may be unobtrusive outside, the Louis is rather remarkable inside, showcasing modern European design that looks and feels effortlessly natural instead of making a "statement." The rooms are relatively large but carefully planned to maximize space (with concealed closets that pull out from the wall) and provide an aura of calm elegance. They're filled with custom loomed fabrics and carpets, fine wood and stone finishes, and handmade furniture—in short, you feel like you've stepped into a spread from *Architectural Digest*. The Market View rooms with Juliet balconies overlooking the market square are the best; other rooms face a quiet inner courtyard. Louis is known for its exeptional Japanese restaurant, **Emiko,** just off the lobby, and its splendid summer roof terrace (the perfect place to relax with a cocktail). The breakfast buffet goes beyond the norm too, with Asia and Middle-Eastern inspired plus vegan options and green smoothies.

Viktualienmarkt 6. www.louis-hotel.com. ℂ **089/41119080.** 72 units. 185€–699€ double. Breakfast buffet 28.50€. Parking 26€. **Amenities:** Restaurant, bar, bikes, sauna roof terrace, Wi-Fi (free). U-/S-Bahn: Marienplatz.

Mandarin Oriental ★★★ Impeccable. That's the word that describes this lovely, luxurious boutique hotel across from the Hofbrauhaus and minutes away from everything in central Munich. In terms of personalized service and guest comfort, it can't be beat. The rooms are fairly large, and some have views over the red tiled roofs of Munich and its church spires. The decor here is traditional and ultra-comfortable, accessorized with fine antiques, prints, and paintings and other Asian décor accents. The large marble-tile bathrooms here are noteworthy with Moulton Brown toiletries, big walk-in showers, and roomy bathtubs. The hotel's **Matsuhisa** restaurant (see p. 348), run by celebrity chef Nobu, offers top-end Japanese-Peruvian cuisine. In the summer, the rooftop terrace, the tallest spot in the Altstadt, opens up its lovely heated pool and features a swanky terrace restaurant China Moon, offering Asian and international fare. The terrace restaurant also opens briefly during Oktoberfest, offering Bavarian specialties each afternoon.

Neuturmstrasse 1. www.mandarinoriental.com/munich. ℂ **089/290980.** 73 units. Doubles 625€–755€ and up. Breakfast not included in all rates. Parking 27€. **Amenities:** 2 restaurants; bar; bikes; concierge; exercise room; outdoor pool (seasonal); spa, Wi-Fi (18€/day). U-/S-Bahn: Marienplatz.

Near the Hauptbahnhof

Anna Hotel ★ This boutique with a mega-modern decor is all wood floors and slatted windowblinds, stylish furniture, and eye-catching light fixtures, in a mod color scheme accented with white, slate, and bright pinks and purples. Bathrooms are sleek, with rainshower fixtures; windows are sound-proofed. The top floor suite features floor-to-ceiling windows with a panoramic view across the city. It's an excellent spot for a glam experience in Munich in a top location between the old town and the train station.

Schützenstrasse 1. www.annahotel.de. ℰ **089/599940.** 75 units. 205€–380€ double. Breakfast 22€. Parking in public garages nearby; rates vary. **Amenities:** Restaurant; bar, Wi-Fi (free). U-Bahn: Karlsplatz or Hauptbahnhof.

Creatif Hotel Elephant ★

The area around the train station is not the most picturesque section of Munich by any stretch, but it's here that you can find centrally located, value-packed hotels like this one. The family-run Creatif Hotel Elephant is one of the better options for travelers who are on a budget but still want a bit of spark in their accommodations. The rooms here are not large but they were recently redone and have a bright, simple, contemporary look and top-quality beds. The refurbed bathrooms are small, too, but completely adequate. If you're looking for a clean, comfortable, no-frills place that's a cut above the average, this is a good choice.

Lämmerstrasse 6, Leopoldvorstadt. www.creatif-elephant-hotel.de. ℰ **089/555785.** 83 units. 59€–160€ double. Buffet breakfast included. Parking in public garages nearby; rates vary. **Amenities:** Wi-Fi (free). U-/S-Bahn: Hauptbahnhof.

Eden-Hotel-Wolff ★

If you're arriving in Munich by train and want a nice, convenient, midrange hotel right across the street from the train station, this is your best option. From the outside, this large rose-colored hotel, founded in 1890, looks a bit forbidding, but the interior has been redone with a pleasantly modern look. Most of the rooms are fairly large, and all are decorated in a comfortable, unobtrusive style that varies from room to room; many have stylishly rustic distressed-wood accent walls and neutral color schemes. Bathrooms are larger than average, with tub and shower combinations.

Arnulfstrasse 4–8. www.ehw.de. ℰ **089/551150.** 210 units. 198€–340€ double. Breakfast included. Parking 18€. **Amenities:** Restaurant; bar; concierge; exercise room; room service; spa, Wi-Fi (free). U-/S-Bahn: Hauptbahnhof.

Hotel Jedermann ★★

Jedermann means "everyman," and that translates here into a range of affordable rooms in different sizes and configurations (several rooms can be connected) and a convenient if not particularly picturesque location within easy walking distance of the train station. This pleasant, family-run hotel, established over 50 years ago, offers plain but comfortable rooms with solid wooden beds, usable work desks, and decently sized closets. Most of the rooms have roomy, shower-only bathrooms. Cheaper rooms with in-room showers but toilets down the hall also are available. The hotel serves a particularly large breakfast buffet. All in all, for central Munich this is a fantastic deal in terms of value, room size, and location.

Bayerstrasse 95. www.hotel-jedermann.de. ✆ **089/543240.** 55 units. 49€–280€ double. Breakfast included. Parking 8€. **Amenities:** Wi-Fi (free). U-/S-Bahn: Hauptbahnhof.

Wombat's City Hostel Munich ★★   Clean, safe, friendly and centrally located near the main train station, Wombat's is by far the best hostel in Munich. That's partially thanks to the relaxed but professional staff, who keep the maintenance standards high. We also laud the Wombat for offering a tad more style than most hostels. The glass-roofed, plant-filled central atrium with its hammock and brightly colored modern furniture is a nice spot for hanging out, as is the bar, which sells inexpensive drinks and food. There are bathrooms with toilets and showers in the 6-bed dorm rooms and double rooms. As in all hostels, rooms are stripped down to the essentials, but the minimalist look is warmed by polished wood floors, wood-framed beds, wooden tables, and storage areas painted with bright, lively colors. There are no curfews at Wombat's and the front desk is open 24/7. You'd be hard-pressed to find better value in this central a location.

Senefelderstrasse 1. www.wombats-hostels.com/munich. ✆ **089/59989180.** From 19€ dorm bed, from 88€ double with bathroom. Buffet breakfast 4.50€. Parking 15€. **Amenities:** Bar, laundry room, free Wi-Fi in lobby. U-Bahn: Hauptbahnhof.

Schwabing & the Englischer Garten

Gästehaus Englischer Garten ★★   From the ivy-covered walls of the main villa to the homey mixture of antiques, old-fashioned beds, and Oriental rugs, you get charm with a capital "C" at this long-established guesthouse. The service is as kindly as the atmosphere; in fact, our only complaint about the place is that the bathrooms are small, with showers only. You can save a few euros by renting one of the rooms that share bathrooms. For those looking at longer stays, the guesthouse rents out 15 small apartments in a more modern annex across the street; each has a kitchenette. On nice mornings, you can eat breakfast outside in the back garden.

Liebergesellstrasse 8. www.hotelenglischergarten.de. ✆ **089/383-9410.** 25 units. 91€–215€ double, 103€–207€ apt. Breakfast 9.50€. Parking 20€. **Amenities:** Wi-Fi (free). U-Bahn: Münchener Freiheit.

La Maison ★   Shades of black and white and fuscia accent lighting permeate the sleek furnishings of this trendy place in a convenient corner of Schwabing near many restaurants and bars, and a few blocks from the park. Rooms are modern and continue the black, charcoal, and white theme, most with floor-to-ceiling windows and some with balconies.

Furnishings with velvet touches make the public spaces feel opulent and more cocktail club than hotel, but it's a great place for both business and leisure travelers, and attracts both. This is a great place if you want to stay in a real neighborhood with more locals than tourists, without being too far from the main attractions.

Occamstrasse 24. www.hotel-la-maison.com. © **089/33035550.** 31 units. 190€–260€ double. Breakfast 15€. Parking 15€. **Amenities:** Restaurant; bar; Wi-Fi (free). U-Bahn: Münchener Freiheit.

Near Theresienwiese (Oktoberfest Grounds)

Hotel Uhland ★ This family-run hotel occupies a handsome Art Nouveau-style building that's over a century old and located just a block from Theresienwiese, the Oktoberfest fairgrounds. Hotel Uhland is the sort of old-fashioned hotel that provides solid comfort, friendly service and great value. There's nothing hip or flashy about it, but that is part of its quiet charm. The rooms are furnished in a functional style. You can walk to the main train station in 10 minutes and Marienplatz is one stop away on the U-Bahn. During Oktoberfest the rates jump to the high end of the price range; book well in advance if that's when you'll be staying.

Uhlandstrasse 1. © **089/543350.** www.hotel-uhland.de. 30 units. 95€–224€ double. Buffet breakfast included. Parking 16€. Closed Dec. 24–26. **Amenities:** Wi-Fi (free). U-/S-Bahn: Theresienwiese.

Pension Westfalia ★ Located directly across the street from the Theresienwiese, where Oktoberfest is held, this budget pension occupies two floors in a building that dates from 1895. The rooms are comfortable if spare, with high ceilings and big windows to let in lots of light. You can save money by booking a room with a shared bathroom. The proprietor, Peter Dieritz, and his staff are friendly and helpful. There's an U-Bahn station at the corner and Marienplatz is only two stops away.

Mozartstrasse 23. © **089/530377.** www.pension-westfalia.de. 19 units. 68€–82€. Buffet breakfast included. Parking: free, first-come, first-serve. **Amenities:** Wi-Fi (free). U-Bahn: Goetheplatz.

WHERE TO EAT IN MUNICH

Munich is a city that loves to eat—and eat *big*. Homemade dumplings are a specialty, and so are all kinds of sausages (*Weisswurst* in particular) and *Leberkäse,* a large loaf of sausage eaten with freshly baked pretzels and mustard. *Schweinbraten,* a braised loin of pork served with potato dumplings and rich brown gravy, is Bavaria's answer to the north's *sauerbraten* (pot- or oven-roasted marinated beef). Inexpensive sausages, soups, and snacks are sold from outdoor stalls all around the Viktualienmarkt. As in the rest of Germany, seasonal food is huge, with asparagus specials hitting menus in the spring, chanterelle mushrooms in late summer, and pumpkin in the autumn and winter.

In the Altstadt

Alois Dallmayr ★ GERMAN/CONTINENTAL In business for almost 300 years, Alois Dallmayr is the most famous delicatessen in Germany, and one of the most elegant. Downstairs you can buy fine food products; upstairs in the cafe-bistro you can order a tempting array of dishes, including herring, sausages, smoked fish, and soups and, of course, *Kaffee und Kuchen* (coffee and cake). The Restaurant is a more sophisticated dining venue, featuring daily fixed-price menus. This is also a good place to buy fine food for a picnic.

Dienerstrasse 14–15. www.dallmayr.de. © **089/2135100.** Main courses cafe-bistro 15€–43€; restaurant fixed-price menus 60€–119€. Mon–Wed 11:30am–7pm; Thurs–Fri 11:30am–8pm; Sat 9am–4pm. U-Bahn: Marienplatz.

Andechser am Dom ★ GERMAN/BAVARIAN Andechser is always packed, so be prepared to be seated at a communal table and make new friends over a glass of beer or two. This brewery-restaurant run by beermeister Sepp Krätz attracts a wide range of diners and drinkers, and it is generally loud and occasionally boisterous. The food is typical Bavarian, not haute cuisine by any stretch, but filling and tasty. Try the *Kloster Schmaus*—sausages, dumplings, and vegetables served in the pan they're cooked in. Another house specialty is *Schweinsbraten* (pork roast) in a dark beer sauce; pork knuckles with crackling are another favorite, and apple strudel is the must-have dessert.

Weinstrasse 7A. www.andechser-am-dom.de. © **089/298481.** Main courses 8.50€–18€. Sun–Tues 10am–midnight, Thurs–Sat 10am–1am. U-/S-Bahn: Marienplatz.

Augustiner Grossgaststätte ★ BAVARIAN/GERMAN Located in the Altstadt on Munich's main pedestrian-only shopping street, this famous beer hall and restaurant has cavernous rooms and a genuinely good-natured and *gemütlich* (comfortable/cozy) atmosphere. Specialties include dumpling soup and roast duck with red cabbage. The house beer, Augustiner Brau, comes from one of Munich's oldest breweries, which owns the restaurant. Expect busloads of tourists mixed in with locals.

Neuhauser Strasse 27. www.augustiner-restaurant.com. © **089/2318-3257.** Main courses 10€–22€. Daily 9am–midnight. U-Bahn: Karlsplatz/Stachus.

Hofbräuhaus am Platzl ★★ GERMAN It's not for the refined, the prissy, or the faint of heart, but it is an absolutely unique Munich experience and has been for almost 200 years. What makes it special is its enormous size and at times raucous, beer-fueled atmosphere. Yes, it's touristy—some nights there seem to be more foreign tourists here than Germans—and if you can't go with the flow (and the din), don't even step inside because you'll probably hate it. You don't have to eat; you can just order a beer and one of the giant pretzels sold by dirndled Frauleins who parade around the room like cigarette girls of yore. In the *Schwemme* (tap room) on the ground floor, you sit on benches at bare wood tables as a band plays and the Germans periodically burst into song, swaying back and forth in unison; a big beer garden is on this level, too. Upstairs there are a number of smaller, somewhat quieter dining rooms. The beer is Hofbrau, served by the *mass* (equal to about a liter and costing 8.40€); *Weissbier* (a light beer) is the only beer served in a smaller glass. The food is heavy and hearty with a menu that includes *Weisswürste* and several other sausages, *Schweinbraten* (roasted pork), *Spanferkel* (roast suckling pig), and the big favorite, *Schweineshaxn* (ham hocks). You gotta love it—or you won't.

Am Platzl 9. www.hofbraeuhaus.de. © **089/290-1360.** Main courses 8€–18€. Daily 9am–11:30pm. U-/S-Bahn: Marienplatz.

Nürnberger Bratwurst Glöckl am Dom ★ BAVARIAN   A short walk from Marienplatz, across from the cathedral (Dom), this is the coziest and friendliest of Munich's local restaurants. You sit on wooden chairs at shared tables. *Nürnberger Schweinwurstl mit Kraut* (pork sausages with cabbage, a specialty from Nuremberg) is the dish to try. Hot dogs will never taste the same again after you've tried one of these delectable little sausages. It's also a prime spot for casual beer-drinking and people-watching in the city center, favored by both tourists and locals alike.

Frauenplatz 9. www.bratwurst-gloeckl.de. © **089/295-264.** Main courses 6€–19€. Mon–Sat 10am–1am, Sun to 11pm. U-/S-Bahn: Marienplatz.

Matsuhisa ★★★ JAPANESE/PERUVIAN   Chef Nobi Matsuhisa, the man behind acclaimed Nobu restaurants around the world, opened the first and only German outpost of his Matsuhari restaurant here in Munich in 2015. Cuisine is primarily Japenese and Peruvian, but a slew of additional South American and Asian influences, often incorporated into inventive sushi and sashimi options, pop up depending on the season. In addition to the restaurant's signature Black Cod, expect anything from tuna, salmon, or lobster tacos to jalapeno-infused yellowfin tuna sashmi to lamb with Peruvian Anticucho sauce.

In the Mandarin Oriental, Neuturmstrasse 1. www.mandarinoriental.com. © **089/ 29098875.** Reservations recommended. Main courses 32€–87€. Daily noon–2:30pm, 7–11pm. U-/S-Bahn: Marienplatz.

Spatenhaus ★★ BAVARIAN/INTERNATIONAL   If you want to experience a Munich beer restaurant without the noise and tourist-overload found at the Hofbräuhaus—and with better food—try Spatenhaus, a well-known brewery restaurant with big windows overlooking the opera house. It serves Bavarian specialties such as veal sausages with potato salad and grilled calf's liver with roast onions; the *Bayerische Teller*

Chilean sea bass, with a Japanese/Peruvian twist, at Matsuhisa in the Mandarin Oriental hotel.

(Bavarian plate) comes loaded with various meats, including pork and sausages. And if you've had enough German food for the time being, there are a handful of well-prepared Italian dishes on the menu as well. Wash down your meal with the restaurant's own beer, Spaten-Franziskaner-Bier. The first floor dining room is more casual than the room upstairs.

Residenzstrasse 12. www.spatenhaus.de. ✆ **089/290-7060.** Main courses 9.50€–28€. Daily 9:30am–12:30am. U-Bahn: Marienplatz.

Around Viktualenmarkt

Beim Sedlmayr ★★ GERMAN/BAVARIAN   It's a bit difficult to find this restaurant because it's tucked away on a sidestreet near Marienplatz and the Viktualienmarkt, but if you sleuth it out, you'll be treated to one of the more authentic Bavarian dining experiences in Munich. Expect to be seated at a communal table, and expect the service to be cordial but a bit brusque, because the overworked waitresses here have a lot of territory to cover. "At Sedlmayr" serves mouthwatering renditions of traditional Bavarian favorites, like roast pork with cracklings and dumplings, grilled *Kalbsbraten,* mushrooms served with dumplings and a creamy herb sauce, and *Kaiserschmarrn* (a kind of bread pudding with a crispy caramelized base and topped with warm apple sauce). The menu is only in German, so do a little homework before you arrive; if you aren't sure what to order, ask your server. The dining may be communal, but it's still a good idea to reserve in advance.

Westenriederstrasse 14. www.beim-sedlmayr.de. ℐ **089/226219.** Main courses 8€–23€. Daily 9am–11pm. U-/S-Bahn: Marienplatz.

Prinz Myshkin ★★ VEGETARIAN   If German sausages and meat dishes are getting to you, give this popular vegetarian restaurant near Marienplatz a try. The menu includes freshly made salads, Asian-inspired vegetarian entrees, and vegetarian *involtini* and several vegan options. The casseroles, soups, and pizzas generally are excellent. An airy, attractive place, it's reasonably priced and offers one of the healthier options in this part of town.

Hackenstrasse 2. www.prinzmyshkin.com. ℐ **089/265-596.** Main courses 13€–18€, 7.50€ fixed-price lunch (Mon–Fri). Daily 11am–12:30am. U-/S-Bahn: Marienplatz.

Riva ★ PIZZA/PASTA   So you want a simple Italian meal and you don't want to spend a fortune in Munich's pricey Altstadt—where do you go? To Riva, just outside Marienplatz on Tal, next to the Isartor. This is an uncomplicated and uncluttered place, simple but nicely designed. Okay, maybe the music is too loud, but Riva also serves as a bar where a young crowd comes for cocktails. The menu is limited to pizza, pasta, and a few salads. You can order a reasonably priced glass of wine to go with your meal and leave quite contented, without having drained your bank account.

Tal 44. www.riva-tal.de. ℐ **089/220240.** Main courses 8€–13€. Mon–Sat 8am–1am; Sun noon–1am. U-/S-Bahn: Marienplatz.

Zum Alten Markt ★ BAVARIAN/INTERNATIONAL   This snug, friendly eatery is located on a tiny square on the east side of the Viktual-ienmarkt, Munich's big outdoor produce market. In winter, the wood-panelled dining room hung with deer antlers makes you feel as if you've stepped into a hunting cabin—an upscale one serving fine wine, how-ever. In summer, tables are set up outside. You might begin with home-made cream of carrot soup or black-truffle tortellini in cream sauce. The chef makes a great *Tafelspitz* (boiled beef), and you can also order classic dishes such as roast duck with applesauce or roast suckling pig. Always classy, consistently good, and never pretentious, this spot is a favorite among locals.

Dreifaltigkeitsplatz 3. www.zumaltenmarkt.de. ℐ **089/299995.** Main courses 13€–17€. Mon–Sat 11am–midnight. U-/S-Bahn: Marienplatz.

Zum Dürnbräu ★ BAVARIAN   This traditional Bavarian restaurant has a history dating back some 500 years, making it perhaps the oldest restaurant in Munich. Specialties include several beef dishes (tongue,

Tafelspitz, fillet), goose in season, and pork. You can get simple omelets or soup, too. The interior is charming with dark wood-panelled walls and candles at night, but in summer the favorite spot is is its lovely beer garden. Note that, while "bräu" is still part of its name, this former brewery no longer produces beer.

Dürngräugasse 2 (off Tal). www.zumduernbraeu.de. ⓒ **089/222-195.** Main courses 9.50€–20€. Daily 9am–midnight. U-/S-Bahn: Marienplatz.

Königplatz & Museumviertel

La Fabbrica ITALIAN   This fun, canteen-style space mixes an industrial feel with a bright and lively vibe: multi-colored chairs, a red wall and bar flanked by exposed silver pipes, and silver-potted herbs hanging from walls. It's known for its pizza, served in regular, gluten- or lactose-free versions, or choose from salads, pasta, or lasagna—none of the options are particularly inventive, but for this price in this location, you'll get a hearty meal in a bustling, casual space with friendly service.

Katharina-von-Bora Str 8a. www.fabbrica-muenchen.com. ⓒ **1517/1200400.** Main courses 7€–10€. Mon–Fri 11:30am–2:30pm and 7pm–late; Sat 7pm–late. U-Bahn: Königsplatz.

Schelling Salon GERMAN/BAVARIAN   Dating from 1872, this tavern is known for its Bavarian *Knödel* and billiards, and it's been a tradition since 1872, having survived World War II bombings. In days of yore, you could see everybody from Lenin to Brecht playing billiards here. The menu offers snacks and hearty fare, easily washed down with mugs of beer. The menu is old school, but covers everything from a simple slice of bread and emmentaler or ham, to goulash soup, salads (including a Russian salad), *Wiener Schnitzel,* sausage platters, and smoked trout with potato salad and creamy horseradish. Breakfast is also served until 2pm. There's even an billiard museum, only open Sundays 2 to 4pm (2€), tracing the history of pool since the days of ancient Egypt.

Schellingstrasse 54. www.schelling-salon.de. ⓒ **089/2720788.** Breakfast 3€–5€; snacks/main courses 4€–13€. Thurs–Mon 10am–1am. U-Bahn: Universität.

Schwabing

Café Ignaz ★ VEGETARIAN   A Schwabing institution for nearly 3 decades, Café Ignaz offers creative fare for both vegetarians and vegans. A variety of grains, rice, couscous, and pastas turn up in the ever-changing daily offerings, and there are also pizzas with imaginative toppings. For dessert, try one of the soy-based cakes or pastries. During Happy Hour (Mon and Wed–Fri 3–5pm), you can order one of the restaurant's main courses for 7.50€.

Georgenstrasse 67. www.ignaz-cafe.de. ⓒ **089/2716093.** Main courses 8€–13€; 2-course lunch menu 8€. Wed–Mon 8am–11pm, closed Tues, also closed Mon in Aug. U-Bahn: Josephsplatz.

Georgenhof ★ GERMAN/INTERNATIONAL This pleasant Schwabing eatery and wine bar has a comfortably rustic interior with a wood-fired grill, but if the weather is nice, sit outside in the beer garden under the chestnut trees. The menu reflects seasonal specialties such as *Spargel* (asparagus) in May and June, chanterelle mushrooms in late summer, and in the fall, pumpkin soup and game dishes like *Rehpfeffer* (venison) with egg *Spätzle* (German short egg pasta) or tagliatelle with venison ragout. Grilled lamb and steak are also smart choices here. For dessert, try the simple but delicious apple pie—its crust is made from a cinammon-infused beer batter, served warm with vanilla ice cream.

Fredrichstrasse 1. www.georgenhof-muenchen.de. *©* **089/393101.** Main courses 11€–24€. Daily 11 am–1am. U-Bahn: Universität.

Tantris ★★★ INTERNATIONAL Munich's most famed gastronomic pilgrimage site has been awarded a Michelin star every year for more than 40 years, and if you are a deep-pocketed foodie, you should reserve your table now. This is a show spot, designed by an architect with a retro-70s interior. You will be in the hands of professionals throughout your meal, and can expect smooth, fluid, fluent service from beginning to end. The cuisine created by Chef Hans Haas changes seasonally (and daily) and is outstanding in terms of freshness, subtlety of taste, and presentation. The multi-course tasting menus are the best way to sample the culinary magic of Tantris. On a tasting menu you might find crustacean variations with curry cream, saddle of venison with red cabbage and mushrooms, turbot with bean ravioli, or banana-chocolate cake with sour cream. The excellent sommelier can recommend the perfect wine accompaniment to each dish (wine pairings are not included in the prices listed below). Your dining experience will be unforgettable, but do be prepared to pay a small fortune for it. *Note:* Tantris is in a slightly out-of-the-way spot so you'll need to take a taxi to get there.

Johann-Fichte-Strasse 7. www.tantris.de. *©* **089/3619590.** Reservations required. Fixed-price 4-course lunch menus 80€–190€, fixed-price dinner menus 150€–180€. Tues–Sat noon–3pm and 6:30–10:30pm. Closed Dec 22–27, Jan 1–15, public holidays, annual holidays in Jan and May. U-Bahn: Dietlindenstrasse.

South of the Altstadt

Das Maria ★ INTERNATIONAL Trendy while being friendly and casual, *Das Maria* lures everyone—from hip young things and families with kids to office workers and neighborhood residents. Perhaps it's because they offer breakfast and brunch until 6pm every day (on weekends the brunch menu expands even more), or because you have so many options (go healthy with detox tea or live it up with a prosecco). Even dinner is full of choice: Enjoy a snack-sized homemade hummus and tabouleh, feast on a Schnitzel with potatoes, or go exotic with a coriander-and-cilantro-infused organic chicken with turmeric rice. Inside you'll perch on oversized stools with comfy pillows under Moroccan lamps, but in clement weather try to snag an outdoor table. Reservations are not required, but if you want to eat at a peak time (lunch or dinner weekdays, or anytime on the weekend), call ahead and book.

Klenzestr. 97. www.dasmaria.de. © **089/20245750.** Main courses 7€–10€. Tues–Fri 8:30am–10:30pm, Sun–Mon 9am–7pm. No credit cards. U-Bahn: Frauenhoferstrasse

Glockenbach ★★ MODERN EUROPEAN   This stylish but casual and unpretentious two-story bisto-restaurant-bar located south of the train station in the Glockenbach neighborhood serves great breakfasts until noon during the week, and until 5pm on weekends. At lunch and dinner, things switch up to imaginative fusion cuisine, served for a very reasonable price. A short but well-focused menu changes daily for lunch and weekly (and seasonally) for dinner. You might find curried chicken breast; Knödel with mushrooms, cherry tomatoes, and egg; pasta with calf's-liver Bolognese; or ocean perch fillet with potato salad. This is an excellent spot to enjoy a good, inexpensive lunch, a classy cocktail, or a delicious dessert. It stays open until roughly midnight or later and morphs into more of a bar atmosphere after the kitchen closes.

Müllerstrasse 49. www.glockenbach.com. © **089/45240622.** Main courses 12€–19€, 9.80€ fixed-price lunch (Mon–Fri), 35€–70€ fixed-price dinner. Daily 10am–3pm and 7–10pm, bar until roughly midnight. U-Bahn: Sendliger Tor.

Kochspielhaus ★ PIZZA/PASTA/BURGERS   Touting the freshness of its local ingredients, this urban-chic corner restaurant near the Isartor offers a casual menu with an artisanal twist. Their long list of crisp thin-crust pizzas all feature housemade dough, fermented for 48 hours; they also have a range of salads, handmade pastas, and hefty burgers served in house-baked spelt buns. (The veggie burger is a winner—in fact the place is overall a good choice for vegetarians.) Their mozzarella and ricotta cheeses are particularly luscious, and save room for the Nutella pizza for dessert. Breakfast is another specialty, with an extensive breakfast menu featuring everything from Spanish omelettes to an Asian mini salmon teriyaki burger, for those who are tired of the traditional German breakfast buffet. Even if you don't have time for a meal, you can always pick up an artisanal treat at the attached bakery, **Bachspielhaus.**

Rumfordstrasse 5. www.kochspielhaus.de. © **089/54802738.** Pizzas 10€–15€, other main courses 10€–17€. Sun–Mon 7am–8pm, Tues–Sat 6:30am–10pm. U-Bahn: Frauenhoferstrasse.

Rue des Halles ★★★ FRENCH   This is one of those restaurants that you leave smiling and feeling like you've discovered something special—and you have. This airy spot in Haidhausen is Munich's oldest French restaurant, or "brasserie de Paris," as it refers to itself. It opened in 1983 and hasn't lost any of its charm or culinary acumen. And you don't have to pay a fortune here to enjoy a memorable meal with a glass or two of wine. The menu is wisely limited, but you will find something that suits your fancy, with fish, meat, and vegetarian options all available. If you want to share something special, start with the *fruits de mer* (seafood) platter, with oysters, langoustines, whelks, shrimp, and crab; the *moules* (mussels) *mariniere de Normandy* are also great, and so is the Breton boullabaisse The meat dishes with various sauces are French classics cooked to perfection: roast breast of guinea fowl with Roquefort sauce; beef cheeks confit with a Madeira sauce; duck with currant sauce; medallions of veal with green pepper sauce; and mustard-and-herb crusted rack of lamb. All of these entrees are served with seasonal vegetables. The desserts, too, are French classics: A selection of cheeses, tarte tatin (apple tart), crème brulee, and warm chocolate cake with crème anglais are tops on my list. This is not a Michelin-starred restaurant, but you will savor every bite of your meal, the lively bistro atmosphere, and the friendly professionalism of the staff. All in all, highly recommended. Late at night this turns into a stylish spot to grab a late drink and small bite.

Steinstrasse 18. www.rue-des-halles.de. *©* **089/485675.** Main courses 18€–24€; fixed-price menu 23€–52€. Daily 6–11pm, cold dishes until 1am. U-Bahn: Max-Weber-Platz.

West of the Altstadt

Gandl ★★ ITALIAN/FRENCH
At this attractive neighborhood bistro, the lunch menu leans toward Italian, but at night the cooking becomes more traditionally French and German. The Italian dishes include homemade pastas, such as spaghetti with truffles, papardelle with fish-ragout, and lasagna. Dinner offerings change often and seasonally, but you'll typically find fare such as entrecote with arugula salad, grilled fillet of salmon, or lamb in red-wine sauce. Delicious salads (including large main-course versions) and soups are always on the menu, too. Eat on the terrace if

The Englischer Garten's beer garden, beside the Chinese Pagoda.

MUNICH beer GARDENS & beer HALLS

Munich is famed for its breweries and beer halls, many of which have outdoor beer gardens where you can quaff their brews and order hearty Bavarian food at reasonable prices. If you'd rather nibble than dine, order typical beer garden snacks like a home-made *Brezeln* (pretzel), *Radl* (large white radishes), or another Munich specialty, *Obatzda*, a mix of soft cheese, butter, and paprika served with bread. For a glass or mug of beer, expect to pay 5€ to 8€, depending on its size. **Note:** Most beer gardens require you to pay a deposit for the mug of beer, which you get back when you return the empty mug. Oom-pah-pah bands, zither players, or accordionists sometimes add to the jovial atmosphere. The beer halls and gardens are typically large and casual, with communal seating (so try not to be shy!).

Two of the city's most famous beer halls, the **Hofbräuhaus am Platzl** and **Augustiner Grossgaststätte,** are described in the "Where to Eat" section, above. Beyond those, we recommend the following:

One of Munich's largest and most popular beer gardens, **Biergarten Chinesischer Turm ★★★**, Englischer Garten 3 (www.chinaturm.de; © **089/383-8720;** U-Bahn Giselastrasse), is located in the Englischer Garten (see p. 333) at the foot of the Chinese pagoda. Also in the English Garden, a 5-minute walk north of the Chinesescher Turm, you'll find the **Seehaus ★**, a lovely beer garden adjacent to the Kleinhesseloher See lake (Kleinhesselohe 3, www.kuffler.com/en/seehaus; © **089/381-6130;** U-Bahn Münchner Freiheit). Ignore the restaurant, but do hit the beer garden, which is open daily from May to October from 10am to 1am. South of the city center, in the Tiergarten, **Gaststätte zum Flaucher ★★**, Isarauen 8 (www.zumflaucher.de; © **089/723-2677;** Bus 52), has tables set in a tree-shaded garden near the zoo,

overlooking the Isar River. This beer garden is open daily from May to October from 10am to midnight; November to April, it's open Friday, Saturday, and Sunday from 10am to 9pm.

While autumn in Munich is all about **Oktoberfest,** the largest beer festival in the world, spring is celebrated with **Starkbierzeit,** a lesser-known beer festival that heralds the end of Lent and the opening of the city's beer gardens. One of the best places to celebrate Starkbierzeit is the brewery-restaurant-beer garden **Paulaner am Nockherberg ★★**, 77 Hoch Strasse (www.nockherberg.com; © **089/14599120**), in southeast Munich. Paulaner serves the original Starkbier, a sweet, strong brew called Salvator, and pairs it with a traditional dish of crisp-skined ham hocks served with sharp mustard. Their beer garden is a convivial spot with old chestnut trees and a playground for the kids. To reach Paulaner, take the U-Bahn to Kolumbusplatz, then bus 54 to Silberhornstrasse and streetcar 25 to the Ostfriedhof stop.

the weather's nice and don't be in a rush because the service is relaxed and unhurried. Located in a pleasant residential area behind the National Theatre, Gandl is frequented mostly by locals—a good sign indeed.
St.-Anna Platz 1. www.gandl.de. © **089/2916-2526.** Main courses 15€–25€; 40€–60€ fixed-price menus. Mon–Sat 9am–1am. U-Bahn: Lehel.

SHOPPING

You'll see a whole lot of shopping going on in Munich. A seemingly endless network of shopping streets rays out from **Marienplatz** and wide,
pedestrian-only **Kaufingerstrasse** and **Neuhauser Strasse.** You can
find anything you want here, but it's unlikely that you'll find any bargains.
What you will find is high-quality, for this is a shopping society that does
not spend its money on junk.

The best streets for elegant boutiques and specialty shops are **Briennerstrasse, Maximilianstrasse** (which also has the leading art galleries), **Maffeistrasse,** and **Theatinerstrasse.** On these streets, all the
top European couturiers and Germany's and Munich's own designers
have shops: Jil Sander, Joop, Bogner, Max Dietl, Rudolph Moshammer,
et cetera. Antiques devotees with deep pockets find what they want on
Ottostrasse. The biggest concentration of shops selling secondhand
goods is on **Westenriederstrasse,** between the Viktualienmarkt and
Isartor. The streets radiating out from the **Gärtnerplatz** roundabout
contain a mix of chain stores and trendy independent boutiques.

When you're shopping, remember that you will almost always pay
more for items imported from the U.S., and less for items made or manufactured in Germany and the European Union.

Crafts

Bayerischer Kunstgewerbe-Verein ★★★ The Bavarian Association of Arts & Crafts is a showcase for Bavarian artisans, selling all kinds
of excellent handicrafts: ceramics, glasses, jewelry, woodcarvings, pewter, and seasonal Christmas decorations. Pacellistrasse 6–8. www.kunst
handwerk-bkv.de. © **089/2901470.** U-Bahn: Karlsplatz.

Münchner Puppenstuben und Zinnfiguren Kabinette ★★ This
is Germany's oldest miniature pewter foundry, dating from 1796, and it
still creates traditional Christmas decorations of a type once sold to the
Bavarian royal family. This store is one of the best sources in Germany

---

Christmas Market in Marienplatz

Beer-drinkers in Munich have their festival, called Oktoberfest. And holiday
shoppers have theirs, called the **Christkindlmarkt,** or Christmas Market. From
late November through December,
Marienplatz, the main square of the inner
city, overflows with stalls selling toys,
tree ornaments, handicrafts, and a
mouthwatering array of traditional
snacks and sweets, including gingerbread, sugarcoated almonds, fruitcakes,
smoked meats, and piping hot *Glühwein,*
a spiced red wine. Even if you don't plan
to buy anything, the atmosphere itself is
guaranteed to put you in a festive mood.

for dollhouses, furniture, bird cages, and small figures of people, all cunningly crafted from pewter or carved wood. Some figures are made from 150-year-old molds that are collector's items in their own right. Maxburgstrasse 4. www.mini-kabi.net. ✆ **089/293797.** U-Bahn: Karlsplatz.

Prinoth ★★ Most of the woodcarvings sold here are produced in small workshops in the South Tyrol. The selection is wide-ranging, and because the shop is 6km (4 miles) west of Munich's tourist zones, prices are reasonable compared to those of shops closer to the Marienplatz. You'll find a variety of Nativity figures, angels, Madonnas, and other traditional pieces. Guido Schneblestrasse 9A. www.prinoth.de. ✆ **089/560378.** U-Bahn: Laimerplatz.

Department Stores

Kaufhof ★ This store carries everything, from men's, women's, and children's clothing to housewares, cosmetics, and much more, all at surprisingly reasonable prices, given the center-of-things location. Marienplatz. www.galeria-kaufhof.de. ✆ **089/231851.** U-/S-Bahn: Marienplatz.

Ludwig Beck ★★ Sometimes called the "Bloomingdale's of Munich," this upscale store on Marienplatz sells high-end clothing for women and men, along with cosmetics, housewares, and has what is reputedly the best classical CD selection in Germany. Am Marienplatz 11. www.ludwigbeck.de. ✆ **089/236910.** U-/S-Bahn: Marienplatz.

Eyeglasses

Pupille ★ If you wear glasses, you probably know that many of the most fashionable and well-made frames are made in Germany. They're less expensive here, and you'll find styles that never make it to the U.S. At Pupille's, shelf after shelf of eyeglasses come in all styles and sizes. Gärtnerplatz 2. www.pupille.de. ✆ **089/2017067.**

Bavarian Fashion

Dirndl-Ecke ★ "Dirndl Corner" stocks a large selection of high-quality Bavarian dirndls (traditional German dresses), folk art, and handicrafts. Am Platzl 1/Sparkassenstrasse 10. www.indra-trachtenmoden.de. ✆ **089/220-163.** U-/S-Bahn: Marienplatz.

Loden-Frey ★★★   This is the place for high-quality *loden,* a waterproof wool used for durable and long-lasting coats, jackets, and hats. Maffeistrasse 7. www.loden-frey.de. ✆ **089/210390.** U-/S-Bahn: Marienplatz.

Jewelry & Watches

CADA-Schmuck ★★   Herbert Kopp, a jewelry designer, has attracted lots of media attention for the distinctive handmade jewelry that's sold here. His chic creations come in 18-carat gold or sterling silver. There is a large collection of rings, earrings, necklaces, pendants, cufflinks, and brooches. Maffeistrasse 8. www.cada-schmuck.de. ✆ **089/2554270.** Tram: 19.

Hemmerle ★★   The founders of this conservative jewelry shop made their fortune designing bejeweled fantasies for the Royal Bavarian Court of Ludwig II. All pieces are limited editions, designed and made in-house by Bavarian craftspeople. The company also designs its own high-end wristwatch, the Hemmerle. Maximilianstrasse 14. www.hemmerle.de. ✆ **089/2422600.** U-/S-Bahn: Marienplatz.

Porcelain

Porzellan-Manufaktur-Nymphenburg ★★★   One of Germany's most famous porcelain factories is located on the grounds of Schloss Nymphenburg (see "Day Trips from Munich," p. 362), about 5 miles (8km) from central Munich. You can visit its exhibition and sales rooms Monday to Friday 10am to 5pm. If you're short on time, you can stop by a branch in Munich's center at Odeonsplatz 1 (✆ **089/282428;** U-Bahn Odeonsplatz). Nördliches Schlossrondell 8. www.nymphenburg.com. ✆ **089/1791970.** Bus: 100.

Toys

Obletter's ★★   Established in 1825, this is one of the largest emporiums of children's toys in all of Germany. The vast inventory contain everything from folkloric dolls to computer games. Karlsplatz 11. www.obletter.de. ✆ **089/55089510.** U-Bahn: Karlsplatz.

ENTERTAINMENT & NIGHTLIFE

Something is always going on in Munich. As southern Germany's cultural capital, Munich is renowned for its opera and symphony concerts and theater, but you can also just sit back in a leafy beer garden or in a beer hall and enjoy the music and the local scene; there are also plenty of bars and dance clubs for late-night partying. To find out what's happening in Munich, pick up a copy of **Monatsprogramm,** a monthly program guide, at the tourist office in the Hauptbahnhof; visit **www.muenchen.de** and click on "Events"; or go to **www.muenchentickets.**

de. The best way to buy tickets is to go directly to the venue's box office, or to the ticket office in the tourist office in the Hauptbahnhof.

The Performing Arts

Altes Residenztheater (Cuvilliés Theater) ★★★ Part of the Residenz palace, this historic theatre is the most beautiful in Germany (see p. 322). The **Bavarian State Opera** and the **Bayerisches Staatsschauspiel** perform smaller works here, in keeping with the tiny theater's intimate character. Residenzstrasse 1. www.bayerischesstaatsschauspiel. de. ✆ **089/21851940.**

Bayerischen Staatsoper ★★★ Performing at the beautiful neo-classical **Nationaltheater,** a component of the Residenz palace that has been restored to its 1830s grandeur, the **Bavarian State Opera** is one of the world's great opera companies. Every year it mounts a full season of grand operas with the world's greatest singers and a superlative orchestra. The productions are often anything but traditional, however. The Nationaltheater is also the home of the **Bavarian State Ballet.** Attending an opera or ballet here may be worth it just to sit in such a gorgeous space. Nationaltheater, Max-Joseph-Platz 2. www.bayerische.staatsoper.de ✆ **089/21851920.** U-/S-Bahn: Odeonsplatz.

Bayerisches Staatsschauspiel ★★ The Bavarian State Theater, which is also housed in a part of the Residenz complex, is known for its performances of the classics by Goethe, Schiller, Shakespeare, and others. Max-Joseph-Platz. www.bayerischesstaatsschauspiel.de. ✆ **089/21851920.** U-/S-Bahn: Marienplatz or Odeonsplatz.

Deutsches Theater ★★ This late-19th-century venue is mainly for musicals, but operettas, ballets, and international shows are staged as well. Schwanthalerstrasse 13. www.deutsches-theater.de. ✆ **089/55234444.** U-Bahn: Fröttmaning.

Münchner Philharmoniker ★★★ One of Europe's great orchestras, the Munich Philharmonic Orchestra performs in Philharmonic Hall in the modern Gasteig Cultural Center. Gasteig Kulturzentrum in the Haidhausen district, Rosenheimerstrasse 5. www.muenchnerphilharmoniker.de. ✆ **089/480985500.** S-Bahn: Rosenheimerplatz. Tram: 18 to Gasteig. Bus: 51.

Live Music

Jazzclub Unterfahrt ★★★ This is Munich's leading jazz club, attracting artists from throughout Europe and North America. The bar opens daily at 7:30pm; live music is Tuesday to Sunday 8:30pm to 1am, Friday and Saturday 7:30pm to 3am. Einsteinstrasse 42. www.unterfahrt.de. ✆ **089/4482794.** Cover 5€–32€. U-Bahn: Max-Weber-Platz.

Mister B's ★   This small club hosts a slightly older, mellower crowd than the rock and dance clubs. Blues, jazz, and rhythm-'n'-blues combos take the stage Thursday to Saturday. Herzog-Heinrichstrasse 38. www.misterbs.de. ℭ **089/534901.** Cover 7€–20€. U-Bahn: Goetheplatz.

Schwabinger Podium ★   This staple of the Schwabing scene offers varying live music acts, which on some nights attracts a jazz crowd; Monday nights are reserved for a local jazz outfit. Otherwise, expect cover bands and local acts. It's open Sunday to Thursday 8pm to 1am and Friday and Saturday 8pm to 3am. Wagnerstrasse 1. www.schwabinger-podium.com. ℭ **089/399482.** Cover 7€. U-Bahn: Münchner Freiheit.

Nightclubs & Dance Halls

Bayerischer Hof Night Club ★   Down below the tony Bayerischer Hof hotel you'll find some of Munich's most sophisticated entertainment. Within one very large room is a piano bar, where a musician plays Friday and Saturday nights. Behind a partition that disappears after 10pm is a stage for the dance bands that play every night. Entrance to the piano bar is free, but there's a cover charge to the nightclub Friday to Sunday nights. The club and bar are open nightly until 3am. Daily happy hour is 7 to 8:30pm, with drinks starting at 6€. In the Bayerischer Hof hotel, Promenadeplatz 2–6. www.bayerischerhof.de. ℭ **089/21200.** Cover to nightclub Fri–Sat 5€–50€. U-/S-Bahn: Marienplatz.

Nachtgalerie ★   The "Night Gallery" contains two dance halls rocking to party music and hip-hop along with house, electronica, or even rhythm 'n' blues. The club, which mostly attracts 20- and 30-somethings, also hosts various theme nights. Nachtgalerie is open Friday and Saturday 10pm to 5am. Landsbergerstrasse 185. www.nachtgalerie.de. ℭ **089/32455595.** Cover 10€. S-Bahn: Hirschgarten.

The Bar & Cafe Scene

Alter Simpl ★★   Back in the 1890s, Frank Wedekind, who penned the play *Spring Awakening,* led a circle of artists who congregated here. Nowadays, it's a spacious "beer cafe" that's popular with students and has a great selection of food. It's open Sunday to Thursday 11am to 3am, Friday and Saturday 11am to 4am. Türkenstrasse 57. www.eggerlokale.de. ℭ **089/2723083.** U-Bahn: Universität.

Café Puck ★   A dark-paneled retreat for students, artists, and workers, this cafe plays a variety of roles for its diverse crowd. It's a bar to students; a restaurant to the locals, who like the daily menu of German, American, and Asian dishes; and a spot where everyone can enjoy a big American breakfast. Café Puck is open daily 9am to 1am. Türkenstrasse 33. www.cafepuck.de. ℭ **089/2802280.** U-Bahn: Universität.

Havana Club ★★   This lively singles bar fueled by rum-based cocktails is open Monday to Thursday 6pm to 1am, Friday and Saturday 6pm to 3am, Sunday 7pm to 1am. Herrnstrasse 30. www.havanaclub-muenchen.de. ✆ **089/291884.** S-Bahn: Isartor.

Ned Kelly's Australian Bar ★   A pub/bar combo, Ned Kelly's offers live music, Irish and Australian drinks and food, and coverage of sporting events, especially soccer. Both bars are open Monday to Thursday 4pm to 1am, Friday and Saturday 11am to 2 or 3am, and Sunday noon to 1am. Frauenplatz 11. www.kiliansirishpub.com. ✆ **089/24219899.** U-/S-Bahn: Marienplatz.

Sausalitos ★   For the best margaritas in town, the kind Hemingway used to slurp down in Havana, head to this welcoming Mexican cantina. If you're in your 20s, you'll fit right in. During happy hour daily from 5 to 8pm, mixed drinks are half-price. It's open Monday to Thursday and Sunday 11am to 1am, Friday and Saturday 11am to 2:30am. Im Tal 16. www.sausalitos.de. ✆ **089/24295494.** U-/S-Bahn: Marienplatz.

Schumann's Bar am Hofgarten ★★   Munich's most legendary bar has an international fan club, lots of pizazz, a history that goes forever, and slick new premises. Schumann's is open Monday to Friday 5pm to roughly 2 or 3am, Saturday and Sunday 6pm to 3am. Odeonsplatz 6–7, at the corner of Galerie Strasse. www.schumanns.de. ✆ **089/229060.** U-Bahn: Odeonsplatz.

Gay & Lesbian Nightlife

Munich's gay and lesbian scene is centered around the blocks between the Viktualienmarkt and Gärtnerplatz, particularly on Hans-Sachs-Strasse.

Bau ★★★   Covering two floors and drawing an international crowd, mostly men, this is Bavaria's largest gay bar. It's open nightly 8pm to 3am. Beethovenstrasse 1. www.bau-munich.de. ✆ **089/269208.** U-Bahn: Sendlinger Tor.

Kraftwerk ★   This cafe-restaurant-bar has been a popular hangout for over a decade. It serves a late breakfast, there's a happy hour on Wednesday from 7 to 9pm, and you can order food (salads, sandwiches, soups) throughout the day. It's open Sunday to Thursday 10am to 1am, Friday and Saturday 10am to 3am. Thalkircher Strasse 4. ✆ **089/21588881.** U-Bahn: Sendlinger Tor.

NY Club ★★   This club is currently the most stylish and modern gay dance club in town, with a beautifully designed lounge and a high-tech dance floor. Look for special events and gay parties by searching the club's website. Sonnenstrasse 25. www.nyclub.de. ✆ **089/62232152.** Cover from 5€. U-Bahn: Sendlinger Tor.

Spectator Sports

FC Bayern Munich ★★   While in Munich, you're bound to see the red-and-white checkered emblem of Munich's most famous football team, FC Bayern Munich, which plays in snazzy Allianz Arena northeast of the city center (take the U6 line to Fröttmaning). Founded in 1900, Bayern Munich reached its heyday in the 70s, when they won the European Cup 3 times. Bayern's roster currently includes many German national team stars, such as Thomas Muller and Manuel Neuer, as well as other international stars like Arjen Robben and Arturo Vidal. FC Bayern plays from late August to late May on alternate weekends. Buy tickets online in advance, as Bayern's 20 million European fans make sell-outs common. Allianz Arena, Werner-Heisenberg-Alle 25. www.fcbayern.de. ✆ **089/699310.**

DAY TRIPS FROM MUNICH

Dachau Concentration Camp Memorial Site (KZ-Gedenkstätte Dachau) ★★★

In 1933, shortly after Hitler became chancellor, Himmler and the SS set up the first German concentration camp on the grounds of a former ammunition factory in the small town of Dachau, 10 miles (15km) northwest of Munich. The list of prisoners at the camp included everyone from communists and Social Democrats to Jews, homosexuals, Gypsies, Jehovah's Witnesses, clergymen, political opponents, trade union members, and others. The camp was presented to the public, and shown off to visitors, as a labor camp where political dissidents and "social and sexual deviants" could be "rehabilitated" through work—hence the chilling and cynical motto that greeted prisoners as they entered the gates of the camp: *arbeit macht frei* (work gives you freedom).

Between 1933 and 1945, more than 206,000 mostly male prisoners from 30 countries were imprisoned at Dachau. (And Dachau was just one of dozens of concentration camps established by the Third Reich throughout Germany.) At least 30,000 people were registered as dead during that period. However, thousands more were murdered here, even if their deaths weren't officially logged. After the SS abandoned the camp on April 28, 1945, the liberating U.S. Army moved in to take charge the following day. When they arrived, they discovered some 67,000 living prisoners—all of them on the verge of death—at Dachau and its subsidiary camps.

GETTING THERE

You can get to the camp/memorial by taking the frequent S-Bahn train S2 from the Hauptbahnhof to Dachau (direction: Petershausen), then

Visiting the former concentration camp at Dachau is a sobering experience.

bus no. 726 to the camp. The bus stop is marked with the name of the memorial, so you can't miss it. Expect to spend about 30 minutes to get there from Munich's main train station.

EXPLORING DACHAU

The reality of what happened at Dachau—where prisoners were stripped of all human rights and dignity, turned into slave laborers, and tortured, beaten, shot, hung, starved, lethally injected, and used for medical experiments—is the reality of the barbarism that took hold of German society during World War II and led to the Holocaust. Dachau is not an easy place to visit, but it is an important place to visit. Taking one of the 2½-hour tours, offered in English, is perhaps the best way to gain and overall understanding of the camp and how it worked. At the **Visitor Center** you can book a tour, rent an audioguide, and visit the bookstore. Then expect to spend at least 2 to 2 to 3 hours visiting the grounds. Guided tours (2½ hours) in English are available daily at 11am and 1pm.

Much of the camp was destroyed after the war, but not all. A museum with a permanent exhibition is housed in the large building where prisoners were registered and "processed." Here, photographs, text panels (all translated into English) and documents tell the story of the camp, how it was run, who was incarcerated and killed, and who some of the personnel were—for Dachau was a training camp for Germans who wanted to work their way up the Nazi ladder. An English version of a 22-minute documentary film, *The Dachau Concentration Camp*, is shown at 10am, 11:30am, 12:30pm, 2pm and 3pm.

The grounds have a bleak, haunted quality. Two barracks have been rebuilt to give visitors insight into the living conditions the prisoners endured, but these are of course sanitized versions. The camp, built to house a couple hundred prisoners, ended up holding thousands, and by the end of the war, prisoners who hadn't worked or starved to death or executed were dying of typhus and other diseases. You will also see the roll-call yard, where prisoners were brutally mustered; a bunker that was used as a camp prison and torture area; the camp road; security installations, and the crematorium area. There are Protestant and Catholic chapels (claiming to be "outside politics," neither denomination actively protested Hitler's policies at the time), a Jewish Memorial, and an International Memorial.

There are still political and controversial elements to be considered at Dachau. The German government, for instance, has refused to acknowledge that the gas chambers at Dachau were used for killing prisoners, although a survivor of the camp has testified that they were. Another controversy surrounds the International Memorial, which was erected to show versions of all the different identification badges that prisoners were forced to wear. When the memorial was dedicated in 1968, however, there were objections that homosexuals were criminals and should not be represented in the memorial. The pink triangle homosexuals were forced to wear was removed from the memorial and has never been replaced, even though some 6,000 gays were imprisoned here and subjected to unusually (even for Dachau) harsh treatment. If there is one lesson to be learned at this moving memorial, it is that there is no hierarchy to suffering. Every single inmate at Dachau deserves the right to be remembered.

KZ-Gedenkstätte Dachau. Alte-Römerstrasse 75. www.kz-gedenkstaette-dachau.de. ℭ **08131/669970.** Free admission; guided tours 3€; audioguides 3.50€. Daily 9am–5pm.

Schloss Nymphenburg (Nymphenburg Palace) ★★★

One of the most sophisticated and beautiful palaces in Europe, Schloss Nymphenburg served as a summer residence for Bavaria's royal family, the Wittelsbachs. (Their official Munich residence was the Residenz, see p. 322, which you can also visit.) Located 8km (5 miles) northwest of Munich, an easy 20-minute tram ride, Nymphenburg's palace and grounds require at least half a day if you want to see everything.

GETTING THERE

You can get to Schloss Nymphenburg by taking the S-Bahn to Laim and then the bus marked "Schloss Nymphenburg." Another option is to take the U-Bahn to Rotkreuzplatz, then the tram to Romanplatz (from there it's a 10-minute walk west to the palace entrance). From central Munich, you can also easily reach the palace in about 20 minutes by taking tram 17 to Romanplatz.

EXPLORING NYMPHENBURG PALACE

There's a lot to see at Nymphenburg, but you'll probably want to begin in the main palace, which was begun in 1664 and took more than 150 years to complete. In 1702, Elector Max Emanuel decided to enlarge the original Italianate villa by adding four large pavilions connected by arcaded passageways, and later architects imposed a French style over the original Italian baroque. Nevertheless, it's a relatively modest palace, without the "room-after-room" feel of a Versailles. There are no guided tours, but you can rent an audioguide; you can easily view it in less than an hour, which gives you more time to explore the gardens and outlying pavilions.

Highlights include the **Great Hall,** the most beautiful of the grand public rooms decorated in a vibrant splash of rococo colors and stuccowork. The great stucco-master Johann Baptist Zimmermann (see the

The Bavarian royals' elegant summer palace, Schloss Nymphenburg.

Wieskirche, p. 287) added these frescoes in 1756, featuring mythological nymphs (as in Nymphenberg) paying homage to the goddess Flora. The south pavilion displays Ludwig I's famous **Gallery of Beauties** painted between 1827-1850 by Josef Karl Stieler. The beauties include portraits of Ludwig's daughter-in-law, Marie of Prussia, who gave birth to his grandson Ludwig II in a bedchamber nearby, and of Lola Montez, the raven-haired dancer whose affair with Ludwig I caused a scandal.

To the south of the palace buildings, the rectangular block of low structures that once housed the court stables now holds the **Marstall-museum,** which displays a dazzling collection of ornate, gilded coaches and sleighs, including those used by Ludwig II (the "Mad" King who built Neuschwanstein, see p. 294). The **Porzellansammlung (Porcelain Collection;** entrance across from the Marstallmuseum) contains superb pieces of 18th-century porcelain, including miniature copies of masterpiece paintings from the Alte Pinakothek.

A canal runs through the 500-acre **Schlosspark,** stretching all the way to the so-called **Grand Cascade** at the far end of the formal French-style gardens. In the English-style park, full of quiet meadows and forested paths, stands the **Badenburg Pavilion,** with an 18th-century swimming pool; the **Pagodenburg,** decorated in the Chinese style that was all the rage in the 18th century; and the **Magdalenenklause (Hermitage),** meant to be a retreat for prayer and solitude.

Prettiest of all the buildings in the park is **Amalienburg ★★★**, built in 1734 as a hunting lodge for Electress Amalia. The interior salons, designed by the Belgian-born architect François de Cuvilliés (see the Cuvilliés Theater, p. 323) are a riot of flamboyant colors, wall paintings, and more glorious Johann Baptist Zimmermann stuccowork. In the delightful Hall of Mirrors, take a closer look at the gilt cherubs festooning the walls and ceilings—they're all busily hunting and fishing, as if to prove that this rococo gem is really just a simple hunting lodge. Really. Schloss Nymphenburg, Schloss Nymphenburg 1. www.schloss-nymphenburg.de. ⓒ **089/179080.** Palace grounds free. Admission to all attractions Apr to mid-Oct 11.50€ adults, 9€seniors, children under 18 free; mid-Oct to Mar 8.50€ adults, 6.50€ seniors, children under 18 free. Apr to mid-Oct open daily 9am–6pm; mid-Oct to Mar daily 10am–4pm. Badenburg and Magdalenenklause closed mid-Oct to Mar.

Chiemsee & Neues Schloss ★★

Chiemsee, known as the "Bavarian Sea," is one of the most beautiful lakes in the Bavarian Alps, an hour south of Munich by train. Resorts line the shores and sailboats swarm the water in summer, but the main sttractions are its two islands, **Fraueninsel** and **Herreninsel,** the latter being where Ludwig II built his Versailles-style palace **Neues Schloss.**

GETTING THERE

Frequent daily trains make the hour-long trip from Munich's Haupt-bahnhof to **Prien Bahnhof,** on the Munich-Salzburg train line. Prien is on the western shore of the lake. By car, it's a 90 km (62-mile) drive from Munich via the A8 motorway; scenic routes via the A94 or B304 are more direct but slower, taking about an hour and a half.

Once you've arrived in the area, you'll need to take a boat to get to the islands. Lake steamers operated by **Chiemsee-Schifffahrt Ludwig Fessle** (www.chiemsee-schifffahrt.de, ☎ 08051/6090) offer a range of excursions, from a 2½-hour grand tour of the lake (12.40€ adults, 6.20€ children 6-15) to a 20-minute trip directly from Prien to Herreninsel (round-trip 7.80€ adults, 3.90€ children 6-15). Local bus service runs from the Prien train station to the docks, but in the summer there's also a vintage narrow-gauge train, operated by the steamer company; train fare (3.80€ adults, 1.90€ children) can be included in your boat ticket.

EXPLORING CHIEMSEE'S ISLANDS

The smaller of the two islands, **Fraueninsel ★** (also sometimes called Frauenchiemsee) is a picturesque place to wander, with a fishing village, gardens, and a Benedictine convent, **Frauenwörth Abbey,** that was founded in 782, which makes it the oldest in Germany. The abbey's stout white bell tower, topped with an onion dome, is the island's most visible

Neues Schloss, Ludwig II's never-finished homage to Versailles.

landmark. Guests are welcome to visit the Romanesque church, with its ancient frescoes; the oldest building in the complex, the gatehouse, also has some fine frescoes, and in summer hosts an art exhibit. Guided 45-minute tours of the abbey (3€) leave from the main gate, but they are only conducted in German.

Day-trip visitors on a more limited schedule may decide to spend their time at the lake entirely on **Herreninsel** (also sometimes called Herrenchiemsee), visiting the lake's biggest attraction: **Neues Schloss ★★** (also known as Königschloss). Begun by King Ludwig II in 1878, it was intended as an homage to French king Louis XIV's palace at Versailles, although of course once Ludwig got going his version of Versailles became bigger and even more opulent. This was the third of Ludwig's trio of fantasy castles, along with **Schloss Linderhof** (p. 303) and **Neuschwanstein** (p. 294), and it was never finished; work stopped upon his death in 1886, with only the center of the palace completed. Nonetheless, the palace and its formal gardens, surrounded by woodlands of beech and fir, remain one of the grandest and most fascinating of Ludwig's castles.

Visitors can only see the palace on guided tours, which last around 30 minutes; German-language tours run continuously, and there are two **English-language tours** per hour in summer, one per hour in winter.

Tours begin in the **vestibule,** presided over by a pair of enameled peacocks, Louis XIV's favorite bird. From there, you proceed up the sumptuously decorated **State Staircase,** with its white marble statues and vividly colored frescoes. Room after room reveals a dizzying level of rococo ornamentation, with gilded woodwork and huge crystal chandeliers hung from frescoed ceilings. Practically every inch of the **State Bedroom** has been gilded. Set behind a golden balustrade, a dais holds not a throne but a richly decorated bed, its purple-velvet draperies weighing more than 135 kilograms (300 lb.). Presumably this was where King Ludwig would have elegantly reclined while receiving state visitors, although in fact he never lived to use this chamber. Note the ceiling fresco, depicting the descent of Apollo to Mount Olympus—the god's features bear a strong resemblance to Ludwig's hero, Louis XIV.

The **Great Hall of Mirrors** is the palace's most splendid room, and the most authentic replica of its counterpart at Versailles. Its 17 arches contain enormous mirrors reflecting 33 crystal chandeliers and 44 gilded candelabras. The vaulted ceiling is covered with 25 paintings depicting the life of—who else?—Louis XIV. The **Dining Room** also fascinates visitors because of its so-called magic table, which could be lowered through the floor to be cleared and relaid between courses. Over the table hangs an immense chandelier of Meissen porcelain, the largest in the world (and the palace's most valuable item). But perhaps the most poignant detail is the fact that the dining table is so small—ideal for a bachelor king to dine by himself.

If all this makes you curious about Ludwig's eccentric personality, Neues Schloss also has a **museum** on the grounds that documents his life story with state robes, ornate furniture, and other royal showpieces to gawk at. Your combination ticket also allows you to visit the nearby **Old Palace,** a former Augustinian monastery where Ludwig lived (in surprisingly simple quarters) while Neues Schloss was under construction; exhibits also explore the building's role as the site of the 1948 conference that wrote the constitution for the new Federal Republic of Germany.

Neues Schloss Chiemsee, Herreninsel. www.herrenchiemsee.de. © **08051/68870.** Combination tickets to Neues Schloss, Ludwig II Museum, and Augustinian Monastery adults 8€, seniors and students 7€, children under 18 free. Apr to mid-Oct open daily 9am–6pm (last tour at 5pm or 4:50pm); late Oct to Mar daily 9:40am–4:15pm (last tour at 3:50 depending on boat schedules).

8

MUNICH | Day Trips from Munich

9

HEIDELBERG, STUTTGART, & THE NECKAR VALLEY

Even the curmudgeonly Mark Twain, visiting the idyllic Neckar Valley, was moved to describe it as the "perfection of the beautiful." Along the Neckar River's meandering, 370km (222-mile) long course lie some of the most enticing, legend-steeped landscapes in Germany. Above its swiftly moving waters stand storied castles, many in picturesque ruin, whose lords once controlled river trade. Vineyards carpet some areas, while others are covered in dense woodlands.

Against the medieval/Renaissance backdrops of Heidelberg and Tubingen—among the very few German towns to escape World War II unscathed—centuries-old universities remain leading centers of science and medicine, while the student population keeps dozens of hospitable, dark-paneled taverns thriving along the old town lanes. In Stuttgart, the Mercedes star twirls atop the train station tower, a welcoming beacon in this business-minded, culturally rich city.

HEIDELBERG ★★★

89km (55 miles) S of Frankfurt

This ancient university town near the edge of the Black Forest enjoys a reputation for wine and romance, song and student life, fun and frivolity. It drew 19th-century German Romantics, who praised and painted it; Mark Twain, who cavorted in its lively streets in *A Tramp Abroad;* and fans of the 1924 Sigmund Romberg operetta *Student Prince*, set in Heidelberg (with a rousing chorus, "Drink, drink, drink" that is still an anthem for many young residents and their visitors). A little less poetically, this attractive city of 135,000 inhabits also housed a U.S. army base for many decades after World War II, helping ensure its popularity with Americans. The **Altstadt** (Old Town) looks much as it did a century or two ago, with architectural landmarks from the later Middle Ages and early Renaissance. Yet Heidelberg is young at heart, home to the oldest university in Germany, dating to 1386; some 28,000 students impart a palpable energy to the narrow lanes and lively drinking inns of the Altstadt.

FACING PAGE: **A deer sculpture gazes down from the entrance of Heidelberg Castle.**

The twin-towered Alte Brücke (Old Bridge) crosses the Neckar in Heidelberg.

Essentials

ARRIVING The nearest major airport is Frankfurt (see chapter 12), with a direct bus link to Heidelberg. A shuttle bus between Frankfurt and Heidelberg (www.ics-logistik.de, ℭ **0621/651620**) costs 20€ per person. Heidelberg's **Hauptbahnhof** has frequent service to regional towns and major cities, from Frankfurt (trip time: 1 hr.) and Munich (about 3½ hours). For information, visit **www.bahn.de**. Motorists should take the A5 Autobahn from the north or south.

GETTING AROUND Heidelberg is crisscrossed with a network of trams and buses, many of which intersect at the **Bismarktplatz.** Bus nos. 31 and 32 travel frequently between the railway station and the Universitätsplatz, in the Altstadt. Another handy route from the train station to Altstadt hotels, especially those clustered around the Marktplatz, is no. 33, with a stop at Rathaus/Bergbahn. Bus or tram fares are 2.30€ for a single ride, 6€ for a day ticket. You can buy tickets from machines at most stops or from the driver.

VISITOR INFORMATION The **Heidelberg Tourist Bureau,** in front of the Hauptbahnhof at Willy-Brandt-Platz 1 (www.heidelberg-marketing. de; ℭ 06221/19433), is open April to October Monday to Saturday 9am

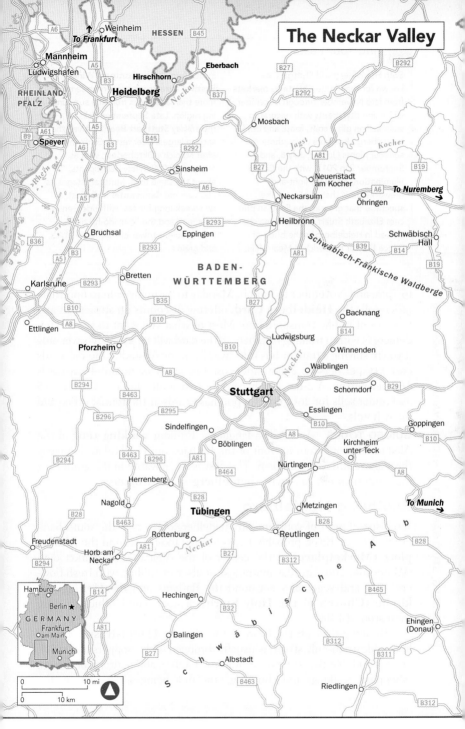

The Neckar Valley

Both Heidelberg and Stuttgart are known for their large **Christmas markets** from late November through December, which line city streets with decorated stalls selling gifts, craft, food, and drink. Heidelberg also lights up on three summer nights (June 3, July 8, and September 2 in 2017) with the **Castle Illumination,** a splashy light-and-fireworks show that duplicates the spectacle that greeted the Scottish princess Elizabeth Stuart in 1613 when she arrived in Heidelberg as the bride of Prince Elector Frederick V. Meanwhile, in late August, the **Stuttgart Wine Festival** attracts wine lovers to sample more than 350 wines from the surrounding region. Late September kicks off the 16-day **Stuttgart Beer Festival,** the second largest beer fest in Germany after Munich's Oktoberfest, with as many as 20,000 thirsty participants; about the same time, Stuttgart stages its 200-year-old **Cannstatter Volksfest,** a two-week-long fun fair, with rides, entertainment, and the 26-m (86-ft.) high Fruchtsaule, a tower of fruit, vegetables, and grains.

to 7pm, and November to March, Monday to Saturday 9am to 6pm. The office sells the **Heidelberg Card,** offering discounts on attractions and free use of public transportation. Most of what you want to see in Heidelberg is within walking distance, so the card will be a money-saver only if you're staying a tram or bus ride away from the Altstadt. One-day cards cost 11€ per person; 2-day cards cost 13€ per person; and 4-day cards 16€ per person. A 2-day family card for two adults and two children 15 and under sells for 26€. You can purchase cards at the tourist office and many hotels.

GUIDED TOURS   An English-language, 1½-hour **walking tour** of the Altstadt sets out from in front of the Rathaus on Martktplatz Thursday through Saturday at 10:30am. The cost is 8€, payable to the guide. For more information, go to **www.heidelberg-marketing.de**.

Exploring Heidelberg

You'll spend most of your time in Heidelberg on or near the south bank of the Neckar River, probably not venturing too far beyond the **Marktplatz (Marketplace)** at the center of the Altstadt. On market days (Wednesday and Saturday mornings), stalls over-spilling with fresh flowers, fish, and vegetables surround the Rathaus and the **Heiliggeistkirche (Church of the Holy Spirit),** a stark, late-Gothic structure from around 1400.

Running through the heart of the city, the **Hauptstrasse,** a mile-long pedestrian-only street, is usually thronged with shoppers and strollers. It's said that the street is for "Kaufen, Laufen, and Saufen," or loosely, "shopping, walking, and chugging," the first being a reference to the

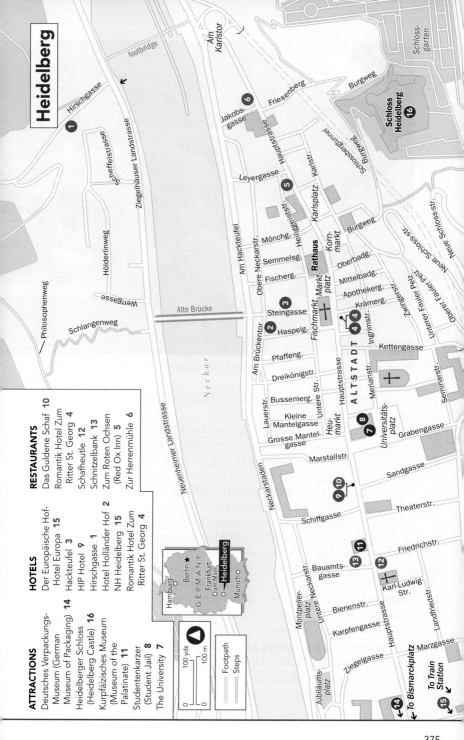

Heidelberg

ATTRACTIONS

Deutsches Verpackungs-
Museum (German
Museum of Packaging) **14**
Heidelberger Schloss
(Heidelberg Castle) **16**
Kurpfälzisches Museum
(Museum of the
Palatinate) **11**
Studentenkarzer
(Student Jail) **8**
The University **7**

HOTELS

Der Europäische Hof-
Hotel Europa **15**
Hackteufel **3**
HIP Hotel **9**
Hirschgasse **1**
Hotel Holländer Hof **2**
NH Heidelberg **15**
Romantik Hotel Zum
Ritter St. Georg **4**

RESTAURANTS

Das Guldene Schaf **10**
Romantik Hotel Zum
Ritter St. Georg **4**
Schafheutle **12**
Schnitzelbank **13**
Zum Roten Ochsen
(Red Ox Inn) **5**
Zur Herrenmühle **6**

0 ____ 100 yds
0 ____ 100 m

Footpath
Steps

GERMANY
Hamburg
Berlin ★
Frankfurt
am Main
Heidelberg
Munich

Neckar

footbridge

Hirschgasse

Scheffelstrasse

Ziegelhäuser Landstrasse

Hölderlinweg

Werrgasse

Schlangenweg

Philosophenweg

Alte Brücke

Am Karlstor

Jakobs-
gasse

Friesenberg

Burgweg

Schloss
Heidelberg

Leyergasse

Hauptstrasse

Karlsplatz

Karlstr.

Burgweg

Schlossbergtunnel

Burgweg

Neue Schloss-str.

Heiligeiststr.

Mönchg.

Semmelsg.

Fischerg.

Am Hackteufel

Obere Neckarstr.

Steingasse

Haspelg.

Am Brückentor

Pfaffeng.

Dreikönigstr.

Bussemerg.

Kleine
Mantelgasse

Grosse Mantel-
gasse

Lauerstr.

Untere Str.

Marstallstr.

Neckarstaden

Schiffgasse

Neuenheimer Landstrasse

Fischmarkt

Markt-
platz

Rathaus

Korn-
markt

Oberbadg.

Mittelbadg.

Apothekerg.

Krämerg.

Ingrimstr.

Kettengasse

ALTSTADT

Hauptstrasse

Merianstr.

Universitäts-
platz

Grabengasse

Sandgasse

Theaterstr.

Zwingerstr.

Unterer Fauler Pelz

Oberer Fauler Pelz

Seminarstr.

Neue Schloss-str.

Heu-
markt

Friedrichstr.

Bauamts-
gasse

Karl-Ludwig-
Str.

Montpellier-
platz

Untere Neckarstr.

Bienenstr.

Karpfengasse

Hauptstrasse

Marzgasse

Landfriedstr.

Ziegelgasse

Jubiläums-
platz

To Bismarckplatz

**To Train
Station**

1
6
5
3
2
4
4
7
8
9
10
9
10
11
13
12
14
15
16

375

Photo op in Heidelberg: Pose with the Bridge Ape for good fortune.

many shops along the street and the last to the many places to have a beer, or for that matter, sip a coffee.

Cross the gracefully flowing Neckar River on the **Alte Brücke (Old Bridge),** a handsome, twin-towered stone span from 1788 (destroyed in 1944 by German troops trying to halt the advance of the Allied army and rebuilt two years later). It's almost mandatory to pay homage to the raffish **Brückenaffe (Bridge Ape)**—touch the mirror he's holding for wealth, his outstretched fingers to ensure a return to Heidelberg, and the mice that surround him to ensure progeny. From the opposite bank continue up the **Schlangenweg (Snake Path)** to the **Philosophenweg (Philosophers' Way),** a 2km (1.25-mile) walking trail that provides memorable views of the castle, the river, and the Altstadt. The amble ends at the **Philosophengärtchen (Philosophers' Garden),** where the valley's mild climate nurtures Japanese cherries, cypresses, lemons, bamboos, rhododendrons, gingkos, yucca trees, and other warm-weather plants.

Deutsches Verpackungs-Museum (German Museum of Packaging) ★★ MUSEUM   This quirky collection stashed in a former church is a lot more charming and intriguing than the name might suggest. Shelves are filled with such curiosities as the world's first tinned food, prepared and packaged for Napoleon's army in 1810, and cigarettes disbursed in specially made packets for the maiden voyage of the *Titanic.* You'll see how, during World I, a popular British import cigarette, House of Lords, was repackaged as Herrenhaus, while some of the best-selling chocolates of the era were wrapped as bombs. Signage is mostly in German, but one of the helpful English-speaking staff will often join you to show off the highlights.

Hauptstrasse 22. www.verpackungsmuseum.de. ✆ **06221/21361.** Admission 3.50€. Wed–Fri 1–6pm, weekends 11am–6pm.

Heidelberger Schloss (Heidelberg Castle) ★★★ HISTORIC SITE

Perched enticingly above the Altstadt, set amid woodlands and terraced gardens that were once known as the Eighth Wonder of the World, Heidelberg's half-ruined castle is the epitome of German romanticism. Even in ruin it's one of the great Renaissance landmarks of northern Europe. Visitors enter the castle through **Elizabeth's Gate,** the portal that the young prince elector Frederick V in 1613 had built overnight as a surprise for his bride Elizabeth, the teenaged daughter of English King James I. (Their marriage was cause for months-long celebrations in both England and Germany.) The entrance, with its elaborately carved vines and a bestiary of forest animals, was part of extensive restorations that included an expansion of the Friedrichsbau, the palace where the young royals took up residence. Though the match of Frederick and Elizabeth was encouraged for its many political advantages, the couple was well suited and remained romantically devoted to one another until Frederick's death in 1632, at the age of 36; they had 11 children together.

Laid waste in 1690 by the French troops of Louis XV, the castle was finished off by a disastrous lightning strike. Enough gables and arches remain, however, to suggest the grandeur of the place, and a multi-language audio-guide does a good job of filling in the missing pieces. Among the many carvings on the remaining façades, look near the entrance for a carved image of Frederick IV, known as "Snazzy Pants" for the elaborate flared britches he is wearing. Another elector left his mark with an inscription ending in "ludovicus.com," leading pundits to refer to it as a reference to a website from the Middle Ages. An especially noteworthy relic is the **Great Cask,** or the Heidelberg Tun, a symbol of the exuberant life of the prince electors. The vulgar vessel was built in 1751 to store more than 208,000 liters (55,000 gal.) of wine. (Mark Twain's sardonic judgment: "An empty cask the size of a cathedral could excite but little emotion in me.") The Chemist's Tower houses the **Apothekenmuseum** (Pharmaceutical Museum), which quite engagingly spotlights the importance of German pharmaceutical research (much of it conducted at Heidelberg University) with utensils, laboratory equipment, and a re-created chemist's shop from the 18th and 19th centuries.

You can reach the castle by several routes. The **Bergbahn** (mountain train) whisks you up from the Kornmarkt in a flash (tickets to the castle include the train ride). A paved road gradually winds up the **Neue Schlossstrasse** past houses perched on the hillside, while the steeper **Burgweg** walk climbs uphill from Kornmarkt.

Schlossberg. www.schloss-heidelberg.de. ℭ **06221/872-7000.** Admission 7€ (includes tram ride). Castle precincts open 24 hr. 1-hr. guided tours in English 5€; audio tours 5€. Daily 8am–6pm. Guided tours in English, Apr–Oct Mon–Fri hourly 11:15am–4:15pm, Sat–Sun hourly 10:15am–4:15pm; Nov–Mar Mon–Fri 11:15am, 12:15pm, 2:15pm, and 4:15pm, Sat–Sun hourly 11:15am–4:15pm.

Heidelberg University ★★ HISTORIC SITE   Germany's oldest university, officially known as the Ruprecht-Karls-Universität Heidelberg, was founded in 1386. With an academic staff of 15,000 and 27,000 students, the university is historically centered around the Universitätsplatz, though its 12 faculties teaching 100 disciplines are scattered throughout the city and outskirts. The small **University Museum** honors the contributions of founder Ruprecht I of the Palantine (as a great swath of southwestern Germany was then known), who in 1386 wished to establish a center of learning and intellectualism within his holdings, and Karl Friedrich of Baden, who in 1803 helped revive and finance the flailing institution. Displays tout the university's many distinctions and achievements, not the least of which is producing 55 Nobel Prize winners. One flight up is the **Great Hall,** a richly paneled and ornamented room installed for the university's 500th anniversary in 1886. The huge painting of Athena, goddess of Wisdom, and ceiling frescoes honoring the disciplines of law, medicine, science, and philosophy could have been distracting when the Great Hall was used for lectures, though they provide a suitably lavish backdrop for university-related ceremonies now held here. The museum and Great Hall share a building with the Student Jail at Augustinergasse 2 (www.uni-heidelberg.de; ℭ **06221/543554**); a combined ticket to all three sights costs 3€ adults, 2.50€ students and children 14 and under. They are open April to October, Tuesday to Sunday 10am to 6pm, and November to March, Tuesday to Sunday 10am to 4pm.

On the ornately carved red sandstone façade of the **University Library,** on the corner of Plöck and Grabengasse, an image shows the god Prometheus, protector of mankind, pulling back the veil of knowledge—a good metaphor for what lies beyond the doors. Most treasured of the 3 million volumes is the *Codex Manesse,* an early 14th-century illustrated manuscript of courtly love songs; pages from a rare facsimile edition are on display in the foyer (www.ub.uni-heidelberg.de; ℭ **06221/544227;** open Monday to Friday 9am to 10pm, Saturday 9am to 5pm).

Among the university's many academic holdings is the **Prinzhorn Collection,** a stash of more than 5,000 drawings, paintings, carving, and textile works by patients of Hans Prinzhorn, who practiced at the university's esteemed psychiatric clinic in the 1920s and 30s. Prinzhorn was one of the first psychiatrists to use art as a way to help patients express their fears and relive traumatic experiences. Rotating exhibitions show pieces from the collection, which attracted the attention of Jean Dubuffet and many other European artists of the time. Works are displayed in a small gallery in the Psychiatric Clinic, Vosstrasse 2 (www.prinzhorn. uni-hd.de; © **06221/564492**); it's open Tuesday to Sunday 11am to 5pm (Wednesdays until 8pm); admission is 2€.

Kurpfälzisches Museum (Museum of the Palatinate) ★ MUSEUM
In the salons of the baroque Palais Morass, Heidelberg's very long history comes to the fore with artifacts that include a cast of the jawbone of Heidelberg Man. This early human lived in Europe and Africa until 250,000 years ago and is thought to be the direct ancestor of homo sapiens; the original jawbone (stored at the university) was unearthed near Heidelberg in 1907. Nearby are some remarkably well-preserved wooden beams from a Roman-era bridge across the Neckar. Other displays may or may not help you understand the complex, strife-torn history of the Palatinate, as this large swath of southwestern Germany was once known, but the collection's standout, the **Altar of the Apostles** by Tilman Riemenschneider from 1509, alone justifies the price of a ticket. If you're traveling on to Würzburg (see p. 245), you'll see more of this master carver's work and admire his uncanny talent for embellishing religious scenes with emotion and compassion.
Hauptstrasse 97. www.museum-heidelberg.de. © **06221/5834020.** Admission 3€ adults, 1.80€ students and children 17 and under. Tues–Sun 10am–6pm. Bus: 31, 32, or 35.

Studentenkarzer (Student Jail) ★★ HISTORIC SITE Count Palatinate Ruprecht I, founder of the University of Heidelberg in 1386, had the foresight to install some rough cells where unruly and drunken students could be incarcerated. (If street laughter and shouting disrupt your sleep in an Altstadt hotel, you may wish the practice were still in force.) Prisoners bedecked the walls and even the ceilings with graffiti and drawings, including portraits and silhouettes, until the jail closed in 1914. Despite a certain rowdy element, even the acerbic Mark Twain commented that "idle students are not the rule" in Heidelberg, and in most cases, spending time in one of the cells was considered a rite of passage. In fact, scholars who were nearing graduation but had never been jailed often went out of their way to be incarcerated. A common ploy was to throw a brick through the window of the police station, then

For centuries, a night in the Student Jail was a rite of passage for Heidelberg students.

wait out front to be arrested. That was good for at least a night or two behind bars, during which time inmates were allowed to have lavish meals and unlimited amounts of beer delivered and to enjoy visits from young women.

Augustinergasse 2. www.uni-heidelberg.de. © **06221/543593.** Admission 3€ adults, 2.50€ students and children 14 and under. Ticket includes entry for the University Museum and Old Auditorium. Apr–Oct daily 10am–6pm; Nov–Mar Mon–Sat 10am–4pm. Bus: 31, 32, or 35.

Where to Stay in Heidelberg
EXPENSIVE
Der Europäische Hof-Hotel Europa ★★★ Heidelberg's best hotel, and one of the finest in Germany, seems to do everything right and makes it all seem effortless. Lounges are comfortably plush and attractive; guest rooms, ranging over an old wing and a newer extension, are enormous and beautifully furnished with a nice mix of old-fashioned comfort and contemporary accents, lit by crystal chandeliers and equipped with sumptuous marble baths. Service is unfailingly attentive while unobtrusive and personable. A multilevel, rooftop spa includes a large indoor pool and state-of-the-art gym, and the wood-paneled grill room serves sophisticated French fare. You'll pay a bit more to stay here

than in other Heidelberg lodgings, but you'll be staying in such style as you won't find many other places in the world.

Friedrich-Ebert-Anlage 1. www.europischerhof.com. ©**06221/5150.** 118 units. 148€–384€ double. Breakfast included. Parking 19€. Tram: Bismarktplatz. **Amenities:** 2 restaurants; bar; babysitting; concierge; health club & spa; indoor pool; room service; Wi-Fi (free).

MODERATE

Hackteufel ★★   A guesthouse right in the heart of the Altstadt offers spruce and comfortable lodgings between the Marktplatz and the Old Bridge. Each of the 12 cozy rooms is different, but most are extra large and embellished with wood floors, beams, dormers, and plenty of nice traditional wood furnishings; number 12 is a cross-beamed garret with a castle view and number 8 is a commodious suite with a terrace. Downstairs, a handsome restaurant and wine bar serves snacks and drinks throughout the day and traditional specialties at mealtimes.

Steingasse 7. www.hackteufel.de. © **06221/905380.** 12 units. 120€–170€ double. Buffet breakfast included. **Amenities:** Restaurant, bar; Wi-Fi (free). Bus 33.

HIP Hotel ★★   As if Heidelberg isn't transporting enough, these over-the-top yet extremely comfortable accommodations are done up in the style of cities around the world. Paris surrounds you in the loft-like, red-velvet ambiance of a posh garret, while Zermatt comes with log walls and a Technicolor alpine scene beyond the cute, gingham curtained window. In Malolo (that's an island in Fiji) you can walk on pure white sand and drift off to sleep to the sound of crashing waves. Excellent beds and snazzy plumbing ensure this place is more than just a fun gimmick, though you might need some serious mental adjustment to relax in Down Under, where tables, drapes, and doors are all upside down.

Hauptstrasse 115. www.hip-hotel.de. © **06221/20879.** 27 units. 150€–240€ double. Buffet breakfast included. **Amenities:** Restaurant; bar; room service; Wi-Fi (free). Bus: 31, 32, or 35.

Hirschgasse ★★★   Many stories surround this lovely guest house on the north side of the Neckar. One spring day in 1472, as one tale goes, singer, poet, and doctor Johann von Soest was enjoying a beer in the garden when he set eyes on the young lady of the house, was bedazzled, and asked for her hand in marriage on the spot. In the 19th century, the house became a famous Mensuren, or fencing, fraternity that included Count Bismark; it hosted famous feasts, fueled by as many (as one participant boasted) as 78 measures of beer. These days the only danger you're likely to face is becoming entrenched in a deep armchair or plump sofa covered in Laura Ashley fabric in one of the beautiful, country-house style guest rooms. Many have separate sitting areas and most have huge windowed bathrooms in which deep soaking tubs are standard issue.

Downstairs is a charmingly wood-paneled *stube* where Bismark himself carved his name into one of the 200-year-old tables; there's also the elegant Michelin-starred Le Gourmet dining room, and that same romance-sparking garden.

Hirschgasse 3. www.hirschgasse.de. ✆ **06221/4540.** 118 units. 140€–185€ double. Breakfast included. Free parking. **Amenities:** 2 restaurants; bar; babysitting; concierge; room service; Wi-Fi (free). S-Bahn: Karlstorbahnhof.

Romantik Hotel Zum Ritter St. Georg ★

This tall old house with a glorious German Renaissance façade right on the Marktplatz is a Heidelberg landmark, built in 1592 as the lavish home of a wealthy cloth merchant; by the end of the next century the old inn was already a Heidelberg institution. Its name refers to a carving of St. George on horseback, tucked beneath one of the tall gables (and duplicated above a mantel on the ground floor). The large, high-ceilinged rooms and suites in the front of the house do justice to the surroundings; others off the rambling back corridors are smaller and perfectly comfortable, done in an unremarkable but pleasing contemporary style. A stay here puts you right in the heart of the Altstadt, and just a flight of stairs away from the Ritter's wonderful in-house restaurant (see p. 383).

Hauptstrasse 178. www.ritter-heidelberg.de. ✆ **06221/1350.** 37 units. 118€–176€ double. Buffet breakfast included. **Amenities:** Restaurant; room service; Wi-Fi (free). Bus: 31, 32, or 35

INEXPENSIVE

Hotel Holländer Hof ★

A tavern was doing a brisk business at the foot of the Old Bridge by the 16th century; by the 17th century, the premises had been expanded into an inn with a series of evocative names, among then The Sword, the Black Eagle, and the Bear. In the 19th century it became the Hollander Hof, so named because rooms in front of the house were popular with Dutch skippers (those in the rear sheltered students and pilgrims). Those front-facing rooms are still the prize, with tall windows that frame the glittering river and green hills beyond. Some of the smaller single accommodations are as cozily snug as a captain's berth, and larger rooms are wrapped in the same homey ambiance, with polished-wood wardrobes and desks and fluffy duvets on the good beds.

Neckarstaden 62. www.hollaender-hof-de. ✆ **06221/60500.** 60 units. 84€–175€ double. Buffet breakfast included. **Amenities:** Bar; Wi-Fi (free). Bus: 31, 32, or 35.

NH Heidelberg ★

A courtyard once piled high with kegs of beer is now the glass-filled atrium of these smart lodgings just outside the Altstadt in the restored former Heidelberg Brewery (plus a modern wing). Bright, commodious rooms are all nicely done in traditional décor, or with an upbeat contemporary look with lots of white surfaces and bursts of bright color. The Bräustüberl, serving Bavarian specialties, is the most popular of the three in-house restaurants; perks also include a spa and health club. This business-oriented hotel often has good weekend and summer deals.

Bergheimer Strasse 91. www.nh-hotels.com. ℂ **06221/13270.** 174 units. 85€–175€ double Buffet breakfast included. Parking 15€. **Amenities:** 3 restaurants; bar; health club and spa; room service; Wi-Fi (free). Tram: 22. Bus: 35.

Where to Eat in Heidelberg

By far the most popular place to eat in Heidelberg, and the least expensive, is the University canteen, the **Zeughaus-Mensa im Marstall,** between the Hauptstrasse and the river at Marstallhof 3 (www.student enwerk.uni-heidelberg.de), open daily for lunch and dinner, served cafeteria-style from 11am to 10pm. There are several delicious hot dishes, as well as salads and soups, and beer and wine is available. The public is welcome, though we pay a little more than the students do.

EXPENSIVE

Zur Herrenmühle ★★ GERMAN/INTERNATIONAL   A 17th-century grain mill with thick walls, antique paneling, and heavy beams is irresistibly atmospheric when candlelight flickers amid all the polished wood and starched linens, and the cuisine does justice to the surroundings. Fresh fish, grass-fed lamb, and homemade pastas appear in classic Mediterranean and elegant German preparations served with more formality than is the norm in Heidelberg restaurants. Its vine-covered courtyard is the city's most atmospheric setting for summertime meals.

Hauptstrasse 237. www.herrenmuehle-heidelberg.de. ℂ **06221/602909.** Main courses 18€–26€. Mon–Sat 6–11pm. Closed last 2 weeks of Mar. Bus: 33.

MODERATE

Das Guldene Schaf ★ GERMAN   A long series of paneled and frescoed rooms seems to go on forever behind the welcoming Hauptstrasse entrance, capturing the atmosphere of the inn's 250 -ear history. The menu is heavily laden with schnitzels, bratwursts, and other local favorites like *Gulyassuppe,* a hearty goulash, and *Maultaschen* (traditional Swabian ravioli). Pair your choice with a bottle from one of Heidelberg's most extensive cellars of international wines and a big selection of beers.

Hauptstrasse 115. www.schaf-heidelberg.de. ℂ **06221/20879.** Main courses 10€–12€. Daily 11am–1am. Bus: 31, 32, or 35.

Romantik Hotel Zum Ritter St. Georg ★★★ GERMAN/INTERNATIONAL   An atmospheric and rather splendid dining room occupies the ground floor of this Renaissance-era landmark, where high-ceilings, paneling, frescoes, and Persian carpets provide lovely old world surroundings for a menu to match. Rumpsteak with cream sauce, roasted venison, calf's livers with apples and onions, *Kurpfälzer* (a so-called farmer's treat of liver dumplings and sausages served on potatoes and sauerkraut) are among the many local specialties served. One of the advantages of staying upstairs (see p. 382) is lingering late over a schnapps or another glass of wine after a meal in this welcoming space.

Hauptstrasse 178. www.ritter-heidelberg.de. © **06221/1350.** Main courses 10€–23€. Daily noon–2pm and 6–10pm. Bus: 31, 32, or 35.

INEXPENSIVE

Schafheutle ★★ CAFE   Heidelberg's favorite stop for *Kaffeeundkuchen* (coffee and cake) flows through a string of airy, glittery rooms that open to a large garden with warm-weather seating. Everyone who finds their way here—businesspeople, families, sightseers—feels a bit grand and pampered in the refined, brightly lit surroundings. A well-starched staff delivers rich pastries along with sandwiches, salads, and other light fare.

Hauptstrasse 94. www.cafe-schafheutle.de. © **06221/14680.** Main courses 5€–10€. Mon–Fri 9:30am–7pm, Sat 9am–6pm. Bus: 31, 32, or 35.

Schnitzelbank ★★ GERMAN   The well-worn tables in a tiny, dark room are workbenches from a time when the premises were a barrel factory. These days the business is wine, with an emphasis on local varieties and sold by the glass, plus the namesake schnitzels. The blackboard is also usually filled with a few mainstays like *Schäufele* (pickled and slightly smoked pork shoulder), *Leberknödel* (liver dumplings), and *Saumagen* (literally, sow's stomach, but actually a spicy meat-and-potato mixture)—dishes you're not going to find at a lot of other places. Local epicures are regulars.

Bauamtsgasse 7. www.schnitzelbank-heidelberg.de. © **06221/21189.** Main courses 8€–12€. Daily noon–11pm. Bus: 31, 32, or 35.

Zum Roten Ochsen (Red Ox Inn) ★★ GERMAN   For six generations, the Spengel family has welcomed everybody from Bismarck to Mark Twain in Heidelberg's most revered student tavern. It seems that every student who has attended the university has left his or her mark (or initials) on the walls, and every visitor in town eventually finds his or her way here, too, joining such past guests as Marilyn Monroe, John Wayne, and John Foster Dulles. Guests dine well if not elegantly on *Kartoffelsupp* (potato soup), *Käsespätzle mit zeilben* (cheese spaetzel with onions), rumpsteak, and other solid basics, which taste all the better when accompanied by a huge selection of beer. A pianist plays everything from show tunes to German drinking songs in the background.

Hauptstrasse 217 www.roterochsen.de. © **06221/20977.** Main courses 8€–17€. Apr–Oct, Mon–Sat 11:30am–2pm and 5pm–midnight; Nov–Mar, Mon–Sat 5pm–midnight. Bus: 33.

Shopping

Heidelberg flashes its big sweet tooth at **Heidelberger Zuckerladen** (Sugarland), Plöck 52 (www.zuckerladen.de; ✆ **06221/24365**), a quirkily old-fashioned place where a husband-and-wife team dispenses licorice, Maltesers, and lots of other candy that you probably haven't tasted for a long, long time. The old-fashioned dentist's chair in the window will hopefully deter you from over-indulging. **Chocolaterie St. Anna No. 1,** St. Anna Gasse 1 (www.chocolaterie-st-anna.de; ✆ **06221/4340087**) dispenses handmade chocolates, along with international brands and, in the café, steaming cups of rich hot chocolate. **Scheuring's Tabakladen,** Hauptstrasse 172 (www.scheuringstabakladen; ✆ **06221/23794**) has been selling tobacco, rolling papers (many Germans still roll their own cigarettes), cigars, and international newspapers for 120 years; the politically incorrect figure in the window is a souvenir that a onetime proprietor brought home from the Chicago World's Fair in 1893. At **Anja's Schloss,** next to the entrance to the castle at Neue Schloss Strasse 50 (✆ **06221/659-5092**) you can find distinctive souvenirs, such as a hot pink cuckoo clock (or maybe just a nice print of the castle).

Nightlife

Come nightfall, many students seems to heed the call to "Drink, drink, drink," and there are many places to partake. **Zum Sepp'l,** Hauptstrasse 213 (www.zum-seppl.de; ✆ **06221/23085**) is a famous drinking club, open since 1634. The cramped rooms are nicely filled with photographs and carved initials of former students, along with memorabilia that ranges from old Berlin street signs to Alabama license plates. Meals cost 8€ to 18€. It's open Monday to Friday noon to 11pm, and Saturday and Sunday 11:30am to 3:30pm and 5pm to midnight. Another old tavern, this one from 1703, **Schnookleloch,** Haspelgasse 8 (www.schnookeloch-heidelberg.de; ✆ **06221/138080**) also shows off its provenance with lots of old photos on the paneled walls. It's open all day, and late into the night, with meals and lunch and dinner and piano music on Wednesday through Saturday evenings. Meals cost 8€ to 16€.

    Dorfschänke, Lutherstrasse 14 (www.dorfschnke-hd.com; ✆ **06221/ 419041**), doesn't have the same pedigree as these other old taverns, having only opened in 1908, but it's been packed ever since and accompanies its beer selections with Flammkuchen, a square pizza with onions and cheese—a bit like tarte flambée. It's open daily, 5pm to midnight; meals cost 8€ to 18€. **Vetter's Alt Heidelberger Brauhaus,** Steingasse 9 (www.brauhaus-vetter.de; ✆ **06221/165850**) attracts a crowd of regulars and is known for its friendly service; the real draw is the house ale, with an alcohol content of 33%, said to be the world's strongest beer. Solid meals, from 8€ to 15€, help soak up all that alcohol. At **Destille,** Untere Strasse 16 (www.destilleonline.de; ✆ **06221/22808**), Schnapps is the drink of choice, especially the Warmer Erpel (Warm Duck), served flaming. A thick cloud of smoke fills the space (smoking is allowed under certain circumstances in some Heidelberg bars), as does loud rock. It's open into the wee hours and is usually packed. **Cave 54,** Krämergasse 4 (www.cave54.de; ✆ **06221/27840**) is a legendary jazz club that's hosted the likes of Ella Fitzgerald and Duke Ellington since 1954, when a group of students decided to open it as an alternative to university-sponsored events; the atmospheric room at the bottom of a spiral staircase still hosts regular shows and jam sessions every Tuesday.

River Excursions from Heidelberg

From Heidelberg, you can float up the Neckar River past wooded hillsides and the occasional castle to **Hirschorn** and **Eberbach,** two picturesque riverside towns. Boats are operated by the **Rhein-Neckar-Fahrgastschiffahrt GmbH,** Stadthalle, Heidelberg (www.rnf-schiff fahrt.de; ✆ **06221/20181**). Round trip between Heidelberg and Hirschhorn is 21€, and between Heidelberg and Eberbach, 25€. There are usually four or five round trips daily, and you need not return on the same boat, so you can get off in both towns and wander around a bit before making the return trip.

You can also follow the river on a section of the **Neckar Valley Cycle Path,** which runs from Villingen-Schwenningen north for 375km (233 miles) to the confluence of the Rhine at Mannheim. Along the way, you'll pass castles, manor houses, vineyards, country inns, and old towns; a popular outing from Heidelberg follows the river through vineyards and the Odenwald Forest toward Eberbach, about 35km (21 miles) east. You can rent a bike from **Radhof,** at the Hauptbahnhof, for about 18€ a day (www.fahrrad-heidelberg.de).

EXPLORING HIRSCHHORN ★
26km (16 miles) east of Heidelberg

As Mark Twain wrote in 1878, "Hirschhorn is best seen from a distance, down the river. Then the clustered brown towers perched on the green hilltop, and the old battlemented stone wall stretching up and over the grassy ridge and disappearing in the leafy sea beyond, make a picture whose grace and beauty entirely satisfy the eye." In fact, that's mostly what brings visitors to town—the experience of standing on the deck of a boat and admiring that view of the town and castle, then scrambling up medieval lanes to the castle to admire the view from up high.

The medieval townscape of Hirschhorn, best viewed from a river boat.

Overlooking the town and the river from a fortified promontory, **Hirschhorn Castle ★** is mostly an 18th-century reconstruction, with some 14th-century battlements cascading down the hillside to become part of the town walls. From the 13th through the 16th century the sturdy fortress and its tall tower was the fiefdom of the knights of Hirschhorn, who made a fortune by controlling fishing and rafting on the river. Their coat of arms, shaped like a stag horn, is said to have been inspired both by their namesake deer *(Hirsch),* which still roam the surrounding woods, and by the shape of the river when seen from the castle. The castle is now a hotel but sections are open to visitors daily from 9am to 6pm, closed from mid-December through January; tower entrance is 2€.

Hirschhorn's **tourist office** is at Untere Gasse 1 (✆**06272/1742**), open May to September Tuesday to Friday 8am to noon and 2 to 5pm, Saturday 9am to 1pm; October to April hours are Monday to Friday 8am to noon and 2 to 5pm.

EXPLORING EBERBACH ★
35km (21 miles) east of Heidelberg

The imperial city of Eberbach, established in 1227, commands a point where the Neckar River twists to make a wide bend to the south. Not much remains of **Burg Eberbach,** the early castle and fortifications, except a jumble of ruined walls and arches about 1km (⅔ mile) above the town. A hike up to the ruins, however, is well worth the exertion for endless views over the river and Odenwald forest. Half-timbered and frescoed houses surround the **Alter Markt,** or old market square; the most fabled is **Haus Thalheim,** at Kellereistrasse 36, where it's assumed that Great Britain's Queen Victoria was conceived. In 1818 the house was home to her parents, Prince Edward and the German-born Princess Victoria of Saxe-Coburg-Saalfeld, who were living in Germany to save money after their lavish lifestyle ran them into deep debt. They allegedly rushed back to England just before Victoria's birth, though local lore claims the queen was actually born aboard the family's yacht when it was still moored in the Neckar.

From Burg Eberbach, a 3km (2-mile) forest path leads to **Katzen-buckl,** a stone tower built during the Victorian era of the Grand Tour. At 626m (2,053 ft.), it's the highest point in the Odenwald Forest.

The Eberbach **tourist office** at Leopoldplatz 1 (www.eberbach.de; *©* **06271/87242**) is open May to October Monday to Friday 8am to 5pm, Saturday 10am to noon; November to April, hours are Monday to Thursday 8am to 5pm, Friday 8am to noon.

STUTTGART ★★

126km (78 miles) SE of Heidelberg

At first glance, this city of about 600,000 seems to be all about business. The neon-lit logos of manufacturers light up the sky high above miles of business and industrial parks that are ground zero for German engineering. Wide, motorway-like boulevards cut through the city center, and if you have any doubt about where civic pride might lie, just look up to see the huge Mercedes star twirling atop the tower above the clean-lined, 1920s-era main train station. Stretching north of the station, a vast construction zone will transform this ever-changing city with **Stuttgart 21,** a new underground terminus for high-speed trains, and **Europaviertel,** an emerging quarter for offices, housing, shops, and parkland.

In Stuttgart, even the central train station bears an automotive logo.

Yet, in that German way of never getting too far away from nature, a lot of greenery takes the hard edges off all this industry and business. The forested banks of the Neckar River cut a swath right through town, with what's known as the "Green U" girdling the city center. Add in several much-respected art collections and a lot of high-brow culture (the Stuttgart Ballet is especially renowned) and you've got a city well worth slotting into your itinerary.

Essentials

ARRIVING **Stuttgart Echterdingen Airport** (www.flughafen-stuttgart. de; ✆ 0711/9480) is 14km (9 miles) south of the city near Echterdingen. The airport has connections with most major German and European cities; S-Bahn trains to Stuttgart (27 minutes, €3.40) leave from below the arrivals level of Terminal 1. A taxi to the city center costs about 30€. Stuttgart has **rail** links to all major German cities, with frequent connections. Direct trains connect Stuttgart to Heidelberg (45 min.), Munich (2½ hr.), and Frankfurt (1½ hr.). The train station is directly north of the historic area. For information, visit www.bahn.de or call ✆ 01805/996633. Access by **car** is via the A8 Autobahn east and west, or the A81 north and south.

GETTING AROUND A single ride between points within Stuttgart's historic core on the city's bus or U-Bahn costs 2.20€. Rides to the outlying districts begin at 2.60€. A 1-day *Tageskarte* (day ticket) costs 6.30€. For more information, visit **www.vvs.de** or call ✆ 0711/19449.

VISITOR INFORMATION Stuttgart's main tourist information office, the **i-Punkt,** is across from the main entrance of the train station at the foot of Königstrasse in the city center (www.stuttgart-tourist.de; ✆ 0711/22280). It's open year-round Monday to Friday 9am to 8pm, Saturday 9am to 6pm, and Sunday 10am to 6pm. Another office is at the airport, in Terminal 3, level 2 (✆ 0711/7828–5831) is open Monday to Friday 8am to 7pm, Saturday 9am to 1pm and 1:45 to 4:30pm, and Sunday 9am to 1pm and 1:45 to 5:30pm.

GUIDED TOURS Between April and October, every day at 11am, the tourist office organizes a 90-minute English-language guided **walking tour** through the city's historic core. Beginning on the sidewalk in front of the tourist office (Königstrasse 1A; www.stuttgart-tourist.de; ✆ 0711/22280). It costs 8€; children 4 and under can tag along for free. Stuttgart's double-decker, open-top, hop-on, hop-off **Citytour buses** are a handy way to get around this far-flung city, with stops at the Mercedes-Benz Museum and nine other sights. The commentary (available in English with headphones) is informative, despite a tiresome staged dialogue. A ticket good for 24 hours costs 15€, and allows two kids under 14 to travel with each adult free of charge. Trips begin in front of the i-Punkt Tourist Information Office at Königstrasse 1A; you can buy tickets there, at the airport tourist office, or on the bus. For more information, go to www.stuttgart-citytour.de or call ✆ **0711/222-8100.**

Exploring Stuttgart

At first glance it may seem that in busy Stuttgart "Geld regiert die Welt," or "Money makes the world go 'round!" Nevertheless, it's easy to plunge into the heart of the city to see its gracious, easygoing side. Do so via the **Königstrasse,** the city's pedestrian shopping street that stretches south for almost a mile from the train station. Just to the east is a generous sweep of parkland and squares that, on a nice day, tempt office workers to linger on the lawns and in the surrounding cafes. The expansive **Oberer Schlossgarten** (Upper Palace Garden) and adjoining **Schlossplatz** (Palace Square) are flanked by such landmarks as the Staatstheater (State Theater); the glass Landtag (State Parliament); and two art museums, the **Staatsgalerie** (p. 395) and **Kunstmuseum Stuttgart** (p. 393). Commanding the largest parcel of real estate on two sides of the Schlossplatz is the Versailles-like **Neues Schloss** (New Castle), commissioned in 1746 by Duke Carl Eugen von Württemberg, who demanded that his architects build "a proper residence which is convenable to my royal dignity and the amplitude of my royal household." Ongoing delays and some disastrous fires must have frustrated the heck out of his grace, who by 1762 insisted that at least the Mirror Gallery be completed in time for his birthday celebrations. Today the palace houses government ministries.

The 18th-century Schlossplatz is Stuttga elegant centerpiece.

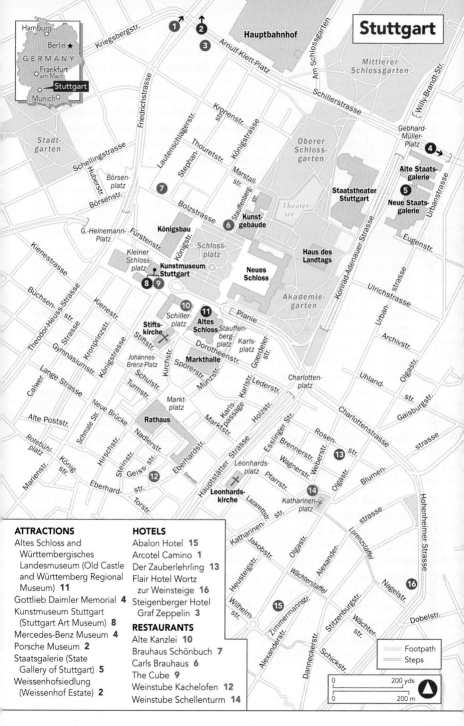

Stuttgart

ATTRACTIONS

Altes Schloss and
  Württembergisches
  Landesmuseum (Old Castle
  and Württemberg Regional
  Museum) **11**
Gottlieb Daimler Memorial **4**
Kunstmuseum Stuttgart
  (Stuttgart Art Museum) **8**
Mercedes-Benz Museum **4**
Porsche Museum **2**
Staatsgalerie (State
  Gallery of Stuttgart) **5**
Weissenhofsiedlung
  (Weissenhof Estate) **2**

HOTELS

Abalon Hotel **15**
Arcotel Camino **1**
Der Zauberlehrling **13**
Flair Hotel Wortz
  zur Weinsteige **16**
Steigenberger Hotel
  Graf Zeppelin **3**

RESTAURANTS

Alte Kanzlei **10**
Brauhaus Schönbuch **7**
Carls Brauhaus **6**
The Cube **9**
Weinstube Kachelofen **12**
Weinstube Schellenturm **14**

Footpath
Steps

0 — 200 yds
0 — 200 m

Adjoining the Schlossplatz is **Schillerplatz,** where a statue honors Germany's beloved 18th-century playwright, philosopher, and poet. Behind him rises the venerable **Altes Schloss** (Old Castle; see below), where a series of fortresses and castles have stood since the 10th century. From there, Kirchstrasse leads south into **Marktplatz,** where vendors still gather, as they have for centuries, to sell flowers and vegetables. The square is now, however, surrounded by the bland 1950s-era Rathaus and other nondescript postwar buildings. You may want to step briefly inside the **Rathaus,** however, to see one peculiar feature: its paternosters, elevators with small open compartments that travel slowly in a continuous loop, letting passengers jump on and off at their desired floors. Safety concerns aside, these contraptions are much beloved, some of the last in operation around Germany.

To the east of the Marktplatz lies one of the city's oldest remaining neighborhoods, a pleasantly bohemian enclave of gabled houses and narrow cobbled streets known as **Bohnenviertel,** or Bean Town—so named because the tanners and dyers who once lived here could afford to eat little else but beans.

Altes Schloss and Württembergisches Landesmuseum (Old Castle and Württemberg Regional Museum) ★

One of Stuttgart's oldest standing structures, this moated castle was built for the dukes of Württemberg in the 13th century. In the 10th century, Luidolf, Duke of Swabia, had created a stud farm here to breed and raise cavalry horses, protecting his holdings with a moat—and giving the city its name, from *stuotengarten* meaning "stud garden." A 16th-century redo in the Renaissance style made the medieval castle into a royal palace, with four wings surrounding a vast courtyard with columned arcades and a staircase so grand that a rider on horseback could ascend it to the Knight's Hall. Royalty decamped for the Neues Schloss (New Castle) in the mid-18th century, but they left behind a spectacular knickknack: two rams that lock horns every hour on the hour on the clockface high above the courtyard. Behind the massive castle doors these days you'll find a treasure trove of all things Swabian (Swabia being the ancient land of which Stuttgart was long the capital). Cases show off the crowns of royalty, ivory figures carved by local cave dwellers some 35,000 years ago, and an 18th-century automaton of a wind-up gold-leafed bird that struts and prances. A playful curiosity from the personal collection of the dukes of Württemberg is the world's oldest known card game, richly decorated and as much a rarity when it was created in 1430 as it is now.

Schillerplatz 6. www.landesmuseum-stuttgart.de. ⓒ **0711/2793498.** Admission 4.50€ adults, 3€ students, children 13 and under free. Tues–Sun 10am–5pm. U-Bahn: Schlossplatz.

Gottlieb Daimler Memorial ★   Gottlieb Daimler converted the garden house behind his villa just outside Stuttgart into a workshop; it was here that the world's first internal-combustion engine began spinning in 1883. (Daimler and his partner, Wilhelm Maybach, worked in such secrecy that a suspicious gardener became convinced his boss was a counterfeiter and summoned the police to the premises.) Daimler was soon fitting his engine onto bikes and into coaches, and eventually moved his workshop to a nearby factory, where his mechanics perfected the automobiles that were eventually manufactured by Mercedes-Benz. Daimler's workshop now houses drawings, photographs, and models of an airship and motorboat that he invented.

Taubenheimstrasse 13, Bad Cannstatt-Stuttgart. ℰ **0711/569399.** Free admission. Tues–Fri 2pm–5pm, Sat–Sun 11am–5pm. U-Bahn: Kursaal.

Kunstmuseum Stuttgart (Stuttgart Art Museum) ★★   A filigreed glass cube surrounding a rough-hewn limestone inner core, designed by Berlin architects Hascher and Jehle, is the dramatic setting for 19th- and 20th-century works by artists from southern Germany. Among many other works, the museum has the world's most important collection of works by Otto Dix (1891–1969), whose paintings often depict the brutality of war. Especially evocative is his *Gross Stadt (Metropolis)*, in which a lonely, crippled veteran looks on from the sidelines as upper-class partygoers dance and cavort, epitomizing the decadence and social inequality so pervasive in Germany in the 1920s. Make it a point to see the exterior of the museum at least twice during your stay in Stuttgart—once by day, when the cube is all shimmering glass, and once at night, when the rough, beautifully illuminated limestone walls of the interior loom out like a large sculpture.

Kleiner Schlossplatz 1. www.kunstmuseum-stuttgart.de. ℰ **0711/2162188.** Admission 6€ adults, 4€ students, children 12 and under free. Tues–Sun 10am–6pm (Fri until 9pm). U-Bahn: Schlossplatz.

Mercedes-Benz Museum ★★   MUSEUM   All curves and glass, this automotive showcase designed by Dutch superstar architects Ben van Berkel and Caroline Bos is as sleek and aerodynamic as the automobiles to which it pays homage. Among the 160 vehicles parked on nine floors are the Daimler Reitwagen, the world's first motorized bicycle, from 1885; a fleet of buses and trucks; Mercedes-built race cars; and, of course, the automaker's sleek icons of luxury car travel. The well-polished beauties are arranged along a ramp down which visitors descend past a timeline that places Mercedes vehicles in the context of world events, from the Wright Brothers' first flight to Albert Einstein's discovery of the theory of relativity. You'll learn that the three-pointed star represents the company's goal to introduce motorization "on land, on water,

Mercedes-built race cars at the sleek Mercedes-Benz Museum.

and in the air," and that the Mercedes was named after the daughter of Emil Jellinek, a wealthy businessman who in the 1890s introduced the European public to the cars that Carl Benz and Gottlieb Damlier manufactured. (Ironically, Mercedes herself never learned to drive.) There's a self-congratulatory ring to all the hype, not surprisingly, but so what? Even if you're not a car buff, you may begin to daydream about slipping into a creamy leather driver's seat and speeding off into the nearby Black Forest.

Mercedesstrasse 100, Stuttgart-Bad Cannstatt. www.museum-mercedes-benz.com. ✆ **0711/1730000.** Admission 8€ (4€ after 4:30pm), 4€ ages 15–17 (2€ after 4:30pm, free for children 14 and under. Tues–Sun 9am–6pm. S-Bahn: 1 (direction Kirchheim) to Neckarpark; then follow signs.

Porsche Museum ★   Bold, dynamic, eye-catching—and that's just the architectural statement that houses these 80 legendary cars, the legacy of Ferdinand Porsche. One of Germany's great automotive pioneers, Porsche set up a factory in Zuffenhausen, an industrial suburb of Stuttgart, in 1931, launching a business that would become world famous for its sporty serial autos and racing cars. (The Volkswagen was also launched here in 1936 and was often called the "Rounded Porsche.") Exhibits are designed to be viewed in 90 minutes, with the cars set off in stark displays at center stage. Vehicles on display include Formula 1 champions and the legendary Porsche 911, the company's two-door flagship. Tours of the factory show how a car comes together, with gigantic robotic claws lowering finished bodies onto drivetrains and chassis. You'll also see how fenders, engines, and dashboards are made and fitted into place to create what many consider to be the world's most beautiful automobiles.

Porscheplatz 1. www.porsche.com/museum. © **0711/91125685.** Admission 8€ (4€ after 5pm), 4€ ages 15–17 (2€ after 5pm), children 14 and under free. Factory tours in English, times vary (check with information desk). Museum Tues–Sun 9am–6pm. S-Bahn: Neuwirtshaus/Porscheplatz.

Staatsgalerie (State Gallery of Stuttgart) ★★ MUSEUM   This renowned collection was amassed in large part by members of the House of Württemberg and opened to the public in 1843. Works span some 550 years; among early masterpieces is Hans Memlings's *Bathsheba at her Bath* (from around 1440), a brilliant piece of portraiture in which the artist captures beads of moisture on his subject's brow and her long hair twisted into a knot. The Old Masters galleries adjoin the New State Gallery, a controversial 1984 addition with an undulating façade designed by British architect James Stirling. Airy spaces surrounding a glass rotunda house a collection of 19th and 20th century works that is one of Europe's great repositories of modern art. Picasso's *Inclined Head of a Woman* and Matisse's *La Coiffeur* are among many early 20th century works, with Mondrian, Gris, Braque, and many other European artists of the time well represented. Curators worked throughout the latter 20th century to reconstitute collections lost to World War II and Nazi purges, with admirable results: Max Beckmann's *Self Portrait with Red Scarf* is one of relatively few early works of the artist to survive, and the museum also has a sizable number of other works by the Bauhaus school and Blue Rider group, once vilified by the Nazis.

Konrad-Adenauer-Strasse 30–32. www.staatsgalerie.de. © **0711/470400.** Admission 8€ adults, 6€ students, free admission Wed. Wed and Fri–Sun 10am–6pm; Tues and Thurs 10am–8pm. U-Bahn: Staatsgalerie.

Weissenhofsiedlung (Weissenhof Estate) ★★ NEIGHBORHOOD Just outside the city center, this appealing modern neighborhood was built on a hillside in the Killesberg quarter for a building exhibition in 1927. The goal was to introduce the public to home design that, in keeping with the austerity of the post-World War I years, would be functional and reduce costs while simplifying housekeeping and improving living conditions. Walking through the well-maintained neighborhood, you see much-coveted houses created by such leading 20th-century architects as Ludwig Mies van der Rohe, Le Corbusier, and Hans Scharoun. The sleek, white row houses show off a straightforward, non-extravagant style that was then being promoted by the Bauhaus school of art and design.

Hit the Heights

The 217m (712-ft.) **Fernsehturm (Television Tower),** capped with a red-and-white transmitter, soars above a forested hillock south of central Stuttgart. It was built in 1956 using radically innovative applications of aluminum and pre-stressed reinforced concrete, and served as a prototype for larger towers in Toronto and Moscow. An elevator ride delivers you to an observation platform (as well as a mediocre and expensive restaurant) and displays that detail the tower's construction. Aside from providing a good view, the top of the Fernsehturm (as someone once said of the Eiffel Tower) is one of the few places in Stuttgart you don't have to look at the damned thing. The entrance is at Jahnstrasse 120, Stuttgart-Degerloch (www.fernsehturm-stuttgart.com; ✆ **0711/232597**). Admission is 7€ adults, 4€ children; the tower is open Monday to Thursday 10am to 11pm, and Friday to Sunday 9am to 11pm. Take the U15 from the Hauptbahnhof to Ruhbank (Fernsehturm).

For a more bucolic view, climb to the top of the 510m (1,670-ft.) **Birkenkopf,** west of the city. Topped off with debris dumped here after World War II, it's the tallest hill in Stuttgart—a reminder that bombing attacks leveled 60% of the city, sparing not a single landmark. After the 20-minute walk to the top, still covered in jagged stone architectural fragments, you'll be rewarded by a panorama of the rebuilt city and the surrounding Swabian Hills, covered with vineyards and woods. The German text of a plaque translates as, "This mountain piled up after World War II from the rubble of the city stands as a memorial to the victims and a warning to the living." Bus 92 from the Hauptbahnhof will drop you at the trailhead.

A climb up 350m (1,155 ft.) high **Karlshöhe,** on the southwest edge of town, comes with a reward: a beer and plate of sausages in the summertime beer garden. The climb begins on Tübingerstrasse and heads uphill via Stäffeles (stepped streets) before continuing through vineyards to the summit. From the Hauptbahnhof, take the U14 to Österreichischer Platz and walk south to Tübingerstrasse.

All the houses were required to have flat roofs; many also incorporate such modern features as roof gardens and combined living and sleeping spaces, sometimes set off by folding screens and equipped with beds that fold down from closets. Visitors were not unanimously swept away by this new approach to domesticity. Many thought the kitchens, corridors, and servants' rooms were cramped, and the large expanses of glass turned out to be unsuitable for Stuttgart winters (and ruinous to frugal household heating budgets). Even so, the estate is a lovely place to wander, with its clean lines and soothing homogeneity. A semi-detached house designed by Swiss-French architect Le Corbusier is now the **Weissenhofmuseum,** combining displays of the history of the estate with living quarters, furnished and decorated as the architect intended. Weissenhofmuseum: Rathenaustrasse 1–3. www.stuttgart.de/weissenhof. ✆ **0711/257-9187.** Tues–Fri 11am–6pm, weekends 10am–6pm, Sunday noon to 5pm. Free admission. Take U-Bahn line 7 to Killesberg-Messe stop and walk northeast around the Messe.

Where to Stay in Stuttgart

Long gone is one of Stuttgart's most beloved lodgings: a bomb shelter beneath the Marktplatz that for a couple of decades after World War II served as a popular hotel, where patrons could forgo natural light and other luxuries in favor of the camaraderie of sitting around in cramped spaces and eating home-cooked meals. Replacing it on the Stuttgart hotel scene are outlets of just about every chain that operates in Europe. Many of these business-oriented hotels offer bargain rates in weekends.

EXPENSIVE

Der Zauberlehrling ★★★   This Bohemian outpost of designer chic in two old houses in the offbeat Bean Quarter is as reliable as any of Stuttgart's business-oriented hotels, just a lot more fun and atmospheric. The 17 rooms and suites at the "Magic Ring" provide such embellishments as a rooftop garden and outdoor tub in the Sunrise suite or a waterbed, claw-foot tub, and nautical bric-a-brac in the Titanic. The Chalet, with white beams, skylights, open fire, and bathtub for two is an especially romantic urban aerie. Rooms vary in size and price, but designer baths, high-tech lighting, and fashionable furnishing in tasteful-yet-edgy colors are standard in all.

Rosenstrasse 38. www.zauberlehrling.de. ✆ **0711/2377770.** 17 units. 140€–280€ double. Buffet breakfast included. Parking 15€. **Amenities:** Restaurant; bar; room service; Wi-Fi (free). U-Bahn: Charlottenplatz.

Flair Hotel Wortz zur Weinsteige ★   This family-run inn in a centuries-old house and nearby annex, the "Little Castle" is the closest thing to old-fashioned Germanic coziness you'll find in Stuttgart. Behind beautifully carved wooden doors festooned with local grape varieties, many rooms have polished headboards, big armoires, and generous, ceramic-tiled bathrooms; others are more adventurous, with free-standing round tubs and jazzy leather headboards. Several units have multiple beds and pullout couches for families. In a cozy restaurant with a terrace, the Scherle family shows off the kind of hospitality that has made their inn a local favorite since the years just after World War II.

Hohenheimer Strasse 28–30. www.zur-weinsteige.de. ✆ **0711/236-7000.** 35 units. 140€–220€ double. Buffet breakfast included. Parking 9.50€. **Amenities:** restaurant; Wi-Fi (free). U-Bahn: Turlenstrasse/Burgerhospital.

MODERATE

Arcotel Camino ★★   All sorts of welcome touches, such as commodious arm chairs, lots of reading lamps, and roomy desks, along with a huge buffet breakfast, make this business hotel on the outskirts of the city center a lot more pleasant than the location on a busy roadway might suggest. (The vast new Europaviertel quarter is under construction across the street, so one day the surroundings might be more welcoming.) This oasis of calm is tucked onto a hillside above the traffic with many rooms overlooking a leafy residential neighborhood. While the only handy convenience nearby is the huge Milano shopping complex across the road, a friendly ground-floor bar and restaurant means you can stay put, while a session in the in-house sauna and steam room can nicely top off a day. Heilbronner Strasse. www.arcotelhotels.com. © **0711/258580.** 168 units. 119€–139€ double. Buffet breakfast included. Parking 18€. **Amenities:** restaurant; bar; exercise room; room service; steam room and sauna; Wi-Fi (free). U-Bahn: Stadtbibliothek.

Steigenberger Hotel Graf Zeppelin ★★ Stuttgart's business-oriented hotels don't get any more luxurious than this quietly dignified postwar mainstay next to the Hauptbahnhof, named for the local count who pioneered dirigible travel in the late 19th century. Acres of deep carpeting, heavy drapes, soundproof windows, and sleek beech-wood furnishings lend a soothing and quiet hush to the commodious, well-equipped accommodations, while the rooftop pool, fitness center, and spa facilities provide an added touch of relaxation. Arnulf-Klett-Platz 7. www.stuttgart.steigenberger.com. © **0711/20480.** 155 units. 125€–2225€ double. Buffet breakfast included. Parking 20€. **Amenities:** 3 restaurants; bar; babysitting; gym; indoor pool; room service; spa; Wi-Fi (free). U-Bahn: Hauptbahnhof.

INEXPENSIVE

Abalon Hotel ★★ Straightforward German efficiency comes to the fore in this hillside lair, where the entrance is at street level and rooms, as well as a handy parking garage, are on floors below. Design is functional, while the light-filled atrium lobby, leafy roof terraces off some rooms, and streamlined built-ins with lots of work and storage space lend flair to the bright and comfortable surroundings. A few units are set up for families and have kitchenettes. A nice buffet breakfast is served in a pleasant glassed-in garden; another unusual perk is two drinks of your choice a day. Though the quiet neighborhood is just outside the city center, Schlossplatz and many other sights are an easy, 15-minute stroll away. Zimmermanstrasse 7–9. www.abalon.de. © **0711/21710.** 40 units. 79€–159€ double. Buffet breakfast included. Parking 9.50€. **Amenities:** Wi-Fi (free). U-Bahn: Turlenstrasse/Burgerhospital.

Where to Eat in Stuttgart

Stuttgarters enjoy their pleasures, and you will want to join them in digging full-heartedly into Swabian cuisine. Topping a list of favorites are *Käsespätzle,* noodles with cheese, the local equivalent of mac n' cheese. *Spätzel* noodles show up alongside almost any main course, including the beloved *Zwiebelrostbraten,* thinly sliced beef steak, pan-fried and

A refined modern version of the traditional Stuttgart dish *Maltaschen*.

topped with fried onions. ***Maultaschen*** is a large ravioli that's usually stuffed with spinach, meat, and onions; it's said that medieval monks invented Maultaschen for fast days when meat was not allowed, since the meat was concealed within the pasta so God could not see it. ***Linsen mit Spätzel,*** lentils with noodles and Frankfurters, is so popular that few restaurants would not dare include it on the menu, sometimes with some fancy variations.

The beverage of choice in Stuttgart is **Trollinger,** a soft red wine with just a hint of pear, made from the most common grape grown in the Württemberg region around the city. (Riesling is another local favorite). An especially atmospheric place to try a glass is century-old **Weinhaus Stetter,** in Bohenviertel at Rosenstrasse 32 (www.weinhaus-stetter.de; ✆ **0711/240163;** Mon–Fri 11am–11pm, Sat noon–3pm and 5:30– 11pm), where you can soak up the alcohol with solid Swabian cooking and take a bottle or two home from the adjacent shop.

On the sweet side, sink your teeth into a ***Stuagerder Rossbolla*** at least once while you're in Stuttgart—a round chocolate praline filled with vanilla cream that looks suspiciously like something a horse might leave behind on the street. As the story goes, two market women got into an argument, and one picked up a pile of horse manure and flung it at the other. Some of the dung became lodged in the teeth of the victim, who declared she'd leave there until the police arrived. The spectacle inspired a local confectionery chef to duplicate the image, with tastier results.

EXPENSIVE

The Cube ★★ GERMAN/CONTINENTAL   The top floor of the stunning Kunstmuseum (p. 393) is a glassed-in aerie where, even before a glass of wine, diners on the chocolate-colored banquettes set on stone floors can be excused for feeling they're floating over the city rooftops. The menu is light and airy, too, with fish and salad choices inspired by the Pacific Rim, several fish and beef *tartare* preparations, and Mediterranean-inspired pastas. This being the heart of Swabia, you can also count on the kitchen for a good *Zwiebelrostbraten* (fried steak with onions) or its meat-heavy kin. These stylish surroundings are especially appealing as a break from the art circuit at lunch, when prices dip to an excellent value and the daytime views are transporting. Reservations are a good idea at any time.

Kleiner Schlossplatz 1. www.cube-restaurant.de. ✆ **0711/280-4439.** Main courses 12€–20€. Daily 11:30am–midnight. U-Bahn: Schlossplatz.

MODERATE

Alte Kanzlei ★★ SWABIAN   A 16th-century house on a corner of Stuttgart's most atmospheric square, the cobbled Schillerplatz, once served as a pantry and storeroom for the adjacent Alte Schloss (Old Castle). Later in the 16th century it became a sort of record office, the Alte Kanzlei (Old Chancery), for the kingdom of Württemberg. Today the bright, atmospheric, high-ceilinged rooms are open all day, with a casual cafe and an adjacent warm-weather terrace that serves breakfast, coffee, and light meals. The pleasant dining room is a bit more formal but no less relaxed. The blond-wood furnishings on bare oak floors are soothingly contemporary, but the lunch and dinner menus are traditionally Swabian. Meals often begin with *Fladelsuppe,* literally, pancake soup, beef broth flavored with strips of salted, crepe-like pastry, move through staples like *Linsen und Saiten* (lentils and sausage), and end with some variation of Strudel.

Schillerplatz 5A. www.alte-kanzlei-stuttgart.de. ✆ **0711/294457.** Main courses 10€–20€. Daily 10am–midnight (Fri and Sat until 1am). U-Bahn: Schlossplatz.

Weinstube Schellenturn ★★ SWABIAN   In the days when this old tower in the city walls was a prison, prisoners wore *schellen* (bells) sewn into their clothing so wardens could hear them if they decided to make a run for it. These days no one's eager to hurry away from these rustic, round, low-ceilinged rooms, their floors sagging a bit with centuries of use (you might still get a whiff of grape must, as the tower was used to store wine in the 19th century). Beams and rough stone walls create an atmospheric setting for a changing menu that, depending on the season, might offer herb-crusted lamb, sautéed trout, roast duck, and such Swabian favorites as *Schweinefilet mit Käsespätzle* (pork chops with noodles and cheese). This might be not be light-as-a-feather fare, but the freshness of the market produce shines through, right down to the rich desserts with seasonal fruits.

Stauffenbergerstrasse 1. www.carls-brauhaus.de. © **0711/259-74611.** Main courses 10€–15€. Sun–Thurs 10am–midnight, Fri–Sun 10am–1am. U-Bahn: Schlossplatz.

INEXPENSIVE

Brauhaus Schönbuch ★ SWABIAN This modern take on an old-fashioned *bierstub* looks like a Scandinavian design statement, with bright light, long blonde-wood communal tables, and simple benches and chairs. The food that the busy kitchen serves, however, is unmistakably old world, with big cutlets of *Schweinschnitzel* (the pork version of *Wienerschnitzel*) that hang over the edge of the platters, and *Swiebelrostbraten,* fried T-bone steak, served with mountains of fried onions and *spätzel* on the side. The beverage of choice is beer, with a huge selection served on tap or in bottles. You'll probably share your table with some good-natured regulars, who in nice weather clamor for a place on the large terrace.

Bolzstrasse 10. www.brauhaus-schoenbuch.de. © **0711/722-30930.** Main courses 8€–15€. Mon–Sat 11am–1am, Sun 11am–midnight. U-Bahn: Börsenplatz.

Carls Brauhaus ★ SWABIAN This Stuttgart institution, run by the venerable local Dinkelacker brewery, serves dozens of kinds of beers in sprawling rooms that could only be described as "rustic modern," with lots of black glazed tiles and wide plank floors. Stylish as the scene is, it's worth forgoing the designer-chic ambiance for a seat on the Schlossplatz out front, one of the choicest spots in town on a warm day. The German fare, of the reliable würst and schnitzel variety, is solid but humbly upstaged by the voluminous beer list and the friendly vibes of this popular gathering spot.

Stauffenbergerstrasse 1. www.carls-brauhaus.de. © **0711/259-74611.** Main courses 8€–15€. Sun–Thurs 10am–midnight, Fri–Sun 10am–1am. U-Bahn: Schlossplatz.

Weinstube Kachelofen ★★★ SWABIAN Lots of wood paneling and the namesake Kachelofen (tile stove) set a cozy mood that never lets up. Service is friendly (the Greek-German proprietors treat every diner as a personal guest). The tasty traditional fare is as good as local cooking gets, with daily specials that usually include *Maultaschen,* served with minced pork and various other fillings, *Rostbraten mit Spätzel* (roast beef with noodles), and *Schweinebacke* (pig cheeks in a Trollinger wine sauce). A wine list filled with local choices rounds off a meal.

Stauffenbergerstrasse 1. www.carls-brauhaus.de. © **0711/259-74611.** Main courses 8€–15€. Sun–Thurs 10am–midnight, Fri–Sun 10am–1am. U-Bahn: Schlossplatz.

Shopping

The mile-long **Königstrasse** claims to be Germany's longest pedestrian shopping strip, lined with hundreds of retail shops. Treasure hunters may want to try the weekly Saturday morning **flea market** on the Karlsplatz between the Neue Schloss (New Castle) and Altes Schloss (Old Castle), where tables are piled with clothing, books, furniture, household items, art, and just about everything else. **Breuninger,** Marktstrasse 1–3 (www.breuninger.de; ✆ **0711/2110**), one of Germany's largest and glitziest department stores, is known for high-design housewares, furnishings, and fashion (it was also the first department store in German to install elevators and to offer a store credit card).

Markthalle Stuttgart (Dorotheestrasse 4; www.stuttgart-tourist. de/en/a-market-hall; ✆ **0711/480-410**) is the city's great epicurean treasure trove, an Art Nouveau market hall where 45 halls are stocked with local produce, cheese, and meats, as well as food and spices from around the world. It's open Monday to Friday, 7am to 6:30pm, and Saturday, 7am to 5pm. It also has three restaurants, the most atmospheric being **Marktstuble** (✆ **0711/245531**), where Swabian favorites made with ingredients from the market are served beneath drawings and photos of old Stuttgart.

Soaking in Stuttgart

While Bad Cannstatt is these days best known for the headquarters of Mercedes-Benz and Porsche (with their attached museums), the "Bad" part of the name should not be forgotten. Underlying the district and other parts of Stuttgart is one of Europe's largest flows of mineral waters, and the city has more thermal baths than any European city except Budapest. Thermal bathing establishments channel the warm waters into huge indoor and outdoor pools, surrounded by whirlpools, waterfalls, massage jets, and all sorts of other hydro-features. They also have saunas and steam rooms where regulars gather to chat, snooze, and relax. First time visitors should be aware that the German practice of Freikörperkultur (FKK) is the norm. That is, while swimming suits are worn in the pools (though some baths offer suit-optional swimming some evenings), saunas and steam rooms are usually "textile free"—you'll be sweating it out next to nude members of both sexes. Two popular bathing establishments, both easy to reach from the city center on the U-Bahn 2 line, are **Das Leuze Mineral Spa,** Am Leuzebad 2 (✆ **0711/2169-9700,** open Monday and Tuesday 8am to 9pm, Wednesday to Friday 8am to 11pm, Saturday 7am to 11pm, and Sunday 7am to 9pm), and **MineralBad Cannstatt,** Sulzerrainstraße 2, (✆ **0711/2166-6270**), open daily 9am to 9:30pm. At both, you'll pay about 8€ to swim and soak and an extra 6€ to use the saunas and steam rooms.

The MineralBad Cannstadt spa, built over the thermal waters of Stuttgart suburb Bad Cannstadt.

The Performing Arts

The **Staatstheater** (State Theater), Oberer Schlossgarten (www.staats theater-stuttgart.de; ✆ **0711/202090**), is home to the highly regarded **Stuttgart Ballet** and the **Staatsoper** (State Opera). Classical and other concerts are given in the **Liederhalle,** Schloss-Strasse (www.liederhalle-stuttgart.de; ✆ **0711/2167110**), home to the Stuttgarter Philharmoni-ker and the Radio Symphony Orchestra. The magazine *Lift,* available at newsstands, lists all the happenings around Stuttgart; it's also available online at www.lift-online.de.

TÜBINGEN ★★

47km (29 miles) S of Stuttgart

It's easy to see the appeal of this centuries-old university town, with its cream-colored towers, red roofs, and half-timbered houses, all topped by a turreted castle. There's more here, though, than just unspoiled medieval ambiance. As you climb the steep cobbled lanes you'll be walking in the footsteps of such luminaries as Aloysius Alzheimer, the psychiatrist who identified the condition that now bears his name; the humanitarian

Tübingen's medieval streets reveal a rich history.

physician Albert Schweitzer; the philosopher Georg Wilhelm Friedrich Hegel; and former Pope Benedict XVI. A young Hermann Hesse went home from his job at a bookstore in Tübingen's Lower Town to wallow in self-doubt while immersing himself in Eastern philosophy and Greek mythology. For all its medieval beauty, Tübingen is young at heart, steeped in university life and youthful energy. Centuries-old lecture halls line the streets, and students crowd the Marktplatz and other squares. Given the university's world-renowned medical, science, and theology faculties, consider this: You'll probably also be walking among some of the most influential movers and shakers of the future.

Essentials

ARRIVING   The Stuttgart–Tübingen train line offers service about every half hour. Tübingen also has good rail ties to other major cities in Germany, including Frankfurt (2½ hr.), Berlin (6½ hr.), and Hamburg (8½ hr.). The station is across the Neckar River, a 5-minute walk from the Altstadt. For information, go to www.bahn.de or call ✆ **01805/996633.** Access by car is via Rte. 27 south from the east-west A8 Autobahn, or via Rte. 28 east from the north-south A81 Autobahn.

VISITOR INFORMATION   The Tübingen tourist office (www.tuebingen-info.de; ✆ **07071/91360**) is near the river, between the train station and the Eberhardsbrücke, the bridge into the Altstadt.

A WALKING TOUR OF TÜBINGEN

START: **The Eberhardsbrücke bridge.**

FINISH: **Holtzmarkt**

TIME: **2 to 4 hours, depending on the length of visits to the museums.**

The enticing medieval and Renaissance warren of the Altstadt beckons you to cross the **Eberhardsbrücke** (the main bridge across the Neckar).

1 Neckar Island

Narrow man-made **Neckar Island** floats midstream at the foot of the Altstadt, reached from steps off the Eberhardsbrücke. The island provides a picturesque overview of the rooftops and towers that tumble down the hillside from the Hohentübingen (High-Tübingen Castle) at the top. Making the scene all the more idyllic is the island's **Platanenallee,** a promenade shaded with plane trees planted in 1828.

From the north end of the bridge, follow Neckargasse to Bursagasse and turn left to find:

2 Hölderlinturm

Note how the upper and lower town walls line the riverbank, with a narrow walkway between them. Rising next to the lower wall is the yellow Hölderlinturm, originally a watchtower, later home to the Romantic poet Frederich Hölderlin (1770–1843). Though Hölderlin is little read outside Germany these days, he had a profound effect on early 19th-century literature. His youthful promise was cut short when he went into a mental decline, in part brought on by an ill-fated affair with the wife of one of his employers. His treatment at Tübingen proved ineffective, and for the next 36 years until his death he lived in a modest room in this tower, then the home of carpenter Ernst Zimmer and his family. The house, with a few effects of the poet and his host family, is open Tuesday to Friday 10am to noon and 3 to 5pm, Saturday and Sunday 2 to 5pm. Admission is 2.50€ adults, 1.50€ students and children.

Continue on Bursagasse to Bursagasse 1 and:

3 The Burse

One of the city's most imposing half-timbered buildings, the Burse dates from around the time of the university's founding in 1477. Its dormitories then housed students as young as 12. By the early 19th century, the building had become a renowned teaching hospital; the university's clinics, many of which now top hillsides east of the city, are still some of the leading medical facilities in Europe.

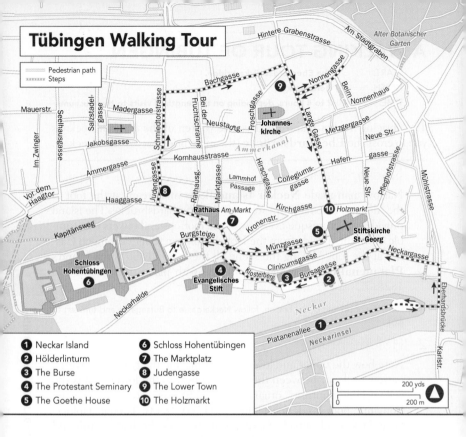

Tübingen Walking Tour

Pedestrian path
Steps

Hintere Grabenstrasse
Am Stadtgraben
Alter Botanischer Garten

Bachgasse
Nonnengasse
Beim Nonnenhaus

Mauerstr.
Seelhausgasse
Salzstadel-gasse
Madergasse
Schmiedtorstrasse
Bei der Fruchtschranne
Froschgasse

9

Neustadtg.
Johannes-kirche
Lange Gasse
Metzgergasse
Neue Str.

Im Zwinger
Jakobsgasse
Kornhausstrasse
Ammerkanal
Hirschgasse
Hafen-gasse
gasse
Pfleghofstrasse
Mühlstrasse

Ammergasse
Lammhof Passage
Collegiums-gasse
Neue Str.

Vor dem Haagtor
Haaggasse
Rathausg.
Marktgasse
8

Rathaus Am Markt
Kirchgasse
10 Holzmarkt

7
Kronenstr.

Kapitänsweg
Burgsteige
5
Stiftskirche St. Georg
Neckargasse

Münzgasse
Clinicumsgasse
Bursagasse
Ebenhardsbrücke

Schloss Hohentübingen
6
Klosterberg
3
2

4
Evangelisches Stift

Neckarhalde
Neckar

Platanenallee **1**
Neckarinsel
Karlstr.

1 Neckar Island
2 Hölderlinturm
3 The Burse
4 The Protestant Seminary
5 The Goethe House
6 Schloss Hohentübingen
7 The Marktplatz
8 Judengasse
9 The Lower Town
10 The Holzmarkt

0   200 yds
0   200 m

Continue on Bursagasse, which becomes Klosterberg, to Klosterberg 2 and:

4   The Protestant Seminary

When the Protestant Reformation swept through Germany in 1534, this monastery was converted to a seminary to train theologians in the new religion. Room, board, and tuition was free and awarded to boys who showed the most promise as future ministers. Despite the investment, many of the young scholars never became men of the cloth. Among its later students was Georg Wilhelm Friedrich Hegel (1770–1831), who became one of the great philosophers of the Age of Enlightenment. The Seminary is now a dormitory and classroom for students of Protestant theology, many of whom, since the late 1960s, are female.

Klosterberg runs into Neckarhalde, near its intersection with Münzgasse. Turn right to find:

5   The Goethe House

At Münzgasse 15, Wolfgang von Goethe spent 14 days of 1780 in the house of publisher Johann Friedrich Cotta. Supposedly the man of letters passed most of his time in Tübingen drinking, a fact that prompted some students in recent years to post a sign near the house, "Goethe puked here." This parody of a German tendency to chronicle every action of its great figures is typical of a youthful irreverence that makesTübingen, lovely and steeped in history as it is, more than just another pretty place.

Backtrack up Münzgasse. A slight jog right takes you to Bergsteige, which leads to:

6 Schloss Hohentübingen

Passing through the **Lower Castle Gate,** an imposing structure from 1608 that resembles a Roman triumphal arch, a steep road leads to Schloss Hohentübingen, or High-Tübingen Castle (www.tuebingen.de, ✆ **07071/297-7384**). You can take your mind off the climb by pausing to soak in views over the Neckar Valley, to the limestone mountains known as the Swabian Alb (or Alps). Begun in the 11th century, this fortress was rebuilt in the 17th century with four palatial wings surrounding a courtyard; they're still protected by ancient dry moats and punctuated with round lookout towers. A colony of bats inhabits the castle cellars and at night the winged creatures most poetically flit around the towers and turrets. The vast chambers now house classrooms and laboratories, along with a set of museums. The town's great prehistoric treasure trove is in the **Archeological Collection:** ivory figurines of horses, water birds, and half-lion, half-man creatures that were discovered in a nearby cave in 1931 and are some of the world's earliest known works of art. Other castle museum collections include the laboratory of biologist Friedrich Miescher, whose research in the 1860s led to the identification of DNA, and plaster casts of the Laocoön and other famous classical works. The castle museums are open Wednesday to Sunday 10am to 5pm (until 7pm on Thursdays). Admission to the collections is 3€.

Go back down Bergsteige and bear left to find:

7 The Marktplatz

Still the scene of a fruit and vegetable market on Monday, Wednesday, and Friday, Tübingen's Marktplatz lies at the heart of the Altstadt. Overlooking the cobbles is the **Rathaus,** built in 1435 with practical and high-minded functions: It was part warehouse as well as the seat of the court of justice. Colorful frescoes on the façade portray some of the town's notable citizens, among them Count Eberhard the Bearded, founder of the university in 1477. Among present-day officials who frequent the Rathaus is popular mayor Boris Palmer, a prominent member of the Green Party who as a boy worked in the market stalls that spread out beneath his windows.

Just west of the Rathaus, follow Haaggasse to:

8 Judengasse

Pretty as this little street is, the cobblestones bear witness to a long history of persecution. Jews settled in the neighborhood as early as the 13th century, and mikvehs, or ritual baths, have been found in the foundations of many of the houses. The community was persecuted during the plague years of 1348–49 and evicted in the 15th century but was thriving again by the 19th century. Under the Nazis, many Tübingen Jews were forced to emigrate after their businesses and synagogues were destroyed on Kristallnacht (Crystal Night, a reference to shattered glass) in 1938 and many others were deported to death camps in 1942 and 1943.

At its north end, Judengasse leads to:

9 The Lower Town

The Ammercanal runs through the Lower Town, once a quarter of tanners, dyers, and artisans. The strong currents of the canal not only carried away offal and other waste products of the tanning process but also powered mills. These days, flower-bedecked paths lined with shops and cafes follow the fast-moving waters, crossed by the Krumme Brücke and other picturesque spans. You can still see some remnants of the quarter's workaday past, such as the huge, half-timbered **Duke's Barn** on Bachgasse, where the cavernous ground floor once housed wine presses; the house at Lange Gasse 15 was once an abattoir, or slaughterhouse, which dumped its carcasses in the adjacent canal. The **Nonnenhaus,** or House of the Nuns, on Nonnengasse, was a convent until the Protestant Reformation, then in the 16th century became the home of medicine and botany professor Leonard Fuchs. (The fuchsia, a flower Fuchs never actually saw, was named in his honor.) Fuchs' house had a terribly modern convenience for the time: a gallery leads from the upper story to a latrine that emptied directly into the canal below.

Walk south on Lange Gasse to Kirchgasse to find:

10 The Holzmarkt

Tubingen's longtime Holzmarkt (Lumber Market) is still a busy gathering spot. The steps of the adjacent **Stiftskirche** (Collegiate Church) provide a convenient perch to sit, while the church's stone window frames, beautifully carved with figures of St. George and other saints, are an elegant backdrop to the comings and goings. A plaque on the square honors Hermann Hesse (1877–1962), the novelist and Nobel Prize recipient who came to Tübingen in 1895 to work as an apprentice at a book shop.

Outlying Sights

Bebenhausen Monastery ★ RELIGIOUS SITE   A beautifully preserved abbey, set amid rolling hills in a nature reserve just outside Tübingen, richly evokes monastic life in the Middle Ages. The romantically
rambling assemblage of chapels, cloisters, half-timbered halls and barns,
and quaint farmyards was founded in 1183 and soon, under the Cistercian monks, became one of the wealthiest monasteries in Germany. In
the summer at least, it's easy to imagine the appeal of a life spent in
prayer and contemplation amid the gentle countryside and such Gothic
interiors as the elegant refectory bathed in warm sunlight. Wintertime
visits more realistically convey the harshness of life in the vast unheated
spaces, where hours were spent in prayer on frigid stone chapel floors,
dormitories were unheated and subarctic, and the "warm room," where
monks were allowed to read and pray near a fire for one hour a day, provided the only respite. The monastery was dissolved in 1684; in the early
19th century, the setting drew the attention of the kings of Wittenberg,
who created a royal hunting lodge. Some of their Gothic and even Art
Nouveau interiors remain and include a luxurious bathroom and kitchen
from around 1915.

Schlossraum 22a, Bruchsal. www.schlosser-und-gaerten.de. © **07251/742-770.**
Admission 4.50€ monastery, 6€ palace, combined 8€. Monastery: Apr–Oct Mon
9am–noon and 1–6pm, Tues–Sun 9am–6pm; Nov–Mar Tues–Sun 10am–noon and
1–5pm. Palace (by guided tour only, in German): Apr–Oct Tues–Fri 11am–6pm, Sat–
Sun 10am–5pm; Nov–Mar Tues–Fri 2pm–4pm, Sat–Sun 11am–5pm. Palace kitchen:
Apr–Oct weekends 11am–5pm. From Tübingen, take bus 826 or 828.

Hohenzollern Castle ★★ CASTLE   While it seems it might be
impossible to match the vision of King Ludwig II of Bavaria, who created
the almost ridiculously romantic Neuschwanstein Castle (see p. 294),
Friedrich William IV of Prussia (1795–1861) came close. While hiking
through the Swabian Alps in 1819, his highness climbed up the ruins of
one of his family's ancestral seats. It was, he wrote, "like a pleasant dream
. . . especially the sunset we watched from one of the Castle bastions."
As king of Prussia, 30 years later he decided to restore the ruin. Friedrich
was a bit more sane than mad Ludwig, but he had a similar passion for
the romanticism of the Middle Ages, as well as the means to create his
own neo-Gothic fantasies. Among his other projects, Friedrich helped
finance the completion of the German Gothic masterpiece **Cologne
cathedral** (see p. 531). Hohenzollern seems to float mid-air on the
heights of a Swabian peak, with enough towers, turrets, gables, and cren-
ellations to satisfy anyone dreaming of knights and damsels. Though
Friedrich never inhabited his mountaintop fiefdom, the castle is still in
the hands of the hereditary princes and princesses of Prussia, who use
the vast halls to display the royal crown and a glittering array of other gold

Hohenzollern Castle, Friedrich of Prussia's 19th-century fantasy of a hilltop Gothic castle.

and silver, along with a painting collection. The views across the surrounding peaks and rolling green valleys below are the showstopper, though. By car take A81 toward Stuttgart, exit Empfingen onto B27 toward the castle; it's a 20-minute walk from the car park, or you can take a shuttle bus. By train from Tübingen, go to Hechingen, then take a taxi to the castle.

Burg Hohenzollern, 20km from Tübingen. www.burg-hohenzollern.com. ☎ **07471/ 2428.** Admission: grounds 7€ adults, 5€ children 6–17; grounds and interior (by guided tour only, in German), 12€ adults, 6€ children 6–17. Mid-Mar to Oct daily 10am–5:30pm, Nov to mid-Mar daily 10am–4:30pm.

Where to Stay in Tübingen

Hospitz Hotel ★   The surrounding streets, climbing up toward the castle gate, are a lot more charm-laden than these almost hostel-like, barebones accommodations in a couple of attached, pink-hued houses that have been rebuilt from their foundations up. Every once in a while a rough old beam or dormer stands out to add a touch of historic color, but for the most part, the clean, modern décor of the decent-sized, well-equipped rooms is more geared to efficient comfort than style or romantic ambiance. The few perks include valet parking, though spaces are limited.

Neckarhalde 2. www.hotel-hospiz.de. ☎ **07071/9240.** 50 units. 110€–115€ double. Buffet breakfast included. Parking 7€. **Amenities:** Wi-Fi (free).

Hotel am Schloss ★★   The most atmospheric place to stay in town is this steep-gabled yellow house next to the Lower Castle Gate, greeting guests, temperatures permitting, with a cascade of bright flowers tumbling out of the window boxes. Some rooms are in two nearby, similarly charming houses of the same antique vintage (none have elevators). While you'll enjoy picturesque facades and Old Town views from the windows, the rooms themselves are a bit more functional. In some you'll find the occasional armoire, draped bed, or handsome replica of an illuminated manuscript, but the overall décor leans towards a clean-lined, blonde-wood, white-fabric aesthetic. The

Hotel Am Schloss is the most atmospheric place to stay in Tübingen.

in-house Mauganeschetle restaurant, which takes up most the ground floor of the main building, serves solid Swabian fare; in summer, its aerie-like terrace supplies memorable dining experiences.

Burgsteige 18. www.hotelamschloss.de. ✆ **07071/92940.** 35 units. 110€–135€ double. Buffet breakfast included. Parking 7€. **Amenities:** Restaurant; bar; Wi-Fi (free).

Krone Hotel ★★   In 1885, the Schlagenhauff family opened their inn in an 18th-century house near the river. Since then, several generations have added floors and wings, making the most of a choice spot between the Hauptbanhof and the Old Town. The rooms are pleasant and refined, with a soothing mix of traditional and contemporary style, accented with colorful art and the occasional antique. A couple of handsome ground-floor lounges are grouped around a fireplace, while a spa and fitness room are tucked away on the top floor. Ludwig's cafe, in a glass atrium, and the hushed, paneled Uhlandstube, are popular with shoppers and business folks.

Uhlandstrasse 1. www.krone-tuebingen.de. ✆ **07071/13310.** 65 units. 139€–159€ double. Buffet breakfast included. Free parking. Closed Dec 23–31. **Amenities:** 2 restaurants; bar; room service; gym; spa; Wi-Fi (free).

Where to Eat in Tübingen

Simply follow the student hordes to the cheapest places in town to eat and drink. Favorites are **Weinhaus Beck,** next to the Rathaus at Am Markt 1 (www.weinhaus-beck.de; ✆ **07071/22772**) with local wines by the glass (you can bring your own food from the stalls in the adjacent market), and **Neckarmüller,** Gartenstrasse 4 (neckarmueller. de; © **07071/27848**), with its huge beer garden overlooking the river.

Wirtshaus Lichtenstein ★ INTERNATIONAL/SWABIAN This atmospheric old place near the Marktplatz is a favorite with homesick American students studying at the university, who come to dig into big, juicy hamburgers and pastrami sandwiches. Even so, the creaky wooden floors and homey seating alcoves are best suited to the classic Swabian grub, like *Käsespätzle,* noodles with cheese, and *Maultaschen,* the local meal-in-itself ravioli stuffed with meat and onions.

Wienergässle 2. www.wirtshaus-lichtenstein.de © **07071/639-4523.** Main courses 7€–12€. Mon–Sat noon–3pm and 6–11pm.

Wurstküche ★★ GERMAN/SWABIAN The "sausage kitchen" makes no pretense to fine dining, but this handsome old white house on the site of an old city gate between the upper and lower towns is a classic Tübingen stop for big platters of hearty Swabian fare. One memorable house specialty that carnivores should not pass up is the *Hausgemachte Fleischkuchle,* or deep fried dumplings filled with meat. That, *Rinderbraten* (beef roast), and other dishes are served on red-clothed tables in a cozy paneled room or on a shady terrace out front in good weather.

Am Lustnauer Tor 8. www.wurstkueche.com. © **07071/92750.** Main courses 13€–20€; fixed-price 3-course lunch 19€. Mon–Sat 11:30am–11pm.

THE BLACK FOREST & BODENSEE

10

S ituated in the extreme southwest of Germany, this is the epitome of "picture-book Germany": a tapestry of deep forest and open farmland, picturesque villages and isolated farms, where nature and culture coexist in harmony. Although the cultural hubs of Baden-Baden and Freiburg are always bustling, the region's romantic appeal reveals itself in quieter locations. Nature lovers flock to the hills to explore miles and miles of hiking trails, wellness devotees love the lavish spa hotels, and foodies appreciate the above-average concentration of Michelin-starred restaurants—enough to dub this region "the secret epicurean capital of Germany."

ESSENTIALS
Arriving

BY AIR   International airports serve the Black Forest area from **Stuttgart** (see p. 388) and the Euro-Airport at **Basel/Mulhouse** in Switzerland, 70km (43 miles) south of Freiburg. **Freiburger Reisedienst** (www.freiburger-reisedienst.de; ✆ **0761/500500**), offers hourly service between Freiburg and EuroAirport Basel-Mulhouse; tickets (19€ adults, 10€ for children under 13) are available from the driver, in cash only. For Lake Constance, the most convenient international airport is **Zurich** airport in Switzerland, 70km (43 miles) southwest of Konstanz; the closest regional airport is **Friedrichshafen** on the northern shore of the lake.

BY TRAIN   Trains run north and south through the Rhine Valley, with fast, frequent service to Freiburg and Baden-Baden. Konstanz is on the main Konstanz-Singen-Villingen-Offenburg rail line, with frequent connections to the major cities of Germany and Switzerland. For information see **www.bahn.de** or call ✆ **01805/996633.**

BY BUS   Long-distance bus services connect the area with many other German and European cities. **Flixbus** (www.flixbus.de; ✆ **030/ 300137300**) and **Meinfernbus** (meinfernbus.de; ✆ 030/300137300) connect with destinations all over Germany as well as some international destinations. Check **www.busliniensuche.de** for all options.

BY CAR   Motorists should take the **A5** Autobahn, which runs through the Rhine Valley, or the **A81,** which runs the length of the Schwarzwald

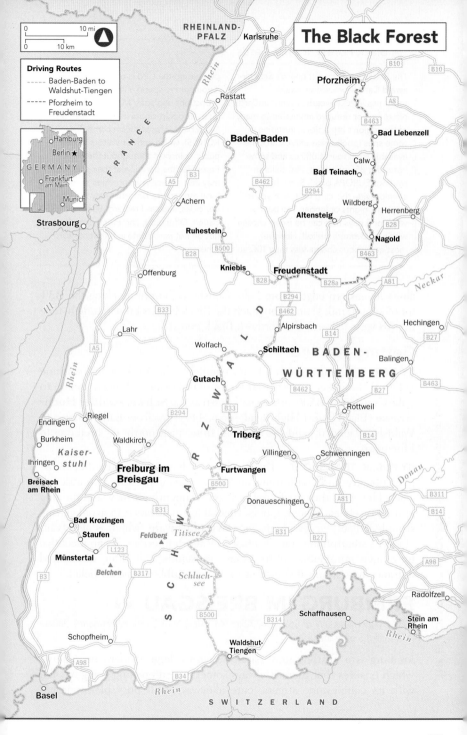

Black Forest Tourist Cards

The Black Forest tourist board's **Schwarzwald Card** (www.schwarzwald-tourismus.info/service/SchwarzwaldCard) offers free or reduced admission to many of the region's attractions, including some spas (pools areas only). Cards are available from tourist offices and some hotels for 35€ per adult, 25€ children (without EUROPA park). Some hotels even provide this card for free if you're staying 2 nights or longer. The pass is valid for 3 days that can be freely chosen within a 12-month period. However, most attractions charge less than 10€, so purchasing the card is only really worth it if you plan to spend a lot of time visiting attractions and spas. Many rural communities also participate in the **Konus Card** (www.blackforest-tourism.com/info/KONUS), which entitles visitors to free public transport throughout the Black Forest for the duration of their stay. It may also reduce entrance fees at some local attractions. Unfortunately the bigger cities, such as Freiburg, Baden-Baden, Offenburg, and Pforzheim, do not do not participate in the Konus card scheme.

along its eastern edge. From Lake Constance, continue along the **B31** for 65km (40 miles) until you reach the Black Forest. From Munich, take the **A8** west to reach the northern Black Forest.

Getting Around

BY CAR The north-south B3 runs parallel to the A5 through the Rhine Valley. B31 runs east-west from Freiburg to Donaueschingen and on to Lake Constance. B500, otherwise known as the **Schwarzwalder Hochstrasse** (Black Forest High Road; see p. 449) runs from Baden-Baden to Waldshut-Tiengen, and B294 runs from just north of Freiburg to Pforzheim.

BY PUBLIC TRANSPORT The Black Forest has a very good public transport infrastructure, with trains and buses serving even remote little villages. However, they might not run very frequently, or may stop running at a relatively early hour. Check timetables in advance to avoid getting stranded. The journey planner at **www.efa-bw.de**, which is also available as a smartphone app, also has an English interface. As an incentive to reduce automobile traffic some museums will offer discounted entrance fees simply if you show them your public transport ticket.

FREIBURG IM BREISGAU ★★

208km (129 miles) SW of Stuttgart, 70km (44 miles) N of Basel (Switzerland), 280km (174 miles) S of Frankfurt

Freiburg is a bustling university city with a large student population, which ensures that there is always something interesting going on. Yet, with its cobblestone streets, cute alleyways, and busy plazas, it has

A university town, Freiburg has a diverse cultural scene.

preserved the charms of a small town. The old city center is car-free (but watch out for trams and bicycles), which makes it a relaxing place to stroll, and street performers add an element of entertainment at just about every corner. Numerous street cafes offer the best vantage points to people-watch. Best of all, Freiburg makes an ideal jumping-off point for exploring the mountains of the Black Forest, as well as the rolling vineyards and orchards of Kaiserstuhl and Markgräflerland.

Essentials

VISITOR INFORMATION

The **tourist information** office is located at Rathausplatz 2–4 (www. freiburg.de; © **0761/3881880**). From June to September it's open Monday to Friday 8am to 8pm, Saturday 9:30am to 5pm, and Sunday 10am to 3.30pm. The rest of the year, it closes earlier—weekdays at 6pm, Saturday at 2:30pm, and Sunday at noon.

GETTING AROUND

Freiburg is well served by **buses and trams,** the latter running in the inner city, operated by **Südbaden Bus GmbH** (www.suedbadenbus.de; © **0761/3680388**). A one-way fare costs 2.20€; a 24-hour day pass is

5.60€. A 3-day welcome pass, available for 25€, includes a round-trip cable car ride to Schauinsland, the local mountain (see p. 421). For schedules and information, or to buy passes, go to VAG Plus-Punkt, Salzstrasse 3 (© **0761/4511500;** www.vag-freiburg.de), in the Altstadt, or to the Radstation, the round modern building by the train station.

Bicycles also can be rented at the Radstation (www.freiburgbikes. de; © **0761/2023426**), daily from June to September, Monday to Saturday in spring and fall, and Monday to Friday from December to March. City, trekking-, mountain- and e-bikes are available. 1 day rental starts at 14€, additional days from 10€.

Exploring Freiburg

Start your explorations in the Altstadt, or historic center. The **Alte Rathaus,** which houses the tourist information office, dates to 1557-59, when it was assembled from several other, even older buildings. The fountain on the Rathausplatz shows the legendary Franciscan monk Berthold Schwarz, who dabbled in alchemy and is said to have discovered an explosive black powder, a forerunner of gunpowder. Around the corner, the **Haus zum Walfisch** with its bright red façade and late Gothic oriel window above the portal dates back to 1515, when it was commissioned

On Münsterplatz, the red Historisches Kaufhaus anchors a row of historic facades.

by the treasurer of Maximilian I. Even before it was finished, in 1529 it gave shelter to the philosopher Erasmus of Rotterdam, after he fled Basel during the turbulence of the Reformation.

At nearby Münsterplatz, across from Freiburg cathedral (see below), look for the conspicuously colorful **Historische Kaufhaus (Customs House),** a Gothic structure with oriel windows at each end. Above the massive supporting arches the facade is decorated with the statues of four emperors of the Habsburg dynasty, of whom all but one visited Freiburg during his reign. The building is now used as an event hall and can only be viewed when functions are hosted inside.

A Hans Baldung *Madonna and Child* **at the Augustiner Museum.**

Augustiner Museum ★★★
MUSEUM   Set within the ancient walls of a remodeled priory church, this museum of ecclesiastical art has been strikingly designed to showcase items as art rather than simply as religious artifacts. The most amazing pieces are the gargoyles and waterspouts that were rescued from Freiburg Münster during recent renovations. The museum also holds paintings, altarpieces, and Freiburg Münster's original stained-glass windows. The Renaissance collection contains some of the few surviving works by Matthias Grünewald, (whose masterpiece, the multi-paneled Isenheim Altar, can be viewed at the Unterlinden Museum in nearby Colmar, France—see p. 426), as well as pieces by Lucas Cranach the Elder and Hans Baldung. Note: In some parts of the building, remodeling may still be in progress.

Augustinerplatz. www.augustinermuseum.de. ℂ **0761/2012531.** Admission 7€ adults, children 18 and under free. Tickets good for same-day free entry at the Museum of Modern Art and the Natural History Museum. Tues–Sun 10am–5pm.

Freiburg Münster ★★ CATHEDRAL   You get a sense of the magnificence of this rusty red stone cathedral long before you reach the doors and catch glimpses of its spire, a masterpiece of filigree stonework that has risen above the roofs of Freiburg for almost 8 centuries. (Miraculously, it survived World War II bombing, thanks to some sound

THE BLACK FOREST & BODENSEE

Freiburg im Breisgau

13th-century engineering and the use of lead anchors.) Those early masterminds never saw the church completed, however, as it took 4 centuries before the last stones were put in place, during which time the cathedral's style had morphed from Romanesque to Gothic. The riot of carvings over the main portal are lessons in stone, intended to teach the illiterate parables from the Old and New Testaments. Inside, look at the brightly-colored stained-glass windows lining the aisles, which were paid for by the city's various guilds—try to spot pretzels, tools, and other signs of their crafts incorporated into the designs. (Some of the original windows were moved to the Augustiner Museum—see p. 419.) Two of the great masterpieces of Germanydesigns. portal are lessons in stone, intended to teach the illiterate parables from the Old and New Testaments.g is now used as a hour (2 hr. journey time), 11-panel piece (various panels are opened and closed at different liturgical seasons) celebrates the Coronation of the Virgin with numerous scenes from her life, all rendered with Baldung's characteristic bright colors and tranquil facial expressions. In a side chapel you'll find another smaller altarpiece by Hans Holbein (1497–1543), probably the greatest German artist of his time. Unfortunately, only two of Holbein's panels remain, portraying the Adoration of the Shepherds and the Three Magi; other panels were apparently destroyed during the Protestant Reformation. Resting against one of the Renaissance pillars along the aisle you can see a carved 16th-century pulpit, with stairs winding around the curve of the column. The figures below the stairs are likenesses of the townspeople, including the sculptor.

Münsterplatz. www.freiburgermuenster.info. © **0761/202790.** Cathedral admission free; choir and chapels 2€ adults, 1.50€ students, children 14 and under free; tower 2€ adults, 1.50€ students, 0.50€ children 12 and under. Cathedral open Mon–Sat 10am–5pm, Sun 1–7:30pm (except during service). Choir and chapels open Mon–Fri 10am–11:30am and 12:30pm–4pm, Sat 10am–11:15am and 12:30pm–3:30pm, Sun 1–4pm. Tower open Mon–Sat 10am–4:45pm, Sun 1–5pm.

Museum für Neue Kunst ★★ MUSEUM   This is not the Guggenheim and there are other, much bigger and better museums and galleries of modern art nearby. However, what makes Freiburg's modern art museum interesting is its selection of artists, all of whom have some connection to Freiburg or southwest Germany. The museum's collections include examples of Expressionism; *Neue Sachlichkeit*, or "new realism"; and pieces from the artistically challenging period of the '30 to '50s, when modern art was politicized and viewed as "un-German" and depraved. Julius Bissier, who was born in Freiburg, is featured prominently.

Marienstrasse 10A. www.museen.freiburg.de. © **0761/2012581.** Admission 3€ adults, children under 18 free. Tues–Sun 10am–5pm.

HIT THE HEIGHTS (& DEPTHS) AT
schauinsland

Towering above Freiburg, Schauinsland (1284m/4213ft) is the highest mountain in the vicinity and well worth a visit for the fabulous views of Freiburg, the Black Forest, Kaiserstuhl, and the Vosges and on clear days, even the Alps. To get to the top, follow Schauinslandstrasse (L124).to Horben, 9km (5 miles) south of Freiburg, where you can catch the cable car **Schauinsland-Bahn** (www.schauinslandbahn.de; © **0761/4511777**). A round-trip ticket costs 12€ adults, 7.50€ children 6 to 14. You can also drive all the way to the top, but it is a very windy, small road. Once youalso drive all the way to the top, but it is a very windy, smtour The **Bergwerkmuseum ★★★** (© **0761/26468**) silver mine, for years the main source of Freiburg's riches. Mined for some 800 years, it has about 100km (60-odd miles) of shafts, the earliest of them dug by hand. Guided tours take between 45 minutes (6€) and 2½ hours (20€); the longer ones involve a lot of climbing and walking. (Families with small children are not permitted on the longer tours; ages 4-12 cost 4€). The climate below ground is often damp and temperature is a constant +8(deg)C (46°F). Hard hat, headlamp and protective gloves are supplied. It's open daily 11am-3:30pm in July and August; in May, June, September, and October it's open only Wednesdays, Saturdays, and Sundays, 11am to 3:30pm.

Halfway up the hillside (a 15-minute walk from the cable car parking lot) you can also tour a well-preserved 400-year old farmhouse, **Schniederlihof ★** (Gegendrumwepg 3, Oberried, © **0170/3462672**), which is furnished just as it was when the last inhabitant died more than a century ago. Admission is 3.50€ adults, 2.50€ children; it's open from May to October, Tuesday to Friday noon-4pm., Saturday and Sunday 11am-4pm.

Where to Stay in Freiburg

Freiburg has a large number of hotels, many of them older buildings, which means the rooms and especially the bathrooms are rather small. The situation will change dramatically within the next couple of years, as several new hotels are presently under construction. The following is a selection of more individualistic hotels.

The Alex Hotel ★★★ This newly refurbished, smart little boutique hotel is located in a residential side street just a 5-minute walk from the train station, yet away from all the bustle of town. Minimalist chic décor in a subdued sand-and-white color scheme makes the most of the smallish rooms. A cozy fireplace lounge and wine-bar with an outdoor terrace provide a quiet space for relaxation.

Rheinstrasse 29. www.the-alex-hotel.de. © **0761/296970.** 39 units. 90€–126€ double. Buffet breakfast 8€. Parking 5€ outside, 10€ garage. **Amenities:** wine bar; Wi-Fi (free).

Fireplace lounge at the Alex Hotel.

Best Western Premier Hotel Victoria ★★★ Just 200 meters (650 ft) from the train station, yet close to the old town, this family-run hotel is extremely conveniently located. The historic hotel, which was established in 1875, has been completely modernized to the highest eco-standards, with solar panels and energy-saving devices. Inside, determinedly modern décor sweeps away any sense of an old-fashioned railway hotel, from the lobby's sleek black marble to the design-conscious rooms, full of opaque glass light fixtures, accent walls, and pale woods (including hardwood floors in some rooms). Almost unique in Freiburg, rooms have air-conditioning. In the basement there is a small spa and fitness studio. There are two bars, a non-smoking bar in the main building and a smokers' lounge in the basement. (There is not a whiff of smoke anywhere in the actual hotel.)

Eisenbahnstrasse 54. www.victoria.bestwestern.de. **℡ 0761/207340.** 66 units. 127€–199€ double. Breakfast 15€. Parking 12€, garage 14€. **Amenities:** Bar; smoking lounge; airport transfers 100€; concierge; room service; sauna; gym; roof terrace; local transport tickets; Wi-Fi (free).

Hotel Kreuzblume ★★ In this quaint boutique hotel, each room is creatively decorated with unique origami artwork. The building is old and rooms and bathrooms are small, but they have all recently been renovated. The hotel is centrally located in one of Freiburg's prettiest alleyways, not far from the cathedral, so there is no escape from the bells, but otherwise the hotel is in a perfect location.

Konviktstrasse 31. www.hotel-kreuzblume.de. 📞 **0761/31194.** 8 units. 120€–150€ double. Buffet breakfast included. Parking 12€ public garage. **Amenities:** Restaurant; Wi-Fi (free).

Rappen ★★ A classic Freiburg hotel, located right on the Münsterplatz facing the cathedral, the Rappen offers hospitable old-world ambience that does not feel staid or stale. Most of the rooms have recently been modernized, though with an understated simplicity—rich-grained wood built-ins, wrought-iron bedsteads, rattan chairs, hardwood floors—that feels quite in keeping with the hotel's character. A few do share bathrooms. Rooms in the main building face the market square; families may want to consider their large family apartment, which has two separate bedrooms and a sleep-sofa (no view, alas). The central location suits those who really want to be in the middle of it all—but be warned, the market bustle (not to mention the church bells) starts up early and is not easily ignored. Access is via a side entrance.

Münsterplatz 13. www.hotel-rappen-freiburg.de. 📞 **0761/31353.** 18 units, 13 with bathroom. 129€–160€ double. Buffet breakfast included. Parking in nearby garage €12. **Amenities:** Restaurant; wine bar; room service; Wi-Fi (free).

Where to Eat in Freiberg

Eichhalde ★★★ FRENCH/GERMAN A little bit off the beaten path, this is a special find. At one point the restaurant was Michelin star decorated, but the owners didn't like all the fuss and returned the star. The quality of food hasn't changed, however (and the price tag is still high-end). A very imaginative cuisine utilizes unusual ingredients to create dishes such as sautéed pulpo with eggplant confit, or Swiss chard roulade and saffron aioli. Fixed price menus, including a vegetarian one, are available at both lunch and dinner. The red-tile-floored dining room has an ambiance that is unpretentious yet classy, without any sense of stuffiness. The restaurant is located in the residential neighborhood of Herdern, near the Botanical Gardens, a 20-minute walk from the town center (or take Bus 27).

Stadtstrasse 91. www.restaurant-eichhalde.de. 📞 **0761/54817.** Reservations required. Main courses 18€–35€; fixed-price menus 32€–69€. Tues–Sat noon–2pm and 6–10pm. Closed 2 weeks in mid-Apr.

Grosser Meyerhof ★ GERMAN A real, traditional German Wirtshaus in the center of the Altstadt, Grosser Meyerhof is as authentic as it gets, and a great place for absorbing the local spirit. Despite the baroque exterior, think of it as a homey food-pub rather than a fine-dining restaurant—traditional food of the schnitzel and sausage variety, inexpensive with plentiful portions. Staff is friendly and flexible, if not always too attentive. The wood-paneled dining room is always packed and can get pretty noisy, which is normal in this kind of establishment. They also have regular entertainment evenings (cabaret, music, et cetera) in a small theater downstairs. During the summer the beer garden is a nice place to relax at the end of the day.

Grünwälderstrasse 1. www.grosser-meyerhof.de. ℭ **0761/3837397.** Main courses from 9.20€. Mon–Sat 10.30am–midnight.

Lichtblick ★★ CONTEMPORARY/INTERNATIONAL   Striking a modern note on a cobbled Altstadt street, this small bistro-style restaurant offers creative, seasonal cuisine made with fresh, regionally sourced ingredients. There are a lot of Italian influences, but also German, French, or Asian—the menu is always a surprise. The service can be a little inconsistent, but the food is delicious and excellent value. Reservations are recommended. Options include a good range of vegetarian dishes, such as orange polenta with goat cheese and vegetable ratatouille, or balsamic sautéed mushrooms with gnocchi. Meat options include prime rib with rosemary potatoes and ratatouille or whole grilled sea-bass.

Konviktstrasse 41. www.lichtblick-freiburg.de. ℭ **0761/29280940.** Main courses 14€–30€. Mon–Thurs 11:30am–3pm and 6–11pm, Fri–Sat 11:30am–11pm, Sun 5–11pm.

Schwarzwälder-Hof ★★ REGIONAL/GERMAN   In a stout 16th-century inn that was once the city's mint, this traditional family-run restaurant serves good quality regional cuisine without trying to be too fancy. The menu isn't huge, but offers enough variety—apart from schnitzel and steak they also have some fish and vegetarian options and daily changing specials. Among the more interesting choices are lamb baked in an herb crust with a slice of polenta, or puff pastry filled with mushroom ragout and herbed pasta as a vegetarian option. Try the Kirsch and sparkling wine sorbet for dessert. The hotel also offers pleasant

black forest **TREATS**

The famous **Schwarzwalder Kirschtorte** (Black Forest cherry cake), a thick chocolaty cake flavored with cherry preserves, is one of the specialties of this corner of Germany. Being so close to France and Switzerland, it's something of a culinary crossroads. If you want to sample other regional specialties, look for **Zwetchgentorte** (plum pastry), **Zwiebelkuchen** (onion tart), **Schwarzwald Schinken** (Black Forest smoked ham), meat and poultry dishes with creamy sauces, and wild game such as venison and boar. Most restaurants make their own **Hauswurst** (sausage) and fiercely guard the recipe.

guestrooms, simply decorated in classic wooden furniture and parquet floors (doubles 99€-130€).

Herrenstrasse 43. www.schwarzwaelder-hof.com. © **0761/38030.** Main courses 14€-21€. Mon–Sat 7am–11pm, Sun 7am–9pm. Lunch 11:45am–2pm, dinner 6–10pm.

Entertainment & Nightlife
PERFORMING ARTS FESTIVALS

The summer in Freiburg is festival season, biggest among them the **Zeltmusik festival** (www.zmf.de) emphasizes jazz, but includes other musical styles as well. Summer also brings a series of **chamber-music concerts** to the Historisches Kaufhaus (see p. 419) on Münsterplatz, and a program of **organ recitals** to the Freiburg Cathedral (see p. 419). October sees a week-long **Blues Festival** (www.freiburg-bluesfestival. de) featuring both German and international artists, who not only give performances, but also workshops. More information about all venues and events listed above, including program schedules and ticket sales, is available from **Freiburg Tourist Board** (see p. 416), or check the local paper: **www.badische-zeitung.de/freizeit.**

NIGHTLIFE

Freiburg has a thriving bar and club scene that goes on into the wee hours. **Jazzhaus,** Schnewlinstrasse 1 (www.jazzhaus.de, © **0761/2923446**), hosts pop, folk, blues and jazz shows by international, regional, and local bands. Located near the train station, the club is open Wednesday to Sunday 7pm until 1am, with a cover of 10€ to 29€. **Café Atlantik** (Schwabentorring 7, www.cafe-atlantik.de, © **0761/33033**), a typical student haunt that serves cheap food from 11am-midnight, has a lively bar scene until 2am in the evenings, and often live music on weekends that runs until 5am. The micro-brewery **Hausbräuerei Feierling** (Gerberau 46, www.feierling.de, © **0761/243480**), with a pleasant shaded beer garden across the street, has a lively ambience and is a good place to meet locals. For a more sophisticated experience try the non-smoking cocktail-bar **Hemingway** or the basement **Smoker's Lounge,** both in the Hotel Victoria (Eisenbahnstrasse 54, www.hemingway-freiburg.de; © **0761/20734501**), open daily from 6pm-2am.

The **Markthalle** food court in the center of town (Grünwälderstrasse 4, www.markthalle-freiburg.de) stages live music on Friday evenings, turning this place into an upbeat after-work party. Access is from Martinsgässle, right by Schwabentor, or from Grünwälderstrasse.

Day Trip to the Kaiserstuhl ★★

Just west of Freiburg, on the other side of the A5 motorway, lies the "mini-mountain massif" of Kaiserstuhl. With their highest peaks barely reaching above 550m (1805ft), they are geologically not related to the

THE french CONNECTION

While you're so close, why not slip across the French border to visit the beautiful historic towns of Colmar and Strasbourg? With their quaint narrow streets, half-timbered houses, and cute little shops, they're well worth the detour. **Strasbourg** is particularly noteworthy for its grand old Gothic cathedral and amazing automaton clock (still in working order). Just over on the other side of the Rhine from Breisach you can also stop to see the UNESCO World Heritage city of **Neuf-Brisach,** noted as the best preserved fortified city designed by Marquis Vauban, the most eminent military engineer of the 17th century.

To reach Colmar by car, cross the Rhine Bridge to enter France and follow the D415 for 25km (15 mi); Strasbourg is another 73km (45 miles) on the N83 north to the A35.

Or even better, you can go by boat. **Breisacher Fahrgast Schiffahrt** offers excursion cruises to both Colmar and Strasbourg. Check **www.bfs-info.de**; or call ✆ **7667/94201** for current schedules.

Black Forest or the Vosges mountains in France, but present the last visible remains of ancient volcanic activity in the rift valley of the Rhine. These hills are blessed with extremely fertile soil and the sunniest climate in Germany. Even Mediterranean species of plants and animals that exist nowhere else this far north can be found here. The rolling hills are draped in vineyards and orchards with pretty little wine villages sprinkled between, creating a quintessential rural idyll. The area is only 16km (10 miles) across in any direction, making it easy to explore on a day's outing from Freiburg. But those who want to linger, or combine visiting Kaiserstuhl with a side trip to Colmar (see above), will find a number of nice country hotels and wineries for food and lodging.

GETTING THERE The main town, **Breisach am Rhein,** is easily reached by a local train that runs hourly from Freiburg. To access the northern Kaiserstuhl, take the regional train to Riegel and switch to the local train (Kaiserstuhlbahn). For schedules see **www.efa-bw.de**.

If you're **driving** from Freiburg, take the B31A west, which turns into the B31 after crossing the A5. Breisach is 15 km (10 miles) west of Freiburg. If you're driving on the A5, turn off at exit 64a to go west on B31, or exit 59 at Riegel to access the northern Kaiserstuhl.

VISITOR INFORMATION There's a tourist office in Breisach at Marktplatz 16 (www.breisach.de; ✆ **07667/940155**), open Monday to Friday 9am to 12:30pm and 1:30 to 6pm, and Saturday 10am to 3pm (closes an hour earlier November to Easter).

EXPLORING THE KAISERSTUHL

The most notable town in the Kaiserstuhl is **Breisach,** an ancient town that overlooks the Rhine. During WWII the town was almost completely destroyed, but much of it has been reconstructed. From here, you may want to drive on to **Burkheim,** 10km (6 miles) north of Breisach, and **Endingen** on the northeastern edge of the hills, two charming little villages with well-preserved historic town centers. Nearby **Riegel** is home to the internationally renowned **Kunsthalle Messmer,** Grossherzog-Leopold-Platz 1 (www.messmerfoundation.com; © **07642/9201620**), a gallery for modern art housed in a former brewery building.

Museum für Stadtgeschichte ★ MUSEUM   Housed in Breisach's historic Rheintor building, a city gate built in 1678 and designed by the Marquis de Vauban (1633-1707), this old-fashioned museum (don't expect high-tech gadgets) focuses on Breisach's fascinating history from its Neolithic beginnings to the present day. (You'll quickly learn that, as a crucial river port and border post, the town has landed on the frontline of innumerable territorial conflicts.) One of the most interesting exhibits is a detailed model of Breisach with its full defense fortifications from 17th and 18th century.

Rheintorplatz 1, Breisach. www.breisach.de. © **07667/832161.** Open Tues–Fri 2pm–5pm, Sat–Sun 11:30am–5pm. Admission adults 2€, children 12 and up 1€.

St. Stephan's Minster ★★ CHURCH   Breisach's iconic landmark towering on top of Münsterberg is visible from afar. Note the mismatched towers, one Romanesque and one Gothic in style—like many big

St. Stephan's Minster in Breisach Am Rhein is visible for miles in the Kaiserstuhl.

medieval churches, St. Stephan's was built over several centuries, from the 12th to the late 15th century, during which time architectural styles changed. The minster's greatest treasure is the carved high altar, created in 1523–1526 by Hans Loi, which vividly depicts the coronation of Mary. Its other treasure is the highly ornate silver reliquary of the city's patrons, Gervasius and Protasius—look for the side showing the historic skyline of Breisach. The minster is a steep 15-minute walk from the town center.

Münsterplatz 3. www.st-stephan-breisach.de. (© **07667/203.** Admission free. Open daily 9am–6pm in summer, 9am–5pm in winter, except during services.

WHERE TO EAT & STAY IN BREISACH

Kaiserstühler Hof ★★ REGIONAL/INTERNATIONAL   Just up from the market square this traditional, family-run establishment is classy and rather pricy. Quality of food is consistent and it is served in a comfortable atmosphere with country charm. There are several different dining rooms to choose from, the most formal of which is **Kaiserstühler-Hof** (entrance Richard Müller Strasse 2). The wine bar **Zur Alten Post** and the **Postgarten-Wintergarten,** are more relaxed and also serve coffee and cake in the afternoon (entrance from the pedestrian zone Neutorstrasse 1). The best space is the cozy courtyard, weather permitting. The menu varies with the season, but may include things like duck with port marinated figs, glazed chicory and polenta patties, or tuna steak with fennel and tomato ragout, with olive oil and lime vinaigrette and steamed potatoes. Unfortunately, vegetarians won't find much, if anything, on the menu. The wine-bar offers a limited menu. Fixed price menus range from 34€ for the daily menu to 98€ for a 6-course dinner including a selection of wines to match each course. They also offer decent, but somewhat dated rooms, at prices of 80€-140€ for a double room.

Richard-Müller-Strasse 2, Breisach. www.kaiserstuehler-hof.de. (© **07667/83060.** Kaiserstühler-Hof and Postgarten-Wintergarten open noon–2pm and 6pm–11pm (kitchen closes 9:45pm); Zur Alten Post wine bar open 11am–midnight, closed Sun night and Mon.

Kapuzinergarten ★★★   Located a little bit up a hill, about 400m north of the minster, this recently renovated hotel offers a range of rooms in different sizes, including some for families. A very comfortable, warm, and homey atmosphere prevails, with lots of pine and some antique furniture; the owners are extremely friendly and helpful. Upper rooms have the best views; many rooms have their own balcony/terrace. The biggest rooms on the top floor are spacious maisonette apartments (157€ to 167€). A rich breakfast buffet is served, and the hotel's restaurant prides itself on its "slow food" quality, featuring seasonal dishes made with locally sourced fresh produce (main courses 17.50€ to 29€, with a

Farm-to-Table Eating at the Straussenwirtschaften

As you explore the backroads of Kaiserstuhl and Markgräflerland you will notice signs adorned with besoms that have colorful ribbons tied to the twigs. These odd brooms point towards a **Straussenwirtschaft,** or **Straussie** for short. These unique little farmhouse eateries are as authentic as it gets, when it comes to discovering local wines and specialties. They are often very rustic, simple, and homey—you might be seated at the same table with other guests, and menu choices are limited—but everything is real, home-cooked food with ingredients picked fresh from the field. Typical dishes include **Flammkuchen** (a kind of very thin, crispy pizza with a cream fraiche topping), schnitzel, cold meats, and other local and seasonal specialties. In April/May asparagus and wild garlic (called Bärlauch) are prominent while later in the year it's pumpkin or seasonal meats. A few more prestigious wineries offer a more refined cuisine, with prices that vary accordingly; most wineries offer tastings and guided tours. Some may also distill their own fruit brandies, the most famous of which is Kirsch, made from cherries, but they can be made from virtually any kind of fruit. Straussies have limited opening times (most likely to be open Thursday to Sunday) and are closed during the winter months. Some offer inexpensive guest rooms or holiday flats but they may not accept credit cards. Check www.straussi.net for details.

3-course fixed menu at 35€). Likewise, the wine list features wines that come from wineries in the immediate vicinity.

Kapuzinergasse 26, Breisach. www.kapuzinergarten.de. © **07667/93000.** 43 units, some wheelchair-access. 81€–99€ double. Buffet breakfast included. **Amenities:** restaurant, WiFi (free).

SPORTS & OUTDOOR PURSUITS IN THE KAISERSTUHL

A great way to explore the area is to rent a bicycle and follow one of the regional cycling routes, such as the **Kaiserstuhl Radweg,** which ambles pleasantly through villages and orchards in a 64km (40 miles) circuit. Both touring bicycles and E-bikes (electric bikes) can be rented in Breisach at **Fun-Bike,** Metzgergasse 1, © **07667/7733** opposite the tourist office, or **Verkehrsbüro Endingen,** Adelshof 20, © **07642/689990.** Prices run about 10€ per day for a regular bike and 20€-30€ for an E-bike.

Walking is another good option. The whole area is criss-crossed with well-marked trails and themed routes 5km to 16km (3–10 miles) in length, which lead through vineyards and villages, ancient hollows, and woodlands. Detailed maps and information for both walking and cycling routes are available from local tourist offices.

Excursion to Markgräflerland ★★★

Just south of Freiburg, the vineyard-covered hills of Markgräflerland, ripple down to Basel, just across the Swiss border. Speckled with quaint

The Story of Dr. Faustus

The **Löwen Inn** on Staufen's market square is where the real Dr. Faustus—a medieval alchemist—is said to have met his demise in 1528, while trying to make gold for his patron, the cash-strapped Lord of Staufen, owner of the local castle. Alas, his experiment failed dramatically, and Dr. Faustus blew himself up in his room. The townspeople had no doubt as to what had happened: the devil must have come to get the Professor. The familiar story was first dramatized in literature by Christopher Marlowe, and later by Goethe. The **castle** up on the hill was not blown up by Faustus, but by the Swedes, in 1632, during the Thirty Years' War. It can be reached via a short, but steep walk through the vineyards. Follow the walking signposts towards **Burgruine**.

little villages and many excellent wineries, the region can be easily explored on the scenic **Belchen Circuit,** a 120km (75-mile) round-trip loop. Although it can be done in a day, taking two or more days would be more relaxing and enjoyable.

From Freiburg head south on the B3, take the by-pass around Bad Krozingen, and turn onto L123 east towards Staufen/Münstertal. In 3km (2 miles) you will see the landmark castle of **Staufen,** which has a pretty Altstadt with cute shops and historic buildings. Continue east through **Münstertal** to the beautiful Baroque Abbey of St. Trudpert (see p. 431).

The L123 gradually leads up the valley, climbing steeply as it approaches the pass at Wiedener Eck. Ahead of you is **Belchen Mountain ★★★**, one of the highest mountains in the Black Forest and, in many people's opinion, the most beautiful. On clear days there are amazing vistas from the top: the Alps to the south and the Vosges to the west, across the Rhine. The road runs right past the base station of the Belchen cable car (www.belchen-seilbahn.de; © **07673/888280**). A round-trip ticket up the mountain costs 7.60€ adults, 5.40€ children, family ticket 20€. After a 5-minute ride to the mountain station, a 10-minute walk gets you to the summit. There's also a trail to the summit from the cable car base station, which takes about 1 hour.

Follow L123 south to Aitern/Utzenfeld and turn right onto the B317, through Schönau. In Wembach turn right onto the L131, now heading west towards Neuenweg, crossing Belchen's southern flanks. Stop to enjoy the scenery from the terrace of hotel **Haldenhof** before heading down to **Badenweiler** (see below). To return to Staufen or Freiburg you can either take the B3, or head north on a back road (L125) via the wine villages of **Britzingen** and **Laufen,** to sample the excellent local wines at the Winzergenossenschaft.

Badenweiler ★★ TOWN   Pretty little Badenweiler has been a spa town for centuries. It all started with the original **Roman Bath** (www.badruine-badenweiler.de/en/home), which has been partly excavated and turned into a museum, open daily year-round. Admission is 2€ (children under 5 free). It's located within the town's attractive **Kurpark,** a 200-year-old arboretum with the remains of an old castle towering above. Here you'll find many beautiful, old exotic trees from all corners of the earth. Also in the park, the **Cassiopeia Therme ★★★** (www.baden weiler.de/Cassiopeia-Therme; © **07632/799200**) is a small jewel of a spa. Though it has only 2 indoor and 1 outdoor pools, the classic design and park setting, with views of the surrounding hills and castle, really makes this place special. Apart from the pools and sauna area there is also a Roman-Irish bath, which follows a set procedure. Extensive renovations are planned for the second half of 2016, so check opening times before you go. A pool-only day pass costs 14€ adults, 10.50€ children under 16, while a pool-and-sauna ticket is 25€. Children under 12 aren't permitted in the sauna area; Wednesday is "women only" sauna day.

Schladerer Distillery ★ DISTILLERY   The Rhine Valley is full of fruit farms, and what better to do with the excess than to turn it into schnapps? At least that is what the locals think. Staufen is home to Schladerer, a distillery of nationwide fame and the region's largest producer of Kirsch and other fruit brandy specialties. During the main tourist season from May to October they offer a guided tour of their facilities at 2pm. Of course, there is also a nice gift shop on site. *Note:* A new visitor center is being built in 2016, and tours may be suspended during construction, so call ahead.

Am Schiessrain 1, Staufen. www.schladerer.de. © **07633/83257.** Reservation required. Admission 5€ adults, children under 18 free.

St. Trudpert Abbey ★★ CHURCH   Founded as a hermitage by an Irish missionary during the first half of the 7th century, this rural outpost quickly grew into a large Benedictine abbey, which is still an active abbey for the nuns today. The original church was ransacked and burnt by marauding Swedes during the Thirty Years' War in 1632. The present church was rebuilt in Baroque style in the 18th century. Visitors are welcome to attend prayer services or to attend regular retreats or spiritual hikes. Some sparely decorated but modern guestrooms are available for 18€-30€ per person per night, with or without meals.

St. Trudpert 6, Münstertal. www.kloster-st-trudpert.de. © **07636/78020.** Admission free. Visit website for schedule of services.

Vita Classica Therme ★ POOLS/SPA   Bad Krozingen's large, popular, spankingly modern thermal spa makes for a handy day out from Freiburg if you want a quick taste of Black Forest spa culture. In some ways, is a bit too big—there are many indoor and a couple of outdoor pools, and when it is very busy one can easily feel a bit lost navigating among them. Try to choose a weekday when there will be fewer crowds. There's also an extensive spa and sauna area offering massages, spa, and beauty applications (must be reserved in advance). Children under 16 are not allowed in the sauna area.

Herbert-Hellmann-Allee 12, Bad Krozingen. www.bad-krozingen.info/Vita-Classica. ✆ **07633/4008140.** Adult day pass 14.80€ or 23.90€ incl. saunas; children 11.80€.

BADEN-BADEN ★★

104km (65 miles) W of Stuttgart, 111km (69 miles) N of Freiburg, 173km (108 miles) S of Frankfurt, 180km (113 miles) NW of Konstanz

The Romans already loved this spot for its hot thermal waters and beautiful location on the edge of the Silva Nigra, as they called the Black Forest. They were the first to build elaborate bath houses here - one for soldiers and another one, the Emperor's Bath, for the upper classes. But although Baden-Baden, then known as Aquae, flourished during their reign, the city's real heyday did not emerge for another 1500 years, during the 18th and 19th centuries, when aristocracy and literati from all over Europe discovered the town and turned it into their summer playground. Wilhelm I, Queen Louise of Prussia, Queen Victoria, Dostoyevsky, and the Russian Tsar, to name but a few, visited here regularly. The air of grandeur still echoes through the town, most notably in the architectural legacy, the manicured parks, high-end shops, and first-class restaurants.

Today, Baden-Baden is as popular as ever. The city's many cultural highlights, museums, galleries, concerts—and of course, its famous spa and casino—have lost none of their appeal, while nature lovers appreciate the town's gorgeous setting and easy access to the surrounding hills.

Essentials

ARRIVING

BY TRAIN Baden-Baden is on two major rail lines, the Frankfurt-Basel line and the Karlsruhe-Konstanz line. Travelers coming from Stuttgart or Munich have to change in Karlsruhe or Mannheim. From Frankfurt the journey takes approximately 1 hour and 30 minutes. For information visit www.bahn.de or call ✆ **01805/996633.** The railway station is at Baden-Oos, northwest of town; regrettably, it's an expensive 10-minute taxi ride from the town center, but city bus 201 makes the run every 10-minutes during the day.

BY CAR Access to Baden-Baden is via the A5 Autobahn north and south or the A8 Autobahn east and west. The drive south from Frankfurt takes 2 hours; from Munich, it's about 4 hours, depending on traffic.

VISITOR INFORMATION

Baden-Baden's **tourist office** is at Schwarzwaldstrasse 52 (www.baden-baden.com, ✆ **07221/275200**). It's open Monday to Sat 9am to 6pm

SPA CULTURE IN THE black forest

"Spa culture" has ancient roots, dating in the Black Forest back to Roman times. Ever fond of a good steam, the Romans were the first to develop an elaborate bath culture. The Black Forest is richly blessed with hot springs and the occupying Romans lost no time in constructing elaborate bath temples around these springs. The remains of these can still be seen in **Baden-Baden** (see p. 432) and in **Badenweiler** (see p. 430).

After the fall of the Roman Empire, repeated cycles of war and invasions wreaked havoc on the Black Forest. The once glorious spas fell into decline—yet, the knowledge of the water's healing virtues survived. Finally, in the late 18th and early 19th centuries, spa culture experienced a true renaissance. Ornate bath houses were constructed once again, mostly for the benefit of the European elite, who flocked to Baden-Baden, Badenweiler, and **Bad Wildbad** (see p. 449), to "take the waters" and enjoy the good life. Alas, this era abruptly came to an end with the onset of the great wars in the 20th century.

Half a century later, spa culture was resurrected once again—but with radically changed demographics. No longer a privilege of the rich, the thirteen spas of the Black Forest have been turned into modern balneo-temples, with saunas and steam baths, heated outdoor pools, whirlpools and massage jets that are affordable and open to anyone. The baths are still used for therapeutic purposes, but mostly people simply come for the relaxation.

These pools are not meant to be "aqua fun parks," but oases of peace—thus, they are often frequented by an older crowd (50+). Although many spas allow children 7 or older (and occasionally even younger), they are expected to be well-behaved. If you're looking for family fun, the Galaxy pool at the **Badeparadies** in Titisee (see p. 464), or any the public indoor and outdoor swimming pools found throughout the region, would be a better choice.

Unfamiliar with German spa and sauna etiquette? It is important to know the rules (which, however, may vary slightly from one establishment to another). The most important and universal rule is that saunas are always taken in the nude ("textile-free" areas). Bring a big towel to sit on and rinse your seat when leaving. Sauna areas are separate from the regular pools and access costs extra. Spa applications and massages must always be reserved in advance. They are very popular—book early to avoid disappointment!

Many spas have a little shop at the facility, where flip-flops or bathing suits can be purchased. Towels and bath robes are usually available for rent at the cash register.

and Sunday 9am to 1pm. There's also an information point at the Trinkhalle, Kaiserallee 3, open Monday to Saturday 10am to 5pm, Sunday 2pm to 5pm.

GETTING AROUND

Baden-Baden is serviced by a network of buses, whose routes coincide at the Leopoldsplatz, in the city center. A one-way fare within Baden-Baden is 2.40€, and a day pass, good for 24 hours of unlimited public transport for up to five people, is 10.10€. Visit **www.stadtwerke-baden-baden. de** or call ✆ **07221/277650** for details.

Exploring Baden-Baden

The center of Baden-Baden activity is **Lichtentaler Allee,** the park-like promenade along the bank of the Oosbach River (affectionately called the Oos—pronounced *Ohs*), which runs through the center of town. As you stroll along the riverbank, you'll be amazed at the variety not only of exotic shrubs and trees, but also of the rhododendrons, azaleas, and roses. At the north end of the park are the buildings of the **Kurgarten,** including the classical **Kurhaus,** now used as an entertainment complex (see p. 441). A 10-minute walk west, at the foot of the Florentinerberg gardens, you'll find the ruins of the old Roman baths and the Friedrichs-bad spa complex.

Caracalla-Therme ★★★ BATHS   Part of the same complex as the historic **Friedrichsbad** (see p. 435), this large and luxurious modern spa facility includes a large indoor pool and two outdoor pools with smaller whirlpool baths and a current-channel pool, as well as a large sauna area.

Baden-Baden's spa choices range from historic baths to the modern Caracalla-Therme.

Medicinal treatment includes mud baths, various types of massages, and whirlpools. The slightly radioactive water, rich in sodium chloride, comes from artesian wells 1,800m (6,000 ft.) under the Florentiner Mountain. The pool temperatures range from 65°–100°F (18°–38°C). Bathers usually begin in cooler pools, working up to the warm water. The sauna area's temperatures range from 135° to 203°F (57°–95°C). You must wear bathing suits in the pools, but everyone goes nude in the saunas. Children under 7 are not allowed in the sauna area (childcare facilities are available). Children aged 7 to 14 must be accompanied by a parent.

Römerplatz 1. www.carasana.de. © **07221/275940.** Admission 15€ for 1 hr. 30min, 19€ for 3 hr., 23€ for a day pass. Additional time charged 0.70€ per 10 min. Daily 8am–10pm. Bus: 201.

Friedrichsbad ★★★ BATHS   Friedrichsbad, also known as the Old Baths, was built from 1869 to 1877 at the behest of Grand Duke Friedrich von Baden. This is not a thermal spa, but rather an Irish-Roman bath, which follows a specific protocol of 17 stations, with pools of various temperatures, brush massages, and showers, taken in a specific sequence. It takes about 2 hours to complete the program, followed by a 30-minute period of rest and relaxation. Note: this is a "textile-free," e.g., nude, experience. On Mondays, Thursdays, and Saturdays men and women bathe separately, except at two of the stations.

Römerplatz 1, www.carasana.de. © **07221/275920.** Admission 25€ w/o soap-brush massage (3 hr.), 37€ w/ soap-brush massage (3 hr. 30min), 49€ w/ soap & cream massage (4 hr.). Additional time charged 0.50€ per 10 min. Children under 14 not allowed. Daily 9am–10pm.

Roman Bath Ruin ★ RUIN/MUSEUM   One of the original Roman bath houses, the soldier's bath, is located underneath the historic **Friedrichsbad** (see below). The original floor and wall heating system can still be observed and with the help of modern technology (computer/video animation) one can get a realistic glimpse of the Roman bath culture. Audio guides in different languages are included in the entrance fee. Access is from the parking garage below Friedrichsbad.

Römerplatz 1. www.carasana.de/de/roemische-badruinen. © **07221/275934.** Admission 2.50€ adults, 1€ children 14 and under. Open mid-Mar to mid-Nov 11am–noon and 3–4pm.

Sammlung Frieder Burda ★★ MUSEUM   The Frieder Burda museum of modern art is housed in a purpose-designed center designed by architect Richard Meier, who also designed the Getty Center in Los Angeles. The hypermodern building is quite stunning in itself and provides the perfect setting for this type of art. Regularly changing exhibitions are based on Frieder Burda's extensive private collections and frequently feature German Expressionists of the postwar era. Curation is

The Richard Meier-designed Frieder Burda art museum in Baden-Baden.

very thoughtful, providing lots of cultural context. Information is provided in German and French only, however, except for exhibition flyers, which are available in English.

Lichtentaler Allee 8B. www.museum-frieder-burda.de. © **07221/398980.** Admission 13€ adults; 11€ students, children under 8 free. Combination ticket w/ Staatliche Kunsthalle 18€, students 14€. Tues–Sun 10am–6pm.

Staatliche Kunsthalle ★★ MUSEUM   This neo-classical gray stone building, located right next to the Frieder Burda museum, presents changing art exhibitions on a particular theme or topic, which are accompanied by a program of related events. There is also a studio space for young, contemporary artists. Most information is presented in German, but exhibition catalogues are bilingual German and English.

Lichtentaler Allee 8a. www.kunsthalle-baden-baden.de. © **07221/30076400.** Admission 7€ adults, 5€ children 9 and older. Open Tues–Sun 10am–6pm, closed Mon except public holidays. Closed Dec 24 and 31.

LA8 Kulturhaus/Museum für Kunst und Technik des 19. Jahrhunderts ★ MUSEUM/EVENT SPACE   Along the same "museum mile" stretch of Lichtentaler Allee, this modern museum is cleverly tucked into the garden behind a staid-looking 19th-century villa. Within this mixed venue, also used for conferences and events, a sleek glass-walled exhibition space mounts biannually changing exhibitions that focus on the interface between art and technology in the 19th century.

Lichtentaler Allee 8. www.la8.de. ℘ **07221/5007960.** Admission 7€ adults, 5€ students 10 and older. Open Tues–Sun and on public holidays (incl. Mondays) 11am–6pm. Closed Dec 24 and 31.

Stadtmuseum ★ MUSEUM   At the south end of museum row, this small but interesting city museum covers Baden-Baden's history, starting with the Romans. A significant part of it deals with its rise to fame and fortune during the 19th century. Changing special exhibitions highlight various cultural or historic themes relevant to the town's past. English audioguides will be available soon.

Lichtentaler Allee 10. www.baden-baden.de. ℘ **07221/275233.** Admission 5€ adults, 4€ children 6 and older. Open Tues–Sun 11am–6pm. Closed Mon.

Trinkhalle (Pump Room) ★ HISTORIC BUILDING   Situated in the Kurgarten spa gardens, this stately pump house with its splendid neoclassical foyer dates to 1839–42. The frescoes depict scenes of Black Forest legends. Aristocrats once converged here "to take the waters" (although making a splashy public appearance was probably more the point); today's visitors can try a taste of the mineral-rich waters as well. For those in need of a stronger boost to their vital spirits, there is an elegant little coffee house on site.

Kaiserallee 3. No phone. Free admission. Apr–Oct daily 10am–6:00pm.

Where to Stay in Baden-Baden

Brenners Park-Hotel & Spa ★★★   This is a true luxury Grand Hotel, steeped in old-school tradition and deservedly rated as one of the top 10 hotels in Germany. It regularly hosts the most illustrious guests from all around the world. Both the standard rooms and suites are elegantly furnished in classic style with plenty of period detail and marble bathrooms. Each room has its own balcony overlooking the beautiful Lichtentaler Allee park. Despite all this classic luxury the hotel does not feel staid, but simply elegant—which however, does not come cheap. The hotel's private spa is housed at Villa Stephanie, a separate villa within the hotel grounds with somewhat more modern rooms, fitted to make longer stays even more comfortable. Spa, beauty treatments, cosmetic surgery, and naturopathic health care are available on site. The hotel's top restaurant (see p. 439) is one of the region's best.

Schillerstrasse 4–6. www.brenners.com. ℘ **07221/9000.** 110 units. 320€–720€ double. Breakfast included. Valet parking 26€. **Amenities:** 3 restaurants; bar; babysitting (on request); gym; indoor pool; spa; room service; Wi-Fi (free).

Hotel am Markt ★   Located on the market square in the old town center, this family-owned boutique hotel is very convenient to the spa and within easy walking distance to the main sites in Baden-Baden. Behind the historic 18th-century façade, recently renovated rooms have a surprisingly modern flair, with minimalist design and a few bold splashes of color. Everything is spic and span and the staff is extremely friendly and helpful. Beware of the church bells, however—Baden-Baden's chief church, the Stiftkirche, is right opposite. If you are driving, finding it without a GPS navigator can be a challenge due to the narrow one-way streets in the neighborhood. **Note:** There is no elevator, so it's not suitable for people with mobility issues.

Marktplatz 18. www.hotel-am-markt-baden.de. ✆ **07221/27040.** 23 units. 95€–105€ double. Breakfast included. Parking 4€. **Amenities:** Room service; Wi-Fi (free).

Hotel am Sophienpark ★★   Just off Leopoldsplatz, this neo-classical grand-dame hotel blends tradition and modernity in a modest, yet tasteful way. As soon as you enter you are struck by the ornate wrought-iron original staircase, which is a piece of art in itself. Downstairs public rooms maintain the hotel's old-world style, while updated guest rooms blend modern art, padded headboards, and flat-screen TVs with quietly classic furnishings. The hotel's super central location is very convenient to all the major sites in town, yet once inside, rooms that overlook the hotel's private park are an oasis of calm. Due to the surrounding one-way systems it is not easy to find the hotel by car; request detailed instructions in advance. There is only a smallish breakfast room and no restaurant, but with so many excellent restaurants nearby that is no problem.

Sophienstrasse 14. www.hotel-am-sophienpark.de. ✆ **07221/3560.** 73 units. 160€–240€ double, 249€–340€ suites. Breakfast included. **Amenities:** Room service; laundry service; Wi-Fi (free).

Hotel Merkur ★★   A lovely and well maintained boutique hotel in a quiet side street, yet close to almost everything, the Merkur offers good value for money. All rooms are finished in a modern style with hardwood floors, leather chairs, and a calming earth-toned color palette; bathrooms are up to date. Standard rooms are a little on the small side, but the superior doubles and suites are very comfortable. The new annex does not have an elevator, so if mobility is an issue, request a room in the main building. The staff is very friendly and helpful and breakfast is plentiful. The hotel has its own little restaurant, **Sterntaler,** which is highly recommended for its very good regional cuisine and reasonable prices (main courses 12€ to 24.50€).

Merkurstrasse 8. www.hotel-am-sophienpark.de. ✆ **07221/303300.** 37 units. 108€–258€ double. Breakfast included. Parking 9€. **Amenities:** restaurant; bar; conference room; business center; laundry service; ticket service; Wi-Fi (free).

Quellenhof Sophia ★   This is an older hotel, which has benefitted greatly from a recent change in management. Although furnishings look dated—think built-in headboards, brass lamps, and overstuffed chairs—for the price this hotel offers incredibly good value. Rooms are spacious and comfortable, but the bathrooms are a bit small. The location right in the center of town is perfect. Unique about this hotel is the thoughtful range of amenities—you can rent everything you need for a visit at the thermal bath, a bike, walking sticks, or even borrow a tie or a handbag for a visit to the casino.

Sophienstrasse 27-29. www.quellenhof-sophia.de. © **07221/9229100.** 52 units. 95€–120€. Buffet breakfast included. **Amenities:** Cafe-bistro; restaurant; hairdresser; children's play room; limited parking 12€ per day; room service; Wi-Fi (free).

Where to Eat in Baden-Baden

Brenners Restaurant ★★★ GERMAN/CONTEMPORARY   Baden-Baden certainly does not lack upscale restaurants and top chefs, but even among this rarified breed, Brenners Park Restaurant stands out. Paul Stradner, its highly skilled and talented chef, is among the youngest 2-star chefs in Germany. But it is not just his incredible skill at re-creating traditional dishes with an innovative twist that make dining here so exciting—it is the whole experience, the ambiance of an elegant dining room overlooking the hotel's gorgeous private park, along with perfect service. Both à la carte and fixed-price menu options are available, even for vegetarians. The menu changes frequently, but may include items

Old World elegance at the Brenners Restaurant.

such as glazed sweetbread of veal with truffled jus, parsley root, and mushrooms, or the spiral of Hokkaido pumpkin with sweet chestnuts, Brussels sprouts, wild broccoli, and Styrian pumpkin seed oil. This is a formal dining experience and formal evening attire is expected. The hotel has two other, less formal, but also excellent restaurants: the **Wintergarten** serves traditional Black Forest cuisine, while the bistro-style **Rive Gauche,** set in the park itself, serves lighter Mediterranean and north African-inspired cuisine.

In Brenner's Park Hotel, Schillerstrasse 4/6. www.brenners.com. ℭ **07221/9000.** Reservations required. Main courses 45€–72€. Fixed 7-course gourmet menu 165€, vegetarian 130€. Wed–Sun 7–11pm. Closed mid-Jan to mid-Feb.

Löwenbräu ★ GERMAN/BAVARIAN   Similar to its sister establishment, the Löwenbräu in the heart of Munich, this is a typical Bavarian food pub, with dirndl-clad waitresses serving rustic, hearty cuisine of the sausage and schnitzel variety. Nothing sophisticated about it, but you won't leave hungry and you won't break the bank either. Pork shank is especially popular. They also offer basic vegetarian options in the same category, such as potato pancake with vegetables or dumplings with creamy mushroom sauce. The restaurant is housed in a historic building that dates back to 1723, when it served as student accommodations. Some of its more famous residents include the Russian writer Fyodor Dostoyevsky and composer Franz Liszt. Today the hotel **zum Goldenen Löwen** occupies the building above the restaurant, and offers nicely renovated, modern rooms, with doubles running about 95€ to 120€ per night. It can get a bit noisy, especially at weekends, but otherwise, this is a nice, centrally located mid-range hotel.

Gernsbacher Strasse 9 (in the Altstadt). www.loewenbraeu-baden-baden.de. ℭ **07221/22311.** Main courses 15€–35€. Daily 10am–11pm.

M10 ★★ REGIONAL/GERMAN   This intimate café/restaurant, with its simple menu of very good regional food in a cozy ambience, offers extremely good value for money. At lunchtime they serve a couple of very reasonably priced specials, one of which is always vegetarian or vegan. In the afternoon they serve coffee and delicious cake and in the evenings the menu features regional cuisine, such as venison in juniper cream sauce and herbed spätzle, with a cranberry, pear, and carrot side dish. For dessert try the home-made cinnamon-parfait with warm caramelized orange fillets.

Marktplatz 10. www.marktplatz10.de. ℭ **07221/3952421.** Lunch specials 9€, dinner main courses 15€–23€. Tues–Sun 11am–11pm. Closed Mon.

Rizzi ★★ INTERNATIONAL/CONTEMPORARY   This stylish wine bistro and restaurant is trendy and, well, ritzy—a place where young and not-so-young professionals enjoy the good life. It can get pretty busy here, especially before or after a theater show, which is not the best time to visit. At quieter times food and service are excellent. Their extensive menu features "the best of" almost any corner of the planet: from organic Scottish salmon sashimi with Wakame salad, ginger, wasabi, and teriyaki sauce, to pumpkin-orange cream soup with organic salmon tempura, or beef carpaccio with lime oil, winter truffle shavings, and parmigiano reggiano. The house Rizzi burgers are made with grass-fed Nebraska beef and served with roasted onions, cheddar cheese, lettuce, grilled bacon, and hot sauce. Of course, the ubiquitous schnitzel isn't amiss either. There's something for everyone, with organic-quality vegan and vegetarian options also available. The outdoor seating area, surrounded by greenery on the banks of the River Oos and in the heart of Baden-Baden, is a perfect place in the summer.

Augustaplatz 1. www.rizzi-baden-baden.de. ✆ **07221/25838.** Main dishes 18€–32€. Daily noon–1am.

Entertainment & Nightlife
PERFORMING ARTS

Baden-Baden has a busy annual schedule of concerts, dance, and dramatic performances. The centerpiece for most of the resort's cultural activities is the oft-photographed **Kurhaus ★★**, Kaiserallee 1 (www.kurhauscasino.de, ✆ **07221/353204**). Originally built in the 1870s as the focal point of the resort, the Kurhaus does not contain spa facilities, as its name implies, but is rather a stylish venue for all kinds of different events. In the same building is Baden-Baden's casino, the **Spielbank ★★** (see "The Casino" below).

The town's renowned resident orchestra, the **Philharmonie Baden-Baden,** performs mostly in the elegant interior of the **Festspielhaus ★★★**, in the Alter Bahnhof (see below for ticket information).

Dating to 1862, the **Theater am Goetheplatz ★★**, Goetheplatz (www.theater.baden-baden.de; ✆ **07221/932700**) has been fitted with state-of-the-art technology without losing any of its beautiful rococo charm. Apart from the impressive main hall it also has a couple of smaller stages, one dedicated to youth theater and the other for more intimate or even solo performances.

Every summer, the verdant core of Baden-Baden is home to several outdoor concerts, many of which focus on jazz or classical music, often informal late-afternoon or early-evening affairs organized at short notice by the tourist office. More elaborate concerts, many of them performed by the Philharmonie Baden-Baden, are part of the resort's **Musikalischer Sommer Festival,** usually conducted during an 8-day period in mid-July.

For tickets to any cultural or musical event within Baden-Baden, contact either the tourist office at the Trinkhalle (✆ **07221/275200**), which sells tickets on its premises, or the **Ticket Service** at the tourist information (Schwarzwaldstrasse 52; ☎ **07221/275233**).

THE CASINO

Spielbank ★★   Located in the Kurpark, Germany's oldest casino is no mean gambling hall. Instead, the interior, with its huge chandeliers, enormous mirrors, plush carpets, and ornate ceilings, rather resembles a ballroom at a palace. As a place for exclusive and high-strung socializing the casino has been a popular place since the day it first opened its doors, in 1824. Dostoyevsky, a frequent visitor to the casino, wrote *The Gambler* during his stay in Baden-Baden. The city's most glamorous party scene now congregates every Friday and Saturday at the casino's **Bernstein Club ★★**, which blends partying and gambling from 9pm to 3:30am. The regular rules of admission to the Casino and dress code apply: To enter you must carry a valid passport and be at least 21 years old; men must wear tie and dinner jacket, women must be in evening wear. We less glamorous types may content ourselves with guided tours of the historic gambling rooms, offered daily before the casino opens.

Kaiserallee 1. www.casino-baden-baden.de. ☎ **07221/30240.** Casino admission 5€, no obligation to play. Open daily (except public holidays) 2pm–2am (Fri and Sat until 3:30am). 40-min guided tours daily Apr–Nov 9:30am–noon, Nov–Apr 10:30am–11:30am. Tours cost 7€ adults, 3€ children 16 and under.

Sports & Outdoor Pursuits

SPECTATOR SPORTS

Horse Racing   Races take place at the historic track at Iffezheim, 12km (8 miles) northwest of Baden-Baden. The racing season consists of three events, organized by the **Internationaler Club:** the Spring Meeting (a week in late May or early June), the Grand Week (the last 8 days of August) and the Sales & Racing event (3 days during the 3rd week of October). For tickets and information go to **www.baden-racing.com**.

OUTDOOR PURSUITS

BALLOONING   For an entirely new perspective on the area, go hot-air ballooning. **Ballooning 2000** offers rides between the Black Forest and the Vosges. Contact pilot Rainer Keitel (www.ballooning2000.de; ☎ **07223/60002**) for details. A 2-hour champagne breakfast trip over the Rhine Valley goes for 253€ per person.

CYCLING   Many easy, medium and difficult routes for both touring cyclists and mountain bikers are available. Detailed maps and information are available from the tourist office. Public rental stations can be found near several public transport hubs. You can rent city, trekking, and mountain bikes, or book guided cycling tours, from Klaus-Peter Müller, Eisenbahnstrasse 1a (rent-a-sportsman.de; ☎ **07221/3730006**).

ROCK CLIMBING For a more up-close-and-personal experience, **rock climbing** at all levels can be enjoyed on the Battert rocks directly above the city. For a climber's guide, contact the **German Alpine Club,** Flugstrasse 17 (www.alpenverein.de; ✆ **07221/17200**).

WALKING It takes about 3 hours to walk the entire 10km (6-mile) scenic **Eberstein Rundweg** circuit, crossing Battert and visiting both Hohenbaden and Ebersteinburg castle ruins along the way. The best place to start is at the **Wolfsschlucht** pass just outside of Ebersteinburg, 6km (4 miles) northeast of Baden-Baden (take bus 244) and follow trail markers for Ebersteinburg-Rundweg.

Another scenic option is to hike up **Merkur Mountain** 668m (2200ft), the local Hausberg that overlooks the town. A **funicular railway** takes you to the top in just 5 minutes, where a cafe js open daily 10am to 6pm (sometimes later in summer), and you can take the lift to the top of the observation tower for even better views. To get to the funicular, take bus 204 or 205 to Merkuriusberg.

THE BLACK FOREST ★★★

Although called "black," this very green region possesses some of the country's purest nature and most stunning scenery. Dark and uncharted in the days of the Romans, the area has long since been cultivated and inhabited, but still retains plenty of sky-bound pine and beech trees blanketing the mountainsides.

It's not a huge area, some 200km (125 miles) from north to south and only about 70km (40 miles) wide, easily seen in one day. It's lovely to see out of a car window, but even lovelier to explore on foot; all along the roadsides are signposts leading to well-maintained trails, for longer and shorter walks. Another way to enjoy the Black Forest is to spend a few hours at one of its many thermal spas (see p. 433), which tend to be more informal and relaxing than those in more fashionable spa towns.

At the northern end, **Pforzheim** makes a convenient touring base, especially for those making a one-day drive-through. If you plan to spend more time here, however, the somewhat more charming **Freudenstadt,** located in the eastern-central Black Forest, makes a better option for access to Kinzig Valley and other destinations in the central parts of the region. If you plan to drive the **Black Forest High Road** (see p. 449), your starting point will be Baden-Baden (see p. 432).

Essentials

ARRIVING

BY TRAIN Trains pull into **Pforzheim** at least once an hour from Munich (trip time: 3 hr.), Frankfurt (trip time: 2 hr.), and Stuttgart (trip time: 1hr.). It's also a 1½-hour direct trip from Freiburg. You can also take a train directly to **Freudenstadt,** which gets hourly service from Munich

(4-4½ hrs.) and Frankfurt (3 hr.); from Freiburg, however, the trip to Freudenstadt entails a change in Karlsruhe and can take up to 4 hours. For information visit **www.bahn.de**, or call ✆ **01805/996633.**

BY CAR   **Pforzheim** lies just off the A8 motorway between Munich and Karlsruhe. From Stuttgart, the drive can take between 45 and 90 minutes; from Frankfurt, it's around 2 hours; and from Munich, around 3 hours. **Freudenstadt** is about an hour's drive southwest of Pforzheim via B294, an hour's drive southeast of Baden-Baden via B500, and a 1½-hour drive northeast of Freiburg via the A5 and A8.

VISITOR INFORMATION

In **Pforzheim,** there's a tourist office at Schlossberg 15 (www.pforzheim.de/tourismus.html; ✆ **07231/393700**), open Monday to Friday 10am to 5pm, Saturday 10am to 1pm. Along the **Black Forest High Road** (see p. 449) the National Park headquarters at Ruhestein (www.schwarzwald-nationalpark.de; ✆ **07449/92998444**) is open Monday to Friday, 8:30am to 5pm. The visitor center in **Kniebis** is at Strassburger Strasse 349 (www.kniebis.de/html/besucherzentrum.html; ✆ **07442/7570**). Just off the main route, at the base of Feldberg, the region's highest peak, **Haus de Natur** (Dr.-Pilet-Spur 4, Feldberg, www.naz-feldberg.de; ✆ **07676/933630**) is an excellent source of information as well.

GETTING AROUND

The Black Forest has a number of themed auto routes, the granddaddy of them all being the **Schwarzwaldhochstrasse** (Black Forest High Road, or Ridgeway, Rte. B500; www.schwarzwaldhochstrasse.de), which runs almost the entire length of the Black Forest, from Baden-Baden to Waldshut-Tiengen. Another unforgettable route, the **Schwarzwald Panoramastrasse** (Black Forest Panorama Road; www.schwarzwald-panoramastrasse.de), winds through the southern half of the region from Waldkirch near Freiburg to Hinterzarten just west of Titisee. Other themed routes include the **Uhrenstrasse** (Clock Road; www.deutsche-uhrenstrasse.de,), and the **Deutsche Fachwerkstrasse** (German Half-timber Road; www.deutsche-fachwerkstrasse.de). Check their websites for information. Drivers are advised to be extremely careful, as the roads are often tight and in summer frequently shared by cyclists.

Exploring the Upper Black Forest

Two good bases for exploring the region are **Pforzheim,** at the north end of the Black Forest, and **Freudenstadt,** which lies in the heart of the Schwarzwald. Whichever you choose for your base, make sure you get out into the countryside and villages, to truly understand why this is such a favorite vacation region for the Germans themselves.

black forest DARK AGES

Just about 18km (11 miles) to the northeast of Pforzheim, in the rural hamlet of Maulbronn, lies **Kloster Maulbronn ★★** (www.kloster-maulbronn.de; © **07043/926610**), one of the region's most evocative sights. This ancient monastery is considered to be one of the best-preserved medieval monasteries north of the Alps and has been declared a UNESCO World Heritage site. Most of its more than 30 buildings were constructed between 1150 and 1390, within an encircling wall that protected the monks and their allies from outside attackers. The most prominent building is the compound's **church,** which combines aspects of Romanesque and Gothic architecture, and has influenced the design of later ecclesiastic architecture throughout central and northern Europe.

Most visitors arrive by car or taxi from the center of Pforzheim, but there's also a bus that departs for Maulbronn from Pforzheim central bus station (ZOB) at hourly intervals throughout the day. The monastery is open March to October, daily 9am to 5:30pm; from November to February it's open Tuesday to Sunday, 9:30am to 5pm. Admission is 7.50€ adults, 3.80€ students and children 6 and older. Family discounts are available.

EXPLORING PFORZHEIM ★

An important mercantile center during the Middle Ages, known for jewelry and clock making, Pforzheim city was severely damaged during World War II and was hastily rebuilt as a car-friendly, modern functional town—thereby losing most of its character. There is not much left of the historic town except for the former **Schloss- und Stiftskirche St Michael** (Castle and Monastery Church) ★, Schlossberg 10 (www.pforzheim-schlosskirche.de; © **07231/102484**), which has been partially restored. The original church was built in stages from the 1200s to the 1400s, and as a result has both Romanesque and Gothic architectural features. It's open daily 8:30am to 6pm. The most interesting museum is the **Schmuckmuseum ★★★** (Museum of Jewelry), Jahnstrasse 42 (www.schmuckmuseum.de; © **07231/392126**), which highlights Pforzheim's historic jewelry-making tradition with a collection spanning 5,000 years. The museum is open Tuesday to Sunday 10am to 5pm. Admission is 3€, free for children under 14. For insights into the role of technology with regard to the region's ubiquitous clock- and jewelry-making traditions, visit **Technisches Museum ★★**, Bleichstrasse 81 (www.technisches-museum.de; © **07231/392869**). A replica of a clock-making workshop from the early 1800s gives a vivid impression of the craftsmanship. The museum is open every Wednesday 2 to 5pm, and Sunday 10am to 5pm. Admission is free, and donations are appreciated.

PFORZHEIM TO FREUDENSTADT: EXPLORING THE ENZ & NAGOLD VALLEYS ★★

By car one can take a wonderful 180km (112 miles) round-trip drive through these valleys, following the B463 south from Pforzheim. You'll pass through **Bad Liebenzell,** an old, if not necessarily well-preserved, spa town (p. 463) with a history that dates back to the 11th century. Just 5km (3 miles) down the road, the hamlet of **Hirsau** was once a powerful ecclesiastic center; its ancient abbey ruins are a haunting reminder of that past (see p. 447). Next in line is **Calw** (p. 447), hometown of Hermann Hesse and a picturesque village lined with historic half-timbered buildings.

Just off the main route the hamlet of **Bad Teinach-Zavelstein** is worth a detour, especially in late March and April, when the meadows around the castle ruin of Zavelstein blossom with crocuses. Bad Teinach's mineral waters can be enjoyed at the newly renovated luxury wellness and spa **Hotel Therme** (see p. 460). Another interesting side trip is a visit to **Neubulach,** where one of the Black Forest's most productive silver mines (see p. 447) once operated; time here seems to have stood still since then.

Back on the B463, another 21km (13 miles) south lies **Nagold,** a lively market town with an old town center. Across the Nagold River, the ruin of **Hohennagold castle** overlooks the town. Like so many castles in the area it was destroyed by French troops during the Thirty Years War. From here, another detour (take the B28 west out of Nagold) goes 16km (10 miles) to the fairytale hilltop village of **Altensteig,** probably the most romantic town in the northern Black Forest. Go to the top of the hill to really appreciate its quaintness. Crowned with an old castle and beautiful Rococo style church, this medieval town seems like a museum. (**Note:** Those with mobility issues might find the steps and rises a bit difficult.)

The quaint spa town of Bad Liebenzell, on the Nagold River south of Pforzheim.

Continuing south on B463, you will pass through **Dornstetten,** which also has a beautiful old town center, and end your drive in **Freudenstadt** (see p. 446).

Besucher Bergwerk Hella-Glück Stollen ★★ SHOW MINE Since the Nebulach mine's closure in the 1920s, some of the shafts have been turned into a show mine. The Hella-Glück Stollen is easy to access and has level flooring, but the Untere Stollen (lower mine) is more adventurous, requiring visitors to climb up and down ladders to get from one level to another. (Clothing may get dirty and wet and the ground is uneven and slippery.) Long after the mine had been abandoned, the medical profession learned that its dust-free interior is beneficial in the treatment of asthma. A therapy center is now located in one of the old shafts.

Nebulach-Ziegelbach. www.bergwerk-neubulach.de. ✆ **07053/7346.** Guided tours 4.50€ adults, 2.50€ children. Tours Apr–Nov Tues–Fri 2pm and 3pm, Sat–Sun 11am–4pm.

Hesse Haus ★ MUSEUM **Hermann Hesse** (1877–1962), who won the Nobel Prize for literature in 1946, is commemorated in his hometown of Calw with a statue at his favorite place on **Nikolausbrücke,** the bridge over the River Nagold, where he used to spend his time fishing as a boy. A museum on the market square houses all kinds of Hesse memorabilia, honors his literary legacy, and highlights the stations of his private life. It also displays some of the author's artwork and paintings, which are rarely seen.

Marktplatz 30, Calw. www.hermann-hesse.com. ✆ **07051/7522.** Admission 5€ adults, 3€ students and children over 12. Apr–Oct 11am–5pm (closed Mon), Nov–Mar 11am– 4pm (closed Mon and Fri).

Kloster Hirsau ★★ CHURCH/MUSEUM In medieval times Kloster Hirsau was one of the most powerful abbeys in southern Germany. Although its origins date back to a humble hermitage in 8th-century, the Abbey reached its pinnacle during the 11th century with the founding of St. Aurelius and St Peter and Paul. The church of St Aurelius still gives a good impression of the monumental architecture of what was once the largest Romanesque church in Germany. The abbeys, however, were destroyed by French troops in 1692 and were never rebuilt. The site is open to the public and can be freely explored. In July and August they provide a very evocative setting for a series of classical concerts, and during the annual **Medieval Fair** (www.mittelalter-hirsau.de) in June, the Middle Ages are resurrected for a weekend of jousting and chivalry. An interesting on-site museum details the history of monastic life at the Abbey and its role as a political power center. A model of the complex in its former glory gives a good impression of its impressive architecture.

Calwer Strasse 6, Hirsau. www.kloster-hirsau.de. ✆ **07051/59015.** Open Apr–Oct Tues–Sun 1–4pm, Sat–Sun noon–5pm. Admission 3.50€ adults, 2.50€ children 18 and under.

Exploring Freudenstadt ★

A relative youngster in this neck of the woods, Freudenstadt wasn't founded until 1599, when Duke Frederic of Württemberg decided to establish a residence in the eastern provinces of his territories. At the time, this was a remote, uninhabited wilderness, and the city architect, Heinrich Schickardt, didn't think much of the idea. Still, he had to comply, and he designed a city layout around a central square, surrounded by three rows of houses, with the Duke's castle to take center stage. Construction started—but then the Duke suddenly died. His successor had little interest in the project, and the castle was never built, leaving Freudenstadt with the largest market square in all of Germany. Freudenstadt's most remarkable building is its **Stadtkirche ★** church (✆ **07441/6554;** admission free). Note how its two wings meet at right angles in the corner of the huge market square. This was the city architect's clever way to fit the church into the main square without giving it the central spot, which was reserved for the castle—you know, the one that never got built.

This story is well told at the **Freudenstadt Stadtsmuseum ★** (Marktplatz 65, ✆ **07441/890254;** admission free), as well as the story of the town's rebuilding after a devastating fire in 1632, and another fire in the closing days of WWII. Unlike Pforzheim, Freudenstadt was rebuilt

The Stadtkirche and wide-open market square in Freudenstadt.

gourmet HAVENS

Looking at Freudenstadt one would never guess that one of Germany's number one gourmet destinations lies just up the road, in the tiny village of **Baiersbronn** (6km/ 4 miles northwest of Freudenstadt, along the B462). Baiersbronn just happens to have the highest concentration of Michelin-starred restaurants per square mile than any other place in Germany. The most famous are **Hotel Bareiss** in Mitteltal (see p. 457) and the **Schwarzwaldstube** at **Hotel Traube Tonbachtal** in Tonbachtal (see p. 459). If you are planning to sample their sublime cuisines you should make reservations well in advance. Their success, however, seems to have inspired other chefs in these otherwise tranquil backwaters, and it is almost impossible to find a bad restaurant in the neighborhood. If scoring foodie trophy restaurants is on your radar, here are some of our other personal choices in Baiersbronn:

Restaurant Schlossberg, Hotel Sackmann, Murgtalstr. 602 (www.hotel-sackmann.de; ✆ **07447/2890**).
Restaurant Andreastube, Hotel Engel Obertal, Rechtmurgstrasse 28 (www.engel-obertal.de; ✆ **07449/850**).

Schwarzwaldhotel Tanne, Tonbachstrasse 243 (www.hotel-tanne.de; ✆ **07442/8330**).
Hotel Lamm, Mitteltal, Ellbachstr. 4, Baiersbronn-Mitteltal (www.lamm-mitteltal.de; ✆ **07442/4980**).

close to the original plans; by 1954 it was ready for the tourism boom, a recovery that has been dubbed "the miracle of Freudenstadt."

From Freudenstadt, it's worth taking an afternoon's excursion to **Bad Wildbad ★**. Once a glamorous spa town, where royalty and all its entourage came to stay for weeks or months on end, the town has lost its glamour, but not its nostalgic charm. The Moorish-style **Palais Thermal Spa** (p. 462) is one the most highly rated spas in the Black Forest. Also of note is the **Kurpark arboretum ★**, which was established some 300 years ago in the English landscape gardening style, as was the fashion of the day. The scenic route to Bad Wildbad, which is about 50km (31 miles), follows the B462 north through Baiersbronn to Schönegründ, the L350 east to Seewald, and north on the B294 to Bad Wildbad.

Driving the Black Forest High Road ★★★
Baden-Baden to Waldshut-Tiengen 244km (152 miles)

Planned during the Nazi era, the B500 was created as Germany's first touristic route, to cater to the emerging class of affluent motorists. The panoramic high route was to lead from Baden-Baden in the north to Waldshut-Tiengen in the south, with glamorous hotels at intermittent intervals. The route was never completed; what's here today is a northern part from Baden-Baden to Freudenstadt and a southern section from Triberg to Waldshut-Tiengen (a short wriggle through the upper part of

Kinzig Valley connects the two ends). You can drive this road in either direction, but north to south is the more scenic option, since you're continually looking south toward the high mountains, and later the Alps. To get the most out of this drive, plan on at least a couple of days for sightseeing stops and nature walks.

NORTHERN SECTION: BADEN-BADEN TO FREUDENSTADT

As you head south out of Baden-Baden, the road climbs steadily past Geroldsau and reaches the ridge at **Bühlerhöhe,** the site of a once and future luxury hotel (the grand reopening is scheduled for 2017). Just a stone's throw away, a string of low-key ski-areas—Sand, Mehliskopf, Hundskopf, and Unterstmatt—come to life in the winter, but look rather forlorn during the summer months.

The first real highlight is **Mummelsee ★**, a pretty little tarn at the base of Hornisgrinde Mountain (1264m/4150 ft), the highest peak of the northern Black Forest. Unfortunately, easy access to this beautiful lake has rather ruined its ambience, especially at weekends, when the place is swarming with day-trippers and souvenir-hunters. Continue south past Seibleseckle (more ski-lifts) to **Ruhestein,** where you'll find the headquarters of the new **Black Forest National Park ★** (www.schwarzwald-nationalpark.de; © **07449/92998444**). Created as a "re-wilding" project, where nature can regenerate of its own accord (thus protecting some rare habitats and species), the park will take some time before it resembles anything like "wilderness," after centuries of exploitation, but it is a start. Here, you can detour on a very small winding road (Rte. 5370) to the romantically situated **Allerheiligen Abbey** (ruins) and **Waterfalls** (see p. 451).

Returning to the B500, continue to **Schliffkopf ★★★**, perhaps the route's most accessible panoramic outlook. Look for the big Schliffkopf Wellness Hotel (see p. 462), where you can park your car and walk to an observation platform; a trail to Schliffkopf's summit (1053m/4355 ft) is only about a 10-minute hike. These stunning 360° views are not to be missed if the weather is clear.

Some 3km (2 miles) farther, look for signs pointing to **Lotharpfad ★★**, a half-mile trail built to demonstrate the havoc wreaked by a deadly storm on December 26, 1999. The trail leads through unrestored thickets of fallen trees, dramatically bearing witness to the storm.

As the road snakes along the heights of the central ridge, you can turn off at the Alexanderschanze pass onto the B28 to the ski village of **Kniebis,** where you'll find the **Schwarzwaldhochstrasse Information Center** (Strassburger Strasse 349; www.kniebis.de; © **07442/7570**). From here the road leads down to **Freudenstadt** (see p. 446),

A scenic waterfall tumbles downhill near ruined Allerheiligen Abbey.

where the northern part of the Schwarzwaldhochstrasse officially ends.

Allerheiligen Abbey and Waterfalls ★★★ CHURCH/NATURAL SIGHT Mark Twain was one of the first visitors to this romantic spot and told the story of his walk from Ottenhöfen to Oppenau in *A Tramp Abroad*. The beautifully situated and very atmospheric abbey ruins are freely accessible; a small museum on site illustrates its history. Then follow the lane along the innocuous-looking Lierbach stream, which quite unexpectedly turns into a wildly tumbling fall. The trail to the bottom is about 2km (1.2 mile) long. (Path may be slippery in wet conditions; it's closed in winter.) The hotel where Twain stayed no longer operates as a hotel, but is a nice place for coffee and cake.

Kloster Allerheiiligen, Oppenau. www.klosterhof-allerheiligen.de. Admission free.

CENTRAL SECTION: FREUDENSTADT/TRIBERG/TITISEE

From **Freudenstadt,** take the B294 south to **Lossburg,** once one of the starting points of the St. James' pilgrim routes to Santiago de Compostella. The road now follows the upper Kinzig Valley, the most interesting valley in the Central Black Forest. You'll pass through **Alpirsbach** (see p. 453), the site of an amazingly intact ancient abbey, well-preserved **Schiltach** (see p. 454) at the confluence of the Schiltach and Kinzig rivers, and **Wolfach** (see p. 456) with another cluster of intriguing museums.

About 5km (3 miles) past Wolfach, follow the B33 south through the beautiful **Gutach Valley.** This is the Black Forest heartland, home of such world-famous icons as the cuckoo clock and the *Bollenhut,* a hat with big red bobbles stuck to the top (traditionally worn by unmarried women). Gutach, the first village down that road, is home to the **Vogtsbauernhof,** a very interesting rural life museum (see p. 455). Continue south past Hornberg to **Triberg** (see p. 452)—welcome to cuckoo-clock central! **Warning:** Triberg is overrun with tour buses in summer, and the traffic tie-ups on the road to Triberg can be horrendous.

Cuckoo clocks aside, Triberg also has a good town museum (see p. 454), one of Germany's loveliest churches (see p. 453), and the **Wasserfälle Gutach (Gutach Falls)** ★, Germany's highest waterfall outside the Alps, which drops some 163m (535 ft) in seven misty stages. You can only see them via a footpath (clearly signposted from a parking area near the Gutach Bridge), about an hour's hike roundtrip. Admission to the falls is 4€ adults, 3.50€ students and ages 8 to 17, collected near the café and gift shop at the bottom of the falls.

The world's biggest cuckoo clock, at Eble Uhren-Park in Triberg.

In Triberg the road officially becomes the B500 again and starts to climb up to the ridge once more. Past Schönwald the road reaches **Furtwangen,** an otherwise dull town with an amazing clock museum (see p. 454). Next the road dips down to **Hinterzarten** and **Titisee,** the busiest resort towns in the Hochschwarzwald. The road skirts the beautifully situated **Lake Titisee,** the Black Forest's largest natural lake, and then a few miles further south, **Schluchsee,** a much larger reservoir that's even more popular for water sports. Between the two lakes, however, it would be a shame not to visit **Feldberg,** the highest peak of the Black Forest range (almost 1493m/4900 ft). To get there, turn off the B500 at Bärental and take the B317 to the signposted turn-off to Feldberger Hof. The **Haus der Natur** ★★ (www.naz-feldberg.de; ✆ **07676/933630**) serves as a nature interpretation center and tourist office in one. (Admission to its exhibits costs 3€ adults, 2€ children 6 and older). A cable car takes people to the top of **Seebuck,** the peak just below Feldberg; to reach Feldberg from there, walk across the saddle, an open expanse with fabulous views.

Return to Bärental and rejoin the B500 past Lake Schluchsee. At Häusern, you may want to take another detour down the side road (signposted) to **Sankt Blasien** (see p. 456).

If you ever wanted to see the guts and bolts of a cuckoo clock from the inside, here is your chance. In 1980 the world's first "walk-in cuckoo clock," with a clockwork measuring an impressive 3.50m x 3.30m, opened its doors just north of Triberg in the village of **Schonach** (Untertalstrasse 28, ☏ **07722/2689**). Guided tours cost 2€. In an act of cuckoo clock one-up-manship, in 1994 a competitor from **Triberg** built an even bigger version, with a clockwork measuring 4.50m x 4.50m, which made it into the Guinness book of records. This clock, which is a much more commercial set-up, can be seen at **Eble Uhren-Park,** along the B33 in Schonachbach. If you are in the market for a cuckoo clock (or any kind of timepiece), you have a good chance of finding it in the huge adjacent showroom. Opening times are Easter through October, Mondays to Saturdays 9am to 6pm, Sundays 10am to 6pm; the rest of the year it's open Monday to Saturday 9am to 5.30pm, Sundays 11am to 5pm. Adults pay 2€; it's free for children under 10 accompanied by their parents.

Alpirsbach Kloster ★★★ CHURCH Almost unique in this part of the world, this ancient Benedictine abbey, founded in 1095, is very well preserved; although no longer a monastery, it is still used as a church. During the summer an excellent series of classical music concerts is held here. The on-site museum tells the history of the abbey and monastic life in the Middle Ages. Nowadays Alpirsbach is more readily associated with the beer that the monks used to brew, still produced (though no longer by monks) at the **Alpirsbach Brauwelt** brewery (Marktplatz 1; www.alpirsbacher.de; ☏ **07444/67149**). An interesting brewery museum details the brewery's history and the brewing process; a guided tour runs daily at 2:30, for 7€ adults, 3€ children 6–15. Check out the gift shop, which sells not only beer but a plethora of surprising items made with beer, from shampoo to beer mustard.

Info-Zentrum Kloster, Alpirsbach. ☏ **07444/51061.** Abbey admission 5€ adults, 2.50€ children. Open mid-Mar to Nov, Mon–Sat 10am–5:30pm, Sun 11am–5:30pm, with guided tours at 11:30am, 12:30pm, 1:30pm, 3pm. Nov to mid-Mar, open Thurs–Sun 1pm–3pm, guided tours at 1:30pm.

The Benedictine abbey at Alpirsbach dates back to the 11th century.

Deutsches Uhrenmuseum (German Clock Museum) ★★ MUSEUM Not just a collection of clocks, this museum puts them into their historical, social, and often political context. You'll see everything from folding sundials to elaborately carved grandfather clocks to peppy alarm clocks, from gem-encrusted aristocratic showpieces to the durable mass-produced items that made it possible for everybody to be on time (and to be slaves to the clock!). Although unfortunately there isn't as much information in English as there is in German, this museum is unique and fascinating and well worth a stop.

Gerwigstrasse 11, Furtwangen. www.deutsches-uhrenmuseum.de. ✆ **07723/920800.** Open daily Apr–Oct 10am–6pm, Nov–Mar 10am–5pm. Admission 6€ adults, 5€ children.

Schiltach ★★ TOWN This appealing half-timbered Black Forest town is well worth a stop, even more so because of its cluster of museums. Start in the central Marktplatz at **Museum am Markt ★** (✆ **07836/ 5875**), the town museum, which focuses on the history of Schiltach, the typical occupations of its inhabitants, and working conditions in the 19th century. Across the street, the original town pharmacy is now the **Pharmacy Museum ★** (✆**07836/360**), full of old bottles, powder boxes, and other paraphernalia. Walking into this "shop" is like taking a trip back in time. Located on the Kinzig River, Schiltach thrived as a mill town, a story told at the **Schüttemühle ★★** museum housed in the old wood mill (Hauptstrasse 1, ✆ **07836/5875**). Fittingly, its theme is wood: forestry, rafting, and all the wood-related trades and crafts that once dominated life in the Black Forest. Then take a leap into the modern age by visiting the **Aquademie-Water-Bath-Design Museum ★★** (Auestrasse 9; www.hansgrohe.de/268.htm; ✆ **07836/513272**), the museum-cum-showroom of Schiltach's renowned Hansgrohe company, producers of bathroom fixtures. It even has changing exhibitions on various related topics. Who knew bathrooms could be so interesting? One can easily spend a couple of hours here.

www.schiltach.de. Admission free to all museums except Pharmacy Museum (2€ adults, 1€ children 6 and older). All museums open daily Apr–Nov, variable hours rest of year.

Schwarzwald-Museum Triberg ★★ MUSEUM This surprisingly good Triberg museum houses all sorts of Schwarzwald paraphernalia, from traditional costumes (including some impressive headdresses) to clocks, barrel organs, blown glass vessels, and of course, wood carvings. There are displays of original artisan workshops and an exhibit about the Schwarzwaldbahn railway, opened in 1873, which led to the development of Triberg as a winter sports resort (the European figure skating championships were held here in 1925). An interesting exhibit of minerals can be seen in the basement.

Wallfahrtstrasse 4, Triberg. www.schwarzwaldmuseum.de. © **07722/4434.** Admission € 6 adults, €4 students and ages 5–17. Family discounts available. Open daily Apr–Sept 10am–6pm; Oct–Mar Tues–Sun 10am–5pm.

Vogtsbauernhof ★★★ OPEN-AIR MUSEUM   Set around a lovely river meadow, this fascinating collection of historic farmhouses (some as much as 400 years old) were dismantled and brought here to be reassembled. Each one is unique and reflects the building style of the area where it originated, from thatched roofs to elaborate timbered balconies. Six houses are fully and authentically furnished, with various outbuildings (a bakery, a storehouse, a mill, a forge) set around them. In summer the museum offers an extensive program of workshops to demonstrate traditional crafts such as spinning and weaving, as well as such events as folk music performances in full traditional costume. During July and August free guided tours in English are available daily at 1pm. Depending on one's interest, one can spend hours exploring these old farms. The museum has its own train stop. (**Note:** the location is Gutach im Schwarzwald, NOT im Breisgau)

At the open-air Vogtsbauernhof museum, traditional crafts such a broom-making are demonstrated.

Wählerbrücke 1, Gutach im Schwaarzwald. www.vogtsbauernhof.de. © **07831/ 93560.** Open mid-Mar to early Nov daily 9am–6pm (until 7pm in Aug); last admission 1 hr before closing. Admission 9€ adults, 8€ students, 5€ ages 6–17, families 20.50€–28.50€.

Wallfahrtskirche Maria in der Tanne (Church of Our Lady in the Fir Tree) ★★ CHURCH   An exquisite small pilgrimage church sits on the western edge of Triberg, an 8-minute walk from the center. According to legend, in 1644 a young girl was cured of her eye affliction by the waters of the spring that bubbles up next to the church. A year later a young man was also cured at the site; in gratitude he placed a statue of Mother Mary into the hollow of a fir tree. In the late 17th century a wooden church was built to commemorate the miracles; by the early 18th century a bigger stone church was built to accommodate the growing numbers of pilgrims. The restrained, simple white exterior belies the rich baroque ornamentation inside, including a beautifully ornate high altar that's among the most significant baroque altars in southwest Germany.

Clemens-Maria-Hofbauer Strasse, Triberg © **07722/4566.** Open year-round, daily from 8am to 7pm. Admission free.

Wolfach ★★ TOWN   Set charmingly at the meeting of the Wolf and Kinzig rivers, this town offers two of the Black Forest's more unusual museums. At the **Dorotheenhütte** ★★ (Glashüttenweg 4; www. dorotheenhuette.info; © **07834/83980**) you can visit one of the last active glassblowing workshops in the Black Forest. The on-site museum provides an overview of the history of glassmaking, while the workshop lets you watch the traditional process of making glass bottles and goblets—you can even have a go yourself. Of course, there is a gift shop, too. Admission is 5€ adults, 3€ children 6 to 18; a guided tour costs another 1€. Then, a 10-minute drive up the Wolf River in Oberwolfach, you can marvel at nature's mysteries at the superb **Mineralien und Mathematik Museum (Museum for Minerals and Mathematics)** ★★★ (Schulstrasse 5, Oberwolfach; www.mima.museum; © **07834/9420**). This unique museum investigates interactively the mathematics of nature, e.g. the complex designs of crystalline structures. Models, art, and computer simulations are all used to throw light onto the subject. This fascinating and unique learning space is open daily (closed November to mid-December); admission is 5€ adults, 3€ children 6 and up. Guided tours are available, but they must be booked in advance.

SOUTHERN SECTION

The southernmost part of the Black Forest is the most sparsely populated region. After **Sankt Blasien,** a small village known mostly for the over-sized dome of its cathedral (see below), the road soon starts to descend to the Rhine Valley and reaches the beautiful old twin town of **Waldshut-Tiengen,** on the border to Switzerland, at the end point of the B500.

Sankt Blasius Cathedral ★   St. Blasien's history goes back to the Middle Ages, when it started as a hermitage during the 9th century. Badly damaged during the peasant uprising in the 16th century, it finally succumbed to a fire in 1768. Over the ruins, this replacement church was a bold Enlightenment statement with its immense dome, 36 meters (118 ft) in diameter. The new church opened in 1781, but by 1806 the monastery was dissolved in a wave of secularization. Monks no longer live here, but it still functions as a cathedral, and in the summer it hosts a series of classical concerts.

Fürstabt-Gerbert-Str. 16, Sankt Blasien. www.dom-st-blasien.de. © **07672/678.** Admission free. Open daily 8am–6:30 pm, except during mass; closes 5pm in winter.

Where to Stay & Eat in the Black Forest

Most of your options, especially in the countryside, will be inns and guesthouses that offer both food and guest rooms. If you plan to spread your Black Forest High Road drive over more than one day, here are some characterful and welcoming places to stay. Look through the list as well for your best dining options along the drive.

FREUDENSTADT

Hotel Bären ★   This conveniently located family-run hotel in a 19th-century building near the Marktplatz offers good value. Although recently renovated, rooms are conservatively furnished in plain colors and trim built-ins, without pretensions or frills. The restaurant is kept in rustic traditional style, as is the food that is served there. The menu consists of hearty German/Swabian dishes that won't leave you hungry. Main courses are from 14€ to 22€.

Langestrasse 33, Freudenstadt. www.hotel-baeren-freudenstadt.de.© **07441/2729.** 36 units. 82€–120€ double. 15€ children 3–6, 25€ children 7–13. Free parking. **Amenities:** Restaurant; room service; Wi-Fi (free).

Hotel Bareiss ★★★   This classy hotel is a family business that has built its reputation over several generations. The hotel is a large complex with a wide range of individually decorated, sophisticated, and supremely comfortable rooms and suites. Many rooms have balconies overlooking the landscaped grounds. There is a large luxurious wellness area with several indoor and outdoor pools, a fitness room, and saunas. Beauty and spa treatments are available. Many different packages, including wellness and yoga specials, and even cooking classes can be booked. Unlike many other high-end hotels in this category, Bareiss regards itself as a family hotel and welcomes children—they have several different children's spaces, an adventure playground, and a treehouse, and they provide entertainment and games for their youngest guests. The hotel has several restaurants, decorated in different styles. Although the quality of food at all the restaurants is top-notch, the elegant **Bareiss** restaurant, which has 3 Michelin stars, is a destination in and of itself. You'll need to make reservations well in advance, and appropriate dinner attire is required; note that the Bareiss restaurant is closed for a month in summer and for 3 weeks in February. To get here from the center of Baiersbronn, head northwest (L401) towards Mitteltal, following signs pointing to Hotel Bareiss (5km/3 miles). *Note:* Credit cards are accepted at the à la carte restaurants, but not for paying the hotel bill.

Hotel Bareiss' resort amenities include pools, a spa, and a top-notch restaurant.

Gärtenbühlweg 14, Baiersbronn/Mitteltal. www.bareiss.com. ℰ **07442/470.** 127 units. 240€–305€ per person double. Breakfast and dinner included. Parking 14€ (garage). **Amenities:** 5 restaurants; 2 bars; smoker's lounge, babysitting; bikes; children's programs; exercise room; 4 pools (2 indoor); room service; spa; outdoor tennis court (lit), Wi-Fi (free).

Hotel Hohenried im Rosengarten ★★

Located about a 15-minute walk south of Freudenstadt's town center, this charming chalet-style hotel offers great value for a relaxing stay. Spacious rooms are simply decorated with white walls and traditional country furniture; many have a balcony. The hotel has a tidy indoor pool and a lovely garden with more than 2,000 rosebushes. A nice perk is the fact that visitors staying 2 nights or longer receive a complementary guest card (Schwarzwald Plus card), which offers free entrance to many attractions in the northern Black Forest. (See www.schwarzwaldplus.de.)

Zeppelinstrasse 5–7, Freudenstadt. www.hotelhohenried.de. ℰ **07441/2414.** 25 units. 80€–140€ double. **Amenities:** Restaurant; bar; exercise room; indoor pool; room service; sauna; massage on request; Wi-Fi (in some rooms; free); free garage parking.

Hotel Traube Tonbach ★★★ Located in another valley, but also part of Baiersbronn, this is another top-notch hotel and gourmet restaurant. A family-run business, they pride themselves on providing personal and attentive service. In both a main building and a more modern annex, the Traube has many different room types, in styles both traditional (warm wood accents, country fabrics) and modern chic (hardwood floors and neutral color schemes); all have balconies or terraces. The restaurants, too, range from rustic and cozy to high-end and elegant, culminating in the renowned **Schwarzwaldstube** restaurant, which, under longtime chef Harald Wohlfahrt, has 3 Michelin stars. Unusually, it offers a full vegetarian tasting menu. If you want to eat here, make your reservations well in advance; formal attire is required. With a large wellness and spa area, the Traube offers special packages including yoga and gourmet retreats; there's even a cookery school offering classes throughout the year. *Note:* Credit cards are not accepted for paying the hotel bill.

Tonbachstrasse 237, Baiersbronn/Tonbach. www.traubetonbach.de. ☎ **07442/4920.** 153 units. 239€–499€ double. Buffet breakfast and afternoon snack included; half-board available. Parking 11€. **Amenities:** 4 restaurants; bar; babysitting; bikes; children's center; health club and spa; 3 pools (2 indoor); whirlpool, saunas, room service; Wi-Fi (free).

Warteck ★ In the historic town center, this traditional restaurant-with-rooms offers a conservative German/Swabian cuisine in a rather formal wood-paneled setting. Although not the most creative, food is of good quality, but prices are quite steep. Apart from a wide range of meat dishes they also offer a variety of fish dishes, such as loup de mer with sunchoke puree, or monkfish medallions with sesame vegetables and Canadian wild rice. Unfortunately, they don't provide much choice for vegetarians. The restaurant's hotel offers 13 recently renovated doubles, costing from 98€ to 105€, including breakfast.

Stuttgarter Strasse 14, Freudenstadt. ☎ **07441/91920.** www.warteck-freudenstadt. de. Reservations recommended. Main courses 20€–43€. Tue–Sat noon–2pm and 6–9pm, Sun lunchtime only.

PFORZHEIM

Parkhotel Pforzheim ★★ For a somewhat typical modern business and conference hotel, this one is well-run, modern, clean, and pleasant, with a nice riverside location. Rooms are spacious, bright, and comfortable, decorated in corporate-style blond woods and neutral color schemes. A spa and wellness area on the top floor has saunas, a Jacuzzi, and a steam room. Downstairs, the **Parkrestaurant** serves a large and varied menu of German and international food, including items such as salmon and king prawn skewer with spring onion and coconut chilli risotto, or lamb roast in thyme jus with ratatouille and potato gratin; there are vegetarian options as well. Main courses cost around 14€ to 30€. In Pforzheim, this is about as upscale a dining experience as you are likely to find, but don't set your hopes too high.

Deimlingstrasse 32-36. www.parkhotel-pforzheim.de. © **07231/1610.** 208 units. 152€–177€ double. Buffet breakfast included. Parking 10€. **Amenities:** 2 restaurants; bar; exercise room; Jacuzzi; room service; sauna; Wi-Fi (free).

ALONG THE BLACK FOREST HIGH ROAD

Bergseestüble ★★   This friendly little Triberg guesthouse is located by a little lake, right next to Maria in der Tanne church (see p. 456). If you don't mind church bells in the morning this is a great budget option. They offer 3 doubles with a kitchenette and a small breakfast table, and 2 family apartments. The cooking facilities are not suitable for anything ambitious, but nice if you don't want to go out for every cup of tea or sandwich. Rooms are simple but tastefully decorated, with good-sized bathrooms. Somewhat unusually, they do not serve breakfast in the restaurant. If you order breakfast (not included in the room rate), they place a basket filled with bread rolls, lunch meats, ham, cheese, yogurt, jam, and coffee or tea outside your room, so you can have breakfast in your room. The small restaurant is very good, offering freshly prepared and tasty dishes, although the choice is limited. If you are not looking for a fine dining experience, it's the best option in town. Reservations recommended.

Clemens-Maria-Hofbauerstrasse 19, Triberg, www.bergseestueble.com © **07722/ 916444.** 5 units. 59€ double, 74€ triple, loft apartment 64€ with double occupancy. Breakfast basket 8€ per person. **Amenities:** Restaurant; playground; Wi-Fi (free).

Hotel Imbery ★★   A lovely traditional family-run hotel in a convenient location in Hinterzarten, the Hotel Imbery's cheery country-style rooms are spacious, well-appointed, and very clean. Bathrooms are not super modern, but perfectly functional. This isn't a fancy hotel, but very good value for money with friendly and helpful staff. The pleasant restaurant serves German regional food, including vegetarian options. The breakfast buffet is plentiful.

Rathausstrasse 14, Hinterzarten. © **07652/91030.** www.hotel-imbery.de. 28 units. 72€–116€ double. Breakfast included. **Amenities:** Restaurant; sauna; lounge; bike/ ski storage; Wi-Fi (free).

Hotel Therme Bad Teinach ★★   Set in the charming village of Bad Teinach-Zavelstein, Hotel Therme with its on-site spa facilities is the best option in this region for a relaxing and classy sojourn. This classic spa hotel looks a bit stern from the outside, with its stone columns and paved courtyard, but don't let that put you off. In 2015 a new wing was added with chic loft-like rooms, most of which overlook the lovely park.

Rooms in the main building, which still sport a more dated traditional look, are less expensive. Renovations of the outside spa areas should be completed in 2016. Sleek indoor spa areas are all new and accessible free of charge to hotel guests. Book the half-board option to save some money on dinner.

Otto-Neidhart-Allee 5, Bad Teinach. www.hotel-therme-teinach.de. ✆ **07053/290.** 119 units. 145€–255€ double. Breakfast included. Parking 7.50€ (garage). **Amenities:** 2 restaurants, bar, spa, saunas, gym, room service, Wi-Fi (free).

Park Hotel Adler ★★★   If you really want to stay somewhere fancy in the Black Forest, this is the place. Like an apparition from another era, Adler hotel exudes 5-star elegance. Set in a well-kept park-like estate, the hotel offers a long roster of leisure activities (badminton, anyone?) and a superb spa with an indoor and outdoor pool, outdoor Jacuzzi, sauna, steam room, beauty salon, and gym. Each room is individually decorated, with rich-toned designer fabrics, eclectic furnishings, and witty accents. Room types range from generous singles to a family suite with space for up to 3 children. A word of warning: There is no air-conditioning, and Wi-Fi may not work reliably in all the rooms. Both of the hotel's restaurants serve fine creative cuisine—you won't find any schnitzels here! The menu changes seasonally, but may include such delicacies as pheasant with juniper, rose hips, and sweet chestnuts, or venison with parsnips, rowan berries, and shallot crullers. Vegetarians might choose from truffle tagliatelle or pumpkin ravioli with sage butter, almond nougat, fermented nuts, and Belper knolle cheese shavings. If you intend to eat at the hotel, book a half-board package in advance to get a discount on the fixed-price menu.

Adlerplatz 3, Hinterzarten. www.parkhoteladler.de. ✆ **07652/1270.** 56 units. 199€– 299€ double. Buffet breakfast included. Parking 12€, in underground garage 15€. **Amenities:** 2 restaurants; bar; cafe, babysitting; gym; indoor pool; room service; spa, beauty salon, WIFI (free).

Romantik Parkhotel Wehrle ★★   A wellness hotel with old-world charm and landed gentry flair, this hotel is right on Triberg's busy main street, 1 mile from the train station, with additional lodgings in three other villas grouped around an adjacent park. Main building rooms have traditional Biedermeier or "rural baroque" furnishings, while the newer guest villa rooms go for a sleeker modern style. Parkside rooms are quieter and slightly more expensive; some have direct access to the spa area, which is also open to non-hotel guests (9:30am to 6pm). The spa has a sauna, a Turkish bath, and a steam room, as well as a pool and a gym. Wellness packages are an especially good deal, including a fixed price dinner menu as well as spa use and overnight accommodations. As restaurants in Triberg go, this is the closest you will find to fine dining.

Menu offerings change seasonally, but local trout is a house specialty that is always available. Food quality is good, but quite expensive (tasting menus 35€-65€) and not particularly imaginative. Vegetarian options are boring.

Gartenstrasse 24, Triberg. www.parkhotel-wehrle.de. ✆ **07722/86020.** 50 units. 155€—179€ doubles. Children 5–12 25€, 12–15 35€. Buffet breakfast included. Free parking outdoors; 6€ in garage. **Amenities:** 3 restaurants; bar; gym; 2 indoor pools; saunas, steam bath, whirlpool, room service; spa; Wi-Fi (free).

Schliffkopf Wellness Hotel ★★★ If you want to stay in nature, this place is unbeatable for its gorgeous views and a location almost at the highest point of the Schwarzwaldhochstrasse. Although the boxy modern building looks a bit dated and not exactly beautiful on the outside, the inside has been smartly renovated recently with a casual modern décor in earth tones. Many rooms have balconies, and top floor rooms have some amazing views. This is a wellness hotel, fitted with a small spa area, pool, and sauna; massages, beauty treatments, and yoga sessions are available. The hotels' restaurants carry out the wellness theme, offering lighter options alongside hearty meals; lactose- or gluten-free and vegetarian /vegan options are available on request.

Schwarzwaldhochstrasse, 1, Schliffkopf. www.schliffkopf.de. ✆ **07449/9200.** 70 units. 99€–146€ per person in double. **Amenities:** 2 restaurants, bar, lounge, spa, saunas, indoor and outdoor pool, room service, Wi-Fi (free).

Trescher's Schwarzwaldhotel am See ★★ A large lakeshore resort complex, Trescher's has a picture-book setting right on Lake Titisee. Ample-sized rooms are conservatively decorated in soft, soothing colors; some rooms have their own balconies and the suites and apartments are especially spacious. Not all rooms have views of the lake, but the fine-dining restaurant (evening wear expected) has glorious picture windows and a nice terrace over the lake. The pools and sleek spa area are beautiful and very relaxing, but unfortunately they close in the evening. At weekends a minimum stay of 2 nights is required, but a 2-night stay earns you a guest card that gives free admission to many local attractions.

Seestrasse 10, Titisee-Neustadt. www.schwarzwaldhotel-trescher.de. ✆ **07651/8050.** 84 units. 81€–140€ per person double. Buffet breakfast included. Outside parking free, garage parking 15€ (reservation required) **Amenities:** 3 restaurants; bar; wine bar; exercise room; indoor pool; outdoor pool; private beach; spa and wellness area, sauna; room service, mountain bikes; Wi-Fi (free).

Black Forest Spas

The Black Forest area is rich in hot mineral springs, which have been developed at a number of spas. Along with these, many excellent "wellness hotels" in the region also have spa facilities—check out **Trescher i, Hotel Bareiss** (p. 457), and **Traube Tonbach** (p. 459), above.

Palais Thermal ★★★ SPA This exquisite spa is a bath temple with exotic ambience. The historic baths on the ground floor comprises

The sleek indoor pool and wellness area at Hotel Traube Tonbach.

several different pools of different temperatures, with whirlpools and massage jets. On the upper floors is the sauna area and small, more intimate baths and jacuzzi-type pools. Downstairs, in the regular pool area, clothing is **optional,** the upper floors and sauna area are textile-free. This is not a spa for the prudish!

Kernerstrasse 5, Bad Wildbad, www.palais-thermal.de, ✆ **07081/3030.** Mon–Fri noon–10pm, Sat–Sun 10am–10pm. Admission Mon–Fri adults 16€ for 2h, additional hours 2€; day pass 21.50€; weekends add 1.50€ on all prices.

Paracelsus-Therme und Sauna Pinea ★ SPA   Blessed with seven hot springs, Bad Liebenzell was destined to become a spa town—which it has been, since at least the 15th century. However, it never reached the fame and fortune of some of the other spa towns in the region. The modern spa complex has been completely renovated in 2012. It has an indoor and an outdoor pool, whirlpools, and various massage jets as well as steam rooms and saunas with a separate outdoor pool and a terrace with views of the ancient castle above the town. On Thursdays the sauna is for women only.

Reuchlinweg 4, Bad Liebenzell, www.paracelsus-therme.de; ✆ **07052/408603.** Open daily 9am–10pm. Day pass 12€ pools only, 18.50€ with sauna. A 2-hr pass 9.50€ pools, 13.50€ with sauna; 3-hr pass 10€ pools, 16€ with sauna. Children under 5 not permitted.

Wunderhiking in the Black Forest

The best way to see the Black Forest is on foot. The region offers an idyllic blend of charming villages, bucolic countryside and pine clad mountains with comfortable lodgings and excellent food waiting at the end of the day. The entire mountain range is crisscrossed by an excellent, well-marked and maintained network of trails. The most famous long-distance trail, the **Westweg**, runs more or less parallel to the B500, along the entire length of the Black Forest, from Pforzheim to Basel. Inaugurated in 1900, it is one of Germany's oldest routes, a classic long-distance hill walk. But there are also many shorter routes, including **Schluchtensteig** in the southern Black Forest, which explores the area's most impressive gorge, the Wutachschlucht;

or **Zweitälersteig,** a circular route that starts and ends in Waldkirch, north of Freiburg. You'll also find charming wine trails that amble through vineyards and wine villages on the edge of the mountains. The tourist board offers some of these as "hiking-without-luggage" packages, each route sectioned into day stages of approximately 20-27km (12-16 miles). Accommodations are pre-booked and your main luggage is transferred from hotel to hotel, so you only have to carry a day pack. The terrain is not particularly demanding, although at times it can be quite steep. Tourist offices in every town and village can advise you on walking trails, long or short. For more information see: **www.blackforest-tourism.com/discovery/hiking**.

Sports & Outdoor Pursuits

AQUA PARKS   In the lake area around Titisee and Schluchsee, it's not enough just to swim in the lake—big chlorinated swimming pools and aqua parks have been built on the lakeshores as well. **Aqua Fun ★★** on Schluchsee (Freiburger Strasse 16, ✆ **07656/7731,** 4€ adults, 2.70€ children, open May–Sept 9am–7pm) has a huge outdoor pool with a waterslide, current-channel pool, massage jet, and whirlpool, as well as a playground and beach ball area. On Titisee, **Schwimmbad Titisee ★** (Strandbadstrasse, ✆ **07651/8272,** 3.50€ adults, 1.90€ children 17 and under, open May to mid-Sept 9am–7pm) has an outdoor pool, a sandy beach, cabanas, showers, and refreshment stands; you can rent stand-up paddle boards and kayaks for €10 per half-hour. Titisee's newest attraction, **Badeparadies Schwarzwald ★★★** (Am Badeparadies 1, www.badeparadies-schwarzwald.de, ✆ **0080004444333,** day passes 20€–25€) goes one better, giving water lovers year-round fun in a huge indoor glass complex with tropical island design, complete with restaurants and pool-bars, waterslides for kids, and a quieter adult space for relaxation; there's also a sauna and wellness area for ages 16 and up.

BOATING   On Lake Titisee, the Black Forest's largest natural lake, both **Drubba** (Seestrasse 37; en.boote-titisee.de, ✆ **07651/9812948**) and **Schweizer-Winterhalder** (www.bootsbetrieb-schweizer-titisee.de;

(✆ **07651/8214**) operate hourly 25-minute excursions on lake steamers that circumnavigate the lake, from June through September. Fares are 5€ adult, 2.50€ ages 4-12. Or if you prefer, you can also rent pedal boats or electric boats, from 6€ per half-hour.

CYCLING   Marked bicycle routes and trails run throughout the Black Forest region. Some routes would require pretty strong legs, as they run through the mountains, but e-bikes are available, making it a bit easier on the uphill sections. The most leisurely routes follow the rivers, such as the **Kinzigtal Radweg** (total length 90 km/59 miles—see www. kinzigtal.com for details), the **Nagold Radweg** (103 km/64 miles; see www.fahrrad-tour.de/Nagold) and **Enztal Radweg** (around 100km/62 miles; see www.enztalradweg.de). The Enztal and Nagold trails can be done as day routes from Pforzheim. The best multistage bicycle routes are the **Schwarzwald Panorama Radweg** (280km/174 miles), which runs the entire length of the Black Forest from Pforzheim to Basel, and the **Südschwarzwald Radweg** (264 km/164 miles), a circuit through the southern Black Forest. Multi-stage bicycle tours can be booked as packages, with luggage forwarding; for details, see www.schwarzwald-tourismus.info for details.

A SWISS detour

From Waldshut-Tiengen it is an easy 80km (50 miles) ride to Lake Constance, curving just a little into Switzerland. Head east via Schaffhausen, a little Swiss enclave on the northern shore of the Rhine. Schaffhausen has a lovely old town center and an interesting history/culture/art museum, **Museum zu Allerheiligen** ★★ (Klosterstrasse 16, www.allerheiligen.ch; ✆ **41 052/6330777**), set in a lovely old abbey complex. Admission costs F12 adults, free for ages 25 and under.

Just west of Schaffhausen, in Neuhausen, make a detour to see the **Rhine Falls,** the biggest falls in continental Europe (for more information, go to www.rheinfall.ch/en/). Frequent boat tours provide an even more impressive view of the falls (www.rhyfall-maendli.ch; ✆ **41 052/67248 11**).

About halfway along route 13, the picturesque Upper Rhine town of **Stein am Rhein** is a true gem, with almost all the old houses in its historic town center featuring elaborately painted facades and oriel windows. Its one must-see

attraction is **Museum Lindwurm** ★★★ (Understadt 18; www.museum-lindwurm. ch, ✆ **41 052/7412512;** open March to November), which offers a window into the past in an 1850 patrician townhouse decorated in then-fashionable Biedermeier style. Admission costs F5 adults, F3 students

Note: To use Swiss motorways (green signs) you will need a toll tag known as "vignette," which are available at gas stations near the border. There is no charge for minor roads such as Route 13.

LAKE CONSTANCE/BODENSEE ★★

The combination of a mild climate, gorgeous scenery, interesting sights and history—not to mention the excellent food and wealth of watersports—make Lake Constance (Bodensee) a top vacation spot. The lake shares its 260km (160-mile) shoreline between three nations, Austria, Germany, and Switzerland, which all contribute to the region's cultural and historical heritage. Artists and writers in particular have long been drawn to the sublime beauty of the region, with its charming old towns, framed by vineyard-covered hills and orchards, dotted around the shore.

Essentials

VISITOR INFORMATION

The tourist office in **Konstanz** is at Bahnhofplatz 43 (www.konstanz-tourismus.de; ✆ **07531/133030**). **Lindau's** is at Alfred-Nobel-Platz 1 (www.lindau-tourismus.de; ✆ **08382/260030**). Both of these are open daily April to October, Monday to Friday the rest of the year. **Meersburg Tourismus,** at Kirchstrasse 4 (www.meersburg.de; ✆ **07532/440400**), is open Monday to Friday year-round.

GETTING AROUND

BY TRAIN   Frequent local trains run along the north shore, connecting Überlingen, Friedrichshafen, and Lindau. While Konstanz is a useful rail hub to other parts of the country, local boat service is a more scenic way to get from Konstanz to other towns on the lake.

BY BUS   Regional bus service along Lake Constance is offered by **RAB Regionalverkehr Alb-Bodensee GmbH** (www.zugbus-rab.de, ✆ **07541/30130**). Bus service around the town of Konstanz is provided by **SBG Südbaden Bus GmbH** at Radolfzell (www.suedbadenbus.de; ✆ **07732/994724**).

BY BOAT   Perhaps the best (if not always the fastest or cheapest) way to get around this region is via ferry service and lake cruises, which operate between Konstanz, Mainau Island, Meersburg, Lindau, and Bregenz, Austria. The entire trip from one end of the lake to the other takes no less than 4 hours. The operator is **Bodensee-Schiffsbetriebe,** Hafenstrasse 6 (www.bsb-online.com; ✆ **07531/3640389**). The timetable for ferries changes every month, so check locally. The cost is 5€ to 19€. A catamaran also runs between Konstanz and Friedrichshafen; contact www.der-katamaran.de; ✆ **07531/3639320.**

BY CAR   Coming from Schaffhausen and Stein am Rhein (see p. 465), take route 13 (Swiss) along the Rhine. Otherwise, take the B33 via Radolfzell. From Munich take the A96 Autobahn west to Lindau. From Friedrichshafen follow the B31 east around the lake.

REGIONAL TRANSPORT PASS For destinations around the lake, the easiest solution is to buy a **Euregiokarte** day pass which covers the whole region, including Swiss and Austrian destinations around the lake. Day passes are valid on buses, local trains, and ferries. The card's pricing system divides the lake into 3 zones: Depending on where you want to go you can get a 1-, 2-, or all-zones pass. A family discount is available for up to 2 adults traveling with up to 4 children. Euregiocard holders also receive discounts on admission at some of the attractions around the lake. See www.euregiokarte.com or call ✆ **41 0512/234920** for details.

SPECIAL EVENTS

Throughout the summer, many festive events take place at towns all around the lake. The season is kicked off by the month-long **Bodensee Festival** in April and May (www.bodenseefestival.de, ✆ **07541/ 2033300**), which, following a different theme each year, offers a mix of concerts, theatrical productions, films, and exhibitions at various locations around the lake. Ticket prices vary; some are even free. A fountain flows with wine instead of water at the **Winzerfest** wine festival in Meersburg the first weekend in July (www.meersburg.de). Konstanz' main event is the open-air **Sommernächte** festival (www.sommer-naechte.com; ✆ **07531/993399**) in early August, where an eclectic mix of bands performs in the city gardens, followed later in August by the one-day **Rock Am See Festival** (www.rock-am-see.de; ✆ **07531/ 908844**), which since 1985 has been drawing big names in rock music (in recent years Kings of Leon, the Hives, and Green Day) to the lakeside Bodensee-Stadion in Konstanz. On a weekend in early September the focus turns to wine again in Meerburg for the **Bodensee Weinfest** (Lake Constance Wine Festival; see www.meersburg.de), while at the other end of the lake Lindau hoists its steins for a city-wide **Oktoberfest** (www.lindau-tourismus.de).

Exploring Around Lake Constance

The three key towns around the lake, where most of the activity takes place, are Konstanz, Friedrichshafen and Lindau, but smaller towns like Meersburg or Überlingen should not be ignored. These tiny historic towns hold plenty of interest to warrant a visit, or even an overnight stay. Beginning in Konstanz, we'll move around the lake clockwise, visiting various town on the German shore.

EXPLORING KONSTANZ (CONSTANCE) ★★★

Konstanz is one of the oldest settlements around the lake, with origins that date back to Neolithic Age times. The strategic advantage of the location at the bay of the Rhine was not lost on the Romans either, who established an important trading point and military outpost here in their effort to defend their borders against the Alemannen. From 1414–1418 Konstanz played host to what was probably the most important event of the Middle Ages, the pivotal Council of Constance, whose task it was to end the schism and reform the church. As many as 15,000 people descended on the town and stayed for a full four years—mostly nobles and bishops with their entire entourage attending to their needs.

During WWII the town managed to escape devastation and thus much of its historic town center has been preserved. The charming, narrow alleyways and hidden corners are fun to discover. Today Konstanz is not only a commercial center, but also a university town, with a vibrant, buzzing energy.

The best way to see Konstanz is from the water. The shoreline is fascinating, with little inlets that weave in and out around ancient buildings and city gardens. Several pleasure ships offer tours along the city shoreline, across the lake to **Meersburg,** and several other destinations.

Not surprisingly, the focal point of Konstanz is its harbor. At the north end of the harbor stands the massive brown-roofed **Konzilgebäude (Council Building),** where the Council of Constance met. The building was originally constructed as a storehouse in 1388, but came to be used for meetings. Restored in 1911, the hall is decorated with murals depicting the history of the town. On the harbor in front is a giant, rather audacious monument of the courtesan **Imperia,** who is said to have held both the king and the pope in her hands, during those fateful years of the Council. Just north of here, the lovely **city gardens** are the site of outdoor concerts in summer.

The towers of the **basilica** rise behind the city garden. The first church was built here in 585, one of the first Christian sites north of the Alps. After extensive remodeling during the 9th–10th century it became the grandest Romanesque church of its time. During the 13th–15th century it was embellished with Gothic elements, but the neo-Gothic spire was not added until 1856. If you are feeling energetic you can climb the 193 steps (40m) to admire the view of the lake, the city and the Alps from the top.

Mainau Island ★★★ GARDEN   The unusual, almost subtropical island of Mainau lies 6km (4 miles) north of Konstanz, in an arm of the Bodensee known as the Überlingersee. Here, palms and orange trees grow and fragrant flowers bloom year-round (in the greenhouse), practically in the shadow of the snow-covered Alps. The lake regulates the temperatures and, protected from harsh winter winds, the island enjoys a mild microclimate where vegetation can grow year-round. The most delicate of tropical plants are given greenhouse protection. The late

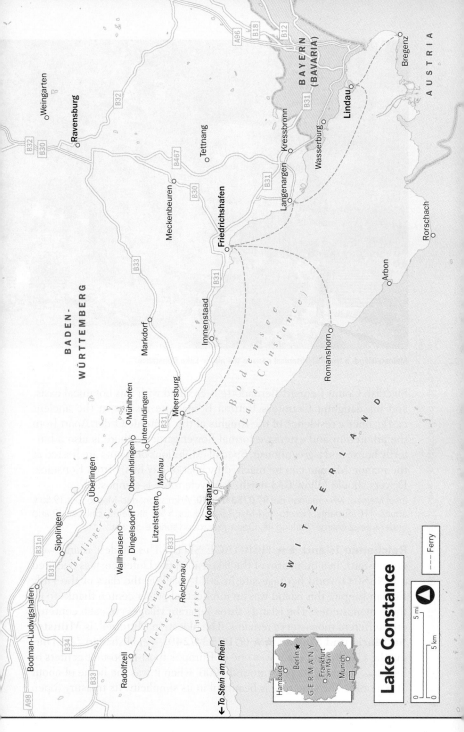

469

Mainau Island, a tropical botanical oasis in the alpine Lake Constance.

Swedish Count Lennart Bernadotte is credited with this botanical oasis, and his daughter Countess Bettina Bernadotte resides in the ancient castle, once a residence of the Knights of the Teutonic Order. Apart from the arboretum and extensive formal flower gardens, there is also a butterfly house and a greenhouse. Special exhibitions or events are hosted at the manor. Mainau can be reached by boat or city bus 4 from Konstanz. Drivers should follow B33 north. A bicycle route is signposted.

Insel Mainau, www.mainau.de; © **07531/3030.** Admission: mid-Mar to Oct 19.50 € adults, 11€ students, Nov to mid-Mar 9.50€ adults, 5.50€ students, children 12 and under free of charge. Parking 4€. Open year round sunrise–sunset.

Reichenau Island ★★ HERITAGE SITE   This modest island west of Konstanz, in a quiet arm of the lake called the Untersee, was declared a UNESCO world heritage site in 2011. Back in the days of the Holy Roman Empire this island was an intellectual power center, thanks to its three monasteries. The island's three separate villages are each centered on a different monastery's remains. The oldest, in Mittelzell, is **Münster St. Maria und Markus ★★** (© **07534/249**), established in 724. During the Carolingian era it was one of Europe's most important centers of learning, reaching its peak around 1000, when it was the home of about 700 monks. The structure is beautiful in its simplicity. Its treasury (open

May-October, admission 2€ adults, 1€ students) displays several reliquaries, including the original St. Mark reliquary, as well as a rare 9th-century book of Gospels. Niederzell's **Stiftskirche St. Peter and St. Paul ★**, founded a few years later in 799, was extensively remodeled at various points in its history; during a 1990 restoration, a series of Romanesque frescoes were uncovered in the apse and are now on view. In Oberzell, the dignified **Stiftskirche St. George ★**, founded in 888, looks rather plain on the outside, but the inside reveals elaborately painted walls covered in charmingly naive medieval frescoes. All three churches are open daily year-round; admission is free. Stop in Mittelzell's **Museum Reichenau ★★** to fill in more of the historic context, with its displays of art and artifacts. Today, the island is a bucolic center for vegetable cultivation, a heritage that makes sense once you visit the **Kräutergarten (Herb Garden) ★**, based on a layout designed by 9th-century abbot Walahfrid Strabo, author of the classic poem "Liber de Cultura Hortulum." It's next to the cathedral in Mittelzell.

www.reichenau-tourismus.de. ℂ **07534/92070.** Museum Reichenau: www.museum reichenau.de, ℂ **07534/999321;** admission 3€ adults, 1.50€ children 7 and up; open Apr–Oct daily 10:30am–4:30pm (until 5:30pm July–Aug); Nov–Mar Sat–Sun 2–5pm.

EXPLORING ÜBERLINGEN ★★

42km (26 miles) N of Konstanz, 15km (9 miles) W of Meersburg, 24km (15 miles) W of Friedrichshafen

Überlingen, founded in the 1200s, is sometimes touted as a German version of Nice, because of its sunny weather and long lakeside promenade. But it does not really need any such pompous comparisons—thanks to a very well-preserved medieval town center, it possesses a charm that is all its own. Be sure to make time to stroll the **city gardens,** a botanical gem first established in 1875 that has been steadily embellished ever since with the addition of exotic plants from all over the world, such as Atlas cedar, handkerchief tree, and sequoias growing alongside bananas, fig trees, and cacti.

Franziskanerkirche ★ CHURCH   Overlooking the lakeside landing plaza, this church's modest exterior give you no clue that inside is a lavishly baroque interior, thanks to an 18th-century remodeling during the era when Rococo had become wildly fashionable. The church is sometimes used as a setting for classical concerts.

Landungsplatz 5, Überlingen. ℂ **07551/9471529.** Admission free. Open daily 10am–5pm.

Münster St. Nikolaus ★★ CHURCH   The most important of Überlingen's monuments is the minster, a surprisingly large gothic medieval structure that required 200 years to build. The larger of its two towers

lake living ON STILTS

In Unteruhldingen, about halfway between Überlingen and Meersburg, a unique and fascinating outdoor museum is dedicated to preserving ancient traces of a very special civilization: dwellings built on stilts above the lake waters, which date back to about 4500 B.C. The remains of these dwellings, which have been found submerged all around Lake Constance, have collectively been declared a UNESCO World Heritage site.

At the **Pfahlbauten Museum ★★★** (Strandpromenade 6, Uhldingen-Mühlhofen, www.pfahlbauten.de, ℂ **07556/928900**), some of these dwellings have been reconstructed to allow visitors to get a real glimpse of this distant past. Beside a cluster of stilted houses set over the lake waters (today on sturdy platforms, not stilts, linked by wooden causeways), a Neolithic shore settlement of reed-roofed huts has been reconstructed as well, with ancient tools and artifacts. Museum staff demonstrate Bronze Age crafts, as well as how to make fire—the Stone Age way. A Time Trail looping around the museum grounds leads you past 20 stations explaining in chronological order the early development of civilization along the shores of the lake.

To get there, take bus 7395 from Meersburg or Friedrichshafen to Unteruhldingen/Meersburger Strasse and follow the signs (about a 5-minute walk). Drivers should follow the B31 to Unteruhldingen, park by the tourist information, then walk or take the shuttle to the museum. Admission is 9€ adults, 7€ students, 6€ ages 6-15. The museum is open mid-March to mid-Sept 9am to 6:30pm.

functioned during wars as a military watchtower and was later capped with an eight-sided Renaissance lantern. The severely dignified exterior is offset by an elaborate and intricate Gothic interior. Take special notice of the main altarpiece, a riot of figures carved in the early 1600s by Jorg Zürn.

Münsterplatz, Überlingen. ℂ **07551/92720.** Admission free. Open daily 8am–6pm.

Ratssaal ★ HISTORIC BUILDING   On the opposite side of the square is Überlingen's Ratshaus, built in the late 1400s. The band of figures painted on its façade represents the different social classes and guilds in the Holy Roman Empire, from Emperor, to king and dukes, down to merchants and farmers. Most of its interior is devoted to municipal offices, except for the main Ratssaal (hall), whose slightly vaulted wooden ceiling, carved beams, and paneled walls make it the most beautiful public room in town.

Münsterstrasse 15-17, Überlingen. Admission free. Open Wed and Thur 11am; can also be viewed on guided city tour.

Stadtmuseum ★★ MUSEUM   Überlingen's town museum is housed in one of the town's most imposing buildings, the Reichlin-von-Meldlegg

Haus, which artfully emulates the style of the Florentine Renaissance. Displays present everyday objects, art, and artifacts that illustrate life in Überlingen through the centuries. There is also a chapel and a wonderfully ornate rococo ballroom.

Krummeberggasse 30, Überlingen. www.museum-ueberlingen.de. © **07551/991079.** Admission 5€ adults, 1€ children, children 5 and under free. Open Tues–Sat 9am–12:30pm and 2pm–5pm, Sun 10am–3pm (Nov–Dec closed Sun). Closed Christmas to mid-Mar.

EXPLORING MEERSBURG ★

56km (35 mi) N and E from Konstanz (40 min by ferry), 14km (9 miles) E of Überlingen, 20km (12 mi) W of Friedrichshafen.

Like the towns of Italy's Lake District, this village on the northern shore of Lake Constance cascades in terraces down the hillside to the water. Meersburg, with its almost intact old town center and castles towering above, is one of the premier tourist spots on the shores of Lake Constance. In the pedestrianized center, the streets become narrow promenades and steps wander up and down the hillside. From the dock, large and small boats set out for trips on the water, and there is a beautiful spa right on the lakefront (see p. 485).

Altes Schloss ★★ CASTLE/MUSEUM   Meersburg's landmark, the old castle, dates from 628 and is the oldest intact German castle. All the relics of a warring age are here—clubs, flails, armor, helmets, and

Meersburg cascades down terraced hillsides to the lake shore.

axes—along with 35 fully furnished rooms, decorated with pieces from various epochs. The bishops of Konstanz lived in this castle until the 18th century, when they moved to the Neues Schloss (see below). The baron of Lassberg, an admirer of medieval romance, then took over and invited Annette von Droste-Hülshoff (1797–1848), his sister-in-law and Germany's leading female poet, to come and stay. She had the castle turned into a setting for artists and writers. You can visit her luxuriously furnished chambers, as well as the murky dungeons and the castle museum with its medieval jousting equipment. Next to the castle is the **Castle Mill** (1620), with a 9m (30-ft.) wooden water wheel, the oldest of its kind in Germany.

Schlossplatz 10. www.meersburg.com. ℂ **07532/80000.** Admission 9.50€ adults, 7.50€ students, 5.50€ children 6–13. Open Mar–Oct daily 9am–6:30pm, Nov–Feb daily 10am–6pm.

Neues Schloss ★ CASTLE/MUSEUM   After visiting the old castle it comes as a bit of a culture shock to leave the medieval sphere and enter the highly manicured Baroque era of the new castle, designed by Balthasar Neumann, the leading architect of the 18th century. The ceiling paintings and frescoes were done by other prominent artists and craftsmen. Elegant stucco moldings grace the ceilings and walls. The castle is often used as an elegant venue and the Spiegelsaal, or Hall of Mirrors, is the setting for an international music festival in summer.

Schlossplatz(www.neuesschlossmeersburg.de. ℂ **07532/8079410.** Admission 5€ adults, 2.50€ children 12 and under. Open Apr–Oct daily 9.30am–6pm, Nov to mid-Mar Sat–Sun and public holidays noon–5pm.

EXPLORING FRIEDRICHSHAFEN ★

117km (80 miles) E from Waldshut-Tiengen, 19km (12 miles) E of Meersburg, 22km (14 miles) W of Lindau

At the northeastern corner of the Bodensee, near the lake's widest point, Friedrichshafen today is a mostly modern city, almost completely rebuilt after World War II. Friedrichshafen is not the prettiest place to stay on the lake, but very convenient for its central location and easy access; it also has a clutch of museums that are good for a rainy day. Driving here from Konstanz should take about 90 minutes, or 1 hour if you take the car ferry to Meersburg.

Friedrichshafen does have one of the longest waterfront exposures of any town along the lake; the best thing to do in town is to stroll the lake-fronting **Seepromenade,** with its sweeping view that extends on clear days all the way to the Swiss Alps. Even better views can be had from the top of the observation tower by the harbor. Cycling along the broad Seestrasse is a delight.

Dornier Museum ★★ MUSEUM

Friedrichshafen has not one but two museums dedicated to aviation and technology; this one is located at the airport (take the local train or bus 8, 7586, or 7394). This museum focuses on the achievements of Claude Dornier, who studied and trained under Count Ferdinand von Zeppelin (see p. 476) and went on to develop many spectacular aircrafts, some of which are exhibited here.

Claude-Dornier-Platz 1, www.dornier museum.de. ⓒ **07541/4873600.** Admission 9.50€ adults, 4.50€ children 6–16. Open May–Oct daily 9am–5pm; Nov–Apr Tues–Sun 10am–5pm.

Largely rebuilt after WWII, busy Friedrichshafn blends old and new.

Schlosskirche ★ CHURCH

Set prominently on a lakeshore point of land, the town's architectural highlight is this twin-towered baroque church, built in 1702. It's worth stepping inside to admire its ornate white plasterwork and the intricate carved pulpit and altarpiece. Check to see if a concert or service is happening soon—the church is known for its sonorous acoustics. In the 1800s the palatial ecclesiastical buildings attached to it, once part of the church's monastery, were converted into a palace for the kings of Württemberg. Today, they're privately owned.

Schlossstrasse 33. www.schlosskirche-fn.de ⓒ **07541/21308.** Open Easter–Oct daily 9am–6pm; rest of the year, open for services only.

Schulmuseum ★ MUSEUM

Kids especially may enjoy this nostalgic little museum tracing the development of education between 1850, when schools were run by the church, to modern times, when the state took over their administration. The museum is near the Schlosskirche in the historic heart of town. Look for reconstructions of schoolrooms from periods in the 19th and 20th centuries.

Friedrichstrasse 14. www.friedrichshafen.de. ⓒ **07541/32622.** Admission 3.50€ adults, 1.50€ children. Apr–Oct daily 10am–5pm; Nov–Mar Tues–Sun 2–5pm.

Zeppelin-Museum ★★★ MUSEUM   In a handsome white Bauhaus-style building overlooking the harbor (formerly the harbor railway station), this fascinating museum pays tribute to Count Ferdinand von Zeppelin, a pioneer of early aviation technology and engineering. In 1900, this native of Konstanz invented and tested the aircraft that bore his name and soon became a sensation in transatlantic transportation. The museum's centerpiece is a re-creation of the giant zeppelin *Hindenburg,* including a full-scale replica of its passenger cabins. Tragically, the airship exploded in a catastrophic fire in New Jersey in 1937, possibly because of sabotage, thus dooming the technology to obscurity. Besides the extensive technological exhibits the museum also houses a large art collection that ranges from medieval wood carving to impressive modern canvases by Otto Dix.

Seestrasse 22. www.zeppelin-museum.de. ✆ **07541/38010.** Admission 9€ adults, 4€ children 6–16. May–Oct daily 9am–5pm; Nov–Apr Tues–Sun 10am–5pm.

EXPLORING LINDAU ★★

20km (12.5 miles) E of Friedricshafen, 180km (113 miles) SW of Munich.

Located on the eastern end of the Lake, Lindau is actually in Bavaria, rather than Baden-Württemberg. Crossing the causeway to an island city symbolized by lions may give the brief impression that you're in Italy. Yet Lindau doesn't need comparisons to Venice to impress the visitor. From its origins in the 9th century, and throughout the Middle Ages as a free imperial town of the Holy Roman Empire, Lindau became the center of trade between Bavaria and Switzerland. In 1804 it officially became part of Bavaria and welcomed the **lion statue** (a symbol of Bavaria) that keeps watch at the harbor entry. Apart from being a tourist hot-spot with an ancient history, Lindau is also the unlikely meeting place of the world's intellectual elite, as it plays host to an annual meet of Nobel laureate scientists from all over the world (www.lindau-nobel.org).

REBIRTH OF THE zeppelin

The zeppelin fell out of favor in 1937 when the *Hindenburg* blew up in New Jersey, but its post-millennium sibling glides peacefully over Lake Constance. (Don't worry. The new zeppelin is much smaller and rises with inert helium gas, not the explosive hydrogen used by the *Hindenburg*.) The airship, named *Bodensee*, can climb to about 2,300m (7,500 ft.). The newer vessel carries 12 passengers and a crew of two, as opposed to the *Hindenburg*, which carried 100 aboard. Cruising at approximately 54kmph (33 mph) over the scenic lake, it offers a range of flights lasting from 30 minutes (220€ per person) to 2 hours (795€ per person). For more information and takeoff points along the lake, visit **www.zeppelinflug.de**.

The 13th-century Mangturm, with its tall yellow-striped roof, overlooks Lindau's historic harbor.

Today you can wander at will through the charming maze of winding narrow streets lined with houses that have stood the test of time. At the harbor stand two **lighthouses:** One, Mangturm, was built in the 1200s, the other in 1856. Each tower is some 37m (120 ft.) tall and can be climbed by the athletic via narrow spiral staircases. The reward is a panoramic vista of the lake, framed by the Alps, both Swiss and Austrian.

Pedestrianized **Maximilianstrasse,** in the center of the town, is the main street of the Altstad, where you'll see the stepped gables of the **Alte Rathaus** (see p. 478). Farther down the street, just north of Maximilianstrasse is the town's most familiar landmark, the round **Diebsturm (Thieves' Tower),** with its turreted roof, which in medieval times was the city jail. Next to it is the oldest building in Lindau, the 11th-century **St. Peter's Church ★,** which houses a war memorial chapel and a group of frescoes by Hans Holbein the Elder.

Heading back east towards the causeway, you'll pass the Marktplatz and go by the Münster and St. Stephen's Church, both baroque, then come to a strange pile of rocks known as **Heathen's Wall,** part of an earlier fortification dating to Roman times. Beyond this is the **Stadtgarten (Town Garden),** which, although peaceful during the day, livens up at night when the wheels of the town's casino begin to spin.

A peak INTO AUSTRIA

Right over the border in Austria, **Pfänder Mountain** ★★★ towers above Lindau and its neighboring Austrian town of Bregenz. To get there, take the local train, or in summer a boat, from Lindau to Bregenz. Here a cable car swiftly takes you up to the top at 1064m (3500ft). It is a fabulous vantage point for enjoying the view across Lake Constance and the Swiss and Austrian Alps; on a good day you may be able to see as many as 240 other mountain tops. Atop the peak, you'll also find a couple of Alpine-style chalet restaurants where you can relish the views over a beer or some lunch, as well as an alpine zoo (admission free) with red deer, ibexes, marrnots, and all sorts of other mountain creatures, and a falconry that offers regular shows. Marked hiking trails go off in all directions. The round-trip cable-car ride costs 12.50€ adults (7.30€ one-way), 10€ for ages 16 to 19 (5.800€ one-way) and 6.30€ for kids ages 6 to 15 (3.70€ one-way. Family discounts are available. For information see: www.pfaender.at/en.

Alte Rathaus ★ HISTORIC BUILDING   Erected in 1422, Lindau's city hall features the stepped gables typical of that period, but the building's facade also combines many later styles of architecture. The frescoes decorating the wall represent scenes from a session of the 1496 Imperial Diet which was held in the council hall here. The interior, once used as a council hall, is now the **historic library** ★★★ and city archive, which dates to 1524. Among its many treasures of ancient books it holds one of the few preserved original German Lutheran Bibles, dating to 1534. (Entrance on the southern side of the building, only accessible with a guided tour).

Bismarckplatz 4. www.lindau-tourismus.de. Open Apr to mid-Oct daily 2–5:30pm; rest of year closed Mon.

Haus zum Cavazzen ★★ MUSEUM   Now the city museum, this was once the handsomest patrician house on Lake Constance, with its baroque painted exterior and high hipped roof. This municipal art collection displayed here includes exhibits of sculpture and painting from the Gothic, Renaissance, and baroque periods. Some of the rooms are furnished with period pieces showing how wealthy citizens lived in the 18th and 19th centuries. Among the rarities is a collection of mechanical musical instruments (can only be viewed during a guided tour).

Am Marktplatz 6. ✆ **08382/944073.** Admission 3€ adults, 1.50€ students and ages 6–15; guided tours 3€. Open mid-Mar to Aug daily 10am–6pm, Sept to mid-Oct Tues–Fri 11am–5pm, Sat 2–5pm.

Where to Stay Around Lake Constance

It's easy enough to get from town to town around Lake Constance; it makes sense to base yourself in one town according to which hotel suits you. The larger towns of Konstanz and Friedrichshafen may offer more choice, while the smaller more historic towns have the edge on atmospheric charm. Many of these hotels also have prime restaurants for the area, so look through the list to find dining options as well.

Adara Boutique Hotel ★★★ On the northern side of Lindau island, near the market square, this charming small hotel has 16 individually decorated guest rooms. Their minimalist gray-and-white décor perfectly sets off the original wooden beams and posts and rough stone walls incorporated into the decor. Bathrooms are a touch narrow and in some rooms the ceiling is quite low. Unusually for such a historic building, it does have an elevator. Its restaurant is one of the better dining spots in the area; see p. 482 for details.

Alter Schulplatz 1, Lindau. www.adara-lindau.de. ✆ **08382/943500.** 16 units. 150€–235€ double. Breakfast included. No parking. **Amenities:** restaurant, bike storage, Wi-Fi (free).

Barbarossa ★ Very centrally located in the old part of Konstanz, this hotel is housed in a charming old building, with its historic character preserved. The rooms vary greatly in size, but have all recently been done up in highly individual style, uncluttered and chic, with hardwood floors and witty designer accents. No two rooms are the same. The basic rooms are quite small, but the larger family rooms sleep 3 or 4 people. There is a roof terrace for relaxation as well as a library/guest lobby on the first floor. Car access is a bit difficult due to its location in the old town, making it necessary to park and unload at a car park nearby. Spaces in the parking garage must be reserved. The hotel has its own wine bar and restaurant with tables out on the plaza in front of the hotel.

Obermarkt 8–12, Konstanz. www.hotelbarbarossa.de. ✆ **07531/128990.** 53 units. 99€–160€ double. Parking 9€ (garage). Breakfast included. **Amenities:** Restaurant; bar; room service; Wi-Fi (free).

Hotel Bayerischer Hof and Hotel Seegarten ★★ These two related hotels are located right next door to each other, in a prime harborside location on Lindau. Bayerische Hof is a traditional 5-star hotel and Hotel Seegarten is its 4-star cousin. Both hotels are very plush, and the very nice new wellness and pool area at Bayrischer Hof is open to guests from both hotels. The staff is attentive and service is courteous and efficient. Rooms are quite large and furnished conservatively in soft tones of green and yellow. The nicest rooms, overlooking the harbor, are of course the most expensive; views from some of the other rooms are not quite as enchanting. Most rooms at Bayerischer Hof have A/C, and some rooms offer disabled access.

Seepromenade, Lindau. www.bayerischerhof-lindau.de. ✆ **800/223-5652** in the U.S. and Canada, or 08382/9150. 105 units. 169€– 297€ double. Buffet breakfast included. Parking 12€ or14€ (garage) **Amenities:** 2 restaurants; bar; sauna, spa and wellness, exercise room; indoor and outdoor pools; room service; Wi-Fi (free).

Hotel Bürgerbräu ★★★   Located not far from the Überlingen train station in an old half-timbered building, this cozy, pleasant hotel is within easy reach of the town center. Service is very friendly; rooms are spotlessly clean and comfortable, with a functional modern look, although some are a bit cramped. The bathrooms were remodeled in 2014. The breakfast is excellent and copious—they even cook eggs and pancakes to order. The restaurant is an excellent choice even if you're not staying here, with a young, creative, and ambitious chef who serves a regional, seasonal and contemporary cuisine (main courses 12€ to 30€, tasting menu 59€). The restaurant is closed Monday and Tuesday.

Aufkircher Strasse 20, Überlingen. www.buergerbraeu-ueberlingen.com. © **07551/92740.** 12 units, 99€–114€ double. **Amenities:** Restaurant; room service; Wi-Fi (free).

Hotel City Krone ★   Very centrally located in Friedrichshafen's pedestrian zone and close to the waterfront, this hotel offers smartly designed modern rooms, many with hardwood floors, and quirky accents such as the quotes stenciled onto the walls in some rooms. Bathrooms are sleekly up-to-date. The standard rooms are a bit small, but better room categories are spacious enough. Rooms on the upper floors have the best views. There is a spa and wellness area, with a small indoor pool; massages should be reserved early. A friendly, attentive staff creates a relaxed and laid-back ambience throughout the hotel. The very generous breakfast buffet is included in the rate. Unfortunately there are not a lot of parking spaces.

Schanzstrasse 7, Friedrichshafen. www.hotel-city-krone.de. © **07541/7050.** 111 units. 99€–159€ double. Buffet breakfast included. Parking 6€. **Amenities:** Spa; sauna; bar; Wi-Fi (free).

Hotel-Garni Brugger ★   This unpretentious, family-run bed & breakfast hotel on Lindau island is located near the Stadtpark and close to everything else. Rooms are a bit bland and functionally furnished, but clean. The bathrooms are rather small, but have recently been modernized. This is a decent and affordable option, with a small wellness area and sauna.

Bei der Heidenmauer 11, Lindau. www.hotel-garni-brugger.de. © **08382/93410.** 23 units. 94€–130€ double. Buffet breakfast included. Parking 9€. **Amenities:** sauna; bike storage; Wi-Fi (free).

Romantik Hotel Residenz am See ★★   It is not the building, but rather the setting that is romantic about this modern Meersberg hotel, which looks out over Lake Constance. Its location is also very convenient to the spa (see p. 484), which is just down the road. This is the top hotel in town and its two restaurants, one of which carries a Michelin star, are in a class of their own in Meersburg. The rooms, which come in many different categories and sizes, are furnished in a classy contemporary style with some designer pizzazz, but you may not notice, since all rooms have their own balcony or terrace overlooking the lake. Although Wi-Fi is available, the signal is sometimes poor as Meersburg generally is poorly covered. Both the rooms and public areas are decorated with artwork, which adds a nice individualistic touch. Both restaurants are very popular. Reserve early if you want to dine here.

Uferpromenade 11, Meersberg. www.hotel-residenz-meersburg.com. © **07532/ 80040.** 24 units. 150€–288€ double. Continental breakfast included. Parking (garage) 10€, outdoor parking 7€. **Amenities:** 2 restaurants; bar, room service, bike rental, Wi-Fi (free).

Seehotel ★ Bauhaus architecture gives this Friedrichshafen hotel an almost futuristic ambiance. Located very close to both the station and the lakefront, the hotel has recently been renovated. Although the rooms are not exactly big, they are quite comfortable, fitted out in a minimalist look with stark white walls and sleek blond-wood built-ins. Most rooms, especially on the upper floors have lake view and some have air-conditioning, which is rare in Germany. Bathrooms are modern, but also a bit small. There is a small wellness area with a sauna and steam bath on the top floor and a roof terrace with a gorgeous view across the lake. The restaurant isn't bad either.

Bahnhofplatz 2, Friedrichshafen. www.seehotelfn.de. © **07541/3030.** 132 units. 99€–139€ double. Breakfast included. Free outside parking; 12€ inside. **Amenities:** Restaurant; bar; room service; spa, Wi-Fi (free).

Steigenberger Inselhotel ★★★ This high-end hotel is unbeatable for both its location—on a private island facing Konstanz to one side and the lake to the other—and for its historic ambiance: It is housed in a 13th-century Dominican monastery. Now it's a 5-star hotel, complete with its own lakeside gardens and dock. The best thing about it, though, are the unbeatable views across the lake. Room décor is contemporary without being flashy, in restrained color schemes; the more spacious double rooms have a sitting area and some have a balcony. All rooms have A/C, which is an advantage during the summer.

Auf der Insel 1, Konstanz. www.konstanz.steigenberger.com. © **800/5908410** in the U.S. and Canada, or 07531/1250. 102 units. 302€–390€ double. Buffet breakfast included. Parking 16€. **Amenities:** 2 restaurants; bar; bike rental; exercise room; room service; sauna; Wi-Fi (free).

Villa Barleben ★ This beautiful converted Belle Epoch Villa is located on the Konstanz lakeshore across the bridge, about 15 minutes' walk from the station. It's an utterly charming and nostalgic boutique hotel that feels more like a home; rooms have been lovingly decorated with throw pillows and houseplants and an eclectic mix of furnishings, each room having its own individual character. Because of the age of the building, some rooms have the sink in the room, rather than in the bathroom, and the bathrooms are very small. Standard rooms face the park, comfort rooms face the lake. There is a lovely garden with beach chairs for relaxing right across from the lake. During the summer the terrace is

Sweeping lake views reward guests at the Steinberger Inselhotel in Konstanz.

used as a restaurant, with a small and somewhat pricey menu, but the ambiance is very romantic.

Seestrasse 15, (Navigator: Säntisstrasse 1), Konstanz. www.hotel-barleben.de. *℗* **07531/942330.** 9 units, 95€–325€ double. Breakfast 15€. Free parking. **Amenities:** Restaurant (summer); Wi-Fi (free).

Where to Eat Around Lake Constance

Adara ★★ CONTEMPORARY   This boutique hotel (see p. 479) and restaurant in Lindau is still an insider's tip. After a 5-year closure for extensive renovations, the hotel reopened in 2014 and has already made its mark on the local gastronomic scene. The young and dynamic kitchen team creates delightful and innovative dishes based on fresh, regional, and seasonal produce sourced from local suppliers. The menu offers a good balance between meat, fish and vegetarian dishes. It might include such delicacies as sea-bass in an herb crust on a bed of fennel-orange and potato pie, or roasted artichoke hearts with cherry tomatoes, mixed mushrooms and wild herb salad. No less delicious is the Tiramisu with marinated berries.

Alter Schulplatz 1, Lindau. www.adara-lindau.de. *℗* **08382/943500.** Main courses 10€–28€, vegetarian and small dishes 10€–15€. Fixed price menu 3-course 38€, 4-course 48€. Closed Jan–Mar. Closed Mon.

Café im Neuen Schloss ★★ CAFE   Not your typical museum cafeteria, the café in Meersberg's baroque castle is run by the same people
who own the hotel and gourmet restaurant **Traube Tonbach** in Baiersbronn (see p. 459), who make it a great place to have lunch, or coffee
and cake, even if you are not interested in the castle. The café can be
accessed freely, without having to pay the castle entrance fee. Although
not a full-scale restaurant, it offers daily changing lunch options and delicious cakes. The quality of food is excellent and prices are quite humane.
The best place to enjoy your meal is on the terrace, with views of the
lake. (Terrace is open during the summer, weather permitting.)
Schlossplatz 12, Meersberg. www.neuesschlossmeersburg.de. © **07532/80794120.**
Open mid-Mar to Dec daily 9:30am–6:30pm, Dec to mid-Mar Thurs–Mon 10am–5pm.
No credit cards.

Graf Zeppelin Haus ★ INTERNATIONAL/REGIONAL   The exclusive location right on the waterfront and inside the multi-purpose event
space couldn't be better. Café Ferdinand is a perfect place to indulge in
the afternoon coffee and cake ritual while enjoying magical views across
Lake Constance, while the full-scale restaurant serves lunch and dinner.
While the food isn't fancy or imaginative, it is tasty and of good quality,
prepared with fresh, regional produce. The daily changing lunch special
frequently includes vegetarian items. The menu features steak, fillets,
and schnitzel variations as well as some fish dishes; vegetarian options
include spätzle and rösti, Swiss-style potato pancakes.
Olgastrasse 20, Friedrichshafen. www.gzh.de/de/gastronomie/restaurant.php
© **07541/6033930.** Main courses 13€–27€. Cafe daily 10am–6pm; restaurant summer Tues–Sun 11am–10:30pm, winter Tues–Sat 11am–2pm and 5:30–10:30pm, Sun
11am–6pm. Closed Mon.

Hafenhalle ★ REGIONAL   The location of this beer-garden/restau-
rant, right by the Konstanz harbor, could not be better. It is the perfect
place to enjoy views across the lake over a nice cool beer on a warm summer night. The beer-garden serves standard beer-garden fare of the sausage and schnitzel variety. The indoor restaurant serves a slightly more
varied menu. Don't expect haute cuisine, but this is a relaxed place with
decent quality food at reasonable prices, which is not that easy to come
by in Konstanz. The restaurant menu has some vegetarian options such
spinach gnocchi. Meat dishes include pork medallions with spätzle,
creamy mushroom sauce, and roasted onions, or wild boar braised in red
wine, red cabbage, and dumplings. Typical Bodensee fish dishes also
feature strongly. From Easter to October they have free music in the beer
garden on Sundays.
Hafenstrasse 10, Konstanz. www.hafenhalle.com. © **07531/21126.** Main courses
8.50€–26€. Mon–Fri 5pm–1am, Sat–Sun and holidays 10am–2am.

Hotel-Restaurant Maier ★★ REGIONAL   This nice little family-run hotel and restaurant is located in the suburb of Fischbach, 6km (4 miles) west of Friedrichshafen via the B31. For lunch they serve a small, weekly changing menu, with a 2-course fixed-price option available Mondays to Thursdays. Evening fixed-price menus are available with 3 or 4 courses. The menu changes with the seasons, but might include rump steak in burgundy jus with caramelized "Höri Bölle" (a specialty red onion), pumpkin, and potato pancake (Rösti). Vegetarians might enjoy pumpkin risotto with fried goat cheese and beet sauce. The hotel has 49 rooms; doubles cost 84€ to 139€, including breakfast and free parking. Most rooms are air-conditioned.

Poststrasse 1–3, Fischbach. ℰ **07541/4040.** www.hotel-maier.de. Reservations recommended. Main courses 10€–28€. Daily 5:30–10pm; Sat–Thurs also 11:30am–2pm.

Marrakesh Moroccan Restaurant ★★ MOROCCAN   This restaurant is a hidden gem, even though its location right across from the Konstanz train station inside the Halm Hotel couldn't be more central. But one would never expect to find such a place under the cover of a somewhat faded Belle Epoch grand hotel. Styled like something out of the Arabian Nights, with a soaring painted ceiling, gigantic mirrors, and richly patterned walls, it feels quite unreal at first. Interestingly, the decor is not a modern fancy, but was part of the original design, in an era when orientalism was a fashion statement. The restaurant serves both Moroccan and regional cuisine. The Moroccan menu features Marrakesh specialties as well as a range of tagine dishes. (A tagine is an earthenware pan with a pointed top, used to braise meats for perfect tenderness.) The spicing is delicate and often sweet, with fruit, raisins, and nuts regularly used. It's a rare pleasure to come across this type of exotic cuisine in Germany. Try the Tagine Aloush with cinnamon-quince confit and flat bread, or the Tagine Agel of braised veal with dates, figs, apricots, almonds, and walnuts. If you prefer German cooking ask for the regional menu and you will find all the usual suspects. Vegetarian dishes are better in the Moroccan variation.

Bahnhofplatz 6, Konstanz. www.hotel-halm.de/de/hotel-konstanz. ℰ **07531/1210.** Main dishes 16€a25€. Tues

LAKE CONSTANCE SPAS

Bodensee Therme Konstanz ★   The most family friendly spa on the lake, in Konstanz, even has a separate family area for parents and children with child-sized installations. It is also joined to the outdoor/aqua-fun pool, making it ideal for both parents and children. The spa area includes whirlpools, a current-channel pool, massage jets, saunas (textile free), and indoor and outdoor pools with views of Lake Constance.

Zur Therme 2, Konstanz. (Navigator: Wilhelm-von-Scholz-Weg 2). www.bodensee-therme-konstanz.de. ℰ **0753/363070.** Pool area: adults 8.50€ for 1.5hrs, 10.50€ for

3 hrs, 12€ day pass. Family pass 25€ for 3 hrs, 31.50€ all day. Pool area plus sauna: 20.50€ for 3.5hrs, 26.50€ day pass. Children under 6 not permitted in sauna area. Open daily 9am–10pm, saunas 10am–10pm.

Bodensee-Therme Überlingen ★★ SPA/POOLS   Located near the station and set on the lakefront, this is a family oriented pool. Children's areas have waterslides and outdoor pools; there are also adult spaces, a 25-meter lap pool, and a separated sauna and wellness area. If you like your peace and quiet, avoid the first Friday of the month (family day with reduced entrance fees) and public holidays, or any time school is out. They also offer special adult events, including full moon sauna nights. Uniquely, the sauna area has both indoor and outdoor saunas—to cool off after the outdoor sauna, you can jump right into the lake. Book massages and treatments well in advance.

Bahnhofstrasse 27, Überlingen. www.bodensee-therme.de. ℂ **07551/301990.** Pools only day pass 13€ adults, 11€ ages 15–21, 8€ children under 15. Pools plus sauna day pass 22.50€ for all ages. Open daily 10am–10pm, Fri and Sat until 11pm. Tues is women-only in the panorama sauna.

Thermen und Freibad ★★ SPA/POOLS   A 5-minute walk east of the harbor lies Meersburg's thermal spa with an adjacent outdoor pool and access to the lake. Here you can lie on the grass on a strip of sand, or immerse yourself in any of three outdoor swimming pools. A sauna, built in the style of the ancient lake dwellings (see p. 472) is also on-site, plus refreshment stands and a bistro.

Uferpromenade 9–11, Meersburg. www.meersburg-therme.de. ℂ **07532/4402850.** Pools only day pass 14€ adults, 10.50€ children; children 3 and under free. Pools plus sauna 18€ adults for 3 hrs, day pass 22€. After 8pm entrance reduced. Open Mon–Thurs 10am–10pm, Fri–Sat 10am–11pm, Sun 9am–10pm. Monday is women-only day in the sauna.

Entertainment & Nightlife

PERFORMING ARTS

Konstanz offers the richest array of nightlife in the area, with numerous classical music offerings throughout the year. The concert season of the **Südwestdeutsche Philharmonie Konstanz** (www.philharmonie-konstanz.de; ℂ **07531/900810**) runs September to June, followed by a **summer music festival** held mid-June to mid-July. Germany's oldest active theater, the **Stadttheater Konstanz,** Konzilstrasse 11 (www.theaterkonstanz.de; ℂ **07531/900150**), has been staging plays since 1609 and has its own repertory company. Ticket prices depend on the production.

CASINOS

In the main room of the **Konstanz Casino,** Seestrasse 21 (www.casino-konstanz.de; ℂ **07531/81570**), you can try your luck at blackjack, seven-card stud poker, or roulette. Slot machines are in a side room. Entry requires a passport as proof of age, and there's a cover charge of 3€. Men are required to wear jackets and ties. The casino is open daily 2pm to 2am and until 3am Friday and Saturday. There's a restaurant on the premises, open Tuesday to Sunday from 1pm to 11pm.

The old wooden building of Lindau's **Spielbank Casino,** Chelles-Alle 1 (www.spielbanken-in-bayern.de; © **08382/27740**), has been replaced by a weird, futuristic-looking blob-like building. Among its amusements are the inevitable slot machines, from noon to 2am, and blackjack and roulette from 3pm to 2am (Fri–Sat until 3am). The building also acts as a venue for music shows and cabarets. The bet ceiling is 12,000€ for roulette. Admission is free. A passport is required as proof of age (minimum age 21). Men should wear a jacket and tie.

Sports & Outdoor Pursuits

BEACHES Konstanz's lakeside **beaches** are open from June to August daily 9am to 8pm, and from 10am to 7pm in May and September. The biggest beach is **Eichwald** (www.sw-lindau.de/freizeit/eichwaldbad), about a half-hour walk away along Uferweg (to the right as you face the harbor). Admission is 3€ for adults, 2€ for children. **Lindenhofbad** beach has an area for sunbathing and free access to the water, but no pools. To get there, take the regional train to Enzisweiler and walk towards the lake on Badstrasse. If you're driving, follow the signs to B31; stay on B31 until you see the exit marked Schachen. A special experience for the nostalgic is the **Aeschbacher Bad,** the only remaining historic wooden bath-house on Lake Constance. The pale green wooden complex built on stilts over the lake serves as a retreat for locals seeking to escape the rambunctiousness prevalent at more family-oriented bathing spots around the lake. The bath-house is located on the mainland, just over the bridge and train tracks, at Lotzbeckweg 3; it is open in summer from 10am to 7pm.

BICYCLING Another excellent way to see the lake and its surroundings is by bike. Some hotels offer bicycle rentals or you can rent one at **Kultur-Rädle,** right by the Konstanz train station (Bahnhofsplatz 29, www.kultur-raedle.de, © **07531/27310**). Prices are 13€ per day for a regular trekking bike, or 25€ per day for an e-bike. If you're in Friedrichshafen, rent bikes at **Fahrradverleih Friedrichshafen,** near the harbor at Eckenerstrasse 16 (www.radverleih-friedrichshafen.de; © **07541/22465**), from 14€ to 24€ a day depending on the type of bike. In Lindau, bicycle rentals are available at **Unger's Fahrradverleih,** Inselgraben 14 (www.fahrrad-unger.de, © **08382/943688**), close to the train station. Prices range from 6€ to 18€ per day. It's open Monday to Friday 9am to 1pm and 3 to 6pm, Saturday and Sunday 9am to 1pm.

BOATING   At the little dock next to Lindau's rail bridge, you can rent a **paddleboat** for 12€, a motorboat for 30€–40€, or an electric boat for 25€ per hour from **Bootsvermietung Hodrius** (*©* **08382/297771;** www.bootsverleih-lindau.de).

SWIMMING   Besides the pools at the spas listed above (see p. 484), **Hotel Bad Schachen** (Bad Schachen 1, www.badschachen.de; *©* **08382/2980**) west of Lindau in Lindenhofbad, has a beautiful art nouveau indoor pool and wellness area with saunas and steam bath. Admission 29€ for a day ticket. Adults only.

11

FRANKFURT

ometimes nicknamed "Mainhattan" because of its skyscraper skyline, Frankfurt-am-Main is a fast-paced and cosmopolitan metropolis A major banking city since the Rothschilds opened their first bank here over 200 years ago, it has long been the financial center not only of Germany but also of the entire European Union, as the home of the Central Bank of the European Union, the ECB. For many travelers, this is their first introduction to Germany, since Frankfurt's airport is the country's main transatlantic and international hub. Visitors looking for a romantic or atmospheric piece of Old Germany will not find much; the medieval Altstadt (Old Town) is fairly small. But while Frankfurt may not be a place you fall in love with on first sight, it is a city that grows on you fast, even on a short stay.

There are cultural riches here: Along the **Museumsufer (Museum Embankment)** is the world-class **Städel** collection, with paintings by Monet, Renoir, German Expressionists and the leading lights of the European Renaissance. There are city museums dedicated to film, modern art, sculpture, and more, as well as the preserved home of one of Germany's greatest writers, **Goethe.**

What's more, Frankfurt is an outward-looking place. It may only have three-quarters of a million inhabitants, but that population is more diverse than almost anywhere else in Germany (which, luckily, leads to a more varied dining scene as well). An increasingly hip nightlife scene centers around the edgy **Bahnhofsviertel,** popular with the young and young-at-heart who like to stay up into the small hours. The cobbled streets of **Alt-Sachsenhausen,** south of the River Main, feel like one big open-air bar on the weekend.

ESSENTIALS

Arriving

BY PLANE **Flughafen Frankfurt/Main** (www.frankfurt-airport.com; ✆ **0180/6372-4636**) lies 11km (7 miles) from the city center. Europe's busiest airport and Germany's major international gateway, this airport

FACING PAGE: Frankfurt's skyscrapered profile has earned it the nickname "Mainhattan."

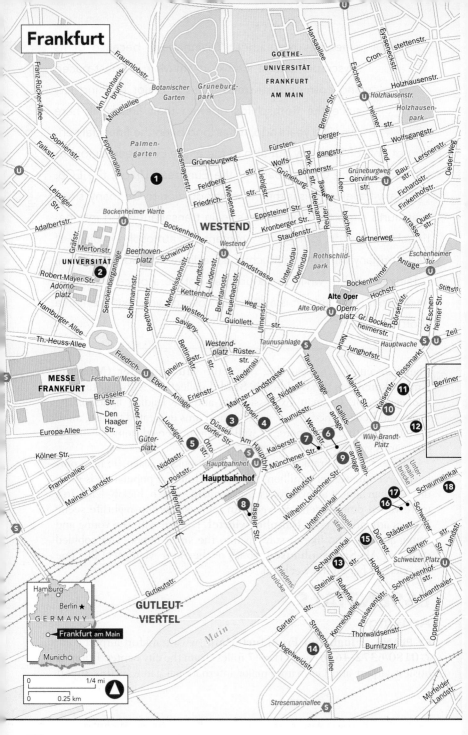

Frankfurt

GOETHE-UNIVERSITÄT FRANKFURT AM MAIN

WESTEND

UNIVERSITÄT

MESSE FRANKFURT

Alte Oper

Hauptbahnhof

GUTLEUT-VIERTEL

Botanischer Garten

Grüneburgpark

Palmengarten

Rothschildpark

Holzhausenpark

Bockenheimer Warte

Festhalle/Messe

Berliner

Willy-Brandt-Platz

Schweizer Platz

Hauptwache

Opernplatz

Westendplatz

Güterplatz

Düsseldorfer Str.

Main

Franz-Rücker-Allee
Frauenlobstr.
Am Leonhardsbrunn
Miquelallee
Zeppelinallee
Siesmayerstr.
Sophienstr.
Falkstr.
Leipziger Str.
Adalbertstr.
Gräfstr.
Mertonstr.
Senckenberganlage
Robert-Mayer-Str.
Adornoplatz
Hamburger Allee
Th.-Heuss-Allee
Schumannstr.
Beethovenstr.
Beethovenplatz
Schwindstr.
Arndtstr.
Lindenstr.
Kettenhofweg
Mendelssohnstr.
Brentanostr.
Feuerbachstr.
Westend
Savigny-
Bettinastr.
Rheinstr.
Friedrich-Ebert-Anlage
Brüsseler Str.
Den Haager Str.
Europa-Allee
Kölner Str.
Frankenallee
Mainzer Landstr.
Niddastr.
Poststr.
Güterplatz
Ludwigstr.
Ottostr.
Düsseldorfer Str.
Am Hauptbhf.
Mainzer Landstrasse
Mosel
Elbestr.
Taunusstr.
Niddastr.
Rüsterstr.
Niedenau
Westendstr.
Guiollett-str.
Ulmenstr.
Taunusanlage
Kaiserstr.
Münchener Str.
Gutleutstr.
Baseler Str.
Hafentunnel
Gutleutstr.
Frankfurt am Main
Gartenstr.
Schaumainkai
Steinlestr.
Rubensstr.
Passavantstr.
Kennedyallee
Stresemannallee
Thorwaldsenstr.
Burnitzstr.
Vogelweidstr.
Friedensbrücke
Holbeinsteg
Untermainkai
Wilhelm-Leuschner-Str.
Weserstr.
Gallusanlage
Mainzer Str.
Untermainanlage
Taunusanlage
Neue Mainzer Str.
Junghofstr.
Hochstr.
Bockenheimer Anlage
Eschenheimer Tor
Stiftstr.
Gr. Bockenheimerstr.
Börsenstr.
Gr. Eschenheimer Str.
Rossmarkt
Zeil
Kaiserstr.
Untermainbrücke
Schaumainkai
Schweizer Str.
Städelstr.
Dürerstr.
Gartenstr.
Holbeinstr.
Schneckenhofstr.
Schwanthalerstr.
Oppenheimer Str.
Mörfelder Landstr.
Stresemannallee

Frauenlobstr.
Grüneburgweg
Fürstenbergerstr.
Wolfsgangstr.
Liebigstr.
Feldbergstr.
Friedrichstr.
Eppsteiner Str.
Kronberger Str.
Staufenstr.
Westend Landstrasse
Unterlindau
Oberlindau
Bremer Str.
Wolfsgangstr.
Park Str.
Böhmerstr.
Jordanstr.
Telemannstr.
Reuterweg
Leerbachstr.
Gervinusstr.
Grüneburgweg
Bauernstr.
Lersnerstr.
Fichardstr.
Finkenhofstr.
Querstrasse
Gärtnerweg
Eschenheimer Anlage
Bockenheimer Landstr.
Holzhausenstr.
Eysseneckstr.
Cronstettenstr.
Croneckstr.
Holzhauserstr.
Hansaallee
Eschersheimer Landstr.
Wolfsgangstr.

Hamburg
Berlin ★
GERMANY
München

0 ___ 1/4 mi
0 ___ 0.25 km

1 2 3 4 5 6 7 8 9 10 11 12 13 14 15 16 17 18

490

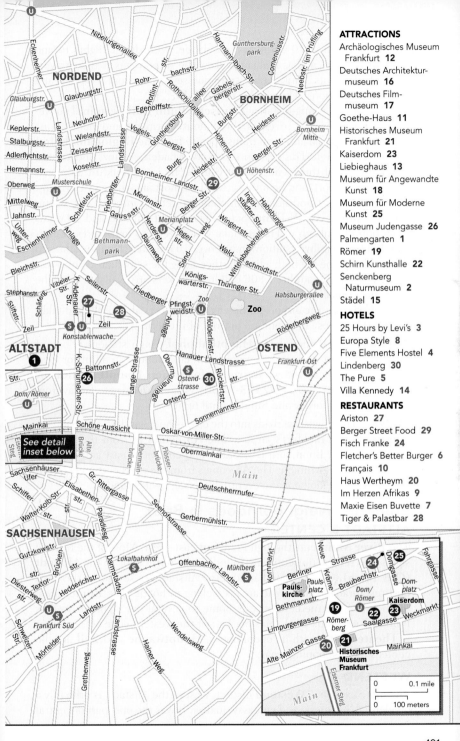

ATTRACTIONS

Archäologisches Museum Frankfurt **12**
Deutsches Architektur- museum **16**
Deutsches Film- museum **17**
Goethe-Haus **11**
Historisches Museum Frankfurt **21**
Kaiserdom **23**
Liebieghaus **13**
Museum für Angewandte Kunst **18**
Museum für Moderne Kunst **25**
Museum Judengasse **26**
Palmengarten **1**
Römer **19**
Schirn Kunsthalle **22**
Senckenberg Naturmuseum **2**
Städel **15**

HOTELS

25 Hours by Levi's **3**
Europa Style **8**
Five Elements Hostel **4**
Lindenberg **30**
The Pure **5**
Villa Kennedy **14**

RESTAURANTS

Ariston **27**
Berger Street Food **29**
Fisch Franke **24**
Fletcher's Better Burger **6**
Français **10**
Haus Wertheym **20**
Im Herzen Afrikas **9**
Maxie Eisen Buvette **7**
Tiger & Palastbar **28**

serves more than 110 countries worldwide, with direct flights to and from many U.S. and Canadian cities. The airport has a full array of stores, restaurants, banks, a bus terminal, several car-rental offices, and two railway stations. There's also **free Wi-Fi.**

The airport's long-distance **Deutsche Bahn Rail Terminal** conveniently links directly to cities throughout Germany and neighboring countries. Regional and local trains operate from the **Regionalbahnhof** below Terminal 1. This station serves Wiesbaden, Mainz, and central Frankfurt. What this means is that you can fly into Frankfurt, hop on a train at the airport, and be on your way to almost anywhere in Germany.

The simplest and quickest method for getting into the city center from the airport is by **S-Bahn** (*Schnellbahn,* light rail). **S8** and **S9** trains (direction Offenbach or Hanau) take you directly to Frankfurt's Hauptbahnhof (main railway station) in just over 10 minutes (Hauptwache and Konstablerwache are both a little farther along the same line). A one-way ticket costs 4.65€ adults, 2.80€ children. Tickets are available from the RMV ticket machines.

A **taxi** from the airport to the city center costs about 30€ and takes about 20 minutes. Taxis pull up in front of the terminals.

BY TRAIN   Frankfurt's large **Hauptbahnhof** (main station) is one of the busiest train stations in Europe, with connections to all major German and European cities. **Tourist Information Hauptbahnhof,** by the main entrance (© **069/2123-8800**), is open Monday to Friday from 8am to 9pm, Saturday and Sunday until 6pm.

BY CAR   The major fast roads into the city—the A3 and A5 autobahns—intersect near Frankfurt's airport. The **A3** comes in from the Netherlands, Cologne, Bonn, and Düsseldorf and continues east and south to Nuremburg and Munich. The **A5** comes from the northeast and continues south to Heidelberg and eventually Basel, Switzerland.

Frankfurt Neighborhoods in Brief
ALTSTADT & CENTER

The **River Main** cuts through Frankfurt east–west. Most of the historic sights and several museums are found on the north bank in the **Altstadt (Old Town).** Concentrated around the Altstadt are several of the city's best restaurants, though the area is lacking in hotels. The **Römer** area, the heart of the medieval city, is home to several key sights as well as Frankfurt's famous Christmas market. At the western edge of the center is **Theaterplatz,** with its opera house. **Hauptwache** and **Zeil** are the center's main shopping areas.

WESTEND

The more exclusive **Westend** district, west of the Altstadt, is primarily a residential, business, and embassy quarter. It was the only part of central

A promenade runs along the Main River, which cuts east-west through Frankfurt.

Frankfurt not destroyed by Allied bombing in World War II. Away from its busy boulevards, it's leafy and quiet, with lots of business-oriented hotels. The natural history museum and botanical gardens are the only major Westend sights; for almost everything else, you'll take a 10-minute U-Bahn ride into the Altstadt and beyond.

OSTEND

Quiet, leafy, and well off the tourist trail, Frankfurt's **Ostend (East End)** is nevertheless well connected by S- and U-Bahn to the center. There's not much in the way of nightlife, but it makes a good base for anyone who likes a genuine local atmosphere.

SACHSENHAUSEN & MUSEUMSUFER

South of the river you'll find two major districts of interest. To the east is **Sachsenhausen,** a popular entertainment quarter famous for its traditional apple-wine taverns. The heart of it, **Alt-Sachsenhausen** (Old Sachsenhausen) has cobbled streets and oozes atmosphere. A couple of streets (notably Brückenstrasse and Wallstrasse) house niche fashion boutiques. West of Sachsenhausen, the **Museumsufer (Museums Embankment)** is home to many of Frankfurt's best museums. The art-stuffed **Städel** is here, as is the sculpture collection at the **Liebieghaus.**

BAHNHOFSVIERTEL

The **"Station Quarter"** has long been considered a neighborhood to avoid, especially after dark. It still retains its edge, certainly, and Frankfurt's seedy red-light district radiates out from **Moselstrasse** between Taunusstrasse and Kaiserstrasse, for about a block in every direction. Yet around here you'll also find the most exciting new restaurant and bar openings. Locals pour into the area after dark on weekends. It is stocked with well-regarded hotels, too, especially at the budget end (though light sleepers should *always* request a room away from the street around here). As you walk out of the station, busy **Baselerstrasse** on your right heads south toward the River Main and the Museum Embankment. Wherever you are around here, don't walk deserted alleyways after dark; the Bahnhofsviertel's busier streets are bustling well into the small hours.

Getting Around

ON FOOT   You can easily get everywhere around the **Altstadt**—including to the **Museumsufer** on the opposite bank of the river—on foot. From the station area, the **Altstadt** is a 20-minute walk or a couple of stops by S-Bahn or U-Bahn (see below).

BY PUBLIC TRANSPORTATION   Frankfurt's metro, train, bus, and tram services are excellent. (Hardly surprising, then, that the city is in the European top 10 for annual public transport trips per capita.) The network comprises a modern **U-Bahn** (subway), **S-Bahn** (*Schnellbahn,* faster urban light rail), **Strassenbahn** (streetcar/tram), and **buses,** all operated by **RMV** (**Rhein-Main-Verkehrsverbund;** www.rmv.de; ✆ **069/2424-8024**). All forms of public transportation can be used interchangeably at a single price based on fare zones. Once purchased, tickets are good for a single journey. Buy at ticket counters or from coin-operated machines found in U-Bahn stations and next to tram and bus stops. The ticket machines have screens in English to guide you through the process. Connected travelers can also buy using the **RMV app** (Android and iOS).

A one-way single ticket *(Einzelfahrkarte)* within the city center costs 2.80€ for adults, 1.65€ for children ages 6 to 14 (1.80€/1€ if the journey is less than 2km: a *Kurzstreckenfahrkarte,* or "short-haul ticket"). Children 5 and under travel free on the RMV network. The fine is 60€ for anyone else caught riding without a ticket; it will be enforced whether you plead ignorance or not. See p. 495 for discount travel card information.

The most useful **bus** line for visitors is **route 46,** which connects the main station to museums along Schaumainkai and the Museums Embankment, south of the River Main.

BY TAXI   To call a cab, dial ✆ **069/230001** (www.taxi-frankfurt.de). You can also get a cab at one of the city's designated taxi stands, or by

Save Big on Transportation & Museum Costs

Three special tickets help you save money on public transportation and museum admission in Frankfurt. A transport **Tageskarte** (day ticket) good for unlimited travel inside Frankfurt's central zone costs 7€ for adults, 4.20€ for children, and 11€ for a group of up to 5 adults and children. You can buy this ticket from the ticket machines or via the RMV app. It's the best discount ticket for travelers who don't plan to visit many museums.

The **Frankfurt Card,** available at the airport's Terminal 1 Welcome Center and city tourist offices, allows unlimited travel anywhere within the greater Frankfurt area (including from Frankfurt Airport); a 20% reduction on the tourist office's sightseeing tour; discounts in some shops and restaurants; and half-price admission to many museums, including MMK and the Goethe-Haus. The cost is 10.50€ for a 1-day card and 15.50€ for a 2-day card. For a group of up to 5 adults and children traveling together, the card

is an even better deal: 20.50€ for 1 day, 30.50€ for 2 days. This is the card to buy if you'll be whizzing around the city on public transportation and dropping into just a couple of museums.

The best discount card for museum hounds is the **MuseumsuferTicket.** This allows free admission for 34 Frankfurt museums—everything we recommend in this chapter except the botanical gardens, including the Städel and temporary shows at the Schirn—for 2 consecutive days. The ticket costs 18€ for adults, 10€ for children and students ages 6 to 18, or 28€ for a family of 2 adults and their children or grandchildren. Considering admission to just the Städel costs 14€, this represents a fantastic deal for anyone planning to visit more than a couple of museums while in Frankfurt. The ticket is sold at all 34 participating museums, as well as Frankfurt's tourism information offices. See **www.museumsufer-frankfurt.de** for further details.

hailing one on the street (the car's roof light will be illuminated if it's available). Taxis charge by the distance, number of passengers, and any waiting time, without extra surcharges for luggage. The initial charge is 2.80€ (rising to 3.30€ between 10pm and 6am); each kilometer costs 1.75€ (rising to 1.85€ between 10pm and 6am). There's a 7€ flat-rate supplement for taxis carrying more than 4 passengers.

VISITOR INFORMATION

Tourist Information Hauptbahnhof, by the main entrance to the train station (© **069/2123-8800**), is open Monday through Friday 8am to 9pm, Saturday and Sunday 9am to 6pm. In the Altstadt, **Tourist Information Römer,** Römerberg 27 (© **069/2123-8800**), is open Monday through Friday 9:30am to 5:30pm, Saturday and Sunday 9:30am to 4pm.

The city tourism website **www.frankfurt-tourismus.de** is loaded with useful information for first-time visitors. The best city blog for new openings, events, and offbeat ideas is **www.stadtkindfrankfurt.de** (in German).

[FastFACTS] FRANKFURT

Dentists & Doctors

Almost all dentists and doctors speak English. If you prefer to select from a preapproved list, contact your consulate.

Drugstores **Apotheke-an-der-Hauptwache,**

Schillerstrasse 4 (www.apotheke-an-der-hauptwache.de; © **069/913-0700**) is a centrally located and well-stocked pharmacy, open Monday through Friday 9am to 7pm, Saturday 10am to 6pm. Posted in the window is the local rota for out-of-hours pharmacy

service. Similar detailed information is posted on their website (click on "Notdienstkalender" in the right-hand margin).

Emergencies Dial

© **110** for the police; © **112** for a fire, first aid, and ambulance.

Internet Access The

MyZeil shopping mall (see p. 516) has free, reliable WiFi, as does the **Schirn** (p. 505) and **Frankfurt Airport** (see p. 489). Most hotels offer free WiFi to guests.

Post Office There's a

post office at the **Hauptbahnhof,** opposite platform 23, open Monday to Friday 7am to 7pm, Saturday 8am to 4pm.

Safety Frankfurt is a

relatively safe city, but you should still stay alert, just as you would in any urban area. Take particular care around the Hauptbahnhof at night.

Toilets There are many

public facilities in central Frankfurt, especially in the Altstadt.

EXPLORING FRANKFURT

As with just about every city in Germany, you have to figure World War II into the equation of modern-day Frankfurt. After major destruction in World War II, Frankfurt was rebuilt in a way that salvaged a small portion of its once-extensive Altstadt, but otherwise turned, in architectural terms, to the future instead of the past. A major rebuilding project to reinstate a larger section of the medieval city—between the half-timbered **Römerberg** and the **Kaiserdom** (Cathedral)—is due to be unveiled by the end of 2017. It will include precise reconstruction of the **House of the Golden Scales,** one of the city's iconic Renaissance buildings, completely destroyed in 1944.

You can easily explore Frankfurt's compact Altstadt on foot. Nearly all the main sights lie within the boundaries of the old city walls, which today form a semicircle of narrow parkland around the center. Other sights are just across the river along the **Museumsufer (Museum Embankment),** where several marquee museums are located along **Schaumainkai,** the street that runs directly parallel to the River Main.

If you plan to see a lot of museums while here, the heavily discounted **MuseumsuferTicket** is a no-brainer; see p. 495. *Note:* **Monday** is the wrong day for museum hounds to come to Frankfurt. Most of the top places of interest are closed.

A good way to see Frankfurt, especially if your time is limited, is by guided tour. A **daily walking tour** is offered by the city tourist offices. This 2-hour tour, in German, picks up passengers at 2pm from TouristInfo Römer (Römerberg 27, in the Altstadt). An additional tour in English leaves from the Römer at 2:30pm (daily Apr–Oct, weekends only Nov–Mar). The tour covers the center of the city and includes the Goethe-Haus and the rooftop observation platform of the 200-metre (656-ft.) Main Tower. The cost is 14€ for adults, 12€ for students (with a 20% discount for Frankfurt Card holders; see p. 495). Reserve tickets by calling ✆ **069/2123-8800.** From April through November the tourist offices also operate themed walks on weekends at 10:30am.

Frankfurt on Foot ★ (www.frankfurt onfoot.com; ✆ **01520/846-4200**) runs a daily walking tour of the old center,

always led by native English speakers. The tour begins from the Römerberg at 10:30am and lasts 3 to 4 hours. It costs 12€ for adults, 10€ for seniors and students. The same folks can also arrange private and themed tours on demand.

On Saturdays, Sundays, and holiday afternoons throughout the year, you can hop on the **Ebbelwei-Express** (www. ebbelwei-express.de; ✆ **069/2132-2425**), an old, colorfully painted streetcar, and ride all through Frankfurt and over to the apple-wine taverns of Sachsenhausen (see p. 518). The entire route takes about an hour and costs 8€ for adults and 3.50€ for children up to 14. The fare includes a glass of apple wine (or apple juice). You can buy tickets from the conductor. Catch the trolley at Römer, Willy-Brandt-Platz, or the main train station; service starts about 1:30pm and ends about 5:30pm.

Exploring the Museum Embankment (Museumsufer)

Several of Frankfurt's best and most-visited museums are found across the river from the Altstadt along the Main embankment on a street called Schaumainkai. The **Eisener Steg ★**, an old iron bridge, spans the river, connecting the Altstadt to the eastern end of the Museumsufer.

Deutsches Architekturmuseum (German Architecture Museum) ★ MUSEUM This specialist collection isn't for everyone, but will intrigue those with an interest in architecture or urban planning. The permanent collection focuses on the development of architecture from Paleolithic huts to the skyscraper. The story is told in a series of 25 scale models showing key stylistic developments over the centuries, from ancient Sumerian city planning to Bath's Royal Crescent and New York's Chrysler Building. Also on display is a collection of 19th- and 20th-century architectural plans, displays on international modern architecture, and a rolling program of temporary exhibits.

Schaumainkai 43. www.dam-online.de. ✆ **069/212-38844.** Admission 9€ adults, 4.50€ students and children. Tues–Sun 11am–6pm (Wed until 8pm). U-Bahn: Schweizer Platz.

THE FRANKFURT skyline

Many visitors never take the time to look up—thereby missing one of Frankfurt's great points of interest. Admittedly, the city doesn't have the icons of New York or Chicago, or the towering colossi of China and the Middle East. But this is the closest thing in continental Europe to a modern skyscraper city. You'll find several interesting examples in the Bankenviertel (Banking Quarter), along and around Neue Mainzer-strasse—known jokingly as "Bankenklamm" (bank gorge) or "Little Wall Street." Some of Frankfurt's most Instagram-friendly pinnacles include the following.

Commerzbank Tower   Completed in 1997 on the edge of the old center, the 259m (849-ft.) Commerzbank Tower was the tallest building in Western Europe for over a decade, until London's 310m (1,004-ft.) Shard took over in 2011. Its 49th-floor observation deck offers a spectacular panorama of Frankfurt and the entire region. Among the building's many environmental innovations are "sky gardens" which flood the tower with natural light. Free tours run on the last Saturday of every month. You'll need to book 4 months ahead; email hochhaus-fuehrungen@commerzbank.com.

Main Tower   The 54th-floor observation deck at Neuer Mainzerstrasse 52 is the highest publicly accessible point in Frankfurt. Opened in 1999, the tower tops out at 200m (656 ft.); views extend northwest across the city to the Feldberg mountain. Admission is 6.50€ adults, 4.50€ students and senior citizens (Frankfurt Card holders, p. 495, get a 20% discount). Hours are Sunday to Thursday 10am to 9pm (7pm winter), Friday to Saturday 10am to 11pm (9pm winter). See **www.maintower.de**.

Messeturm   The postmodern design of this 256.5m (842-ft.) tower near the Messe (convention center) incorporates classic Art Deco skyscraper elements, a pyramid, and Frankfurt's traditional building material, red sandstone. Its designer, German-American Helmut Jahn, is also known for Berlin's futuristic Sony Center.

Deutsches Filmmuseum (German Film Museum) ★★ MUSEUM

Deutsches Filmmuseum is one of the two top movie museums in Germany (the other is in Berlin; p. 80). Over 2 floors, galleries chronicle the history of the German and European filmmaking industry with examples of moviemaking equipment and models illustrating how special effects are shot. The history-focused collection traces the evolution of movie technology from crude 18th-century "peep shows" and later moving panoramas to the 1834 **Zoetrope,** Emile Reynaud's 1882 **Praxinoscope,** a replica of Edison's 1889 **Kinetoscope,** and the Lumière brothers' **Cinematograph** from 1895. A small theater shows pioneering early cinema, mostly French and British. The upper floor examines the craft of modern moviemaking, with a large interactive green-screen, costumes—including Darth Vader's head and an *Alien*—plus a host of iconic clips playing on a loop.

Schaumainkai 41. www.deutsches-filminstitut.de/en/filmmuseum. © **069/961-220220.** Admission 7€ adults, 5€ students and children. Tues–Sun 10am–6pm (Wed until 8pm). U-Bahn: Schweizer Platz.

ECB Tower   The newest (2015) monolith on the Frankfurt skyline stands alone in the Ostend district, on the banks of the River Main. At 185m (607 ft.) and with an apparent "bend" in its twin-towered design, it houses the European Central Bank.

Kronenhochhaus   Also known as the Westend Tower (or Westendstrasse 1), this distinctive 208m (682.2-ft.) tower gets its name from its bill-shaped crown. A giant sculpture at its entrance, *Inverted Collar and Tie* by Claes Oldenburg and Coosje van Bruggen, reminds us that bankers can also have a sense of humor.

Silberturm (Silver Tower)   At 167m (547 ft.), the modernist seat of Deutsche Bahn is notable for its aluminum exterior, giving it a silver sheen. It has the only rounded corners found on a Frankfurt skyscraper.

Deutsche Bank Towers   These twins have been nicknamed *Soll und Haben*, meaning Debits and Credits, which apparently seems funny to Frankfurt's bankers. Initially built between 1979 and 1984, the 158m (518 ft.) towers were later rebuilt from within as "green towers," which now use half the electricity.

Skyper   At 153m (502-ft.), this is Frankfurt's shortest skyscraper. Its quarter-circle floor plan blends in with the Siberturm across Taunusstrasse and a 1913 neoclassical block at its foot.

Japan Center   Completed in 1996 and rising 115m (377.2 ft.) above Taunustor, the Japan Center features a hanging roof and a red granite, square-paneled facade whose proportions are based on a traditional Japanese tatami mat.

Europaturm   At 337m (1107 ft.), a tad taller than the Eiffel Tower, this needle-shaped structure north of the city center has been Frankfurt's highest structure since it was built in 1979. Used as a communications tower, it is not open to the public.

Liebieghaus ★★ ART MUSEUM   Housed in a rustic 19th-century villa with an Art Nouveau extension, this important museum displays superb sculpture of the human face and traces the development of its form over a 4,000-year period. There's an intimacy and expressiveness in some of the sculptures that is both timeless and somehow elevating. Each item is beautifully displayed, which adds to the aesthetic pleasure of a visit. The Liebieghaus collection includes noteworthy pieces from ancient Egypt, Greece, and Rome, and from medieval and Renaissance Europe. In the medieval section, look for the 11th-century carving of the Virgin and Child created from applewood in Trier (probably). Farther down the timeline there's an expressive 16th-century Madonna created by Tilman Riemenschneider, the brilliant woodcarver from Würzburg (for more on his work, and where it's found, see p. 252); Andrea della Robbia's polychrome terracotta altarpiece of the Assumption (ca. 1500); and Chinese and Khmer stone carvings. Give yourself at least an hour to see the major works. The museum's **garden café** makes a pleasant spot to pause for a coffee.

Schaumainkai 71. www.liebieghaus.de. © **069/605098-200.** Admission 10€ adults; 8€ seniors and students; 18€ family ticket. Tues–Sun 10am–6pm (Thurs until 9pm). U-Bahn: Schweizer Platz.

Museum für Angewandte Kunst (Museum of Applied Arts) ★

MUSEUM   Two buildings—one the early 19th-century Villa Metzler, the other a 1985 structure designed by architect Richard Meier—house this substantial collection of European, Asian, and Islamic decorative arts. The museum has outstanding collections of glassware (including 15th-century Venetian pieces), German rococo furnishings, and porcelain. A series of rooms in the older wing place objects and furniture in their historical context, from a Georgian dining room to rooms with Biedermeier and Jugendstil styling.

Schaumainkai 17. www.museumangewandtekunst.de. © **069/212-21386.** Admission 9€ adults, 4.50€ students; free last Sat of month. Tues–Sun 10am–6pm (Wed until 8pm). U-Bahn: Schweizer Platz.

Städel ★★★ ART MUSEUM   Frankfurt's most august art gallery, which celebrated its 200th birthday in 2015, is also one of the top museums in Germany. Its collection brings together noteoworthy painting,

Modern art in the Städel, one of Europe's top museums.

johann wolfgang **VON GOETHE** (1749–1832)

"That is the true season of love; when we believe that we alone can love, that no one could ever have loved as much before, and that no one will ever love in the same way again."

Romanticist, poet, playwright, philosopher, scientist, Goethe is the towering figure in German literature. His book *The Sorrows of Young Werther* was a seminal inspiration for the Romantic movement. His epic *Faust* inspired such composers as Mozart, Liszt, Beethoven, and Mahler. Goethe's nonfiction writing heavily influenced Hegel, Nietzsche, Jung, Darwin, and others. Never afraid of controversy, he favored a highly sexualized writing style at a time of repressive social mores; some of his poems were suppressed from publication in his lifetime. *Werther*, one of his first works, was criticized as glorifying suicide. His poem "Der Zauberlehrling" was adapted for "The Sorcerer's Apprentice" segment in the 1940 animated Disney film *Fantasia*.

sculpture, and drawings from medieval to modern Europe, and a photography collection that covers the spectrum of photographic art. The top floor **Old Masters galleries** house a roll-call of Western painting; highlights include 17th-century Dutch artists including Rembrandt; 16th-century German painters Dürer, Grünewald, and Memling; and an outstanding collection of Flemish primitives, including Jan van Eyck's **Lucca Madonna** (1437), with exquisite detail on the carpet and folded robes. A large multicolored 1509 altarpiece and an impish nude *Venus* represent the work of Lucas Cranach the Elder. A small Dutch Golden Age room houses one of the Städel's most famous works, Jan Vermeer's **The Geographer** (1669), a precise interior and portrait rich in symbolism. A high-quality **Italian Renaissance and Mannerist collection** has Raphael, Tintoretto, Carpaccio, Rosso Fiorentino and a Botticelli portrait of Simonetta Vespucci. The "modern art" floor features French Impressionists such as Renoir, Degas and Monet, along with German painters of the 19th and 20th centuries, including Tischbein's famous 1787 **Portrait of Goethe in the Roman Campagna** in Italy. (Goethe was heavily influenced by his wide-ranging Italian wandering.) A vast **basement gallery** houses postwar painting and sculpture, from Francis Bacon and Alberto Giacometti to contemporary art, photography and installations. Highlights include a few Cubist panels and 20th-century German Expressionists, including a large Ernst Ludwig Kirchner collection. Art lovers should allow at least 2 hours to tour the Städel.

Schaumainkai 63. www.staedelmuseum.de. ✆ **069/605-0980.** Admission 14€ adults, 12€ students. Tues and Fri–Sun 10am–6pm; Wed–Thurs 10am–9pm. U-Bahn: Schweizer Platz.

Exploring Altstadt

Archäologisches Museum Frankfurt ★ MUSEUM   This archaeology collection is displayed inside the city's former Carmelite church, an atmospheric Gothic building with a faintly frescoed cloister annex. The collection focuses on the prehistory and ancient history of settlements in the Main Valley. Notable exhibits include basalt and sandstone carvings from the Roman era.

Karmelitergasse 1. www.archaeologisches-museum.frankfurt.de. ⓒ **069/212-35896.** Admission 7€ adults, 3.50€ students and children. Tues–Sun 10am–6pm (Wed until 8pm). U-Bahn: Willy-Brandt-Platz or Römer.

Goethe-Haus ★ HISTORIC HOME   Johann Wolfgang von Goethe (1749–1832), Germany's greatest writer, was born in this spacious house and lived here until 1765, when he moved to Weimar. Creaking floorboards and original furnishings make it easy to conjure up the feeling of a prosperous, tranquil home life in bygone days. The interior decoration reflects eclectic baroque, rococo, and neoclassical styles of the 18th century. Paintings of friends and family adorn the walls. The room where Goethe wrote is on the top floor; the room next door displays one of his cherished childhood possessions, a puppet theater. Annexed to the

Goethe Haus, the boyhood home of Johann Wolfgang von Goethe.

house, the modern, glass-fronted **Goethe-Museum** is mostly of interest to Goethe specialists, as it contains a library of books, manuscripts, graphic artworks, and paintings associated with Goethe and his works. Highlights includes some extraordinary vistas of Rome, painted in the 1790s by Goethe's friend Jacob Philipp Hackert.

Grosser Hirschgraben 23–25. www.goethehaus-frankfurt.de ✆ **069/138-800.** Admission 7€ adults, 3€ students, 1.50€ children. Mon–Sat 10am–6pm; Sun 10am–5:30pm. U-/S-Bahn: Hauptwache.

Historisches Museum Frankfurt ★ MUSEUM   This wide-ranging city museum looks at Frankfurt's history in a broad sense, from **early-medieval remains of the city walls** in the basement—dating to the period when Frankfurt was ruled by Staufer emperors—to a series of eclectic collections amassed by eminent burghers over the ages, encompassing everything from antique coins to faïence pottery. It's shocking to view side-by-side **models of the Altstadt** from around 1927 and the burned-out pile of rubble from 1946. Rebuilding Frankfurt's center has been a subject for local polemics ever since. The latest project—re-creating the Coronation Route between the cathedral and Römer—will include a revamp to this very museum, scheduled for completion in 2017. Most of the museum remains open in the meantime.

Fahrtor 2. www.historisches-museum.frankfurt.de. ✆ **069/212-35154.** Admission 7€ adults; 2€ students and seniors. Tues–Sun 10am–5pm (Wed until 9pm). U-Bahn: Römer.

Kaiserdom (Imperial Cathedral) ★ CHURCH   The famous dome-topped west tower of the Kaiserdom (also known as Bartholomäus-Dom/Cathedral of St. Bartholomew) dominates the Altstadt. The highly ornamented tower dates from the 15th century and is built of red sandstone. Construction on the cathedral began in the 13th century and went on to the 15th, but the structure wasn't entirely completed until 1877. The church gained cathedral status in the 14th century when it became the site of the election of the emperors (called Kaisers in Germany) of the Holy Roman Empire. Between 1562 and 1792, the Kaisers also were crowned here, so the church became known as the Kaiserdom. (Previous coronations had taken place in Aachen Cathedral; p. 545.) Destroyed by Allied bombs in 1944, the cathedral was painstakingly rebuilt in 1953. The layout is a fairly simple Gothic hall-church with three naves and a transept. The **Dommuseum** in the church's 19th-century cloister exhibits coronation robes of the imperial electors. The oldest vestments date from the 1400s. The cathedral also hosts a series of classical and organ music concerts; see **www.domkonzerte.de** for details.

Domplatz. ✆ **069/1337-6186.** Church free; Dommuseum 4€ adults, 2€ children. Church open Sat–Thurs 8am–8pm, Fri noon–8pm; Dommuseum open Tues–Fri 10am–5pm, Sat–Sun 11am–5pm. Free guided tours Tues–Fri 3pm. U-Bahn: Römer.

Museum für Moderne Kunst (Museum of Modern Art) ★★
ART MUSEUM   The Germans are great collectors of modern and contemporary American art from the New York School; museums reverentially displaying the works of Andy Warhol and other big-name American artists are found all over the country. This is one of them. Its contemporary and modern collection has just the right mix of top-quality work and indecipherable nonsense—though which specific pieces fall into which category is very much a matter of opinion. Big, bold works by Americans Roy Liechtenstein, Claes Oldenburg, and Warhol tend to steal the show from the modern German artists, including Joseph Beuys and Florian Hecker, whose works are also on permanent display. Regular high-profile contemporary shows (and site-specific installations) occupy a large part of the exhibition space, so a visit serves as a useful tool to tune in on current trends in international contemporary art. Absolutely not in doubt is the quality of the museum building itself, a postmodern structure designed by Austrian architect Hans Hollein. A triangular white-marble palace full of hidden stairwells and secret vistas, it stands in stark contrast to everything in the surrounding streets.
Domstrasse 10. www.mmk-frankfurt.de. © **069/212-30447.** Admission 7€ adults, 3.50€ students. Tues–Sun 10am–6pm (Wed until 8pm). U-Bahn: Römer/S-Bahn: Hauptwache.

Museum Judengasse ★ MUSEUM/HISTORIC SITE   While the main center of Frankfurt's Jewish Museum is closed through 2018 for large-scale redevelopment, this smaller Judengasse site (reopened in 2016 after a major revamp of its own) has a significant location: This was where Frankfurt's **Jewish ghetto** stood, an overcrowded alleyway established in the 15th century and inhabited for almost 400 years. Only archaeological traces remain, as do paintings, ritual items, and other everyday objects displayed to illuminate Frankfurt's significant Jewish history before 1800. (The new museum will take the story forward from 1800.) Beside the building is the **Jewish cemetery** and a **Holocaust memorial** marking the spot from where around 12,000 of the city's 26,000 Jews were transported to their deaths during World War II. The rest mostly fled; by 1945, Frankfurt's official Jewish population was 160.
Neuer Börneplatz. www.juedischesmuseum.de. © **069/2127-0790.** Admission 6€ adults, 3€ seniors and students. Tues 10am–8pm, Wed–Fri 10am–6pm, Sat–Sun 11am–6pm. U-Bahn: Konstablerwache.

Römer and Römerberg ★★ HISTORIC SITE   As early as the Stone Age, people occupied this high ground that was later settled by the Romans. After Germanic tribes conquered the Romans, their settlement fell into ruins and was forgotten until construction workers in the 20th century stumbled across its ancient remains. But from then to now, this area in Frankfurt's Altstadt has played a prominent role in the life of the city. The Altstadt centers around three Gothic buildings with stepped gables, known collectively as the **Römer**—the German word for Roman, and perhaps an oblique reference to the Holy Roman Empire and its Holy Roman Emperor, who was once crowned in the nearby Kaiserdom. These houses, just west of the cathedral, originally were built between 1288 and 1305 and then bought by the city a century later for use as the **Rathaus (Town Hall).** After his coronation in the Kaiserdom, a new emperor and his entourage paraded westward to the Römer for a banquet. In the **Kaisersaal (Imperial Hall),** on an upper floor of the center house, you can see romanticized images of 52 emperors, painted in the 19th century to celebrate the thousand-year history of the Holy Roman Empire. Medieval city officials and their families used to watch plays and tournaments from a specially

Half-timbered Gothic buildings in Römerberg, the heart of Frankfurt's Altstadt.

built gallery added in the 1460s to the **Alte Nikolaikirche,** a small chapel opposite the city hall. (The chapel's 35-bell carillon plays at 9:05am, 12:05pm, and 5:05pm.) **Römerplatz,** the square in front of the Römer, is one of Frankfurt's most popular spots, with rebuilt half-timbered buildings housing cafes and restaurants. For a month from late November, the site becomes the heart of Frankfurt's giant **Christmas Market,** where Alpine-style wooden huts sell all kinds of festive trinkets—plus (of course) Glühwein and hot Apfelwein.

Römer. **Kaisersaal:** ✆ **069/21234814,** admission 2€; open daily 10am–1pm and 2–5pm. U-Bahn: Römer.

Schirn Kunsthalle ★ ART MUSEUM   Frankfurt's premier venue for one-off art shows and exhibitions has an offbeat, contemporary edge to its programs. Recent headliners have included "Sturm-Frauen," a retrospective of early–20th-century female avant-garde artists. The building also has excellent free Wi-Fi.

Römerberg. www.schirn.de. ✆ **069/299882-112.** Admission 7€–11€ adults; 5€–9€ students and seniors. Tues–Sun 10am–7pm (until 10pm Wed–Thurs). U-Bahn: Römer

Exploring Westend

Palmengarten ★★ PARK/GARDEN   In recent years, renewals and reconstructions have enhanced Frankfurt's 19th-century botanical gardens: They're now home to a perennial garden, an expanded rock garden, and a beautiful rose garden. A huge gallery that serves as an exhibition hall for flower shows and other exhibitions surrounds the 1869 **Palm House.** The vast glass **Tropicarium** is split into dry and humid areas, with individual zones maintained at different temperatures and humidity levels to accommodate desert, savannah, rainforest, and mangrove vegetation. The **Sub-Antarctic House** houses plants from southern Chile, Argentina, and New Zealand. Collections of orchids, palms, succulents, waterlilies, and many others are also on display. In the park area, there's a small lake where visitors can row boats. In summer, concerts are staged in the band shell; evening events include open-air dancing, jazz, and fountain illumination.

Siesmayerstrasse/Palmengartenstrasse. www.palmengarten.de. ⓒ **069/21233939.** Admission 7€ adults; 2€ children 12 and under. Daily 9am–6pm (Nov–Jan closes 4pm). U-Bahn: Bockenheimer Warte or Westend.

Senckenberg Naturmuseum ★ MUSEUM   The city's grand 1817 natural history museum may have been rebranded as a "world of

On summer nights, the Palmengarten's fountains are brilliantly lit.

struwwelpeter: **A VERY NAUGHTY BOY**

He's a memory now, but up until World War II, the image of Struwwelpeter, with his enormous shock of hair and Edward Scissorhands-length fingernails, was ingrained in the nightmares of every German child and many children throughout the world. (Struwwelpeter's grotesque hair and fingernails were the result of his bad-boy behavior.) Published in 1844, Struwwelpeter was the creation of Heinrich Hoffmann (1809–94), a Frankfurt psychiatrist who wrote gruesomely moralistic children's short stories. The illustrated story became one of the most popular "children's books" in Germany and was translated into 14 languages (in England, Struwwelpeter became "Shockheaded Peter"). The entertaining **Struwwelpeter Museum,** Schubertstrasse 20 ✆ **069/747-969**), displays original sketches and illustrations with copies of the book (and its classic image of Struwwelpeter) from many different countries. Admission is free; the museum is open Tuesday to Sunday 10am to 5pm.

biodiversity" but it's a fairly un-diverse bunch that grab most people's attention: The large entrance hall's colossal casts of **dinosaur skeletons** (and some originals, too). All the classics are present: T-Rex, Triceratops, Iguanadon, Stegasaurus (a personal favorite). Some skeletons are cast from fossils in New York's American Museum of Natural History. The museum also has a fine **fossil collection** of its own, which includes trilobites, Archaeopteryx, and casts of 150 million–year-old footprints left by a sauropod. The excellent gallery devoted to marine dinosaurs has useful explanations in English. The full-sized skeleton collection of more recent Earth dwellers includes a Mammoth, blue whale, Orca, and hippo.

Senckenberganlage 25. www.senckenberg.de. ✆ **069/75420.** Admission 9€ adults; 7€ seniors; 4.50€ students. Mon–Fri 9am–5pm (Wed until 8pm); Sat–Sun 9am–6pm. U-Bahn: Bockenheimer Warte.

Parks & Gardens

Despite such a soaring skyline, Frankfurt is remarkably green. Both banks of the River Main provide a riverside retreat for lunch breaks, and are often the venues for summertime events. The entire ring where the city ramparts once ran is now a green, shady oasis popular with joggers, the **Grüne Gurtel (Green Belt)** ★. **Bethmann Park** ★, with its Chinese and rose gardens, lies along this route, reachable by tram no. 12.

Farther north and west, the city's two major parks can be found next to one another: the **Palmengarten** botanical garden (see p. 506) and, on the grounds of the Rothschild family's former castle, **Grüneburg Park,** the city's largest, and a popular sunbathing haunt in summer.

Grüneberg Park, the city's largest, is on the grounds of a former Rothschild family castle.

Especially for Kids

Several Frankfurt museums appeal particularly to children. One obvious choice is the **Senckenberg Naturmuseum** ★ (p. 506), whose grand hall is populated with lifesize dinosaurs (skeletons and casts), including Stegosaurus and T-Rex. The rest of the collection is child-friendly and educational. It's also open on a Monday, unlike almost every other city museum. Attached to the **Schirn Kunsthalle** (p. 505), **MiniSchirn** has activities aimed at children ages 3 and up.

The early evening variety show at **Tigerpalast** (p. 520) features acrobats and magicians. Children ages 12 and under get half off the ticket price. **Oper Frankfurt** (p. 520) offers free tickets to some performances for children ages 8 to 18 accompanying an adult to the opera.

Sports-loving kids will relish a chance to experience the loud and lively atmosphere at a German *Fussball* (soccer) game. Though not as famous as big European teams such as Real Madrid, Liverpool, or Barcelona, **Eintracht Frankfurt** ★ (www.eintracht.de) is one of the major historic names in the German league. Founded in the late 19th century, *Die Adler* ("the eagles") are probably best known for a defeat—in the 1960 European Cup Final, when a 3–7 loss to Real Madrid was judged at the time to be the best soccer match ever played. Eintracht plays

September to May, alternate weekends, at the **Commerzbank Arena** (S-Bahn line 8 or 9 to Stadion; 15 min. from central Frankfurt). Buy tickets for home printing as far ahead as you can (they include a return S-Bahn fare) at **www.eintracht.de/en/tickets**. Many games sell out fast. To get kitted out in local colors before the game, visit **Eintracht Shop,** Bethmannstrasse 19 (closed Wed and Sun). Failing that, wear black and red.

WHERE TO STAY IN FRANKFURT

Finding a room, not to mention one at an affordable price, depends partly on the city's busy trade-fair schedule. On average, there is one major event a month; the local promotion office maintains a schedule online at **www.messefrankfurt.com**. It's best to reserve well in advance. At any time, **weekend rates in hotels are significantly cheaper**— Friday through Sunday nights are the time to pick up a bargain, when rooms often cost a fraction of their midweek price. Last-minute accommodation apps including Hotel Tonight usually have several offers on weekends.

Most of Frankfurt's accommodations lie around the **Westend** convention area and the train station. The station can be considered central, although reaching the old city on foot requires a walk through the less-than-picturesque **Bahnhofsviertel** in front of the main station. This is not the most scenic part of Frankfurt, but it is lively at night, well stocked with good restaurants, and convenient for transport links. Consider hotels in **Ostend** or south of the River Main to get a more sedate perspective that many casual visitors miss.

Note: Many Frankfurt hotels do not have parking facilities. We note those that do; in other cases, you'll have to park in nearby public lots or garages, where rates vary.

Expensive

The Pure ★★   White on white on more white (with dark oak flooring and orange accents thrown in): That about sums up the decor at this Zen property. If you like contemporary minimalist décor, warm designer lighting, and airy, high ceilings, you'll think this place is stunning (most do). Iin the end, no matter how trendy it is, a good hotel must provide efficient service and a good bed—and The Pure is a winner here as well.
Niddastrasse 86. www.the-pure.de. © **069/710-4570.** 50 units. 99€–423€ double. Breakfast included. **Amenities:** Restaurant; bar; fitness center and sauna; Wi-Fi (free). U-Bahn/S-Bahn: Hauptbahnhof.

Villa Kennedy ★★★   Perhaps the best address in Frankfurt, this place is tucked away south of the Main, just a short walk from the

The courtyard garden at Villa Kennedy.

Museum Embankment. Rooms inside the early 20th-century villa build-ing are large and elegant, making liberal use of natural materials and subtle tones. You'll pay a little extra for a terrace and garden view. A peaceful courtyard garden and full spa give the place a feeling of serenity that's not easy to find in bustling, businesslike Frankfurt.

Kennedyallee 70. www.villakennedy.com. ✆ **069/717120.** 163 units. 210€–345€ double. Breakfast 35€ (some rates include B&B). Parking 32€. **Amenities:** Restau-rant; bar; concierge; health club; spa; indoor pool; room service; Wi-Fi (free). U-Bahn: Schweizer Platz.

Moderate

25 Hours Hotel by Levi's ★   One of the hippest addresses in Frank-furt's increasingly fashionable Bahnhofsviertel, this high-concept hotel has rooms themed on the world's best-known jeans, with each of the 6 floors taking a different decade from the 20th century as a starting point for a riff on denim-influenced design. Every room is quirky, with an authentic vintage feel matching the inspiration; if you want more space, pay the extra for an XL unit (about 40€ over the price of the smallest rooms).

Niddastrasse 58. www.25hours-hotels.com. ✆ **069/2566-770.** 76 units. 79€–300€ double. Breakfast 18€. **Amenities:** Restaurant; bike rental (free); Wi-Fi (free). U-Bahn: Hauptbahnhof.

Europa Style ★   There's a gaggle of affordable hotels close to the main rail station, but few match the Europa Style for service and value. Rooms are spacious, with modern furnishings themed loosely around iconic European locations, bold-print feature walls, and beds with comfortable mattresses. A well-stocked minibar—soft drinks, beer, chocolate—is thrown in for free. Light sleepers should request a Superior room; these face the back rather than busy Baselerstrasse (and cost 20€ or so more). The **Europa Life** hotel shares the same building, with slightly reduced comforts but the same welcoming owners.

Baselerstrasse 19. www.hoteleuropa-frankfurt.de. © **069/2380-589.** 31 units. 88€– 139€ double. Breakfast included. **Amenities:** Bar; minibar (free); Wi-Fi (free). U-Bahn/S-Bahn: Hauptbahnhof.

Lindenberg ★★★   Built in 1874, this elegant townhouse offers relaxed, quietly upscale accommodations in the serene eastern quarter of Frankfurt. Rooms are large, with high ceilings, period stucco coving, parquet floors, pile rugs, and proper double beds. Bold colors and contemporary fittings ward off any chance of a dated feeling to the place, including in the (fairly petite) tiled bathrooms. Communal areas include a fully equipped kitchen and a parlor with midcentury–modern Scandinavian-inspired styling. The whole place has an open, homey feel—if you like concierge desks and tipping the bellhop, this isn't for you. In 2016, the same owners inaugurated a second Lindenberg, in Sachsenhausen; if it's even half as good as their first, it also deserves a place on your shortlist.

Rückertstrasse 47. www.das-lindenberg.de. © **069/430-591530.** 10 units. 99€– 228€ double. Breakfast 6€–9€. **Amenities:** Kitchen; gym; Wi-Fi (free). S-Bahn: Ostendstrasse.

Inexpensive

Five Elements Hostel ★★   Though billed as a hostel, this place also throws in some of the best features of a budget hotel, notably rooms with ensuite bathrooms (and good water pressure). Private rooms are spacious and basic, but that doesn't translate as "plain and uninteresting": There's an industrial-chic feel to the décor, where bold colors contrast with occasional bare concrete surfaces. Beds are budget, but comfortable. Reception staff is friendly and full of advice on where to go, especially for night owls. The area is a little seedy—this was traditionally Frankfurt's red-light area, and some old habits die hard—but is an increasingly popular zone for bars, clubs, and hipster restaurants. Light sleepers should request a room which does not overlook Moselstrasse. Room rates vary widely based on demand: Book well ahead and away from trade-fair periods for an enticing deal.

Moselstrasse 40. www.5elementshostel.de. © **069/2400-5885.** 45 units. 38€–240€ double with bathroom. Breakfast 4.50€. **Amenities:** Bar; Wi-Fi (free). U-Bahn/ S-Bahn: Hauptbahnhof.

WHERE TO EAT IN FRANKFURT

In recent years, Frankfurt has become—along with Berlin and Munich—one of Germany's best dining cities, with restaurants that offer an array of well-executed world cuisines (occasionally at steep prices). There are, however, many places where you can eat well for less. The *Apfelwein* (apple wine) taverns in Sachsenhausen on the south bank of the Main, tend to serve traditional Hessian dishes such as *Rippchen mit Kraut* (pickled pork chops with sauerkraut), *Haspel* (pigs' knuckles), and *Handkäs mit Musik* (strong, cheese with vinegar, oil, and chopped onions; not recommended for honeymooners). See p. 518 for specific recommendations. One condiment unique to Frankfurt is *grüne Sosse,* a green sauce made from herbs and other seasonings, chopped hard-boiled eggs, and sour cream, usually served with boiled beef (*Tafelspitz*) or poached fish.

As well as our favorites below, consider lunchtime grazing at the buzzing **Kleinmarkthalle** (see p. 518).

Ariston ★★ GREEK   Behind a handsome 19th-century facade is the best Greek restaurant in Frankfurt. Both food and décor are elevated above typical "taverna" level. Menu offerings are rooted in the simple, bold flavors of the Mediterranean and reliably good, with a special shout-out to the grilled lamb with lemon marinade and rosemary potatoes. There is also a catch-dependent fish and seafood list. Every morning except Sunday, Ariston doubles as an elegant cafe-bar.

Heiligkreuzgasse 29 (at Klingerstrasse). www.ariston-restaurant.de. *©* **069/9203-9950.** Main courses 18€–24€. Mon–Sat 10:30am–1am; Sun noon–midnight. U-Bahn/S-Bahn: Konstablerwache.

Berger Street Food ★★★ SUSHI   Flavor and freshness burst from the dishes at this fantastic little sushi bar with indoor and outdoor tables (and boxed food to go, too). Maki, nigiri, and futomaki rolls come in "fusion" combinations that pinch ingredients from various Asian cuisines, notably Vietnamese. The likes of a salmon, avocado, and flying fish roe "inside-out roll" are freshly made while you wait, and beautifully

FRANKFURTER VERSUS hot dog

At traditional taverns in Sachsenhausen and around the city, real **Frankfurters**—smoked sausages made with pork and seasonings—are almost always on the menu. The oldest-known recipe dates from 1487. The local product has been labeled "genuine Frankfurt sausage" since about 1900 to distinguish it from the American hot dog (hot dogs are for sale in Frankfurt, too, but always under the name "hot dog"). Unlike hot dogs, Frankfurters are long, skinny, and usually served in pairs; like all German sausages, they contain no fillers.

presented. Spring rolls—wrapped in ricepaper, with fillings such as chopped shrimp, spring onion, and cilantro—really zing. They also make their own fruit cocktails, served with or without a shot of liquor. No credit cards.

Bergerstrasse 83. www.bergerstreetfood.de. © **069/8580-1714.** Portions 2.50€– 8.50€. Mon–Sat 11:30am–10:30pm; Sun 1:30–10:30pm. U-Bahn: Merianplatz.

Fisch Franke ★ SEAFOOD   It's a long way from Frankfurt to the sea, but this place manages to pull off a light-and-airy seafood bistro atmosphere just right. Catch-fresh specials are often the best way to go, but evergreen classics on the menu also include broiled salmon with Hollandaise sauce and spinach or shrimp tagliatelle with Mediterranean vegetables. This is also a good place to sample local freshwater fish such as pike-perch and catfish.

Domstrasse 9 (at Berliner Strasse). www.fischfranke.de. © **069/296261.** Main courses 13€–27€. Mon–Fri 9am–9pm, Sat 9am–5pm. U-Bahn: Römer.

Fletcher's Better Burger ★★ FAST FOOD/AMERICAN   What a burger bar should be: Brash, Fast, and Fresh. Fletcher's serves up the best patty in the city, cooked to order with quality beef and crispy salad sandwiched in a lightly toasted bun. The Coke comes in real bottles, not from bottomless soda dispensers. Seating is at communal benches: This is a place for a very satisfying taste of home, not a romantic meal for two.

Münchenerstrasse 11. www.fletchers-frankfurt.de. © **069/2400-7558.** Main courses 6.50€–12€. Mon–Fri 11:30am–10pm; Sat–Sun noon–11pm. U-Bahn: Willy-Brandt-Platz. Also at: Ohmstrasse 57 (© **069/7807-9514**) and Nordwestzentrum (© **069/ 1302-7611;** closed Sun).

Français ★★★ FRENCH   It's a dress-up affair at the Français— "smart casual" is the official lingo, but men may feel most comfortable in a coat and tie—which is only appropriate for the dining experience at this well-heeled restaurant inside the grand Steigenberger Frankfurter hotel. Many consider this some of the best French food in Germany; chef Patrick Bittner's cooking is creative and beautifully presented. To sample his full range, go for a seven-course tasting menu (also comes in a five-course version). Your starter might be Alsatian goose liver with apricots and artichokes or a black salsify soup with tiger prawns, followed by Scottish partridge with grapes and radicchio, or Breton turbot with celery red onions. (The menu changes monthly.) The unpasteurized cheeseboard is legendary, and an expert sommelier is on hand. An evening here represents a major splurge in refined surrounds. Reservations are essential.

In the Steigenberger Frankfurter Hof, Am Kaiserplatz. www.restaurant-francais.de. © **069/215118.** Main courses 36€–48€; lunch menu 49€/59€ for 2/3 courses; dinner menu 104€/135€ for 5/7 courses. Tues–Fri noon–1:45pm and 6:30–9:30pm; Sat 6:30– 9:30pm. U-Bahn: Willy-Brandt-Platz.

Haus Wertheym ★ HESSIAN/GERMAN Old-fashioned, atmospheric, and a relatively inexpensive taste of old Frankfurt—that's the vibe in this half-timbered house on a cobblestoned street just off the Römer. A beamed ceiling is hung with everything from wrought-iron pendant lamps and antique serving spoons to hokey maxims carved into wood. It's a bit touristy, but also reliable and lots of fun. The menu focuses on traditional dishes such as Frankfurter sausages, pork Schnitzels (breaded cutlets), and *Rippchen* (pickled pork chop) served with a slab of smoky Speck ham. Waitstaff squeeze the most out of a limited number of large tables: Expect to eat communally at busy times. No credit cards.

Fahrtor 1. www.haus-wertheym.de. ✆ **069/281432.** Main courses 12€–22€. Daily 11am–11pm. U-Bahn: Römer.

Im Herzen Afrikas ★★ EAST AFRICAN A relatively recent arrival on the dining scene, this popular and lively place delivers knockout Eritrean and Ethipioan cuisine at very affordable prices. It's an especially welcome spot for vegetarians in this carnivorous city. The selection of Eritrean specialties includes *schiro* (spicy garbanzo beans and tomato) and *timtimo* (lentils, tomato, and onion), all served with homebaked *injera* flatbread (also available gluten-free). To get a taste of the best of the place's meat and meat-free cooking, order a mixed multi-dish platter at 10€ per person.

Gutleutstrasse 13. www.im-herzen-afrikas.de. ✆ **069-2424-6080.** Main courses 6€–10€. Tues–Sat 6pm–1am; Sun 4–10pm. Closed 2 weeks Dec–Jan. U-Bahn: Willy-Brandt-Platz.

Maxie Eisen Buvette ★ AMERICAN/DINER Mainhattan's homage to a hip Manhattan deli-diner is a good spot for a lunch or informal dinner. The menu is heavy on NYC favorites, including pastrami on rye (served here with pickled cabbage) and a well-executed Caesar salad—though Hessian and Oriental ingredients also feature. Hungry diners might prefer the chipotle chicken wings with a side of nutmeg fries. For anyone with a sweet tooth, there's New York cheesecake and homemade lemonade. The wine list is short but very carefully selected: Plenty of folk just stop in to drink and snack.

Münchenerstrasse 18. www.maxieeisen.com. ✆ **069/7675-8362.** Main courses 10€–12.50€. Mon–Wed 11:30am–11pm; Thurs–Sat 11:30am–midnight; Sun noon–6pm. U-Bahn: Willy-Brandt-Platz.

Tiger & Palastbar ★★★ INTERNATIONAL What came first, the first-class variety show or the first-class restaurant? Well, this 190-seat venue has been playing two shows a night for 25 years, but the gourmet restaurant only really took off in 1997 when it was first awarded a Michelin star (it has held two stars since 2013). Eating here can be pricey, but if you combine it with watching the show (see p. 520), it gives

The Tiger Restaurant offers gourmet dining before or after a cabaret show.

you a unique and high-caliber dining–entertainment experience that goes way beyond regular supper-club level. Several seasonal multicourse menus show off chef Christoph Rainer's culinary talents (or you can order à la carte). In season, you might encounter a fresh "fruits of the sea" menu featuring hamachi, Arctic char, and a medley of other fresh fish, for example. There is an entire vegetarian menu, as well. Another option is to eat in the larger and less elaborate **Palastbar**—kind of like business class as opposed to first-class. Reservations are required for either.

Heiligkreuzgasse 16–20. www.tigerpalast.com. ℰ **069/9200-220.** Tiger main courses 35€–65€, fixed-price menus 98€–120€ (dinner and show packages from 125€ per person). Palastbar main courses 22€–38€. Tiger Tues–Sat 7pm–midnight. Palastbar Tues–Sun 5pm–11pm. S-Bahn/U-Bahn: Konstablerwache.

Cafés

Brot und Seine Freunde ★ This wonderland of baked goods sells freshly made sandwiches (around 5€), cakes by the slice and a decent espresso, from a corner bar that echoes 1950s America. Kornmarkt 5. www. brotundseinefreunde.de. ℰ **069/2097-8885.** Mon–Fri 7am–7pm; Sat 8am–6pm; Sun 10am–5pm. S-/U-Bahn: Hauptwache.

Café Karin ★ An unpretentious cafe with art-filled walls, old wooden tables and daily newspapers, this is a good place to stop for coffee, a glass of wine or beer, or a light meal (5€–9€ a dish). Grosser Hirschgraben 28.

www.cafekarin.de. ✆ **069/295-217.** Mon–Sat 9am–7pm; Sun 10am–7pm. S-/U-Bahn: Hauptwache.

Laumer ★ A classic German *Kaffeehaus* with a large garden and modernist interior, Café Laumer serves some of the best pastries in town, at a relaxed pace. It's had plenty of time to perfect the recipes—it's been around since 1919. Bockenheimer Landstrasse 67. www.cafelaumer.de. ✆ **069/727912.** Daily 8am–7pm. U-Bahn: Westend.

Schirn Café ★ Beside the Schirn art museum (p. 505) in the heart of the Altstadt, this light-filled steel, glass, and granite cafe-bar has a brunch menu served Sundays 10am to 6pm. At other times, it's a light-bites menu with the likes of squid salad. Römerberg. ✆ **0172/3753111.** Tues and Fri–Sun 10am–7pm; Wed–Thurs 10am–10pm. U-Bahn: Römer.

FRANKFURT SHOPPING

As you might expect, this big, modern, wealthy and international city serves as a shopping magnet for the entire region. Stores are generally open Monday through Saturday 9 or 10am to 6 or 6:30pm. Of course, Sunday sees most everything closed.

The Top Shopping Streets & Areas

Zeil—the "Golden Mile" and reputedly Germany's busiest shopping boulevard—is a pedestrian zone that runs between the Hauptwache and Konstablerwache. It's loaded with boutiques of all kinds, shoe retailers, countless clothing chains, and fashionable department stores including a large **Peek & Cloppenburg ★** (www.peek-cloppenburg.de). Once the site of the city's 14th-century cattle market, it is also home to **MyZeil ★** (www.myzeil.com), which from an architectural standpoint is more than just a mainstream mall. Designed by Italian architect Massimiliano Fuksas and opened in 2009, its spider-web glass facade caves inward, creating an inner funnel of glass and metal that creates a sense of movement within the space. Ride

Riding the 6-story escalator up through the ultra-modern MyZeil mall.

to the top of the six-story escalator, the longest shopping mall escalator in Europe, to appreciate its impressive architecture. The mall also has reliable free Wi-Fi.

Nearby **Kleidoscop** ★, Töngesgasse 38 (www.kleidoscop.de; ✆ **069/9776-1428**), is *the* place in town to hunt down women's fashions by hot local designers. Items tend to be from the avant-garde end of the scale: original but eminently wearable.

Schillerstrasse, on the section between the Börse (stock exchange) and Eschenheimer Turm, has high-toned, but mostly affordable fashion boutiques, accessories and linens.

West of the Hauptwache towards the Alte Oper, **Goethestrasse** is populated by exclusive stores evocative of Paris and Milan. Ready-to-wear couture jewelry and lingerie are the mainstays—think Jimmy Choo, Hermes, Armani, and the like. Running parallel to Goethestrasse, **Grosse Bockenheimerstrasse**—traditionally nicknamed *Fressgasse,* or "Pig-Out Alley"—is lined with wine dealers, delis, and butcher shops, most of which look back on a long and venerable past. These days, street-front space is shared with a few marquee brands, including Apple, Hugo Boss, and Porsche Design.

Many book dealers are located just west of the Hauptwache and around **Goetheplatz.** Antiques, old books, and etchings, plus modern and traditional commercial art galleries, arc on **Braubachstrasse** near the Römer and Dom, and at the southern end of **Fahrgasse.**

Lying just outside the center, **Bergerstrasse** is a strip of indie stores, small cafes, stationers, end-of-line clothing sale shops, and porcelain. Bohemian female fashion shoppers are well served by the likes of **Mi.na** ★ (no. 112; www.mina-schuhe.de; ✆ **069/4800-5172**); **Aries** ★ (no. 63; ✆ **069/448825**); and hippie-chic **Schick & Schock** ★ (no. 12; www.schick-schock.de; ✆ **069/9441-0050**). To get there, take the U-Bahn to Höhenstrasse.

South of the river, **Brückenstrasse** (around the corner of Wallstrasse) has a small but select group of boutiques selling one-off designer womenswear in retro and contemporary styles. Nothing much opens in this part of town before 11am. Stores here are best visited on a Saturday, when you can combine a stop at the trendy **Markt im Hof** (see p. 519).

Frankfurt's Best Markets

Bornheim Market ★ A colorful and bustling weekly market, frequented almost exclusively by local shoppers, its stalls hawk produce, freshly baked bread and pastries, honey, flowers, cheese, and more. Wednesdays and Saturdays from 8am to late afternoon. Bergerstrasse (at Saalburgstrasse). No phone. U-Bahn: Bornheim Mitte.

Flohmarkt (Flea Market) ★ Selling everything from old printers' blocks and posters to vintage bric-a-brac, bike locks, and secondhand

SACHSENHAUSEN & ITS apple-wine TAVERNS

Sachsenhausen, the district south of the River Main, has long been known for its taverns where **Apfelwein,** not beer, is the local drink. At an apple-wine tavern, everyone sits together at long wooden tables—and sooner or later, the singing starts.

Apfelwein (pronounced *ebb*-el-vye in the local dialect) is a dry, alcoholic, 12-proof apple cider. The "wine" is poured from a blue-and-gray stoneware jug (a *Bembel*) into glasses embossed with a diamond-shaped pattern (the *Gerippte*). The first sip may pucker your whole being, and convince you that you're drinking vinegar. If taking an Apfelwein straight is too much for you, try a *Sauergespritzt* (sour spritzer), a mixture of Apfelwein and plain mineral water, or a *Süssgespritzt* (sweet spritzer), Apfelwein mixed with lemonade-like mineral water.

Although available year-round, Apfelwein also comes in seasonal versions. *Süsser* (sweet), sold in the autumn, is the dark, cloudy product of the first pressing of the apple harvest. When the wine starts to ferment it's called *Rauscher,* which means it's darker and more acidic. You're supposed to drink Süsser and Rauscher straight, not mixed.

The Apfelwein taverns in Sachsenhausen traditionally display a pine wreath outside when a new barrel has arrived. Several are *Gartenlokale,* meaning they have tables outside in good weather. As well as drinks, the taverns usually serve traditional meals; hard rolls, salted bread sticks, and pretzels for nibbling are often on the tables, too. What you eat, including the snacks, goes on your tab.

To find a tavern, you could simply roam the cobblestoned streets of **Alt-Sachsenhausen**—there's no shortage of joints along **Neuer Wall** and **Klein Rittergasse.** Some of our favorite traditional Sachsenhausen taverns are **Fichtekränzi,** Wallstrasse 5 (www.fichtekraenzi.de; © **069/612-778**), open daily; **Atschel,** Wallstrasse 7 (www.atschel-frankfurt.de; © **069/619-201**), open daily; and **Dauth Schneider,** Neuer Wall 5–7 (www.dauth-schneider.de; © **069/613533**), open daily. Hours vary by establishment and season, but apple-wine taverns are generally open from midafternoon til midnight.

If you want to take home a typical Apfelwein souvenir, you'll find everything you need—including a stoneware Bembel—at **Maurer,** Wallstrasse 5 (www.keramik-maurer.de). For just a taste of apple wine as you view the city sights, ride the **Ebbelwei Express** (p. 497).

books, this flea market runs alternate Saturdays from around 8am to 2pm along the Main River on the Sachsenhausen side. The best place to begin is the south end of the Eisener Steg bridge. Follow stalls and tables westward from there. Schaumainkai. No phone. U-Bahn: Römer or Schweizer Platz.

Kleinmarkthalle ★★ It calls itself "Frankfurt with heart"—but in truth, it's all about the stomach. Bread, fresh produce, preserves and butcher's stalls share the city's covered market with spice vendors, bakers, cheesemongers, and florists. For anyone feeling peckish, there are authentic German sausages to go for a couple of euros, as well as a sushi bar and an Italian deli— **Valentino ★** (*©* **069/46092-361**)—that knocks out fresh pasta with a homemade sauce for around 9€ a plate. Market hours are Monday to Friday 8am to 6pm, Saturday 8am to 4pm. An der Klein-markthalle (entrances at Ziegelgasse and Hasengasse). www.kleinmarkthalle. de. S-/U-Bahn: Konstablerwache.

Markt im Hof ★ Local "Creative Quarter" hipsters, farm-direct regional produce, and organic street-food trucks set up shop in a former stables courtyard. Runs Saturdays from 10am to around 5pm. Wallstrasse 9–13. www.marktim hof.de. U-Bahn: Schweizer Platz.

The traditional Apfelwein tavern Altschel in Sachsenhausen.

ENTERTAINMENT & NIGHTLIFE

Frankfurt may be big and cosmopolitan, but it can sometimes lack the spit and spirit that animates the nightlife in places like Berlin or even nearby Cologne. It's not dull, certainly, but parts of town are geared to bankers rather than the young and young at heart. But that's not to say you won't be able to find somewhere to go after dark.

In recent years the **Bahnhofsviertel** (p. 494) has become the heart of a trendy, rapidly changing nightlife scene. Around here you'll find most of Frankfurt's lively new openings on the bar and club scenes (and even buzzing restaurants; p. 512)—and not all of them aimed just at the under-30s. It's a pretty inclusive scene. Remember, though: The Bahn-hofsviertel remains an edgy neighborhood, only a few blocks from the city's red-light district. You should not wander quiet alleys alone in the small hours. Stick to busy boulevards and nighttime hotspots.

For listings and general news about what's happening, pick up *Journal Frankfurt* (1.80€; www.journal-frankfurt.de) at newsstands all over the city. *Frizz* (www.frizz-online.de/stadtmagazin/frankfurt) and culture-focused *Strandgut* (www.strandgut.de), both free and available at the tourist office, also have listings. To purchase tickets for major cultural events, go to a venue's own box office (*Kasse*) or website, or to the **Tour-istInfo** office at the main train station or in the Römer. One of the best places for first-time visitors to spend an evening is at an **apple-wine tavern** in Sachsenhausen (see p. 518).

The Performing Arts

Alte Oper ★★   When the Alte Oper (Old Opera House) opened in 1880, critics hailed the building as one of the most beautiful theaters in Europe. Destroyed in the war, the Alte Oper didn't reopen until 1981. Today the theater, with its golden-red mahogany interior and superb acoustics, is the site of frequent symphonic and choral concerts, though no opera. The season runs September through June. Opernplatz. www. alteoper.de. ✆ **069/1340-400.** U-Bahn: Alte Oper/S-Bahn: Taunusanlage.

English Theatre Frankfurt ★   This long-established theater presents touring English-language musicals, comedies, and dramas from Tennessee Williams and Roald Dahl to works by contemporary playwrights. Tickets cost 25€ to 50€, with substantial reductions for students (not available on Saturdays). Gallusanlage 7. www.english-theatre.org. ✆ **069/242-31620.** U-Bahn: Willy-Brandt-Platz.

Oper Frankfurt ★★   Frankfurt's premier showcase for opera is also one of Germany's top spots, with a season that runs mid-September to early July. Tickets cost 15€ to 165€. Children ages 8 to 18 can go free with a full-paying adult to some performances. Untermainanlage. www.oper-frankfurt.de. ✆ **069/212-49494.** U-Bahn: Willy-Brandt-Platz.

Tigerpalast ★★   At Frankfurt's most famous cabaret, shows take place in a small theater, where guests sit at tiny tables to see about eight different variety acts (you can also have dinner before or after the twice-nightly shows; see **Tiger** gourmet restaurant, p. 514). Each show—a kind of small-scale vaudeville Cirque de Soleil with everything from gymnasts and acrobats to magicians and musicians—lasts 2 hours with a break for drinks and snacks. You don't need to know German to enjoy it, making it excellent family-style entertainment. Tickets cost 60€ to 66€; it's half-off for children 12 and under and a 25% discount for students aged 30 and under. Heiligkreuzgasse 16–20. www.tigerpalast.de. ✆ **069/920022-0.** U-Bahn: Konstablerwache.

Bars & Clubs

Aber ★★   Less achingly hip than many recent arrivals in this part of town: The music is lower, the clientele older. Fine wines, a good gin range, classic cocktails like a Negroni or a Dark and Stormy, and a sophisticated vibe. There's also a short restaurant menu. Gutleutstrasse 17. www. aber-frankfurt.de. ✆ **069/2648-6360.** U-Bahn: Willy-Brandt-Platz.

Gibson ★   Live rock and indie music venue with DJs and electronic music on Fridays and Saturdays. Zeil 85–93. www.gibson-club.de. ✆ **069/407-662580.** S-/U-Bahn: Hauptwache or Konstablerwache.

Harvey's ★   Popular and relaxed cafe and bar named after San Francisco gay rights campaigner Harvey Milk. With outdoor seating in summer, it draws a mixed gay-straight crowd and occasionally features live bands on weekends. Bornheimer Landstrasse 64. www.harveys-ffm.de. ✆ **069/4800-4878.** U-Bahn: Merianplatz.

Karlson ★   On weekdays, this place serves a younger crowd with cocktails in low lighting. On Fridays and Saturdays, they turn up the volume with electronic music after 11pm. Karlstrasse 17. www.karlson-club.de. S-/U-Bahn: Hauptbahnhof.

Luna ★   Often packed with young professionals, this is the sort of place where singles mix while mixologists—bartenders who know a thing or two about grasshoppers, juleps, champagne fizzes, and tropical coladas—work their magic. Closed Sundays. Stiftstrasse 6. www.luna-bar.de. ✆ **069/8477-6572.** S-/U-Bahn: Hauptwache.

Naïv ★   Dark wood, granite, low-watt pendant lighting, and a 10-page menu with German and international bottled beers. Naïf offers four of their own tap "house brews," plus wine, Prosecco, gin, vodka, and rum long drinks, outdoor seating, and food platters. Fahrgasse 4 (at Fischerplätzchen). www.naiv-frankfurt.de. ✆ **069/2100-6230.** U-Bahn: Römer.

Plank ★   Cozy corner bar that's become a mainstay of the Bahnhofsviertel. Daytime coffee; cocktails, wine, and bottled beers after dark. The party spills out onto the street in summer. Closed Sundays. Elbestrasse 4 (at Münchenerstrasse). www.barplank.de. ✆ **069/269-58666.** S-/U-Bahn: Hauptbahnhof.

A SPA TRIP TO BAD HOMBURG ★

20km (12 miles) N of Frankfurt

Bad Homburg has one of Germany's most attractive spas, still basking in some grandeur left over from turn-of-the-20th-century Europe. The town's natural mineral springs are thought to treat various disorders, especially heart and circulatory diseases. This popular watering spot has attracted regular folk and royalty from all over the world since Roman times. King Chulalongkorn of Siam (Thailand) was so impressed that he paid for a Buddhist temple to be built in Bangkok and transported to the **Kurpark** in 1910. Czar Nicholas II laid the foundation stone of an onion-domed Russian chapel nearby.

The name of the town itself entered into popular culture after a visit by England's King Edward VII. As Prince of Wales, he visited the spa and returned home with a new hat style, which he called the "Homburg." It became one of the West's most popular styles of male headgear: Famous wearers included Al Pacino's character in *The Godfather*.

The Buddhist Temple, a gift from the King of Siam, in Bad Homburg's Kurpark.

Essentials

ARRIVING   From Frankfurt, take the S-Bahn (line S5) from Frankfurt Hauptbahnhof to Bad Homburg for 4.55€ each way. The trip takes 20 to 25 minutes. See **www.rmv.de** for timetables. It's a 10-minute walk from Bad Homburg station to the center or the Kurpark (Spa Park). Access by car from the north or south is via the A5, exiting at Bad Homburg.

VISITOR INFORMATION   **TouristInfo im Kurhaus,** Louisenstrasse 58 (www.bad-homburg-tourismus.de; ✆ **06172/178-3710**) is open Monday to Friday 10am to 6pm and Saturday 10am to 2pm. The station info-point (Am Bahnhof 2; ✆ **06172/178-37120**) operates similar hours.

Taking the Waters

The **Kurpark (Spa Park)** ★ is a verdant, carefully landscaped oasis amid an otherwise commercial-looking town; its immaculately tended gardens are filled with brooks, ponds, arbors, and flowers. Bad Homburg's historic spa facilities sit within the Kurpark in the **Kur Royal (Kaiser-Wilhelms-Bad)** ★ (www.kur-royal.de; ✆ **06172/178-3178**), open daily 10am to 10pm. Entrance is 25€ per person for 2 hours, 40€ for 4 hours, 60€ for a full day. Patrons have access to a range of facilities, including thermally heated pools, saunas, steam baths, cold pools, and herb-enriched vapor baths. Massages, aromatherapy baths, and skin treatments require additional fees (36€–80€).

A nearby modern recreation area, **Taunus Therme ★**, Seedammweg 10 (www.taunus-therme.de/en; ℭ **06172/40640**), has thermal pools, a sauna, a hammam area, and a fitness center, plus two restaurants and bars, for a somewhat lower price: 14.70€ for 2 hours, 17.30€ for 3 hours, 19.40€ for 4 hours, and 26.20€ for a full day. Prices are a couple of euros higher on weekends and holidays. This large complex is open daily 9am to 11pm. Additional therapies and beauty treatments are available Monday through Thursday 9:30am to 12:30pm and 2:30 to 6pm, Friday 9:30am to 12:30pm.

Exploring the Rest of Bad Homburg

The town center has a sprawling pedestrian-only district with many shops, restaurants, and cafes. At the high end of the town is pretty **Marktplatz ★**.

Schloss Homburg ★ PALACE   The residence of the ruling Landgraves of Hesse-Homburg was begun in 1680 and finally completed in 1866. Its commissioner, Landgrave Friedrich II von Homburg, preserved the **White Tower** from the medieval castle that stood on the site, building his baroque palace and formal **gardens** around it. In the late 19th century, the palace became a summer residence for Prussian kings and, later, German emperors. The interior contains 18th-century furniture and paintings.

www.schloesser-hessen.de. ℭ **06172/9262-148.** Admission 4€ adults, 2.50€ seniors and children. Tues–Sun 10am–5pm (Nov–Feb until 4pm).

WHERE TO EAT IN BAD HOMBURG

Bad Homburg's spa complexes include on-site restaurants where you can have lunch. If you end up staying a little later in town before heading back to Frankfurt, here's our recommendation for an early dinner.

Flamm's ★   This lively local restaurant specializes in *Flammkuchen,* a thin, pizzalike flatbread, usually wood-fired with cream or crème fraiche in place of pizza's tomato paste. The dish is a specialty of Alsace, France, and southern Germany; tasty versions served here include the likes of French salami and Gruyère cheese and seasonal specials like the Christmas Flammkuchen, with goose breast, red cabbage, and chestnuts.

Elisabethenstrasse 38. www.flamms.de. ℭ **06172/23733.** Main courses 7€–9€. Open daily from 5 or 6pm (closed 2 weeks Dec–Jan).

COLOGNE & THE RHINELAND

F ew rivers claim such an important role in the growth of a nation as the Rhine. It rises in Switzerland and ultimately flows through the Netherlands in its progress to the sea, but most of its 1,370km (850 miles) snake through the mountains and plains of Germany. For more than 2,000 years, it has been a chief trade route, its deep waters enabling seagoing vessels to travel downstream from the North Sea as far as Cologne (Köln).

Rhine commerce brought wealth and power to several of Germany's most important cities, especially along the northern stretch from Bonn up through Cologne and Düsseldorf. All three cities, along with nearby Aachen, are within day-trip distance from each other, making it possible to choose one for a base and still sample the cultural riches of the others.

Farther south, between Koblenz and **Mainz,** the winding river cuts through steep vine-covered hillsides dotted with towns whose names are synonymous with fine German wine. Here you'll also find the **Lorelei,** the legendary rock from which a siren lured men to their doom. The saga of the Nibelungenlied comes to life here, from the *Siebengebirge* (Seven Mountains) near **Bonn,** where Siegfried slew the dragon, to **Worms,** where Brunhild plotted against the slayer.

Roadways along the Rhine tend to be heavily trafficked, so allow adequate time. Main roads hug both the left and right banks, with many car ferries to take you across. The most scenic stretch for driving is the mid-Rhine between Koblenz and Mainz. High-speed trains connect all the major cities, including Cologne, Bonn, and Mainz.

COLOGNE (KÖLN) ★★

It's difficult not to like Cologne. Visitors to this lively metropolis on the Rhine, Germany's fourth-largest and oldest city, are often struck by the cheek-by-jowl juxtaposition of the very old with the very new. You can see Roman ruins in an underground parking garage, an ornate Gothic cathedral beside a concrete museum complex, and a humble Romanesque church wedged in among luxury shops. On a 10-minute walk in Cologne, you could traverse 2,000 years of history.

Cologne—spelled *Köln* in Germany and pronounced *koeln*—offers far more than Germany's largest and most famous cathedral, although

FACING PAGE: **A view of the scenic Middle Rhine valley, near Boppard.**

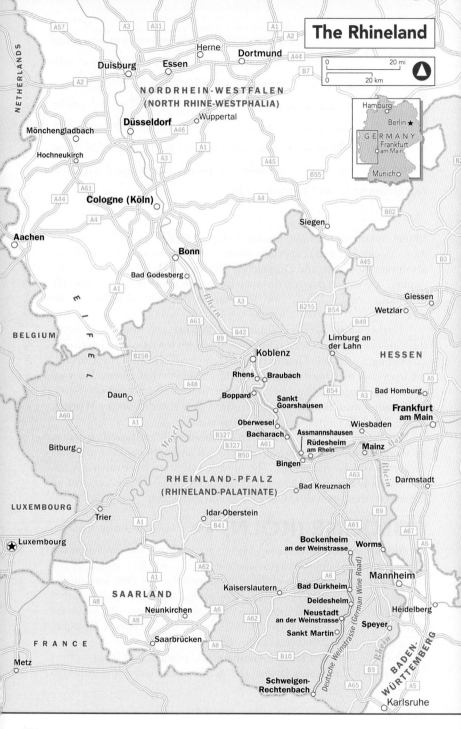

The Rhineland

Rosenmontag, the climax of Carnival season in Cologne.

that is reason enough to visit. The range of museums and the quality of their collections make Cologne one of the outstanding museum cities of Germany. Music, whether it's a symphony concert in the modern philharmonic hall, an opera at the highly regarded opera house, or a boisterous outdoor concert in the Rheinpark, is likewise a vital component of life here.

Cologne traces its beginnings to 38 B.C., when Roman legions set up camp. As early as A.D. 50, the emperor Claudius gave the city municipal rights—his wife, Agrippina the Younger, was born here. In addition to its

carnival **IN COLOGNE**

Many cities throughout Germany have Christmas markets, but only the traditionally Catholic cities celebrate carnival—a time when the weather may be gray, but spirits are high. Cologne's Carnival, the city's "fifth season," is one of the most eagerly anticipated events in Germany. The season officially lasts from New Year's Eve to Ash Wednesday. During this period, Cologne buzzes with masked balls, parades, and general delirium, particularly around **Rosenmontag**—the carnival's climax, which takes place on the day before Shrove Tuesday. Natives call their celebration *Fasteleer* or *Fastelovend*. We highly recommend visiting at this time—just make sure to book a room in advance. For upcoming events, see **www.koelnerkarneval.de**.

substantial Roman legacy, the city boasts 12 major Romanesque churches. Older than the cathedral, the churches drew medieval pilgrims from all across Europe to what was known as "Holy Cologne," one of the most important pilgrimage cities in medieval Christendom. From the early 1700s on, the city's name took on another meaning, as the birthplace of eau de Cologne.

Like Munich, Cologne is a city that likes to have fun, and a huge student population keeps it buzzing. When the weather turns warm, visitors and citizens stroll the Rhine promenades and flock to outdoor taverns and restaurants to enjoy the pleasures of a *Kölsch*, Cologne's unique beer.

Essentials
ARRIVING

BY PLANE Cologne's airport, **Flughafen Köln–Bonn** (www.koeln-bonn-airport.de), is located 14km (9 miles) southeast of the city. Direct flights arrive from most major European cities. The fastest and simplest way to get into the city from there is by taking an **S-Bahn train** (line S-13) from the airport train station directly to Cologne main train station. The trip takes around 15 minutes; the fare is 2.80€. A **taxi** from the airport to the center costs about 27€.

BY TRAIN Cologne is a major rail hub; reaching the city from anywhere in Germany, or the rest of Europe, is easy. Frequent daily trains arrive from Berlin (trip time: 4¼ hr.), Frankfurt (1¼ hr.), and Hamburg (4 hr.). Cologne's **Hauptbahnhof** (main train station) is in the heart of the city. For schedules, visit **www.bahn.com**.

BY CAR Cologne is easily reached from major German cities. It's connected north and south by the **A3** Autobahn and east and west by the **A4** Autobahn.

The Neighborhoods in Brief
ALTSTADT

The major sights of Cologne, including the mighty cathedral and the most important museums, are located in the **Altstadt (Old Town),** the restored but much altered medieval core of the city. The Altstadt spreads in a semicircle west from the Rhine to a ring road that follows the line of the 12th-century city walls (demolished, except for three gateways, in the 19th century). The center of the Altstadt is the **Innenstadt (Inner City),** the historical heart of Cologne, where the Romans built their first walled colony. Everything in this area is walkable by day or night.

BELGISCHES VIERTEL (BELGIAN QUARTER)

Called the **Belgian Quarter** because its street names refer to Belgian cities and provinces, this inner-city neighborhood just west of the

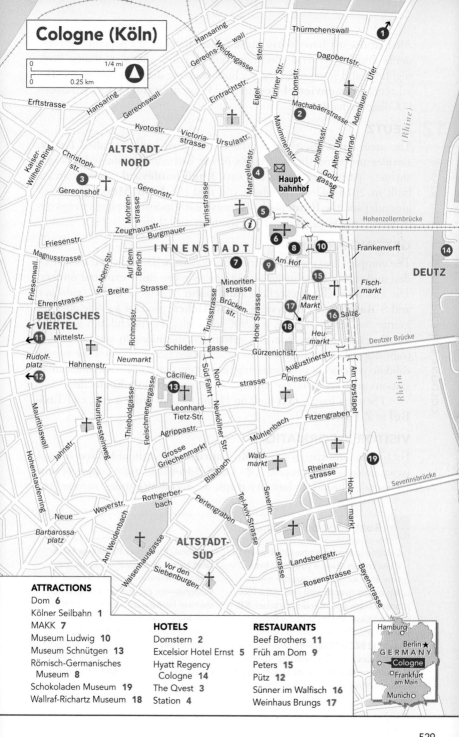

Cologne (Köln)

ALTSTADT-NORD

INNENSTADT

BELGISCHES VIERTEL

DEUTZ

ALTSTADT-SÜD

Hauptbahnhof

Hohenzollernbrücke

Deutzer Brücke

Severinsbrücke

ATTRACTIONS

Dom **6**
Kölner Seilbahn **1**
MAKK **7**
Museum Ludwig **10**
Museum Schnütgen **13**
Römisch-Germanisches
  Museum **8**
Schokoladen Museum **19**
Wallraf-Richartz Museum **18**

HOTELS

Domstern **2**
Excelsior Hotel Ernst **5**
Hyatt Regency
  Cologne **14**
The Qvest **3**
Station **4**

RESTAURANTS

Beef Brothers **11**
Früh am Dom **9**
Peters **15**
Pütz **12**
Sünner im Walfisch **16**
Weinhaus Brungs **17**

GERMANY
Hamburg
Berlin ★
Cologne
Frankfurt
  am Main
Munich

Altstadt doesn't have tourist attractions. However, it's popular with students and has several good non-touristy cafes and restaurants, lively nightlife, and some of Cologne's hottest young designer boutiques. The adjacent **Friesenviertel**—centred on Friesenplatz and Friesenstrasse—is Cologne's party zone.

DEUTZ

The area across the river, on the Rhine's east bank, is called **Deutz.** Besides providing the best views of the cathedral-dominated Cologne skyline—particularly from the vast **Rheinboulevard** stone staircase built in 2016—Deutz is where you find the **Köln Messe** (trade-fair grounds) and the **Rhinepark.** The city's early industrial plants were concentrated in Deutz, and many of them are still there.

GETTING AROUND

The compact and pedestrian-friendly Altstadt, where you find the cathedral and most of the major attractions, is most easily explored on foot. The city also has an excellent **Stadtbahn** (tram), **U-Bahn** (subway), and **S-Bahn** (light rail) system. A **CityTicket,** good for a single one-way journey within the center, is 1.90€ for adults, 1€ for children ages 6 to 14. Purchase tickets from the automated machines in stations and at tram stops (labeled *Fahrscheine*), or at station ticket windows. Be sure to validate your ticket upon entering the system; validation machines are in stations and on trams. For information, visit **www.kvb-koeln.de**.

There's a handy **taxi** rank on Heumarkt. To order a cab, call **Taxi-Ruf** at ✆ **0221/2882.**

VISITOR INFORMATION

For tourist information go to **Köln Tourismus,** Kardinal-Höffner-Platz 1 (www.cologne-tourism.com; ✆ **0221/346430**), right opposite the cathedral. The office has city maps, an accommodations service, and

---

Boat Trips on the Rhine

Cologne is a major embarkation point for Rhine cruises. Even if you don't have time for a long cruise, you can enjoy a trip on the river aboard one of the local boats. From April through October, **KD** (Köln-Düsseldorfer Deutsche Rhein-schifffahrt), Frankenwerft 35 (www.k-d. com; ✆ **0221/2088-318**), offers several boat tours from Cologne. The KD ticket booth and boarding point is right on the river, a short walk south from the cathedral. The 1-hour **Panorama Rund-fahrt** tour is a pleasant way to see the stretch of Rhine immediately around Cologne—not particularly scenic, since the river hereabouts is pretty industrial-ized, but you will get a view of the Cologne skyline with its spires. The tour departs daily at 10:30am, noon, 1:30pm, 3pm, 5pm and 6pm. Tickets cost 9.80€ for adults, 6€ children ages 4 to 13.

Rhine cruise boats afford a fine panorama of Cologne Cathedral.

information on attractions and tours. It's open Monday to Saturday 9am to 8pm, Sunday 10am to 5pm.

Exploring Cologne

Cologne cathedral and all the city's major museums are found in the **Altstadt**. *Note:* Museums in Cologne are generally closed on Monday. However, several of the best remain open until 10pm on the **first Thursday of every month**.

Dom (Cathedral) ★★★ CATHEDRAL   This enormous structure—the largest cathedral in Germany and all northern Europe—is the star of Cologne, the city celebrity with top billing. Considering how much time passed during its construction, it's a wonder that the Gothic facade is so stylistically coherent. More than 600 years elapsed from the laying of the cornerstone in 1248 to the placement of the last finial on the south tower in 1880. Upon completion, Cologne cathedral was the tallest building in the world, its twin filigreed spires rising to a height of 157m (515 ft.). Overwhelming is the simplest way to describe it—as you'll discover when you step inside.

The cathedral was built to enshrine holy relics—in this case, relics of the Three Kings, or Magi, which had been stolen from a church in Milan by Emperor Frederick Barbarossa. These relics, which drew pilgrims to Cologne throughout the Middle Ages, are still housed in the **Dreikönigschrein (Shrine of the Three Magi),** at the end of the cathedral choir. The giant reliquary is a masterpiece of goldsmith work dating from the end of the 12th century. The **Choir,** which can be visited only on guided tours, was consecrated in 1322 and contains original, richly carved oak stalls, screen paintings, and a series of statues made in the cathedral workshop between 1270 and 1290. The famous **Three Kings windows** in the clerestory were installed in the early 14th century. There are also some magnificent Renaissance-era stained-glass windows in the north aisle, and German artist Gerhard Richter's darkly shimmering stained-glass windows in the south transept, installed in 2007. Another treasure is the **Gero Cross,** hanging in a chapel on the north side of the choir, a rare monumental sculpture carved in Cologne in the late 10th century and reputedly the oldest large-scale crucifix in the Western world. On the south side of the choir, don't miss seeing Stephan Lochner's altarpiece, **Adoration of the Magi** (ca. 1445). The painting is a masterpiece of the Cologne school—Italian in format, Flemish in the precision of its execution.

The Gothic clerestory of Cologne Cathedral.

The cathedral's **Schatzkammer** (**Treasury**) is rather disappointing; you aren't missing much if you skip it. If, on the other hand, you're in reasonably good shape, climb the 509 stairs of the 14th-century **South Tower** for an inspiring view of the city and the Rhine.

Domkloster. www.koelner-dom.de. ✆ **0221/9258-4730.** Admission to cathedral free; treasury and tower 8€ adults, 4€ children and students, 16€ family; tower only 4€ adults, 2€ children and students, 8€ family. Tour of choir 8€ adults, 6€ students and children. Daily 6am–7:30pm (tourist visits easiest Mon–Sat 10am–6pm, Sun 1–4:30pm); tower 9am–4pm (May–Sept until 6pm); treasury 10am–6pm. English-language cathedral tour Mon–Sat 10:30am and 2:30pm, Sun 2:30pm. Bahn: Hauptbahnhof/Dom.

Kölner Seilbahn (Cologne Cable Car) ★ VIEW/RIDE   For a fun, family-friendly panoramic view of the the city, take a ride on the first cable-car system in Europe designed to span a major river. In operation since 1957, the enclosed gondolas cross the river beside the Zoobrücke (Zoo Bridge) between the Rheinpark in Deutz and the zoo. You get a great view of the massive cathedral and Rhine river traffic. The trip takes about 15 minutes each way.

Riehler Strasse 180. www.koelner-seilbahn.de. ✆ **0221/547-4184.** Round-trip 6.50€ adults, 3.70€ children ages 4–12. Mar 20–Oct daily 10am–6pm. Bahn: Zoo/Flora.

MAKK: Museum für Angewandte Kunst Köln (Museum of Applied Arts) ★ MUSEUM   The treasures on display in this museum include furniture, home decor, and crafts from the Middle Ages to the present day. There's a strong narrative theme to the ground-floor **Winkler Galleries,** which examine the interplay of art, design movements such as Bauhaus, and wider history, notably war and industrialization. Exhibits, largely from the 20th century, include furniture by Finnish architect Alvar Aalto and American architect Frank Lloyd Wright, Arne Jacobsen chairs, and work by German architect Mies van der Rohe, American designer Charles Eames, and others. Upper floors are dedicated to **Jugendstil interiors,** and there's temporary exhibition space, which could be showing anything from radio design to 20th-century fashion.

An der Rechtschule. www.museenkoeln.de. ✆ **0221/221-23860.** Admission 6€ adults, 3.50€ children 6–12. Tues–Sun 11am–5pm (1st Thurs of every month until 10pm). Bahn: Hauptbahnhof or Appellhofplatz.

Museum Ludwig ★★ ART MUSEUM   Dedicated to 20th-century and contemporary art, Museum Ludwig opened in 1986 in a choice location right behind the cathedral. It's a vast, echoey space, with one of the world's largest collections of **Picasso** paintings, ceramics, and works on paper. A substantial, high-quality **Pop Art** collection focuses on the aesthetics of consumerism. **Max Beckmann** (1884–1950), Minimalism, Surrealism, Constructivism, Expressionism, and abstract art are further strong points of the collections. Contemporary works include monumental pieces by Xu Bing and Brits Gilbert and George. Give yourself at least an hour.

Heinrich-Böll-Platz. www.museenkoeln.de. © **0221/221-26165.** Admission 13€ adults, 8.50€ students, children 18 and under free. Tues–Sun 10am–6pm (1st Thurs of every month until 10pm). Bahn: Dom/Hauptbahnhof.

Museum Schnütgen ★★ ART MUSEUM   The medieval period in Cologne—starting in the 12th century and lasting into the 16th, when the Renaissance hit town—saw a blossoming of art and architecture that was nothing short of amazing. This was the period when construction of the massive cathedral began, and when the city's 12 Romanesque churches (see p. 536) were built. Cologne was a major pilgrimage site, and ecclesiastical art flourished through woodcarvers, stonecarvers, stained-glass makers, and painters. Art in this period was part of a belief system that reflected Christianity as the word of God, not just pretty images to look at (though they are that, too). This is the art that you will see in the strangely undervisited Schnütgen, housed in a forbidding-looking modern building that incorporates the graceful Romanesque church of **St. Cäcilien** (St. Cecilia, patron saint of music). A must for anyone interested in Cologne's medieval heritage, the museum houses a small, splendid sampling of sacred art from the early Middle Ages to the baroque. Prized among the woodcarvings displayed in St. Cecilia is the **Kalverienberg,** a large oak scene created in the Netherlands in the 1430s. Expressive sculptures and images in stained glass give an idea of the artistic blessings bestowed upon "Holy Cologne."

Cäcilienstrasse 29. www.museenkoeln.de. © **0221/221-23620.** Admission 6€ adults, 3.50€ students. Tues–Sun 10am–6pm (Thurs until 8pm; 1st Thurs of every month until 10pm). Bahn: Neumarkt.

Römisch-Germanisches Museum (Roman-Germanic Museum) ★★ MUSEUM   Local history is inextricably bound up with the history of Rome. In fact, Cologne first earned official status at the behest of Empress Agrippina the Younger (ca. A.D. 14–59), who was born here. This museum was built around the magnificent **Dionysius Mosaic,** produced in a Rhineland workshop in the 3rd century and discovered in 1941 by workers digging an air-raid shelter. Towering over the mosaic, which extols the joys of good living (something Kölner are still good at), is the **Tomb of Lucius Poblicius,** constructed around A.D. 40 for a Roman officer. It is the largest antique tomb ever found north of the Alps. The museum's less-showy exhibits explore themes in the lives of ancient Romans in Cologne: religious life, trade and industry, the cult of the dead, and so on. Upstairs is a superlative collection of **Roman glassware,** a renowned collection of jewelry, gravestones from the earliest years of Christianity in Cologne, and the **Philosophers' Mosaic,** which depicts several Ancient Greek thinkers. On the lower level, devoted to

Roman daily life, there's an ancient black-and-white mosaic floor covered with swastikas. Centuries before the symbol became ominously identified with the atrocities of the Third Reich, the swastika—probably Indian in origin—was a symbol of good luck and happiness, and was known in Latin as the *crux gammata.* You need at least an hour to see the museum.

Roncalliplatz 4. www.museenkoeln.de. ✆ **0221/221-24438.** Admission 9€ adults, 5€ students. Tues–Sun 10am–5pm (1st Thurs of every month until 10pm). Bahn: Hauptbahnhof.

Schokoladen Museum (Chocolate Museum) ★★ MUSEUM

This enlightening museum traces the history and culture of chocolate, as far back as Europeans' first encounter with *cacao* around the time of Prussian explorer Alexander von Humboldt's journey to South America (1799–1804). There are child-friendly displays about chocolate cultivation, a working Lindt mini-production line, a chocolate fountain, and some gloriously surprising facts: Côte d'Ivoire's annual production is about double that of the entire Americas combined, for example. Exhibits also introduce in an accessible way such issues as the role of chocolate in Spain's conquest of Mesoamerica, 21st-century fair trade, sustainability, commodity pricing, and producer cooperatives. And there's a store, of course. A big one.

Holzmarkt. www.chocolatemuseum-cologne.com. ✆ **0221/931-8880.** Admission 9€ adults; 6.50€ children, students and seniors 65 and over; 25€ family. Tues–Fri 10am–6pm, Sat–Sun 11am–7pm (Jul–Aug and Dec also Mon 10am–6pm). Bahn: Heumarkt.

Wallraf-Richartz Museum ★★★ ART MUSEUM

The Wallraf-Richartz Museum is the city's greatest repository of fine art from the Middle Ages to the late 19th century. The first floor traces western art's origins in medieval Italy, with an outstanding collection of paintings by the **Cologne School** (most done between 1330 and 1550). Many of the panels and altarpieces depict legends from the lives of martyred saints who became identified with the "Holy Cologne" of the Middle Ages, St. Ursula in particular. Excellent labeling provides succinct explanations of the means, motivation, and methods behind highlighted works. A memorable collection of 17th-century **Dutch and Flemish paintings** holds pride of place on the second floor, including major works by Rubens and Rembrandt. In addition to important French and Spanish works, the museum boasts a rich collection of **19th-century paintings,** with major pieces by the German Romantic painter Caspar David Friedrich, Gustave Courbet, Edvard Munch, Auguste Renoir, and Camille Pissarro, among scores of others. Give yourself about 2 hours if you want to browse through all the galleries.

Obenmarspforten. www.museenkoeln.de. ✆ **0221/221-21119.** Admission 8€ adults, 4.50€ students. Tues–Sun 10am–6pm (1st and 3rd Thurs of every month until 10pm). Bahn: Rathaus or Heumarkt.

COLOGNE'S romanesque CHURCHES

Cologne has a dozen important Romanesque churches, all within the medieval city walls. During the Middle Ages, these churches were important destinations for the pilgrims who flocked to "Holy Cologne" to venerate relics of the Three Kings and various Christian martyrs. Eleven churches were devastated during World War II, but all twelve churches were later restored, often with interior changes; together they represent the rich architectural legacy of early medieval Cologne. If you have the time, and an interest in architectural history, Cologne's Romanesque churches are worth seeking out. Keep in mind, however, that not all of them are open daily. (Consult **www. romanische-kirchen-koeln.de** for more details.)

Let's start with the patron saint of Cologne, **St. Ursula,** whose 12th-century church ★ on Ursulaplatz (Bahn: Hauptbahnhof or Hansaring) stands on the site of a Roman graveyard. Legend has it that St. Ursula was martyred here with her 11,000 virgin companions in about 451. (An alternate telling of the tale suggests just 11 companions.) The story inspired countless medieval paintings and sculptures. The **shrine room of St. Ursula** (2€ admission) is a remarkable sight, its niches full of medieval sculpted wooden busts while the upper walls and ceiling are decorated with bones.

St. Panteleon, Am Pantaleonsberg 2 (Bahn: Barbarossaplatz), built in 980, has the oldest cloister arcades remaining in Germany. Elliptically shaped and twin-towered **St. Gereon,** Gereonsdriesch 2–4 (Bahn: Christophstrasse/Mediaark), contains the tomb of St. Gereon and other martyrs, with 11th-century mosaics in the crypt. **St. Severin,** Severinstrasse 1 (Bahn: Chlodwigplatz), originated as a 4th-century memorial chapel; the present church dates from the 13th to the 15th centuries.

Consecrated in 1065, **St. Maria im Kapitol,** Kasinostrasse 6 (Bahn: Heumarkt), stands on the site where Plectrudis, the wife of Pippin, built a church in the early 8th century; note its cloverleaf choir, modeled on that of the Church of the Nativity in Bethlehem. **St. Aposteln,** Neumarkt 30 (Bahn: Neumarkt), and **Gross St. Martin** ★, on the Rhine in the Altstadt (Bahn: Rathaus), also have the cloverleaf choir design.

St. Georg, Am Waidmarkt (Bahn: Poststrasse or Severinstrasse) is the only remaining Romanesque pillared basilica in the Rhineland; it contains an impressive forked crucifix from the early 14th century. **Cäcilienkirche (St. Cecilia's Church),** Cäcilienstrasse 29 (Bahn: Neumarkt), is the site of the **Museum Schnütgen** (see p. 534). **St. Andreas,** near the cathedral (Bahn: Hauptbahnhof), contains a wealth of late-Romanesque architectural sculpture. The remaining two Romanesque churches are set right on the Rhine: **St. Kunibert,** Kunibertskloster 2 (Bahn: Hauptbahnhof), and the smallest of the twelve, **St. Maria Lyskirchen,** Am Lyskirchen 12 (Bahn: Heumarkt), both of 13th-century origin.

Where to Stay

The city of Cologne levies an **additional 5% tax** on accommodation prices which is not (usually) included in the quoted room rate. Business travelers are exempt (you just need to fill out a form). *Note:* Prices can go above the usual maximums when there's a major trade fair in town.

Domstern ★ Small, friendly, affordable, and very handy for the station, this hotel is also unbelievably peaceful, considering how close you are to the chaos of the Altstadt. Rooms are midsized, with modern furnishings, firm mattresses, good water pressure in the showers, and thoughtful little extras like power sockets with U.S. fittings. Scattered about the place are old photos and drawings of Cologne, before World War II wreaked its havoc. The buffet breakfast is a cut above, with eggs available fresh to order however you like them.

Domstrasse 26. www.hotel-domstern.de. © **0221/16800-80.** 16 units. 89€–119€ double. Breakfast included. Parking 10€. **Amenities:** Wi-Fi (free). Bahn: Hauptbahnhof.

Excelsior Hotel Ernst ★★★ Walk out of the train station in Cologne and you stare up, mesmerized, at the enormous cathedral, one of the architectural wonders of Europe. You can see it from some of the rooms in the Excelsior, founded in 1863 and the grand dame of Cologne hotels. But that's not the only masterpiece on view: The breakfast room contains a Gobelins tapestry, and the walls of the public areas are hung with works by the likes of Van Dyck. Guest rooms are swank (especially deluxe units in the Hanse wing), with high ceilings, French windows (many with

A marble Pieta in St. Georg's church, one of Cologne's Romanesque beauties.

Juliet balconies), fine linens, and regal furnishings, plus such nice perks as a complimentary minibar. Bathrooms throughout are large, marble, and luxurious.

Trankgasse 1–5. www.excelsiorhotelernst. com/en. © **0221/2701.** 140 units. 198€– 490€. Breakfast 20€–31€. Valet parking 27€. **Amenities:** 2 restaurants; bar; concierge; exercise room; room service; sauna, Wi-Fi (free). Bahn: Hauptbahnhof.

Hyatt Regency Cologne ★★ For sure, you'll forgo some of the "only in Cologne" vibe. But if you like a full-service hotel with a plethora of amenities, this is your best bet. Even the most basic room is large, with king bed, electrical outlets everywhere, and a spacious travertine bathroom. You'll pay a little more for the best view in Cologne, across the Rhine to the cathedral and Rathaus tower. You can enjoy the same panorama at breakfast, which is extensive but expensive; if you search online, you'll find it bundled into value B&B packages at more palatable prices. Service is impeccable.

Kennedyufer 2A. www.cologne.regency.hyatt.com. © **0221/828-1234,** or 800/633-7313 from North America. 307 units. 135€–370€ double. Breakfast 25€–32€. Parking 29€. **Amenities:** Restaurant; bar; concierge; exercise room; indoor pool; room service; sauna, Wi-Fi (free). Bahn: Deutz Messe or Deutzer Freiheit

Station ★ Station lodgings put you on the wrong side of the tracks in much of Europe. But not here: Almost beside Cologne cathedral, with all the main sights in Cologne just a few minutes' walk away, this hostel has a better location that most city hotels, and for a fraction of the cost. The rooms are bright and comfortable, if spare, with good beds and strong showers. The staff is friendly and helpful and there's no curfew. Minimum 2 nights for stays including a Saturday.

Marzellenstrasse 44–56. www.hostel-cologne.de. © **0221/912-5301.** 50 units. 48€–62€ double. Breakfast 3€–9€. Parking in nearby garages, prices vary. **Amenities:** Bar; Wi-Fi (free). Bahn: Hauptbahnhof/Dom.

The Qvest ★★★ In 2014 the city's neo-Gothic former archive building was converted to a design hotel quite unlike anything else in the city. Much of the 19th-century framework remains—parquet floor, Revival-style ceramic tiles, stucco, and leaded window panes. On top of that sits a well-chosen veneer of Scandinavian and Bauhaus modernism, including original furniture by Arne Jacobsen, Gropius, and others. Rooms are spacious and high-ceilinged, though cupboard space is a bit tight. The location, in the old cloister of St. Gereon church, makes for a silent night.

Gereonkloster 12. www.qvest-hotel.de. © **0221/278-5780.** 34 units. 170€–320€ double. Breakfast included. Parking 30€. **Amenities:** Restaurant; bar; Wi-Fi (free). Bahn: Christophstrasse/Mediapark.

Where to Eat

Although several highly rated restaurants have established themselves in recent years, Cologne is not a city particularly known for its gourmet dining. Rather, it's a place for conversation and drinking, generally over enormous portions of typical Rhineland fare in crowded restaurants that are *gemütlich* (cozy) rather than elegant.

To eat and drink as traditional Kölner do, visit an old-style tavern-restaurant, or **Brauhaus.** Local menus generally feature *Halver Hahn* (a rye bread roll and Dutch cheese), *Tatar* (finely minced raw beef mixed with egg yolk, onions, and spices and served on bread or a roll), *Kölsch Kaviar* (smoked blood sausage served with raw onion rings), *Matjesfilet mit grünen Bohnen* (herring served with green butter beans and potatoes), *Hämchen* (cured pork knuckle cooked in vegetable broth), *Himmel und Äd* (apples and potatoes boiled and mashed together and served with fried blood sausage), and *Speckpfannekuchen* (pancakes fried in smoked bacon fat).

Kölsch: Cologne's Trademark Beer

Even if you don't really like beer, you might like Kölsch (pronounced *koehlsch*), a dry, frothy, top-fermented beer that's brewed only in Cologne. Tap Kölsch has an alcohol content of about 3% (most other types of German beer have an alcohol content ranging from 4% to 6%). If you go to any of the taverns in town, you can order a Kölsch from one of the blue-aproned waiters, called a *Köbes*. Waiters serve the beer in a tall, thin glass, called a *Stangen,* which they bring you in a carrier called a *Kölschkranz.* Expect to pay about 2€ a pop, .50€ less outside the Altstadt.

BRAUHAUS DINING

Früh am Dom ★ GERMAN/RHINELAND   This vast, busy Brauhaus near the cathedral has a good combination of atmosphere, economy, and proximity to the major sights. Expect straight-up Köln specialties, such as *Hämchen* (smoked pork knuckle with sauerkraut and potato), *Sauerkrautsuppe* (sauerkraut soup), and *Kölsche Kaviar* (blood sausage with onion). Früh-Kölsch, the tavern's tap beer, has over a century of brewing tradition. No credit cards.

Am Hof 12–18. www.frueh.de. ℂ **0221/2613-215.** Main courses 9€–22€. Daily 8am–midnight. Bahn: Hauptbahnhof.

Peters ★ GERMAN/RHINELAND   This large Brauhaus is packed to the rafters on weekends and holidays, and with good reason. Its wood-paneled rooms serve up classic fare from Cologne, and they brew some of the city's best Kölsch to wash it down. *Kölsche Kaviar* (blood sausage with onion), *Himmel und Åd* (mashed potatoes and applesauce with blood sausage), and *Hämchen* (smoked pork knuckle) are all good. Portions are enormous, but tables—seating is communal—can be a tight squeeze when the place is full.

Mühlengasse 1. www.peters-brauhaus.de. ℂ **0221/257-3950.** Main courses 10€–17€. Daily 11:30am–midnight. Bahn: Rathaus.

Pütz ★ GERMAN/RHINELAND   A neighborhood brewery-restaurant near the Belgian Quarter and university, Pütz is small and non-touristy—the sort of place where locals come for a good meal and a glass of Kölsch. Consequently it's more "authentic" than some larger brewery-restaurants in the Altstadt, and less expensive. The food is all traditional Kölner fare: herring filets (in cream or freshly marinated) with fried or boiled parsley potatoes and onions; homemade goulasch with brown bread; *Himmel und Åd* (mashed potatoes and applesauce with blood sausage and fried onions); or *Mettwurst,* a smoked, minced pork sausage. The atmosphere is unfussy, with wooden tables and brick walls.

Engelbertstrasse 67. ℂ **0221/211166.** Main courses 9€–17€. Mon–Sat noon–1am; Sun 4:30pm–1am. Bahn: Rudolfplatz.

OTHER FARE

Beef Brothers ★ FAST FOOD/AMERICAN   If you're the kind of traveler who commits to eat according to local traditions, look away now. From its home in the Belgian Quarter, Beef Brothers was at the front leading native Kölner toward appreciation of the beefburger. This isn't junk, though: One of the brothers in question previously worked as a chef at the five-star Excelsior Hotel Ernst (see p. 537). Burgers are fresh, portions are big, relishes are homemade, and there's a fridge stocked with cold Kölsch, German craft beers, and soft drinks. The food is a little salty—but that's no bad thing, right? Reservations not accepted.

Aachener Strasse 12. www.beef-brothers.de. ✆ **0221/2983-4736.** Main courses 3.50€–8€. Mon–Thurs noon–10pm, Fri noon–midnight, Sat 1pm–midnight, Sun 1–10pm. Bahn: Rudolfplatz.

Sünner im Walfisch ★ RHINELAND/GERMAN   Set back from the Rhine in the Altstadt, this 17th-century step-gabled inn with a black-and-white stone façade is a good choice for atmospheric dining—especially if you are interested in trying the traditional dishes of Cologne. Think *Himmel und Äd* (fried blood sausages with fried onions, mashed potatoes, and applesauce) or Rhenish *Sauerbraten* (braised pork with raisin sauce and potato dumplings). There are *Flammkuchen* as well. No credit cards.

Salzgasse 13. www.walfisch.de. ✆ **0221/257-7879.** Main courses 10€–18€. Mon–Thurs 5pm–midnight; Fri–Sun noon–midnight. Bahn: Heumarkt.

Weinhaus Brungs ★★ RHINELAND/GERMAN   A typical 16th-century merchant's house now houses a Rhineland restaurant where Rhenish and other German specialties are elevated beyond "Brauhaus" level. So, alongside *Sauerbraten* with potato dumplings, there's 30-hour slow roast beef or classics like *Wienerschnitzel* (breaded veal scallop). The standout wine list is strong on Rieslings from the Moselle, Rheingau, and Pfalz wine regions. Round out your meal with homemade chocolate mousse and a shot of aged *Trester,* Germany's answer to grappa. Ask for a seat on the gallery, up an 18th-century staircase and adorned with Renaissance-era wood paneling, for a real feeling of old Cologne.

Marsplatz 3–5. www.weinhaus-brungs.de. ✆ **0221/2581-666.** Main courses 12€–23€. Daily noon–11:30pm. Bahn: Heumarkt.

Shopping

Some of the first *Füssgänger* (pedestrian) shopping zones in Germany were in Cologne, and they now present a seemingly endless and interconnected conglomeration of downtown shops and shopping arcades.

Hohe Strasse, the main north-south street in Roman times, is now one of Cologne's busiest commercial drags, jammed every day except Sunday with shoppers, musicians, snack shops, chain stores, and fruit sellers. Still-busier **Schildergasse** is where you find international men's fashions, fine leather bags and purses, and French, German, and Italian designer shoes.

Eau de Cologne

Any kind of perfumed water is often now called "eau de Cologne," or simply "cologne," but *Echt Kölnisch Wasser* (real eau de Cologne) remains the official designation of origin for the distinctive fragrances created in the city of Cologne. **4711 Haus ★**, Glockengasse 4 (www.4711.com; ✆ **0221/9250450**), sells an orange, bergamot-, and lavender-scented water first created (originally as a tonic to drink) by the Mühlens family in 1792. Their flagship store even has an eau de Cologne fountain if you want to freshen up. The street number assigned by occupying French forces eventually became the brand name for their product. **Farina,** Obenmarspforten 21 (www.farina1709.de; ✆ **0221/294-1709**), sells a lighter *Kölnisch Wasser* first developed in 1709 by Italian chemist Giovanni Maria Farina.

To the west of here, just beyond busy Neumarkt, **Apostelnstrasse** and particularly **Mittelstrasse** are known for high-end designer boutiques. Here you'll find **Apropos ★**, Mittelstrasse 12 (www.apropos-store.com; ✆ 0221/2725-1915), stuffed with designer fashion (men's and women's) by the likes of Valentino and Louboutin. **Filz Gnoss ★**, Apostelnstrasse 21 (www.filz-gnoss.de; ✆ **0221/257010**), is a long-established family business that manufactures and sells all manner of personal and household accessories made out of felt. You'll find comfortable felt slippers, hats, phone cases, bags, coasters, chair coverings, and more.

For cutting-edge, young clothing and jewelry designers (and likely the next big thing), take the Stadtbahn to Friesenplatz and make for the **Belgian Quarter:** Antwerpenerstrasse, Brüsselerstrasse, and Maastrichterstrasse are a good starting point. Pretty much everything around here is indie, handmade, and original. You can check out the latest openings at **www.chicbelgique.de**. Designers Eva Gronbach and Chang13° are just a couple of the names to have emerged in recent years from Cologne's hippest neighborhood.

Nightlife & Entertainment

One of Germany's major cultural centers, Cologne offers a variety of performing arts and nightlife options. You can purchase tickets at a venue's box office *(Kasse)*; at the **Kölm Tourismus** office (see p. 530); or at **KölnTicket,** Roncalliplatz 4, next to the cathedral (www.koelnticket.de; ✆ **0221/2801**), whose website is a good guide to what's coming up.

PERFORMING ARTS

Kölner Philharmonie ★★   Completed in 1986, and located behind and below the Roman-Germanic Museum, Cologne's philarmonic hall plays host to fine orchestras, both local and touring. The **Gürzenich-Orchestra Cologne** and the **WDR Symphony Orchestra** are both resident.   Bischofsgartenstrasse 1. http://en.koelner-philharmonie.de. ✆ **0221/280280.** Bahn: Hauptbahnhof.

Oper Köln ★★   The Rhineland's leading opera house—designed by Wilhelm Riphahn and opened in 1957 after the original opera house was destroyed by Allied bombs—is undergoing a major refurbishment that should keep it closed through late 2016. Along with improving the acoustics and bringing the technical and stage infrastructure up to state-of-the-art standards, the project renewed the plaza and adjacent Schauspielhaus (Theater), all part of Riphahn's postwar architectural ensemble. Check the website for updates. Offenbachplatz. www.oper.koeln/en. ✆ **0221/221-28400.** Bahn: Neumarkt.

THE BAR & LIVE MUSIC SCENE

Pretty much any **Brauhaus** (see "Brauhaus Dining," p. 539) has a section where you're welcome to sit and quaff a Kölsch or two without ordering food. Bar snacks are served and the atmosphere is usually lively.

If you're looking for more action than that, the **Friesenviertel** (around Friesenplatz and Friesenstrasse) is the place to party til the small hours. Cocktail bars, dance bars, and nightclubs all fuse into one hedonistic haze after dark.

Elements ★   Bringing a touch of class to Cologne's nightlife-central, Elements offers signature and classic cocktails (around 10€) and a good gin list. Closed Sunday and Monday. Friesenstrasse 16. www.elements-cologne.de. ✆ **0151/212-77685.** Bahn: Friesenplatz.

Gebäude 9 ★   Underground indie acts from Germany, Europe, and North America are the staple at this 500-capacity former industrial warehouse. Deutz-Mühlheimer Strasse 127. www.gebaeude9.de. ✆ **0221/589-19414.** Bahn: KölnMesse Osthallen.

Gloria ★★   If you're looking for a LGBT venue with food, drink and music, this long-established and straight-friendly cafe and cabaret stage should be at the top of your list. The bar opens Monday through Saturday noon to 7pm, before performances. Apostelnstrasse 11. www.gloria-theater.com. ✆ **0221/660630.** Bahn: Neumarkt.

Loft ★   Eclectic international ensembles, jazz musicians, and other solo artists perform most nights of the week at this intimate music hub created in a musician's apartment. The website has details of who's performing and opening hours. Wissmannstrasse 30. www.loft-koeln.de. ✆ **0221/952-1555.** Bahn: Ehrenfeld Liebigstrasse.

Papa Joe's "Klimperkasten" ★   This jazz, cabaret, and piano bar has live music every night beginning around 8pm. There's no admission charge. Alter Markt 50–52. www.papajoes.de. ✆ **0221/258-2132.** Bahn: Rathaus.

Zum Köbes ★   This neighborhood bar serves Kölsch fresh from the Reissdorf brewery. There's also a traditional Brauhaus food menu, but you're welcome to simply sit and drink. Closed Monday. Cleverstrasse 2 (at Thürmchenswall). www.essen-im-koebes.de. ✆ **0221/800-64548.** Bahn: Ebertplatz.

AACHEN (AIX-LA-CHAPELLE) ★★

64km (40 miles) W of Cologne

The Imperial City of Aachen (Aix-La-Chapelle to French speakers) is forever connected with the ancient legacy of Emperor Charlemagne (748–814), who in 800 was crowned Emperor in Rome and became the first emperor of western Europe after the demise of ancient Rome. Charlemagne ("Karl der Grosse" in German) selected this spot—at the frontier where modern Germany, Belgium, and the Netherlands now meet—as the center of his vast Frankish empire. Visitors come to visit Charlemagne's cathedral, where subsequent Holy Roman emperors were crowned; the Altstadt with its impressive Rathaus; and to relax in the hot mineral baths that have been a big draw since Roman times. It's easy to visit on a day trip from Cologne, but don't dismiss the idea of an overnight.

Essentials

ARRIVING

The trip from Cologne to Aachen's **Hauptbahnhof,** on the edge of the Altstadt, takes 35 to 55 minutes; trains depart frequently all day. For schedules, visit **www.bahn.com**. If you're traveling by car, it's about 1 hour from Cologne via the A4 autobahn.

VISITOR INFORMATION

The **Aachen Tourist Service,** Friedrich-Wilhelm-Platz (www.aachen.de; ✆ **0241/1802950**) is open Monday to Friday 9am to 6pm, Saturday 9am to 3pm (Jan-Mar until 2pm). From April through December, 90-minute **guided walking tours** of Aachen's Altstadt are offered in English every Saturday at 11am, departing from the tourist office; the cost is 8€. The city also offers **free Wi-Fi** in the center of the Altstadt; you can get a 24-hour pass at the tourist office (see www.aachenwifi.de).

Exploring Aachen

Aachen's **Altstadt** (Old Town), the area you want to explore, is enclosed by a busy ring road, beside which the main train station stands. From the station, it's a 15-minute walk north to the cathedral precincts. Along the way, you'll pass the giant **Theater Aachen** (Theaterplatz 1), a postwar reconstruction of the city's original 1825 theater, opera, and concert hall. Nearby, right behind the tourist office, is the **Elisenbrunnen ★**, a colonnaded neoclassical building that sits atop one of Aachen's famous thermal springs. The smell that accosts you as you get near isn't bad drains; it's sulphur-rich water that spills out into shallow pools behind the building, where you'll find the **Elisengarten,** small landscaped gardens where recent archaeological excavations of Aachen's Roman and medieval past are on view in a glass-walled pavilion. Just north of the cathedral you'll find the **Marktplatz,** the historic area's main square, where Aachen's **Rathaus** is located.

Carolus Thermen ★★ SPA   Not everything in Aachen revolves around Charlemagne. For over 2,000 years, the warm mineral-rich waters that flow from thermal springs below the town have been frequented for health and relaxation (okay, probably including by Charlemagne). This modern baths complex in the Stadtgarten, just outside the ring road, has outdoor and indoor thermal pools (most around 35°C/95°F), whirlpool baths, a cold plunge pool, and a wet steam room. Pay extra and you can use the Scandinavian sauna complex, too. A locker is included with your admission, but if you need to rent a towel, it's an extra 4€. Outdoor terraces make this place a delight in summer; it's even better on a cold winter's night, when you can swim outside under floodlights as a fog of steam whirls around you like something out of a Tolkein tale. No children 5 and under.

Passstrasse 79. www.carolus-thermen.de. ✆ **0241/182740.** Admission: up to 2½ hr. 12€–13€ without sauna, 26€–28€ with sauna; full day 18€–19€ without sauna, 36€–38€ with sauna. Daily 9am–10:30pm.

Centre Charlemagne ★ MUSEUM   Opened in late 2015, this multimedia exhibit (handily located just off the Marktplatz) presents a historical overview of Aachen. The approach is unashamedly didactic; it is well worth starting your visit here, with an audioguide, to give the other city sights their proper context. Displays—some original and some reproductions—trace the city's origins to way before Charlemagne. Hot thermal springs were the catalyst for settlement in prehistory, a geological feature that was properly exploited by the Romans, in the town they named Aquae Granni. (The name Aachen is simply an old Germanization of the Latin word for water.) Exhibits continue through the career of Charlemagne, when Aachen was the center of Europe's most powerful empire, and later events such as the Great Town Fire of May 1656 (when the entire medieval city was

At the new Centre Charlemagne, multimedia exhibits tell Aachen's history.

swept away) and World War II, when Aachen was the first German city to fall to the Allies, in October 1944.

Katschhof 1. www.centre-charlemagne.eu. ☎ **0241/432-4956.** Admission 5€ adult, seniors and students 3€, family ticket 10€. Tues–Sun 10am–6pm.

Dom (Cathedral) ★★★ CHURCH Between A.D. 792 and 805, as part of his now vanished palace, Emperor Charlemagne built what's called the **Palatine Chapel,** or the **Octagon.** This eight-sided, two-tiered, domed structure clad in multicolored marble is the first part of the cathedral that you enter, and the oldest. Consecrated by the Pope in 805, it was the first large church building to be constructed in western Europe after the demise of the Roman Empire. **Charlemagne's throne,** the simple stone *Königsstuhl,* one of the most venerable monuments in Germany, sits on the chapel's upper level and can only be seen on a guided tour.

From 936 until 1531, when the ceremony moved to Frankfurt, Holy Roman Emperors were crowned in this cathedral. Stylistically it's an amalgamation of classical, Byzantine, and pre-Romanesque architecture. Much sympathetic restoration work has been done over the centuries, including the cupola mosaic, depicting a scene from the Book of Revelation in Byzantine style but redone in the 19th century. The soaring Gothic style, imported from France, was used when the cathedral's **Choir and Sanctuary** were constructed in the 14th century. Visitors aren't allowed to enter this section, but can view its two major treasures: the **Charlemagne Reliquary,** an ornate gold box crafted around 1215 for the emperor's remains; and the stunning gold **Pulpit of Henry II** (ca. 1014), decorated with antique bowls, ivory carvings, chess figures, and reliefs of the evangelists. The **Domschatz (Cathedral Treasury)** is worth visiting to see the famous silver and gilt bust of Charlemagne and other religious treasures.

Klosterplatz 2. www.aachenerdom.de/en. ☎ **0241/47709127.** Cathedral free (1€ for permission to take photos); Domschatz 5€ adult, 4€ students and seniors; guided tour 4€ (45 min., approx. hourly from opening until 5pm; English language tour 2pm). Cathedral open Mon–Fri 11am–7pm, Sat–Sun 12:30–7pm (Jan–Mar until 6pm). Treasury open Mon 10am–1pm; Tues–Sun 10am–6pm (Jan–Mar until 5pm).

Rathaus (Town Hall) ★ HISTORIC BUILDING Some 500 years after Charlemagne's death (in 814), the Aachen Rathaus was built on the site of the emperor's ruined palace. (Part of the ancient palace structure can still be seen in exposed brickwork belonging to the so-called **Granus Tower** at the east side of the upstairs hall.) After the devastating Great Town Fire of 1656, the blackened facade of the building was redone in the baroque style and decorated with stucco statues of 50 German rulers, 31 of whom had been crowned in Aachen. Standing in relief in the center are the "Majestas Domini," the two most important men of their time in the Holy Roman Empire, Charlemagne and Pope Leo III. Inside, on the second floor, you can visit the vaulted **Coronation Hall** where coronation banquets took place from 1349 to 1531, after which the coronation site was moved to Frankfurt. The hall is decorated with the **Charlemagne frescoes,** painted in 1847–51 by Alfred Rethel and illustrating the victory of Christian Franks over the Germanic "heathens."

Marktplatz. www.rathaus-aachen.de. ℂ **0241/18029-60.** Admission 5€ adults, 3€ students and children. Daily 10am–6pm (closed for city events; see website for calendar).

Where to Stay in Aachen

While Aachen is an easy daytrip from nearby **Cologne** (p. 525), it has a completely different pace and atmosphere from its bigger neighbor. Staying overnight gives you a chance to sample the local food, soak in the spa waters, and experience its surprising nightlife (see p. 548).

Bensons ★   Bland European chain hotels have snapped up many of the best locations right in the center. This independent near the station—convenient and quiet, but unromantic—more than compensates with the kind of intimacy and personal touch that few chains can match. It's our top pick in Aachen. Rooms are spacious, bright, and modern, with bold accent colours and white laminate flooring. Some bathrooms are a little small. The breakfast buffet is above the norm for this price category. No elevator.

Bahnhofstrasse 3. www.bensons.de. ℂ **0241/160411-10.** 14 units. 99€–165€ double. Buffet breakfast 10€. **Amenities:** Wi-Fi (free).

Where to Eat in Aachen

Van den Daele ★, Büchel 18 (www.van-den-daele.de; ℂ **0241/35724**), with its wood paneling, stained glass, wrought iron, and Delft-style tiles, is the most atmospheric place in Aachen to stop for *Kaffee und Kuchen.*

Printen, a traditional Aachen sweet.

---

sweet specialty: **PRINTEN FROM AACHEN**

Aachen is famous for the *Printe*, a cakelike cookie made with honey and spices, soft or hard, and often frosted with white or dark chocolate (*krauter* are the unfrosted version). A box of Printen makes a great gift…if there are any left by the time you get home. **Printenbäckerei Klein ★**, Franzstrasse 91 (at Aureliusstrasse; www.printen.de; ℂ **0241/474350**), the last authentic bakery left in the center, sells this delicious local treat in a variety of sizes and containers. Another tasty, sweet Aachen specialty, **Reisfladen** are baked tarts filled with sweetened, milky rice.

AKL ★ LEBANESE/TURKISH   It's quite a challenge to spend much over 10€ here. The menu is loaded with eastern Mediterranean classics, including a *meze* of kibbeh (spiced meatballs), falafel, and Lebanese samosa, served with dips including hummus and tahini (sesame paste). Shish kebab is flamegrilled to order, and there's schwarma, too. The best way to enjoy AKL's food is to take a seat next door in **Egmont**—a café-bar with grunge Art Nouveau décor, cocktails, and a long tea list including fruit, black, green and rooibos teas—then pop next door and order your food. They bring it round as soon as it's prepped. No credit cards. Pontstrasse 1–3. www.akl-orient.de. ℂ **0241/4686-4844.** Main courses 7€–11€. Mon–Sat noon–11pm.

Elisenbrunnen ★ CAFE/GERMAN   A long-established institution, this cafe-restaurant behind the Elisenbrunnen is a convenient spot to relax with a coffee, pastry, or light meal—especially if the weather's nice and you can sit outside on the terrace overlooking the gardens. Inside, it's casual dining, including fresh salads, soups, baked potatoes with various toppings, or heartier Rhineland fare. There's also a kids' menu and a short vegetarian menu. Friedrich-Wilhelm-Platz 14. www.eb-aachen.de. ℂ **0241/9431-3490.** Main courses 7€–18€. Daily 9:30am–11pm.

Ratskeller ★★ CONTEMPORARY GERMAN   The creative, modern cuisine served here beneath the Rathaus is perfect for a special occasion. Today, the medieval cellar has an attractive, formal look, with whitewashed masonry walls and a black granite floor. Chef Maurice de Boer focuses on international-style gourmet cooking using fresh local ingredients, such as a goose liver tart served with chicory; scallops and cardamom crème; or duck breast with ratatouille and artichoke. Reservations are essential. Unusually for such an upscale place, credit cards are not accepted. Am Markt (below the Rathaus). www.ratskeller-aachen.de. ℂ **0241/35001.** Main courses 25€; fixed-price 3-/4-course menu 45€/55€. Daily noon–3pm and 6–10pm.

aachen's DECADENT SIDE

Beneath a conservative exterior, Aachen has some downright eccentric, fun bars. Walking through the frosted glass front door at **Grotesque ★★**, Rennbahn 1 (ⓒ **0241/ 4758-6835**), transports you to 1920s Europe, complete with period furnishings, mustachioed host, and a gramophone record crackling away in the background. The bar majors in absinthe, a wormwood and anise spirit whose supposed—and now thought largely mythical—hallucinatory effects saw it banned in Europe and North America for almost a century. The bar list has around 25 to choose from, including classics like Lemercier Amer alongside several anise-free absinthes. Be cautious: Some absinthes contain over 70% alcohol, although you drink it diluted with water dripped over a sugar cube, in 1920s style. There's also wine, a fine gin list, and German and Belgian beers.

DÜSSELDORF ★★

40km (25 miles) N of Cologne (Köln), 230km (143 miles) NW of Frankfurt

Wealthy Düsseldorf began as a settlement on the right bank of the Rhine, but today it's spread out on both sides—the older part on the right, and the upscale residential, commercial, and industrial part on the left. Parks and esplanades line the riverbanks; it's the most elegant metropolis in the Rhine Valley.

Like many other German towns, Düsseldorf has an Altstadt (Old Town), a thick ribbon of cobbled lanes in the city center, but it also has the Rhine Valley's most famous—and maybe most expensive—shopping street, **Königsallee,** which is lined with high-end designer shops to make your credit card ache. Outstanding art and museums are also part of the package: The city's post-WWII painting collection includes over 100 panels by Paul Klee alone. Nightlife centers around the Altstadt and Düsseldorf's signature **Altbier,** the local copper-colored, semisweet beer—one of the best brews in Germany.

This is a seriously fun city to visit, especially in summer when Düsseldorfers live outside—eating, drinking, and partying on the Rhine banks. For art lovers, there's easily enough to fill a weekend here. If you like art *and* beer… Düsseldorf is made for you.

Essentials

ARRIVING

BY PLANE **Düsseldorf Airport** (www.dus.com), 6km (4 miles) north of the city, has regularly scheduled connections to several global airports, including New York. It's also a hub for Lufthansa-owned **Eurowings,** a budget airline serving destinations across Germany and Europe, and **Air**

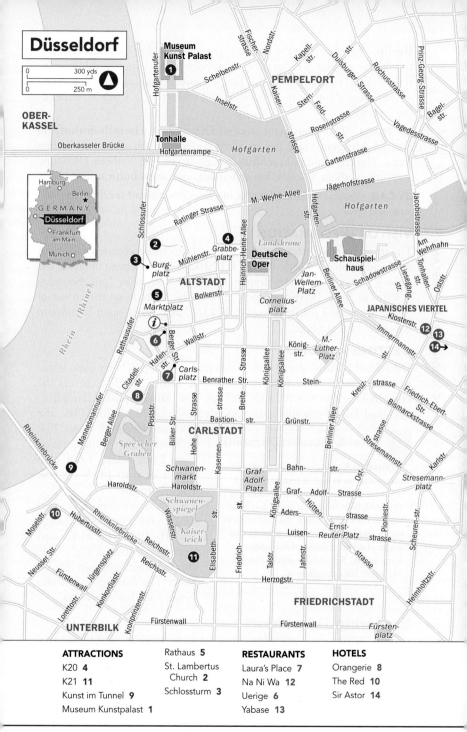

Düsseldorf

0 — 300 yds
0 — 250 m

OBER-KASSEL

Oberkasseler Brücke

GERMANY
Hamburg
Berlin ★
Düsseldorf
Frankfurt am Main
Munich

Rhein (Rhine)

Museum Kunst Palast ①

PEMPELFORT

Hofgartenufer

Fischerstrasse
Nordstr.
Kapell-str.
Duisburger Strasse
Rochusstrasse
Prinz-Georg-Strasse
Bagel-str.

Scheibenstr.
Kaiser-strasse
Stern-Feld-strasse
Rosenstrasse
Vagedesstrasse

Tonhalle
Hofgartenrampe
Inselstr.
Gartenstrasse

Hofgarten

Jägerhofstrasse

Schlossufer
Ratinger Strasse
M.-Weyhe-Allee
Hofgarten-str.
Hofgarten
Jacobistrasse

② ④
Burgplatz ③
Mühlenstr.
Grabbe-platz
Heinrich-Heine-Allee
Landskrone
Deutsche Oper
Schauspiel-haus
Schadowstrasse
Am Wehrhahn
Tonhallen-str.
Liesegang-str.
Oststr.

ALTSTADT
Bolkerstr.
⑤
Marktplatz
Jan-Wellem-Platz
Berliner Allee
JAPANISCHES VIERTEL
Klosterstr. ⑫ ⑬
Immermannstr. ⑭→

ⓘ
⑥
Rathausufer
Berger Str.
Wallstr.
Cornelius-platz
König-str.
M.-Luther-Platz

Hafen-str. ⑦
Carls-platz
Benrather Str.
Königsallee
Königsallee
Stein-strasse
Kreuz-strasse
Friedrich-Ebert-Strasse

Citadell-str. ⑧
Breite strasse
Bastion-str.
Grünstr.
Bismarckstrasse
Karlstr.

Mannesmannufer
Berger Allee
Poststr.
Bilker Str.
Hohe strasse
Kasernen-strasse

CARLSTADT

Spee'scher Graben

Rheinkniebrücke

⑨
Haroldstr.
Schwanen-markt
Haroldstr.
Graf-Adolf-Platz
Bahn-str.
Ost-strasse
Stresemannstr.
Stresemann-platz

⑩
Moselstr.
Hubertusstr.
Rheinkniebrücke
Reichsstr.
Schwanen-spiegel
Wasserstr.
Graf-Adolf-Strasse
Königsallee
Aders-strasse
Luisen-strasse
Ernst-Reuter-Platz
Pionierstr.
Scheuren-str.

Neusser Str.
Fürstenwall
Jürgensplatz
Konkordiastr.
Kaiser-teich
⑪
Elisabeth-str.
Friedrich-str.
Talstr.
Jahnstr.
Herzogstr.
Helmholtzstr.

Lorettostr.
Kronprinzenstr.

UNTERBILK
Fürstenwall
Fürstenwall
FRIEDRICHSTADT
Fürsten-platz

ATTRACTIONS
K20 **4**
K21 **11**
Kunst im Tunnel **9**
Museum Kunstpalast **1**

Rathaus **5**
St. Lambertus Church **2**
Schlossturm **3**

RESTAURANTS
Laura's Place **7**
Na Ni Wa **12**
Uerige **6**
Yabase **13**

HOTELS
Orangerie **8**
The Red **10**
Sir Astor **14**

Berlin. The easiest way to get into central Düsseldorf from the airport is to take the regular S-Bahn (line 11) service to the Hauptbahnhof (main train station; 12 min.). One-way fare is 2.60€. A **taxi** ride to central Düsseldorf takes about 20 to 30 minutes and costs from 20€ to 25€, depending on traffic.

BY TRAIN The main train station, **Düsseldorf Hauptbahnhof,** on Konrad-Adenauer-Platz, has frequent connections to all major German cities. The trip time to Frankfurt by high-speed ICE is about 1½ hours; to Munich, about 5 hours. For schedules, visit **www.bahn.com**.

BY CAR Access to Düsseldorf is by the A3 north and south or the A46 east and west.

VISITOR INFORMATION

The main **Tourist Information Office,** Immermannstrasse 65B (www.duesseldorf-tourismus.de; ✆ **0211/17202-844**), is almost opposite the railway station. It's open Monday to Friday 9:30am to 7pm, Saturday 9:30am to 5pm. There's another office in the Altstadt, on the corner of Marktstrasse and Rheinstrasse (✆ **0211/17202-840**), open Monday to Saturday 10am to 6pm.

GETTING AROUND

Düsseldorf is fairly spread out, so you may rely (in part) on public transportation. You're most likely to use the **U-Bahn,** which connects the Hauptbahnhof to the Altstadt and Kö. The **Strassenbahn** (streetcar) has good links from the station to Medienhafen (lines 706, 708, and 709) and Unterbilk (lines 704, 708, and 709). A single ticket costs 2.60€ adults, 1.60€ children ages 6 to 14. See **www.rheinbahn.de**.

There are convenient **taxi** ranks in Burgplatz and at the station. The Rhine river makes navigating easier than it might be in the pedestrianized, mazelike Altstadt. The riverside Rheinufer promenade has city views.

Travel & Museum Discounts

A **DüsseldorfCard** offers free use of public transportation as well as free or reduced entrance to city museums, and reductions on city tours, boat rides, and opera and ballet tickets. Valid for 24 hours, the card costs 9€ for an adult or 18€ for a group/family (two adults plus two children 14 and under, or three adults). For 48-hour validity it costs 14€ adult, 28€ group/family.

Exploring Düsseldorf

On the east bank of the Rhine, Düsseldorf's **Altstadt (Old Town)** is centered around a handsome **Marktplatz (Market Square)** and a Gothic **Rathaus (Town Hall)** ★, which dates to 1573. North of the Rathaus on Burgplatz are two of the city's most famous landmarks, the

The twisted spire of St. Lambert's Church.

twisted spire of **St-Lambertus Basilika (St. Lambertus Church)** and the **Schlossturm (Castle Tower),** both of 13th-century origin. East of the historic center, **Königsallee ★**—"Kö" to Düsseldorfers—runs north-south along an ornamental canal, shaded by trees and crossed by bridges. One bank is lined with office buildings, the other with exclusive shops, cafes, and restaurants (see "Shopping," p. 556). Above the northern end of Kö stretches the **Hofgarten,** a huge, rambling park where you can wander along paths or sit and relax amid trees, gardens, fountains, and statues, almost forgetting you're in the very center of the city. Among the monuments is one to the poet **Heinrich Heine** (1797–1856), a native of the city who eventually emigrated to Paris to escape German conservatism and censorship.

K20: Kunstsammlung am Grabbeplatz ★★★ ART MUSEUM Düsseldorf's weekend-break draw is built upon the number and variety of its art spots, and this museum houses a 20th-century collection of exceptional quality. Contents of the softly lit main galleries read like a checklist of **European avant-garde** movements and the men (the collection is dominated by male artists) who shaped them. There's Cubism,

Frank O. Gehry's innovative Neuer Zollhof buildings in the trendy MedienHafen district.

post-Impressionism, abstract expressionism, surrealism, Futurism. Mirò, De Chirico, Picasso, a notable group of works by Paul Klee, Braque, Matisse, Kandinsky, Magritte, Chagall, Mondrian, Dalí, Bacon, August Macke, and Pierre Bonnard. And that's just a few. **Joseph Beuys,** who died in Düsseldorf, has a room of watercolors and drawings to himself. Also here is the **Henckel Gallery,** dominated by 2 giant canvases—one by Jackson Pollock, the other Robert Rauschenberg.

Grabbeplatz 5. www.kunstsammlung.de. © **0211/8381-204.** Admission 12€ adults, 2.50€ children ages 6–18. Tues–Fri 10am–6pm (until 10pm 1st Wed of every month, free admission after 6pm); Sat–Sun 11am–6pm. U-Bahn: Heinrich-Heine-Allee.

K21: Kunstsammlung im Ständehaus ★ ART MUSEUM Formerly the home of the Rhineland Parliament, this exceedingly grand neo-classical building overlooking the Kaiserteich lake now houses the state's contemporary art collection. Both rotated permanent exhibits and limited-run installations are on show. (Recent temporary hits include Tomás Saraceno's 2016 *In Orbit,* wherein museum visitors could romp around on a steel mesh suspended 25m/82 ft. above the atrium.) Expect absolutely anything from the mapcap to thought-provoking from the cutting edge of international contemporary art.

Ständehausstrasse 1. www.kunstsammlung.de. © **0211/8381-204.** Admission 12€ adults, 2.50€ children ages 6–18. Tues–Fri 10am–6pm (until 10pm 1st Wed of every month, free admission after 6pm); Sat–Sun 11am–6pm. U-Bahn: Graf-Adolf-Platz.

Docklands Reborn?

As is de rigueur for every design-conscious city, Düsseldorf has a once-dilapidated but now trendy post-industrial neighborhood: **MedienHafen**. This was a flourishing warehouse sector in the 19th century. Today it is often a showcase for modern architecture, especially in the office buildings and other works of Frank O. Gehry. Düsseldorf's most striking example of his work is the trio of "organic-looking" high-rises at **Neuer Zollhof** ★. With their wavy lines, they can easily be spotted along the waterfront. For the best view of these avant-garde buildings, including Gehry's controversial architecture, walk down the water-bordering promenade, Am Handelshafen, beginning at the **Rhein Turm (Rhine Tower)** ★★, and heading toward Franziusstrasse.

Kunst im Tunnel ★ ART MUSEUM   There's no art space quite like this anywhere in Europe. The subterranean, concrete, elliptical gallery runs parallel to the adjacent Rhine for around 140m/459 feet. The "tunnel" name is no arty metaphor: This is a disused section between roads that ran below the pedestrian embankment. Its ever-changing program is contemporary and eclectic, with a focus on young German artists. The website lists current and forthcoming shows. Its glass-fronted **KIT Café** is a pleasant spot for drinks or a snack in summer.

Mannesmannufer 1b. www.kunst-im-tunnel.de. No phone. Admission 4€ adults, children 17 and under free (also free admission 2nd Sun of every month). Tues–Sun 11am–6pm. Tram: 706, 708, or 709 to Landtag.

Museum Kunstpalast ★ MUSEUM   Just north of the Hofgarten, the city's principal fine art collection is housed behind a sublime façade that mixes rationalist and historical architectural styles—almost all that remains from the original Ehrenhof building designed in the 1920s by Wilhelm Kreis. The **foyer** also has a monumental stained glass window (1926) by Johan Thorn Prikker. One of Hitler's infamous "Degenerate Art" propaganda exhibitions was staged at the museum in 1938, and in fact, it had around 900 works of modern art that were confiscated by the Nazi regime. What remains, however, is an enjoyable trot through European art history, from Romanesque woodcarvings and panels by **Cranach the Elder** (ca. 1472–1553) to 20th-century German Expressionism (including **Ernst Ludwig Kirchner**) and even the op-art of **Bridget Riley.** Along the way, galleries include Dutch Masters (notably some fleshy Rubens paintings); a number of works bequeathed in the 17th and 18th centuries by various Electors Palatine, who resided in Düsseldorf; 19th-century street scenes and family portraiture; and the Romantic paintings of the **Düsseldorf School** and **Caspar David Friedrich** (1774–1840).

Ehrenhof 4–5. www.smkp.de/en. ✆ **0211/566-42100.** Admission 5€ adults, 1€ children ages 7–17. Tues–Sun 11am–6pm (until 9pm Thurs). U-Bahn: Tonhalle.

Where to Stay

Accommodation rates can go sky-high during **trade fairs.** It's worth consulting the tourist office (see above) to find out if any coincide with your plans.

Orangerie ★   This place has a sublime location, in a tiny cobbled square in a part of the Altstadt dating to the 17th century. Interiors are contemporary, with bold colors and light wood. Rooms come in two grades: There's little difference in room size, but deluxe units (30€–40€ extra) are bigger all-round, with bigger bathrooms and sharper furnishings. Those on the fourth floor (especially corner room no. 41) are our favorites.

Bäckergasse 1. www.hotel-orangerie-mcs.de. ℂ **0211/866800.** 27 units. 130€–250€ double. Breakfast included. Parking in nearby garages, prices vary. **Amenities:** Wi-Fi (free). Tram: 704 or 709.

The Red ★★   If you're traveling as a family, or mixing business in Medienhafen with some Altstadt tourism, this place has an ideal location; everything except the main train station is walkable. The **serviced apartments** are inside a handsome red-brick former customs house, originally built in 1901. The inside, by contrast, is pure 21st century: Light-filled units have plenty of space, even in the smallest "Studio" units, leather furnishings, light-oak floors, and up-to-date gadgetry. Many look directly at the Rheinturm.

Hubertusstrasse 1 (at Moselstrasse). www.the-red.de/en. ℂ **0211/5421-710.** 23 units. 135€–205€ apartment. Parking 15€. **Amenities:** Kitchenette; Wi-Fi (free). Tram: 708 or 709 to Landtag.

Sir Astor ★★   There's an enjoyable quirkiness to the décor here, inspired (apparently) by a fusion of African and Scottish elements. Animal prints, yes; but also a "tartan" carpet and argyle-pattern woolen cushion covers. It really works, providing each of the individually decorated rooms with its own personality. Some units are small by North American standards, and soundproofing between some could be better.

Kurfürstenstrasse 23. www.sir-astor.de. ℂ **0211/936090.** 21 units. 80€–100€ double. Breakfast included. Parking 11€. **Amenities:** Wi-Fi (free). U-Bahn: Hauptbahnhof.

Where to Eat

For a taste of old Düsseldorf, most traditional brewhouses (see "Altbier in the Altstadt," p. 556) serve a full menu of hearty fare. Expect the likes of *Erbensuppe* (seasonal vegetable soup with pieces of pork knuckle) followed by *Sauerbraten* (beef marinated in vinegar then roasted). On another note, Düsseldorf has the largest Japanese community in Germany, so you can head to the so-called **Japanese Quarter** (around Immermannstrasse, Oststrasse, and Klosterstrasse) to eat lighter and spicier than the native norm.

Laura's Deli ★★ HEALTH FOOD/DELI This modern spot is perfect for a healthy, light lunch, particularly for vegetarians and vegan travelers, who can struggle with Düsseldorf's hearty, meat-heavy cuisine. Carefully sourced, often organic, ingredients appear in a range of tasty, modish dishes such as chicken bone broth or daily, seasonal "superfood" salads. There's also gluten-free dining, including the likes of wheat-free zucchini pasta served with a pesto of tomatoes, cashews, and pine nuts. No reservations.

Carlsplatz 1. www.laurasdeli.de. ✆ **0211/8693-3880.** Main courses 6.50€–14€. Mon–Fri 8:30am–6:30pm, Sat 9am–6pm. Tram: 704 or 709.

Na Ni Wa ★★ JAPANESE/ASIAN This place is busy and quick: Fresh and fast food done well, borrowing flavors from across Asia but remaining predominantly Japanese. Ramen-style noodle soups take center-stage, with up to 30 combos available, always including *tokusei miso* (a rich, chilli-spiked broth with soya noodles plus sliced and ground pork). Pair it up with a portion of *gyoza* (fried dumplings; 4.50€) to satisfy even the biggest appetite. Singles or pairs are often seated at the open-kitchen counter; there are also tables for families and larger groups. No reservations (lines build at peak times), no credit cards.

Oststrasse 55. www.naniwa.de. ✆ **0211/161799.** Main courses 8€–10.50€. Wed–Mon 11:30am–10:30pm. Tram: 707 to Klosterstrasse.

Uerige ★ GERMAN/RHINELAND An atmospheric old Brauhaus, Uerige welcomes everyone from lively afternoon drinking buddies to young families out for a meal together. There's a basic menu of classic Brauhaus specialties, including multiple types of *Wurst* (sausage), plus rotating daily specials—the likes of *Erbensuppe* (a thick soup-stew of seasonal vegetables and pork knuckle), goulash, or cabbage stuffed with minced beef. From 6:30pm onward, there's an additional short menu of more substantial dishes, such as *Haxe mit Sauerkraut* (pork knuckle served with pickled cabbage) and *Wienerschnitzel* (breaded veal escalope). And of course, there's plenty of fine Altbier to wash it down.

Bergerstrasse 1. www.uerige.de. ✆ **0211/866990.** Main courses 5€–17€. Daily 10am–midnight. U-Bahn: Heinrich-Heine-Allee.

Yabase ★★ JAPANESE In a city that has earned a rep for its Japanese food, this place is probably the best in town for sushi, futomaki, miso, and the rest. Alongside the sushi and sublime sashimi, there's grilled fresh fish, the odd surprise (including eel tempura), and warm udon and soba noodle dishes such as *kakiage* (with fried shellfish and vegetables)—as well as sake and shochu to eash it down. Prices are a little elevated—it's Japanese food *and* it's Düsseldorf, after all—but the quality lives up to the pricetag. Go at lunchtime if you want a taste of

Altbier in the Altstadt

The **Altstadt**'s narrow streets and alleyways, between Königsallee and the Rhine, are jampacked with restaurants, nightclubs, and some 200 song-filled **beer taverns** (earning the area the nickname "the longest bar in the world." The copper-colored local brew, **Altbier** (or just "Alt" for short), is still crafted on a small scale right in the center, by a handful of venerable breweries. Altbier is served cold, but only lightly sparkling.

At any beer hall, take a seat and you will be served. The waiter keeps track of how much you have drunk by marking your beermat. Düsseldorf's oldest brewery-bar is **Schumacher ★**, Oststrasse 123 (www.schumacher-alt.de;

© **0211/828-9020**). **Uerige ★**, Berger Strasse 1 (www.uerige.de; © **0211/866990**), sells its own super Altbier, and has a separate room for watching sports on the big screen. If you're hell-bent on an Altbier crawl, add in **Zum Schlüssel ★**, Bolkerstrasse 43 (© **0211/828955**; www.hausbrauerei-zum-schluessel.de), too. All also offer platters of hearty Rhenish food.

To tour the Altstadt breweries in the company of an expert guide, book an **Altbier Safari ★** (www.altbier-safari.de). The 2-hour walk runs daily and costs 24.50€ per person, including beers. Buy tickets at one of the city tourist offices.

their food at more affordable prices. You'll need to book on weekends; it's very popular.

Klosterstrasse 70. www.yabase-ddf.com. © **0211/362677.** Main courses 10€–30€; sushi 2.50€–7€/pc.; set menu 40€–45€ evening, 10€–26€ lunch. Tues–Fri noon–2pm and 6:30–10:30pm; Sat noon–10:30pm; Sun 6–10pm. Tram: 707 to Klosterstrasse.

Shopping

It's a wonder Düsseldorf doesn't collapse under the weight of its retail outlets. Stores are *everywhere*. And Düsseldorfers are the kind of shoppers who get world-famous architect Daniel Libeskind to design them a mall—the **Kö-Bogen,** Königsallee 2 (www.koebogen.info). If you love to shop, you've come to the right place.

HAUTE KÖ-TURE At first glance, Düsseldorf is a city of high fashion and high prices, with all the famous international names in fashion sold on the opulent east side of the Königsallee, in the city center bordering the Stadtgraben canal. A large concentration of designer shops is found at the **Kö Galerie,** Königsallee 60 (www.koegalerie.com). At the nearby **Schadow Arkaden,** Martin-Luther-Platz (www.schadow-arkaden.de), fashion isn't quite so haute—but neither are the prices. The covered space also hosts a Sunday **antiques market** approximately once a month.

CARLSPLATZ & HOHE STRASSE Düsseldorf's main market has operated in **Carlsplatz** since the Middle Ages. Vendors at covered stalls hawk everything from fresh produce and takeout bratwurst to candy, fresh flowers, gluten-free snacks, and fried shrimps to go. **Kauf Dich Glücklich,** Carlsplatz 4 (www.kaufdichgluecklich-shop.de; ✆ **0211/8693-0291**), is a reliable stop for young, affordable fashion. Its name translates as "shop your-self happy"—which doubtless chimes with the locals. Running south from Carlsplatz, as far as Schwanenmarkt, **Hohe Strasse** has a freewheeling selection of local designers' boutiques, antique shops, general stores, and restaurants.

UNTERBILK Lorettostrasse is the hip heart of Düsseldorf's indie shopping scene in the neighborhood known as Unterbilk, just south of the city center. **Boutiquechen** (no. 22; www.boutiquechen.de; ✆ **0211/6954-0955**) sells wom-en's designerwear and accessories, while **Null Zwo Elf** (no. 4; www. nullzwoelfshop.de; ✆ **0211/989-4540**), is the place for edgy, youth-oriented streetwear. **RomantikLabor** (no. 32; www.romantiklabor-shop. de; ✆ **01636/313030**) has a unique selection of handcrafted, quirky gifts. At the southern end, by the Bilker Kirche, a couple of cafes provide good hipster-watching possibilities. *Note:* Nothing much gets going around here until after 11am.

Altbier, Düsseldorf's signature brew.

The Performing Arts

Classical music has long had an illustrious association with this city, once home to Brahms, Mendelssohn, and Schumann (though there are no specific tourist sites relating to them in Düsseldorf). Therefore, it's not surprising that both the **Düsseldorfer Symphoniker** and its home, the **Tonhalle ★★**, Ehrenhof 1 (www.tonhalle-duesseldorf.de; ✆ **0211/ 8996-123**), are world famous. Though originally built as a planetarium, the Tonhalle is perhaps Germany's most successful modern concert hall after Berlin's Philharmonie. **Deutsche Oper am Rhein,** Heinrich-Heine-Allee 24 (www.rheinoper.de; ✆ **0211/8925-211**), is one of the city's renowned opera and ballet companies.

BONN ★

72km (45 miles) S of Düsseldorf, 27km (17 miles) S of Cologne, 174km (108 miles) NW of Frankfurt

Until 1949, Bonn was a sleepy little university town, basking in its 2,000 years of history. Then suddenly it was shaken out of this quiet life and made capital of the Federal Republic of Germany. All that changed again in 1991, after the reunification of Germany, when Berlin reassumed its role as the official capital.

Bonn did not return to being a sleepy little university town, however. Several ministries still remain in Bonn (defense and agriculture) and Bonn still serves as the second official residence of all major German political figures and bureaus. Bonn is also still Germany's United Nations city, with 18 U.N. organizations calling Bonn their home. Bonn has a mixed population of young and old, conservative and liberal, due to the existence of the university and several corporations' head offices. The city has a more quiet nightlife than Hamburg or Berlin, but tourists who are interested in the arts, history, or relaxation will find everything they want here.

Bonn is also within sight of the **Siebenbirge (Seven Mountains),** a volcanic mountain range rising up on the eastern bank of the Rhine. The local wine produced on these slopes is known as *Drachenblut* (Dragon's Blood) and is better than most German reds.

A statue of Bonn's most famous native son, Ludwig von Beethoven, on Münsterplatz.

Essentials

ARRIVING

BY PLANE The nearest airport is **Flughafen Köln/Bonn** (see p. 528), which is served by direct flights from most European cities. Buses run directly from the airport to Bonn's main rail station every 30 minutes daily 5:40am to 10:30pm.

BY TRAIN The **Bonn Hauptbahnhof** is on a major rail line, with connections to most German cities. There are frequent daily trains to Berlin (trip time: 5 hr.) and Frankfurt (trip time: 2 hr.), and service to Cologne every 15 minutes (trip time: 20 min.). For information, go to **www.bahn.de**.

BY BUS   Long-distance bus service connects with such cities as Munich, Stuttgart, Aachen, Brussels, and London. For information, call **Eurolines Touring** (www.eurolines.de; ✆ **06196/2078-501**). Regional bus service is provided by **Regionalverkehr Köln GmbH at Meckenheim** (www.rvk.de; ✆ **0180/6131313**).

BY CAR   Access is by the A565 autobahn connecting with the A3 Autobahn from the north or south. Frankfurt is about a 2-hour drive away.

VISITOR INFORMATION

The **Bonn Tourist Office,** Windeckstrasse 1 (www.bonn.de, ✆ **0228/ 775000**), is open Monday to Friday 10am to 6pm, Saturday 10am to 4pm, and Sunday 10am to 2pm.

GETTING AROUND

At the **Reisenzentrum** under the Bonn railway station, you can pick up a free map outlining the city's transportation network. The office is open Monday to Saturday 5:30am to 10pm and Sunday 6:30am to 10pm. Bus or S-Bahn/U-Bahn tickets cost 1.90€ to 11.30€. You can also purchase a day ticket costing 7€ to 24€.

Exploring Bonn

From the 13th century to the 18th century, Bonn was the capital of the prince-electors of Cologne, who had the right to participate in the election of the emperor of the Holy Roman Empire. The city is also proud of its intellectual and musical history—Beethoven was born here; composer Robert Schumann and his wife, pianist Clara Schumann, lived here; and Karl Marx and Heinrich Heine studied in Bonn's university.

But what you may notice first are relics of a more recent era—the **Government Quarter,** along the west bank of the Rhine, a complex of modern, rather nondescript white buildings. The two most impressive, both along Koblenzerstrasse, are the former residences of the president and chancellor. These empire-style villas are reminiscent of the older Bonn, before it became an international center of diplomatic activity. They are not open to the public. Running north along the Rhine from the government buildings is a tree- and flower-lined promenade, which ends at the **Alter Zoll.** This ruined ancient fortress makes a fantastic viewing point from which visitors can see across the Rhine to the **Siebenbirge (Seven Mountains),** a volcanic mountain range rising up on the eastern bank of the Rhine. A local wine produced on these slopes is known as *Drachenblut* (Dragon's Blood) and is better than most German reds.

Beethoven Haus ★★ HISTORIC HOUSE   Located in the old section of town, just north of the marketplace, Beethoven House is Bonn's pride and joy. Beethoven was born in 1770 in the small house in back, which opens onto a little garden. On its second floor is the room where he was born, decorated only with a simple marble bust of the composer. Many of Beethoven's personal possessions are in the house, including manuscripts and musical instruments. In the Vienna Room, in the front of the house overlooking the street, is Beethoven's last piano (it was custom made, with a special sounding board to amplify sound for the hearing-impaired composer).

Bonngasse 20. www.beethoven-haus-bonn.de. ✆ **0228/981750.** Admission 6€ adults, 4.50€ students and children, 12€ family ticket. Apr–Oct daily 10am–6pm; Nov–Mar Mon–Sat 10am–5pm, Sun 11am–5pm. Tram: 62 or 66.

Haus der Geschichte der Bundesrepublik Deutschland (House of History of the German Republic) ★ MUSEUM

All the sweep and drama of Germany's modern history is brought to life in this museum, in artifacts, photographs, and other displays. Exhibits trace the history of Germany after 1945, up to the breakdown of law and order in the eastern sector which eventually led to reunification. In 2001 Emilie Schindler, the 93-year-old widow of German industrialist Oskar Schindler (subject of the 1993 film *Schindler's List*) donated a trove of his documents to the museum, including excerpts from the diary of one of hundreds of Jews whom Schindler saved from the Nazi death camps. The donation also includes a photo album of the making of the Spielberg movie and a congratulatory letter from then American president Bill Clinton.

Willy-Brandt-Allee 14. www.hdg.de. ✆ **0228/91650.** Free admission. Tues–Fri 9am–7pm, Sat–Sun 10am–6pm. U-Bahn: Heussallee/Museumsmeile.

Kunstmuseum Bonn ★ MUSEUM

This triangular structure, flooded with light, contains one of the most important art collections along the Rhine. The highlight is 20th-century art, including works by Rhenish expressionists, most notably August Macke. There are also works by Kirchner, Schmidt-Rottluff, Campen-Donk, Ernst, Seehaus, and Thuar.

Friedrich-Ebert-Allee 2. www.kunstmuseum-bonn.de. ✆ **0228/776260.** Admission 7€ adults, 3.50€ children, 14€ family ticket. Tues–Sun 11am–6pm (Wed until 9pm). U-Bahn: Heussallee.

Where to Stay in Bonn

ApartmentHotel Kaiser Karl ★★

Kaiser Karl is one of Bonn's gems, with more style and atmosphere than other luxury leaders. Constructed in 1905 as a private town house, it was converted in 1983 into a stylish four-story hotel. The attractive decor includes lacquered Japanese screens, English antiques, Oriental carpets, Venetian mirrors, and Edwardian potted palms. Each beautifully furnished room has a sleek bathroom. Apartments are serviced, and there are discounts available for longer stays.

Vorgebirgstrasse 56. www.apartment-hotel-bonn.de. ✆ **0228/98141999.** 42 units. 70€–149€ double; 84€–113€ apt. Breakfast buffet 15€. Parking 12€. **Amenities:** Café; lounge; laundry; room service; Wi-Fi (free).

Dorint Venusberg Bonn ★★★   This elegant and intimate hotel, built in a style evocative of a French country home, is surrounded by the beauty of the Venusberg nature reserve, part of the larger Kottenforst, about 2.5km (1½ miles) southwest of Bonn. It is the grandest choice for Bonn. About half the units offer private balconies overlooking the hills. Bathrooms are well accessorized.

An der Casselsruhe 1. http://hotel-bonn.dorint.com/de. ℂ **0228/2880.** 85 units. 80€–184€ double. Breakfast included in most rates. Parking 12€. **Amenities:** 2 restaurants; babysitting; concierge; access to nearby health club; Jacuzzi; room service; sauna; Wi-Fi (5€ per hour).

Günnewig Bristol Hotel ★★   Near Poppelsdorf Castle, this somewhat sterile, Cold War–era concrete-and-glass tower is still a suitable address. The good-size rooms with desks, ample chairs, and satellite TV are the best in Bonn, featuring double-glazing on the windows, along with fashionable and well-equipped bathrooms. The staff is also excellent.

Prinz-Albert-Strasse 2. www.guennewig.de/hotel-bristol-bonn. ℂ **0228/26980.** 116 units. 116€–217€ double. Breakfast included. Parking 15€. **Amenities:** 3 restaurants; bar; babysitting; indoor pool; room service; sauna, Wi-Fi (free).

Hotel Domicil ★★   This modern and convenient hotel is an oasis of charm and grace in a rather drab section of Bonn. In the front, a glass-and-steel portico stretches over the sidewalk. The interior is one of the most elegant in the capital, reminiscent of an exclusive London town house. The handsomely designed and spacious rooms range in décor from Belle Epoque to Italian modern. It's 4 blocks north of the cathedral, near the Hauptbahnhof.

Thomas-Mann-Strasse 24–26. www.bestwestern.com. ℂ **800/780-7234** in the U.S., or 0228/729090. 44 units. 105€–225€ double. Buffet breakfast included. Free parking. **Amenities:** Restaurant; bar; babysitting; Barber; Jacuzzi; room service; sauna; Wi-Fi (free).

Ringhotel Rheinhotel Dreesen ★   Out in the spa town of Bad Godesberg, this noble structure sits directly beside the river, with rooms opening onto river panoramas. Across the river, guests can see the national park areas of Siebengebirge (Seven Mountains) and Drachenfels (Dragon's Rock), where, according to legend, Siegfried slew the dragon. Bedrooms are elegant and comfortable, each tastefully furnished and ranging from midsize to spacious, with first-class bathrooms. Bikes are available for cycling tours along the banks of the Rhine or else in the Kurpark, center of the town's 18th-century spa district. Freshly prepared meals with quality ingredients are served in the on-site bistro and restaurant. Bad Godesberg is 6km (4 miles) south of central Bonn, a 20-minute drive (via B9) or tram ride (no. 16).

Rheinstrasse 45, Bad Godesberg. www.rheinhoteldreesen.de. ℂ **0228/82020.** 72 units. 145€–250€ double. Buffet breakfast included. Free parking. **Amenities:** Restaurant; bar; room service; Wi-Fi (16€ per day).

Sternhotel One of the best of Bonn's moderately priced hotels, the Sternhotel offers an informal atmosphere in a handy location next to the Rathaus. Despite the vintage yellow stucco façade, within all is trim and modern, with lots of built-ins. Rooms are comfy, if a little compact, and bathrooms are well equipped.

Markt 8. www.sternhotel-bonn.de. © **0228/72670.** 80 units. 145€–185€ double; 240€–275€ suite. Buffet breakfast included. Parking in nearby garages, rates vary. **Amenities:** Exercise room; sauna; Wi-Fi (free).

Where to Eat in Bonn

A weekly food market, **Wochenmarkt,** on the square of the same name, is held Monday to Saturday. You can enjoy a good lunch here, buying cooked food as you walk along inspecting the produce and various flea market items.

Em Höttche GERMAN Em Höttche enjoys a long and colorful history, going all the way back to 1389. With a prime location next to the Rathaus, it's fed thousands over the centuries with its rib-sticking fare—perhaps changing the recipes every 100 years or so. The interior has been restored, with carved-wood paneling, natural brick, old beamed ceilings, decoratively painted plaster, and curlicue chandeliers. Favorite dining spots are tables set inside the walk-in fireplace. On the a la carte list, you'll find specialties for two, including various steak dishes. Complement your meal with a carafe of local wine—the best buy in the house. However, the drink of choice for most visitors is *Kölsch,* a famous Rhineland beer for which the establishment is well known.

Markt 4. www.em-hoettche.de. © **0228/690009.** Reservations suggested. Main courses 12€–21€. Daily 11am–1am.

Halbedel's Gasthaus ★★ GOURMET An easy trip south of the city center (take tram 16), the gracious 18th-century spa town of Bad Godesberg is an appropriate setting for this Michelin-starred restaurant. Here, amid many nostalgic souvenirs and antique tables and chairs, the courtly owners will welcome you to their turn-of-the-20th-century villa. Chef Rainer Maria Halbedel prides himself on using mostly German-grown produce, much of it from the restaurant's own farm.

Rheinallee 47, Bad Godesberg. www.halbedels-gasthaus.de. © **0228/354253.** Reservations recommended. Main courses 42€–48€; fixed-price menu 90€–125€. Tues–Sun 6–10:30pm. Closed 3 weeks July–Aug.

Zur Lese GERMAN This restaurant's polite service and outdoor terrace with a sweeping view over the Rhine attract many local residents, especially in the afternoon, when visitors drop in for coffee, cakes, and glasses of wine after strolling in the nearby Hofgarten. Elegant, well-prepared lunches are also offered. Dinner is served in the cafe. A menu of German specialties (with English translations) includes veal with horseradish sauce and Argentinian rumpsteak. The food is home-style and hearty, with no pretense.

Adenauerallee 37. www.zurlese.de. ✆ **0228/223322.** Reservations recommended. Main courses 12€–27€; fixed-price menu 34€–40€. Tues–Sun noon–midnight, Mon noon–2:30pm and 6–10pm.

The Performing Arts

Bonn has always struggled with the perception that it can't compete with the larger arts communities in Hamburg and Berlin, and consequently it compensates (or overcompensates) with an impressive roster of cultural events. Bonn's **Theater-Kasse,** Windeckstrasse 1 (www.theater-bonn. de; ✆ **0228/775000;** S-Bahn Hauptbahnhof), is a well-known and highly resourceful ticket agency associated with the city's tourist office. It has information and access to tickets for virtually every sporting, entertainment, and cultural venue in Bonn.

One of the most visible cultural assets of Bonn is "La Scala of the Rhineland," the **Oper der Stadt Bonn,** Am Boeselagerhof (www.theater-bonn.de; ✆ **0228/778008;** S-Bahn Hauptbahnhof), where ballet and opera are performed at regular intervals from September to June. Tickets are 55€ and upwards, depending on the event.

The **Klassische Philharmonie Bonn (Bonn Symphony Orchestra)** performs in Beethovenhalle, Wachsbleiche 16 (www.klassische-philharmonie-bonn.de; ✆ **0228/654965;** S-Bahn Hauptbahnhof), September to June; tickets cost 15€ to 65€. On a more intimate scale, chamber music is sometimes presented within a small but charming concert hall within the **Beethoven Haus** (see p. 559).

The **BeethovenFest Bonn,** a rekindling of both the nostalgia and the music associated with Bonn's greatest musical genius, takes place from early September to early October. Visit **www.beethovenfestbonn. de** for information.

The **Pantheon Theater,** Bundeskanzlerplatz (www.pantheon.de; ✆ **0228/212521;** bus 610), stages jazz and pop concerts, comedy shows, and political cabaret. Nearly every weekday there is a performance of some sort.

THE RHINELAND ★★★

For over 2,000 years the Rhine has played a huge role in the history of Germany and Europe, serving as a means of transportation, communication, and cultural exchange between the south and the north. Whoever was in power sought to dominate the Rhineland, from the Romans to medieval popes and emperors to today's well-heeled wine tourists. Today, however, the ships that ply these waters are more often excursion vessels, as tourists on deck gape at the river's spectacular scenery. And when these invaders come ashore, they do so not to wage war but to enjoy the region's famed wines.

As one of the great trade routes of medieval Europe, the Rhine gave rise to a number of historic cities such as Mainz, Worms, and Speyer, any of which would make good bases for your Rhineland explorations. However, the region's greatest charms today lie outside the cities, in the wine villages and scenic landscapes along the river. Whether you visit those on day trips from the city or choose to stay there overnight, don't miss out on that quintessential Rheinland experience. We'll give you options for lodging and dining in both city and country.

Essentials

ARRIVING

BY PLANE   The nearest airport is at **Frankfurt** (see p. 489), 35km (22 miles) from Mainz. There is direct rail service from the airport (S-8 train) to Mainz, about a half-hour trip. For information, call the Mainz Railway Station at © **06131/151055.** From the airport, you can also rent a car, which may be your best option if you're planning to tour the countryside.

BY TRAIN   From Frankfurt, an express train takes 30 minutes to reach **Mainz,** while the S-Bahn arrives in 40 minutes. There are also train connections to Mainz from Heidelberg (trip time: 1 hr.), Cologne (trip time: 2 hr.), and Munich (4½ hours).

BY CAR   The main highways into this region are the A 61 (which runs from Koblenz southeast to Speyer), the A63 from the southwest, the east-west A60 (connecting via A67 to the A3 near Frankfurt), and the east-west A6, which runs through the southern Rhineland on its way from Saarbrücken to Heidelberg.

GETTING AROUND

BY TRAIN   To reach Rüdesheim and the **Rheingau,** you'll need to change trains at Mainz for the Wiesbaden-Koblenz line (total trip time from Frankfurt: 1 hr.). **Worms** also enjoys good rail connections, via the main Mainz-Mannheim line (27 min. express or 40 min. local trains from Mainz). The train south to **Speyer** takes 1 hr from Mainz, 33 min. from Worms (also 1½ hrs. from Frankfurt, 3½-4 hr. from Munich). .For rail information and schedules, call © **01805/996633** (www.bahn.de).

BY BUS   Bus service for the northern part of this region is provided by **ORN Omnibusverkehr Rhein-Nahe GmbH,** at Mainz (© 06131/ 5767470; www.orn-online.de); for the southern part, **BRN Busverkehr Rhein-Neckar GmbH** at Worms (© **06241/207312;** www.brn.de).

BY CAR   One useful road to know is **Route 9,** which runs north and south through Mainz, Worms, and Speyer. North of Mainz, it continues along the west bank of the Rhine, while **Route 42** follows the east bank. To cross the Rhine, however, can be a challenge, since there are no bridges between Koblenz and Wiesbaden; there is, however, a handy ferry at Bingen (call ☏ **06722/2972** for ferry information). Farther south, the officially designated German Wine Road is **Route 271,** which you can access by taking Route 47 west from Worms.

Sailing Up the Middle Rhine ★★★

The most scenic section of the Rhine, with the legendary Lorelei rock and many hilltop castles, is the **Middle Rhine (Mittelrhein),** between Koblenz and Rüdesheim. Known also as the Rhine Gorge, this stretch of the river with its vineyards, forest, and castle-topped crags, has been designated a UNESCO World Heritage Site.

While routes 9 and 42 follow the river banks, the best views are almost inevitably from the water. Even if you're not taking a luxury cruise (see box below), you can enjoy the sights along the Middle Rhine on an excursion boat departing from Koblenz. **KD Cruises** (www.k-d.de; ☏ **0261/31030** in Koblenz, ☏ **06722/3808** in Rüdesheim) offers daily services along the Middle Rhine, with 16 landing stages between Koblenz and Rüdesheim, as well as services on up the Rhine to Bonn, Cologne,

---

cruising **THE RHINE**

Increasing numbers of travelers are opting for views of some of the most legendary panoramas in Germany directly from the deck chairs of yachts and cruise ships. We highly recommend one in particular.

Viking River Cruises, 5700 Canoga Ave., Woodland Hills, CA 91367 (☏ **800/ 304-9616;** www.vikingrivers.com), is the world's largest river cruise line. It maintains a total of 38 river cruisers, each designed for between 100 and 230 passengers. Efficient and, in some cases, infused with touches of luxury, the cruises traverse the muddy waters of the Rhine between Amsterdam and Basel (Switzerland), traveling for between 8 and 12 nights. Along the way, they view the many castles of the Rhine river valley, adding on options such as guided tours of Marksburg and Heidelberg castles, Cologne, and the lush landscape of the

southern Black Forest. The 12-day cruise offers additional overnight stops in Bruges, Ghent, and Amsterdam as well as Kinderdijk and its famous windmills.

The per-person rate, depending on the onboard accommodations and the season, ranges from $2156 to $4606 double occupancy. Onboard attendants deliver commentaries in several languages (including English) of the sights and monuments en route. Food is served at tables for between four and eight diners, cruise-ship-style. All meals, onboard lodgings, and shore excursions are included in the price.

Pfalzgrafenstein, a medieval toll castle, fortifies its own island in the River Rhine.

and Düsseldorf. The journey takes about 6½ hours from Koblenz to Rüdesheim; there's usually a morning and an afternoon sailing in each direction. To make a round-trip loop, you may want to disembark at one of the earlier stops to give yourself more time to walk around before catching the return boat.

SIGHTS ALONG THE MIDDLE RHINE

From Koblenz south to Alsace, the Rhine Valley's sheltered sunny slopes covered with vineyards make it look almost like a northern extension of Italy. This part of the Rhineland has been fundamentally formed by the culture of wine, as reflected in its economy, traditions, and festivals.

As you head south from Koblenz, highlights are:

The fortress of **Marksburg,** one of two surviving medieval fortifications on the Middle Rhine, towers above the town of **Braubach** on the right (west) bank. **Rhens,** on the left (east) bank, is where the German Emperors were enthroned after being elected in Frankfurt and crowned in Aachen Cathedral (see p. 545). **Oberspay** and **Niederspay,** now incorporated into a single town, contain more timber-framed houses than anywhere on the Middle Rhine. **Boppard,** located below a horse-hoe loop in the river, originated as a Roman way-station and was replaced in the 4th century by a military fort. Across the river on the right bank is **St. Goarshausen,** with its castle of Neu-Katzenelnbogen.

As you continue towards Oberwesel, the valley landscape begins to transition from soft clay-slate to hard sandstone, creating a series of narrows, the most famous of which is the **Loreley,** the most over-rated rock formation in the world. This stretch of river, which was hazardous for shipping, inspired legends of the Lorelei, a golden-haired beauty who sat on the rocks combing her hair, apparently so entrancingly that she lured sailors to their deaths. This area is also reputed to be the place where the fabulous treasure of the Niebelungs, immortalized in Wagner's operas, lies hidden. Looking at the Loreley today, you may scratch your head and wonder what all the fuss was about.

Oberwesel, on the river's left bank, has preserved a number of fine early houses, as well as two Gothic churches, the medieval Schönburg castle, and its medieval town wall. **Kaub** and its environs contain a number of monuments, among them the **Pfalzgrafenstein castle,** the town wall of Kaub itself, and the terraced vineyards, created in the Middle Ages. **Bacharach,** at the entrance of the Steeger Valley, contains many timber-framed houses and retains its medieval appearance.

Just before river curves east toward Mainz and Wiesbaden, you'll pass through the 5km (3-mile) long **Binger Pforte (Bingen Gate),** a section of the river widened in the 19th and 20th centuries. If you're not heading back to Koblenz on a later boat, this may be an excellent place to get off, and spend a little more time in the **Rheingau** (see below).

The Rheingau ★★★

Legend says that when God was looking for a place to set up Paradise, the sunny slopes between the Taunus Mountains and the Rhine nearly won the prize. Today the Rheingau is the kingdom of another god: Bacchus. Vineyards on terraced hillsides have produced wine here since the times of the Romans, who recognized the area's perfect conditions: wind-sheltered south-facing slopes that get plenty of sunshine and comparatively little rain. Nearly every town and village along the river's north bank from Wiesbaden to Assmannshausen is a major wine producer.

If the place names here seem familiar—Bingen, Johannesburg, Rüdesheim, Oestrich—it's because they're featured on the labels of many wines. Rheingau wine grapes produce a delicately fruity wine with a full aroma. Eighty percent of this wine comes from the Riesling grape, and wine fans consider Rheigau Riseling to be among the best white wines made anywhere.

What may be even more important to visitors, though, is the cheerful character of the Rheingau wine villages and their people. Rüdesheim and Assmannshausen are the most visited towns.

VISITOR INFORMATION

The **Stadt Verkehrsamt,** Geissenheimer 22 in Rüdesheim (www. ruedesheim.de, © 06722/906150) is open April to October Monday to Friday 8:30am to 6:30pm, Saturday and Sunday 10am to 4pm; the rest of the year, it's open Monday to Friday 10am to 4pm. During Christmas market (the weeks before Christmas) they are also open Saturday and Sunday 11am to 3pm.

RHINE FERRIES

There are no bridges along this twisty, superbly scenic stretch of the Rhine, but there are **ferryboats** (www.bingen-rudesheimer.de, © 06722/ 3080810) crossing the river between Bingen and Rüdesheim. The car ferry costs 4.20€ per car, passengers 1.80€ (.80€ children), pedestrians 2€ (1€ children). Ferries run roughly every 20 minutes from 5:30am to 12:45am (November to April, the ferry stops running at 9:45pm). There's also a passenger ferry which runs hourly between 7am and 10pm (9am to 5pm November to April); fares are 2.50 one-way, 4.50 round-trip (half-price for children 6 to 14 years old).

EXPLORING THE RHEINGAU

Route 42 is the connecting highway for the Rheingau, running along the river's north bank from just west of Wiesbaden (take the highway 643 bridge from Mainz) all the way to Assmannshausen.

With its old courtyards and winding alleyways lined with half-timbered houses, **Rüdesheim** is the quintessential Rheingau wine town. The vineyards around the village date back to the Roman times and produce a full-bodied Riesling and *Sekt* (sparkling wine). Every year in August, when Rüdesheim celebrates the harvest with its annual **wine festival,** the old taverns on narrow **Drosselgasse (Thrush Lane)** are crowded with visitors from all over the world. Drosselgasse has been called "the smallest but the happiest street in the world."

Wine taverns throng narrow Drosselgasse in Rudesheim.

Overlooking the riverside road, in the stout stone medieval fortress of Brömserburg Castle, the **Rheingauer Weinmuseum,** Rheinstrasse 2 (www.rheingauer-weinmuseum.de; © **06722/2348**) traces the history of the grape with a exhibition of wine presses, glasses, goblets, and drinking utensils from Roman times to the present. Admission is 5€ for adults, 3€ for children, 10€ families, with an extra charge for wine tastings. The museum is open March to October daily 10am to 6pm.

Looming on a hill halfway between Rüdesheim and Assmannshausen, the **Niederwald Monument** is a huge statue of Germania, erected by Bismarck in 1883 to commemorate the unification of Germany. A cable car runs to the peak from both towns (www.seilbahn-rudesheim.de), costing 7€ round-trip up and down, or 8€ from one town to the other. Views from the top are delightful. Look for the small island at the bend of the Rhine with a stone tower at its east end—that's the **Mäuseturm (Mouse Tower),** where, according to legend, the greedy archbishop of Mainz was devoured by a swarm of hungry mice.

Another 5km (3 miles) northwest of Rüdesheim, the old village of **Assmannshausen** is built on the slopes of the east bank of the Rhine. Its half-timbered houses and vineyards seem precariously perched on the steep hillsides, and the view of the Rhine Valley from here is awe-inspiring. While Riesling is the wine of choice in Rüdesheim, Assmannshausen is known instead for its fine burgundy-style wine.

WHERE TO EAT & STAY IN THE RHEINGAU

Berg's Alte Bauernschanke Hotel ★★   The winegrower owners have turned two of the oldest half-timbered mansions in town into a hotel and restaurant. Rooms are nicely furnished in rustic traditional style; some rooms have original beams and other architectural features. The restaurant offers a refreshing mix of traditional schnitzels and spätzels with several salads and vegetarian-friendly fare, plus small plates designed to go well with the growers' red wine. Main courses cost 8€ to 19€.

Niederwaldstrasse 23, Assmannshausen. www.altebauernschaenke.de. © **06722/ 49990.** 54 units. 95€–170€ double. Buffet breakfast included. **Amenities:** Restaurant; bar; spa; sauna; room service; Wi-Fi (free). Closed Dec 16–Jan 31.

Gasthof Krancher ★   Located next to the family's own vineyards, this homey half-timbered guesthouse also serves regional German food, mostly Rhinelander specialties; there's a beer garden in season. Rooms are bright and modern, with blond wood built-ins, while the restaurant retains a wood-beamed rustic look.

Eibinger-Oberstrasse 4, Rüdesheim. www.gasthof-krancher.de. © **06722/2762.** 34€–42€ double. Breakfast included. **Amenities:** Restaurant, bar; Wi-Fi (free).

Hotel und Weinhaus Felsenkeller ★   The beautifully carved 17th-century facade of this hotel-restaurant suggest the traditional ambience you'll find within. Sample Rhine wine in a room with vaulted ceilings and murals or, if the weather is nice, enjoy regional Rhineland cuisine on the terrace. Upstairs, the rooms have a crisp modern look, with updated bathrooms.

Oberstrasse 39–41, Rüdesheim. www.felsenkeller-ruedesheim.de. ✆ **06722/94250.** 60 units. 85€–125€ double. Buffet breakfast included. **Amenities:** Restaurant, bar, free Wi-Fi in public areas. Closed Nov–Easter.

Krone Assmannshausen ★★★   This distinguished hotel offers the most luxurious accommodations in the entire Rüdesheim am Rhein district. It's on the banks of the Rhine, surrounded by lawns, gardens, and a pool. Its origins can be traced back 400 years. The inn is a great big gingerbread fantasy with fairy-tale turrets and wooden balconies evocative of the Romantic architecture of the 16th century. A small second-floor lounge is virtually a museum, with framed letters and manuscripts of some of the famous people who have stayed here—Goethe, for one, and also Kaiser Wilhelm II. There's a stack of about 40 autograph books dating from 1893 signed by writers, painters, diplomats, and composers. You may stay in a medieval, Renaissance, or postwar building. The spacious rooms have an old-inn character, with traditional furnishings. The elegant restaurant offers main courses for 18€ to 40€, or 45€ to 50€ for a 3-course fixed menu.

Rheinuferstrasse 10, Assmannshausen. www.hotel-krone.com. ✆ **06722/4030.** 65 units. 150€–245€ double. Breakfast included. Parking 10€. **Amenities:** Restaurant; babysitting; outdoor pool; room service; Wi-Fi (free). Closed Jan–Mar.

Mainz ★

100km (62 miles) SE of Koblenz, 180km (112 miles) SE of Cologne, 40km (25 miles) SW of Frankfurt, 92km (57 miles) NW of Heidelberg

The ancient city of Mainz occupies some prime real estate on the left bank of the Rhine, across from the Rhine's confluence with the Main River. When the Romans first arrived here in 57 B.C., there may have already been wine-producing vines in the area, but the Romans made the most of what they found: The regions of the Rheingau and Rheinhessen became widely known for fine viticulture.

At the beginning of the Christian era, a bridge connected the settlement on the Rhine's left bank with the Roman fortifications opposite. In the 8th century, the town became a primary archbishopric. Over the centuries, church politics and a series of wars shuffled control of the city back and forth between the French (who called it "Mayence") and various German factions.

Carnival in Mainz

The most celebrated merrymaking in festive Mainz is the **All Fools capers** at **Carnival** each spring, on the Monday and Tuesday before Ash Wednesday, where merrymakers act like fools, jesters, and clowns. This festival is broadcast throughout Germany the way the Macy's Thanksgiving Day parade is throughout the U.S.

Today Mainz is a bustling, cosmopolitan city, with a university and a prosperous business sector. It stands not only at the meeting of two rivers, but at the meeting of several highways and train lines, making it a good base for exploring this region.

VISITOR INFORMATION

Touristik Centrale, Brückenturm am Rathaus (www.touristik-mainz. de, © 06131/242888), is open Monday to Friday 10am to 5pm, Saturday 10am to 3pm. Trams and buses fan out across the city from the Hauptbahnhof from 5am until around midnight. Fares start at 2.30€ and vary depending on how far you go.

EXPLORING MAINZ

Most visitors will be interested in the relatively compact **Altstadt,** which has been restored tastefully and carefully; it's about a 15-minute walk southeast from the station to the **Marktplatz,** where you'll find Mainz's cathedral (see below) and the Gutenberg Museum (see p. 572). The main shopping street, pedestrianized **Am Brand,** is a couple blocks north of the Marktplatz, running east toward the Rhine, where landscaped **riverside promenades** lead north. Antiquity buffs might also like to visit the remains of the **Roman amphitheather,** which is just a 10-minute walk south of the Altstadt.

Dom und Diözesan Museum (Cathedral and Diocesan Museum) ★

CHURCH   Above the roofs of the half-timbered houses in the Altstadt rise the six towers of St. Martin's Cathedral, seat of the Archbishop of Mainz and the most important Catholic cathedral in the country after Cologne's. It dates from A.D. 975 but was continually rebuilt and restored, reaching its present form mainly in the 13th and 14th centuries. Below the largest dome, a combination of Romanesque and baroque styles, a transept separates the west chancel from the nave and smaller east chancel. Many of the supporting pillars along the aisles of the nave are decorated with carved and painted statues of French and German saints. Among other impressive furnishings in the sanctuary are rococo choir stalls and an early 14th-century pewter baptismal font. The cathedral's **Diocesan Museum** houses a collection of religious art, including reliquaries, medieval sculpture, and works by the Master of Naumburg, the

Graceful Mainz Cathedral, founded in 975 but mostly built in the 13th and 14th centuries.

anonymous 13th-century artist who sculpted many of the statues in cathedrals across Northern France and Germany. In the 1,000-year-old cathedral **crypt** is a contemporary gold reliquary of the saints of Mainz. Domstrasse 3. © **06131/253344.** www.dom-mainz.de and www.dommuseum-mainz.de. Cathedral free; Diocesan Museum 2€ adults, 1.50€ students and seniors, family ticket 2€–4€. Cathedral open Mar–Oct Mon–Fri 9am–6:30pm, Sat 9am–4pm, Sun 12:45–3pm and 4–6:30pm; Nov–Feb Mon–Fri 9am–5pm, Sat 9am–4pm, Sun 12:45–3pm and 4–5pm. Museum open Tues–Fri 10am–5pm; Sat–Sun 11am–6pm.

Gutenberg Museum ★★ MUSEUM   Across from the east towers of the cathedral, a rose-colored stepped-gable Renaissance building once owned by the Holy Roman Emperors now houses this memorial to the city's most famous son, 15th-century printer Johannes Gutenberg. (The museum's exhibits are in a modern addition behind the old house.) In the rebuilt Gutenberg workshop, visitors can trace the history of printing, beginning with the hand press on which Gutenberg printed his 42-line-per-page Bible from 1452 to 1455. The collections cover the entire spectrum of the graphic arts in all countries, past and present, as well as printing, illustration, and binding. Two Gutenberg Bibles are the most popular exhibits. Liebfrauenplatz 5. © **06131/122640.** www.gutenberg-museum.de. Admission 5€ adults, 3€ students and seniors, 2€ ages 8–18, children 7 and under free; families 10€. Tues–Sat 9am–5pm, Sun 11am–5pm.

Landesmuseum Mainz (Provincial Museum of the Central Rhineland) ★ MUSEUM   It's worth a visit here to get a visual history of Mainz and the middle Rhineland, ranging from prehistoric times to the present. The Lapidarium shows one of the most important collections of Roman monuments in Europe, including tombstones of Roman soldiers and civilians of the 1st century A.D. and the towering Column of Jupiter, erected in Mainz at the time of Nero, around A.D. 65 to 68. (There's a true-to-life replica of the column in front of the Parliament building.) The Landesmuseum also has an impressive collection of antiquities from the Near East, assembled by Prince Johann Georg, an avid arts collector from the late 19th century. But there's lots more here, from medieval jewelry to 18th-century porcelain to Biedermeir furniture to Picasso and Rothko paintings. The Landesmuseum's baroque building (look for the gilded horse rearing atop its pediment) is a 10-minute walk north of the cathedral.

Grosse Bleiche 49–51. © **06131/23295557.** www.landesmuseum-mainz.de. Admission 6€ adults, 5€ seniors and students, children under age 6 free. Tues 10am–8pm; Wed–Sun 10am–5pm.

Stephenskirche (Church of St. Stephen) ★ CHURCH   There's one main reason to visit this reconstructed medieval Gothic church, which is a 10-minute walk southwest of the cathedral: to see the

Original Bibles at the Gutenberg Museum, which honors the inventor of the printing press.

stained-glass windows by Marc Chagall, installed in 1978. Predominantly using deep shades of blue, these nine stained-glass windows were created by Chagall, a Russian Jew, as a symbol of German-Jewish reconciliation after the Holocaust. The scenes depicted are all from the old Testament, to show the commonalities between Judaism and Christianity.

Kleine Weißgasse 12. www.st-stephan-mainz.de. © **06131/231640.** Church admission free. Mon–Sat 10am–5pm, Sun noon–5pm (Nov–Feb closes 4:30pm).

WHERE TO STAY IN MAINZ

Note that because Mainz was bombed heavily in World War II, there are very few historic properties here—most of the city's best hotels are in modern buildings, many of them operated by international chains.

Favorite Parkhotel ★ Set in isolated privacy within a park on a hillside above the Rhine, a 12-minute walk from Mainz's Altstadt, this family-run three-story hotel was established in the early 1960s, and enlarged in 2005 with a five-story modern wing. Accommodations in the old wing are preferred for their solid sense of comfort, pastel colors, and a conservative sense of modernity. Rooms within the newer wing are trendier and monochromic, but still very comfortable. The morning breakfast buffet is substantial, a reflection of the good service and food in the hotel's gourmet-conscious **Stadtpark Restaurant,** and its *Bierkeller*-style cohort, the **Bierkutscher.** Then, of course, there is an outdoor beer garden (open May to late Sept daily noon–10pm).

Karl Weiser Strasse 1. www.favorite-mainz.de. © **06131/80150.** 120 units. 175€–205€ double. Buffet breakfast included. Parking 15€. **Amenities:** 2 restaurants; babysitting; bikes; concierge; exercise room; Jacuzzi; indoor pool; room service; sauna; Wi-Fi (free).

Hilton Mainz ★★ Occupying two desirable plots of land near the center of town, the Hilton is one of the most imaginatively designed and strikingly modern hotels along the Rhine Valley. Its twin sections are sheathed in reflective glass and soaring spans of steel, and connected by a glass-enclosed walkway over the traffic below. The labyrinthine interior has sun-flooded atriums with live plants and acres of marble flooring. The spacious rooms are the most artfully decorated in the region with modern furniture and stark colors. It's a 5-minute walk from the cathedral.

Rheinstrasse 68. www.hilton.com. © **800/445-8667** in the U.S. and Canada, or 06131/2450. 437 units. 185€–300€ double. Breakfast not included in lower rates. Parking 20€. **Amenities:** 3 restaurants; bar; babysitting; concierge; exercise room; room service; sauna; Wi-Fi (14.95€ per day).

Hilton Mainz City ★★ In the historic zone of Mainz, about a 3-block walk from the rail terminus, this Hilton is particularly lively. Although the rooms are about the same in both Hiltons, we prefer the relatively subdued atmosphere here and the more personal staff. We also like the architectural touches, including an ancient wall discovered during reconstruction. The wall was preserved and now frames the courtyard terrace. Rooms are a bit cookie-cutter, but tasteful and spacious, each with a deluxe bathroom. They're priced according to view and location; those on the top cost the most money because of their panoramic views and balconies. The least desirable are on the lower floors, facing a park.

Münsterstrasse 11. www.hilton.com. ✆ 06131/2780. 128 units. 140€–290€ double. Buffet breakfast included. Parking 20.50€. **Amenities:** Restaurant; 2 bars; babysitting; concierge; exercise room; room service; Wi-Fi (14.95€ per day).

Hotel Mainzer Hof ★ Mainzer Hof is six floors of modernity directly on the Rhine, almost at the point where some of the boats dock. This hotel is a clean-cut, convenient stopover, and only a 10-minute walk from the Hauptbahnhof. The medium-size rooms have simple, if somewhat dated, furnishings, with built-in wood headboards and bedside cabinets. Most rooms have views overlooking the Rhine.

Kaiserstrasse 98. www.hotel-mainzerhof.de. ✆ 06131/97240. 86 units. 75€–123€ double. Buffet breakfast included. Parking 8€. **Amenities:** bar; exercise room; room service; sauna; Wi-Fi (free).

Hyatt Regency Mainz ★★★ Opening onto the Rhine, this deluxe palace has eclipsed the two Hiltons and now reigns supreme. It is the best hotel south of Cologne, done in a strikingly modern architectural style that cleverly incorporates bits of a 19th-century red sandstone fort. A glittering 21st-century aura prevails in the public rooms, restaurants, and guest accommodations. The room furnishings are monochromatic and modern, with a tendency towards sleek metal rather than wood. The more desirable units open onto the Rhine, and these have even larger bathrooms. The public facilities are among the best in this part of Germany, with a wine bar and the **Bellpepper** restaurant, featuring a grand terrace along the Rhine. In summer a beer garden goes full blast.

Templerstrasse 6. www.mainz.regency.hyatt.com. ✆ 06131/731234. 268 units. 125€–255€ double. Breakfast not included in all rates. Parking 22€. **Amenities:** 2 restaurants; bar; babysitting; concierge; exercise room; indoor pool; room service; spa; Wi-Fi (free).

WHERE TO EAT IN MAINZ

Bistrorante L'Angolo ITALIAN This casual Italian-inspired trattoria is known for its congenial staff and its excellent pizza and pasta. You can also order freshly made salads, with shrimp or prosciutto, and main courses with a Roman accent, such veal scallopini, grilled salmon, or saltimbocca. Reasonable prices and a full bar generally keep this place packed. The location is convenient, on the southern end of the Altstadt, just down the street from Frankfurter Hof concerts (see below).

Augustinerstrasse 8. www.l-angolo.de. ✆ 06131/231737. Pizzas and pastas 8€–16€; main courses 14€–24€. Mon–Sat 11am–10:30pm, Sun noon–10:30pm.

Geberts Weinstuben ★★ PALATINATE   This traditional *Wein-stube* is housed in one of the oldest buildings in Mainz, built in 1879, located at the north end of the Rhine riverbank promenade. The sleek purple-and-white décor, with crystal chandeliers and gilt-framed mirrors, evokes images of Mozart playing at Austrian salons. But people flock here primarily for the food. The menu, which was reinvented in 2007 when the original owner's son, Frank Gebert, took over, includes local dishes sourced by local farmers. Steak dishes and fish dominate the menu, which includes a prix-fixe option and wine pairings.

Frauenlobstrasse 94. www.geberts-weinstuben.de. ✆ **06131/611619.** Reservations required. Main courses 18.50€–28€; fixed-price menu 35€. Wed–Sat 11:30am–2:30pm and 6pm–midnight. Closed mid-July to mid-Aug.

Haus des Deutschen Weines ★ GERMAN   Set in Mainz's historic core, one block east of the Marktplatz, this cheery contemporary-looking restaurant focuses on a savory combination of German food and mostly German wines. Said wines run the gamut of virtually every vintage pro-duced within Germany, and the staff is well versed in their compatibility with menu items that include fresh or marinated salmon, venison, calves' liver, a savory version of rump steak, and perfectly grilled fish. Expect lots of emphasis on whatever vegetable is in season at the moment of your arrival. No one will object if you order just wine and a small platter of food; examples include flammkuchen, housemade sausages, or *Spundekäse,* an age-old recipe that mingles local cheese whipped with onions and cream into a soft paste. It's best served with rough-textured bread. They also serve a hearty breakfast.

Gutenbergplatz 3-5. www.hdw-gaststaetten.de. ✆ **06131/221300.** Reservations recommended. Main courses 9€–20€. Daily 10am–midnight.

Weinstube Lösch RHINELAND   This old-fashioned wood-paneled *Weinstube* in the heart of the Altstadt, founded in 1907, has been popular for generations and is rich in tradition. The menu offers regional hot and cold dishes and light salads, plus lots of Rhine wine. The pork *Schnitzel* with mushrooms is particularly savory. Tender rump steak, served with fried onions, is also a huge specialty here. Additional tables are placed out front in summer on the pedestrian mall.

Jakobsbergstrasse 9. www.weinstube-loesch.de. ✆ **06131/220383.** Reservations recommended. Main courses 9€–28€. Tues–Fri 3pm–midnight, Sat 2pm–midnight, Sun noon–11pm (2–11pm mid-Apr to Sept).

PERFORMING ARTS

The cultural center of the city is **Frankfurter Hof,** Augustinerstrasse 55 (www.frankfurter-hof-mainz.de; ✆ **06131/220438**), a handsomely revamped 19th-century hall in the Altstadt which now stages concerts of classical music, jazz, folk, and pop. The center also hosts an annual tent festival featuring an eclectic mix of international performers. Tickets to all events cost 10€ to 75€. Call for scheduled shows, festival dates and performers, and ticket information.

Worms ★

45km (28 miles) S of Mainz, 49km (30 miles) N of Speyer

Before the Romans came, Germanic peoples had made Worms (pronounced *Vohrrms*) their capital. Here, legend has it, Siegfried began his adventures, as recorded in *The Nibelungenlied*. Later on, Martin Luther arrived under less than desirable circumstances: In 1521, he was "invited" to appear before the Imperial Diet at Worms, a court invoked to decide his fate. After he refused to retract his grievances against the Church of Rome, Holy Roman Emperor Karl V declared him an outlaw, but today a huge monument to Luther and other giants of the Reformation stands tall in the Lutherring city park a stone's throw from the cathedral. The city also has a long Jewish history, having the country's oldest Jewish synagogue, Rashi, and the oldest Jewish cemetery.

Worms also makes an excellent base for a tour of the **Deutsche Weinstrasse,** an 80km (50-mile) route through local wine towns (see p. 580).

VISITOR INFORMATION

Worms' tourist office, at Neumarkt 14 (www.worms.de, ©**06241/8537306**) is open year-round Monday to Friday 9am to 6pm; Saturday, Sunday, and holidays it's open 10am to 2pm. Buses traverse the city from 6am to midnight and charge 2€-4€ depending on how far you go, paid directly to the driver.

EXPLORING WORMS

Dom St. Peter ★★ CATHEDRAL   Towering physically and historically above all the other ancient buildings of the city, this majestic basilica is a fine example of High Romanesque style. The east choir, with a flat facade and semicircular interior, is the oldest section, dating from 1132, when it was the church's main sanctuary. The main chancel, built in 1181, glows with the gold and marble of a pillared enclosure around the **baroque high altar** by the famous 18th-century architect Balthasar Neumann. This opulent work was so large that there was no place for a proper transept. Otherwise the cathedral's interior has a quiet elegance, with little decoration other than the rosette window and several memorial slabs and monuments. Well worth seeing is the highly decorated 14th-century **side chapel of St. Nicholas,** with its Gothic baptismal font and new stained-glass windows. This was the setting of history's famous Diet of Worms, an assembly of the Catholic hierarchy, which banished Martin Luther when he refused to renounce his so-called heretical doctrine. (Luther adamantly maintained that religious truth exists in Scripture, not in papal power or edicts.)

Lutherring 9. www.wormser-dom.de. © **06241/6151.** Apr–Oct daily 9am–6pm, Nov–Mar daily 10am–5pm.

Jüdisches Viertel (Jewish Quarter) ★★ HISTORIC NEIGHBORHOOD Before World War II, Worms had one of the oldest Jewish communities in Germany. The cobbled streets and old brick buildings of their neighbhood, once known as "Little Jerusalem," has been carefully restored (you'll find it north of the Altstadt, east of Friedrichstrasse). The still-functioning **synagogue,** just off Judengasse on Synagogenplatz, dates from the 11th century; it was destroyed in 1938 and has since been rebuilt. Behind it is the **Raschi-Haus Museum** (Hintere Judengasse 6), containing memorabilia from the original synagogue and references to the Holocaust. A staff member inside will point you in the direction of the **Judenfriedhof (Jewish cemetery)** ★, off the Lutherring, the oldest preserved Jewish cemetery north of the Alps, with hundreds of tombstones, some more than 900 years old. (Note that the cemetery is closed on Saturdays.)

Ancient mossy graves in the historic Jewish cemetery in Worms.

www.worms.de. © **06241/8534701.** Museum admission 1.50€ adults, .80€ children 13 and under. Museum open Tues–Sun 10am–12:30pm and 1:30–5pm (closes at 4:30pm Nov–Mar). Synagogue open daily Apr–Oct 10am–12:30pm and 1:30–5pm, Nov–Mar 10am–noon and 2–4pm.

WHERE TO STAY IN WORMS

Central Hotel Worms ★ The Central Hotel certainly lives up to its name—the location couldn't be more central, right off the Marktplatz and within walking distance of all major historic monuments. Though modest and unassuming, this is one of the best values in the city. Innkeeper Alexandra Hill rents tidily furnished, if rather small rooms. All contain bathrooms with tub/shower combos. The breakfast buffet is particularly bountiful. Note that the reception area is up a flight of stairs, but there is an elevator for those with mobility issues.

Kämmererstrasse 5. www.centralhotel-worms.de. ✆ **06241/64570.** 19 units. 89€–95€ double. Buffet breakfast included. Parking 6€. **Amenities:** Internet access in lobby. Closed late Dec to late Jan.

Dom-Hotel ★ About a block from the cathedral, this is an ideal choice for the in-and-out traveler. The all-purpose hotel is a white gridlike postwar structure built in a complex of shops and boutiques, overlooking a public square. Rooms are a little boxy and functionally furnished—lots of blond wood, chrome, and black leather—but all are well maintained and contain spick-and-span bathrooms.

Am Obermarkt 10. www.dom-hotel.de. ✆ **06241/9070.** 55 units. From 105€ double. Buffet breakfast included. Free parking. **Amenities:** Restaurant; Wi-Fi (free).

Parkhotel Prinz Carl ★★ Architecturally distinguished in the old Rhinelander style with step gables, this hotel is completely modernized inside, decorated in a warm, elegant style. There are five room categories ranging from standard to deluxe, but all of the accommodations are furnished comfortably and tastefully with mahogany furniture, sitting areas, wall-to-wall carpeting, and sleek bathrooms. In the morning, guests enjoy the most generous breakfast buffet in town. The formal restaurant features first-class and international specialties backed up with an impressive wine list from the Rhineland.

Prinz-carl-Anlage 10-14. www.parkhotel-prinzcarl.de. ✆ **06241/3080.** 90 units. 98€–131€ double. Buffet breakfast 13€. Free parking. **Amenities:** Restaurant; bar; babysitting; bikes; room service; Wi-Fi (free).

WHERE TO EAT IN WORMS

Die Pfälzer ★ PALATINATE This traditional restaurant is exactly what you need after a tough day of sightseeing: a homey vibe with exposed timber, rustic stucco walls, friendly service, and rib-sticking fare. Dishes such as liver-and-blood-sausage dumplings with horseradish sauce will fill you up quick, but salmon with sautéed spinach or green salad with chicken and peaches offer healthier options. Wash it all down with a selection from their extensive wine list, or if you really want to go local, go for a post-meal fruit-infused *Ostbrand* (schnapps).

Peterstrasse 16. www.xn-die-pflzer-v5a.com. ✆ **06242/6989199.** Reservations recommended. Main courses 9€–18€. Tues–Fri noon–2pm and 5–11pm, Sat–Sun 11:30am–2:30pm and 6–11pm.

Landhaus Dubs ★★ CONTINENTAL Set in a modern structure in the country with sweeping views of local vineyards, Landhaus Dubs gives you a dose of country with a sophisticated flair and offers a wide—largely local—selection of wines to choose from. The much-lauded chef Wolfgang Dubs has been a culinary fixture around here since 1969, when he opened his previous restaurant, Rotisserie Dubs. The Landhaus menu, a mix of local specialties and international fare, features everything from Asian-inspired dishes like wild salmon on Thai noodle salad to a Schnitzel served with wild mushroom ragu and *rosti* (shredded fried potatoes).

Am Mühlpfad 10, Osthofen. Take Rte. 9 north for 10km (6 miles) then east on L386 for 5km (3 miles). ℂ **06242/912-5205.** www.dubs.de. Reservations recommended. Main courses 16€–32€; fixed-price menu 50€. Wed–Fri and Sun–Mon noon–2pm and 6–10pm, Sat 6–10pm.

A Driving Tour of the German Wine Road ★★

Germany's oldest designated tourist route, the **Deutsche Weinstrasse,** runs south for 80km (50 miles) from Bockenheim, a small town 14km (8½ miles) west of Worms, to Schweigen-Rechtenbach on the frontier with France. This is a land of old castles (most in ruins) and venerable vineyards. Most of the wines produced here are whites, with special emphasis on clear, aromatic Rieslings and *Weissburgunders.* In every town along the route, you'll find old Rhineland-Palatinate inns and wine taverns, serving hearty local specialties such as *Sauerbraten* (beef marinated in wine vinegar).

Armed with a map (available at the Worms tourist office, see p. 577), you can set out to explore the area beginning in the north at **Bockenheim.** Stop in the square-towered St. Lambert's church, on Kirchgasse; you know you're in wine country when even the medieval wood carvings, like this church's Madonna and Child, prominently feature bunches of grapes. From Bockenheim, follow Rte. 271 directly south 7.2km (4.5 miles) to Grünstadt, where signs point the way west to the village of **Neuleiningen,** 10km (6 miles) away. The ruins of Neuleiningen castle have

---

Going to Ruin

About 3.5km (2 miles) west of Bad Dürkheim on Rte. 37, you can view the remains of the **Monastery of Limburg,** once one of the most impressive Romanesque structures in the country, which stands on a hill overlooking Bad Dürkheim. A small garden restaurant amid the ruins makes a good stop-off for a light lunch. If you're still in the mood

for picturesque ruins, continue west on Rte. 37 for another 17 km (10 miles) to the town of Frankenstein. Turn north on the Diemerstein road for about 1 km to see **Burgruine Diemerstein,** a hilltop ruined castle from the Middle Ages that local legend claims inspired Mary Shelley's classic monster.

Bad Dürkheim lures visitors with a restaurant in the world's largest wine cask.

a splendid view of the upper Rhine valley, as well as a romantic cellar restaurant, **Die Burgschänke** (www.burgschaenke-neuleiningen.de).

From Grunstadt, Hwy. 271 leads south 10km (6 miles) to Kallstadt, where the next stopover at **Bad Dürkheim** is signposted. Lest you doubt Bad Dürkheim's identity as a wine town, the world's largest wine cask, the **Dürkheimer Fass** (St. Michael Allee 1; www.duerkheimer-fass.de) will set you straight; built in 1934, it now houses a restaurant serving traditional Palatine food. Bad Dürkheim is also home to the huge Wurstmarkt festival, held every September to celebrate the twin pleasures of sausage and wine.

From Bad Dürkheim, drive 8km (5 miles) south along 271 to **Deidesheim,** your best bet for tastings in this area. In medieval times, this town was the seat of the bishops of Speyer; their former *Schloss,* now a picturesque ruin, stands amid a lovely park, and some of the wine road's most charming half-timbered buildings surround the Marktplatz. In the old town hall, a **wine museum** (www.die-weinprobe.de) organizes tasting and tours. Our favorite place is the **Basserman-Jordan Wine Estate,** Kirchgasse 10 (www.bassermann-jordan.de; ✆ **06326/6006**), dating from 1775. Admission is free; you can visit the estate

Monday to Friday from 8am to 6pm and Saturday and Sunday from 10am to 3pm.

From Deidesheim, continue along Rte. 271 for another 15 minutes, branching onto the B38 to reach **Neustadt-an-der-Weinstrasse,** the largest town on the Weinstrasse, lying at the foot of the Haardt hills. Pass quickly through its ugly suburbs to reach the heart of the old town, with its narrow, often-crooked streets. There are some 2,000 hectares (5,000 acres) of vineyards within the town limits, and the main streets are lined with taverns and wine shops. For wine tastings, visit **Weingut Probsthof,** Probstgasse 7 (www.weingut-probsthof.de, *C* **06321/6315**) or **Weingut Muller-Catoir,** Mandelring 25 (www.mueller-catoir.de, *C* **06321/2815**), both open Monday to Saturdays, which offer tastings for 12€ and up, depending on the number of wines and length of the tasting.

If you need to cut things short, you can head from here to Speyer (see p. 583), a 26km (16-mile) jaunt from Neustadt east along B39. Otherwise, continue south from Neustadt about 5km (3 miles) to crenellated **Schloss Hambach** (www.hambacher-schloss.de, *C* **06321/926290**), just southwest of the village of Hambach. The movement to unify Germany as a single democratic nation began with a rally here in 1832; exhibits trace the history of that movement. The castle, which also has a full-service restaurant, is open daily 11am to 5pm; admission is 4.50€. Beyond Hambach, the Weinstrasse, now L512, continues south 8km (5 miles) to the sleepy hamlet of **St. Martin,** which for our money is the loveliest village along the wine road, filled with antique houses draped with flowering vines. **St. Martiner Castle** (see p. 583), whose nostalgic ruins still tower over St. Martin, happens to have the best food and lodging along the wine road.

The signposted road, now L507, passes through **Gleisweiler,** a wine-producing hamlet known as the warmest village in Germany (notice the fig trees flourishing in its subtropical climate), and on to **Annweiler,** site of the fabled castle **Burg Trifels ★★** (www.annweiler.de; *C* **06346/8470**), a red sandstone pile set imperiously on a jagged crag. In 1193, Richard the Lionhearted was captured and imprisoned here until he was bailed out with a huge ransom. Burg Trifels is open daily 9am to 6pm (October to March, it closes at 5pm, and it's closed in December). Admission is 4.50€ adults, 3.50€ seniors and students, 2.50€ children.

The B48 leads next 14km (9 miles) southeast to **Klingenmünster,** where you can take a 30- to 40-minute stroll through chestnut forest to the ruins of **Burg Landeck,** one of the most scenic spots along the wine road, with views extending as far as the Black Forest. Past Klingenmünster, B38 and L508 lead 5km (3 miles) through **Bad Bergzabern,** an old spa town full of half-timbered houses, where you can pick up Highway

B38 for the last 10 kms (6 miles) of the Wine Road, ending at **Schwei-gen-Rechtenbach,** a village at the French frontier. In the summer of 1935, local vintners constructed a gargantuan stone arch, the **Deutsches Weintor (German Wine Gate),** marking the southern end of this oft-traveled tourist route. From a gallery atop the gate, you can view miles of vineyards and even see a panorama of the Vosges in France. From the Deutsches Weintor it is a 55km (34-mile) drive northeast along B39 into B9 to Speyer.

WHERE TO EAT & STAY ALONG THE GERMAN WINE ROAD

While in **Neuleiningen,** sample the local fare at **Alte Pfarrey ★,** Untergasse 40, (www.altepfarrey.de, ✆ **06359/86066**), set in a charming former rectory, where fixed-price menus cost 65€ to 179€. It is open for dinner Tuesday through Saturday 6:30 to 9:30pm; lunch is also available Friday to Sunday, noon to 1:30pm.

In **Deidesheim,** the very stylish **Deidesheimer Hof,** Am Markt-platz 1 (www.deidesheimerhof.de, ✆ **06326/96870**) has two restaurants, the gourmet **Schwarzer Hahn ★,** where fixed-price menus go from 118€ to 229€, and the more artfully rustic **St.-Urban ★,** which charges 35€-76€ for fixed-price menus.

If you want to stop overnight along the road, your best best is probably in **St. Martin** at the **St. Martiner Castell ★★,** Maikammer Strasse 2; (www.hotelcastell.de, ✆ **06323/9510**). Double rooms go for around 100€ to 125€ a night, with breakfast included. In its restaurant, main courses are 12€ to 22€ and fixed-price menus are 36€ to 88€.

In Schweigen-Rechtenbach, the **Hotel Schweigener Hof,** Haupt-strasse 2 (www.schweigener-hof.com, ✆ **06342/9250,** open 11:30am-3pm and 5-9pm) serves hearty regional fare; main courses cost 12€ to 27€.

Speyer ★

93km (58 miles) S of Mainz, 47 km (29 miles) S of Worms, 21km (13 miles) SW of Heidelberg

One of the oldest Rhine cities, Speyer celebrated its 2,000th jubilee in 1990. It became a significant religious center early on when the Diet of Speyer, in 1529, united the followers of Luther in a protest against the Church of Rome. With its enormous Romanesque cathedral, not to mention an intriguing old Jewish quarter, it's definitely a place for history buffs.

VISITOR INFORMATION

Speyer's tourist office, at Maximilianstrasse 13 (www.speyer.de, ✆ **06232/142392**), is open Monday to Friday 9am to 5pm, Saturday 10am to 3pm

WATCH ON THE rhine

The Rhine carries more freight than any other river in Europe, and its once famous salmon were caught at the rate of 250,000 annually. But by the 1950s the river had simply become too poisonous for the fish to survive. By the 1970s and 1980s, the fabled Rhine was called "the sewer of Europe."

That has now changed. Billions of euros spent on water-treatment plants led to a cleaner river, and now the salmon are back—though the fish you see today heroically leaping about aren't the same salmon of yore, as new strains had to be imported from Ireland, France, Scotland, and Scandinavia. We must rely on old cookbooks to tell us of the glorious taste of the salmon Rhinelanders once enjoyed.

One species of small crab is not as welcome. This alien amphipod that came from the Danube is now spreading to all the major rivers of Germany, including the Rhine, devouring native species at a rapid rate, and reducing biodiversity.

(closes Saturdays at noon Nov-Mar), and Sunday 10am to 2pm (closed on Sundays Nov-Mar). **Walking tours** in English are available April to November, on Saturday and Sunday at 11am, for 3.60€ per person; the tour leaves from the tourist office.

Exploring Speyer

Dreifaltigkeitskirke (Trinity Church) ★ CHURCH   Constructed from 1701 to 1717, this baroque church is one of the most richly adorned and decorated churches along the Rhine. In fact, it's the only elaborate, baroque-style church that still exists in the Rhine-Main-Neckar region. The interior contains a two-story gallery with a splendid balustrade of wooden-capped vaulting painted by artisans. Johann Peter Grabner, architect to the court of Palatinate, designed the church. *Note:* As we went to press, Trinity Church was closed for renovations into 2017; check the website to see if it has reopened.

Grosse Himmelsgasse 4. www.dreifaltigkeit-speyer.de. © **06232/629958.**

Historisches Museum der Pfalz (Palatinate Historical Museum) ★ MUSEUM   More than your run-of-the-mill Domschatz, or cathedral treasury, this museum is housed in a castle with four wings next door to the cathedral. Inaugurated in 1910, it has some 300,000 artifacts related to the history of the Palatinate and the city of Speyer. Relics date from prehistoric times, with a strong emphasis on the Roman and medieval eras; objects found in the tombs of former emperors under the Dom are fascinating. The most celebrated exhibit is the Bronze Age *Golden Hat of Schifferstadt,* a golden, cone-shaped object used in religious celebrations in ancient times. On-site also is the **Wein Museum (Wine Museum),**

with exhibits showing how the Romans produced their *vino,* including the world's oldest bottle of wine (ca. A.D. 300).

Domplatz. www.museum.speyer.de. ✆ **06232/13250.** Admission 7€ adults, 5€ students and children 6–17, families 14€. Open Tues–Sun 10am–6pm.

Jüdisches Viertel (Jewish Quarter) ★ HISTORIC NEIGHBORHOOD   Speyer was one of the most important centers of Jewish culture along the Rhine, although precious little of that settlement remains today. However, some ruins from the old neighborhood can still be seen near the Palatinate Historical Museum. Enter the ruins through a gatehouse from Judengasse, onto Judenbadstrasse. Here you'll see ruined fragments of the ancient **synagogue,** and in its east wall, the *Judenbad* (called *Mikwe* in Hebrew), a 12th-century ritual bathhouse for women. The masons who constructed the Dom also built this bathhouse, the oldest and best-preserved relic of its kind in the country and a poignant, nostalgic reminder of a vanished culture.

Judengasse. www.christen-und-juden.de/html/synagSP.html. ✆ **06232/291971.** Admission 2€. Open Apr–Oct daily 10am–5:30pm.

Kaiserdom (Imperial Cathedral) ★★ CATHEDRAL   Nothing brings back the medieval German empire as much as the Speyer cathedral, the greatest building of its time. This cathedral, consecrated in the early 11th century, is the largest Romanesque edifice in Germany. Having weathered damage by fires, wars, and restorations, the cathedral was finally brought back to its original shape during a restoration that ran from 1957 to 1961. When you enter the church through the single west door set in a stepped arch, you're at once caught up in the vastness of its proportions; the whole length of the nave and east chancel opens up, lit by the muted daylight from above. The church contains the royal tombs of four emperors, three empresses, and four German kings, as well as a row of bishops' tombs.

Domplatz. www.dom-speyer.de. ✆ **06232/1020.** Admission free. Open Apr–Oct daily 9am–7pm; Nov–Mar daily 10am–5pm.

Technik-Museum (Museum of Technology) ★ MUSEUM   South of the historic city center, in a former aircraft hangar from 1913, you can view a vast array of airplanes, locomotives, vintage automobiles, fire engines, and even automatic musical instruments. For many, the biggest thrill is going inside a 20-ton U-boat once used to terrorize Allied shipping in the Atlantic. Annexed to the museum is the **Marine Museum,** displaying a rich collection of historical model ships. Part of the attraction is a monumental 3-D IMAX cinema.

Am Technik Museum 1. www.technik-museum.de. ✆ **06232/67080.** Admission 15€ adults, 12.50€ children ages 5–14. IMAX tickets 10€ adults, 7.50€ children 5–14. Combined ticket 19€ adults, 15€ children 5–14. Daily 9am–7pm.

The Speyer Museum of Technology occupies a pre-World War I airplane hangar.

WHERE TO STAY IN SPEYER

Goldener Engel Located near the Gothic town gate at Maximilianstrasse, adjoining one of Speyer's finest restaurants, Zum Alten Engel (see p. 587), this inn is the most atmospheric choice in town. Imbued with lots of character in the spirit of old Rhinelander hotels, the larger rooms have many traditional touches and antiques such as baroque free-standing clothes closets. In contrast, the midsize bedrooms are completely modern and up-to-date with hardwood floors, white walls and crisp white linens, and well-maintained en-suite bathrooms.

Mühlturmstrasse 5–7. www.goldener-engel-speyer.de. ℂ **06232/13260.** 46 units. 68€–120€ double. Buffet breakfast included. **Amenities:** Restaurant, bar, Wi-Fi (free).

Rhein-Hotel Luxhof This hotel is imbued with an unusual character. It's modern in style, but somehow retains the spirit of a rambling country inn. The blandly decorated rooms are well designed and compact, often featuring small sitting areas that open onto tiny balconies. All come equipped with well-maintained bathrooms. It's at the Rhine Bridge, just outside of town.

Ketscher Landstr. 2, Hockenheim. www.luxhof.de. ℂ **06205/3030.** 45 units. 95€–118€ double. Buffet breakfast included. Free parking. **Amenities:** Restaurant; bikes; exercise room; sauna; Wi-Fi (free).

WHERE TO EAT IN SPEYER

Zum Alten Engel ★ RHINELANDER   Zum Alten Engel, one of the finest restaurants in Speyer, is animated, loud, convivial, and extremely popular. To reach it, you'll descend a flight of antique masonry steps to a century-old brick-vaulted cellar, flickering with candles and awash with German antiques. Set in Speyer's historic core, it specializes in hearty regional cuisine accompanied by the perfect glass of wine—more than 180 kinds of wine from around Germany and the world are available. Menu items usually include hearty *gutbürgerlich* fare of the kind many locals remember from their childhoods: fried sausages, liver dumplings, a Rhenish version of *Sauerbraten,* pepper steak, veal cutlets, and at least two different preparations of lamb.

Mühlturmstrasse 7. © **06232/70914.** www.zumaltenengel.de. Reservations required. Main courses 9€–26€. Daily 6–11pm. Closed 2 weeks in Aug.

13

THE MOSELLE VALLEY

D riving along the Moselle River, you'll encounter some of the most breathtaking views in Germany. A tributary to the deeper and faster-flowing Rhine, the Moselle River slowly twists and turns, carving a path through the countryside as it cuts through western Germany from France via Luxemburg. It's a quiet area, the landscape its claim to fame, with lush vineyards sloping up the river banks giving way to evergreen forests. Roman ruins and castles dot the area as well, a testament to the wealth that once inhabited the area thanks to medieval trading routes. It's the ideal place to join a relaxing river cruise, go for a restorative hike, or indulge in delicious regional cuisine, including some of Germany's best wines, all grown locally.

The Moselle (*Mosel* in German) springs out of the Vosges hills of France; after reaching Trier, on the western German border, the river snakes along 193 kilometers (120 miles) to Koblenz at such a slow pace, people can easily canoe, kayak, or hop aboard a cruise to enjoy the river at its level. Riverside is the best way to appreciate the valley, though scenic views can be had on several roads connecting the small towns along the river banks. However one chooses to travel downstream, the former Roman city of Trier is a great jumping-off point for the area.

ESSENTIALS
Arriving
The Moselle Valley is most easily accessible from the international airports at **Dusseldorf** (see p. 548) or **Frankfurt** (p. 489), or the domestic airport in **Cologne/Bonn** (p. 528). Trains run more or less hourly between these airports and the region's largest cities, Koblenz and Trier.

Visitor Information
A central tourist information office for the region, **Moselland Touristik,** is located at Kordelweg 1 in Bernkastel-Kues (www.mosellandtouristik. de; © **06531/97330**). The office is open Monday to Friday 9am to 5pm.

FACING PAGE: **Stately Burg Eltz castle, at the north end of the Moselle Valley.**

Getting Around the Moselle Valley

BY CAR

The main route between Trier and Koblenz is quickly traversed via the A1 and A48 autobahns. However, these express highways only skirt the Moselle Valley; to visit its most picturesque towns, you'll need to take smaller roads, such as highways 51 and 49, which each trace the river's path for a long section. To do the entire drive by car would take a few hours, which you could easily stretch into days with stops at each town along the way. Our suggestion: Make it a long weekend and enjoy the small-town atmosphere in Traben-Trarbach for one night before heading on to Cochem for the second, making stops in Bernkastel-Kues and other towns that appeal to you along the way. Or, even better—travel on the water rather than along its banks.

BY BOAT

Water was one of the main draws for the Romans who came to Trier centuries ago, and still today, the town owes its success and much of its majesty to the two rivers who meet here, the Saar and the Moselle. To appreciate the beauty of the landscape, take a day cruise from **Trier** (p. 592) down the Moselle for a waterside view of the historic banks.

Vineyards cover hillsides along the winding course of the Moselle River.

WINE festivals

Wine is what this area survives on, so it's no wonder that the locals celebrate the grapes that give them life in each town. Tastings and festivals in the Moselle Valley begin even before the grapes have ripened, picking up the pace from late summer into early fall. The dates shift each year depending on the weather for harvesting, but September and October are always good times to visit.

The Mosel-Wein-Woche is in Cochem at the **end of May,** followed soon thereafter by the Cochemer Weinlagenfest, also in Cochem, in **late June.** A **July** wine festival attracts tourists to the old wine cellars and taverns of Traben-Trarbach. Cochem has another Weinfest in **the last weekend of August.** In Bernkastel, St. Michael's Fountain flows with wine during the annual **September** wine festival. There's also an **autumn** wine festival in Zell.

Even outside of festival weekends, local vintners host their own tasting events and celebrations. Check directly with the tourist office in each town for times, or simply stop at one of the vineyards along the route. The owners are usually friendly and accommodating and the wine is for sale from them directly.

If you come early enough in the harvest season, you may even be able to taste the first pressed grapes, an extra sweet sparkling wine known as **Federweisser** (though don't expect to take any home with you—the carbonation makes the bottles impossible to cork.)

From Easter to October, boats depart Tuesday to Sunday at 9am from the Zurlauben (city docks) for a 4-hour trip along the Moselle to **Bernkastel** (p. 602), passing vineyards, wine hamlets, historic churches, and semi-ruined fortresses. Participants can spend two hours exploring Bernkastel before returning to Trier on the same boat, arriving back at 7:30pm. The cost is 26€ per person. If you don't have so much time to spare, take a shorter, hour-long trip to the nearby historic hamlet of **Pfalzel.** Boats depart from Trier's docks Easter to October daily at 10 and 11:15am, 12:30, 1:45, 3, and 4:15pm. Round-trip is 8€. You can stay for a walk along the riverbanks in Pfalzel or return on the next boat almost immediately after your arrival.

The Trier tourist office (www.trier-info.de; ✆ **0651/978080**) can give you more information, or visit www.trier-today.de, which has daily updates regarding the excursions offered by a number of boat operators, including **Gebrüder Kolb** (www.moselrundfahrten.de; ✆ **0651/26666**), the best source for boat rides along the Moselle. During the warmer months, Gebrüder Kolb offers excursions from Cochem to nearly all towns on the Moselle, including Traben-Trarbach, Zell and Bernkastel-Kues. Operating between Bernkastel-Kues and Traben-Trarbach, **Mosel Schiffs Touristik** (www.mosel-personenschifffahrt.de) also offers day

The Moselsteig walking trail runs the length of the Moselle Valley.

trips to the wine towns of Zell and Neumagen from late July through early October.

BY TRAIN

Trier (see below) and **Cochem** (p. 610) are on the Wasserbillig-Trier-Koblenz line. Most other towns in this region are not well served by train, however; to get there, you would have to take a bus or taxi from Wittlich or Bullay.

BY BUS

Regional bus service along the Moselle River is provided by **RMV Rhein Mosel Verkehrsgesellschaft** (www.rmv.de, ✆ **01805/7684636**) and **Moselbahn GmbH** (www.moselbahn.de, ✆ **06531/96800**). Mainly used by local commuters, regional bus service is slow and infrequent, but it is designed to complement the train schedules, so it remains a decent option for reaching out-of-the-way places if combined with a train ride.

TRIER ★★

124km (77 miles) SW of Koblenz, 143km (89 miles) SW of Bonn, 193km (120 miles) SW of Frankfurt

Founded under Augustus in 16 B.C., the city known to the Romans as Augusta Treverorumits has some of the best-preserved remnants from

pure nature: **HIKING THE VALLEY**

Some of Germany's purest nature can be found in the region around the border to Luxembourg. Two networks of well-marked trails draw nature-lovers and hikers from around the country for day trips as well as longer excursions.

Moselsteig: 365 kilometers of trails that run the length of the Moselle and then some are divided into 24 stages of varying difficulty. From Perl on the Luxembourg border to the intersection of the Rhine and Moselle in Koblenz, the hikes can run alongside the river, cut through forests, meander around vineyards and cross creeks. (http://www.moselsteig.de)

Saar-Huensruck Steig: Just to the south of the Moselle, this series of connected trails covers over 410 kilometers of hiking paths that are unique in Europe because of the diversity of the landscape they pass through. Catch unusual cliffs or the ruins of Celtic walls on one of the 27 stages that run from 11-24 kilometers long, some of which abut newly-recognized national forest. (http://www.saar-hunsrueck-steig.de)

For more information, contact the regional tourist office, **Moselland Touristik,** at Kordelweg 1 in Bernkastel-Kues (www.mosellandtouristik.de, ☎ **06531/97330**).

the era north of the Alps. For nearly five centuries, well into the Christian era, Trier remained one of Europe's power centers, its grandeur earning it the title Roma Secunda—the second Rome.

Yet according to legend, the city actually dates back much farther. In 2000 B.C., the Assyrians established a colony here and archaeological findings indicate a pre-Roman Celtic civilization, making it Germany's oldest city. The Assyrian buildings and monuments are no longer standing, but architecture dating from the Roman period abounds.

Trier lies only 10km (6 miles) from Luxembourg on the western frontier of Germany, where the Ruwer and Saar rivers meet the Moselle. The city is rich not only in art and tradition but also in wine—it's one of Germany's largest exporters.

Essentials
ARRIVING
BY TRAIN **Trier Hauptbahnhof** has frequent regional connections via the Wasserbillig-Trier-Koblenz "Moselbahn" line and also the Trier-Saarbrücken line. Weekdays, there are hourly express trains to Koblenz (1 hr., 25 min.), direct trains to Cologne (2 hr., 30 min.), and frequent trains to Saarbrücken (1 hr., 20 min.). For information, call ☎ **01806/996633** (www.bahn.de).

BY CAR Access is via the A1 Autobahn north and south, the A48 east, and Rte. 51 from the north and south.

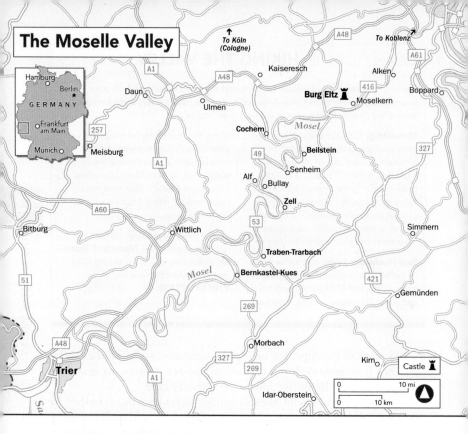

The Moselle Valley

VISITOR INFORMATION

Tourist Information is located at An der Porta Nigra (www.trier-info.de, © 0651/978080), open Monday to Saturday 9am to 6pm and Sunday 10am to 5pm (closed Dec 25–26 and Jan 1).

GETTING AROUND

Trier is a walkable city, with most of the tourist attractions within a short distance of each other. Should you wish to take the bus, purchase tickets on board for 2€ within zone 1 (the city) or pay 5.80€ for an all-day pass. After-hours buses, numbers 81 through 87, run special routes on Monday through Friday from 6:45pm until 2am, as well as on Saturday and Sunday. For information, call © 1805/131619, or visit www.vrt-info.de.

WALKING TOURS

Every day April to October, the tourist office (see above) conducts a 2-hour **walking tour** of the town in German, starting at 10:30am and 2:30pm. From November to March, there's only one tour, at 10:30am on Saturday. The cost is 9.90€ per adult, 5.90€ for children 6 to 14. **Tours**

in English are 75 minutes long and conducted only on Saturday at 1 pm from May to October. It costs 6.90€ per adult, 3.50€ for children 6 to 14.

Exploring Trier
VISITING THE ROMAN RUINS

Trier's extensive Roman ruins, which have earned UNESCO-World Heritage status, can be seen in one relatively easy walk. The **Antiquity Card,** available from the tourist office, grants admission to the Rheinisches Landesmuseum (p. 598) plus two other Roman sights, for 8€ for adults, 5.60€ for students, and 4€ ages 17 and under.

You'll want to start right outside the tourist office at the **Porta Nigra (Black Gate)** (p. 598), the best-preserved Roman structure in Germany and the only surviving piece of the great wall that once surrounded Trier. From there, walk up Simeonstrasse to the Hauptmarkt, then follow Grabenstrasse to Palaststrasse. At the end of Palaststrasse, you'll find Constantine's Throne Room, now known as the **Basilica,** Basilikaplatz (www.konstantin-basilika.de, *©* **0651/42570**), the city's largest surviving single-room structure from Roman times. Though it has largely been demolished, the huge hall is an architectural wonder, designed to create the illusion of grandeur. Two tiers of windows are arranged within high-rising arches in which fragments of the original wall paintings can be seen. Now Trier's main Protestant church, it is open to visitors free of charge, April to October Monday to Saturday 10am to 6pm and Sunday noon to 6pm; November to March hours are Tuesday to Saturday 10am to noon and 2pm to 4pm, and Sunday 1 pm to 3pm.

Next door, take a break from Roman grandeur to admire the 17th-century **Kurfürstliches Palais (Electoral Palace;** *©* **0651/9494202**), a pink-tinted rococo residence built for the archbishops-electors of Trier. (The interior is now administrative offices.) The adjoining **Palastgarten (Palace Gardens),** filled with ponds, flowers, and rococo statues, are a great place to stroll.

Trailing Bacchus into the Underground

Thousands of liters of wine have fermented in cellars beneath the streets of Trier. Some of these underground warehouses date back to medieval times; at least 40 are still in use, spread out throughout the city and surrounding suburbs. The oldest and most venerable is owned by **Vereinigte Hospitien,** an organization that's also involved in running a network of local hospitals and hospices; their offices at Krahnen Ufer Strasse 19 (www.weingut.vereinigte hospitien.de, *©* **0651/9451210**) coordinate tours that include tastings of the vintages. Tours cost from 20€ per person, for 6 samples in a cellar dating back to the 4th century. The Trier tourist office (p. 594) can help arrange a tour either here or at one of the other cellars.

The 4th-century Imperial Baths were among the largest in the Roman Empire.

On the east side of the gardens, return to the Roman era by viewing a trove of antiquities at the **Rheinisches Landesmuseum** (p. 598). At the south end of Palastgarten is another major Roman site, the **Imperial Baths (Kaiserthermen) ★★** (© 0651/44262), built in the early 4th century by Constantine I. Although never completed, the hot baths are among the largest in the Roman Empire, and had rooms for spa services as well as an immense pool (opera performances held there today can hold an audience of up to 650). The baths are open daily April to September 9am to 6pm, October and March 9am to 5pm, and November to February 9am to 4pm. Admission is 4€ for adults and 2.50€ for children.

A short walk east, follow Olestrasse to see where Roman gladiators fought off animals at the amazingly intact 2nd-century **Amphitheater,** Amphitheaterplatz (© 0651/73010), the oldest Roman construction in Trier. Stone seats, arranged in three circles and separated by broad promenades, held at least 20,000 people. Admission is 4€ adults, 2.50€ children, 8€ families. The ruins are open daily April to September 9am to 6pm, October and March 9am to 5pm, and November to February 9am to 4pm.

Der Trierer Dom (Trier Cathedral) ★ CATHEDRAL   In the city center, this cathedral is the oldest bishop's church in Germany. With its rough-hewn stonework, it could be mistaken for a fortress were it not for

the fine architectural details. It's the third church to stand on the site of the former 4th-century palace of the Empress Helena, mother of Constantine; the current building is a mixture of the Romanesque style of its original design from 1035, with later Gothic and Baroque additions. A church in the round, the interior combines Baroque decoration with Gothic vaulting and archways, with Gothic pillars built atop the Roman columns. On the south aisle is a magnificent tympanum depicting Christ between the Virgin and St. Peter. **Die Schatzkammer (Treasury Museum)** contains many important works of art, including the 10th-century St. Andrew's Altar, an unusual portable altar made of wood and covered with gold and ivory. Tours in German are held every Saturday at 2pm from April to October for 5.45 € for adults.

Domfreihof (north of Palace Gardens). www.trierer-dom.de ✆ **0651/9790790.** Cathedral free; treasury 1.50€ adults, .50€ children 15 and under. Cathedral Apr–Oct daily 6:30am–6pm; Nov–Mar daily 6:30am–5:30pm. Treasury Apr–Oct Mon–Sat 10am–5pm, Sun 12:30–5pm; Nov–Mar Tues–Sat 11am–4pm, Sun 12:30–4pm.

Karl-Marx-Haus HISTORIC HOUSE   Karl Marx (1818–83), one of Germany's most influential men of ideas, was born here in Trier, and now

tourists flock to visit this old burgher's house where he was born and lived until 1835, when he left to attend university. The museum has exhibits on Marx's personal history, volumes of poetry, original letters, and photographs with personal dedications. There's also a collection of rare first editions and international editions of his works, as well as exhibits on the development of socialism in the 19th century. In the vicinity of the museum is a study center, **Studienzentrum Karl-Marx-Haus,** Johannestrasse 28 (same phone), for research on Marx and his collaborator Friedrich Engels.

Brückenstrasse 10. www.fes.de. ✆ **0651/ 970680.** Admission 4€ adults, 2.50€ children. Apr–Oct daily 10am–6pm; Nov–Mar Mon 2–5pm, Tues–Sun 11am–5pm.

Liebfrauenkirche ★ CHURCH The oldest Gothic church in Germany, this parish church is right

The Romanesque apse of Trier Cathedral, the oldest bishop's church in Germany.

597

next to the cathedral, separated only by a narrow passageway. The 13th-century structure was built with a cruciform floor plan, giving it the shape of a rose in bloom, with all points equidistant from the central high altar. More pleasing aesthetically than its older neighbor, the church was constructed beginning in 1235. Its structure is supported by 12 circular columns, rather than the typical open buttresses. Sunlight streams through the high transoms.

Liebfrauenstrasse 2. © **0651/9790790.** Free admission. Apr–Oct Mon–Fri 10am–7pm, Sat 11am–4:30pm, Sun 12:30pm–6pm; Nov–Mar Mon–Fri 10am–5pm, Sat 11am–4:30pm, Sun 12:30–5pm.

Porta Nigra (Black Gate) ★★ RUIN   Built around A.D. 180, this is one of the few monuments remaining after the last Roman prefect departed from Trier around 400 A.D. Despite numerous threats to its stability, the gate still stands, assembled from huge sandstone blocks and held together with iron clamps in lieu of mortar. From outside the gate, the structure appears to be simply two arched entrances between rounded towers that lead directly into the town, but invaders soon discovered that the arches opened into an inner courtyard where they were at the mercy of the town's defenders. During the Middle Ages, the Greek hermit Simeon—later canonized as St. Simeon—chose the east tower as his retreat. After his death, the archbishop added a huge double church, which stood here until Napoleon invaded and had it knocked down to restore the original Roman core.

© **0651/75424.** Admission 4€ adults, 2.50€ children, 8€ families. Open daily Apr–Sept 9am–6pm, Oct and Mar 9am–5pm, Nov–Feb 9am–4pm.

Rheinisches Landesmuseum ★★ MUSEUM   One of Germany's most important and outstanding museums, the museum documents 200,000 years of history and houses the world's largest Roman gold coin collection. Roman antiquities are a highlight here, with numerous reliefs from funerary monuments showing daily life in Roman times, including the most popular exhibit, the *Mosel Ship,* a sculpture of a wine-bearing vessel crowning a big burial monument of the 3rd century A.D. Other highlights include mosaics and frescoes, ceramics, glassware, a 2,700-year-old Egyptian casket complete with mummy, an outstanding numismatic collection, and prehistoric and medieval art and sculpture.

Weimarer Allee 1. www.landesmuseum-trier.de © **0651/97740.** Admission 8€ adults, 4€ children. Tues–Sun 10am–5pm.

Where to Stay in Trier

EXPENSIVE

Becker's Hotel ★   Though a bit removed from the action in the suburb of Olewig (take bus nos. 6 or 16), this design hotel and vintner is the place for both food and lodgings. Furnishings are trendy and modern; a wine bar draws a stylish crowd. Beautifully kept and individually decorated bedrooms, most with light-wood furnishings, welcome guests; several rooms open onto private balconies overlooking the vineyards. In summer head here for an alfresco meal on the terrace.

Olewiger Strasse 206, Trier-Olewig. www.weinhaus-becker.de. © **0651/938080.** 30 units. 140€–190€ double; 105€–120€ suite. Buffet breakfast included. **Amenities:** 3 restaurants; bar; room service; Wi-Fi (free; in lobby).

Park Plaza ★★   One of the most well-appointed hotels in Trier, the Park Plaza is just a 3-minute walk from the Dom. Stylish and tastefully furnished, the hotel is a supremely comfortable choice and has many of the standard offerings of a chain, including hypoallergenic rooms and state-of-the-art bathrooms. Extras include everything from the city's best health club (styled in the Roman tradition) to a winter garden lounge. An in-house restaurant specializes in both regional and international cuisine.

Nikolaus-Koch-Platz 1. www.parkplaza-trier.de. © **0651/99930.** 150 units. 112€–162€ double; 192€–332€ suite. Breakfast 17€. Parking 12€. **Amenities:** Restaurant; bar; health club; spa; room service; Wi-Fi (free).

Villa Hügel ★★   This lovely Art Nouveau villa, built in 1914, is tranquilly located with windows overlooking either a private garden with old trees or the city. Rooms are spacious and high-ceilinged, and all contain modern bathrooms. Four double rooms are so large that they're almost suites, making them favorites with families. High tea is on offer every afternoon; a gourmet restaurant on site serves dinner from 6pm–10pm.

Bernhardstrasse 14. www.hotel-villa-huegel.de. © **0651/937100.** 36 units. 128€–188€ double. Buffet breakfast included. Free outdoor parking; 9€ in garage. **Amenities:** Restaurant; bar; Jacuzzi; indoor pool; room service; sauna; Wi-Fi (free; in lobby).

MODERATE

Hotel Petrisberg   A family-run hotel in a pleasant location, the Petrisberg is at the heart of where a forest, a vineyard, and a private park meet; the Roman amphitheater is just a short walk away. Well-maintained rooms offer a view of the lush greenery outside. The ground-floor *Weinstube* is the gathering place for many locals, particularly on weekends.

Sickingenstrasse 11–13, 54296 Trier. www.hotel-petrisberg.de. © **0651/4640.** 35 units. 97€–105€ double; 150€–185€ suite. Rates include buffet breakfast. Free outdoor parking; 5€ in garage. Bus: 6, 7, or 16. A 10-min. walk from the Altstadt. **Amenities:** Wi-Fi (free).

Mercure Porta Nigra ★   Part of a chain, what the six-story Mercure Porta Nigra lacks in charm, it more than makes up for in location. A safe, comfortable bet, it is one of the best choices in Trier, and is a stone's throw from the major sites of the Roman ruins. Most rooms have sitting areas and ornately tiled bathrooms.

Porta-Nigra-Platz 1, 54292 Trier. www.accorhotels.com. © **0651/27010.** 106 units. 105€–139€ double; 246€ suite. Parking 12€. Bus: 2, 3, 12, 13, 14. **Amenities:** 2 restaurants; bar; tennis; gym; room service; sauna; Wi-Fi (free).

pentahotel Trier ★ This chain hotel has comfortable beds and modern amenities, with streamlined furnishings and modern bathrooms. In the heart of the sightseeing zone, near the old Roman monuments, it's serviceable in every way.

Kaiserstrasse 29, 54290 Trier. www.pentahotels.com. ⓒ **0651/94950.** 127 units. 68€–132€ double; 118€–230€ suite. Parking 6€ outdoors; 8.50€ in garage. Bus: 1, 3, 5, 6, 7, 8, 16, or 40. **Amenities:** Restaurant; bar; babysitting; room service; Wi-Fi (free).

Römischer Kaiser ★ Parisian charms inhabit this landmark building from 1895, which has been beautifully restored and updated with modern touches. Right at the Porta Nigra, the hotel also has a notable restaurant whose chefs create both German and international dishes out of first-class ingredients.

Porta Nigra Platz, 54292 Trier. www.friedrich-hotels.de. ⓒ **0651/9770100.** 43 units. 95€–115€ double. Free parking. **Amenities:** Wi-Fi (free).

INEXPENSIVE

Winzer Haeuschen ★ Three tiny houses built in the gardens of a vineyard provide a quiet respite just 15 km (9 miles) outside of Trier. Perfect for families with children, the houses are set a bit apart, offering the bare amenities and comfortable furnishings for a time out as you sleep in the midst of an orchard or rose garden.

WeinKulturgut Longen-Schloeder, Kirchenweg 9, Longuich. www.longen-schloeder.de. ⓒ **06502/8345.** 3 units. 88€–145€ apartment. Breakfast included. Parking free. **Amenities:** garden; self-catering possible.

Where to Eat in Trier

Paulaner ★ GERMAN Newly opened in 2015, this restaurant focusing on Bavarian cuisine replaced the much-loved Pfeffermuehle restaurant in picturesque Zurlauben, a former fishing village just 10 minutes north of the city center. While the elegance of the paneled dining rooms and an airy terrace for summer dining remain, the menu has been adapted to include more standard German fare, like schnitzel with fries or Schweinshaxen. The list of Moselle wines is extensive.

Zurlaubener Ufer 76. www.paulaner-in-zurlauben.de. ⓒ **0651/9936770.** Reservations recommended. Main courses 22€–31€. Daily 11am–10pm.

Schlemmereule ★★ CONTINENTAL A local favorite, this gourmet spot across from the Dom is a culinary highlight under chef Peter Schmalen, who has brought some excitement to bored taste buds in the city. The romantic setting in the 19th-century Palais Walderdorff complex is complimented by a pretty courtyard open for dining in summer. The menu includes both beef steak and tuna steak. A summer specialty is plain old spaghetti, given a sublime twist with fresh truffles, or delectable pikeperch steamed under a golden-brown potato crust. Finish off with the town's best crème brûlée. Schmalen proudly boasts one of the town's finest wine lists, with some marvelous Moselle vintages.

Palais Walderdorff, Domfreihof 1B. www.schlemmereule.de. © **0651/73616.** Reservations required. Main courses 27€–32€. Mon–Sat noon–2:30pm and 6–10:30pm. Closed 1 week in Feb.

Weinstube Kesselstatt ★ GERMAN   A traditional *Weinstube* gets a shot of romance, as it lies within the baroque landmark, Palais Kesselstatt, the former residence of the counts of Kesselstatt. Its wine cellar prides itself on stocking only an excellent selection of Rieslings produced in nearby vineyards; anyone interested in sampling the region's legendary wines should head down to the cellar here. You get not only wine but platters of traditional German food. In summer the shady terrace fills up quickly. Inside, old wooden tables rest under exposed beams. Menu items are made with fresh ingredients and change with the seasons. Try such dishes as slices of duck breast in an herb vinaigrette, or fillet of turbot with vegetables, or even pork medallions in a pepper sauce.

Liebfrauenstrasse 10. www.weinstube-kesselstatt.de. © **0651/41178.** Reservations recommended. Main courses 12€–18€. Daily 10am–midnight.

Zum Domstein ★ RHINELAND   In the shadow of the cathedral, the charming Zum Domstein restaurant and hotel overlooks the flower stands and the fountain in Trier's central plaza. Specialists in a kitsch "Roman" menu that dates back to the time of Emperor Constantin, the kitchen also serves up modern-day fare. Try one of the wine tastings starting at 9€, which will get you three glasses of wine from the Moselle, the Ruwer, or the Saar. Otherwise, taste one of a dozen local and international wines by the glass, or select one of the hundreds of bottles stored in the cellars. The food here is as tempting as the wine; a typically savory offering is fillet of trout in a Riesling sauce or knuckle of lamb with vegetables. All the dishes are redolent of old-fashioned flavors; it is said that some were even served by the Romans, who preferred them with rich sauces. In winter, you'll want to find a spot near the huge tiled stove. They come by the Roman theme honestly: The restaurant sits above one of the oldest cellars in town, the **Römischer Weinkeller (Roman wine cellar),** originally built around A.D. 326. Original Roman artifacts, many connected with food and cooking, decorate the room. Dishes here are prepared according to recipes attributed to Marcus Gavius Apicius, said to have been the foremost chef at the court of Emperor Tiberius.

Hauptmarkt 5. www.domstein.de. © **0651/74490.** Reservations recommended. Main courses lunch 8€–15€, dinner 13€–20€; fixed-price menus in the Roman wine cellar 16€–40€. Open daily 8:30am–10pm.

Nightlife & Entertainment

A university city and the largest in the area, Trier is where people come to get their cultural fill. The cathedral hosts a series of free **organ recitals** in May, June, August, and September; contact the tourist office (see

p. 594) for schedules. **TUFA** (Wechselstrasse 4, www.tufa-trier.de, ℰ **0651/7182412**) presents theater, established touring bands, and the occasional dance party. Across from the cathedral stands **Walderdorffs,** Domfreihof (www.walderdorffs.de, ℰ **0651/9944412**), a cafe by day, but an action-packed bar and dance club at night. The club, which runs Thursday to Saturday, is open 10pm to 4am, although the action doesn't really pick up until after midnight; there's sometimes a cover free, depending on the entertainment. The cafe is open Sunday to Thursday from 9:30am to 1am, Friday and Saturday until 2am. A club with a beer garden, **Exhaus,** Zurmaiener Strasse 114 (www.exhaus.de, ℰ **0651/25191**), has both dancing and bands, usually Wednesday to Saturday. Days vary, but the hours are 8pm to 2am. Call to see what's scheduled. Cover is 8€ to 15€.

BERNKASTEL-KUES ★

48km (30 miles) NE of Trier

Driving alongside the river as it twists and turns, you'll catch glimpses of the quaint riverfront town of Bernkastel-Kues long before you arrive. Though small, it's a must-see village on the wine route with stunning views of vineyards across the river.

Essentials

The nearest **train** station is the Wittlich Hauptbahnhof, 20km (12 miles) west, with a bus or taxi connection to Bernkastel-Kues. To get here by **car,** exit the A1 at Wittlich; it's about a 15-minute drive, via Hwy. 50. Bernkastel's **tourist office** is at Gestade 6 (www.en.bernkastel.de, ℰ **06531/500190**), open daily late April to October, weekdays only the rest of the year.

Exploring Bernkastel-Kues

Home to influential philosopher Nicolas of Cusa (1401–1464), whose seminal works marked a transition in thinking from the medieval to the modern age, charming Bernkastel-Kues still reflects the 15th-century cardinal's time. Centuries-old half-timbered buildings surround the handsome **Marktplatz** and the **St. Michael's Fountain,** which flows with wine during the annual September wine festival. Along the river on the Kues bank, Cardinal Cusa founded the late-Gothic **Cusanusstift** (St. Nicholas Hospital), where his precious library is preserved; his heart is buried under the altar in its lovely chapel (admission free). You can also visit his **birthplace** at Nikolausufer 49.

Atop a rocky promontory 3km (2 miles) to the southeast of the town stands **Burg Landshut.** Once the domain of the archbishops of Trier,

Outdoor dining in Bernkastel's medieval core.

the property dates from the 11th century but was destroyed by fire in 1692. Though still in ruins, the castle with its crumbling tower offers one of the grandest **panoramas** ★★ in the Rhineland and a gorgeous hike through vineyards as you climb the steep slopes on the way.

Where to Stay & Eat in Bernkastel-Kues

Doctor Weinstuben ★ Located in the town center, this half-timbered building from the late 17th century is the most visually arresting hotel in Bernkastel. Opened as a tavern in 1830, it still has many of its original woodcarvings. Its quiet terrace, on-site restaurant, and historical charm makes up for small rooms.

Hebegasse 5. www.doctor-weinstuben-bernkastel.de. ☏ **06531/96650.** 29 units. 119€–155€ double with half-pension. Buffet breakfast included. **Amenities:** Restaurant; bar; bikes; Wi-Fi (free).

Hotel Moselpark ★ One of the largest hotels in the area, this modern three-story hotel on a hill west of the town center boasts the widest range of leisure facilities and activities for its guests, including a fitness studio, dance bar, sauna, and large swimming pool. Streamlined rooms with lots of wood built-ins are nothing spectacular, and the hotel has a less personal feeling, but rooms are spacious and well maintained.

Im Kurpark. www.moselpark.de. ☏ **06531/5080.** 143 units. 80€–110€ double; suites with kitchenette available. Buffet breakfast included. Free parking. **Amenities:** 2 restaurants; babysitting; bikes; exercise room; indoor pool; room service; sauna; 4 indoor and 2 outdoor tennis courts; Wi-Fi (free).

Kloster Hotel Marienhoehe ★★★ About 40 km (25 miles) southeast of Bernkastel, the town of Langweiler—literally translated to The Bore—has little to offer besides a few cows and hiking trails, but this family-friendly spa hotel is the perfect place to relax and take in the scenery. Located just off the Saar-Huensruck Path (see p. 593), this former nunnery atop a steep hill has all the amenities one needs for a luxurious

The pool at Kloster Hotel Marienhohe, a spa hotel in Langweiler, south of Berncastle-Kues.

getaway, from locally-grown cuisine to a pool to childcare. Several hikers' rooms without amenities are available at reduced rates.

Marienhoehe 2-10, Langweiler (Kreis Birkenfeld). www.klosterhotel-marienhoehe. de. ℰ **06768/292990.** 66 units. 145€–320€ double. Buffet breakfast included. Free parking. **Amenities:** Spa services, sauna, indoor pool, babysitting, Wi-Fi (free).

Waldhotel Sonnora ★★★ The Hotel Sonnora, just 18km (11 miles) west of Bernkastel-Kues, is home to one of the most spectacular restaurants in Germany, awarded three Michelin stars. Master chef Helmut Thieltges creates 5- or 7-course menus using fresh, seasonal ingredients, like grilled lobster served with chicory in a lemon-butter sauce in summer or venison and local game in winter. Pair it with wine from one of the most comprehensive wine lists in the area. With only 12 tables, it is often booked months in advance, so be sure to reserve well ahead of your visit. Or consider lunch. An overnight stay is also an option should you book one of the hotel's 20 rooms. Doubles run from 140€ to 300€, including breakfast.

Auf dem Eichelfeld, Dreis. www.hotel-sonnora.de. ℰ **06578/406.** Reservations essential. Main courses 45€–52€; fixed-price menus 168€–198€. Wed–Sun noon–2pm and 7–9pm. Closed late Dec to late Jan and July 15–29.

an overnight stay **AT A VINEYARD**

S. A. Prüm Winery ★★, Uferallee 25–26, Bernkastel-Wehlen (www.sapruem.com, ℂ **06531/3110**), is operated by the Prüm family, who have owned vineyards in this area since 1156. With sculptures in the orchards and a hike cutting around the vineyards, this bed-and-breakfast inn is surrounded by beauty; a patio garden even opens out onto the Moselle. The guesthouse itself contains eight spacious, antique-decorated bedrooms that can be rented for 95€ to 145€ a night for a double. Neatly tiled bathrooms have showers, and there's TV and internet; rates include a buffet breakfast. (**Note:** the hotel is closed at Christmas and in January.) But you don't have to be an overnight guest to enjoy it: Day visitors can book a group hike or take part in a wine tasting at the estate for 15€ (reservations advised). Previously best known for its Rieslings, the winery now offers *Weissburgunder*/Pinot Blanc, which is a delight; it also has a Pinot Noir. Day visits take place Monday to Friday 10am to noon and 2 to 4pm, and Saturday 10am to 4pm.

Zur Post ★★   What seems like a relatively modest inn is in fact one of this winegrowing town's finest. Centrally located in Kues, it was once a stopover for horseback riders on the local postal routes, hence the name. Public areas are more charming than the functional but comfortable rooms; there's an elegantly crafted stairwell flanked by half-timbered walls and a traditional German oak-paneled, beamed dining room. The restaurant serves

The S.A. Prum Winery in Bernkastel also has a guesthouse for overnight stays.

Traveling the Roman Way

Hiking is a favored pastime in this area and a quick look at the map will show that one of the best ways to travel between Traben-Trarbach and its sister Bernkastel-Kues just may be a hike. The two towns lie within a 2- to 3-hour walk over the hill along a marked path that offers fine views of the area. A glass of Riesling in either town at the end of your hike makes for a great reward.

loads of hearty dishes include a selection of grilled cuts of Angus steak with potatoes as you like them, or pork medallions with creamed mushrooms and *Spätzle*. Meals cost 13€ to 28€. Gestade 17. www.hotel-zur-post-bernkastel.de. © **06531/96700.** 42 units. 95€–115€ double; 155€ suite. Buffet breakfast included. Free parking. Closed Jan. **Amenities:** Restaurant; sauna; Wi-Fi (free).

TRABEN-TRARBACH ★★★

60km (37 miles) NE of Trier, 23km (14 miles) NE of Bernkastel-Kues

As a midpoint between Koblenz and Trier, the twin cities of Traben and Trarbach have become the wine capitals of the Moselle Valley region. Vineyards run up steep slopes behind the town, providing a beautiful backdrop. Along the river are garden-like promenades which offer splendid views of the surroundings.

Essentials

If you're arriving by **car,** exit the A1 autobahn at Wittlich; from there it's about 30 minutes, via B50 and B53. Traben's **tourist office** is at Am Bahnhof 5 (www.traben-trarbach.de, © **06541/83980**), open Monday to Saturday from May to October; Monday to Friday from March to May; from November to March it's closed on weekends and Wednesdays.

Exploring Traben-Trarbach

For most visitors, the focus of a stay in Traben-Trarbach will be wine tasting and vineyard visits; the tourist office can supply you with a list of local vintners, as well as visiting hours and prices. If you have time, however, you may also want to take in the ruins of two castles, each high above the cities they once served as outlooks for. Above Trarbach, on the east bank of the river, are the now-diminished remains of the 14th-century **Grevenburg Castle,** the scene of hard-fought battles to gain control of its strategic position above lucrative medieval trade routes. On the opposite bank, above Traben, are the ruins of **Mont Royal,** a 1687 fortress built by the invading Louis XIV, and destroyed by him 11 years later.

As you walk around, you'll notice the twin towns' excellent and well-preserved **Jugendstil architecture,** the German version of Art Nouveau, stemming from the time when architect Bruno Möhring resided here. The fancy **bridge gate** in Trarbach and **Hotel Bellevue** (see p. 607) are just a few of his works.

The ruins of Gravenburg Castle, above the twin towns of Traben-Trarbach.

Where to Eat & Stay in Traben-Trarbach

Hotel Moseltor ★   You'll find this gay-friendly hotel on the outskirts of town at Im Ortsteil Trarbach. Inside this masterpiece of 19th-century fieldstone masonry, a charming combination of new construction and antique elements creates a warm mixture of comfort and convenience. The inviting rooms have neatly kept bathrooms. Chef George Bauer's reputation for light cuisine ingredients has drawn fans from around the area for gastronomic dinners (3-course meals cost 25€–38€; reservations required). The hotel is open year-round, but the restaurant is closed in February and on Tuesday year-round.

Moselstrasse 1. www.moseltor.de. ℰ **06541/6551.** 11 units. 100€–200€ double or suite. Continental breakfast included. Parking 10€ in garage. **Amenities:** Restaurant; room service; Wi-Fi (free).

Romantik Art Nouveau Hotel Bellevue ★★   This Art Nouveau residence on the riverbank is one of the finest hotels along the Moselle. Designed in 1903 by noted architect Bruno Möhring, it features elaborate timberwork, a domed tower, a high-pitched roof, gables, and dormers. Many of the 42 cozy rooms in the main building are furnished with antiques, while 26 more rooms in a nearby building along the riverfront promenade offer a fine view. Inside, chef Matthias Meurer has drawn crowds and acclaim with the **Belle Epoque** restaurant. In summer, sit at an ivy-covered terrace for romantic al fresco dining. In winter, there's a cozy fireplace as well as stained-glass windows and an old-German ambiance.

An der Mosel 11. www.bellevue-hotel.de. © **06541/7030.** 70 units. 145€–170€ double; 150€–380€ suite. Buffet breakfast included. Free outdoor parking; 10€ in garage. **Amenities:** Restaurant; bar; bikes; exercise room; indoor pool; room service; spa; Wi-Fi (free).

ZELL AN DER MOSEL ★

69km (43 miles) NE of Trier, 18km (11 miles) NE of Traben-Trarbach

This old town, along the east bank of the Moselle, is best known for its excellent wine, Schwarze Katze ("Black Cat"). The grape is king here, as you'll quickly realize if you visit during the annual autumn wine festival. Nearby, on the left bank of the Moselle, 8km (5 miles) from Zell, stands the charming little wine village of **Alf.** The surroundings are idyllic, especially if you climb up to the top of Marienburg, which has a fine view over the Moselle and the vineyards of Zell.

Essentials

If you're coming by **car,** exit the A1 Autobahn at Wittlich-Mitte; it's about 35 minutes via B49. Zell's **tourist office,** Balduinstrasse 44 (www.zellerland.de, © **06542/96220**) is open Monday to Friday 9am to 5pm and Saturday 10am to 1pm.

Where to Stay in Zell an der Mosel

Haus Notenau ★   The owners of two buildings in the heart of Zell have converted their furnished apartments into short-term rentals. Comfortable and well maintained, the rooms are cheerful and no-nonsense, with kitchens, and are located either in **Haus Balduin** in the pedestrian district at Baldiun Strasse 60 or at its comparably priced sibling, **Haus Brandenburg,** Brandenburger Strasse 27 (© **06542/5010**).

56856 Zell an der Mosel. www.haus-notenau.de. © **06542/5010.** 20 units. 70€ per apartment per night. **Amenities:** Self-catering possible.

BEILSTEIN ★

84km (52 miles) NE of Trier, 18km (11 miles) NE of Zell an der Mosel

This unspoiled medieval wine town on the east bank of the Moselle has a memorable marketplace dwarfed by the adjacent hillside. Above the town stand the former cloister church with a 13th-century **Black Madonna** of Spanish origin, and the ruins of the 12th-century **Metternich Castle,** also destroyed by Louis XIV's army.

Essentials

If you're traveling by **car,** exit the A48 at either Ulmen (35 minutes via B259) or Kaisersesch (30 minutes via L98). From Zell, Rte. 199 is the most direct road, over the hills, while Hwy. 49 follows the river.

Where to Eat & Stay in Beilstein

Haus Burgfrieden ★   One of two guesthouses owned by the Herzer family, a 5-minute walk from the town center, this hotel's simple but comfortable rooms are modern and well-maintained with neatly kept bathrooms. A dining room on premises features international cuisine with main courses cost 9.50€ to 23€. Guests are able to tour the ruins of the nearby Metternich castle free. No credit cards are accepted.

Im Muhlental 17. www.hotel-burgfrieden.de. © **02673/93639.** 39 units. 42€–69€ per person double. Buffet breakfast included. No credit cards. Free parking. **Amenities:** Restaurant, Wi-Fi (free).

The narrow medieval streets of Beilstein.

Hotel Haus Lipmann ★   A former administration building for the Metternich dynasty that once ruled the area, this structure was converted to an inn in the 18th century. In 2006, a second villa nearby was bought and the hotel expanded, bringing 21st-century amenities to rooms that still appeal to those looking for medieval touches. The half-timbered exteriors are well-kept and oft-photographed. For six generations, the same family has tended the vast riverside vineyards nearby. (Try their Ellenzer Goldbäumchen or their Beilsteiner Schlossberg.) In summer, the most popular place at the inn for drinking and dining is the vine-covered terrace with a statue of Bacchus, overlooking the Moselle. You can also try the antiques-filled tavern or the wood-paneled Rittersaal, with its collection of old firearms and pewter. In the cooler months, fires burn in the tall walk-in fireplace and the tiny open hearth. German food is served. No credit cards are accepted.

Marktplatz 3. www.hotel-haus-lipmann.com. © **02673/1573.** 12 units. 100€–140€ double. Buffet breakfast included. No credit cards. Free parking. Closed Nov–Mar. **Amenities:** Restaurant; bar; room service; Wi-Fi (free).

COCHEM ★

11km (7 miles) W of Beilstein, 92km (57 miles) NE of Trier, 51km (32 miles) SW of Koblenz.

Cochem's highlight is a medieval castle looming over it on a vineyard-covered hill. The village features three medieval gates (the Endertor, Martinstor, and Balduinstor) and several half-timbered houses. Its selection of fine inns and rail and road connections also make it an ideal stop-over between Koblenz and Trier.

Essentials

On the outskirts of town, Cochem's **train station** lies on the Trier-Koblenz rail line, with hourly or semi-hourly service connecting to these cities. For information, call © **01806/ 996633** (www.bahn.de). If you're traveling by **car,** exit the A48 Autobahn at either Ulmen (take B259) or at Kaisersesch. (take L98). Cochem's **tourist office** is located in the Verkehrsamt at Endertplatz 1 (www. cochem.de, © **02671/60040**). It's open Monday to Friday year-round; from May to October they are also open on weekends.

In Vino Veritas . . . with a Little Less Alcohol

Due to the cold winter months Moselle wines have the lowest alcohol content (about 9%) of any white wine in the world. According to the German Wine Institute in Mainz, white wines make up 90% of the region's production, the highest output of any in Germany. Sixty-five percent of the overall grapes are crisp Rieslings, with Müller-Thurgau coming in a distant second at 15%. Be sure to enjoy them young.

Exploring Cochem

The town's biggest attraction is **Reichsburg Cochem ★** (www.burg-cochem.de, © **02671/255**), one of the few castles in the area still remaining intact. The original castle, built in 1027, was laid to ruin by Louis XIV's army in 1689. Atop its ruins, the current castle was rebuilt in 1868 in the neo-Gothic style; its medieval ramparts and turrets overlook the town below and create a dramatic backdrop when you view Cochem from the riverside. To reach the castle from the village, follow signs along the steep footpath from the town center, ascending for about 15 minutes, depending on how long you pause to take in the gorgeous views of

Cochem's castle rises above the medieval town.

the town and the Moselle below. Although you can visit the grounds any-time, to view the interior, you'll need to book a guided tour (offered daily mid-March to November, 9am–5pm). During the winter season, hours vary; be sure to check in advance. Guided tours can be conducted in English. Admission is 6€ for adults, 5€ for students, 3€ for children 6 to 17 years old, and 16€ for a family ticket.

Where to Stay in Cochem

Alte Thorschenke ★   One of the oldest and best-known establish-ments—both a hotel and wine restaurant—along either side of the Moselle, the Alte Thorschenke benefits from its central location. The original part of the building was built in 1332 with timbers and towers that give it its antiquated look today, but with an update and addition of a modern wing in 1960, the inn became a hotel with 35 rooms, six of which have four-poster beds. It has the charms of an older building, complete with creaky staircase, but all rooms, including the romantic Napoleon suite, have modern baths.

Brückenstrasse 3. www.castle-thorschenke.com. ✆ **02671/7059.** 35 units. 75€–130€ double; from 110€ suite. Buffet breakfast included. Parking 6€ in garage. **Amenities:** Restaurant; room service; Wi-Fi (free).

Wine Tasting with the Baron

Guests of the Alte Thorschenke can visit the 500-year-old **Schloss Landesberg,** Ediger-Eller (www.mosel-weinproben. de), about 7km (4½ miles) from Cochem. Here in the old cellars, you can taste some of the best wines produced along the banks of the Moselle. To arrange a visit if you're not staying at the hotel, call *(℃)* **02675/277.**

Villa Vinum ★★   Located directly on the river and close to the train station, this stylish boutique hotel is just a few hundred meters from the city's action but has great views and plenty of space to make up for it. The owners are warm and friendly, often inviting guests to join them for wine in the lounge; the exterior is one of a classical 19th century villa but inside, rooms are smartly modern in both decoration and amenities.
Moselstrasse 18. www.villa-vinum-cochem.de. *(℃)* **02671/9165445.** 12 units. 80€–150€ per night. Buffet breakfast included. Parking 4€. **Amenities:** WiFi (free).

Where to Eat in Cochem

L'Auberge du Vin ★ RHINELAND   Cochem's best regional cuisine is served by the Beth family, who use seasonal offerings fresh from their market-fresh shopping each day. The three- and four-course menus vary based on season, but fresh fish and game dishes, such as venison in autumn or a fillet of pikeperch with fresh asparagus, are standard. Delectable snails, or pigeon breast with "smashed" celery in a red-wine sauce, or saddle of lamb with ratatouille, all might appeal to gourmands. There are three rooms for rent as well, should you wish to spend the night, though check-in must be done by 6pm and check-out no later than 10am. Prices available only upon request.
In the Lohspeicher, Obergasse 1. www.lohspeicher.de. *(℃)* **02671/3976.** Reservations recommended. 3- or 4-course menus 35€–65€. Tues 6–8pm, Fri 6–8:30pm, Sat 7–10pm. Closed Jan–Mar.

Weissmühle im Enderttal ★ GERMAN   Set across the river from the Reichsburg castle, this popular hotel has two restaurants with fine traditional cuisine. Though the menus are the same, the atmosphere is different as you can choose: either the Müllerstube—a dark, wood-paneled room reminiscent of Alpine architecture—or the larger, airier Sommerrestaurant. Locally-grown foods adorn the menu, including a trademark dish of fresh trout from a small nearby lake, stuffed with herbs and baked. With 36 well-furnished bedrooms, each individually furnished in a rustic country style, the inn is also a great base. The price per person for bed-and-breakfast ranges from 49€ to 59€. From Cochem city center, drive toward the A48, following the signs for Koblenz/Trier; the inn is on the left of the road, 1.5km (1 mile) northwest of Cochem.
Endertstrasse 1. www.weissmuehle.de. *(℃)* **02671/8955.** Reservations recommended. Main courses 19€–30€. Daily noon–2pm and 6–8:30pm.

A Side Trip to Burg Eltz ★★★

Burg Eltz ★★★ This stately castle tucked up the Elzbach valley north of the river is a bit out of the way, but it makes for a nice stopover between Cochem and Koblenz. Burg Eltz, built from the 12th century to the 17th century, has been called the most beautiful authentic castle in Germany, even surpassing the more heavily touristed 19th-century Bavarian fairy-tale castles like Neuschwanstein. The original structure has been preserved in all its glory, thanks in part to one family member who joined the French army to keep the "Sun King" Louis XIV from laying it to ruin. The castle has housed different families in four separate residences, with original medieval furnishings that include some fine old paintings and tapestries. A treasury contains works by goldsmiths and silversmiths, armor, weapons, and other objects acquired by the family over the centuries. The castle lies 20km (12 miles) northeast of Cochem; a parking lot less than 800m (½ mile) from the castle can be reached via Münstermaifeld. A bus runs to the castle every 5 minutes and costs 1.50€. Fitter visitors can take a 35-minute uphill hike on a marked path through the valley from Moselkern.

www.burg-eltz.de. ✆ **02672/950500.** Admission 10€ adults, 6.50€ children, 28€ families. Open daily Apr–Oct 9:30am–5:30pm, with regularly offered tours.

THE FAIRY-TALE ROAD

14

Once upon a time, folks in a pretty, rural, and relatively untraveled part of central Germany between Frankfurt and Bremen got together to see how they might put their region on the map. "Let's see, who's lived here that anyone really cares about?" they wondered aloud.

"I've got it!" someone ventured. "How about those Grimm boys? Quiet, mousy types, always had their noses in a book. Cared more about words than they did about people. But they sure told a whopper of a tale. Plus, all those characters they wrote about, Goldilocks, the Pied Piper, Little Red Riding Hood, Hansel and Gretel . . . they all lived in these parts, too."

"*Meine Gütte*, we're on to something," the crowd roared. And that, if you choose to believe it, is how the Fairy Tale Road came to be.

The so-called Fairy-Tale Road (*Märchenstrasse*) meanders for 595km (369 miles) north from Frankfurt through the states of Hesse and Lower Saxony, from Hanau, where the Brothers Grimm were born, to Bremen. Following the entire route is a five-day adventure at least, taking many twists and turns to the towns and villages where the librarian brothers lived, worked, and studied, until they left the region for Berlin in 1840. Along the way are half-timbered houses strung along cobbled lanes, castle towers on the horizon, and green river valleys edged with dark, gnarly forests. This is the land that inspired the tales that still fascinate children and adults around the world. While some towns and villages on the long route have no bona fide association with the Grimms, they are picturesque enough to qualify—you'll find yourself wondering if a witch or wizard might live in that thatched cottage by the road, or if a princess is taking a century-long snooze in the castle tower you see in the distance.

Trains serve a few towns on the route, but getting from place to place by public transport is for the most part inefficient and time-consuming. Unless someone transforms a pumpkin into a coach for you, the only easy way to follow the route is by car, maybe picking up a vehicle in Frankfurt and dropping it in Bremen, or vice versa (see p. 706 for more about rental cars).

Facing Page: **The Bremen Town Musicians, immortalized in bronze on Bremen's Marktplatz.**

A memorial statue of Jacob and Wilhelm Grimm in Hanau, their birthplace.

HANAU ★

20km (12 miles) E of Frankfurt

The Fairy Tale Road officially begins in Hanau, where the Brothers Grimm were born—Jacob Ludwig Carl Grimm on January 4, 1785, and Wilhelm Carl Grimm on February 24, 1786. Their father, Philipp, was a jurist, and the family lived comfortably in a house that—as if one of the demons the brothers wrote about had waved his arm and cast a spell—was blown off the face of the earth in World War II.

While the brothers would feel right at home in many of the beautiful landscapes you'll encounter farther along the Fairy Tale Road, they wouldn't recognize their hometown. These days Hanau is an eastern suburb of Frankfurt (see p. 488), and not a very attractive one at that. You'll probably only want to stop to pay a quick visit to the brothers at their **Nationaldenkmal Brüder Grimm (Brothers Grimm Memorial)**, on Marktplatz (the central square). In a bronze statue grouping erected in 1898, the brothers stand in long frock coats, contently reading and oblivious to all the selfies being composed around them.

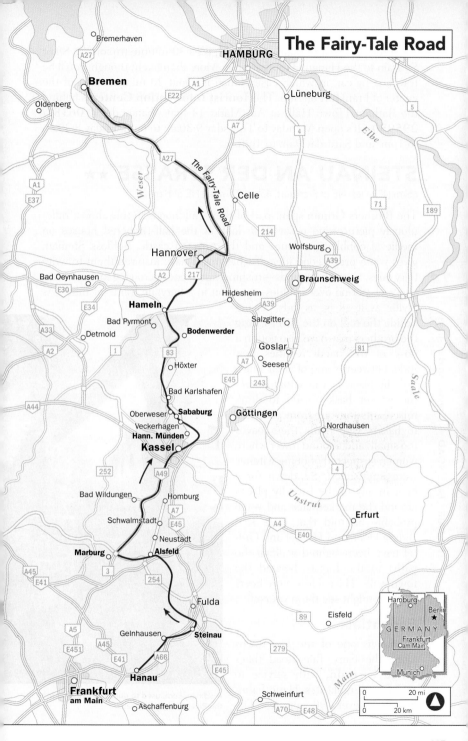

The Fairy-Tale Road

From Frankfurt's main rail station, it's a 30-minute trip on the S8 or S9 train to the Hanau Hauptbahnhof. More than likely, though, you'll be traveling by car, in which case Hanau is about 20 minutes east of the center of Frankfurt on A66. The **Tourist Information Center** is behind the Rathaus (Town Hall) at Am Markt 14 (www.hanau.de; ✆ **06181/ 295950**). It's open Monday to Thursday 9:30am to 6pm, Friday 8:30am to 1pm, and Saturday 9am to 1pm.

STEINAU AN DER STRASSE ★★

65km (40 miles) NE of Frankfurt, 45km (27 miles) NE of Hanau

The Brothers Grimm spent part of their childhoods in this almost ridiculously picturesque town. One look at the half-timbered houses on medieval cobblestone lanes and the turreted castle, Schloss Steinau, gives you a pretty good idea of what might have inspired them to write fairy tales. Even the sounds—rushing water, cocks crowing in farmyards, shoes clattering over cobbles—put you in a fairytale frame of mind. As idyllic as it all is, as lads playing beside the mill on the River Linzig the brothers may have also gotten a dose of the harsh realities that lurks between some of their lines. Still in place is the *schnappkorb,* the wicker basket used to dunk miscreants (anyone from poachers to bakers who made their loaves too small) and a round tower where women suspected of being witches were imprisoned. Sit down for a beer in any of the friendly places around the marketplace and you'll probably be told that little Red Riding Hood and Hansel and Gretel have been sighted walking the paths in the forests beyond the town walls. Have a few more beers and you might see them yourself.

A *schnappkorb,* used to dunk law-breakers in the River Linzig in Steinau.

Essentials

Steinau is one of the few towns along the Fairy Tale Road that's served by **train,** with service to and from Frankfurt's Hauptbahnhof about every 90 minutes. The

A66 deposits you on the outskirts of town. The **Tourist Information Office** is in the center at Brüder-Grimm-Strasse 70 (www.steinau.de; ✆ **06663/96310**). It's open Monday to Friday 8am to 4:30pm and Saturday 9am to 4:30pm.

Exploring Steinau

You'll get a quick lesson in Grimm Brothers storytelling as soon as you step into the **Marktplatz,** where characters from the tales inhabit the four tiers of the **Märchenbrunnen (Fairytale Fountain).** A boy faces the evil spirit he's freed from the bottle, Rumpelstiltskin dances around the fire, the Water Nymph plays with the flounder—all this iconography might inspire a deeper reading of *Grimms' Fairy Tales,* an ideal companion for the trip along the Fairy Tale Road.

While the fountain makes it clear who and what brings Steinau its fame and fortune these days, the town's full name, Steinau an der Strasse (Steinau on the Road) reflects its prominence long before Jacob and Wilhelm Grimm got into the fairy tale business. The timber-pillared market hall inside the **Rathaus** did a brisk business when Steinau was a popular stop on the well-traveled road between Leipzig and Frankfurt. Dozens of the charming, half-timbered old houses along the main street, now known as Brüder-Grimm-Strasse, were once inns that provided travelers with a place to rinse the dust off, rest their road-shaken bones, and water and refresh their horses.

Brüder Grimm Haus & Museum Steinau ★★ HISTORIC HOUSE The Brothers Grimm were brought to live in this large and attractive

Exhibits in the Brüder Grimm Haus, the authors' boyhood home.

house in 1791, when Jacob was five and Wilhelm was six. Their father, Philipp, was a Steinau native who had left for the big town of Hanau, done well, and returned as magistrate. The aristocratic home with high gables and carved timberwork served as a courthouse, with living quarters grouped around a huge kitchen downstairs and offices above, reached via a tower with a spiral staircase. Philipp died of pneumonia in 1796, leaving the family in financial straits, and the brothers left Steinau in 1798 to study in Kassel (see p. 627). Today the downstairs rooms are filled with family memorabilia and portraits, some by older brother Ludwig, while the upper floor is devoted to the fairy tales that made Grimm into a household name around the world. First editions and beautiful illustrations from the many published volumes of the tales are on display, alongside a wall of backlit dioramas, full of wolves and dark forests, as transporting as the stories that inspired them.

Brüder-Grimm-Strasse 80. www.museum-steinau.de. ℂ **06663/7605.** Admission 6€, 3.50€ children, 12€ families. Daily 10am–5pm.

Schloss Steinau ★ HISTORIC BUILDING   Had the Brothers Grimm never left Steinau, they still would have found plenty of inspiration for their tales in this castle of light stone and honey-colored brick that looms picturesquely over the town. Its archways, cobbled courtyards, tall turrets, and expanses of half-timbering look like something out of a fairy tale, though there's no record of a princess ever letting her hair down so a suitor could climb into one of the many towers. For the most part, the counts of Hanau—whose country residence this was—were serious-minded aristocrats who concentrated on trade, commerce, and fortuitous matchmaking to enrich their lands. They acquired the medieval castle through a marriage dowry in the 13th century and later added wings and pavilions in 16th-century German Renaissance style, keeping some noticeable medieval vestiges. One such feature is the dry moat, in which the counts once kept the deer and other beasts that they'd slaughtered for feasts in the Great Hall. On a playful note, the town's noted puppet theater, the **Steinauer Marionettentheater,** performs in the castle's former stables. Performances, mostly of Grimm tales, are staged most weekends at 3pm; tickets cost 7.50€. For more information visit www.die-holzkoeppe.de or call ℂ **06663/245.**

Schloss Steinau. www.schloesser-hessen.de. ℂ **06663/6843.** Admission 4€ adults, 3.50€ children. Mar–Oct Tues–Thurs and Sat–Sun 10am–5pm; Nov–Dec 12 Tues–Thurs and Sat–Sun 10am–4pm. Closed Jan–Feb.

Where to Eat & Stay in Steinau an der Strasse

Brathähnchen Farm ★★ GERMAN/PORTUGUESE   The fellow walking around the rustic, woody room with a sword isn't a knight from a fairy tale but one of the cooks, wielding a skewer to take a roast chicken off the open fire in the big stone hearth. That's what just about anyone who finds their way to the "Roast Chicken Farm" on a hilltop outside

Steinau orders, and diners come from miles around to do so. Kebabs of chicken, lamb, and pork are also roasted to order, and hefty portions of homemade applesauce and roasted potatoes accompany everything. Some of the dishes, like the pan-fried shrimp and roasted spare ribs, show off a dash of the owner's native Portugal. Upstairs are 14 airy, simply furnished bedrooms where everything—bedsteads, bureaus, and fabrics—is white, except for the green countryside outside the windows. Doubles are 80€ a night.

Im Ohl 1. www.brathaehnchenfarm.net. ✆ **06663/228.** Main courses 9€–18€. Daily noon–10pm.

Burgmannehaus ★ Soaking in the lovely medieval ambiance of Steinau works up a thirst for beer, and no better place to have one than the plain rooms and terrace of this old *stube* right on the main square. Many kinds of beer are on tap, and the menu introduces you to some hearty Hessian classics like beef or pork with *grüne soss* (green sauce, with herbs, eggs, oil, and vinegar). In this part of the world many dishes are also served *Mit musik,* a sauce of onions and vinegar, with the "music" referring to the resulting flatulence. Upstairs are eight simply yet utterly charming bedrooms where old-fashioned beds sit atop polished floors, beams crisscross the walls and ceilings, and no view is bad, taking in the cobblestone square, the old surrounding houses, and best of all, the towers of the castle.

Brüder-Grimm-Strasse 49. www.burgmannenhaus-steinau.de. ✆ **06663/911-2902.** 8 units. 70€ double. Rates include buffet breakfast. **Amenities:** Restaurant; bar; room; Wi-Fi (free).

ALSFELD ★★

78km (47 miles) northeast of Steinau

It's thought that the Brothers Grimm may have written "Little Red Riding Hood"—*Rötkappchen* in German—while staying near this beautiful medieval town in the valley of the Schwalm River. That's more conjecture than fact, but the collection of 400 half-timbered houses along crooked lanes behind old walls and towers could certainly inspire a good story or two. The prettiest route from Steinau to Alsfeld takes you north along A66 and B254. The **tourist office** is at Markt 3 (www.alsfeld.de; ✆ **06631/182165**); it's open Monday to Saturday, 10am to 5pm.

Exploring Alsfeld

It may or not be true that a visit here prompted the Grimm Brothers to write about a little girl finding her way to her grannie's house through the dark woods just outside town. In describing Rötkappchen's clothing they certainly could have been talking about the local women, who until quite recently wore short-sleeved bodices, full aproned skirts over many petticoats, and red headdresses. Even without the Grimms, townsfolk have come up with some good yarns of their own over the years. Among them is a popular legend claiming that storks nesting in **Leonhard's Tower,** a 27m-high (89 ft.) defense on the southeast end of the Altstadt, deliver babies to families living on the streets below. The birds allegedly pluck their little bundles of joy from the depths of the **Grabbrünnen,** a nearby well used for dying cloth.

What's known with some certainty is that Martin Luther spent a night in Alsfeld on his way to Worms in 1521. He lodged at an inn called Zum Schwanen on the **Marktplatz** (Marketplace), in what is now the pretty, half-timbered house at number 12. He might have enjoyed the view of the many fine landmarks surrounding the square, including the sturdy, half-timbered **Rathaus,** with an open market on the ground floor. Had Luther been in a celebratory mood, he could have walked along the square to the **Wedding House.** The stone structure was used for dances and weddings in peaceable times, and as a storehouse for salt and food (and as a prison) during the many plagues, occupations, and other hardships that have befallen Alsfeld. On the north side of the Marktplatz is the **Wine House,** where the product that accounted for close to half the town's medieval income was stored and traded. The building was so much a part of public life that it was also used as a place of punishment. Embedded in the stone walls is the pillory, a metal frame in which miscreants were secured by their heads and hands as public humiliation.

MARBURG ★★

50km (30 miles) W of Alsfeld

When the Brothers Grimm came to the university in Marburg in the first years of the 19th century, they were following in well-worn footsteps. By then this lovely town crowding a hillside above the Lahn River had been a draw for pilgrims for almost six centuries. The faithful came to venerate the relics of St. Elisabeth (1207–31) of Hungary, canonized in 1235. The 13th-century **Elisabethkirche** built in her honor lies at the foot of the medieval town that grew up around the church in the only direction it could go—up a steep hillside. So, be prepared for some climbing in Marburg.

Even if you've never set foot in Marburg before, as you wander about the town you may come upon familiar-looking scenes. That's because local artist Otto Ubbeholde depicted Marburg's castle gateway and other landmarks in his illustrations for a 1907 edition of the fairy tales that has been reprinted many times since.

Essentials

Marburg is served by **train** from Frankfurt's Hauptbahnhof, with hourly service in both directions for trips that take about an hour. Traveling by

The medieval Marktplatz and Rathaus of Marburg, where the Grimms came to university in the early 1800s.

car from Alsfeld, follow Rte. B62 west into Marburg. The **Marburg Tourist Office** is at Pilgrimstein 26 (www.marburg.de; ✆ **06421/ 99120**), open Monday to Friday 9am to 6pm, Saturday 10am to 2pm.

Exploring Marburg

As the cranky Jacob Grimm once remarked about Marburg, "I think there are more steps in the streets than in the houses." Free elevators on **Pilgrimstein,** near the tourist office and **Elisabethkirche** (see p. 624), will deliver you from flat ground alongside the river to the precincts of the **Marktplatz,** the marketplace, surrounded by timbered houses. The oldest café here, at number 18, dates from 1323. Towering over the picturesque scene is the **Rathaus,** where a mechanical rooster on the gable crows the hour.

In 1802, Jacob Grimm came to Marburg to attend the town's famous **Philipps University,** founded in 1527 by the House of Hesse. Jacob became despondent without Wilhelm, who joined him in 1803, and the two lodged in a house at **Bärfusserstrasse 35,** a short walk west of the Marktplatz. (Oddly enough, Nazi war criminal Klaus Barbie, the so-called Butcher of Lyon, lived in the same house under an alias from 1946 to 1947.) Jacob was annoyed by the noise and dirt in the narrow streets and complained about barking dogs. Even so, the young brothers flourished in Marburg, where they studied law and developed an interest in folk tales, romanticism, medieval literature, and the German language, passions they would pursue the rest of their lives. Around the corner at **Wendelgasse 4** is the house where Wilhelm went to live when Jacob moved to Paris to study. Wilhelm unhappily wrote his brother, "When you are away I feel a tearing at my heart . . . certainly you cannot know just how fond I am of you."

From there it's an uphill climb to the 13th-century **Landgrave Castle** at the peak of the Old Town, but it's definitely worth the trek for views over the town and a look at the gables and turrets. Famously, Martin Luther and Ulrich Zwingli met in the castle in 1529 at the Colloquy of Marburg to discuss the fine points of ecumenical dogma. (Though Luther reported "We are all still bright-eyed and healthy and living like royalty," they never could reach an agreement on the meaning of the Last Supper.) On your climb up to the castle, pass by **Ritterstrasse 15,** where the brothers' professor and mentor, Carl von Savigny, once lived. In those days, the university had only 170 or so students, who met in their professors' homes to discourse and share a midday meal. The Grimms delighted in Savigny's collection of rare manuscripts of medieval epics and hero's tales. Next to the **Lutherische Pfarrkirche St. Marien,** or St. Mary's Lutheran Church, on Ritterstrasse, with its landmark crooked spire, you can also see a house that Jacob complained about, where "one enters by a door in the roof" (it's still there).

The Philipps University of Marburg now has 25,000 students, who account for a full third of the town's population. The so-called **Old University,** mostly from the latter part of the 19th century, is at the lower edge of the Altstadt, off Reitgasse. Jacob attended a ball in the house at Reitgasse 5, politely calling it "an exceptionally good diversion." A similar sense of decorum prevailed well into the 1960s, when the university mandated that students of the opposite sex could only visit one another in their rooms if they took the door off the hinges. As a sign of how times change, it's now said that if a student should ever come to Marburg a virgin and leave a virgin, the severely leaning tower of Lutherische Pfarrkirche will straighten itself.

Among the many statues you'll encounter as you wander through the Altstadt, at the foot of Wettergasse you'll find a modern bronze statue of the town's beloved **Dientsmann Christian,** a porter who worked at the train station until the 1950s. It's said he managed to consume 5 liters of beer a day while half-heartedly but good-naturedly fulfilling his duties. He's honored with a popular and wise rhyme, "First beer then wine, that's fine, First wine then beer, oh dear."

Elisabethkirche ★★ CHURCH   No sooner had the town's famous saint, Elisabeth, been canonized in 1235 than construction began on her final resting place, which is said to be the first Gothic church in Germany. It wasn't a sense of piety that inspired this huge monument, styled on the great cathedrals in Reims and Amiens. Rather, the town had business in mind: Even before the church was completed in 1283, Marburg had become one of the most important pilgrimage sites in Europe. Elizabeth had succumbed to exhaustion at age 24, by which time she had led a remarkably full life. Daughter of King Andrew of Hungary, she was engaged at birth to marry Ludwig IV, the future count of Thuringia. She moved to court at 4 to be brought up with her future husband, and was married at 14. She was widowed at 21 when Ludwig was killed on a Crusade. She renounced her enormous wealth and splendid lifestyle and spent the rest of her time living in poverty in Marburg, tending to the poor at the hospital she founded. Her bones rest in a gold reliquary, surrounded by statues and paintings exemplifying her life and values. In a baptistery carving, lepers and lunatics raise their hands to Elisabeth as she is carried to heaven. A colorful painting portrays an incident in which Ludwig, learning his wife is tending to a leper in the marital bed, confronts her and discovers a crucifix instead. The piece de la resistance is a magnificent 13th-century stained glass window that presents a colorful visual history of Elisabeth's life and good deeds. A panel at the top shows Mary and Jesus crowning Elisabeth as she takes her place alongside St. Francis.

Elisabethstrasse 3. www.elisabethkirche.de. ✆ **06421/65497.** Admission 2€ for St. Elisabeth's Shrine. Apr–Sept daily 9am–6pm; Oct daily 9am–5pm; Nov–Mar daily 10am–4pm.

Where to Eat & Stay in Marburg

For the past century or so, the place to take a break while climbing around the Old Town has been **Café Vetter,** Reitgasse 4 (www.cafe-vetter-marburg.de; ✆ **06421/25888**). On the outdoor terrace, cakes and coffee come with panoramic views.

Vila Vita Hotel Rosenpark ★★★   A stay at this large and luxurious hotel, set apart from the rest of town on the banks of the Lahn River, is like slipping away to a resort. Large, comfortably appointed guest rooms are a lot more sophisticated than you'd expect to find in a small university city surrounded by rural countryside—if you've had any notions of coming to Marburg to relive your student days, you'll forgo them amid the grown-up pleasures of plush lounge chairs and fine linens. Downstairs is a marvelously hedonistic spa, with steam baths, saunas, ice fountains, aroma cabins, fog showers, a swimming pool, and a cafe. Several in-house restaurants include the cozy, rustic **Zirbelstube.** Elisabethkirche and other sights are about a 10-minute walk away.

Rosenstrasse 18. www.vilavitahotels.com. ✆ **06421/60050.** 233€–313€ double. Buffet breakfast included. Free parking. **Amenities:** 3 restaurants; 3 bars; bikes; room service; indoor pool; spa; Wi-Fi (free).

Flammkuchen, a local specialty, at Weinstube Weidlägen.

Weinstube Weinlädele ★ GERMAN/HESSIAN Marburg is *Flammkuchen* country, and you can find the thin-crusted tartes, baked with white cheese, onions, and *lardons,* at market stalls and restaurants all over town. It's said that no one makes this snack or light meal better than they do at this handsome *stube* with a wooden gallery above the main room You can accompany it with another Kassel specialty, *Ahle Wurst,* a hard pork sausage. Wine is the beverage of choice, whether you're having Flammkuchen or a heavier choice like the excellent *Geschmorte Rinderroulade,* beef in wine sauce. Warm-weather meals are served on a terrace overlooking the marketplace.

Schlosstreppe 1. www.weinlädele.de. ✆ **06421/14244.** Main courses 6€–12€. Daily noon–3pm and 6:30–10:30pm.

Zur Sonne ★★ A half-timbered house with geraniums cascading down the high-gabled facade provides all the historic atmosphere you might want in Marburg, especially if you stay in one of the large doubles overlooking the marketplace. The old guest quarters and two *stubes* on the lower floors have been accommodating guests since 1569. Amenities in the wonderful old lodgings are pretty basic, though the polished, wide-plank floors and rough beams crisscrossing the walls and ceilings are luxuries themselves.

Markt 14. www.zur-sonne-marburg.de. ✆ **06421/17190.** 9 units. 90€–105€ double. Buffet breakfast included. **Amenities:** Restaurant; bar; Wi-Fi (free).

KASSEL ★

100km (62 miles) NE of Marburg

If you're expecting to come to Kassel and walk in the brothers' footsteps from one Grimm landmark to the next, you're in for a disappointment. Kassel (originally Castle, from the Latin *Castella,* or stronghold) was blown to smithereens in World War II and rose from the rubble as a modern manufacturing center. The brothers are certainly still here in spirit, however, and they loom larger-than-life at the **Grimmwelt** (Grimm World Museum; see p. 628). Kassel also has a few other show places, including the spectacular **Bergpark Wilhelmshöhe,** a baroque retreat of royalty at the edge of the city.

Essentials

GETTING THERE   Kassel's two train stations, **Kassel Bahnhof and Kassel-Wilhelmshöhe Bahnhof,** are connected to Frankfurt's Hauptbahnhof by trains that run every 75 to 90 minutes throughout the day. The trip takes 1½ hours. Kassel-Wilhelmshöhe station, a stop on high-speed lines, is west of the center on Willy-Brandt-Platz. By car from Marburg, follow Rte. A49 northeast into Kassel.

VISITOR INFORMATION   The **Kassel Tourist Office** is at Obere Königstrasse 15 (www.kassel-tourist.de; © **0561/7077707**). It's open Monday to Saturday 9am to 6pm. Another office (© **0561/34054**) in the Kassel-Wilhelmshöhe station is open the same hours.

The Grimms in Kassel

The Brothers Grimm came to Kassel as adolescents in 1798, under the patronage of their aunt, a lady in waiting for a Hessian princess. Their mother, Dorothea, had been raised in Kassel and was the daughter of a council member. Jacob and Wilhelm attended the Lyzeum, in those days an undertaking that began at 5am and lasted well into the evening. After a spell at university in **Marburg** (see p. 622), they returned to Kassel in 1805 to take up posts as librarians at the court of Napoleon's youngest brother, Jerome Bonaparte, who was the King of Westphalia. Jacob, as the elder brother, was responsible for the welfare of the rest of family, and the clan hovered so near poverty at times that Wilhelm once

wrote, "We five people eat only three portions and only once a day." The job in Kassel eventually provided a bit of financial security, however, and also gave the brothers time to research and write. They launched their publishing career in Kassel, bringing out their first volume, *Kinder- und Hausmärchen (Children's and Household Tales,* usually known in English simply as *Grimms' Fairy Tales),* with 86 folk tales, in 1812, and a second volume in 1814, with 70 additional tales. They also published a compilation, *Deutsche Sagen (German Legends),* brought out in two parts, in 1816 and 1818. They left Kassel for Göttingen in 1830 when they were passed over for the post of chief librarian.

Exploring Kassel

At the center of Kassel is Königstrasse, the pedestrian shopping street, and the adjacent **Friedrichsplatz.** This lovely 18th-century square manages to bring together the many facets of Kassel. In the middle is a monument to Landgrave Friedrich II, for whom the square is named. A view to the south extends over the green valley of the Fulda River, the surrounding countryside to which Kassel still has deep ties, despite its industrialization. Off to one side of the square is an oak tree, with a stone next to it, that conceptual artist Joseph Beuys planted in 1982 for **Documenta,** the renowned modern art exhibition that Kassel has hosted every 5 years since 1955 (see p. 629). Another piece of art looms at the end of 4.5km (3-mile) long Wilhelmshöher Allee, a park-like boulevard that shoots west from the edge of the center: Atop a rise at the end stands a **statue of Hercules,** watching over Kassel since 1717.

Grimmwelt (Grimm World) ★★★ MUSEUM   The Grimm Brothers are given well-deserved celebrity treatment at this modernist museum of rusticated stone, an architectural statement on a hillside at the edge of the city center. The emphasis in the dramatic galleries, entered through a tunnel of milky paper (to suggest stepping into a book), centers on the tales as a publishing phenomenon. In terms of staying power and readership, the tales are in the same league as the Bible. Clips from theater,

Every 5 years, Kassel hosts the contemporary art world at the Documenta festival, next held in summer 2017.

When the Art World Comes to Kassel

The Documenta, considered the world's most important exhibition of contemporary art, opened in Kassel in 1955 and now takes place every five years. More than 800,000 attendees pour into Kassel for the event, among them in the past such luminaries as Brad Pitt and Queen Beatrix of the Netherlands. Documenta 14 (www.documenta.de) will run from June 10 through September 17, 2017. The main exhibition space is the Freericianum on Friedrichsplatz, though art is on display throughout Kassel at the time, some of it outdoors. For his *7,000 Oaks* project at Kassel's 1982 Documenta exhibition, conceptual artist Joseph Beuys (1921–1986) piled 7,000 basalt stones next to a tree he planted on Friedrichsplatz and encouraged Kassel residents to take a stone, plant another tree elsewhere in town, and place one of the stones next to it. By 1987, the pile was gone and 7,000 new trees were growing around Kassel. Beuys called the endeavor Social Sculpture and expressed his commitment to taking art beyond its usual boundaries to instill creativity in every aspect of life. As he once said, "Every sphere of human activity, even peeling a potato, can be a work of art as long as it is a conscious act." So, consider that when you come across a tree with a stone next to it in Kassel.

opera, comic books, and other media bring home what enormous cultural influence they have had. Pride of place among many volumes, often lavishly illustrated, belongs to the brothers' personal, dog-eared, heavily annotated copy of *Kinder- und Hausmärchen.* The brothers' impact as scholarly etymologists is explored in exhibits that follow their painstaking work from 1838 until their deaths, compiling *Deutsches Wörterbuch*— not just a dictionary but a compendium of the German language. (The last entry Jacob completed was *Froteufel,* a medieval word for demon.) The brothers considered their investigation into language and cultures as "research into roots," a concept illustrated by Chinese artist Ai Weiwei's forest of brilliantly painted tree trunks, one of many abstract interpretations of the tales you'll see here. An honorable nod also goes to the 1,400 correspondents with whom the Grimms met and exchanged letters, many of who passed stories along to the brothers. Among them was Dorothea Viehmann, another Kassel resident and well-known storyteller, who gathered the brothers around her fire and recited more than forty tales and their variations, including "Hansel and Gretel," "Little Red Riding Hood," and "Rumpelstiltskin."

Weinbergstrasse 21. www.grimmwelt.de © **0561/598-6190.** Admission 8€. Tues–Sun 10am–6pm (Fri until 8pm).

Wilhelmshöhe Park ★★ PARK Sprawling across 350 hectares (865 acres) of a steep hillside at the western edge of the city, this exuberant expanse of greenery was laid out in the baroque style in 1701 and expanded many times since. Within the park are dense forests, a faux romantic castle, formal gardens, lakes, fountains, viewpoints, a Chinese village with a pagoda, and a cascade that rushes 350m (1,155 fit.) feet down a hillside. Standing high above it all, mounted on a pyramid atop a 526.2m (1,726 ft) summit, is a copper statue of Hercules. In comparison to such grandiose garden ornamentation, the early 19th century **Schloss,** a summer residence for local royalty, seems almost sedate, massive though it is. The state apartments now house an admirable collection of Old Masters, with a haunting self-portrait of a young, wild-haired, and unkempt Rembrandt. Anyone who visited Germany in the pre-euro days will immediately recognize Albrecht Dürer's *Portrait of Elizabeth Tucher*— the well-attired lady holding her wedding ring used to grace the 20-mark note.

Schlosspark 3. www.wilhelmshoehe.de. ✆ **0561/312456.** Admission 6€. Mar–Oct Tues–Sun 10am–5pm; Nov–Feb Tues–Sun 10am–3pm.

Where to Stay & Eat in Kassel

Autobahnrastätte Knallhütte ★ HESSIAN/GERMAN   One of the Grimm Brothers' most valued Kassel colleagues, Dorothea Viehmann, was born in this inn on the stagecoach road to Frankfurt in 1755 and grew up hearing stories that travelers told to while away the time on long winter nights. In her later years Dorothea passed many of the tales and legends on to the Grimm Brothers (see **Grimmwelt,** p. 628). Today the coach road is an autobahn, but the inn still stands and is now a brewery and tavern with a beer garden and several homey dining rooms. The house-made brew is excellent, as is the *Biersuppe,* a good way to work up to a big platter of *Schnitzel* or rump steak. The inn is 8km (5 miles) south of Kassel off A49; you can take Tram RB from the city center.

Knallhütterstrasse 1, Baunatal-Rengershausen. www.knallhuette.de. ✆**0561/492076.** Main courses 12€–18€. Daily 11am–midnight.

Hotel Gude ★★★   Ever so subtly, a Brothers Grimm theme permeates this bastion of sophistication and good taste at the edge of town. Ghostlike portraits of the brothers appear on a specially clad aluminum screen at the top of the modern façade, behind which is a cinema-worthy penthouse. Entries from the brothers' *Deutsches Wörterbuch* are affixed to the walls of all the rooms, many of which have chic, contemporary sofas and chairs. Specially engineered beds would tempt any princess or prince to fall into a 100-year-long sleep. The **Pfeffermühle** restaurant serves satisfying modern takes on German standards.

Frankfurterstrasse 299. www.hotel-gude.de. ✆ **0561/48050.** 84 units. 89€–134€ double. Buffet breakfast included. **Amenities:** 2 restaurants; bar; sauna; Wi-Fi (free).

STAYING NEARBY

Hotel Schloss Waldeck ★★   West of Kassel, the Edersee reservoir stretches behind a dam on the Eder, a tributary of the Fulda River. The dam gained infamy in May 1943, when Royal Air Force bombers ripped a massive breach in the structure and sent a deadly wall of water crashing through the valley below, killing scores and causing massive destruction. Today the lake glistens placidly below the heights commanded by the castle of the counts of Waldeck, a romantic assemblage of towers and gables that has been a military barracks and a prison. It now houses guests in stylish, smartly designed rooms full of fine wood furnishings that overlook the valley and lake through huge windows. An aerie-like café also overlooks the lake-and-forest scenery. Waldeck is 40km (25 miles) southwest of Kassel on L3215.

Waldeck. www.schloss-hotel-waldeck.com. © **05623/5890.** 45 units. 108€–258€ double. Buffet breakfast included. **Amenities:** 2 restaurants; bar; spa; Wi–Fi (free).

HANN. MÜNDEN ★★

24km (15 miles) NE of Kassel

Surprisingly, this beautiful little town at the confluence of the Werra and Fulda rivers is Grimm-free. It's one of relatively few places in the region where the brothers didn't spend time, though the stone bridges over darting waters and the 700 half-timbered houses would have suited them well. Even the full, no-longer-used name of the town, Hannoversch Münden, glides off the tongue like the language of a fairy tale. Hann. Münden has its own larger-than-life character, though, a folk legend in his own right. That's Dr. Johann Andreas Eisenbarth (1663–1727), an oculist, barber, and traveling surgeon. He was noted, as a famous old German drinking song goes, for "applying cures you may have heard, that help the blind to walk again, the lame to see like no other man."

Essentials

GETTING THERE   Trains travel between Kassel and Hann. Münden throughout the day; the trip takes 15 minutes. If you're driving, avoid the speedy A7 and instead take Rte. 3 for a scenic half-hour drive along the Fulda River.

VISITOR INFORMATION   The **Tourist Information Office** is in the Rathaus on Lotzestrasse (www.hann.muenden-tourismus.de; © **05541/ 75313**). It's open May to October Monday to Friday 8am to 5:30pm, Saturday 10am to 3pm, and Sunday 11am to 3pm; from November to April it's open Monday to Thursday 9am to 4pm and Friday 9am to 1pm.

Exploring Hann. Münden

The great 18th- and 19th-century naturalist and world traveler Alexander von Humboldt praised Hann. Münden as one of the most beautifully located towns in the world. That's on account of the Werra and Fulda rivers, whose waters converge at the edge of town to form the **Weser**

Picturesque Hann. Münden is the southern endpoint of the Weser River Cycle Route.

River. As a popular poem has it, Hann. Münden stands "Where Werra and Fulda unite and embrace, Their name through this kiss they have to replace, And the River Weser thus is born." As you stand at the peninsula just north of the Altstadt and witness the waters flowing into one another, it's easy to see how the phenomenon inspires such a romantic interpretation of hydrology.

The little city's fortified towers and fragments of old wall speak of its importance as a trading center in the Middle Ages, lying as did on a major river route between the south and the North Sea. It's not by accident that one of the most imposing structures in the half-timbered Altstadt is the **Packhof (Warehouse),** overlooking the Werra on Wanfrieder Schlagd, built to store goods transported on the river. A small theater in the courtyard will tell you all you ever wanted to know about Dr. Eisenbarth in spring and summer with a play staged by the **Doctor Eisenbarth Theatre Company** (www.eisenbarth-theater.de), founded in 1957. Performances are every other Saturday evening from mid-May through mid-September. Tickets cost 16€ for adults, 12€ for children 12 to 16, and free for children under 12.

Murals in the lower hall of the **Rathaus** provide a colorful overview of the town history. Among them is a scene showing a young couple with their baby swimming through flood waters, clinging to a raft carrying

Hann. Münden is at the southern end of the Weser River Cycle Route, a mostly flat, well-maintained path that follows the river for 515km (309 miles) between Hann. Münden and Cuxhaven, on the North Sea near Bremerhaven. Scenery ranges from lush river meadows backed by forests to fens and heaths and coastal dunes, and the path passes through many fabled towns and villages on the Fairy Tale Road. Among the half-timbered houses you'll encounter a notorious liar in Bodenwerder (see p. 634), an infamous rat catcher in Hameln (p. 636), and furred and feathered musicians in Bremen (p. 640). Tourist offices in Hann. Münden and other towns along the route provide maps and information, as does the German-language website weser-radweg.de.

their most valuable procession, a fat pig. Floods have been an all-too-regular occurrence in this river town over the centuries, as water gauges on the façade of the Rathaus indicate. Another mural depicts the town's famous physician, Dr. Eisenbarth, with his entourage of musicians and harlequins. Dr. Eisenbarth was especially renowned throughout northern Europe for his skill at removing cataracts, wielding a purpose-made hook to the accompaniment of a band that drowned out his patients' screams. Every day at noon, 3, and 5, the doctor makes an appearance in a revolving clock/chime on the Rathaus gable.

Near the Marktplatz, Eisenbarth died in a half-timbered house at **Lange Strasse 79,** back in 1727 when it was the Wild Man Inn. Down the street at **number 20** is a house with one of the elaborately carved entrances that are typical of the town; this double entrance is especially ornate, carved with scallop shells. The fairest house of them all, however, is in the Altstadt's south end at **Siebenturmstrasse 12,** with 28 mythical sea and river creatures carved into the wood framing.

Where to Stay & Eat in Hann. Münden

Alte Rathausschanke ★ You're not going to bask in luxury in these plain spacious rooms—they're just a notch or two above hostel-standard—but that's not why you'd choose to stay here. Instead, the remarkably reasonable rates place you right on the marketplace, surrounded by the town's plethora of half-timbering. Among the few perks is the use of a washing machine, a most welcome convenience if you've been washing your socks in bathroom sinks. One convenience that's conspicuously absent is an elevator, so ask for a room on a lower floor if you don't care to climb up several flights of rickety stairs.

Ziegelstrasse 12. www.ratsbrauhaus.de. **℃ 05541/75313.** 10 units. 66€–69€ double. Rates include breakfast. Amenities: Wi-Fi (free).

Die Reblaus ★★ GERMAN/EUROPEAN Despite the half timbers and the old sag to the house, the décor is contemporary and the cuisine is a decidedly modern take on German and European classics. You can enjoy a perfectly grilled steak here, but for the most part the menu likes to experiment with such innovations as herb-and-spinach-infused souffles, house-made pasta noodles with walnuts and Gorgonzola cheese, and a delicious *Spinatknödel mit Curry* (spinach dumplings with curry). Ziegelstrasse 32. www.die-reblaus.com. ✆ **05541/954-610.** Main courses 14€–22€. Mon–Sat noon–2:30pm and 6–11pm. Closed Mon Jan–Mar.

Ratsbrauhaus ★ GERMAN   The atmospheric cellars of Hann. Münden's 1605 Rathaus are often full to bursting with patrons who come for a glass two of the town's own Ratsbrauhaus beer, brewed since 1550. At that time it was illegal to drink beer not made in the town, though the output was expensive; it was touted as "liquid bread" and an important part of the diet. Many beer drinkers would argue it still is, though hearty meals are also served in the vaulted cellar and adjacent beer garden. You can help yourself from a buffet table laden with everything from home-baked breads to grilled chops, or order from the menu. Marktplatz 3. www.ratsbrauhaus.de. ✆ **05541/957107.** Main courses 10€–20€. Tues–Sat 6–10:30pm; Sat–Sun 11am–2pm.

An Excursion to Sababurg ★

To get back on the track of the Brothers Grimm, head north from Hann. Münden on B80 for 24km (15 miles) to **Sababurg Castle.** This romantic-looking pile of towers and turrets has no authentic connection to the Grimms, though it is linked to them with a tiny bit of historical conjecture and a lot of romance. By some accounts, the brothers knew of the castle and thought it would be an ideal setting for *Dornroschen,* or Sleeping Beauty. That's really neither here nor there, since they based their popular tale of the princess who slumbers for a century on older Italian and French folk stories. It's still worth a detour to see the castle, which built in 1334 to protect pilgrims on the route to Göttsburen; later it became a hunting lodge for the House of Hesse. It's easy to imagine a maiden slumbering in one of the towers, what with the wild briar roses blooming in the courtyard of the castle (now a hotel) and wild beasts roaming beneath ancient oaks and beech trees in the adjacent **Tierpark Sababurg** ★ wildlife refuge (www.tierpark-sababurg.de, ✆ **05671/766-4990**). Admission is 8€ adults, 4.50€ children 4 to 15; the park is open daily from April to September, 8am to 7pm, October 9am to 6pm, November to February 10am to 4pm, and March 9am to 5pm.

BODENWERDER ★

95km (57 miles) N of Sababurg, 119km (71 miles) N of Hann. Münden

You'll be forgiven if you feel a little nervous about pulling into this pretty little collection of half-timbered houses that cluster along the green

A statue of Baron von Münchausen, who spun his own tall tales in Bodenwerder.

banks of the River Weser. Even the signs announcing Bodenwerder's town limits could be fraudulent. This is the hometown of one of the world's most famous liars, **Lügenbaron (the lying baron) von Münchhausen** (1720–97). It would be hard to find anyone who's ever spun as many tall tales, provided, that is, you don't take politicians into account. If you're driving from Hann. Munden and Sababurg, you can follow the river along scenic Rte. 83. The **Tourist Information office** is at Münchhausenplatz 3 (www.muenchhausenland.de, © **05533/40541**); it's open Monday to Friday 9am to noon and 2 to 5pm, and Saturday 10am to 12:30pm.

The baron's gracious, half-timbered house is now the town's **Rathaus,** at Münchhausenplatz 1. One room is devoted to **Münchhausen-Erinnerungszimmer,** a little museum honoring the most famous resident (© **05533/409147;** admission 3€; open April to October, daily 10am–noon and 2–5pm). Displayed among various editions of Raspe's books is the cannon ball that Munchausen allegedly rode into battle. A small portrait is of Bernardine von Brunn, a young woman whom the delusion-prone baron married in 1794, though she was 57 years his junior. Not surprisingly, he was soon levying charges of infidelity against his bride.

From May to October, on the first Sunday of every month, the **Münchhausenplay** is performed in front of the Rathaus. Locals reenact

c'mon, **BARON,** tell me another

To be fair, the real Baron Münchhausen was not quite the fibber he's been made out to be. He was a soldier who fought in the Russo-Turkish War in the mid 18th century and, upon retiring to Bodenwerder, liked to sit around the fire and talk about his adventures, no doubt embellishing them with each retelling. Many loquacious old soldiers have done the same thing, but Münchhausen had the misfortune of bending the ear of a down-on-his-luck writer, Rudolph Erich Raspe. The Baron was pay dirt for Raspe, who elaborated wildly upon his unwitting subject's exploits in his 1785 hit, *Baron Munchausen's Narrative of his Marvellous Travels and Campaigns in Russia.* Probably the most famous tale is the one in which the baron decides to ride a cannonball into an enemy stronghold, changes his mind midair, and leaps onto a cannonball heading in the opposite direction. Münchausen's adventures have inspired films, plays, novels, radio shows, a board game, even an essay by Friedrich Nietzsche. He has posthumously lent his name to an asteroid belt, a philosophical dilemma, a mathematical theorem, and to Münchausen syndrome, in which a patient feigns illness to draw attention. Moving into the 21st century, Munchausen by Internet is a disorder in which one goes online and presents a fake illness to elicit emotional support.

scenes from Münchhausen's life that, whether truth or fiction, was certainly colorful.

HAMELN ★★

25km (16 miles) N of Bodenwater

It's ironic that a town as pretty and charming as Hameln rests its fame on rodents. Rats are everywhere in Hameln—not in a furry, scurrying, scary sort of way, but on plaques, signs, pavement markers, and little effigies all over town. Proof of Hameln's rodent fixation is the huge golden rat perched atop a footbridge across the River Weser that you'll encounter as you enter town from the south on Rte. 83.

It all began with a most mysterious incident in 1284. As the Brothers Grimm report in "The Pied Piper of Hameln," that's when a *Rattenfänger* (rat catcher) became vengeful after he was not paid for ridding the town of a rat infestation. He lured the town's children onto the slopes of a nearby mountain by playing his pipe and they were never heard from again. Scholars are still debating what might have really happened and what the psycho/cultural implications of the tragic-yet-popular story might be (see p. 639), but one thing's for certain: That long-ago morning turned out to be Hameln's lucky day, for rats and the *Rattenfänger* put Hameln on the map.

Today visitors are lured to this lovely town on the River Weser like rats to the mysterious strains of a rat catcher's flute. In fact, you may well encounter enchanted throngs following a Rattenfänger in colorful tights and a jaunty feathered cap as he leads them past half-timbered houses elaborately carved and ornamented in what's known as the Weser Renaissance style. If you're in town on a summer Sunday at noon, you can watch a half-hour reenactment of the tale on an open-air stage in front of the three-gabled **Hochzeitshaus (Wedding House)** on Osterstrasse.

Essentials

GETTING THERE You can reach Hameln by train with connections through Hannover, about 50 minutes away. Rte. 83 follows the Wesser River into town from the south.

VISITOR INFORMATION Hameln's **tourist office** is at the eastern edge of the Altstadt at Deisterallee 1 (www.hameln.de; ✆ **05151/957823**). From April to September it's open Monday to Friday 9am to 6:30pm, Saturday 9:30am to 4pm, and Sunday 9:30am to 1pm (closed Sundays in April); from October to March, hours are Monday to Friday 9am to 6pm and Saturday 9:30am to 1pm. The well-stocked center screens a jaunty 10-minute film that introduces you to the town and surrounding region.

Exploring Hameln

Rat catcher this, rat catcher that—you just can't escape Hameln's famous man in tights. The so-called **Rattenfängerhaus,** at Osterstrasse 28, is the 17th-century home of a prosperous burgher, brilliantly decorated with stone ornaments, gargoyles, and an inscription telling the town's famous legend. (Inside it's a restaurant—see p. 639). You'll encounter the rat catcher again on the other end of Osterstrasse at the stoutly gabled **Hochzeitshaus (Wedding House),** where he emerges from the clock on the façade three times a day (at 1:05, 3:35, and 5:35pm) to lead a procession of—what else?—rats.

Around the corner, on the side of Marktkirche St. Nikolai on **Pfedermarkt** (Horseman's Square, named for the medieval knights who used to joust here), a stained-glass window portrays the piper in a colorful mosaic. Although this window is from 1984, it replaces an original from 1300 that was the first known reference to the piper, believed to have been created to commemorate a mysterious tragedy involving the town's children. The first written record of a mass disappearance, from 1384, simply states, "It is 100 years since our children left." Also on Pfedermarkt is a memorial of a more recent event: the fall of the Iron Curtain. Under til 1989, the border with Eastern Germany was just to the east of Hameln.

The **Hameln Museum,** Osterstrasse 8–9 (www.hameln.com; ✆ **05151/202**) nicely displays historic texts and illustrations of the Pied Piper tale, along with some wonderfully whimsical products the Piper has inspired over the years, including Pied Piper clothes hangers from

In Hameln, images of the Pied Piper are everywhere.

the early 20th century. An old mill behind the house has been converted to a theater in which the audience sits on corn sacks as "mechanical puppets" creatively re-enact the incidents of that day in 1284, ending with dozens of phantom like night shirts floating off the stage. Galleries also chronicle other notable local events, such as a spate of 16th-century witch-hunts and etchings, and the town's role in the 1866 Battle of Langensalza, which, along with helping to form modern Germany, also introduced medics from an organization that would become the International Red Cross. The museum is open Tuesday through Sunday, 11am to 6pm; admission is 5€, children 6 to 15 3€.

Where to Stay & Eat in Hameln

Hotel Stadt Hameln ★   Over the years these three buildings surrounding a huge courtyard have been a prison, a factory, and a British military headquarters. There's still a slightly institutional air to the complex, just outside the Altstadt next to the river. That's not necessarily a

following the **PIPER**

The Brothers Grimm based their version of "The Pied Piper of Hameln" on 11 sources. Their tale comes to a not entirely unhappy conclusion, in which the children follow a tunnel through the mountain and end up in Transylvania, where one can surmise they live relatively happily ever after. Some scholars see some historical fact in the Grimm's portrayal. It's known that brightly clad, silver-tongued recruiters, known as *lokators*, went from town to town in that era, encouraging parents to save their children from poverty and starvation by sending them to Pomerania and other eastern regions, more or less selling them into slavery. (Intriguingly, surnames in some eastern regions are strikingly similar to those in Hameln.) Other theories posit that the children died of a plague, and the procession with the rat catcher was actually a dance of death, a *totentanz*. It's also been suggested that the young people set off to the Holy Land on one of the Children's Crusades that were not uncommon in the 13th century, or that they were killed in a flood, landslide, or some other natural calamity. Whatever the truth, the tale of the plight of Hameln's children has inspired not just the Brothers Grimm but also Goethe, Robert Browning, Walt Disney, and millions of readers, many of who find their way to this picturesque town to see the scene of the crime for themselves.

drawback—rooms are huge, some bordering on cavernous, while many of the tall windows overlook the river or gabled rooftops across the way, and rose bushes flourish in a former prison factory yard, now a parklike garden. The in-house restaurant and bar spills onto a terrace in good weather. To get there from the Altstadt, take Bus 1 or 2.

Münsterwall 2. www.hotel-stadthameln.de. ℰ **05151/901333.** 82 units. 99€ double. Buffet breakfast included. Parking 10€. **Amenities:** Restaurant; bar; room service; Wi-Fi (free).

Pfanneküchen ★ GERMAN   The same-named specialty, a filled pancake, is a local favorite. Filled with big slices of ham, many kinds of cheese, bacon, fruits, and jams, they're served in 40 savory and sweet variations in these heavily beamed old rooms with a charmingly creaky, overhanging gallery. You can enjoy them as a meal or a snack; they're especially popular as a midafternoon treat on weekends, when the kitchen serves all day.

Hummenstrasse 12. www.pfannekuchen-hamelin.de. ℰ **05151/41378.** Main courses 8–15€. Mon–Fri 11am–3pm and 5–10pm, Sat–Sun 11am–10pm.

Rattenfängerhaus GERMAN   The very name, "Rat-Catcher's House," could kill the most robust appetite, but by the time you've made it as far as this beautiful Dutch Renaissance house from 1603, you'll probably have overcome your musophobia (fear of rats). At any rate, the kitchen is banking on it, dishing up such specials as "Rat Tail Flambe" washed down with Rattenkiller Schnapps. Not to worry—schnitzels and appealing standards are also served in these very pleasant rooms filled with Pied

Piper knickknacks, and coffee and cake are available through much of the day.

Osterstrasse 28. www.rattenfaengerhaus.de. ℂ **05151/3888.** Main courses 8€–22€. Daily 11am–3pm and 6–11pm.

BREMEN ★★

181km (107 miles) N of Hameln

Bremen traces its roots to a fishing village going back to at least the 8th century (Roman historian Ptolemy vaguely, and perhaps inaccurately, refers to a settlement here as far back as A.D. 150). The city is a major port and industrial center and, with nearby Bremerhaven, comprises its own German state. All that's well and good, of course, but anyone who's read the Brothers Grimm also knows that Bremen was the destination of a donkey, dog, cat, and rooster who set out on a journey across the countryside toward this vibrant northern city. In the story, they never made it as far as Bremen, but that doesn't seem to make a difference—the Bremen Town Musicians are treated like honored citizens here. The foursome stands one atop the other in the beautiful Marktplatz, at the center of the Altstadt.

The legendary medieval knight Roland stands guard over Bremen's marketplace.

Nearby rises a statue of the medieval knight and warrior Roland, bearing the "sword of justice" and a shield decorated with an imperial eagle. He was erected in the 15th century (originally in wood) to assert Bremen's trading rights; local legend has it that as long as he stands in the Marktplatz, Bremen will survive as a free city. As you'll soon learn, this combination of whimsy and practicality, of art and commerce, is typical of Bremen.

Essentials

GETTING THERE Bremen Hauptbahnhof lies on major rail lines, with frequent daily trains to and from Hamburg (trip time: 1 hour), Hannover

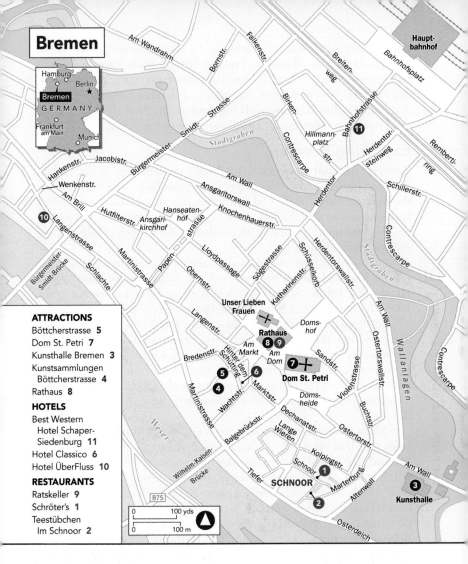

Bremen

Hamburg
Berlin ★
Bremen
G E R M A N Y
Frankfurt
am Main
Munich

Haupt-
bahnhof

Bahnhofsplatz

ATTRACTIONS
Böttcherstrasse **5**
Dom St. Petri **7**
Kunsthalle Bremen **3**
Kunstsammlungen
  Böttcherstrasse **4**
Rathaus **8**

HOTELS
Best Western
  Hotel Schaper-
  Siedenburg **11**
Hotel Classico **6**
Hotel ÜberFluss **10**

RESTAURANTS
Ratskeller **9**
Schröter's **1**
Teestübchen
  Im Schnoor **2**

Unser Lieben
Frauen

Rathaus

Dom St. Petri

SCHNOOR

Kunsthalle

0   100 yds
0   100 m

(1 hour), Berlin (5 hours), and Frankfurt (4 hours and 15 minutes.). For information, go to www.bahn.de or call ✆ **01805/996633.** The train station is one of Germany's few grand, late-19th-century terminals. During World War II, Bremen camouflaged the station by constructing a false park atop it, which apparently fooled Allied bombers—they spared the landmark. Coming from Hameln, the fastest route is via the A27 north and south. The A7 Autobahn runs east and west from Bremen.

VISITOR INFORMATION   Bremen has two central **tourist offices** (www.bremen-tourism.de; ✆ **0421/3080010**), one on the Marktplatz at Langenstrasse 2–4, and the other in the Hauptbahnhof. Hours of the Martplatz office are Monday to Friday 8:30am to 6pm, Saturday 9:30am to 5pm, and Sunday 10am to 4pm. The train station office is open Monday to Friday 9am to 6:30pm, Saturday and Sunday 9:30am to 5:30pm. A 2-hour English-language **walking tour** of the Altstadt departs from the Marktplatz office every Saturday at 3pm; cost is 7.50€.

Exploring Bremen

Bremen's **Altstadt** was encircled by water through most of the Middle Ages and into the early 19th century. The Weser River, which flows along the southern flanks of the Old Town, was channeled into a moat to flow past ramparts around the rest of the city. These defenses are now a park, the **Wallanlagen;** it's laced with ponds and, for a touch of added scenery, a working windmill.

Country folk who once came into the city to sell their goods at the central **Marktplatz** are honored with the **Schweinehirt und seine Herde** (Pig Herder Statue), by local sculptor Peter Lehmann (1921–1995). It's at the foot of **Sögestrasse** (Sow's Street), called that because herders drove their pigs along the lane to the Herdentor, a gate in the city walls, and into the countryside to graze. Look carefully and you'll see a commentary on human nature in the grouping: One shy pig stands close to the herder, one loner remains aloof, two enamored pigs are an inseparable couple, and three gregarious pigs frolic in a group. When arranging a meeting place in Bremen, it's common to "make an appointment with the pigs."

Many of Bremen's great landmarks crowd the **Marktplatz** and the lanes that lead off it. The imposing medieval statue of legendary hero **Roland** (see p. 640) commands attention, standing 5.5 meters (18 feet) tall. Even so, he's a benign presence, with the words "I show you freedom" emblazoned on his shield. During the French occupation, Napoleon was so impressed with the statue that he wanted to have it carted off to the Louvre in Paris. Roland stands in front of two great symbols of Bremen's onetime trading might, the **Rathaus,** with its remarkable façade of gables and statues (see p. 646), and the **Schötting,** the guild house for city merchants. The Schötting's fanciful spires and tall, ornamented windows attest to the wealth that Bremen once possessed as a powerful member of the Hanseatic League. The guild's anthem is proudly displayed on the facade, "Outside and in, risk it and win." That is, you've got to take some chances to make a fortune.

Before following this advice, walk across the square to the bronze statue of the **Bremen Town Musicians** and place your hands on the donkey's knees—it's said to bring good luck. As the Grimms told it, this beloved quartet of old, unwanted farm animals had reached the end of their useful days but made their way toward Bremen, famous city of freedom, to earn their keep as musicians. The statue is by Gerhard Marcks (1889–1981), a proponent of the Bauhaus movement who the Nazis decreed as degenerate.

Another Marktplatz landmark is beneath your feet: What looks like a manhole cover next to the 1960s-era **Haus der Bürgerschaft (State Parliament)** conceals the **Bremer Loch (The Hole of Bremen).** Throw a coin down one of the slots and a Bremen Town musician will bray, bark, meow, or crow in response. The money goes to charity.

BEYOND THE ALTSTADT

Bremen gets especially picturesque in the **Schnoor** quarter, alongside the River Weser at the southeastern edge of the Altstadt. The name comes from "string," *Schnur,* for the rope and cable that neighborhood craftsmen once made in workshops along the narrow alleys. The name could also easily be a reference to the lanes that wind and twist like a piece of string; some are so narrow that it's necessary to walk sideways to pass through them. Neighborhood houses that are usually no more than 55 sq. m (600 square feet) once provided cramped quarters for some of Bremen's poorest residents; they're now the quaint settings for shops and restaurants. To get to the Schnoor, from the southeastern end of the Marktplatz, follow **Balgebrückestrasse.** (This street covers what was

The narrow lanes of the Schnoor neighborhood.

once The Balge, a tributary of the Weser River that was Bremen's medieval harbor.)

East of the Altstadt, **Am Wall** crosses the old ramparts, now the Wallanlagen park. This leafy boulevard is also known as the **Kultur-meile,** or Culture Mile, because lining the broad pavement are such institutions as the **Kunsthalle** (p. 646) and the neoclassical **Theater am Goetheplatz.** Am Wall emerges into the **Viertel,** a slightly Bohemian quarter beloved for its relaxed nightlife and terraced 19th-century houses. Bremen claims these rows of two- and three-story residences with high ceilings are typically Hanseatic, though they might remind you of Chelsea or another London neighborhood. The sensation is reinforced with a walk back toward the Altstadt along the riverside Osterdeich, with more than a whiff of the Chelsea Embankment.

Expressionist wall decoration in Böttcherstrasse.

Böttcherstrasse ★★★ STREET   Bremen's most atmospheric street, the lane of the coopers, or barrel makers, runs between the Marktplatz and the banks of the Weser River and looks like something out of a Nordic fantasy. That's exactly the point. In the 1920s, coffee merchant Ludwig Roselius had the medieval lane knocked down and hired artist Bernhard Hoetger to rebuild the houses in the Brick Expressionist style then popular in Europe, stating "The re-erection of Böttcherstrasse is an attempt to think in a German way." His pro-Nazi views come to the fore in Hoetger's gold relief over the entrance, where Lichtbringer (Bringer of Light) glorifies the victory of "our führer over the powers of darkness." The Führer, however, did not return the compliment; Hitler deemed the curving brick facades "divergent" and "degenerate." Along the short lane, look for **Haus des Glockenspiels** (Glockenspiel House), with its carillon of Meissen bells at noon, 3, and 6pm (see p. 648). Across from the **Kunstsammlungen Böttcherstrasse** (p. 645), a tall house sports an exotic facade that resembles the stern of a galleon; there's even an aquarium imbedded in the lower floor. At the river end of the street stands

Robinson-Crusoe-Haus (Robinson Crusoe House), named for the hero of Daniel Defoe's novel, which begins, "I was born in the year 1632, in the city of York, of a good family, though not of that country, my father being a foreigner of Bremen." Roselius thought the hero who fends for himself so ably when stranded on an island displayed everything that was good about the Bremen character.

Off Marktplatz. www.boettcherstrasse.de. ⓒ **0421/338820.**

Dom St. Petri (St. Peter's Cathedral) ★★ CHURCH

Local tradition dictates that no building in Bremen can rise higher than the city's august cathedral. The city has turned a blind eye to this rule in a few cases, but in one form or another, the church has been a commanding presence on high ground in the Altstadt since 782, when a timber structure was erected. Since then, the church has been built and rebuilt, with craftsmen and architects adding ceiling ribbing, flying buttresses, even some Moorish-looking window frames and column or two. The church also has a long record of misfortune, and 1638 was an especially bad year for the towers—one collapsed entirely, killing eight worshippers, and another was struck by lightning, burned, and crashed into the nave. During all the construction and reconstruction, lead from the roof was stored in a cellar that became known as a *Bleikeller,* or lead basement. It was discovered that bodies left in the chamber remained remarkably well preserved, creating a mummy room where an English countess, two Swedish soldiers, and a murdered student are among the church's most popular attractions. As you enter or leave the church you may see young men, often well dressed, sweeping the steps. It's a tradition that any man who reaches his 30th birthday and is still unmarried come to St. Petri to perform this clean-up duty. He must keep at it until a young woman relieves him of the task with a kiss.

Sandstrasse 10–12. www.stpetridom.de. ⓒ **0421/365040.** Cathedral free; museum and tower 1€ adults, .70€ children, Mon–Fri 10am–5pm; Sat–Sun 2–4pm.

Kunstsammlungen Böttcherstrasse ★★ MUSEUM

Two adjoining houses belonged to the two creators of Böttcherstrasse. The older house, a patrician's townhouse dating to 1588, was owned by Ludwig Roselius, who financed the construction of the street in the 1920s; he filled the house with Northern European art and furnishings from the medieval through baroque periods. The idea was to create the feeling that a 16th-century family was still in residence, and he succeeded with altarpieces, glorious wooden sculptures by Bavarian master carver Tilmann Riemenschneider, and paintings by Lucas Cranach the Elder. Walking though these rooms so rooted in the distant past, it's ironic to note that the Roselius fortune came from a modern commodity: in 1906 Ludwig patented a process for removing caffeine from coffee beans.

14

(Ludwig vowed to add a healthful twist to the business after his coffee importer father died suddenly at age 59, supposedly from drinking too much of his own product.) The house next door was designed by Bernhard Hoetger (1874–1949), the sculptor and architect who created Böttcherstrasse under Roselius' patronage. Like his boss, Hoetger hoped to ingratiate himself with the Nazis, who found his elongated nudes and fantastical animals to be degenerate; some are displayed on the top floors. Most the house is filled with paintings, drawings, and prints of Paula Becker-Modersohn (1876–1907), who lived and worked in Worpswede, a village north of Bremen that has been an artist colony since the late 19th century. Though Becker-Modersohn died young, she is considered a pioneer of modern European art with her imaginative use of color and bold subject matter (she was one of the first women to paint the female nude).

Böttcherstrasse 6–10. www.pmbm.de. ✆ **0421/3365077.** Admission 5€ adults, 3€ children 7–16. Tues–Sun 11am–6pm.

Kunsthalle Bremen ★★ MUSEUM   Bremen's art gallery opened in 1849 and has been expanded many times since. The museum is especially well known for its collection of Impressionist paintings, including several by Max Leibermann (1847–1935). The son of a wealthy banking family, Leibermann used much of his fortune to collect French impressionists. He is known for his portraits of Albert Einstein and other early 20th century celebrities. One of his early works, *The 12-Year-Old Jesus in the Temple With the Scholars* (1879), created a sensation, with one critic commenting that Jesus looked like "the ugliest, most impertinent Jewish boy imaginable." Another Leibermann work, *Riders on a Beach,* was in the news in 2012 when it was found among a trove of paintings confiscated from private collectors by the Nazis. Leibermann earned a solid reputation for his bourgeois subjects rendered in the style of Edouard Manet. His *The Papageienallee* (1902), a scene of promenaders and strollers, hangs in the Kunsthalle galleries among works by Corot, Pissarro, and other Impressionists.

Am Wall 207. www.kunsthalle-bremen.de. ✆ **0421/329-080.** Admission 8€. Tues 10am–9pm, Wed–Sun 10am–5pm.

Rathaus ★★★ LANDMARK   Bremen's 560-year-old Rathaus was built and rebuilt in the early 17th century to suggest might and civic power. The glorious structure on one side of the Marktplatz achieves this effect not with towers and battlements but with glass—a graceful sweep of tall Renaissance windows interspersed with statues of Charlemagne, the electors of the Holy Roman Empire, and ancient philosophers. A medieval hall on the ground floor, supported by massive oak pillars, was once used as a marketplace and theater. Upstairs is the grandest room in

Bremen's ornate gabled Rathaus and cathedral dominate Marktplatz.

town, a **Festival Hall** that is 40m (132 ft.) long and 13m (43 ft.) high. It's the site of the annual Schaffermahl, a banquet for 600 male ship captains and owners that sets up waves of feminist protest every year (the men-only rule was relaxed a few years ago when Chancellor Angela Merkel was invited). The gentlemen dine beneath four colorful ship models that hang from the ceiling as a reminder of the trade that once brought Bremen its enormous wealth. The hall was also used as a courtroom, a function denoted by a huge painting depicting the Judgment of Solomon. Look also for the painting of a ship at sea; walk past it from right to left to enjoy the optical illusion. The Festival Hall reveals another secret in the **Guldenkammer** (Golden Chamber), a room-within-a-room that floats above the main hall, concealed behind wood panels and paintings. In 1905, artist Heinrich Vogeler decorated the intimate chamber in red and gold leather with a riot of bird and flower motifs on the door panels, lampshades, screens, and carpets. The Germans call the effect *gesamtkunstwerk,* basically the fusion of a lot of elements into one pleasing whole, which it is.

Marktplatz. www.rathaus-bremen.de. ⓒ **0421/3610.** Admission 5€ adults, children 11 and under free. For tours, inquire at the tourist office.

Where to Stay in Bremen

Best Western Hotel Schaper-Siedenburg ★   The location between the train station and the Altstadt is certainly convenient, but there's a lot

A Clock with Many Stories to Tell

In the carillon on the façade of the *Haus des Glockenspiels* on Böttcherstrasse (see p. 644), at noon, 3, and 6pm a set of bells strung between two gables send up a chorus of sea shanties, while ten panels revolve for a 15-minute show celebrating the great moments of transportation. While you'll probably recognize **Christopher Columbus,** steamboat inventor **Robert Fulton,** and transatlantic aviator **Charles Lindbergh,** most of the heroes may be unfamiliar. Here's a primer. Eleventh-century Icelandic explorer **Thorfinn Karlsefni** followed Leif Eriksson's route across the Atlantic in an aborted attempted to establish a colony in Newfoundland. German explorer **Hans Pothorst** claimed to have discovered America in 1470, 22 years before an Italian navigator with Spanish employers took all the credit. **Paul König** was a much-lauded captain of a U-boat in World War I. British aviators **John Alcock, George Herbert Scott,** and **Arthur Brown** made the first transatlantic flight, from Newfoundland to County Galway, Ireland, in 1919, while **Hermann Kohl, James Fitzmaurice,** and **Ehrenfried Günther Freiherr von Hünefeld** made the first transatlantic flight from east to west, in 1928. **Hugo Eckener** was the commander of the famous *Graf Zeppelin,* on which he made the first airship flight around the world. Not pictured on the carillon are many other transportation firsts that Bremen has achieved: The paddle steamer *Washington* crossed the Atlantic from New York to Bremerhaven in 1847, inaugurating regular transatlantic steamship service; Bremen aviator Henrich Foche made the first helicopter flight, on June 25, 1936; and in May 1966, Bremen became Germany's first container seaport.

more going for this hotel and an apartment annex just down the street. Rooms are stylishly minimalist, with low-slung wood furnishings, soothing color schemes, and sensible lighting. Many face an interior courtyard that is blissfully quiet in a busy part of town. The marketplace and the historic sections of the Altstadt (Old Town) are an easy walk away.
Bahnhofstrasse 8. www.schaper-siedenburg.de. ✆ **0421/30870;** 800/780-7234 in the U.S. and Canada. 88 units. 106€–120€ double; 120€–158€ apt. Buffet breakfast included. Parking 10€. **Amenities:** Restaurant; bikes; room service; Wi-Fi (free).

Hotel Classico ★★   As if the medieval center of Bremen weren't exotic enough, these rooms are designed to transport guests to other worlds. Nothing is over the top, just subtly playful. The Moulin Rouge room has a hint of Parisian chic with a canopied bed, while the Alexander the Greek is quietly neoclassical. Stylish décor never gets in the way of basic comforts, and among the conveniences is a ground-floor coffee house.
Hinter dem Schütting 1a. www.hotel-classico-bremen.de. ✆ **0421/2440-0867.** 12 units. 89€–99€ double. Parking 15€. Breakfast included. **Amenities:** Cafe; Wi-Fi (free).

Hotel ÜberFluss ★   Can chic design be too much? Every once in while, at this redo of a 19th-century house, a curvaceous chair is just too difficult to get out of—and is one a prude to prefer bathrooms where the walls aren't made of glass? For the most part, though, the aesthetic is a smashing success, with soothing modernist furnishings in neutral-toned surroundings that often afford a glimpse of the River Weser. The sleek, contemporary design comes with a provenance, too: beneath the foundations are the remnants of a city wall from 1184.

Langenstraße 72. www.designhotels.com. ✆ **421/322860.** 51 units. 180€–210€. Breakfast included with some rates. **Amenities:** Restaurant; bar; spa; indoor pool; Wi-Fi (free).

Where to Eat in Bremen

Among Bremen specialties is the *rollo,* a pastry roll filled with meat, cheese, and salad and topped with sauce—a fast-food Germanic cousin to the döner kebab. Another favorite is the Bremen burger, a piece of white fish rolled in breadcrumbs, fried, and served on a roll garnished with mustard and fried onions. Coffee is as popular in Bremen as beer is in other German cities, in keeping with a long tradition: in 1673, Bremen became the first city in German to earn the right to serve coffee in public.

Ratskeller ★ GERMAN/INTERNATIONAL   It only goes to follow that what might be Germany's most famous Rathaus should also have a celebrated Ratskeller. Walk into the paneled and vaulted cellars and order a beer and you're likely to be thrown out on your ear. That's because the wine cellar claims to be one of the largest and best-stocked in Germany, with 1,200 different varieties, including one cask wine dating back to 1653 and a still-drinkable bottled Rüdesheimer Apostkeller from 1727. The culinary offerings are less rare and less refined; best is the informal bistro menu with some local snacks, along the lines of *Bremer Brotzeit vom Brett,* or Bremen Snack from the Wooden Plate, with cheeses and liverwurst, or *Dreierlei vom Hering,* three kinds of grilled herring.

In the Rathaus, Am Markt. www.ratskeller-bremen.de. ✆ **0421/321676.** Main courses 12€–20€. Daily 11am–midnight.

Schröter's ★★ GERMAN/MEDITERRANEAN   The full name is Schröter's Body and Soul, and this Schnoor quarter favorite lives up to the name with good food and plenty of friendly, relaxing ambiance. A warren of rooms winds around a skylit courtyard, combining cool, contemporary chic with old prints and bric-a-brac to supply lots of casual, old world flair. A lunchtime menu keeps things simple with pastas and salads, while in the evening offerings range through many fish and meat dishes and some creatively assembled set-price menus.

Schnoor 13. www.schroeters-schnoor.de. ✆ **0421/326677.** Main courses 12€–22€. Daily noon–11pm.

Teestübchen Im Schnoor ★★★ GERMAN   Look no further for a giant dose of charm than this beautifully restored, high-gabled house in the Schnoor. The four floors connected by a steep, narrow staircase are part tearoom and coffeehouse, with excellent evening meals served as well. Whatever you eat or drink, the polished antiques, old prints, and wonderful uneven walls and floors will remind you of some old Dutch master print. The kitchen, meanwhile, focuses on healthful, local products that appear in hearty stews, flavorful soups, and some creative pastas, along the lines of ravioli filled with beets. Desserts are made fresh daily, and the wine list is as well chosen as the menu and the furnishings.

Wustestatte 1. www.teesteuben-schnoor.de. © **0421/323867.** Main courses 12€–20€. Tues–Sat 10am–10pm, Sun and Mon 10am–6pm.

A Side Trip to Bremerhaven

Only 55km (34 miles) north of Bremen, one of Germany's largest ports lies on the North Sea at the mouth of the Weser River. You'll come here for one compelling reason: to visit the city's fascinating museum of emigration. Trains make the trip from Bremen every 15 minutes; the journey takes 30 minutes. From the Bremerhaven Bahnhof, buses 502, 505, 506, 508, or 509 go to the Havenwelten stop in front of the museum (the bus fare is included in the price of your train ticket).

Bremerhaven's Deutsches Auswanderhaus brings to life the story of German emigration.

Deutsches Auswandererhaus (German Emigration Center) ★★★

MUSEUM   Between 1830 and 1974, more than 7 million Europeans emigrated to the New World from Bremerhaven. Most were German, though many traveled to Bremerhaven from elsewhere in Central and Eastern Europe. Most went to the United States, but also to Canada, Australia, and South America. In Bremerhaven they boarded ships that would take them to new beginnings, away from poverty, wars, and in the 1930s, the Nazi terror. At this museum, a highly imaginative approach brings the experience to life, or at least help us understand what the departures, voyages, and arrival in new lands might have been like. Most fascinating are the reconstructed wharves and ship's quarters. For the three-month transatlantic crossing on an 1854 sailing ship, passengers slept five to a bunk in vermin and flea-infested below-decks dormitories, here they were allotted ½ liter of water a day. Passage had improved considerably by 1887, when the crossing by steamer took just 8 to 15 days, and even more by 1929, when even second- and third-class passengers enjoyed lounges and dining rooms. A research station guides visitors through the process of locating ancestors who passed through Bremerhaven. The museum also pays homage to those who have emigrated to Germany. An arrival that's not noted is that of Elvis Presley, who stepped ashore in Bremerhaven in 1958 along with 1,000 other GIs who were being stationed in Europe.

Columbusstrasse 65. www.dah-bremerhaven.de. © **0471/902200.** Admission 13€ adults, 8.50€ children 4–14. Mar–Oct daily 10am–6pm, Nov–Feb daily 10am–5pm.

HAMBURG
& THE
NORTH

15

Every nation seems to have a north–south divide, and Germany is no exception. Travel up here from even northerly Berlin and you'll notice a difference—the salt-tinged breezes off the North Sea, the distinctive brick-gabled houses favored by Hanseatic merchants and seafarers, a preference for herring and other fish, the long winter nights and long summer days, the palpable presence of Scandinavia. Hamburg is dynamic, energetic, and cosmopolitan, showing off its Hanseatic heritage in atmospheric warehouse districts and a still-thriving port. Lübeck and Lüneburg, meanwhile, preserve the past with their lanes of gabled houses, the realms of merchants who made fortunes off of Lüneburg's salt and Lübeck's trading clout. The island of Sylt is another sort of place altogether, a fragile strip of sand where endless beaches and tidal flats are a cherished getaway.

HAMBURG ★★

285km (177 miles) northwest of Berlin

Hamburg's is a tale of two cities…or three, or four. Germany's second largest city, after Berlin, and Europe's second-largest port, after Rotterdam, Hamburg has so many facets that visitors can step into one fascinating cityscape after another. The copper-roofed tower of old baroque Hauptkirche St. Michael's rises next to glass and steel office buildings. The port, with its wharfs, cranes, dry docks, and a flotilla of ships coming and going day and night, rambles along the banks of the Elbe River as far as the eye can see. A maze of canals laces through Speicherstadt, lined with sturdy brick warehouses where Hamburg merchants once stashed carpets, tea, and the other lucre of trade. These days boldly designed high-rise corporate headquarters—Hamburg is a media capital and industrial center—are the powerhouses of wealth and influence. Elegant 19th-century facades along the shores of the Alster, the shimmering lake at Hamburg's center, and Jugenstil (art nouveau) villas scream bourgeois comforts; smart-phone-toting Armani-clad execs carry on the legacy of the burghers who thrived after Friedrich Barbarossa declared the city a free port in 1193. Then there's Hamburg's underbelly—the infamous

FACING PAGE: **HafenCity, Hamburg's showcase for postmodern architecture.**

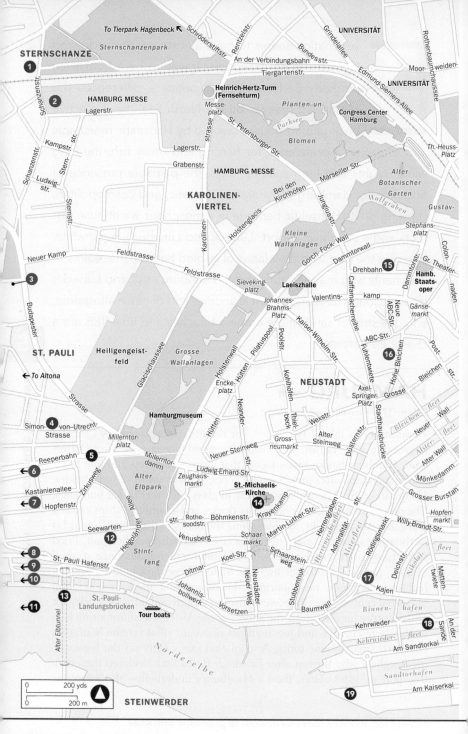

To Tierpark Hagenbeck ↖ Schröderstiftstr.

Rentzelstr.

Schröderstiftstr.

Grindelallee

UNIVERSITÄT

Rothenbaumchaussee

Moor-weiden

STERNSCHANZE

1

An der Verbindungsbahn

Bundesstr.

Edmund-Siemers-Allee

UNIVERSITÄT

Sternschanzenpark

Tiergartenstr.

2

HAMBURG MESSE

Lagerstr.

Heinrich-Hertz-Turm
(Fernsehturm)

Messe-platz

Congress Center
Hamburg

Th.-Heuss-Platz

Schanzenstr.

Messe-strasse

St. Petersburger Str.

Planten un

Parksee

Blomen

Kampstr.

Stern-str.

Lagerstr.

Marseiller Str.

Alter
Botanischer
Garten

Gustav-

Ludwig-str.

Grabenstr.

HAMBURG MESSE

Bei den
Kirchhöfen

Wallgraben

Schanzenstr.

Sternstr.

KAROLINEN-
VIERTEL

Holstenglacis

Jungiusstr.

Stephans-platz

Colon-naden

Gr. Theater

Neuer Kamp

Feldstrasse

Karolinen-

Gorch-Fock-Wall

Dammtorwall

Drehbahn

15

Hamb.
Staats-oper

Budapester

3

Feldstrasse

Sieveking-platz

Laeiszhalle

Valentins-

kamp

Dammtorstr.

Neue
ABC-Str.

Gänse-markt

Caffamacherreihe

ST. PAULI

Heiligengeist-
feld

Glacischaussee

Grosse
Wallanlagen

Johannes-
Brahms-Platz

Kaiser-Wilhelm-Str.

Fuhlentwiete

ABC-Str.

Hohe Bleichen

Bleichen

str.

← To Altona

Strasse

Holstenwall

Pilatuspool

Poolstr.

NEUSTADT

Axel-
Springer-Platz

Grosse

Stadthausbrücke

Bleichen

Neuer

Alster-

fleet

Wall

Alter Wall

Hamburgmuseum

Encke-platz

Hütten

Kohlhöfen

Thiel-beck

Wexstr.

Alter
Steinweg

Düstern-str.

Simon-

4

von-Utrecht-
Strasse

Millerntor-platz

Neander-

Grass-neumarkt

Mönkedamm

Reeperbahn

5

Zirkusweg

Millerntor-damm

Neuer Steinweg

Ludwig-Erhard-Str.

Grosser Burstah

6

Alter
Elbpark

Zeughaus-markt

St.-Michaelis-
Kirche

14

Krayenkamp

Martin-Luther-Str.

Herrengraben

Admiralität-

str.

Rödingsmarkt

Willy-Brandt-Str.

Hopfen-markt

Kastanienallee

7

Hopfenstr.

Heligoländer

Allee

Seewarten-

12

str.

Rothe-soodstr.

Böhmkenstr.

Herrengraben

Alsterfleet

Deichstr.

Nikolai-

fleet

Matten-twiete

Venusberg

Schaar-markt

Schaarstein-weg

8

9

10

St. Pauli Hafenstr.

Stint-fang

Ditmar-

Koel-Str.

Neustädter

Neuer Weg

Stubbenhuk

Baumwall

Kajen

17

Binnen-

hafen

An der

Sande

13

St.-Pauli-
Landungsbrücken

Johannis-
bollwerk

Vörsetzen

11

Alter Elbtunnel

Tour boats

Kehrwieder

Kehrwieder

fleet

18

Am Sandtorkai

Norderelbe

0   200 yds

0   200 m

STEINWERDER

Sandtorhafen

19

Am Kaiserkai

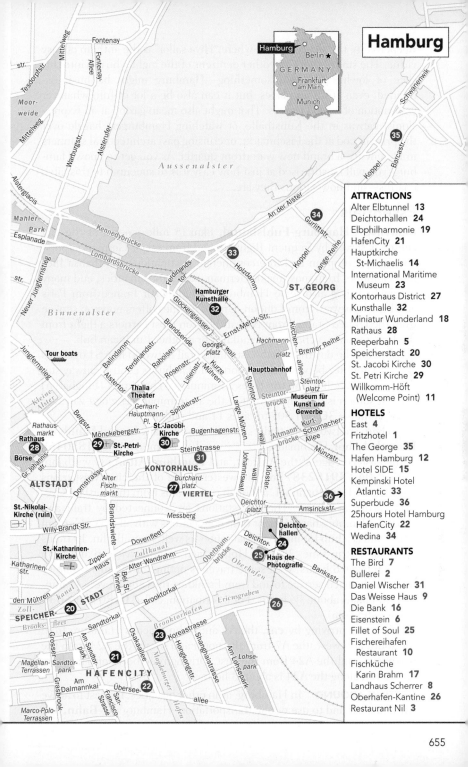

Reeperbahn, the sleazy avenue where "Hiya sailor" is the anthem of easy virtue. The stag partiers and other denizens of the night who dip into this slice of lowlife are onto something—Hamburg might be business-minded, even stuffy in places, but it can also be a lot of fun, whatever your notion of a good time is. That might also mean gazing at an Expressionist canvas in the Kunsthalle, or watching Hamburgers haggle over the price of cod at the Fischmarkt, or cruising past architectural stunners in HafenCity, a brand new waterfront quarter. As you get to know Hamburg, you will be surprised at just how easy it is to succumb to this city's charms—and how various they are.

Essentials

ARRIVING   **Hamburg-Fuhlsbüttel,** 8km (5 miles) north of the city center, is served by frequent flights to and from major German airports and many European and intercontinental destinations. Lufthansa flies into Hamburg from most major German and European cities, and many national carriers also serve Hamburg, including Air France from Paris and British Airways from London. United Airlines offers nonstop service from the United States (from Newark) but on most carriers a flight from the U.S. requires a change in Frankfurt or another European hub.

During the day the S-Bahn (suburban rail network) line S1 operates every 10 minutes between the airport and Hamburg's central railway station, Hauptbahnhof (the trip takes 25 minutes). The airport (Flughafen) S-Bahn station is directly in front of the air terminals. The one-way fare to the center is 3€, or 1.50€ for ages 11 and under.

There are two major **train** stations, the centrally located **Hamburg Hauptbahnhof,** Hachmannplatz 10 (www.bahn.com; © 040/39183046), at the eastern edge of the Altstadt, and **Hamburg-Altona** (www.bahn.com; © 040/39182387) on the western edge of the city. Most trains arrive at the Hauptbahnhof, although some trains from the north of Germany arrive at Altona. The two stations are connected by train and S-Bahn. Hamburg has frequent train connections with all major German cities, and is a hub for international routes as well. From Berlin, 15 trains arrive daily (trip time: 2½ hr.). Hourly high-speed service to and from Munich takes 6 hours, with some travelers opting for the night train (9 hrs.). High-speed service to and from Frankfurt runs about every 45 minutes and takes about 3½ hours. For information, call © **01805/996633** (www.bahn.com).

If you're arriving by **car,** the A1 autobahn reaches Hamburg from the south and west, the A7 from the north and south, the A23 from the northwest, and the A24 from the east. Driving time between Hamburg and Berlin along the A24 is about 3 hours.

GETTING AROUND   In Hamburg, as in other big cities, it's best to arrive without a car and to use public transportation. Hamburg's **U-Bahn,** one of the best subway systems in Germany, connects with the **S-Bahn** surface trains. This combined network is the fastest means of getting around, though buses are also fast and efficient and travel in special lanes throughout the city center. Single tickets for the U-Bahn, S-Bahn, and the bus cost 2.80€ for citywide service and 1.30€ for trips within the center city. A 3-day pass for 1 person costs 17€. Public transport is run by Hamburger Verkehrsverbund (**HVV**), Steinstrasse 12. For information, go to www.hvv.de or call ✆ **040/19449.** Tickets are sold at machines in U-Bahn and S-Bahn stations, on buses, and at railroad ticket counters.

Taxis are available at all hours; call ✆ **040/211211** (www.taxi 11211.de). Taxi meters begin at 2.70€ and charge 1.70€ per kilometer after that.

VISITOR INFORMATION **Tourist-Information,** in the Hauptbahnhof, Kirchenallee exit (www.hamburg-tourism.de; ✆ **040/30051300**), is open Monday to Saturday 8am to 9pm, Sunday 10am to 6pm (phone inquiries are accepted Mon–Sat 9am–7pm). Another office, **Port Information,** near the harbor landing stage in St. Pauli on Landungsbrücken (✆ **040/30051300**), is open April to October daily 8am to 6pm, and November to March daily 10am to 6pm. There is another **tourist office at the airport,** at terminals 1 and 2 (arrivals area), open daily 6am to 11pm.

[Fast FACTS] HAMBURG

Business Hours Most businesses and stores are open Monday to Friday 9am to 6pm and Saturday 9am to 2pm (to 4 or 6pm on the first Sat of the month). Note that most stores are not open on Sunday or in the evenings.

Car Rentals We don't recommend that you rent a car for touring Hamburg, and you can easily reach Lübeck and other outlying towns by train. If you do require a car, you'll find all the major agencies at the airport; see p. 706 for more information on car rentals in Germany.

Consulates The Consulate General of the U.S. is at Alsterufer 27–28 (✆ **040/41171415**); there's also a British Consulate-General at Neuer Jungfernstieg 20 (✆ **040/4480326**).

Doctors & Dentists Ask at the British or American consulates, or go to the large medical center in St. Georg, **Allgemeines Krankenhaus Sankt Georg,** Lohmühlenstrasse 5, 20099 Hamburg (✆ **040/1818850;** U-Bahn: Lohmühlenstrasse), where you'll find an English-speaking staff. If you need a dentist, ask your hotel concierge.

Drugstores Pharmacies that stock foreign drugs include **Roth's Alte Englische Apotheke,** Jungfernstieg 48 (✆ **040/343906;** U-Bahn: Jungfernstieg), open Monday to Friday 8:30am to 8pm and Saturday 9am to 6pm.

Emergencies To call the police, dial ✆ **110;** for an ambulance, an emergency doctor or dentist, or the fire brigade, dial ✆ **112.**

Post Office The post office at the Hauptbahnhof, Hachmannplatz 13, is centrally located. You can make long-distance calls here far more cheaply than at your hotel. It's open Monday to Friday 8am to 8pm, Saturday 8am to 6pm, and Sunday 10am to 4pm. A branch office located at the airport is open Monday to Friday 6:30am to 9pm, Saturday 8am to 6pm, and Sunday 10am to 6pm. For information on either post office, call © **01802/3333.**

Safety   Hamburg, like all big cities of the world, has its share of crime. The major crimes that tourists encounter are pickpocketing and purse/camera snatching. Most robberies occur in the big tourist areas, such as the Reeperbahn and the area around the Hauptbahnhof, which can be dangerous at night.

Toilets   There are decent public facilities in the center of Hamburg, and the Hauptbahnhof has several. Expect to pay about 1€ to use them.

CITY LAYOUT   A couple of things to keep in mind. One, Hamburg is not compact and can't be easily covered on foot; you'll probably have to depend on public transportation or taxis. Two, think water. Hamburg lies on the Elbe River, 109km (68 miles) south of the North Sea, and water seems to be everywhere, from its busy harbor to its central lake (the Alster) to its network of canals. (These canals are commercial and industrial waterways, lined with docks and warehouses; don't fall for the touristic mumbo jumbo that Hamburg is the Venice of the North, because busy, business-minded Hamburg in no way resembles that Italian city.)

The **Alster,** often sparkling with white sails, is divided by bridges into the Binnenalster (Inner Alster) and the larger Aussenalster (Outer Alster). Busy avenues, including the elegant, shop-lined Ballindamm, flank the Binnenalster, as do such noteworthy landmarks as the Colonnaden, an arcade of shops and cafes, and the Hamburgische Staatsoper, the opera house.

The **Altstadt (Old Town)** is south of the Binnenalster, tucked between the lakeshore and the Elbe River waterfront. The Hauptbahnhof is on the eastern fringe of the Altstadt, and the Rathaus, the Renaissance-style city hall, and adjacent Rathausmarkt are on the western edge. Two major shopping streets run between the Hauptbahnhof and the Rathausmarkt, the

Boat tours are a great way to explore sprawling, canal-laced Hamburg.

Spitalerstrasse (a pedestrian mall) and Mönckebergstrasse, paralleling it to the south.

A new district, **HafenCity,** is growing up south of the Altstadt in former docklands that extend 3km (2 miles) along the Elbe River. At the moment much of HafenCity looks like a forest of cranes rising above construction sites, but it's predicted that by 2020 or so a concert hall, bars, slick office buildings, and hundreds of waterfront apartments will have transformed the docklands into the city's new pride and joy.

St. Pauli, west of the Altstadt, is the Hamburg's famous red light district, where shops and clubs line the lurid Reeperbahn, a street where sex is sold over-the-counter, not under.

The Neighborhoods in Brief
CENTRAL HAMBURG

Hamburg's commercial and shopping districts are on the southernmost shores of the **Alster** (the lake at the city center) and in the **Altstadt** (Old City), around the Rathaus (City Hall). Don't look for a lot of historic charm—World War II laid waste to much of it. Notable survivors include the 1920s-era Kontorhaus District (p. 661), Europe's first dedicated office precinct, and such medieval landmarks as St. Petri Church with its skyline-piercing dome. **St. Georg,** an inner city neighborhood running alongside the lake just north of the Hauptbanhof, is one of many old quarters that have been gentrified in recent years. Parts are still a bit dodgy, but leafy streets near the lake, especially the Langhe Reihe, are lined with cafes and restaurants, some catering to gays. Some of the city's most character-filled hotels are in this old neighborhood.

THE WATERFRONT

The Port of Hamburg is the world's fifth-largest harbor, stretching for nearly 40km (25 miles) along the Elbe River. Hamburg has been one of the busiest centers of trade on the Continent for almost ten centuries. **Speicherstadt** (see p. 668), where distinctive red-brick warehouses line canals, is a reminder of this long history. **HafenCity** (see p. 665), Europe's largest inner-city urban development project, extends for 3km (2 miles) along the Elbe River.

ST. PAULI

Hamburg's infamous nightlife and red-light district centers on the neon-lit **Reeperbahn** (p. 666), offering all sorts of pleasures—cafes, sex shows, bars, dance clubs, and music halls. This maritime quarter is a lot less raucous than it once was; these days many habitues are more intent on drinking and dancing than paying for companionship.

ALTONA

Once populated mainly by Jews and Portuguese, this western district is the scene of some great dining and nightlife, as well as the historic **Altona Fischmarkt.**

AROUND THE LAKE

Many villas dating from the 1800s and some stunning *Jugendstil* buildings line the tree-filled streets around the Aussenalster. A particularly attractive lakeside enclave is **Harvestude,** a 19th-century enclave of wealthy burghers; their villas are now occupied by many foreign consulates.

Exploring Hamburg

Hamburg is large and spread out, but geography won't put a damper on your sightseeing. Much of what you'll want to see is in or near the central city, and even if a cold wind off the Baltic Sea deters you from walking it's easy to get around town on the U-Bahn or bus.

Hamburg has far fewer landmarks and stellar museums than Berlin or Munich do. You can probably tick everything off your list in one full day. Even if your appreciation of art is on the low side, you'll want to step into the **Kunsthalle** (p. 662), at least to see the weird creations of the German Expressionists. The façade of the over-the-the-top neo-Renaissance-style **Rathaus** (p. 663) is a must-see, and so is **Hauptkirche St-Michaelis** (p. 661), where you should make the ascent to the dome for a view over the far-flung metropolis at your feet.

The real attraction is the city itself. You can't leave town without catching a glimpse of the Alster, the lake in the city center, and you'll want to see the port—best viewed from the deck of a tour boat (p. 669). Neighborhoods to stroll around are the **Altstadt** with its adjacent lakeside shopping quarter and **Kontorhaus District;** waterside **Speicherstadt,** with its 19th-century warehouses; and **HafenCity,** an emerging quarter where some of the world's leading architects are in a contest to see who can create the most stunning glass tower. Then there's **St. Pauli**—whether you come to this red-light district dedicated to debauchery to partake or observe, you'll never think of Germany as uptight and strictly businesslike again.

IN & AROUND THE ALTSTADT

Deichtorhallen ★★ MUSEUM Two steel-and-glass halls, built as markets between 1911 and 1914, comprise one of Europe's major exhibition spaces for photography and contemporary art. Changing exhibitions have shown the paintings of Andy Warhol, sculptures of Louise Bourgeois, and the fashion photography of Sarah Moon. A collection of fashion and art photography is on permanent view.

Deichtorstrasse 1-2. www.deichtorhallen.de. ✆ **040/321030.** Admission 10€; 5€ Tues after 4pm. Tues–Sun 11am–6pm. U-Bahn: Steinstrasse.

Hauptkirche St-Michaelis ★ CHURCH Anyone stepping into the largest church in Hamburg learns immediately that it's best to leave temptation outside the door: Above the main portal looms a vivid bronze statue of a determined-looking Archangel Michael standing astride the devil, into whose back he is preparing to plunge a lance. Safely past that, you'll want to soak in the sumptuous baroque interior, admire the pipe organs (maybe in play if you come for a morning service or evensong), pay homage at the tombs of esteemed Hamburgers in the huge crypt, and admire the marble font where Johannes Brahms was baptized in 1833. But save your energy for the climb up the 449 steps of the twisting, narrow staircase (there's an elevator as well) for a sweeping view of Hamburg from the top of the copper-roofed tower. The tower has been a beacon for ships sailing up the Elbe since 1669, though it's disappeared from the skyline several times: The ill-fated church was destroyed by a lightning strike in 1750, burned to the ground in 1906, and reduced to rubble.

Michaeliskirchplatz, Krayenkamp 4C. www.st-michaelis.de. ✆ **040/376780.** Free admission. Daily 8am–6pm. U-Bahn: Rodginsmarkt or St. Pauli.

Kontorhaus District ★★★ NEIGHBORHOOD Europe's first dedicated office district was built in the 1920s and 1930s to house the headquarters of trading companies. The ensemble of ten-story, dark-brick office buildings has become an icon of what's known as Brick Expressionism. Most famous of them is Chilehaus, with a sweeping, hand-worked façade of 4.8

The dramatic profile of Chilehaus, among the most impressive buildings of the Kontorhaus District.

million bricks that narrows to a point that, not by accident, resembles the prow of a ship. Original owner Henry B. Sloman made his fortune importing saltpeter from Chile—hence the name. Chilehaus and the adjoining **Sprinkrnhof, Messberghof,** and **Mohlenhof** buildings are built around large, airy courtyards. Even in their bold functionality, they suggest a more gracious era of office life, with handsomely tiled entranceways and spiral staircases. Also standard are the paternosters, elevators in which small open compartments travel slowly in a continuous loop and passengers jump on and off at the desired floors. Safe? Maybe not, but the contraptions are much beloved, and protected, like the entire district, as part of a UNESCO World Heritage Site.

Between Steinstrasse and Klingberg. Foyers and courtyards usually open during business hours. U-Bahn: Messberg.

Kunsthalle ★★★ MUSEUM   A walk through the bright, handsome galleries of one of Germany's outstanding art museums provides a head-spinning look at Western masterpieces. For many Hamburgers, pride of place in the two buildings belongs to the **Bertram altarpiece,** painted for the St. Petri Church in 1379. Its 24 scenes depict the history of humankind as told in the Bible, from creation to the flight into Egypt. Look for some sardonic touches, like the little fox chewing the neck of the lamb next to it, a sad comment perhaps on the fate of the meek. Continue through the Canalettos, Rembrandts, Holbeins, and other old masters to German Romanticism. Among these works is *Wanderer Above the Sea of Fog* by **Caspar David Friedrich** (1774–1840), who often portrayed individuals being rendered insignificant by the landscapes around them He enjoyed a spate of popularity in his lifetime but died in obscurity, was embraced by Impressionists and Expressionists, then forgotten again in the postwar years, partly because his landscapes were a favorite of the Nazis. Hamburg Kuntshalle is one of several German museums responsible for reviving his image. Here you can also see what might be his most striking painting, *The Sea of Ice,* in which jagged shapes seem to advance then recede on the surface of light-infused canvas. His *Waft of Mist* was stolen from a train in 1994 and later returned to the gallery.

A new wing by the late O. M. Ungers, who designed modern museums throughout Germany, houses the **Galerie der Gegenwart** (Art of the Present), with an impressive collection of canvases by Picasso, Warhol, Beuys, Munch, Kandinsky, Klee, Hockney, and many contemporary artists currently making waves in the art world. Among them are installation artist Rebecca Horn, photorealist Gerhardt Richter, and conceptualist Jenny Holzer. A large showing of **German Expressionism** is a credit to the museum's effort to rebuild a collection of art that was banned as "degenerate" and often destroyed by the Nazis.

Glockengiesser Wall. www.hamburger-kunsthalle.de. ✆ **040/428131200.** Admission 12€ adults, 6€ children 4–12, children 3 and under free, 18€ family ticket. Tues–Sun 10am–6pm (Thurs until 9pm). U-Bahn: Hauptbahnhof.

Rathaus ★ LANDMARK   It's new by German standards—late 19th century—but the neo-Renaissance City Hall with 647 rooms makes quite an impression nonetheless, a sandstone testimony to Hamburg's wealth and importance. The 49m (161-ft.) clock tower looms high above the Rathausmarkt and the Alster Fleet, the city's largest canal. Tours through grandiose state rooms embellished with tapestries and glittering chandeliers are given hourly, but this pile is just as satisfyingly admired from the outside—unless you are detail-oriented and might enjoy hearing about the 3,780 pinewood piles upon which the block-long structure rests or the 8,605 souls who perished in the 1897 cholera epidemic and are commemorated by a gurgling fountain. The 16th-century **Börse** (Stock Exchange), Adolphsplatz 1 (✆ **040/361-3020**), stands back to back with the Rathaus; guides conduct free tours (in German) of the Börse on Tuesday and Thursday at 11am and noon. Should this brush with capitalism inspire you to disperse some of your own wealth, cross the Alster Fleet to the **Alsterarkaden,** an arched passageway lined with fashionable clothing and jewelry shops.
Rathausplatz. ✆ **040/428310.** Rathaus tours 3€. Mon–Fri 10am–3pm and Sat–Sun 10am–1pm (no tours during official functions). U-Bahn: Rathausmarkt.

St. Jacobi Kirche ★ CHURCH   A few remaining medieval altars and sculptures evoke the 14th-century founding of this church, dedicated to the apostle James, although most of the Gothic exterior is a 1950s reconstruction. Germany's premier organ manufacturer Arp Schnitger, who made instruments for Johan Sebastian Bach, crafted the massive **pipe organ** with 4,000 pipes in 1693. It's the largest remaining single instrument from the 16th and 17th centuries, when Hamburg was a center for organ-building. Church elders had the foresight to stash the pipes away for safekeeping during World War II, when the church was leveled. To hear the sonorous sounds you may attend Sunday services or, better yet, stop in at noon on Thursdays to enjoy a free concert.
Jakobikirchhof 22, with an entrance on Steinstrasse. www.jacobus.de. ✆ **040/3037370.** Free admission. Mon–Sat 10am–5pm. U-Bahn: Mönckebergstrasse.

St. Petri Kirche ★ CHURCH   Hamburg's favorite church deserves a quick stop just because it's so venerable, founded in 1192 and in continuous use since. The lion-head knocker on the main door dates from 1342, making it the oldest piece of art in Hamburg, though little else in the church can claim similarly notable provenance or artistic merit. One other illuminating work is a painting on a column in the south part of the nave, *Christmas in 1813 in St. Peter's.* It shows Napoleon's troops locking citizens inside the church to let them starve, an act of revenge carried out after the town collectively refused to provide their occupiers with food. The troops stabled their horses in the 16th-century church tower, leaving it in such bad shape that it had to be torn down before it collapsed. The present church itself dates from the mid-19th century, after the earlier structure was razed by a fire. World War II bombers attempted many times to repeat that destruction, but they failed—making St. Peter's one of old Hamburg's proud survivors. The best time to visit is Wednesday afternoon at 5:15, when the organ pumps out a *Stunde der Kirchenmusik* (Hour of Church Music); admission is free.

Speersort 10. www.sankt-petri.de. © **040/3257400.** Free admission. Mon–Fri 10am–6pm, Sat 10am–5pm, Sun 9am–9pm. U-Bahn: Rathausmarkt.

ALONG THE WATERFRONT

Ever since the emperor Friedrich Barbarossa issued an edict granting free-trading privileges to Hamburg in 1189, the city has earned fame and riches from its busy harbor, one of the largest in the world. Hamburg commemorates Friedrich's gesture in early May every year with three days of windjammer parades, fireworks, and other celebrations.

These days most of the maritime activity takes place in a vast swath of riverside docks and warehouses just southwest of the city, where the Elbe splits into two arms as it nears the North Sea. The only real way to see the docklands is on a harbor cruise that departs from the city's main passenger landing stage, **St. Pauli-Landungsbrücken** (see "Organized Tours," p. 669).

Don't, however, board the 19th-century clipper ship ***Rickmer Rickmers*** and expect to get anywhere; docked just east of the landing at Pier 1, the magnificent vessel is now a museum of maritime history (© **040/319-5959;** daily 10am–5:30pm; 3€ for adults, 2.50€ for children ages 4–12).

Alter Elbtunnel (Old Elbe Tunnel) ★ LANDMARK Had you been visiting Hamburg a century ago, first stop on the tour itinerary would have been this engineering marvel, a 1,398-ft-long passageway beneath the Elbe River that connects St-Pauli with shipyards in Steinwerder on the opposite bank. The now-historic passage still provides a memorable way to get from one bank to the other, with huge elevators providing access to and from the 24-meter (80-ft) depths. One tunnel facilitates car traffic, the other bicyclists and pedestrians. Walking is best, as a trip along the glazed-tile passage is enlivened with terracotta tiles depicting maritime creatures found in the Elbe, with rats and old boots appearing alongside fish and crabs.

North entrance off St-Paul Hafenstrasse. www.hamburg-port-authority.de. Free for cyclists and pedestrians, open 24 hrs. Car traffic 2€; one-way only from St-Pauli to Steinwerder, Mon–Fri 9am–1pm; from Steinwerder to St-Pauli, 1pm–6pm. U-Bahn: Landungsbrücken.

Elbphilharmonie ★★★ PERFORMING ARTS VENUE Hamburg's newest landmark is this soaring, dramatic glass tower that rises out of the waters of the Elbe River like a phantom ship. Opening in January 2017,

Hamburg's newest landmark, the dramatic Elbphilharmonie concert hall.

the glassed-in symphony space is built atop a 1960s-era bunker-like warehouse, Kaispeicher A, once used to store cocoa, tea, and tobacco. The complex creates a dramatic interplay between the low waterside warehouse, which now houses parking, studios, shops, and restaurants, and the glistening tower perched on top, with two concert halls, apartments, and a hotel. A long moving sidewalk transports visitors through the lower warehouse in an illuminated, tunnel-like tube to a vast plaza and viewing platform 50 meters (122 ft.) above the city. The NDR Symphony Orchestra under the musical direction of Thomas Hengelbrock is the Orchestra in Residence.

Dammtorwall 46. www.elbphilharmonie.de. © **040/357-6660.** U-Bahn: Baumwall.

HafenCity ★★ NEIGHBORHOOD More than 400 acres of former docklands along the River Elbe are being transformed under Germany's largest urban renewal project since the postwar era. Eventually this will increase the size of the inner city by almost half and double the amount of housing in Hamburg. While it's estimated that it will be at least several more years before finishing touches are put on the streets, plazas, and riverside promenades, some stunning glass towers are already transforming the skyline. Check out the shiplike **Unilever** building at Strandkai 1, and the undulating glass **Elbphilharmonie,** the new philharmonic hall (see p. 683). You can learn about the district's former importance as Sandtorkal, the world's most modern port in the late 19th century, and more at the **HafenCity InfoCenter.**

InfoCenter, Sandtorkai 30. www.hafencity.de. ℂ **040/3690-1799.** Open Tues–Sun 10am– 6pm (May–Sept until 8pm). U-Bahn: U3 Baumwall, Bus: 3 or 6.

International Maritime Museum ★ MUSEUM   In a tribute to Hamburg's longstanding relationship with the sea, ten floors of a formidable old red-brick neo-Gothic warehouse near the waterfront in Hafen-City are stacked chockablock with all things nautical. The vast spaces are literally crammed with memorabilia, and eclectic holdings run the gamut from a 3,000-year-old dugout unearthed on the banks of the Elbe to 47 letters by Lord Horatio Nelson, hero of the Battle of Trafalgar. If the 15,000 menus from ocean liners seem overwhelming, wait until you get to the top floor and come across the 26,000 model ships, stacked tightly side by side in row after row of glass cases, as if moored in the world's most impossibly crowded harbor.

Koreastrasse 1. www.internationales-maritimes-museum.de. ℂ **040/30093300.** Admission 13€, 15€–25€ families. Tues–Sun 10am–6pm. U-Bahn: Überseequartier.

Miniatur Wunderland ★ MUSEUM   Everything is cut down to size in this fantasyland. Wunderland bills itself as the world's largest model railway, but it's a lot more than Lilliputian trains chugging through snowy Alpine peaks—even though there are plenty of such charming scenarios, with 900 trains and a total of 12,000 cars traveling through landscapes from Scandinavian forests to American deserts. Planes descend from the sky and make a smooth landing at Hamburg airport, trucks roar down highways, and fire trucks and police cars race through city streets. Even the miniaturized human activity is fascinating to witness: body builders lift weights, prostitutes stand alluringly in windows, and pop-concertgoers light up cigarettes, making Wunderland one of the few public places in Hamburg where smoking is tolerated.

Kehrwieder 2. www.miniatur-wunderland.de. ℂ **040/3006800.** Admission 12€ adults, 6€ children. Sun 8:30am–6pm, Mon–Fri 9:30am–9pm, Sat 8am–9pm. U-Bahn: Baumwell.

Reeperbahn ★★ NEIGHBORHOOD   The St. Pauli district, just east of the center, is where it all hangs out in Hamburg. St. Pauli's midsection—the "genital zone," as it's sometimes called—is the district's main drag, the Reeperbahn, a 1km (1/2-mile) thoroughfare whose name literally translates as "rope street." This is a reference to the massive amounts of hempen rope produced here during the 18th and 19th centuries for ships in Germany's biggest harbor. Hamburg's first theater opened on the Reeperbahn in 1842, and from there it was all downhill into any manner of licentiousness. By the 1860s, the question, "Whatcha doing, sailor?" became the unofficial motto of an army of prostitutes who set up shop (with the legal sanction of municipal authorities) in the

The world's largest model railway, Miniatur Wunderland.

district. These days, by mid-evening the bars and theaters (legitimate and otherwise) are roaring away and you'll find thousands of women and men in drag, strutting their stuff along the turf. German enterprise has honored these women (and their reputation for a good time) by naming one of Hamburg's native beers in their honor—the famous "St. Pauli Girl."

The most exclusive and expensive area is **Herbertstrasse,** where women display their charms to window-shoppers from behind plate-glass. By city ordinance, this street is open only to men 19 and over (women are officially banned, but this does not seem to be enforced). Less expensive rents can be found on the streets near Herbertstrasse: Gunterstrasse, Erichstrasse, Friedrichstrasse, Davidstrasse, and Gerhardstrasse. If it's erotic theater you're looking for, you'll have to move a few blocks away to **Grosse Freiheit,** a street whose name appropriately translates as "Great Freedom." Any act of sexual expression, with every conceivable permutation, except those that involve animals (bestiality is one of the few things expressly forbidden), is shown in these theaters. Be it joyful, be it disgusting, it's all here, often performed by artists who can barely conceal their boredom.

U-Bahn: St. Pauli; S-Bahn: Reeperbahn.

The "city of warehouses," Speicherstadt.

Speicherstadt ★★★ NEIGHBORHOOD　It was economics, not aesthetics, that inspired what is now one of Hamburg's most intriguing and hauntingly beautiful districts. In the late 19th century German customs law limited the area of the city from which merchants could process, store, and ship wares free of duties. So, a massive district of gabled and turreted brick warehouses, laced with canals, was constructed on heavy oak pilings along a network of canals; more than 16,000 residents were removed from centuries-old neighborhoods to make way for this building spree. All told, the "city of warehouses" comprises more than a million square feet of storage lofts. Ships dropped anchor alongside loading docks, to and from which goods were lifted with giant hoists. Large windows and vents ensured that air circulated to provide a stable climate suitable for storing coffee, cocoa, spices, linen, wool, and other perishable items. Modern container ports on the Hamburg outskirts now render Speicherstadt a quaint relic from the past; these historic warehouses now contain museums, shops, restaurants, and offices. (Changeable tides and frequent flooding renders the neighborhood unsuitable for housing.) The neighborhood is especially magical at night, when the warehouses and bridges are illuminated and their reflections shimmer in the canal waters.
Between Deichtorhallen and Baumwall. U-Bahn: Baumwall.

Willkomm-Höft (Welcome Point) ★ LANDMARK   If you're feeling especially nautical, you can join the cadre of old salts who regularly make the half-hour trip to outlying Wedel. Each day more than 50 arriving and 50 departing ships pass a maritime station that stands on the tip of the peninsula, off which crews first catch sight of the cranes and slipways of the Port of Hamburg. From sunrise to sunset (8am–8pm in summer) arriving ships are greeted with the national anthem of the country where the vessel is registered (the station has recordings of 150 anthems). The stationmaster lowers the Hamburg flag in salute, and the passing ship dips its flag in response. He also keeps a data bank on world shipping and makes a fact-filled announcement that, provided you understand German, tells you the age, weight, ownership, and everything else you might want to know about a ship. While in Wedel, you might want to step into **Schulauer Fährhaus,** a popular waterside stop for a seafood lunch or dinner (Parnastrasse 29, www.schulauer-faehrhaus.de; ✆ 04103/92000; open daily 11am to midnight). In the nearby **Buddelschiff-Museum** (www.buddel.de; ✆ 04103/920016), more than 200 little vessels are carefully preserved in bottles. The museum is open Monday to Friday 10am to 6pm and Saturday 10am to 2pm. Admission is 3€ for adults and free for children.

S-Bahn to Wedel-Schulau; the point is a 15-min walk from the stop.

Organized Tours

Guided tours are a good way to see spread-out Hamburg, and plenty of operators are on hand to show you around. To get a sense of the lay of the land and see the far-flung landmarks and neighborhoods, hop on one of the red double-decker buses operated by **Hamburger Stadtrundfahrten** (www.top-tour-hamburg.de; ✆ 040/6413731) that leave from the main train station, Kirchenallee entrance, every 30 minutes from 7:30 a.m. to 5 p.m. (hourly in winter). The bus makes 28 stops in a 90-minute circuit; tickets good for the day cost 17.50€ for adults, 15€ for children 14 and under.

For a look at Hamburg's port, a fascinating hubbub of maritime activity, climb aboard one of the pleasure craft operated by **HADAG Seetouristik und Fährdienst AG,** Bei den St. Pauli, Fischmarkt 28

The World's Oldest Profession

Hamburg's official line is that the Reeperbahn is the city's second-greatest attraction and asset (after the port). Every officially sanctioned working girl must submit to a medical examination every 2 weeks—and pay income tax on her profits. The district's police station, Davidwache, at the corner of Davidstrasse and the Reeperbahn, provides highly visible and omnipresent police protection. No amount of police presence is going to protect you from paying exorbitant prices for watered-down cocktails or astronomical cover charges, however; a little common sense will help you enjoy a walk on the wild side without losing your shirt.

15

A Bit of Beatlemania

John Lennon once said, "I was born in Liverpool, but I grew up in Hamburg." As Beatles fans know, the group got its start here in the early 1960s, when they played gigs at a string of sleazy St Pauli clubs. When the group returned to Liverpool in 1960 they were billed as "The Beatles: Direct from Hamburg." They soon returned to Germany and introduced such hits as "Love Me Do" in St. Pauli clubs. Though a museum to the Fab Four has been shuttered, the city has not lost interest in the sensation it nurtured. A corner on the Reeperbahn has been designated "Beatles-Platz," where effigies of the five are enshrined in glass (the fifth wheel is bassist Stuart Sutcliffe, who left the group to study art and died of a cerebral aneurism soon afterward). The boys stand in the middle of a circle of paving stones blackened to look like a vinyl record.

(www.hadag.de; © **040/3117070**). The 75-minute tours, in German and English, depart the Landungsbrücken, Pier 3, in St. Pauli at hourly intervals every day April to September 10:30am to 4:30pm, and from October to March 11am to 3:30pm. The fare is 17€ for adults, 8€ for children 13 and under, and 25€ for a family ticket.

Relaxing, but a lot less colorful, are boat tours of the Inner and Outer Alster operated by **ATG-Alster-Touristik,** Am Anleger Jungfernstieg (www.alstertouristik.de; © **040/3574240**). In good weather departures are daily about every 30 minutes from 10am to 6pm, with trips lasting 50 minutes—just about the right amount of time to get your fill of pleasant vistas of the tree-lined shores, church spires, and sailing boats. November to March, tours depart daily at 10:30am, noon, 1:30, and 3pm. Boats leave from the Jungfernstieg quayside (U-Bahn: Jungfernstieg). Trips cost 15€ for adults and 7€ for children 15 and under.

Parks and Gardens

The Alster ★★ Top spot for a jog or power walk is the pedestrian walkway around this lake in the city center. It's about 7km (4 miles) all the way around, but you can do a shorter circuit around the smaller, inner lake, the Binnenalster, in about 1.5km (1 mile). On a nice day you can also take to the waters of the outer lake, the Aussenalster. **H. Pieper** (www.segelschule-pieper.de; © **040/247578**), a boathouse just off Kennedybrucke in front of the Atlantic Kempinski Hotel, rents rowboats, paddle boats, and one-occupant sailing dinghies; prices begin at 15€ to 22€ per hour. This outfitter is open April to late September, daily 10am to 8pm.

Oevelgönne ★ Hamburg sports a beach life, in a matter of speaking, in this sandy stretch along the Elbe River west of the city. On a warm

Walrus swim-by at Tierpark Hagenbeck.

summer day it can seem like most of the population has come out to lie in the sun and splash in the river waters. Even on chilly days a popular outing is to stroll along the banks munching on a wurst from the Strandperle, an old beach kiosk. Passing ships present ongoing entertainment, and another attraction is the Alter Schwede (the Old Swede)—not a grizzled beachcomber (though you'll see those too) but a 220-ton boulder dredged out of the shipping lanes. It's believed to have migrated south during the European Ice Age some 20,000 years ago.

Tierpark Hagenbeck ★★　Hamburg's **zoo,** 5km (3 miles) northwest of the city center, is home to some 2,500 animals, but the flora here is just as appealing as the fauna. The Nepalese temple and Japanese garden are especially transporting, as are the animal enclosures themselves—the Tierpark was the first zoo in the world to recreate environments similar to the creatures' habitats in the wild, separated from onlookers by pools and moats. These have been shored up a bit since 1956, when in one of the biggest "zoo breaks" in history 45 rhesus monkeys escaped from their quarters and ran wild through the streets of Hamburg. There's an adjacent tropical aquarium as well.

Hagenbeckallee at Steilingen. www.hagenbeck.de. ✆ **040/5300330.** Admission 20€ adults, 15€ children 4–16, children 3 and under free, 60€ family ticket. Parking 2.50€. Mar–Oct daily 9am–5pm (closes later in nice weather); Nov–Feb daily 9am–4:30pm. U-Bahn: Hagenbeck's Tierpark.

Wallringpark ★★   While Hamburg has no shortage of greenery, the most beautiful stretches are these four adjacent, meticulously maintained parks and gardens west of the Altstadt and Alster Lake. **Planten und Blomen** (Plants and Flowers), laid out in 1936, contains the largest Japanese garden in Europe, with rock gardens, flowering plants, miniature trees, and winding pathways. The **Alter Botanischer Garten** (Old Botanical Garden), south of Planten and Blomen, nurtures rare plant specimens in greenhouses bursting with tropical flora. The **Kleine** (small) and **Grosse** (large) **Wallanlagen** parks are geared to recreation, with a roller-skating rink, playgrounds, and an ice-skating rink in winter. You can chug through the quartet on a miniature railway and cap off a summertime visit with an evening concert in in the Planten und Bloomen, where colorfully illuminated fountains keep time to classical and pop music; daily from June to August at 10pm.

Where to Stay in Hamburg

You'll probably want to stay near the center of this far-flung metropolis—choice locales are the central city in the Altstadt and around the Alster, and near the waterfront, around the port and St. Pauli. A hotel in any of these spots will put you within easy reach of sights, restaurants, and nightlife. If you need a room last minute, stop by **Hamburg's Tourismus Centrale** (Tourist Information Office) in the Hauptbahnhof (www.hamburg-tourism.de; © **040/30051300**), where a counter can book accommodations. There's a fee of 5€ per reservation. You can use this agency on a last-minute basis, but no more than 7 days in advance of the time you'll need the room. Hotel-booking desks can also be found at the airport in Arrival Hall A.

THE CENTRAL CITY
Expensive
Hotel SIDE ★   Offbeat and postmodern, built around an elliptical atrium, this design statement in steel and glass puts you right in the heart of Hamburg while giving you a break from the typical chain hotel circuit. Neutral-toned bedrooms are not only airy and stylish but also extremely comfortable, with lots of surfaces and places to tuck clutter away, plus commodious, snazzy bathrooms embellished with glass sinks and big windows. Suites float above the city in special glass-enclosed quarters cantilevered above the main structure.

Drehbahn 49. www.side-hamburg.de. © **040/309990.** 178 units. 150€–300€ double. Buffet breakfast included. Parking 30€. **Amenities:** Restaurant; bar; exercise room; indoor pool; room service; spa; Wi-Fi (free). U-Bahn: Gänsemarkt or Stephansplatz.

Kempinski Hotel Atlantic ★★   Madonna, Mick Jagger, Elton John, and a long roster of other notables stay here when in town, as do savvy travelers who feel at home in the surprisingly cozy lounges, sophisticated art deco bar, and guest rooms well stuffed with comfy arm chairs and

The courtyard of the Hotel Atlantic.

plump bedding. No doubt they all enjoy the sweeping staircases, lake views, indoor pool, meticulous service, and atmosphere that is a lot more laid-back than you'd expect from such regal surroundings. With a little internet sleuthing you can book one of the commodious, high-ceilinged guest rooms for not much more than what you'd pay for a business-oriented hotel in Hamburg.

An der Alster 72–79. www.kempinski.atlantic.de. © **040/28880.** 252 units. 179€– 400€ double. Buffet breakfast included. Parking 32€. U-Bahn: Hauptbahnhof. 2 restaurants; bar; bikes; concierge; exercise room; indoor pool; room service; spa; Wi-Fi (free).

Moderate

The George ★★   A handsome library and some other clubby touches play off the English-sounding name, but for the most part these lodgings at the edge of the St. Georg neighborhood give off a chic, contemporary vibe. More than half of the handsome guest rooms open to balconies, as do most of the corner suites. In all, dark carpeting, subdued lighting, and sleek furnishings enhanced with rich fabrics ensure a nice refuge from the busy city. Especially relaxing are the friendly, ground-floor Ciao bar and the top-floor spa and sauna, where a lounge and terrace overlook the Alster.

Barcastrasse 3. www.thegeorge-hotel.de. © **040/2800300.** 125 units. 155€–216€ double. Buffet breakfast included. Parking 16€. **Amenities:** Restaurant; bar; bikes; concierge; health club and spa; room service; Wi-Fi (free). U-Bahn: Uhlandstrasse

Wedina ★★★   You can chose from a lot of options at this stylish and low-key retreat near the shores of the Alster: a choice of pillows and bedding, the style of decor (traditional or soothing minimalist), which of four buildings you prefer (from a 19th-century villa to a sleek concrete-and-glass modern annex), even where you want to enjoy breakfast—in a conservatory overlooking a lovely Italianate garden or, in good weather, the garden itself. Many famous writers like to lay low in these soothing surroundings while in Hamburg on book tours; autographed copies of many modern masterpieces are proudly on display in the library.

Gurlittstrasse 23. www.wedina.de. © **040/2808900.** 59 units. 118€–170€ double. Buffet breakfast included. Parking 20€. **Amenities:** Bar; bikes; Wi-Fi (free). Bus: 6.

Inexpensive

Superbude ★★   It's a little too cool for its own good sometimes—montages made from newspaper clippings on the walls, funky furnishings fashioned from crates, lots of high-tech lighting. But if that's the only snarky thing to be said about an incredibly fair-valued hostel, the place must be okay. And Hamburg's best lodging deal has plenty to commend it. Functional though colorfully stylish lounges and rooms are spotless, fridges are stocked with cheap beer, the breakfast is substantial, the beds are super comfortable, and bathrooms are modern and spiffy. A lot of rooms are cozy doubles and can be let as singles, though young backpackers and young at hearts on a budget often opt for a bunk in a four-bedded room.

Spaldingstrasse 152. www.superbude.de. © **040/3808780.** 64 units. 59€–133€ double. Breakfast not included. Parking 20€. **Amenities:** Cafe; bikes; Wi-Fi (free). U-Bahn: Berliner Tor.

NEAR THE WATERFRONT

Expensive

East ★★   Style has soul in this sophisticated redo of a formidable red-brick early 20th-century iron foundry. Minimalist design is accented with exposed brick, wrought iron, and natural fabrics to create a transporting environment—surprisingly warm and welcoming and vaguely exotic. Nattily curved headboards separate even the smallest rooms into lounging and sleeping areas, while bathrooms, tucked away behind floating curtains, have separate WC and shower cabins with rainfall shower heads. A modernistic candlelit bar, soaring Eurasian restaurant, leafy courtyard, rooftop terrace, and gym and spa provide plenty of in-house diversions, and St. Pauli nightlife is just outside the door.

Simon-von-Utrecht-Strasse 31. www.east-hotel.de. © **040/309930.** 78 units. 155€–290€ double. Buffet breakfast included. Parking 25€. **Amenities:** Restaurant; bar; babysitting; concierge; exercise room; room service; spa; Wi-Fi (free). U-Bahn: St. Pauli.

Moderate

25hours Hotel Hamburg HafenCity ★   If you're smack dab in the middle of Hamburg's new waterfront district, you'd better make the most of your surroundings—and that's exactly what this trendy outpost of a Hamburg-based, design-oriented hotel group does. Shipping crates, old timbers, and stacks of Oriental carpets (a nod to the surrounding warehouses that once stored the bounty of Eastern trade) fill the lounge areas, while bedrooms are cabin-style, varying in size from snug to commodious enough for a captain. The nautical theme is creatively carried out with tattoo-emblazoned wallpaper, crate-like furnishings, portholes, and logbooks in which you can follow the story of seafarers. If all this design gets to be a bit much, head up to the rooftop sauna to chill out while taking in the city below.

Paul-Dessau-Strasse 2. www.25hours-hotel.com. ✆ **040/855070.** 89 units. 135€–165€ double. Buffet breakfast included. Parking 25€. **Amenities:** Restaurant; 2 bars; babysitting; bikes; Wi-Fi (free). S-Bahn: Bahrenfeld.

Hafen Hamburg ★   This waterside complex does not have a lot of designer flash and flair, but its modern, businesslike accommodations put you within easy walking distance of St. Pauli nightlife. Best of all, a room with a view here provides a front row seat for the comings and goings in the busy harbor below, and many city sights are an easy stroll or short U-Bahn ride away. The sprawling complex encompasses a 19th-century seafarers' residence and two modern towers. Rooms in all are functionally comfy and enlivened with nautical prints, but only some have water views—and since that's why you're staying here, make sure to request one when booking.

Seewartenstrasse 9. www.hotel-hafen-hamburg.de. ✆ **040/311130.** 355 units. 100€–200€ double. Buffet breakfast included with most rates. Parking 25€. **Amenities:** Restaurant; 3 bars; sauna; Wi-Fi (free). U-Bahn: Landungsbrücken.

Inexpensive

Fritzhotel ★★   Hamburg doesn't get much more hip than it does in the arty Sternschanze quarter, and here's a hotel that coolly—as in quietly and tastefully—suits the surroundings. Bright, high-ceilinged guest rooms on a floor of a 19th-century apartment house are done in soothing neutrals with bold splashes of color. Some open to balconies, but the quieter ones face a leafy courtyard off the street. There are few amenities—and no bar or restaurant—but fresh fruit and coffee are on hand and the neighborhood, at the edge of lively St. Pauli, is chockablock with cafes and bars.

Schanzenstrasse 101–103. www.fritzhotel.com. ✆ **040/82222830.** 17 units. 95€ double. Buffet breakfast included. Free parking. **Amenities:** Wi-Fi (free). U-Bahn: Sternschanze.

Where to Eat in Hamburg

Hamburg is married to the sea, and all sorts of denizens of the deep end up on the table: lobster from Helgoland; shrimp from Büsum; turbot, plaice, and sole from the North Sea; and huge quantities of fresh oysters. It's no accident that many of Hamburg's best and most popular restaurants are seafood houses—and they're reasonably priced, since seafood is not exorbitantly expensive in this port city.

But Hamburgers are carnivores, too, hence their eponymous contribution to world cuisine, here known as *Stubenküchen* (hamburger steak). A traditional sailor's dish, *Labskaus,* is made with beer, onions, cured meat, potatoes, herring, and pickles. Brace yourself for at least a taste of the city's iconic treat, *Aalsuppe* (eel soup).

Whatever your epicurean appetite, you can probably satisfy it in this city that's long had ties with exotic lands—ethnic restaurants do a brisk business in almost every neighborhood. While dining can be a fine art and a costly pursuit in this expense-account-oriented city, you can also eat well without breaking the bank. No matter how much you spend, in many places your meal will probably be seasoned with an ingredient that Hamburg seems to care a lot about, a generous dash of trendiness.

Dining in the historic arcades, looking over the Alster toward the Rauhaus.

CENTRAL CITY
Moderate
Bullerei ★ MEAT   An old cattle hall in the Schanze meatpacking district, just north of St. Pauli, has been transformed into an industrial-looking dining room geared to some serious meat eating (dried beef hangs in a glass display case and menus are covered in the plastic strips that hang over the doors to meat lockers). Graffiti art, exposed brick walls, and lots of wood furnishings create comfortable surroundings for enjoying pork cheeks, veal knuckles, salty ham, or maybe just some old-fashioned German sausages, even fresh fish—washed down with a selection from the excellent wine list or a wide choice of German beers.
Lagerstrasse 34b. www.bullerei.com. ℂ **040/33442110.** Main courses 18€–30€. Daily 11am–11pm. U-Bahn: Sternschanze.

Die Bank ★★ NORTHERN GERMAN/CONTINENTAL   You'll feel like a robber baron on the marble-columned trading floor of this former bank. Imaginatively backlit photos of money might get you in the mood to part with some yours for the richly satisfying Banker's Plate, an embarrassment of crustacean riches, or foie gras and other traditional French indulgences; you can also dine simply on wurst or steak frites, or explore the kitchen's forays into some adventurous Asian-fusion dishes. The lounge-music-infused space is hopping at all times, with diners crowded onto communal tables and a long, long bar, but stick around after dessert and you'll see this former temple of commerce turned into a rather riotous dance club.
Hohebleichen 17. www.diebank-brasserie.de. ℂ **040/2380030.** Main courses 14€–25€. Mon–Sat noon–3pm and 6:30–10:30pm. U-Bahn: Gasenmarkt.

Inexpensive
Daniel Wischer ★ SEAFOOD   Anyone who grew up in Hamburg remembers stopping for lunch during downtown shopping excursions at this mainstay that's been doing a brisk business since 1924. Many loyal regulars claim the fried fish is the freshest in town, though that's a much-debated subject in Hamburg. Here the platters come with home-made potato salad or French fries and the house special drink, Frass-brause, a soft drink that has a deceptively foamy beer-like head. Real beer is available, too, along with wine. You can order from a cart along the pedestrian street out front and eat standing up with the crowd, but take a seat inside to enjoy the nicely paneled historic main room where a huge swordfish (stuffed, of course) leaps over the tables.
Spitalestrasse 12. www.danielwischer.de. ℂ **040/3891360.** Main courses 7€–15€. Mon–Sat 11am–8pm. U-Bahn: Mönckebergstrasse.

Fillet of Soul ★ INTERNATIONAL   The Deichtorhallen (see p. 661) is a turn-of-the-20th-century gem, two adjoining steel-and-glass structures near the harbor that once served as market halls and these days house temporary art and photography exhibitions. Tucked into a wing of the vast spaces is an intimate, minimalist dining room where chefs in an open kitchen do nouvelle takes on German standards that are works of art in themselves. Expect dishes along the lines of pink-roasted breast of goose with saffron-flavored rice, and pan-fried zanderfish with bacon-studded *Sauerkraut*. Coffee, pastries, and light fare are available in the adjoining cafe throughout the day, and any daytime visit should coincide with a walk through the galleries.

In the Deichtorhallen Museum, Deichtorstrasse 2. www.fillet-of-soul.de. ✆ **040/70705800.** Reservations recommended. Main courses lunch 8.50€–12€, dinner 14€–24€. No credit cards. Cafe and bar Tues–Sun 11am–midnight; restaurant Tues–Sun noon–3pm and 6–10pm. U-Bahn: Steinstrasse.

Oberhafen-Kantine ★ GERMAN   A much battered landmark near the old canal ports tilts and sags as a result of almost constant flooding since it went up in 1925, but it's all the more beloved for its lack of perfect beauty. Adding to the allure is the railway bridge that crosses the roof, just inches from the bricks. Inside the stark but cozy tiled rooms, a simple menu stays close to the building's origins as a dockworker's coffee house, featuring the real hamburger: fried pork patties served between two buns. Homemade potato salad, that time-honored accompaniment, is also served alongside the thick stews.

Stockmeyerstrasse 39. www.oberhafenkantine-hamburg.de. ✆ **040/3280-9984.** Main courses 6€–15€ Tues 5–10pm, Wed–Sun noon–10pm.

Restaurant Nil ★ INTERNATIONAL   The name is a reference to some innovative spicing in such classics as beef bourguignon, but that's about as exotic as this classic French bistro gets. A regular clientele (many are in publishing and the arts) can count on the kitchen to serve heartier northern-style dishes in the colder months, then dip into the south for inspiration come spring. Any time of year, mirrored walls and lots of brass and plush upholstery will probably transport you to Paris.

Neuer Pferdemarkt 5. www.restaurant-nil.de. ✆ **040/4397823.** Reservations recommended. Main courses 18€–22€; fixed-price menu 41€. No credit cards. Wed–Mon 6pm–midnight. U-Bahn: Feldstrasse.

NEAR THE WATERFRONT
Moderate

Fischküche Karin Brahm ★★ SEAFOOD   An unpretentious, brightly lit fish house near the harbor works hard to satisfy Hamburg's unquenchable appetite for seafood, serving the freshest catch in many variations. To get a taste of some local favorites, start with smoked eel and move on to cod, served with potatoes and mustard sauce—but there's plenty else on the large, ever-changing menu. Nothing that comes out of the kitchen is trendy or haute, service is of the no-nonsense school, and there's nothing stylish, cozy, or otherwise notable about the modern surroundings, but fresh ingredients deftly prepared make this a surefire hit with piscivores.

Kajen 12. www.die-fischkueche.de. ℭ **040/365631.** Main courses 15€–40€. Mon–Fri noon–midnight; Sat 4pm–midnight. U-Bahn: Rödingsmarkt.

Inexpensive

The Bird ★ AMERICAN   For better or worse, the hamburger craze that is sweeping Europe has come to Hamburg. That's *hamburger* as in the American beef version, not the fried pork filets that Hamburgers consider to be hamburgers. The taste for fresh beef is in full swing at this clamorous, bare-bones St. Pauli burger joint that claims to be "New York style" but seems a lot more like an American corporate cafeteria. The aged steaks are from Iowa and the burgers are made with beef from local farms. Both are served with house-made fries and a selection of German and imported beers.

Trommelstrasse 2. www.thebirdhamburg.com. ℭ **040/7566-2333.** Main courses 8€–20€. Mon–Wed 6–11pm, Thurs 5–11pm, Fri 5–midnight, Sat 2pm–midnight, Sun 2–11pm. U-Bahn: St. Pauli.

IN ALTONA

Expensive

Das Weisse Haus ★ GERMAN/SEAFOOD   Unlike the Washington landmark with which it shares a name, Hamburg's famous White House is a cramped old fisherman's cottage. That doesn't keep eager diners away, and you'll have to book well in advance for the privilege of submitting yourself to the whims of the kitchen, which, aside from catering to allergies and strong dislikes, sends out whatever it wants, basing meals on what looked good in the market that day. A Hamburg classic, *aalsuppe* (eel soup), often makes an appearance, followed by some creative seafood preparations, though the kitchen is just as comfortable with meat and even vegetarian meals.

Neumühlen 50. www.das-weisse-haus.de. ℭ **04/309016.** Reservations required. 2-course menu 28€; 3-course menu 34€; 4-course menu 42€. Mon–Sat noon–3pm and 6–9pm. U-Bahn: Altona.

Landhaus Scherrer ★★ NORTHERN GERMAN/CONTINENTAL A converted white-brick, cozy-looking brewery in Altona soothes at first sight, surrounded as it is by lawns shaded by trees. Wood paneled walls and low lighting do nothing to disrupt the mellow mood, the inventive menu combines northern German and international flavors to satisfying effect, and the kitchen throws in an emphasis on locavore ingredients. Crispy whole north German duck with seasoned vegetables is a feast for two, but you can dine solo on roast goose with rhubarb in cassis sauce and other hearty classics. You can eat lightly in the adjoining bistro.

Elbchaussee 130. www.landhausscherrer.de. ℭ**040/8801325.** Reservations required. Main courses 28€–39€; fixed-price menu 111€. Mon–Sat noon–3pm and 6:30–10:30pm. Bus: 135.

15

HAMBURG & THE NORTH

Hamburg

Moderate

Eisenstein ★ INTERNATIONAL/PIZZA   The crowd of stylish regulars doesn't let the clamor and clatter deter them from enjoying a fusion of Italian, Mediterranean, and German fare in one of Hamburg's most appealing dining spaces. A restored factory envelops diners in brick walls, rough-hewn timbers, and daylight streaming through huge windows (and candlelight by night). Southern Europe meets the north in dishes like Atlantic cod flavored with Provençal spices and Italian-style thin crust pizza topped with gravlax. An excellent selection of beer and light fare makes this a popular stop on the late-night circuit.

Friedensallee 9. www.restaurant-eisenstein.de. © **040/3904606.** Reservations recommended. Main courses 18€–25€; fixed-price dinners 33€–37€; pizzas 8€–14€. No credit cards. Daily 11am–11pm. U-Bahn: Altona Bahnhof.

Fischereihafen Restaurant ★★ SEAFOOD   A harborside perch near the fish market is a fortuitous locale for this long-standing Hamburg favorite, an institution that's popular with a well-dressed crowd who look like they're used to fancier surroundings. What matters here is freshness, and fish and shellfish are right out of the market stalls. They show up in some simple but memorable renditions, along the lines of Arctic trout with wild garlic, and rare tuna steak with peppercorns and honey-laced soy sauce. A nice view of the Elbe, through large picture windows and from a small terrace in good weather, nicely tops off a memorable meal.

Grosse Elbstrasse 143. www.fischereihafenrestaurant.de. © **040/381816.** Reservations required. Main courses 18€–46€; fixed-price menu 60€. Sun–Thurs 11:30am–10pm; Fri–Sat 11:30am–10:30pm. S-Bahn: Königstrasse.

Shopping

Historically a city of merchants, Hamburg still has a strong commercial bent. Even so, Americans especially will be surprised to learn that most stores close Saturday at 2pm (until 4 or 6pm on langer Samstag, the first Saturday of the month) and remain shut until Monday morning.

TOP SHOPPING AREAS

Hamburg has two main shopping zones. In the old center, pedestrianized **Mönckebergstrasse and Spitalerstrasse** run parallel to one another and connect the main train station with the Rathaus. They are lined with big department stores and lots of outlets of midrange international clothing chains. To the north, elegant shop-lined **Ballindamm** and **Jungfernstieg** flank the Binnenalster, Hamburg's inner-city lake. These waterside promenades are home to fancy department stores, high-end fashion retailers, and jewelry stores as well as some especially posh shopping arcades, most notably the Colonnaden, Hamburger Hof, and Gänsemarkt Passage. Jungfernstieg is a popular place to stroll, in keeping with its name—this was once where prominent families came on Sundays to promenade and show off their unmarried daughters (*jungfer*). **Neuer Wall,** leading inland from the lake off Jungfernsteig, unabashedly flaunts luxury brands along one of the most exclusive shopping strips in Europe.

SPECIALTY SHOPS

Bath & Skin Care

Nivea ★★ This Hamburg native company's flagship is a lotions-filled emporium in the classy Jungfernsteig shopping strip. Jungfernsteig 51. www.nivea.de. © **040/8222-4740.** U-Bahn: Jungfernsteig.

Rigaer Seifenmanufaktur ★ For decades, this fragrant shop has been soothing jangled nerves with handmade soaps and bath oils. Mohlenhofstrasse 5. www.duftseifen.de. © **040/69667333.** U-Bahn: Mönckebergstrasse.

Fashion

Hip Cats ★ Hamburg's favorite stop for men and women's vintage fashion offers clothes from every era, shown on groaning racks amid accessories and furniture. Paul-Roosen Strasse 4. www.hip-cats.de. © **040/3173064.** U-Bahn: St. Pauli.

Jil Sander ★★ Internationally known designer Jil Sander started her line of classically minimalist women's and men's clothing in Hamburg back in the 1970s; it's fitting that her sleek shop should now star among the ritzy retailers on Neuer-Wall. Neuer-Wall 43. www.jilsander.com. © **040/3741290.** U-Bahn: Jungfernsteig.

Gourmet

Mutterland ★★★ This is the place to go to pick up a jar of mustard, some cheese, herring, and just about any other high-quality German foodstuff. Sandwiches, soups, and other light fare is available in a café and to take away, making this a handy stop if you're catching a train at the station, just down the street. Ernst-Merke Strasse 9. www.mutterland.de. © **040/2840-7978.** U-Bahn: Hauptbahnhof.

Wasscherschloss ★★ Probably the most romantic-looking building in the Speicherstadt district (see p. 668), this old warehouse is bounded by water and embellished with steep gables and turreted towers. It's now occupied by a restaurant and pleasant coffee house, as well as an atmospheric shop selling coffees and teas—quite befitting, since the premises once were the offices of a tea and coffee importer. Dienerrelhe 4. www.wasserschloss.de. © **040/5589-82640.** U-Bahn: Baumwall.

Miscellaneous

Manufactum ★★★ With a prime location in the landmark Chilehaus (see p. 661), this shop specializes in everything and anything of quality—clothing, accessories, gardening tools, leather goods, notebooks, all of it from the best European manufacturers. Fischertwiete 2. www.manufactum. de. © **040/3008-7743.** U-Bahn: Messberg.

Stefan Fink ★ Fountain pens are back in style at this St. Georg shop, where rollerballs and other wood-encased writing utensils are also on offer. Koppel 66. www.stefanfink.de. © **040/247151.** U-Bahn: Hauptbahnhof.

Nautical Souvenirs

Captain's Cabin ★ Feeling salty after your harbor cruise? Right by the passenger dock, you can pop into this shop selling ship models, telescopes, barometers, figureheads, lamps, prints, posters, and nautical clothing for the whole family. St. Pauli Landungsbrücken 3. www.captainscabin.de. © **040/316373.** S-Bahn: Landungsbrücken.

Entertainment & Nightlife

Hamburg is famous and infamous for nightlife. You can go high-brow, as the city has excellent opera and dance companies and symphonies; middle-brow in chic bars and homey weinstubs; or low-brow on and around the Reeperbahn, in Hamburg's notoriously sex-oriented St. Pauli district.

Hamburg's gay scene is almost as robust as that in Berlin, and centers in St Georg, just to the east of the Haupthbanhof, with a string of venues along and around two main streets, **Lange Reihe** and **Steindamm.**

Visitor information centers in the Wandelhalle of the Hauptbahnhof (© **040/30051300**) and at St. Pauli-Landungsbrücken are usually littered with fliers announcing goings-on around town; their counters sell tickets to mainstream events. The Ticketmaster affiliate in Hamburg is **Kartenhaus** at Schanzenstrasse 5 (Mon–Fri 10am–7pm, Sat 10am–2pm; www.kartenhaus. de; © **040/435946**).

Nighttime on the Reeperbahn.

THE PERFORMING ARTS

Deutsches Schauspielhaus ★ In a huge and ornate theater opened in 1901, this is one of the largest and most important theaters in the German-speaking world. Its eclectic year-round schedule includes both classics and modern plays—but you'll need to understand German to appreciate fully the genius of these productions. Kirchenallee 39. www.schauspielhaus.de. ℂ **040/248713.** Ticket prices vary, but most are 10€–50€. U-Bahn: Hauptbahnhof.

Elbphilharmonie ★★★ Hamburg's glassed-in symphony space, opening in January 2017, is home to the NDR Symphony Orchestra under the musical direction of Thomas Hengelbrock. Dammtorwall 46. www.elbphilharmonie.de. ℂ **040/357-6666.** U-Bahn: Baumwall.

English Theater of Hamburg ★ The only English-speaking theater in northern Germany, this company's actors present popular plays and the classics. Their season runs September to June. Lerchenfeld 14. www.englishtheatre.de. ℂ **040/2277089.** Tickets 18€–31€. U-Bahn: Mundsburg.

Hamburgische Staatsoper (Hamburg State Opera) ★★★ One of the world's leading opera houses, built after World War II, is known for excellent acoustics and advanced technical facilities. It's home to the **Hamburg State Opera** and the **Hamburg Ballet.** Grosstheaterstrasse 25. www.hamburgische-staatsoper.de. ℂ **040/356868.** Tickets 10€–146€. U-Bahn: Stephansplatz. S-Bahn: Dammtor.

Laeiszhalle Hamburg ★★ This survivor of Germany's romantic age, painstakingly restored after World War II, hosts concerts by the **Hamburg Symphony,** the **Hamburg Philharmonic,** the **NDR Symphony,**

Laeiszhalle Hamburg hosts classical music.

Elbphilharmonie Konzerte, and the **Monteverdi-Chor,** known for its interpretations of baroque and Renaissance music. Touring orchestras also perform here. For tickets, call either the number listed below or the number listed for the Staatsoper (see p. 683). Johannes-Brahms-Platz 1. www.laeiszhalle.de. ✆ **040/357666.** Tickets up to 45€. U-Bahn: Stephansplatz. S-Bahn: Dammtor.

BARS & CLUBS
Cocktail Bars

Le Lion ★★ So intimate you might not get in—try though, by ringing the buzzer hidden inside the lion's head on the door. Better yet, make a reservation to enjoy serious cocktails in a grown-up, subtly lit room. Rauthaustrasse 3. www.lelion.net. ✆ **040/334753780.** S-Bahn: Rathaus.

Dance Clubs

Meanie Bar ★ One of the few places along the Reeperbahn that caters to locals attracts a lot of artists and musicians. Spielbudenplatz 5. www.molotowclub.com. ✆ **040/4301110.** S-Bahn: Reeperbahn.

Molotow ★★ This much-beloved venue in the cellar of the Meanie Bar is the place to dance to funk and alternative. Opening hours may vary, but usually it opens Wednesday and Sunday at 8pm, Thursday to Saturday at 11pm; closing time is usually when the crowd feels like dispersing. Spielbudenplatz 5. www.molotowclub.com. ✆ **040/4301110.** Cover 5€–16€. S-Bahn: Reeperbahn.

Gay Bars

Café Gnosa ★★ Laid-back and art deco-inspired, this gay-friendly bar and restaurant is a popular place to sip coffee or wine and enjoy breakfast and a nice selection of salads and more substantial meals throughout the day. The real reason to come is to mingle with the locals, many of whom have been hanging out here for years. It's open until 1am. Lange Reihe 93. www.gnosa.de. ✆ **040/243034.** U-Bahn: Hauptbahnhof.

Tom's Saloon ★★ Hamburg's landmark gay bar, named for gay icon Tom of Finland (once a regular) has a street-level dance club, a friendly cocktail lounge, and a cellar bar where leather is de rigeur. Men of all ages mix here, and women won't feel comfortable anywhere but the crowded dance floor, and even there aren't a terribly welcome presence. At least one part of this place is open every night 10pm until dawn; every Wednesday to Sunday, additional sections open for greater space. The 5€ cover includes one drink. Pulverteich 17. www.toms-hamburg.de. ✆ **040/ 25328943.** U-Bahn: Hauptbahnhof.

Music Clubs

Club Grosse Freiheit 36/Kaiserkeller ★ The Beatles performed here in the basement Kaiserkeller in their earliest days, and Prince and

Willie Nelson have been on the bill at the larger club upstairs. Today the venue is best known as a cultural landmark, though some of the pop and rock concerts pull in big crowds. Grosse Freiheit 36. www.grossefreiheit36.de. ✆ **040/31777811.** Cover 5€–20€. S-Bahn: Reeperbahn).

Cotton Club ★ Hamburg's oldest jazz club hosts jazz and Dixieland bands from throughout Europe and the United States. Hours are Monday to Saturday 8pm to 1am. Alter Steinweg 10. www.cotton-club.de. ✆ **040/343878.** Cover 6.50€–15€. S-Bahn: Stadthausbrücke.

Fabrik ★ An old ammunition depot turned factory hosts musician of every stripe and mixed programs feature club music, classical, African bands, jazz, and blues, along with film and stage events. Barnerstrasse 36 (5 min. from Bahnhof Altona). www.fabrik.de. ✆ **040/391070.** Cover 10€–35€. U-Bahn: Altona.

A CASINO

Spielbank Hamburg ★ CASINO Hamburg's low-key casino occupies attractive but fairly unremarkable surroundings and offers roulette, blackjack, and poker, played according to international rules. You can also enjoy a drink at the bar, taking in the panoramic view over the roofs and lakes of Hamburg. The minimum stake for roulette is 2€, for blackjack 5€. Men should wear jackets and ties. Everyone needs a passport to get in (you must be 18 or over to enter and gamble). The casino is open daily 3pm to 3am. Stephansplatz 10. www.spielbank -hamburg.de. ✆ **040/4501760.** U-Bahn: Stephansplatz.

Bar Rooms with a View

You can enjoy the spectacle of Hamburg's port while keeping warm and dry and slaking your thirst at 20Up, on the 20th floor of the **Empire Riverside Hotel,** Bernhard-Nocht-Strasse 97 (www.empire-riverside.de; ✆ 040/311190). A similarly dramatic view is to be had from the 14th-floor **Tower Bar** of the Hafen Hotel, Seewartenstrasse 9 (www. hotel-hafen-hamburg.de; ✆ 040/311130). The perspective of the maritime activity and sprawling city is eye-catching by day, and downright dazzling at night.

A Day Trip to Lüneburg ★★

55km (34 miles) SE of Hamburg

This proud old city once provided what all the world wanted, salt. For seven prosperous centuries Lüneburg's salt mines yielded what in the Middle Ages became known as White Gold, making the city a valued member of the Hanseatic League. Streets of gabled brick houses in the distinctive Hanseatic style attest to the onetime wealth, and the heavy salt deposits still put the town on the map as a spa where warm, briny waters sooth weary modern bones.

Trains runs between Hamburg and Lüneburg Bahnhof (www.bahn.de; ✆ **01805/996633**) about every half hour; the trip takes about 45 minutes. Access by car is via B4 from Hamburg. **Lüneburg Tourist Information** is in the Rathaus, Am Markt 1 (www.lueneburg.de, ✆ **04131/ 2076620**). It's open Monday to Friday 9am to 6pm, Saturday and Sunday 9am to 4pm (closed Sat–Sun Dec–Feb).

EXPLORING LÜNEBURG

Years of extracting salt from the earth have taken a toll on Lüneburg, delightfully so. Given the subsidence of the salt dome beneath the town, facades buckle, towers lean precariously, and entire streets seem a little off kilter. (A few medieval landmarks actually toppled over in the 20th century). That only adds to the delight of walking along Am Sande and other old lanes in the Altstadt. **Am Sande** (so named for the sandy ground that predated today's cobbles) is also the name of the city's most beautiful square, where salt merchants once laid out their wares. The **Schütting,** or "Black House," on the western side of the square takes its name from the glazed black bricks that cover its façade.

Nearby rises Lüneburg's most beloved landmark, **St. Johanniskirche,** with its 108-m (350-ft) tall sloping tower. The definite lean of the tower is all a bit of a visual trick, as the corkscrew shape of the structure makes it seem more off balance than it really is. As the story goes, the 14th-century architect was so appalled when he saw the effect of his design that he jumped out of a window of the tower but landed in a hay cart. To celebrate his good fortune the poor fellow retired to a tavern, drank himself into a stupor, fell over, hit his head on the stone hearth, and died. Too bad, as he had much to be proud of. The five-naved church is a masterpiece of Northern Gothic architecture and often resounds with the sounds of a massive pipe organ on which Johann Sebastian Bach once honed his craft.

Another monument to the town's industriousness is the **Alter Kran,** or Old Crane, on the Stintmarkt quayside in the old river port. The

---

The Lüneburg Heath

Lüneburg is also the ideal starting point for excursions into the **Lüneburg Heath,** nearly 775 sq. km (300 sq. miles) of sandy soil mainly covered with brush, heather, and sheep. In late summer, the flowering heath turns from green to purple. You'll find the most dramatic, wind-swept, and bleakly evocative scenery in the center of the heath in the **Naturschützpark Lüneburger Heide** (Luneberg Heath Nature Park; www. naturpark-lueneburger-heide.de), a preserve for plants and wildlife. To reach the park from Lüneburg, drive 35km (22 miles) west, following the signs to Salzhausen. After you cross the bridge over the A7 Autobahn, follow the brown-and-white signs into the park.

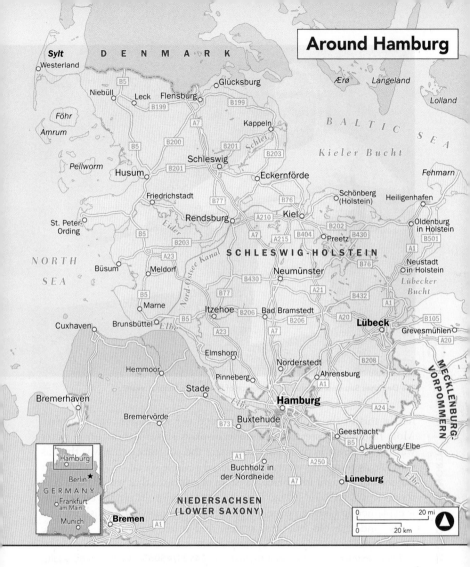

Around Hamburg

sturdy wood and iron device now hanging over the waters of the River Ilmenau is an 18th-century replacement for the medieval original that was used to load the town's precious cargo onto barges. Salt also traveled north to Lübeck and Scandinavia via wagon along the Old Salt Route.

Deutsches Salzmuseum ★★ MUSEUM   You'll again never take salt with, well, a grain of salt after a visit to these exhibits on the site of the old Lüneburg Salt Works, a mainstay of the town's economy from the 12th century until as late as the mid-1980s. The operations finally closed because salt was more readily available from other sources and the vast salt dome upon which Lüneburg sits was on the verge of collapse (you'll

The Deutshes Salzmuseum plumbs the source of Lüneburg's historic wealth.

notice this in the wobbly state of several old structures around town). Most fascinating are the well-done displays showing how briny water was boiled down in huge pans to extract the substance that was then as valuable as gold. This wealth engendered a whole social system of master salters and brought into place a system of salt taxes that would have kept rooms full of IRS and Inland Revenue agents gainfully employed. All this is explained in German panels with some accompanying English translations, and the old buckets, scales, and other equipment are quite fascinating.

Sülfmeisterstrasse 1. www.salzmuseum.de. ✆ **04131/45065.** Admission 6€ adults, 5€ students and children, 19€ families. May–Sept Mon–Fri 9am–5pm, Sat–Sun 10am–5pm; Oct–Apr daily 10am–5pm.

Rathaus ★★ LANDMARK   Luneberg's town hall is a bold presence, with a façade as white as slightly discolored salt and several tiers of statuary representing peace, justice, and all the other virtues of a good citizenry and government. The Gerichtslaube (Great Council Room) is an explosion of ornamentation, with intricate wooden bas-reliefs of town elders that master carver Albert von Soest executed between 1566 and

1584. In the tower are 41 Meissen porcelain bells that ring several times a day. The favorite relic, though, is the preserved leg bone of a wild boar displayed in the main trading hall. It's said that a hunter shot the animal when he came upon it wallowing in a pool some 800 years ago. When he laid the pelt out to dry, he noticed salt crystals embedded in the hairs and bristles, and the discovery led him to more closely investigate the salt pools that would eventually put Lüneburg on the map.

Am Markt 1. ✆ **04131/309230.** Daily 9am–5pm. Guided tours at 10 and 11:30am, and 1, 2:30, and 3:30pm; 5€ adults, 4€ students and children.

Salü Saltztherme ★★ SPA   This thermal bath complex is the place to test the soothing effects of Lüneburg's saline waters. You can do so in a wave pool, a vast indoor/outdoor pool in which you can float as if you were in the Dead Sea, and any number of other water features. Saunas (one outdoors, with a fireplace), steam rooms, and whirlpools enhance the relaxing effects.

Uelzener Strasse 1–5. www.salue.info. ✆ **04131/7230.** Admission from 6€ pools, from 12€ with sauna. Mon–Sat 10am–11pm, Sun 8am–9pm.

LÜBECK ★★★

66km (41 miles) NE of Hamburg

Along the ancient streets of Lübeck's Altstadt you'll find more buildings from the 13th to the 15th centuries than in any other city in northern Germany—more, for that matter, than just about anywhere else in Germany or in Europe. It's said that within an area of 5 sq. km (2 sq. miles) around the Marktplatz stand 1,000 medieval houses. The overall effect of all these high-gabled houses, massive gates, strong towers, and towering steeples is outrageously picturesque. A visit is a dip into the past when Lübeck was one of the founding cities of the mighty Hanseatic League, a confederation that controlled trade along the Baltic as far as Russia.

The Hanseatic merchants decorated their churches with art treasures and gilded their spires to show off their wealth. Much of this remains, earning the city a place on the UNESCO World Heritage list of international monuments. You could work a day trip to Lübeck into your Hamburg itinerary, but the city is so captivatingly picturesque, with quite a bit to see and do, that you might want to spend the night.

Essentials

GETTING THERE   The **Lübeck Hauptbahnhof** lies on major rail lines linking Denmark and Hamburg, and on the Hamburg-Lüneburg-Lübeck-Kiel-Flensburg and Lübeck-Rostock-Stralsund lines, with frequent connections. Trip times are 48 minutes from Hamburg, 3 to 4 hours from

Berlin. For information, visit **www.bahn.de** or call © **01805/996633.** Access to Lübeck by car is via the A1 Autobahn north and south.

GETTING AROUND   The Altstadt and most of the city's attractions can be reached on foot from the Hauptbanhof, about a 15-minute walk from the Marktplatz. You can also take bus no. 1, 5, 11, or 21; fare is 2.20€.

VISITOR INFORMATION   The **Lübeck-Informations-Zentrum** is next to the entrance to the medieval city, Holstentor (Holsten Gate), at Holstentorplatz 1–5 (www.luebeck-tourismus.de; © **0451/8899700**). It's open June to September, Monday to Friday 9:30am to 7pm, Saturday 10am to 3pm, and Sunday 10am to 2pm (the rest of the year it closes at 6pm on weekdays and all day Sunday). *Tip:* If you're going to visit two city museums, save your receipts—you'll get 50% off your admission to the second one by showing your receipt from the first.

SPECIAL EVENTS   Lübeck is the center of the **Schleswig-Holstein Music Festival** (www.shmf.de; © **0451/389570**), with performances during July and August every year.

Exploring Lübeck

The Trave River and connecting canals completely surround the Altstadt, lending this unspoiled collection of medieval and Renaissance houses an island-like appearance. After 13th-century fires destroyed many wooden structures, the city mandated the use of brick, creating a remarkably pleasing uniformity throughout the old town. You'll notice that some of the medieval redbrick buildings are decorated with black glazed bricks. The black glaze comes from salt sprinkled onto the bricks before they were put in the kiln—a measure of the wealth of the builder, for salt was considered to be "white gold."

To reach the Altstadt from the train station, cross the **Puppenbrücke** (Puppets' Bridge) and head east. The bridge got its irreverent name from the seven statues of classical gods and goddesses that stand on its stone railings. You enter the historic district through the **Holstentor** gate (see p. 693). Across from the Holstentor stand the **Salzspeicher** (Salt Lofts), a group of six gabled Renaissance buildings; the oldest dates from 1579, the newest from 1745. Merchants stored salt from nearby Lüneburg in these buildings before shipping it to Scandinavia, where the salt was used to preserve fish. Each of the six buildings is different, reflecting trends in Renaissance gabled architecture.

For an overview of this distinctive-looking city, head to the 750-year-old **Petrikirche** (St. Peter's Church), Schmiedestrasse (© **0451/397-330**), and take the elevator to the top of its tower. From the height, the sprawling conglomeration of brick, gables, and spires looks like a model of a medieval town. The tower is open daily 9am to 7pm (October to March 10am–7pm). Admission is 3€ adults, 2€ students and children.

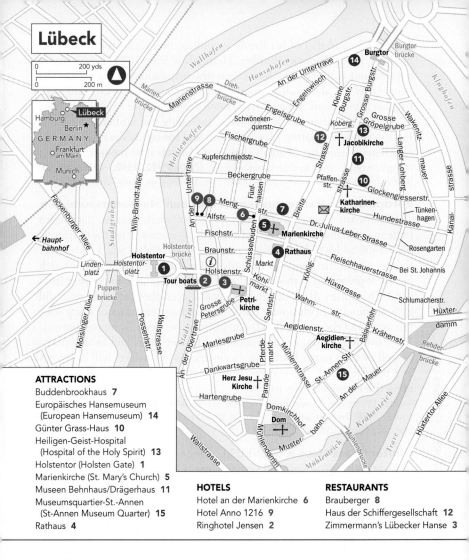

Lübeck

0 — 200 yds
0 — 200 m

Lübeck

Hamburg
Berlin ★
GERMANY
Frankfurt
am Main
Munich

ATTRACTIONS

Buddenbrookhaus **7**
Europäisches Hansemuseum
 (European Hansemuseum) **14**
Günter Grass-Haus **10**
Heiligen-Geist-Hospital
 (Hospital of the Holy Spirit) **13**
Holstentor (Holsten Gate) **1**
Marienkirche (St. Mary's Church) **5**
Museen Behnhaus/Drägerhaus **11**
Museumsquartier-St.-Annen
 (St-Annen Museum Quarter) **15**
Rathaus **4**

HOTELS

Hotel an der Marienkirche **6**
Hotel Anno 1216 **9**
Ringhotel Jensen **2**

RESTAURANTS

Brauberger **8**
Haus der Schiffergesellschaft **12**
Zimmermann's Lübecker Hanse **3**

Buddenbrookhaus ★ HISTORIC HOME Readers well versed in the works of Nobel prize-winning author Thomas Mann (and anyone planning a visit to Lübeck should read at least a couple of his books) might recognize this commodious,stone house with a gabled roof, recessed doorway, and leaded-glass fan over heavy double doors. This is the house Mann (1875–1955) described as the family home in *Budden-brooks*. Mann's grandparents lived here, and the novelist spent much of his childhood in the large gracious rooms, a few of which have been reconstructed. Most galleries in the rebuilt and modernized interior, however, display photographs, letters, and documents chronicling

Mann's life, and that of his family, including their flight from Nazi Germany in 1933. Thomas's brother, Heinrich Mann (1871–1950), also a novelist and author of *Professor Unrat* (the inspiration for the movie *The Blue Angel*) is also well memorialized. Displays are in German with English translations in small type; more accessible are video recordings of Mann and other family members, including the author's speech in Hollywood denouncing McCarthyism, and his son Klaus's moving recollection of returning to bomb-shattered Munich after the war.

Mengstrasse 4. www.buddenbrookhaus.de. ℂ **0451/1224192.** Admission 6€ adults, 3€ students, children 13 and under free, 10€ families. Daily 10am–5pm.

Europaïsches Hansemuseum (European Hansemuseum) ★★

The Hanseatic League, a confederation of 200 market towns, dominated trade in the Baltic Sea and elsewhere along the coast of northern Europe from 1400 to 1800. With its key position on the Baltic Sea, Lübeck was the key city in the league, so it's only fitting that the confederation's rich history is preserved in the city's Castle Friary, a Dominican convent from the 13th century. Rare documents, coins, even the sartorially splendid garb of merchants chronicle the league and its importance, along with the impact of the plague and the many wars between European powers. Most riveting are the reconstructions of trading posts and fishing ports, as well as such major Hanseatic landmarks as the market hall in Bruges and the Steelyard, the league's walled outpost in London, that vividly bring the Hanseatic past to life.

An der Untertrave 1. www.hansemuseum.eu. ℂ **0451/809-0990.** Admission 13€ adults, 7.50€ children under 16, 18€–31€ families. Apr–Oct daily 10am–6pm, Nov–Mar daily 10am–5pm.

Günter Grass-Haus ★ MUSEUM

One of Germany's most esteemed postwar authors was born in Danzing—now Gansk, Poland—in 1927 and lived outside Lübeck for many years. Grass, who died in Lübeck in 2015, is best known for *The Tin Drum*, published in 1959. Anyone who's read the novel or seen the film can't help but think of the eels-in-the-horsehead scene when traveling along the broad, marshy shores of the North Sea around Hamburg and Lübeck. Grass unleashed a torrent of criticism in 2006 when he revealed, in advance of the publication of his autobiography, that he had served in the Nazi Waffen SS at age 17; some critics suggested the Nobel Prize committee should revoke Grass's prize. Grass was also a sculptor, watercolorist, printmaker, and charcoal artist, and renderings of eels and fish fill these rooms in an old printing plant, alongside many of his original manuscripts and the machines, from an Olivetti manual typewriter to computers, on which he wrote them. Some of his elegant bronzes grace the courtyard.

Glockengiesserstrasse 21. www.grass-haus.de. ℂ **0451/1224190.** Admission 6€ adults, 3€ students, 2.50€ children 13 and under. Apr–Dec daily 10am–6pm, Jan–Mar daily 11am–5pm.

Heiligen-Geist-Hospital (Hospital of the Holy Spirit) ★★ HISTORIC SIGHT   Beneath a belfry and four turreted spires is one of the oldest social-welfare institutions in Europe and one of the most important monumental buildings of the Middle Ages. Philanthropic local citizens founded the hospital in 1230. In the early 19th century, when the building was converted to a shelter for elderly men and women, 130 tiny wooden cabins without ceilings were built within its enormous main hall. The cabins remain intact, and you can poke your head inside them. Lübeck has founded charitable organizations throughout its long history. **Glockengiesserstrasse,** a couple of blocks south of Heiligen-Geist, is lined with almshouses. Füchtingshof, at no. 25, was built in the 17th century for the widows of seamen and merchants; step through the ornamented baroque portal (open 9am–noon and 3–6pm) to enter a tranquil courtyard with houses still occupied by widows. The Glandorps-Gang, at no. 41, and the Glandorps-Hof, at nos. 49 and 51, are the city's oldest almshouses, dating from 1612 and built for the widows of merchants and craftsmen (can be viewed only from the outside).
Koburg 11. Free admission. Tues–Sun 10am–5pm.

Holstentor (Holsten Gate) ★★ LANDMARK   The first monument you encounter when you emerge from the train station was for centuries the main entrance to town, looming over a bridge leading into the Altstadt. The twin cylindrical towers rising above a steeped gable are mightily impressive, which is the point—built in the 15th century, the gate was meant to announce Lübeck's power and prestige rather than defend the city. An inscribed motto brings home the city's traditionally non-combative nature, reading "Harmony at home and peace abroad." Within the tower is the **Museum Holstentor,** worth a quick stop to see a made-to-scale replica of mid-17th century Lübeck, along with some beautifully made scale models of Hanseatic *Kogge* (cogs, or single-sail vessels).
Holstentorplatz. www.die-luebecker-museen.de. ℂ **0451/1224129.** Admission 5€ adults, 2€ children under 16. Tues–Fri 10am–4pm, Sat–Sun 11am–5pm.

Marienkirche (St. Mary's Church) ★★ CHURCH   Soaring flying buttresses and towering windows seem to dwarf the rest of Lübeck, all the more so since this assemblage rises on the highest point in the Altstadt. One of Germany's most remarkable and picturesque churches was an easy mark for World War II bombers, who leveled the bell towers in 1942, inadvertently creating a conversation piece—the shattered bells remain embedded in the church floor, a testament to the horror of war. The soaring nave, with the world's tallest brick vaulting, is the setting for summertime organ concerts, a tradition established by esteemed 18th-century master organist Dietrich Buxtehude, one of the most important composers of the German baroque period. Handel and Bach both came

Lübeck's Holsten Gate.

to Lübeck to meet Buxtehude. Handel supposedly left in a hurry, when Buxtehude offered him the post of organ master with the proviso that he marry his eldest daughter. Bach, who walked 400km (250 miles) to meet Buxtehude, seems to have received no such offer and remained in Lübeck three months. Just outside the entrance a rather cherubic devil with shiny horns polished by the touch of many hands sits atop a block of stone. Legend has it that the workers building the cathedral told the devil they were constructing a weinstube, and the devil gladly joined in the construction, knowing the establishment would help bring many souls over to the dark side. When Satan realized he had been duped he attempted to smash the walls with the stone, but workers appeased him by pointing out that the Rathskeller in the adjoining Rathaus would send him many clients.

Schusselbuden 13. www.st-marien-luebeck.de. ✆ **0451/397700.** Free admission. Daily 10am–6pm (closed when services are being conducted).

Museen Behnhaus/Drägerhaus ★ MUSEUM   Two patrician houses portray prosperous Lübeck life in a suites of rooms furnished and decorated in the styles of different periods, from lavish Rococo to restrained neoclassical. On the walls of adjoining galleries is an outstanding collection of 19th and 20th paintings. Among them are several works by Norwegian painter Edward Munch, who lived and worked in Lübeck, as well as German Romantic and Impressionist paintings. Look for the colorful painting of Lubeck's St. Jacobkirch by Austrian artist Oskar Kokoshka (1886–1980) who also lived and worked in Lübeck briefly. *Self Portrait with Family* (1820), by Lübeck native Johan Friedrich Overbeck, eerily evokes a Renaissance painting of the Holy Family; it's one of several works by like-minded artists who left Germany to lead a life of virtue in Rome, taking artistic inspiration from the Renaissance masters. Königstrasse 9–11. museum-behnhaus-draegerhaus.de. *©* **0451/1224148.** Admission 6€ adults, 3€ students and children 6–18, 2€ children 5 and under. Apr–Sept Tues–Sun 10am–5pm; Oct–Mar Tues–Fri 10am–4pm, Sat–Sun 11am–5pm.

Museumsquartier-St.-Annen (St-Annen Museum Quarter) ★★

MUSEUM   A 16th-century Augustinian convent later used as an almshouse and a prison is now the centerpiece of a medieval quarter that also includes a church, a synagogue, and a string of cobblestone lanes and courtyards. The St-Annen Museum and Kunsthall house a wealth of medieval and Renaissance altarpieces and other art, including the Passion altarpiece that Hans Memling (1430–1493) did for Lübeck Cathedral in 1491. Memling, by then wildly popular throughout Northern Europe, was clearly pleasing his market: Not only are the scenes rich in Renaissance finery and decidedly Germanic townscapes in the backgrounds, but the piece is designed in such a way that it affords multiple views, giving the patrons three ways to show the work. An Annunciation scene appears when the triptych is closed; four saints appear on the panels when they are partially open; and when the altarpiece is fully open, three vividly colored panels depict the procession of the cross up Calgary, the Crucifixion, and the Resurrection. Compared to the richness of Memling's scenes, Andy Warhol's print of the Holstentor, part of a fine collection of contemporary art, looks like a mere doodle. St.-Annen-Strasse 15. museumsquartier-st-annen.de. *©* **0451/122-4137.** Admission 10€ adults, 4€ students and children 6–18. Jan–Mar Tues–Sun 11am–5pm, Apr–Dec Tues–Sun 10am–6pm.

Rathaus ★★ HISTORIC BUILDING

With arcades, towers, gables, and redbrick walls embellished with black glazing and coats of arms, this 13th-century monument to the town's importance takes on almost fairytale appearance. It may well be the most picturesque town hall in all of Germany. Tours in English and other languages show off the pompous staterooms' elaborate rococo flourishes and some somber paintings illustrating the virtues of good government. Reminding us of medieval justice are the doors of the large audience hall, once used as a courtroom: The openings are of different heights, so that the acquitted could leave via

Lübeck is the world capital of Marzipan, a sweet almond paste. According to legend, Lübeckers ran out of flour during a long siege and started grinding almonds to make bread. They were so pleased with the sweet results that they've been making Marzipan ever since. To sample Lübeck's famous Marzipan, stop in at **Cafe Niederegger**, Breitestrasse 98 (www.niederegger.de; ✆ **0451/53010**), located right across from the main entrance to the Rathaus since 1806. On the ground floor, you can purchase bars and boxes of Marzipan to take away (an excellent gift idea), or you can go upstairs to the pleasant cafe for dessert and coffee; they also have seating across the street in the arcades behind the Rathaus facing Marktplatz. Niederegger's is open daily from 9am to 6pm.

the tall door, hats on, while those found guilty had to remove their hats and duck as they left through the short door. The Rathaus stands on the north and east sides of the Marktplatz, a large square filled with meat, fruit, and vegetable stalls every Monday and Thursday. In December, the Markt is the site of Lübeck's Christmas Market.

Rathausplatz. www.luebeck-tourism.de. ✆ **0451/1221005.** Tours Mon–Fri at 11am, noon, and 3pm. 3€ adults, 1.50€ children.

Where to Stay in Lübeck

Lübeck spreads well beyond the banks of the Trave River and connecting canals that once formed the perimeter of the old city. You'll find some chains in these outlying areas, but the atmospheric Altstadt is the best place to stay; a hotel here puts you within walking distance of the train station and all the sights you want to see.

Hotel an der Marienkirche ★★   Everything is sparse and uncluttered in this old house across from Marienkirche, where rooms are done in crisp Scandinavian style and neutral tones, with nice bursts of color and contemporary art here and there. All of the rooms are furnished to be allergy free, and some have dust-preventing cork flooring. On the aesthetic side, from some rooms in the front of the house you'll be staring right into the brick towers of Marienkirche. A healthful and substantial breakfast is served in the sunny breakfast room, opening to a small terrace.

Schüsselbuden 4. www.hotel-an-der-marienkirche.de. ✆ **0451/799410.** 18 units. 75€–95€ double. Buffet breakfast included. Parking 7€ nearby. **Amenities:** Wi-Fi (free).

Hotel Anno 1216 ★★★   The name dates the premises, one of the oldest brick houses in Lübeck—and so beautifully restored that staying in this former guildhall and residence seems like a real privilege. The spacious quarters keep the historic surroundings intact, with sleek, contemporary furnishings offsetting heavy timbers, stucco ceilings, frescoes, and other treasures. The handsome singles and doubles are commodious, while three suites installed in former salons are as impressive as the surroundings were meant to be. An excellent breakfast (extra) tops off a stay in these distinctive lodgings; amenities include free phone calls within Europe and to the United States.

Alfstrasse 38. www.hotelanno1216.de. © **0451/4008210.** 11 units. 138€ double, suites 198€–228€. Breakfast around 10€. Parking 7€ nearby. **Amenities:** Wi-Fi (free).

Ringhotel Jensen ★   This gabled 14th-century patrician townhouse on the banks of the Taber has been an inn since 1774, so they've had plenty of time to make a sure stay goes well. The somewhat plain accommodations aren't as historically authentic as the exterior, but they are pleasantly comfortable, and many face the Holstenstor gate. A buffet breakfast is served in a sunny room overlooking the river.

An der Obertrave 4–5. www.ringhotel-jensen.de. © **0451/702490.** 42 units. 93€–115€ double. Buffet breakfast included. Parking 7€ nearby. **Amenities:** Restaurant; room service; Wi-Fi (free).

Where to Eat in Lübeck

Brauberger ★ NORTHERN GERMAN   A short walk from the Marienkirche, drink from the source at this in-town brewery that has been making pale ale since 1225. You'll have to make your way around the huge copper brewing kettles to look for a seat at one of the communal tables in the cavernous, multilevel space. Customers put down their steins long enough to discover some excellent food of the schnitzel and sausage variety. Service, despite a nightly crush, is friendly and fast.

Alfstrasse 36. www.brauberger.de. © **0451/71444.** Main courses 7€–14€. Daily 5pm–midnight.

Haus der Schiffergesellschaft ★ NORTHERN GERMAN   It's hard not to fall under the spell of this former sailors' haunt from 1535, where ship models, lanterns, and other nautical memorabilia hang from paneled walls and ceilings. Seating is at scrubbed-oak plank tables and high-backed wooden booths carved with the coats of arms of Baltic merchants. You can share a table in the main dining hall to enjoy baked black pudding with slices of apple and lamb's lettuce and other local favorites, or take a seat at the long bar. Wherever you sit, take a look at what might be the most charming artifacts of all, revolving lamps painted with scenes in which ships sail across the seas.

Breitestrasse 2. www.schiffergesellschaft.com. © **0451/76776.** Main courses 12€–20€. Daily 10am–midnight. Bar Tues–Sat 5pm–4am.

Zimmermann's Lübecker Hanse ★★ SEAFOOD/GERMAN   Ask Lübeckers where to eat, and they'll probably steer you to this time-honored favorite near Petrikirche, where warmly lit, dark-paneled rooms are an especially welcome and atmospheric refuge on a chilly evening. Fresh

Baltic fish and seafood are the menu standouts (the hearty fish soup is a meal in itself), though chef Patrick Marquand also prepares a lot of beef and game, including an aromatic roast duck and a delicious currywurst made from deer. Desserts couple Lubeck's love of chocolate and the kitchen's skill with pastry.

Kolk 3–7. www.luebecker-hanse.com. ✆ **0451/78054.** Main courses 14€–23€. Tues–Sat noon–3pm and 6pm–midnight. Closed Jan 1–14.

SYLT ★★

193km (120 miles) NW of Hamburg, 20km (12 miles) W of the Danish border

The long, narrow island of Sylt (pronounced *Zoolt*) lies in the North Sea 5 miles off the northernmost coast. Sylt is the largest island of the Frisian archipelago and the fourth largest island in Germany. Even at that, the long, narrow storm-lashed outcropping is small and fragile, only 550m (1,800 ft.) wide at its narrowest point and 38km (24 miles) in total length. Very few international travelers find their way to Sylt, but Germans come in droves to take in the iodine-rich air and enjoy the rain-soaked North Sea climate they call *Reizklima.* Even in midsummer temperatures rarely rise above the low 70s (low to mid-20s Celsius); rain can come at any minute, and winds on the beach are a constant. Accordingly, the Sylt "mink" is yellow oilskin, de rigueur for even the most fashion-conscious residents and visitors.

Despite the rigors, Sylt caters to a sophisticated resort clientele: the island is a second home for some of Germany's wealthiest citizens, and it's also popular with lesbian and gay vacationers. For the most part, Sylt is an expensive place to spend time, especially in the popular summer months. Some northerners, including those from Hamburg, defray the cost by visiting as day trippers (an early start from Hamburg, three hours away by car or train, gives you a full day at the beach). The main attractions for many visitors, no matter what their social status, are walking on 40km (25 miles) of beaches and sweating it out in a waterside sauna, then plunging into the chilly North Sea to cool off.

Adding to the island's allure is a sense of fleetingness, as ongoing erosion eats away at what is essentially an endangered strip of sand jutting into the North Sea. Dunes on the especially vulnerable west coast shift by as much as 3.5m (11 ft.) a year, and with each winter storm and rise in tides, there is less of this northern paradise to enjoy.

Essentials

GETTING THERE   As many as 17 **trains** travel daily between Hamburg and the Westerland Bahnhof on Sylt; the trip takes around 3 hours (give or take 20 minutes depending on stops), with the final portion on a long rail causeway from the mainland. For information, visit www.bahn.de or call © **01805/996633.** If you wish to drive to the island, you'll have to load your car onto the Sylt-bound train at Niebüll on the mainland. No advance booking is necessary; you just arrive and take your chances. An alternative route is via **car-ferry** from the Danish port of Havneby, on the island of Rømo (easily accessible via highway from Germany), landing at List, at Sylt's northern tip. There are at least a dozen daily crossings in summer, significantly fewer in winter. Round-trip passage for a car with a driver and up to three passengers costs 85€; you can make reservations in advance. For information, call the **Rømo-Sylt Line** (www.sylt faehre.de; © **0180/3103030**).

The nearest international airport is at Hamburg. From there you can fly to the regional **Sylt Airport;** (www.flughafen-sylt.de; © **04651/ 920612**). There's also regularly scheduled air service from Berlin, Munich, and Düsseldorf. Airlines serving Sylt are Sylt Air, Air Berlin, and Lufthansa.

VISITOR INFORMATION   Sylt's tourist office is at Keitumer Landstrasse 10B (www.sylt-tourismus.de; © **04651/6026**), open May to October daily 9am to 5pm, November to April Monday to Saturday 9am to 4pm.

GETTING AROUND   Low-lying Sylt is good biking terrain, and Sylt Fahrrad, at Westerland's bahnhof (www.sylt-fahrrad.de; © **04024/424- 9307**) rents bikes and helmets and dispenses maps of Sylt's 136 miles of biking and hiking paths. The shop is open daily, 8am to 7pm (closes at 5pm from October to March). Bikes rent for about 15€ a day. SVG (www. svg-busreisen.de; © **04651/836100**) operates **bus service** around the island, with fares ranging from 1.90€ to 7.10€, depending on distance traveled; family passes begin at 15€ a day and weekly passes cost 31€ and up, depending on the number of zones covered. You can purchase tickets on buses and at the tourist office. **Sylt Taxi** (www.sylt-taxi5555. de; © **04651/5555**) operates a fleet of cars around the island.

Exploring Sylt

The island's main settlement, **Westerland,** has enough concrete and high rises to dispel any notion of Sylt being a remote getaway. In fact, shops and restaurants lining the 5-km (4-mile) seafront promenade are so affluent that the town is known as the "Beverly Hills of the North Sea." Come summer, Westerland's white-sand beach is filled with 4,000 *Strandkörbe,* beach chairs that resemble wicker baskets, and so many sun worshippers crowd the strip that you may long for the lonely cobblestone squares of a Bavarian village. More appealing than Westerland are **Kampen,** a collection of thatch-roofed cottages (albeit some of the most expensive quaint cottages on earth) surrounded by dune cliffs, and similarly lower-key **Wenningstedt-Braderup.**

Strandkörbe **beach chairs crowd Sylt's popular Westerland beach.**

For many travelers who make it as far north as Sylt, it's not the settlements or the island's very few manmade attractions that will be of interest. One compelling reason to come to Sylt is to engage in *Wattwanderungen*—walking in **the Watt,** the shoreline tidelands and mudflats along the Wadden Sea on the east coast. Another reason is to hike or bask on the sandy expanses that ring much of the island's west coast. Top for scenic beauty is **Rote Kliff,** tucked beneath magnificent 50-meter-high (165-ft.) sand cliffs between Kampen and Wennigstedt. Adjoining this stretch of sand is **Buhne 16,** the most popular of the island's many nude beaches. Just about anywhere you venture on the island beyond the beaches and few settlements, you'll find yourself among wild heaths and low-lying tidal flats.

Where to Stay & Eat on Sylt

Alter Gasthof ★ FRISSAN/SEAFOOD   A 200-year-old farm at the northern tip of the island, near the List ferryport, isn't the quaint thatched-roof homestead it once was, but the warm rooms and pleasant terrace are still an atmospheric place to enjoy some typical island cuisine. That means seafood, of course, and specialties are oysters, crayfish, and house-smoked salmon and eel.

5 Alte Dorfstrasse, List. alter-gasthof.com. ✆ **04651/877244.** Main courses 25€–50€. Tues–Sun 1pm–midnight. Closed in Jan.

Landhaus Sylter Hahn ★★   Large guest rooms spread over two houses at the southern end of Westerland have a nice, easygoing island feel with pine bureaus, wicker chairs, and bright fabrics. You'll have to walk to the beach, but it's only a few minutes away, and you can hear the surf from the balconies and terraces off some of the rooms. A delightful garden provides a welcome respite from the beach crowds; an indoor pool and sauna make this a good wintertime choice as well.

Robbenweg 3, Westerland. www.sylter-hahn.de. ✆ **04651/92820.** 20 units. 120€–160€ double. Buffet breakfast included. **Amenities:** Bar; pool; sauna; Wi-Fi (free).

Sol'Ring Hof ★★   If you have pretentions of coming to Sylt and living like the 1 percent, this beautiful, thatch-roofed beach cottage is the place to do it. All of the units (many are two-story) face the sea and a private stretch of beach, while fireplaces and style-magazine worthy décor make staying indoors a treat. The in-house restaurant, one of the island's best, cinches the deal on never leaving the property.

1 Am Sandwall, Rantum. soelring-hof.de. ✆ **04651/836200.** 15 units. From 450€. **Amenities:** Restaurant; bar; spa; beach; Wi-Fi (free).

16

PLANNING YOUR TRIP TO GERMANY

Germans are famously organized. Travelers would be wise to follow their example and do a little advance planning for a trip to Germany, including how to get there, the best ways to get around, and where to stay.

GETTING THERE
By Plane

Lufthansa (www.lufthansa.com; © **800/645-3880** in the U.S., 800/563-5954 in Canada, or 06986/799-799 in Germany) operates the most frequent service from North America, with a nonstop service from around 20 cities. Given the quality of the fleet and service, as well as timeliness, a flight on Lufthansa is a good kickoff to a trip to Germany.

American Airlines (www.aa.com; © **800/433-7300**) flies nonstop from Dallas to Frankfurt daily, and serves other routes including Chicago–Düsseldorf. **Delta Airlines** (www.delta.com; © **800/241-4141**) offers daily nonstop service to Frankfurt from Atlanta, Detroit, and New York's JFK; a nonstop to Munich from Atlanta and Detroit; and connections to Berlin via Amsterdam and Paris. **United Airlines** (www.united.com; © **800/864-8331**) offers nonstops from Los Angeles, New York, Washington DC, San Francisco, and Chicago to Frankfurt; and Charlotte, Washington DC, and Boston to Munich, among others. **Air**

Berlin (www.airberlin.com; ℭ 866/266-5588) flies from Los Angeles, San Francisco, Miami, New York, and Vancouver to Berlin. **Eurowings** (www.eurowings.com), which is owned by Lufthansa, offers a direct flight to Cologne from Boston.

From London, **British Airways** (www.britishairways.com; ℭ 0844/493-0787 from the U.K.) and **Lufthansa** are the most convenient major carriers to the principal German cities, including Cologne and Stuttgart as well as more obvious hubs like Frankfurt, Munich, and Berlin. **BMI Regional** (www.bmiregional.com; ℭ 0870/6070555) serves Düsseldorf, Frankfurt, Hamburg, and Munich from U.K. regional airports Bristol and Southampton. **Ryanair** (www.ryanair.com), **Eurowings** (www.eurowings.com), and **EasyJet** (www.easyjet.com) offer low-cost, point-to-point services from Britain to dozens of German cities.

By Train

Many passengers travel to Germany by train from other European cities. (See "Getting Around," below, for information on purchasing rail passes.) Every single neighboring country has a direct rail link to somewhere (often many places) in Germany.

From **London,** your fastest option is to take the Eurostar to Brussels, and from there a high-speed train to your destination within Germany. Travel time from London to Cologne is between 4¾ hours and 6 hours; from London to Berlin or Munich, between 9 and 10½ hours; and from London to Hamburg, around 9 hours, depending on the precise service. You can buy tickets directly online via **Deutsche Bahn** (www.bahn.com) or use the **Loco2** (www.loco2.com) search and booking engine to purchase rail tickets, in English, in and between several major European countries, including the U.K., Germany, Italy, and France.

GETTING AROUND
By Plane

Germany has such a fast, efficient rail network (see "By Train," below) that you are unlikely to take an internal flight too often. However, if you do prefer to fly, from Frankfurt and other German hubs most destinations in Germany can be reached within an hour. A flight between **Hamburg and Munich** or **Berlin and Munich** will save you significant time over a train trip. Lufthansa and Air Berlin serve both routes.

All German cities with commercial airports have an airport shuttle service, offering reduced fares and fast connections between the airport and the city center; see individual chapters in this book for details.

Lufthansa and Deutsche Bahn (DB/German Rail) also have a joint ticketing system, **Rail&Fly,** which allows you to combine a train and a flight between two destinations on a single discounted ticket. Their **AIRail** program connects several cities in west and northwest Germany directly with Frankfurt Airport; luggage is checked and collected at Frankfurt's dedicated AIRail Terminal. See **www.bahn.com** for more details on where these services operate.

By Train

You'll find that the trains of **Deutsche Bahn** (**DB;** www.bahn.com; ℂ **01806/101111,** 08718/808066 in the U.K.) deserve their good reputation for comfort, cleanliness, and punctuality. Most trains are modern and fast, and all cars are nonsmoking. A snack bar or a dining car, serving German and international cuisine as well as wine and beer, can usually be found on all trains except locals.

Germany's high-speed train, known as the **Intercity Express (ICE),** is among the fastest in Europe, reaching speeds of 320kmph (199 mph) and making transits north to south or across the country in half a day or less. ICE trains have adjustable cushioned seats and air conditioning, and most are equipped with Wi-Fi (for a fee in second class, free in first).

Several thousand slightly slower **InterCity (IC)** passenger trains offer express service between most large and medium-sized German cities. Most have onboard restaurants or catering. A network of **EuroCity (EC)** trains connecting Germany with 13 other countries offers the same high standards of service as those of an IC.

City Night Line (CNL) or **Intercity-Night** trains operate on a Europewide network that includes Warsaw to Cologne via Berlin; Berlin to Zürich, Switzerland, via Frankfurt and the Rhineland; Hamburg to Munich (stopping in Stuttgart, Ulm, and Augsburg); and Hamburg to Zürich via Freiburg. Trains often depart between 10pm and midnight with arrival the next morning between 7 and 8am. Sleeping accommodations in first class include single, double, or three-person compartments with shower and toilet. Standard class offers sleeping cars with washbasin only, as well as berths in four- or five-person couchette compartments. The CNL is equipped with a restaurant and bistro car; a breakfast buffet is included in any sleeping-car fare. Advance reservations are mandatory for sleeping accommodations. Deutsche Bahn issues tickets for the City Night Line and also makes seat reservations; go to **www. bahn.de/citynightline**. Eurail and German Rail Pass holders (see p. 705) have to pay extra for the couchette or sleeper reservation.

Regional and Regional-Express (R/RE) trains connect local stations, towns, and cities nationwide. **S-Bahn** lines are integrated into urban transit networks all over Germany.

Private rail operator **HKX** (www.hkx.de) operates a limited service between Hamburg and Frankfurt, via Cologne and Düsseldorf.

Insider tip: Download the **DB Navigator** app (for Android or iOS), which allows you to quickly check journey times and prices between anywhere and anywhere else in Germany.

DISCOUNTED TICKETS There's no advantage to buying regional and local rail tickets ahead of travel. However, you can **save big** by booking an ICE or IC train in advance. Tickets are generally released **91 days** ahead of departure date. The discounted *Sparpreis* **(saver fare)** could be up to 75% less than the normal flexible ticket price you'd pay if buying your ticket on the day of travel. *Sparpreis* fares start from as little as 19€ per person. (If you are quick and lucky, you could bag London–Frankfurt for 59€.) As tickets are snapped up, the saver price rises steadily. But even a few days before travel, it's worth checking. Note: *Sparpreis* tickets incur a fee to change or refund.

Another discount worth knowing about is the *Schönes-Wochenende-Ticket.* These permit unlimited travel on a single weekend day (a 27-hour period from midnight through 3am the next day) on Regional and Regional-Express trains, although not high-speed services. It costs 40€ per person, with up to 3 additional passengers paying just 4€ each.

Children ages 5 and under travel free on all Germany's trains; they don't need a ticket. Children ages 6 to 14 also do not pay, if accompanied by a parent or grandparent, but they must have a valid (free) ticket. This applies even on ICE trains.

GERMAN RAIL TRAVEL PASSES The **German Rail Pass** offers several options beginning with 3 days and going up to 15 days. For example, 3 days of travel in 1 month costs $302 first class or $224 second class. The **German Rail Twin Pass,** for two adults (who do not have to be married and can be of the same sex) *traveling together* in first or second class represents a 50% saving over single prices. A **German Rail Youth Pass**— around 20% cheaper than the adult pass—is valid only for travelers ages 12 to 25. Up to two kids ages 6 to 11 can also travel free on an accompanying adult's full-priced pass in first or second class.

Passholders **must** reserve (and pay a little extra) in advance for night trains. However, unlike in several other European countries, there are no extra supplements for passholders to travel on high-speed trains. You **can** reserve for IC and ICE trains to get a guaranteed seat, however.

The passes also entitle the bearer to additional benefits. Bonuses include free travel (subject to a 4€ prebooking charge) on **IC buses'** international routes, including Munich–Prague, Düsseldorf–London, and Berlin–Krakow; discounted travel on the Romantic Road motorcoach (see www.touring-travel.eu/en/romantic-road-coach); a discounted pass on **KD German Line** (www.k-d.de) boat trips on the Rhine or Mosel; and a half-price ride on a **Lake Constance steamboat** (www.bsb-online.com), among others.

Travel Times Between Some Major Cities

CITIES	DISTANCE	FASTEST TRAIN TRAVEL TIME	APPROXIMATE DRIVING TIME
Berlin to Cologne	563km/350 miles	4 hr., 15 min.	5¼ hr.
Berlin to Frankfurt	545km/339 miles	3 hr., 45 min.	5 hr.
Berlin to Hamburg	280km/174 miles	1 hr., 50 min.	2¾ hr.
Berlin to Munich	600km/373 miles	6 hr., 10 min.	5 hr.
Frankfurt to Hamburg	500km/311 miles	3 hr., 40 min.	4½ hr.
Frankfurt to Munich	385km/239 miles	3 hr., 15 min.	3¾ hr.
Munich to Cologne	562km/349 miles	4 hr., 40 min.	5½ hr.
Munich to Hamburg	766km/476 miles	5 hr., 40 min.	7 hr.

If your itinerary takes in several European countries, you may also want to consider a multicountry **Eurail Pass.** See **www.eurail.com** for details.

WHERE TO BUY RAIL PASSES Order German Rail Passes from a dedicated site operated by Eurail and DB: **www.germanrailpasses.com**.

By Car

Competition in the European car-rental industry is fierce, so make sure to comparison shop on sites (and apps) including **Kayak** (www.kayak.com), **Skyscanner** (www.skyscanner.net/carhire), and **Rentalcars.com.** Major agencies include **Avis** (www.avis.com; ✆ 800/331-1084), **Budget** (www.budget.com; ✆ 800/472-3325), **Hertz** (www.hertz.com; ✆ 800/654-3001), **Kemwel** (www.kemwel.com; ✆ 877/820-0668), and **Auto Europe** (www.autoeurope.com; ✆ 888/223-5555).

There are some advantages to **prepaying rentals** in your native currency before leaving home. You get an easy-to-understand net price, the rental process is more streamlined, and you can avoid unfavorable changes in currency exchange rates. Remember, however, that if you opt to prepay and your plans change, you'll have to go through some rather complicated paperwork for changing or canceling a prepaid contract. Also note that **diesel fuel** is cheaper than gas/petrol, so opt for diesel if your rental company gives you a choice.

DRIVING RULES In Germany, you drive on the right side of the road. Both front- and back-seat passengers must wear safety belts. Children 3 and younger cannot ride in the front seat. Children ages 11 and under and under 1.5m/4 ft. 11 in. tall must wear a child restraint or sit in an adapted **child seat.** Be sure to ask your rental company to supply one with your vehicle: It's the law.

Easy-to-understand international road signs are posted, but travelers should remember that distances and speeds are in kilometers, not miles. In congested areas, the **speed limit** is about 50kmph (about 30 mph).

On all other roads except the autobahns, the speed limit is 100kmph (about 60 mph).

In theory, there is no speed limit on the autobahns (in the left, fast lane), but many drivers going too fast report that they have been stopped by the police and fined, and the government recommends a speed limit of 130kmph (81 mph). German motorists generally flash their lights if they want you to move over so they can pass. You must use low-beam headlights at night and during fog, heavy rain, and snowfalls, and you must stop for pedestrians in crosswalks. Using a cellphone while at the wheel is illegal; you may incur an on-the-spot fine if caught.

All roads—including the autobahn/freeway—are toll-free.

Note: Drinking while driving is a very serious offense in Germany. Be sure to keep alcoholic beverages in the trunk or another storage area.

BREAKDOWNS/ASSISTANCE   The major automobile clubs in Germany are **Automobilclub von Deutschland (AvD)** (www.avd.de; ✆ **069/ 6606-0**) and the **Allgemeiner Deutscher Automobile-Club (ADAC)** (www.adac.de; ✆ **0800/510-1112**). If you have a breakdown on the autobahn, you can call from one of many emergency phones, spaced about a mile apart. Your rental car will come with instructions on which number to call in the event of an emergency away from the autobahn. The **ADAC** emergency number is ✆ **01802/222222.** In English, ask for "roadside assistance." Thanks to a reciprocal agreement, ADAC road-side assistance is free for AAA members, but you must pay for any parts.

DRIVER'S LICENSES   American drivers and those resident in E.U. coun-tries need only a domestic license to drive. However, in Germany and throughout the rest of Europe, you must also have an international insur-ance certificate or "green card." Any car-rental agency will automatically provide one of these as a standard part of the rental contract, but it's a good idea to double-check all documents at the time of rental, just to be sure that you can identify the card if asked by border patrol or the police.

PARKING   Parking in the center of most big towns is expensive. Look for parking lots and parking garages outside the center, identified by a large P (a little "hat" over the P indicates a covered garage). Most parking lots use an automated ticket system. You insert coins or a credit card to purchase time, either in advance or on departure.

By Bus

An excellent, efficient bus network serves Germany. Many buses are operated by **Bahnbus** (www.bahnbus.com), a conglomerate which is owned by the railway. These are integrated to complement the rail ser-vice. Bahnbus service is particularly convenient during slow periods of rail service, normally around midday and on Saturday and Sunday.

FlixBus (www.flixbus.com, ✆ **030/300-137300**) is an indepen-dent bus operator with a network of well-priced, Wi-Fi-equipped, day and night bus services all over Germany. Useful express connections include Munich–Berlin (7 hr.), Berlin–Cologne (7 hr.), and Hamburg–Freiburg (10½ hr.).

By Boat

The mighty **Rhine** is Germany's most traveled waterway. Cruise ships also run on the River **Main** between Mainz and Frankfurt; on the **Danube** from Nürnberg to Linz (Austria), going on to Vienna and Budapest; and on the **Mosel** between Cochem and Trier. A good place to begin investigating the many options, is **Cruise Critic** (www.cruisecritic.com). Also see the individual chapters in this book for details of boat trips on stretches of the Rhine, Mosel, and Danube.

Canal barge cruises are a good way to see a rarely viewed part of Germany. Many German itineraries focus on Berlin and the Mecklenburg lakes, and the classic Mosel route, from Trier to Koblenz. A good overview of trips, as well as packages, are available from **European Barging** (www.europeanbarging.com; © 888/869-7907).

ACCOMMODATIONS STRATEGIES

In Germany's large cities—like Berlin, Frankfurt, Cologne, and Munich—booking your hotel room ahead is essential, especially if you're going to be in Munich during Oktoberfest or any city during a major event. **Trade fairs** can push up prices significantly, particularly in cities like Frankfurt and Düsseldorf where they are a recurring feature.

Booking ahead isn't as important in the rest of Germany, but it's still a good idea, particularly when you're going to be spending a Friday or Saturday night in places that are popular getaways for Germans, such as Dresden, the Black Forest, the Rhine and Mosel valleys, and Bodensee (Lake Constance).

Tourist information centers, located in or near the main train stations in most German cities and towns, can help you find a room. Some charge nothing; others charge a small fixed fee (usually no more than a few euros); and others charge 10% of the first night's hotel rate, but you get that back at the hotel, so the service ends up costing nothing.

But you shouldn't only be thinking about accommodations in terms of hotels. **Short-term apartment, cottage, and house rentals** can be economical and often provide travelers with more space and a more authentic travel experience. In some places you'll rent through an agency and in others directly from the owner of the property, who may or may not be nearby to offer assistance during your stay. This sector is not as well-developed as in France or Italy, but you will find options that can help you get off the beaten path. Among the companies offering such rentals are **Airbnb** (www.airbnb.com); **Belvilla** (www.belvilla.com); Tripadvisor-owned **Holiday Lettings** (www.holidaylettings.co.uk); **HomeAway** (www.homeaway.com); and HomeAway-owned **VRBO** (www.vrbo.com).

SPECIAL-INTEREST TRIPS & TOURS

SPECIALTY ESCORTED TOURS **Maupintour** (www.maupintour.com; ✆ 800/255-4266) offers escorted tours of German Christmas markets, as well as the Romantic Road and Black Forest. **Reformation Tours** (www.reformationtours.com; ✆ 800/303-5534) leads excursions to cathedrals, monasteries, and sites associated with Martin Luther. **World War II Tours** (www.worldwar2toursofeurope.com; ✆ 702/586-7330) visits naval bases and other sites associated with the war and Third Reich. You can taste beer in Bamberg and sample Oktoberfest in Munich with **BeerTrips** (www.beertrips.com; ✆ 406/531-9109). Grape-lovers can tour Rhine and Mosel vineyards with **Wine Tours of the World** (www.winetoursoftheworld.com; ✆ 888/635-8007).

LEARNING VACATIONS **Road Scholar** (www.roadscholar.org; ✆ 800/454-5768) offers travelers aged 55 and older university-based courses on art, history, culture and other subjects that provide insight into Germany. Fees for the programs, usually around two weeks long, include accommodations, meals, tuition, tips, and insurance. Good sources for language schools in Germany include **Languages Abroad** (www.languages abroad.com) and **GoAbroad.com.**

BIKING Germany has lots of excellent biking terrain. **Classic Adventures** (www.classicadventures.com; ✆ 800/777-8090) leads bike tours along the Romantic Road and other scenic routes including Lake Constance. **Austin Adventures** (www.austinadventures.com; ✆ 800/575-1540) leads bike trips in Bavaria and the Mosel Valley. **Cyclists' Touring Club Holidays** (www.cyclingholidays.org) organizes bike trips through Bavaria and Franconia. **Bike Adventures** (www.bikeadventures.co.uk; ✆ 44-1584/877508) offers one trip that follows the Danube through Germany, Austria, Slovakia, and into Budapest, and plus another that follows the Rhine "from source to sea," covering 750 miles and passing through four countries.

WALKING & HIKING It's estimated that Germany has more than 80,000 marked hiking and mountain-walking tracks. **Deutschen Wanderverband** (www.wanderverband.de; ✆ 0561/938-730) has details about trails, shelters, huts, and contact details for hiking associations in various regions. The **Deutscher Alpenverein** (www.alpenverein.de; ✆ 089/140030) operates over 300 huts in and around the Alps that are open to mountaineers and trekkers; it also maintains a 15,000km (9,300-mile) network of Alpine trails. The best Alpine hiking is in the Bavarian Alps, especially the 1,240m (4,070-ft.) Eckbauer, on the southern fringe of Garmisch-Partenkirchen. **Headwater** (www.headwater.com; ✆ 44-1606/828560) operates a Bavarian walking itinerary that includes Oberammergau and the Zugspitze, Germany's tallest peak.

ATMs

In German cities, you can easily find 24-hour ATMs in airports, train stations, and outside banks. **Cirrus** (www.mastercard.com) and **Plus** (www.visa.com/atms) are the most common networks. Remember that almost all banks impose a fee every time you use your card at an overseas ATM. Despite the fees, ATM withdrawals are usually less costly than transactions made at Bureaux de Change and other commercial exchanges.

Business Hours

Most **banks** are open Monday to Friday 8:30am to 1pm and 2:30 to 4pm (Thurs to 5:30pm). Money exchanges at airports and border-crossing points are generally open daily from 6am to 10pm. Most **businesses** are open Monday to Friday from 9am to 5pm and on Saturday from 9am to 1pm. **Store** hours are tightly regulated by a federal law, the *Ladenschlussgesetz*. This stipulates that shops must remain closed on Sundays and public holidays. Monday through Saturday hours can vary from region to region, but shops are generally open Monday to Friday 9 or 10am to 6 or 6:30pm. Saturday hours are generally from 9am to 1 or 2pm, except in major shopping areas, where Saturday hours follow the Monday-to-Friday times.

Customs

You can take into Germany most personal effects including gadgetry like video and still cameras, a smartphone, and a laptop, provided they show signs of use; 200 cigarettes, 50 cigars, or 250 grams of tobacco; 4 liters of wine or 1 liter of liquor per person 17 and over. Fishing gear, a bicycle, skis, tennis or squash racquets, and golf clubs are all permitted.

For specifics on what U.S. citizens can bring home from Germany (and anywhere else), check *Know Before You Go* online at **www.cbp.gov/travel/us-citizens/know-before-you-go**. For a clear summary of Canadian rules, check the "Travellers" section on the Canadian Border Services Agency website at **www.cbsa-asfc.gc.ca**. U.K. visitors can take home any legal goods, as long as they are for personal rather than commercial use.

Disabled Travelers

Germany is relatively hospitable for travelers with disabilities. Most large cities and many smaller ones provide elevator access to subways, ramps and lifts on buses and streetcars and at museums and other public facilities, and wheelchair-accessible taxis. Local tourist offices can issue permits for drivers to give them access to parking areas for the disabled. Many hotels, especially newer ones, are equipped to meet the needs of those with disabilities, and often have specially equipped rooms. Many restaurants are wheelchair accessible. Keep in mind, though, that throughout the country some historic sights may not be properly equipped for travelers with disabilities.

Organizations that offer assistance to travelers with disabilities include the **Society for Accessible Travel & Hospitality** (SATH; www.sath.org; ✆ 212/447-7284), which offers a wealth of travel resources for all types of disabilities and informed recommendations on destinations, access guides, travel agents, tour operators, vehicle rentals, and companion services. **Access-Able Travel Source** (www.access-able.com; ✆ 303/232-2979) keeps a database on travel agents from around the world with experience in accessible travel; destination-specific access information; and links to such resources as service animals, equipment rentals, and access guides. The "Accessible Travel" section linked from the sidebar at **Mobility-Advisor.com** suggests several travel resources suited to persons with disabilities. Launched in 2015, **Accomable** (www.accomable.com) is an Airbnb-like website listing accessible accommodations worldwide, including in Berlin and Hannover.

Many travel agencies offer customized tours and itineraries for travelers with disabilities. Among them are **Flying Wheels Travel** (www.flyingwheelstravel.com; © **877/451-5006** or 507/451-5005), which operates Danube and Rhine riverboat cruise tours; and **Accessible Journeys** (www.disabilitytravel.com; © **800/846-4537** or 610/521-0339).

Doctors
U.S. travelers will be expected to pay for nonemergency medical care (claim afterwards on your travel medical insurance). Members of the **International Association for Medical Assistance to Travelers** (**IAMAT;** www.iamat.org; © **716/754-4883** or 416/652-0137) can access lists of approved English-speaking doctors. In major towns and cities, the tourist office sometimes keeps a list of local English-speaking doctors.

Drinking Laws
Officially, you must be 18 to consume any kind of alcoholic beverage in Germany. Bars and cafes rarely request proof of age. Drinking while driving, however, is treated as a very serious offense. The **blood alcohol limit** is .05%; for young drivers it's zero.

Electricity
Standard electricity is **220 volts AC** (50 cycles). Much of your electronic gear (including laptops) have built-in converters but you will need a transformer for any device without one. Be sure to pack an **adapter** (a 2-prong plug that fits the standard European socket). Some hotels will supply these, but your safest bet is to travel with a couple in your hand luggage.

Embassies & Consulates
Principal embassies are all in Berlin. The **Embassy of the United States** is at Clayallee 170 (http://de.usembassy.gov; © **030/83050**). The **U.K. Embassy** is at Wilhelmstrasse 70–71 (www.gov.uk/government/world/germany; © **030/204570**). The **Australian Embassy** is at Wallstrasse 76–79 (www.germany.embassy.gov.au; © **030/880-0880**). The **Canadian Embassy** is at Leipziger Platz 17 (www.germany.gc.ca; © **030/203120**). The **Irish Embassy** is at Jägerstrasse 51 (www.embassyofireland.de; © **030/220720**). The **New Zealand Embassy** is at Friedrichstrasse 60 (www.nzembassy.com; © **030/206210**). There are also **U.S. Consulates General** in: **Düsseldorf** (Willi-Becker-Allee 10; © **0211/788-8927**); **Frankfurt** (Giessener Strasse 30; © **069/75350**); **Hamburg** (Alsterufer 27–28; © **040/411-71100**); **Leipzig** (Wilhelm-Seyfferth-Strasse 4; © **0341/213-840**); and **Munich** (Königinstrasse 5; © **089/28880**). **Canadian Consulates** are located in: **Düsseldorf** (Benrather Strasse 8; © **0211/172170**); **Munich** (Tal 29;

© **089/2199-570**); and **Stuttgart** (Leitzstrasse 45; © **0711/2239-678**).

Emergencies
Throughout Germany the emergency number for police is © **110;** for fire or to call an ambulance, dial © **112.** You can also get connected to the police by dialing © **112** anywhere in Europe.

Family Travel
Admission prices for attractions throughout Germany are usually reduced for children ages 6 to 14. Kids younger than 6 almost always get in for free. If you're traveling with children, always check to see whether the attraction offers a money-saving **family ticket,** which considerably reduces the admission price for a group of two adults and two or more children. The same is true for long-distance public transportation: Low-priced family or group tickets are usually available. On **trains,** children ages 6 to 14 travel free, if accompanied by a parent or grandparent (half-off otherwise). Children ages 5 and under always travel free. **Hotels** usually have family rooms, or will put an extra bed in a large double.

Gay & Lesbian Travelers
Germany is one of the most "developed" countries in the world when it comes to gay pride, gay culture, and gay tourism. If you are *schwul* (gay) or *lesbisch* (lesbian), you'll find plenty to do in Deutschland. Berlin, Munich,

Hamburg, Frankfurt, and Cologne all have large gay communities, and gay life flourishes outside the big cities, too. Berlin celebrates its **Christopher Street Day and Parade** (www.csd-berlin.de) around the third weekend in June. **Cologne-Pride** (www.colognepride. de) usually is the first weekend in July. Frankfurt's **Christopher Street Day** (www.csd-frankfurt.de) takes place in the middle of July; Munich's **Christopher Street Day** (www.csdm-uenchen.de) in also mid-July. **Hamburg Pride** (www. hamburg-pride.de) is usually staged in early August.

Gay and lesbian couples (or friends) qualify for family tickets on public transportation in many Germany cities. With most family or *Gruppen* (group) tickets, all that matters is that two (or more) individuals travel together.

Health
Germany should not pose any major health hazards. The heavy cuisine may give some travelers mild indigestion, however; you might want to pack an over-the-counter medicine, or (better yet) eat moderately. The water is safe to drink throughout Germany. However, don't drink from mountain streams, no matter how clear and pure the water looks, to prevent contact with **Giardia** and other unpleasant bacteria (especially if animals are reared upstream).

Pack **prescription medications** in your carry-on luggage and carry them in their original containers, with pharmacy labels—otherwise they might not make it through airport security.

Insurance
For travel overseas, most U.S. health plans (including Medicare and Medicaid) do not provide coverage, and the ones that do often require you to pay for services upfront and reimburse you only after you return home.

Canadians should check with their provincial health-plan offices or call **Health Canada** (www.hc-sc.gc.ca; 🕿 **866/225-0709**) to find out the extent of their coverage and what documentation and receipts they must take home if they are treated overseas.

Travelers from the U.K. should carry their **European Health Insurance Card (EHIC)** as proof of entitlement to free/reduced-cost medical treatment abroad (see www.nhs.uk/ehic). Note, however, that the EHIC covers only "necessary medical treatment"; for repatriation costs, lost money, baggage, or cancellation, travel insurance from a reputable provider should always be sought.

Mail
Street mailboxes are painted yellow. It costs 1.50€ for the first 50 grams (about 1¾ oz.) to send an airmail letter to the United States or Canada, and .90€ for postcards. Small letters or postcards to the U.K. cost .90€. See **www. deutschepost.de**.

Mobile Phones
In Germany, a mobile phone is called a *Handy* (pronounced as it's spelled). If your cellphone is on a GSM system, and you have a world-capable multiband phone (most are these days), you can make and receive calls across Germany and the rest of Europe. Just call your wireless operator and ask for "international roaming" to be activated on your account. Having an **unlocked phone** enables you to install a cheap, prepaid SIM card (found at a local retailer) in Germany. (Show your phone to the salesperson; not all phones work on all networks.) You'll get a local phone number and much lower calling and data rates, plus receiving calls from back home is free.

Buying a phone in Germany is another option. You shouldn't have too much trouble finding one for around 30€ (a little more for a smartphone). Use it. then recycle it or resell on eBay when you get home. It'll save you a fortune versus roaming costs or using hotel telephones.

Money & Costs
The **euro** (€) is the single European currency of Germany and other participating countries. Exchange rates of all Eurozone countries are locked into this common currency. Prices in Germany are moderate, especially compared to those in large cities in the U.S. and Britain, and you generally get good value for your money.

Euro	Aus$	Can$	NZ$	UK£	US$
1€	1.46	1.45	1.56	0.84	1.10

Check a currency conversion website such as **XE.com** for up-to-date exchange rates.

Passports

Citizens of the U.S., Canada, Ireland, Australia, New Zealand, and the U.K. do not require visas for visits of less than 3 months. Your passport must be valid for **at least 3 months** beyond your planned date of departure.

Police

Throughout the country, dial ✆ **110** or **112** for police emergencies.

Safety

Overall, the security risk to travelers in Germany is low. Violent crime is rare, but it can occur, especially in larger cities. Most incidents of **street crime** consist of pickpocketing or theft of unattended items. Take the same precautions against becoming a crime victim as you would in any city.

If your passport is stolen or lost, report it immediately to the local police and the nearest embassy or consulate. If you are the victim of a crime while in Germany, in addition to reporting to local police, contact the nearest embassy or consulate for assistance.

Smoking

Check before lighting up. In general, you cannot smoke in most restaurants and many **bars** in Germany, but these rules vary by federal state. In some places smoking is banned by law and enforced. In other places the federal law is not enforced in bars of a certain size, or after the kitchen closes at restaurants that stay open late, morphing into a barlike setting as the night goes on. Throughout the country, smoking is banned in all **public buildings** and on **transport.**

Taxes

Germany imposes a sales tax on most goods and services known as a **value-added tax (VAT)** or, in German, *Umsatzteuer*. Nearly everything is taxed at 19%, from necessities such as gas to luxury items like jewelry; the tax is factored into the posted price rather than added at the cash register. Food and books are taxed at 7%. VAT is included in the prices of restaurants and hotels. Stores that display a tax-free sticker will issue you a **Tax-Free Shopping** form at the time of purchase. When leaving the country, have your goods and receipts on hand as you get the form stamped by the German Customs Service. You can then get a cash refund at one of the Tax-Free Shopping offices in the major airports, train stations, and bigger ferry terminals; or use a service such as **Global Blue** (www.globalblue.com).

Telephones

To call Germany from home: 1. dial your country's international access code (011 from the U.S. or Canada, 00 from the U.K. or New Zealand, 0011 from Australia), 2. dial the country code for Germany (**49**), and 3. dial the local number (remember to drop the initial 0, which is for use only within Germany). So, for example, to call Berlin Tourism's information line from New York City, you would dial 011-49-30-250025.

To make international calls from Germany, dial 00 (Germany's international access code), the other country's code (1 for the U.S. and Canada, 44 for the U.K., 61 for Australia, and 64 for New Zealand), then the local number you wish to reach.

To make local calls within Germany: To dial a number within the same area code, drop the initial 0. To dial a number within Germany in a different area code, use the 0.

Tipping

If a restaurant bill includes *Bedienung* (it almost always does), that means a service charge has already been added, so just round up a couple of euros.

Guided tour of Neuschwanstein Castle	12€, + 9€ carriage ride
Admission to Cologne Cathedral	free
Watching the Glockenspiel on Munich's Marienplatz	free
Day pass at Caracalla Therme Spa, Baden-Baden	23€
Ticket to the Stuttgart Ballet	10€–116€
Ticket to the Bayreuth Opera Festival	30€–320€
Cover charge at the Cotton Club jazz club in Hamburg	6.50€–15€
1-day pass on Rhine river tour boat (KD Cruises)	30€–36€
Multi-day Rhine river cruise (Viking Cruises)	$2,156–$4,606
Double room at the Bayerische Hof, Munich	270€–380€ per night and up
Double room at Circus Hostel, Berlin	29€–43€ per night
Fixed-price dinner menu at Vau, in Berlin	120€–160€
Traditional Saxon meal at Auersbach Keller, Leipzig	15€–27€
A döner kebab in Berlin	2.50€
A frankfurter sausage in Frankfurt	2€
A hamburger in Hamburg	10€
A stein of beer at the Hofbrauhaus in Munich	8.40€

If not, add 10% or so. **Wait-staff** should be handed the tip directly, rather than expected to pick up your change from the table. **Bellhops** expect around 1€–2€ per bag. Round up **taxi** fares to the next euro—no more is expected. **Room-cleaning staffs** often get small tips in Germany, as do **concierges** who perform some special favors.

Toilets

Use the word *"Toilette"* (pronounced twah-leh-tah). Women's toilets are usually marked with an F for *Frauen*, and men's toilets with an H for *Herren*. Expect to pay 1€ to use some public facilities.

Visitor Information

All cities and nearly all large towns in Germany have **tourist offices;** we include details for these for all places we cover in the indi-vidual chapters. The German National Tourist Board also operates a website with advice and inspiration for travelers: **www.germany. travel**.

Index

A

Ä (Berlin), 132
Aachen (Aix-La-Chapelle),
    543–548
Abandoned Berlin, 90
Aber (Frankfurt), 520
Abteikirche St. Maria
    (Amorbach), 259–260
Accommodations, 708
    best hotels, 10–11
ACUD (Berlin), 127
Aeschbacher Bad, 486
Air travel, 702–704
    Berlin, 61–62
    Black Forest area, 414
    Cologne, 528
    Dresden, 178
    Düsseldorf, 548, 550
    Frankfurt, 489, 492
    Leipzig, 164, 166
    Nürnberg, 200
    The Rhineland, 564
Albertinum (Dresden), 180
Albrecht Dürer House
    (Nürnberg), 203
Albrechtsburg (Meissen), 194
Alexandrowka/Pfingstberg
    (Potsdam), 140
Allerheiligen Abbey and
    Waterfalls, 450, 451
Alpirsbach, 451
Alpirsbach Brauwelt brewery,
    453
Alpirsbach Kloster, 453
Alpspitz region, 298
Alsfeld, 621–622
The Alster (Hamburg), 670
Alstervergnügen (Hamburg), 34
Altar of the Apostles
    (Heidelberg), 379
Altbier, 556
Alte Brücke (Old Bridge;
    Heidelberg), 376
Alte Hofhaltung (Bamberg), 219
Alte Mainbrücke (Old Main
    Bridge; Würzburg),
    250–251
Alte Nationalgalerie (Berlin),
    86–87
Altenburg, 157
Altensteig, 446
Alte Oper (Frankfurt), 520
Alte Pinakothek (Old Masters
    Gallery; Munich), 324
Alte Rathaus
    Freiburg, 418
    Lindau, 478
Alter Elbtunnel (Old Elbe
    Tunnel; Hamburg), 664
Alter Kran (Lüneburg), 686–687
Alter Markt (Eberbach), 387
Alter Simpl (Munich), 360
Altes Museum (Berlin), 87

Altes Rathaus (Old City or Town
    Hall)
    Bamberg, 216–217
    Munich, 320
    Potsdam, 140
Altes Residenztheater (Cuvilliés
    Theater; Munich), 322,
    323, 359
Altes Schloss
    Stuttgart, 392
    Überlingen, 473–474
Altes Schloss and
    Württembergisches
    Landesmuseum (Old Castle
    and Württemberg Regional
    Museum; Stuttgart), 392
Altes Schloss Eremitage
    (Hermitage; Bayreuth), 224
Altstadt (Old Town)
    Bremen, 642
    Heidelberg, 371
    Munich, 315–321
Amalienburg (Nymphenburg
    Palace), 366
Amorbach, 259–261
Ampelmann (Berlin), 121–122
Amphitheater (Trier), 596
Ancestral Gallery (Munich), 323
Andreas Murkudis (Berlin), 121
Anja's Schloss (Heidelberg), 385
Ankerklause (Berlin), 132
Annweiler, 582
Antikensammlungen
    (Antiquities Collections;
    Munich), 327–328
Antiquarium (Munich), 322
Antiquity Card (Trier), 595
Apartment rentals, 708
    Berlin, 95
Apothekenmuseum
    (Pharmaceutical Museum;
    Heidelberg), 377
Apple-wine taverns,
    Frankfurt, 518
Aquademie-Water-Bath-Design
    Museum (Schiltach), 454
Aqua Fun, 464
Archäologisches Museum
    Frankfurt, 502
Archeological Collection
    (Tübingen), 407
Architecture, 19–23
Arnstadt, 157
Art, 23–26
Art galleries, Berlin, 74
Asamkirche (Munich), 318
Assmannshausen, 569
Astra Kulturhaus (Berlin), 130
Astronomical floor clock
    (Munich), 330
ATMs, 710
A Trane (Berlin), 127

Augsburg, 281–288
    exploring, 282
    restaurants and
        accommodations, 286–288
    traveling to, 281–282
    visitor information, 282
Augustiner Grossgaststätte
    (Munich), 355
Augustinerkloster (Erfurt), 159
Augustiner Museum
    (Freiburg), 419
Äussere Neustadt
    (Dresden), 180

B

Bacharach, 567
Bachhaus Eisenach, 163
Bach Museum Leipzig, 166–167
Bad Bergzabern, 582–583
Bad Cannstatt, 402
Bad Dürkheim, 581
Badehaus Szimpla (Berlin), 130
Baden-Baden, 432–443
    accommodations, 437–439
    arriving in, 432
    entertainment and nightlife,
        441–442
    exploring, 434
    getting around, 433–434
    restaurants, 439–441
    sports and outdoor pursuits,
        442–443
    visitor information, 432–433
Badenweiler, 430–431
Badeparadies Schwarzwald, 464
Badeschiff (Berlin), 130
Bad Homburg, 521–523
Bad Liebenzell, 446
Bad Mergentheim, 263
Bad Teinach-Zavelstein, 446
Bad Wildbad, 449
Baiersbronn, 449
Balgebrückestrasse (Bremen),
    643–644
Ballabeni (Munich), 336
Ballooning, Baden-Baden, 442
Bamberg, 215–222
    accommodations, 219–220
    arriving in, 216
    exploring, 216–219
    restaurants, 221
    shopping, 221–222
    visitor information, 216
Bamberger Reiter, 218
Barfussgässchen (Leipzig), 175
Barockviertel (Dresden), 192
Basserman-Jordan Wine Estate,
    581–582
Bau (Munich), 361
Bauhaus-Archiv (Berlin), 70–71
Bauhaus-Museum (Weimar), 148
Bauhaus School, 23
Bauhaus Shop (Berlin), 119

Bauhaus Universität
(Weimar), 148
Baumkronenpfad, 142
Bavarian Alps, 296–306
accommodations, 304–305
restaurants, 305–306
Bavarian National Museum
(Bayerisches
Nationalmuseum; Munich),
329–330
Bavarian State Ballet.
(Munich), 359
Bavarian State Opera
(Munich), 359
Bayerischen Staatsoper
(Munich), 359
Bayerischer Hof Night Club
(Munich), 360
Bayerischer Kunstgewerbe-
Verein (Munich), 356
Bayerisches Nationalmuseum
(Bavarian National Museum;
Munich), 329–330
Bayerisches Staatsschauspiel
(Bavarian State Theater;
Munich), 359
Bayerisches Viertel (Bavarian
Quarter; Berlin), 81
Bayreuth, 222–230
accommodations, 229
arriving in, 223
exploring, 223–228
restaurants, 230
visitor information, 223
Bayreuther Festspiele, 34
Bayreuther Festspiele (Bayreuth
Festival), 224
Beaches, Konstanz, 486
The Beatles, 670
Bebelplatz (Berlin), 79, 81
Bebenhausen Monastery (near
Tübingen), 409
Beckmann, Max, 167
Beelitz-Heilstätten, 142
Beer, 30
Beer gardens and beer halls
Berlin, 131–132
Munich, 355
BeethovenFest Bonn, 563
Beethoven Haus (Bonn),
559–560
Beilstein, 608–610
Belchen Circuit, 430
Belchen Mountain, 430
Bergbahnen (Dresden), 181
Berghain (Berlin), 129
Berg Kolben, 302
Berg Laber, 302
Bergwerkmuseum
(Freiburg), 421
Berlin, 60–143
abandonment issues, 90
accommodations, 95–103
Mitte and eastern Berlin,
99–103
western Berlin, 95–98
arriving in, 61–62
art galleries, 74
day trips from, 135–143

exploring, 70–94
abandoned Berlin, 90–93
for kids, 93–94
Mitte and eastern Berlin
attractions, 75–86
organized tours, 89–93
western Berlin attractions,
70–75
food markets, 116
getting around, 66–69
layout, 62–66
eastern Berlin
neighborhoods, 65–66
western Berlin
neighborhoods, 63–65
money-saving tourist deals, 67
nightlife and entertainment,
123–135
pharmacies, Berlin, 69
restaurants, 103–117
Mitte and eastern Berlin,
107–117
street eats, 108
western Berlin, 104–107
shopping, 117–123
visitor information, 62
Berlin-Brandenburg
International Airport, 61
Berliner Dom, 79
Berliner Ensemble, 126
Berliner Philharmoniker (Berlin
Philharmonic), 124
Berliner Unterwelten, 89
Berlin-Höhenschönhausen
Memorial (Berlin), 84
BERLIN infostore, 95
Berlin International Film
Festival, 33
Berlinische Galerie (Berlin),
75, 78
Berlin Programm, 124
Berlin Walks, 89
Berlin Wall, 87
buying a piece of, 123
Berlin Wall Memorial/
Berliner Mauer
Dokumentationszentrum, 87
Berlin WelcomeCard, 67
Berlin Welcome Card
Museumsinsel, 67
Berlin Zoo (Zoologischer
Garten), 92
Berlin Zoo/Tierpark, 93–94
Bernkastel-Kues, 602–605
Bernstein Club (Baden-
Baden), 442
Best, restaurants, best, 9–10
Besucher Bergwerk Hella-Glück
Stollen, 447
Bethmann Park (Frankfurt), 507
BEX Sightseeing (Berlin), 89
Biergarten Chinesischer Turm
(Munich), 355
Bier- und Oktoberfestmuseum
(Munich), 318–319
Biking
Baden-Baden, 442
Berlin, 68–69
Black Forest region, 465

Freiburg, 418
Hann. Münden, 633
Kaiserstuhl, 429
Lake Constance, 486
Munich, 314, 336–337
Romantic Road, 246
tours, 709
Berlin, 89
Bildergalerie (Picture Gallery;
Potsdam), 138
Birkenkopf (Stuttgart), 396
Black Forest (Schwarzwald),
414–416, 443–465
accommodations and
restaurants, 457–462
arriving in, 443–444
getting around, 444
hiking and walking, 464
regional specialties, 424
Schwarzwald Card, 416
spa culture, 433
spas, 462–463
visitor information, 444
Black Forest High Road,
accommodations and
restaurants, 460–462
Black Forest National Park, 450
Black Madonna (Beilstein), 608
Blaudruckwerkstatt im
Dürerhaus (Erfurt), 161
Blues Festival (Freiburg), 425
BMW Munich Plant, 331
BMW Museum (Munich), 331
BMW Welt (Munich), 330–331
Boating
Lake Constance, 487
Lake Titisee, 464–465
Boat trips and cruises, 708
Berlin, 89
Lake Constance, 466
the Middle Rhine, 565–567
Moselle Valley, 590–591
Bockenheim, 580
Bode Museum (Berlin), 88
Bodensee (Lake Constance),
466–487
accommodations, 478–482
entertainment and nightlife,
485–486
exploring around, 467–478
getting around, 466
restaurants, 482–485
spas, 484–485
sports and outdoor pursuits,
486–487
visitor information, 466
Bodensee Festival, 467
Bodensee Weinfest, 467
Bodenwerder, 634–636
Bohnenviertel (Stuttgart), 392
Bonbonmacherei (Berlin), 118
Bonn, 558–563
Books, recommended, 27
Bornheim Market
(Frankfurt), 517
Born Senf-Laden (Erfurt), 161
Börse (Stock Exchange;
Hamburg), 663
Böttcherstrasse (Bremen), 644

Boutiquechen (Düsseldorf), 557
Brandenburger Tor
    (Brandenburg Gate;
    Berlin), 78
Breisach, 426–429
Breisach am Rhein, 426
Breisacher Fahrgast
    Schiffahrt, 426
Bremen, 640–651
    accommodations, 647–649
    exploring, 642
    restaurants, 649–650
    side trip to Bremerhaven,
    650–651
    traveling to, 640
    visitor information, 641–642
Bremen Town Musicians,
    642–643
Bremerhaven, 650–651
Bremer Loch, 643
Breuninger (Stuttgart), 402
Britzingen, 430
Brockmann & Knoedler
    (Dresden), 191
Brothers Grimm, 616, 618–622,
    627, 639
Brückenstrasse (Frankfurt), 517
Brüder Grimm Haus & Museum
    Steinau (Steinau), 619–620
Buchenwald Concentration
    Camp & Memorial Site,
    152–153
Buddelschiff-Museum
    (Hamburg), 669
Buddenbrookhaus (Lübeck),
    691–692
Bühlerhöhe, 450
Buhne 16 (Sylt), 700
Burg Eberbach, 387
Burg Eltz, 613
Burg Landeck, 582
Burg Landshut (Bernkastel-
    Kues), 602–603
Burgruine Diemerstein, 580
Burg Trifels (Annweiler), 582
Burkheim, 427
The Burse (Tübingen), 405
Business hours, 710
Bus tours, Berlin, 89
Bus travel, 707–708

C

Cäcilienkirche (St. Cecilia's
    Church; Cologne), 536
CADA-Schmuck (Munich), 358
Café am Neuen See (Berlin), 92
Café Atlantik (Freiburg), 425
Café Einstein (Berlin), 132
Café Gnosa (Hamburg), 684
Café Puck (Munich), 360
Café Wintergarten im
    Literaturhaus (Berlin), 132
Calw, 446
Canal barge cruises, 708
Cannstatter Volksfest, 34
Cannstatter Volksfest
    (Stuttgart), 374
Captain's Cabin (Hamburg), 682

Caracalla-Therme (Baden-
    Baden), 434–435
Carnival (Fasching), 33, 315
    Cologne, 527
    Mainz, 571
Carolus Thermen (Aachen), 544
Car travel and rentals, 706–707
Casements and Water Supply
    Conduits (Nürnberg), 201
Casinos, Konstanz, 485–486
Cassiopeia (Berlin), 130
Cassiopeia Therme, 431
Castle Church (Schlosskirche;
    Lutherstadt Wittenberg), 176
Castle Illumination
    (Heidelberg), 374
Castle Mill (Überlingen), 474
Cave 54 (Heidelberg), 386
Cecilienhof Palace (Schloss
    Cecilienhof; Potsdam), 139
Cellphones, 712
Centre Charlemagne (Aachen),
    544–545
Chalet (Berlin), 130
Chapel of St. Anne
    (Füssen), 290
Charlottenburg Palace (Schloss
    Charlottenburg; Berlin), 75
Chiemsee, 366–369
Chiemsee-Schifffahrt Ludwig
    Fessle, 367
Children's Festival (Kinderzeche;
    Dinkelsbühl), 276
Chinesischer Turm (Chinese
    Pagoda; Munich), 333
Chinesisches Spiegelkabinett
    (Chinese Mirror Chamber;
    Bayreuth), 224
Chinesische Teehaus (Chinese
    Teahouse; Potsdam), 138
Chocolaterie St. Anna No. 1
    (Heidelberg), 385
Christmas markets, 34
    Berlin, 117
    Dresden, 191–192
    Frankfurt, 505
    Heidelberg, 374
    Munich, 315, 356
Christmasmarkt, Nürnberg, 201
Church of Our Lady in the Fir
    Tree (Wallfahrtskirche Maria
    in der Tanne; Triberg), 456
CitySightseeing (Munich), 336
C-Keller & Galerie Markt 21
    (Weimar), 157
Clärchens Ballhaus (Berlin),
    128–129
Claudia Skoda (Berlin), 121
Club der Visionäre (Berlin),
    129, 130
Club Grosse Freiheit 36/
    Kaiserkeller (Hamburg),
    684–685
Cochem, 610–613
Cologne (Köln), 525–542
    accommodations, 536–538
    arriving in, 528
    exploring, 531–536
    getting around, 530

    neighborhoods in brief,
    528–530
    nightlife and entertainment,
    541–542
    restaurants, 538–540
    shopping, 540–541
    visitor information, 530
Comedy Café Berlin, 126
Commerzbank Tower
    (Frankfurt), 498
Concentration camps
    Buchenwald Concentration
    Camp & Memorial Site,
    152–153
    Sachsenhausen, 141–142
Constance, Lake (Bodensee),
    466–487
    accommodations, 478–482
    entertainment and nightlife,
    485–486
    exploring around, 467–478
    getting around, 466
    restaurants, 482–485
    spas, 484–485
    sports and outdoor pursuits,
    486–487
    visitor information, 466
Consulates, 711
Cotton Club (Hamburg), 685
Cranach, Lucas, the Elder, 145,
    205, 285, 419, 501, 645
    House (Weimar), 148
Creglingen, 264–265
Criminal Museum
    (Kriminalmuseum;
    Rothenburg), 269–270
Cuckoo clocks, 453
Currywurst (Berlin), 108
Cusanusstift (Bernkastel-
    Kues), 602
Customs regulations, 710
Cuvilliés Theater (Altes
    Residenztheater; Munich),
    322, 323, 359
    CyclingBaden-Baden, 442
    Berlin, 68–69
    Black Forest region, 465
    Freiburg, 418
    Hann. Münden, 633
    Kaiserstuhl, 429
    Lake Constance, 486
    Munich, 314, 336–337
    Romantic Road, 246
    tours, 709
    Berlin, 89

D

Dachau Concentration Camp
    Memorial Site (KZ-
    Gedenkstätte Dachau),
    362–364
Daniel tower (Nördlingen), 278
Danube River
    cruises, 235
    Ulm, 240
Darklands (Berlin), 121
Das Leuze Mineral Spa
    (Stuttgart), 402
DDR Museum (Berlin), 84

Dean (Berlin), 129
Deichtorhallen (Hamburg), 661
Deidesheim, 581, 583
Der Trierer Dom (Trier
    Cathedral), 596–597
Der Verrückte Eismacher
    (Munich), 336
Destille (Heidelberg), 386
Deusches Museum
    (Munich), 337
Deutsche Bank Towers
    (Frankfurt), 499
Deutsche Barockgalerie
    (Augsburg), 285
Deutsche Fachwerkstrasse
    (German Half-timber
    Road), 444
Deutsche Kinemathek Museum
    für Film und Fernsehen
    (German Film and
    Television Museum; Berlin),
    79–80
Deutsche Oper am Rhein
    (Düsseldorf), 557
Deutsche Oper Berlin, 125
Deutsches Architekturmuseum
    (German Architecture
    Museum; Frankfurt), 497
Deutsches Auswandererhaus
    (German Emigration
    Center; Bremerhaven), 651
Deutsches Filmmuseum
    (German Film Museum;
    Frankfurt), 498
Deutsches Historisches Museum
    (German History Museum;
    Berlin), 78–79
Deutsches Museum (Munich),
    331–332
Deutsches Museum
    Verkehrszentrum
    (Transportation Museum;
    Munich), 332, 337
Deutsches Nationaltheater
    (Weimar), 156
Deutsches Salzmuseum
    (Lüneburg), 687–688
Deutsches Schauspielhaus
    (Hamburg), 682–683
Deutsches Theater
    (Munich), 359
Deutsches Uhrenmuseum
    (German Clock Museum;
    Furtwangen), 454
Deutsches Verpackungs-
    Museum (German Museum
    of Packaging; Heidelberg),
    376–377
Deutsches Weihnachtsmuseum
    (German Christmas
    Museum; Rothenburg), 274
Deutsches Weintor (German
    Wine Gate), 583
Deutsche Weinstrasse (German
    Wine Road), 577, 580–583
Diebsturm (Thieves' Tower;
    Lindau), 477
Dientsmann Christian
    (Marburg), 624

Die Schatzkammer (Treasury
    Museum; Trier), 597
Dinkelsbühl, 275–276, 280, 281
Diözesanmuseum St. Afra
    (Augsburg), 284
Dirndl-Ecke (Munich), 357
Disabled travelers, 710–711
Distillery (Leipzig), 175
Doctor Eisenbarth Theatre
    Company (Hann.
    Münden), 632
Doctors, 711
Doctors and hospitals, 69
Dokumentationszentrum
    Reichsparteitagsgelände
    (Nürnberg), 203–204
Dom (Cathedral)
    Aachen, 545
    Cologne, 531–533
Domberg (Erfurt), 159
Dommuseum (Frankfurt), 503
Domplatz (Bamberg), 216
Domschatzmuseum and
    Diözesanmuseum St. Ulrich
    (Regensburg), 232
Dom St. Kilian (Würzburg),
    250, 251
Dom St. Maria (Augsburg),
    282, 284
Dom St. Marien (Erfurt), 159
Dom St. Peter (Worms),
    577–578
Dom St. Peter's (Regensburg),
    231–232
Dom St. Petri (St. Peter's
    Cathedral; Bremen), 645
Domstufen-Festspiele
    (Erfurt), 159
Dom und Diözesan Museum
    (Cathedral and Diocesan
    Museum; Mainz), 571–572
Dom zu Meissen, 194
Donau-Schiffahrt Line, 235
Donauwörth, 279–280
Dorfschänke (Heidelberg), 385
Dornburg, 157
Dornier Museum
    (Friedrichshafen), 475
Dornstetten, 447
Dorothea Michalk
    (Dresden), 192
Dorotheenhütte (Wolfach), 456
Dreifaltigkeitskirke (Trinity
    Church; Speyer), 584–585
Dresden, 177–194
    accommodations, 185–187
    arriving in, 178
    day trips from, 193–194
    exploring, 180–185
    getting around, 178, 180
    nightlife and entertainment, 192
    restaurants, 187–190
    shopping, 191–192
    visitor information, 178
Dresden Cathedral (Kathedrale
    St. Trinitas), 182
Dresden City Card, 180
Dresden Philharmonie, 192

Drinking laws, 711
Driver's licenses, 707
Dr. Pong (Berlin), 133
Duke's Barn (Tübingen), 408
Dürer, Albrecht, 324
    House (Nürnberg), 203
Dürkheimer Fass, 581
Düsseldorf, 548–557
    accommodations, 554
    arriving in, 548, 550
    exploring, 550–553
    getting around, 550
    performing arts, 557
    restaurants, 554–556
    shopping, 556–557
    visitor information, 550
DüsseldorfCard, 550
Düsseldorfer Symphoniker, 557

E

East Side Gallery (Berlin), 87
Eating and drinking, 29–32
Eau de Cologne, 541
Eberbach, 387–388
Eberstein Rundweg circuit, 443
Eble Uhren-Park, 453
ECB Tower (Frankfurt), 499
Eckbauerbahn, 298
Eckbauer peak, 298
Edelweiss (Berlin), 133
Eibsee Sielbahn, 299
Eichwald, 486
Einstein, Albert, 237
Eintracht Frankfurt, 508
Eisbach, 333
Eisenach, 157, 161–164
Elbphilharmonie (Hamburg),
    664–666, 683
Electricity, 711
Elements (Cologne), 542
Elipamanoke (Leipzig), 175
Elisabethkirche (Marburg), 622,
    624–625
Elisengarten (Aachen), 543
Elizabeth's Gate
    (Heidelberg), 377
Embassies, 711
Emergencies, 711
Endingen, 427
Englischer Garten (English
    Garden; Munich), 333, 337
English Theater of
    Hamburg, 683
English Theatre Frankfurt, 520
Erfurt, 157–161
Erfurt Tourist-Information, 158
Erlebniswelt Haus Meissen, 194
Erzgebirgshaus (Berlin), 122
Eschenbräu (Berlin), 131
E.T.A. Hoffmann Theatre
    (Bamberg), 220
Euregiokarte, 467
Europaisches Hansemuseum
    (European Hansemuseum;
    Lübeck), 692
Europaturm (Frankfurt), 499
Exberliner, 124
Exhaus (Trier), 602

F

Fabrik (Hamburg), 685
Fairy-Tale Road
    (Märchenstrasse), 615, 616
Falkenhaus (Würzburg),
    249–250
Fame (Berlin), 130
Families with children, 711
    Berlin attractions, 93
    best for, 13–14
    Frankfurt attractions, 508
    Munich attractions, 337
    suggested itinerary, 53–55
Fasching (Carnival), 33, 315
    Cologne, 527
    Mainz, 571
Fat Tire (Berlin), 89
Faustus, Dr., 430
FC Bayern Munich, 362
Feldberg, 452
Fernsehturm (Television Tower;
    Berlin), 80–81
Fernsehturm (Television Tower;
    Stuttgart), 396
Festivals and special events,
    33–34
Festspielhaus
    Baden-Baden, 441
    Bayreuth, 222, 225
Festung Marienberg
    (Marienberg Fortress;
    Würzburg), 252
Films, 28–29
Fingerhutmuseum (Thimble
    Museum; Creglingen), 264
Fishermen's and Tanners'
    Quarter (Ulm), 239
Flohmarkt (Flea Market)
    Berlin, 120
    Frankfurt, 517–518
    Stuttgart, 402
Flohmarkt am Arkonaplatz
    (Berlin), 120
Flohmarkt Boxhagener Platz
    (Berlin), 120
Food markets, Berlin, 116
Franconia (Würzburg), 250
Frankfurt, accommodations,
    509–511
Frankfurt-am-Main, 489–523
    arriving in, 489–492
    cafés, 515–516
    entertainment and nightlife,
    519–521
    exploring, 496–509
        Altstadt, 502–505
        guides and tours, 497
        for kids, 508–509
        Museum Embankment
        (Museumsufer), 497–501
        parks and gardens, 507
        skyscrapers, 498–499
        Westend, 506–507
    getting around, 494–495
    money-saving tickets, 495
    neighborhoods in brief, 492
    restaurants, 512–516
    shopping, 516–519
    visitor information, 495

Frankfurt Card, 495
Frankfurter Buchmesse (Book
    Fair), 34
Frankfurters, 512
Franziskanerkirche
    (Überlingen), 471
Franz-Liszt-Museum
    (Bayreuth), 226
Fraueninsel, 366, 367
Frauenkirche (Cathedral of Our
    Lady; Munich), 319
Frauenkirche (Church of
    Our Lady)
    Dresden, 181
    Nürnberg, 201
Frauenwörth Abbey
    (Fraueninsel), 367
Frau Tonis (Berlin), 122
Free things to do, best, 11–12
Freiburg im Breisgau, 416–432
    accommodations, 421–423
    day trip to the Kaiserstuhl,
    425–432
    entertainment and nightlife, 425
    exploring, 418–421
    getting around, 417–418
    restaurants, 423–425
    visitor information, 417
Freiburg Münster, 419–420
Freudenstadt, 443, 444, 447,
    450, 451
    accommodations and
    restaurants, 457–459
    exploring, 448–449
    sports and outdoor pursuits,
    464–465
Freudenstadt Stadtsmuseum
    (Freudenstadt), 448
Friedrichsbad (Baden-
    Baden), 435
Friedrichshafen, 474–476
Friedrichstadt Palast
    (Berlin), 127
Fuggerei (Augsburg), 284–285
Fuggerei Museum (Augsburg),
    284–285
Fugger family, 286
Fugger-Stadtpalais (Fugger City
    Palace; Augsburg), 282
Fugger und Welser Museum
    (Augsburg), 286
Fun-Bike (Breisach), 429
Fürstenbaumuseum
    (Würzburg), 252
Fürstengarten (Prince's Garden;
    Würzburg), 252
Furtwangen, 452
Füssen, 288–291

G

Galatea, 389
Galeries Lafayette (Berlin), 119
Gallery of Beauties
    (Nymphenburg Palace), 366
Garmisch-Partenkirchen,
    296–299
Gärtnerstadt (Market
    Gardener's Quarter;
    Bamberg), 218

Gärtner-und Häckermuseum
    (Bamberg), 219
Gaststätte zum Flaucher
    (Munich), 355
Gay Pride festivals, 34
Gays and lesbians, 711–712
    Berlin, 135
    Munich, 361
Gebäude 9 (Cologne), 542
Gedenkstätte Buchenwald,
    152–153
Geigenbau Leonhardt
    (Mittenwald), 301
Geigenbau und Heimatmuseum
    (Mittenwald), 300
Gemäldegalerie (Painting
    Gallery; Berlin), 71, 94
Gemäldegalerie Alte Meister
    (Old Masters Gallery;
    Dresden), 184
Gendarmenmarkt (Berlin), 79,
    81–82
German Clock Museum
    (Deutsches Uhrenmuseum;
    Furtwangen), 454
German Film and Television
    Museum (Deutsche
    Kinemathek Museum für
    Film und Fernsehen; Berlin),
    79–80
German History Museum
    (Deutsches Historisches
    Museum; Berlin), 78–79
Germanisches Nationalmuseum
    (Germanic National
    Museum; Nürnberg),
    204–205
German Museum of Packaging
    (Deutsches Verpackungs-
    Museum; Heidelberg),
    376–377
Gewandhaus (Leipzig), 175
Gewandhausorchester
    (Leipzig), 175
Gibson (Frankfurt), 520
Glanzstücke (Berlin), 122
Gläserne Manufaktur
    (Transparent Factory;
    Dresden), 184–185
Gleisweiler, 582
Glockengiesserstrasse
    (Lübeck), 693
Glockenspiel (Munich), 315, 320
Gloria (Cologne), 542
Glyptothek (Museum of
    Sculpture; Munich), 328
Goethe, Johann Wolfgang
    von, 501
Goethe Gartenhaus
    (Goethe's Garden House;
    Weimar), 148
Goethe-Haus (Frankfurt),
    502–503
Goethe House (Tübingen),
    406–407
Goethe-Museum
    (Frankfurt), 503
Goethe Nationalmuseum
    (Weimar), 148, 150

Goldhelm Schokoladen
Manufaktur (Erfurt), 161
Golgatha (Berlin), 131
Gottlieb Daimler Memorial
(Stuttgart), 393
Government Quarter
(Bonn), 559
Grabbrünnen (Alsfeld), 622
Grafeneckart (Würzburg), 250
Graphische Sammlung (Graphics
Collection; Munich),
326–327
Great Cask (Heidelberg), 377
Great Hall (Heidelberg), 378
Great Hall of Mirrors (Neues
Schloss), 368
Green Gallery (Munich), 323
Green Vault (Grünes Gewölbe;
Dresden), 182
Grevenburg Castle, 606
Gropius, Martin, Martin-
Gropius-Bau (Berlin), 74
Grosse Freiheit (Hamburg), 667
Grosser Spreewald Hafen, 142
Gross St. Martin (Cologne), 536
Grotesque (Aachen), 548
Grotto Courtyard (Munich), 323
Grüneburg Park (Frankfurt), 507
Grüne Gurtel (Green Belt;
Frankfurt), 507
Grüner Markt (Bamberg), 221
Grünes Gewölbe (Green Vault;
Dresden), 182
Günter Grass-Haus
(Lübeck), 692
Gutach, 451
Gutach Valley, 451
Gutenberg Museum
(Mainz), 572

H
HafenCity (Hamburg), 665
Hamburg, 653–689
accommodations, 672–675
arriving in, 656
day trip to Lüneburg, 685–687
entertainment and nightlife,
682–685
exploring, 660–672
organized tours, 669–670
parks and gardens, 670–672
getting around, 656–657
layout, 658–659
neighborhoods in brief, 659
restaurants, 676–680
shopping, 680–682
visitor information, 657
Hamburg Card, 660
Hamburger Dom, 34
Hamburgische Staatsoper
(Hamburg State
Opera), 683
Hamburg Sommer, 33
Hameln, 636–640
Hameln Museum, 637–638
Hanau, 616–618
Handwerkerhof (Nürnberg), 214
Hann. Münden, 631–634

The Hare (Nürnberg), 209
Harvey's (Frankfurt), 521
Haubentaucher (Berlin), 130
Hauptkirche St-Michaelis
(Hamburg), 661
Hauptmarkt (Nürnberg), 203
Hauptstrasse (Heidelberg),
374, 376
Hausbräuerei Feierling
(Freiburg), 425
Haus de Natur, 444
Haus der Bürgerschaft
(Bremen), 643
Haus der Geschichte der
Bundesrepublik
Deutschland (House of
History of the German
Republic; Bonn), 560
Haus der Geschichte
Dinkelsbühl, 276
Haus der Natur, 452
Haus der Stiftung (Erfurt), 158
Haus Thalheim (Eberbach), 387
Haus zum Cavazzen
(Lindau), 478
Haus zum Walfisch (Freiburg),
418–419
Havana Club (Munich), 361
Health, 712
Heathen's Wall (Lindau), 477
Hebbel am Ufer (HAU;
Berlin), 126
Heidelberg, 371–388
accommodations, 380–383
arriving in, 372
exploring, 374–380
getting around, 372
guided tours, 374
nightlife, 385–386
restaurants, 383–384
river excursions from, 386–388
shopping, 385
visitor information, 372, 374
Heidelberg Card, 374
Heidelberg Castle
Illumination, 34
Heidelberger Schloss
(Heidelberg Castle), 377
Heidelberger Zuckerladen, 385
Heidelberg University, 378–379
Heiligen-Geist-Hospital
(Hospital of the Holy Spirit;
Lübeck), 693
Heiliggeistkirche (Church of
the Holy Spirit;
Heidelberg), 374
Heimatmuseum (Füssen), 290
Hekticket (Berlin), 124
Hemingway (Freiburg), 425
Hemmerle (Munich), 358
Herbertstrasse (Hamburg), 667
Herreninsel, 366–368
Herrgottskirche (Chapel of Our
Lord; Creglingen), 264
Herzogin Anna Amalia
Bibliothek (Duchess
Anna Amalia Library;
Weimar), 150

Hesse Haus (Calw), 447
Hiking and walking, 709
Baden-Baden, 443
Black Forest, 464
Kaiserstuhl, 429
Konigshaus Am Schachen, 299
Moselle Valley, 593
Traben-Trarbach and
Bernkastel-Kues, 606
Hinterzarten, 452
Hip Cats (Hamburg), 681
Hirsau, 446
Hirschhorn, 386–387
Hirschhorn Castle, 387
Historical Green Vault
(Dresden), 182
Historic Rock Cut Cellars
(Nürnberg), 201
Historische Kaufhaus (Customs
House; Freiburg), 419
Historisches Festspiel "Der
Meistertrunk," 33
Historisches Museum (History
Museum; Regensburg),
232–233
Historisches Museum der Pfalz
(Palatinate Historical
Museum; Speyer), 584
Historisches Museum
Frankfurt, 503
History of Germany, 16–18
Hitler, Adolf, 198
Munich Documentation Centre
for the History of National
Socialism, 329
Hochzeitshaus (Wedding House;
Hameln), 637
Hofbräuhaus am Platzl
(Munich), 355
Hoffmann, E.T.A., 220
Hofgarten (Munich), 334
Hohennagold castle
(Nagold), 446
Hohenschwangau, 291–294
Hohenzollern Castle (near
Tübingen), 409–410
Hohes Schloss (Füssen), 289
Holbein, Hans, the Elder, 282,
285, 420, 477
Hölderlinturm (Tübingen), 405
Holidays, 35
Holländisches Viertel (Dutch
Quarter; Potsdam), 140
Holocaust memorial
(Frankfurt), 504
Holstentor (Lübeck), 693
Holzmarkt (Berlin), 130
Holzmarkt (Lumber Market;
Tübingen), 408
Holzschnitzerei Franz Barthels
(Oberammergau), 302
Hopfenreich (Berlin), 131
House rentals, 708
H. Pieper (Hamburg), 670
Humboldt University (Berlin), 79
Hut Up (Berlin), 121

I

Ice cream, 336
Ilmenau, 157
Imperial Baths (Kaiserthermen; Trier), 596
Imperial Castle Museum (Nürnberg), 205
Imperial Cathedral (Kaiserdom)
  Bamberg, 217
  Frankfurt, 503
  Speyer, 585
Imperial Hall and Staircase (Munich), 323
Institut für Zukunft (Leipzig), 175
Internationaler Club (Baden-Baden), 442
International Maritime Museum (Hamburg), 666
Isartor (Munich), 315
Itineraries, suggested, 39–58

J

Japan Center (Frankfurt), 499
Japanese teahouse (Munich), 333
Jazzclub Unterfahrt (Munich), 359
Jazzfest Berlin, 34
Jazzhaus (Freiburg), 425
Jewish cemetery (Frankfurt), 504
Jewish ghetto, Frankfurt, 504
Jewish Museum (Jüdisches Museum)
  Berlin, 82
  Frankfurt, 504
Jil Sander (Hamburg), 681
Judenfriedhof (Jewish cemetery; Worms), 578
Judengasse (Tübingen), 408
Jüdisches Museum (Jewish Museum)
  Berlin, 82
  Munich, 319–320
Jüdisches Viertel (Jewish Quarter)
  Speyer, 585
  Worms, 578
Jünemann's Pantoffel-Eck (Berlin), 121

K

Kaffee Burger (Berlin), 129
Kaiserburg (Nürnberg), 203, 205
Kaiserdom (Imperial Cathedral)
  Bamberg, 217
  Frankfurt, 503
  Speyer, 585
Kaiserstuhl, 425–432
  exploring, 426–428
  traveling to, 426
  visitor information, 426
  where to eat and stay in, 428–429
Kaiserstuhl Radweg, 429

Kaiser-Wilhelm Gedächtniskirche (Kaiser Wilhelm Memorial Church; Berlin), 71, 74
Kampen (Sylt), 699
Karl-Heine-Strasse (Plagwitz), 171
Karl-Marx-Haus (Trier), 597
Karl May Bar (Dresden), 192
Karlshöhe (Stuttgart), 396
Karlson (Frankfurt), 521
Karlstor (Munich), 315
Karwendelbahn Mittenwald, 300
Kassel, 627–631
Kater Blau (Berlin), 130
Katharinenkirche (St. Catherine's Church; Nürnberg), 202
Kathedrale St. Trinitas (Dresden Cathedral), 182
Käthe-Kruse-Puppen-Museum (Donauwörth), 280
Katzenbuckl (Eberbach), 388
Kaub, 567
Kauf Dich Glücklich (Düsseldorf), 557
Kaufhaus des Westens (KaDeWe; Berlin), 116, 119
Kaufhof (Munich), 357
Kayak Berlin Tours, 89
KD Cruises, 565
Kinderzeche (Children's Festival; Dinkelsbühl), 276
King Othon's coronation garb (Munich), 330
Klassische Philharmonie Bonn (Bonn Symphony Orchestra), 563
Kleidoscop (Frankfurt), 517
Kleinhesseloher See (Munich), 333
Kleinmarkthalle (Frankfurt), 518–519
Klingenmünster, 582
Klingentor (Rothenburg), 269
Klinger, Max, 167
Kloster Amorbach (Amorbach), 260
Klosteranlage Heilig Kreuz (Donauwörth), 279
Kloster Ettal (near Oberammergau), 302
Kloster Hirsau, 447
Klösterle (Nördlingen), 277–278
Kloster Maulbronn, 445
Klunkerkranich (Berlin), 133–134
Kniebis, 444, 450
Koko von Knebel (Berlin), 121
Kölner Philharmonie (Cologne), 541
Kölner Seilbahn (Cologne Cable Car), 533
Komische Oper Berlin, 125
Konigshaus Am Schachen, 299
Königsplatz (Munich), 327
Königstor (Nürnberg), 202
Königstrasse (Stuttgart), 390, 402

Konstanz. See also Lake Constance
Konstanz (Constance), 467–471
Konstanz Casino, 485–486
Kontorhaus District (Hamburg), 661–662
Konus Card, 416
Konzerthaus Berlin, 125
KonzertKasse36 (Berlin), 124
KPM (Königliche Porzellan-Manufaktur; Berlin), 118–119
Kraftwerk (Munich), 361
Krämerbrücke (Merchants Bridge; Erfurt), 158
Kräutergarten (Herb Garden; Mittelzell), 471
Kriminalmuseum (Criminal Museum; Rothenburg), 269–270
Kronenhochhaus (Frankfurt), 499
Kronentor (Crown's Gate; Dresden), 183
Krumme Lanke (Berlin), 93
Ku'damm (Kurfürstendamm; Berlin), 63, 117
Kumpelnest 3000 (Berlin), 135
Kunsthalle (Hamburg), 662
Kunsthalle Messmer, 427
Kunsthofpassage (Dresden), 192
Kunst im Tunnel (Düsseldorf), 553
Kunstmuseum Bonn, 560
Kunstmuseum Stuttgart (Stuttgart Art Museum), 393
Kunstsammlungen Böttcherstrasse (Bremen), 645–646
Kunsthalle Bremen, 646
Kunst- und Trödelmarkt am Fehrbelliner Platz (Berlin), 120
Kupferstichkabinett (Berlin), 71
Kurfürstliches Palais (Trier), 595
Kurgarten (Baden-Baden), 434
Kurhaus, Baden-Baden, 434, 441
Kurpark, Bad Homburg, 522
Kurpark arboretum (Freudenstadt), 449
Kurpfälzisches Museum (Museum of the Palatinate; Heidelberg), 379
Kur Royal (Kaiser-Wilhelms-Bad; Bad Homburg), 522–523
KZ-Gedenkstätte Dachau (Dachau Concentration Camp Memorial Site), 362–364
K20: Kunstsammlung am Grabbeplatz (Düsseldorf), 551–552
K21: Kunstsammlung im Ständehaus (Düsseldorf), 552

L

Laeiszhalle Hamburg, 683–684
Lake Constance (Bodensee),
    466–487
    accommodations, 478–482
    entertainment and nightlife,
        485–486
    exploring around, 467–478
    getting around, 466
    restaurants, 482–485
    spas, 484–485
    sports and outdoor pursuits,
        486–487
    visitor information, 466
Lake Titisee, 452
LA8 Kulturhaus/Museum für
    Kunst und Technik des 19.
    Jahrhunderts (Baden-
    Baden), 436–437
Landesmuseum Mainz
    (Provincial Museum of
    the Central Rhineland;
    Mainz), 573
Landgrave Castle
    (Marburg), 624
Landwehr Canal (Berlin), 93
Laufen, 430
Learning vacations, 709
Lebensstern (Berlin), 132
Lebkuchen Schmidt
    (Nürnberg), 215
Lechfall (Füssen), 289
Le Croco Bleu (Berlin), 134
Leipzig, 164–177
    accommodations, 171–173
    arriving in, 164, 166
    day trips from, 176–177
    exploring, 166–171
    nightlife and entertainment,
        175–176
    restaurants, 173–175
    visitor information, 166
Leipzig Card, 166
Leipzig Forum of Contemporary
    History (Zeitgeschichtliches
    Forum Leipzig), 169–170
Le Lion (Hamburg), 684
Lenbachhaus (Munich), 329
Lennon, John, 670
Leonhard's Tower (Alsfeld), 622
Lichtentaler Allee (Baden-
    Baden), 434
Liebfrauenkirche, Trier, 597–598
Liebieghaus (Frankfurt),
    499–500
Liederhalle (Stuttgart), 403
Lindau, 476–478
Lindenau, 170
Lindenhofbad, 486
Lindleinturm (Creglingen), 265
Linz (Austria), 235
Liszt, Franz, Franz-Liszt-Museum
    (Bayreuth), 226
Liszt-Haus (Weimar), 150–151
Loden-Frey (Munich), 358
Loft (Cologne), 542
Long Distance Walking
    Trail, 246
Loreley, 567

Lossburg, 451
Lotharpfad, 450
Lower Castle Gate
    (Tübingen), 407
Lübbenau, 142
Lübeck, 689–698
    accommodations, 696–697
    exploring, 690–696
    getting around, 690
    restaurants, 697–698
    traveling to, 689–690
    visitor information, 690
Lucas Cranach the Elder House
    (Weimar), 148
Ludwig Beck (Munich), 357
Ludwig Collection
    (Bamberg), 217
Ludwig II, King ("Mad" King),
    291, 294, 299, 303, 366
Lügenbaron (the lying baron)
    von Münchhausen
    (Bodenwerder), 635
Luna (Frankfurt), 521
Lüneburg, 685–687
Lüneburg Heath, 686
Luther, Martin, 162–164, 176
Lutherhaus (Eisenach), 164
Lutherhaus Wittenberg, 176
Lutherische Pfarrkirche St.
    Marien (Marburg), 624
Lutherstadt Wittenberg,
    176–177

M

Made in Berlin, 123
Mail, 712
Mainau Island, 468, 470
Mainfränkisches Museum
    (Main-Franconian Museum;
    Würzburg), 252
Main Tower (Frankfurt), 498
Mainz, 570–577
    accommodations, 574–575
    exploring, 571–574
    performing arts, 576–577
    restaurants, 575–576
    visitor information, 571
Mainzertor (Mainz Gate;
    Miltenberg), 258
MAKK: Museum für
    Angewandte Kunst Köln
    (Museum of Applied Arts;
    Cologne), 533
Mann, Thomas, 691–692
Männleinlaufen clock
    (Nürnberg), 209
Manufactum (Hamburg), 682
Marburg, 622–626
Märchenbrunnen (Fairytale
    Fountain; Steinau), 619
Marienberg Fortress
    (Festung Marienberg;
    Würzburg), 252
Marienberg Fortress
    (Würzburg), 251
Marienbrücke, 294
Marienkapelle (St. Mary's
    Chapel; Würzburg),
    249, 253

Marienkirche (St. Mary's Church)
    Lübeck, 693–694
    Würzburg, 252
Marienplatz (Munich), 315, 320
Marine Museum (Speyer), 585
Markgräflerland, 429–432
Markgräfliches Opernhaus
    (Margravial Opera House;
    Bayreuth), 226–227
Marksburg, 566
Markthalle (Freiburg), 425
Markthalle IX (Berlin), 116
Markthalle Stuttgart, 402
Markt im Hof (Frankfurt), 519
Marktplatz (Marketplace)
    Alsfeld, 622
    Bremen, 642
    Heidelberg, 374
    Rothenburg, 268
    Steinau, 619
    Stuttgart, 392
    Tübingen, 407
    Weimar, 146, 148
    Würzburg, 249
Marktstube (Stuttgart), 402
Marriage Carousel Fountain
    (Nürnberg), 209
Marstallmuseum (Nymphenburg
    Palace), 366
Martin-Gropius-Bau (Berlin), 74
Mathematisch-Physikalischer
    Salon (Dresden), 183
Mauermuseum Haus am
    Checkpoint Charlie (Berlin
    Wall Museum at Checkpoint
    Charlie; Berlin), 83
Mauerpark (Berlin), 120
Maulbronn, 445
Mäuseturm (Mouse Tower), 569
Maxim Gorki Theater
    (Berlin), 126
Maximilianstrasse
    (Augsburg), 282
Maximilianstrasse (Lindau), 477
Meanie Bar (Hamburg), 684
Meersburg, 468, 473–474
Mehrtagesticket
    (Würzburg), 250
Meissen, 193–194
Meissen porcelain, 190–191
Memorial to Homosexuals
    Persecuted Under Nazism
    (Berlin), 81
Memorial to Sinti and Roma
    Victims of National
    Socialism (Berlin), 81
Memorial to the Murdered Jews
    of Europe (Berlin), 81
Memorium Nürnberg Prozesse
    & Justizgebäude (Nürnberg
    Trials Memorial &
    Courthouse), 205–206
Mercedes-Benz Museum
    (Stuttgart), 393–394
Merkur Mountain, 443
Metternich Castle
    (Beilstein), 608
Michaelskirche (St. Michael's
    Church; Munich), 320

Middle Rhine (Mittelrhein), 565–567
Mies van der Rohe, Ludwig, Neue Nationalgalerie (New National Gallery)/ Hamburger Bahnhof, 74
Mike's Bike Tours (Munich), 336–337
Militärhistorisches Museum (Dresden), 185
Miltenberg, 257–259
  accommodations, 261
Mimi (Berlin), 123
MineralBad Cannstatt (Stuttgart), 402
Mineralien und Mathematik Museum (Wolfach), 456
Miniatur Wunderland (Hamburg), 666
Mister B's (Munich), 360
Mittenwald, 299–301
Möbel-Olfe (Berlin), 135
Mobile phones, 712
Modulor (Berlin), 119
Molotow (Hamburg), 684
Monastery of Limburg, 580
Monastery of the Holy Cross (Donauwörth), 279
Money and costs, 712–713
Monopteros (Munich), 333
Mont Royal, 606
Moriskentanzer (Moorish dancers; Munich), 320
Moritzbastei (Leipzig), 175–176
Moselle Valley, 589–613
  arriving in, 589
  getting around, 590–592
  hiking, 593
  visitor information, 589
  wine festivals, 591
Moselle wines, 610
Moselsteig, 593
Mozart Festival, Würzburg, 249
Mozart Festival (Würzburg), 34
Mummelsee, 450
Münchhausen, Baron, 636
Münchhausen-Erinnerungszimmer (Bodenwerder), 635
Münchhausenplay (Bodenwerder), 635–636
Münchner Philharmoniker (Munich), 359
Münchner Puppenstuben und Zinnfiguren Kabinette (Munich), 356
Münchner Stadtmuseum (City Museum; Munich), 320–321, 337
Munich, 308–369
  accommodations, 338–346
  arriving in, 309–310
  day trips from, 362–369
  drugstores, 314
  entertainment and nightlife, 358–362
  exploring, 315–337
    Altstadt, 315–321
    for kids, 337

museum savings on Saturday and Sunday, 324
organized tours, 336–337
parks and gardens, 333–335
getting around, 313–314
layout, 310–311
neighborhoods in brief, 311–313
restaurants, 346–355
safety, 314
shopping, 356–358
visitor information, 310
Munich Documentation Centre for the History of National Socialism, 329
Munich Walk Tours, 337
Münster St. Georg (Dinkelsbühl), 275
Münster St. Maria und Markus (Mittelzell), 470–471
Münster St. Nikolaus (Überlingen), 471–472
Münstertal, 430
Museen Behnhaus/Drägerhaus (Lübeck), 694–695
Museum am Markt (Schiltach), 454
Museum Brandhorst (Munich), 325–326
Museum der Bildenden Künste (Museum of Fine Arts; Leipzig), 167–168
Museum für Angewandte Kunst (Museum of Applied Arts; Frankfurt), 500
Museum für Moderne Kunst (Museum of Modern Art; Frankfurt), 504
Museum für Neue Kunst (Freiburg), 420
Museum für Stadtgeschichte (Breisach), 427
Museum Holstentor (Lübeck), 693
Museum in der Runden Ecke (Stasi Museum; Leipzig), 84, 168
Museum Island pass (Berlin), 67
Museum Judengasse (Frankfurt), 504
Museum Kunstpalast (Düsseldorf), 553
Museum Lindwurm (Stein am Rhein), 465
Museum Ludwig (Cologne), 533–534
Museum of Architecture (Munich), 326
Museum of Fine Arts (Museum der Bildenden Künste; Leipzig), 167
Museum of the Palatinate (Kurpfälzisches Museum; Heidelberg), 379
Museum Pass Berlin, 67
Museum Reichenau (Mittelzell), 471
Museums, 6
Museum Schnütgen (Cologne), 534

Museumsinsel (Museum Island; Berlin), 86–88
Museumsquartier-St.-Annen (St-Annen Museum Quarter; Lübeck), 695
Museum Stadt Miltenberg/ Museum Burg Miltenberg, 258–259
Museumsufer (Museum Embankment; Frankfurt), 489
MuseumsuferTicket (Frankfurt), 495
Museumsviertel (Museum Quarter; Munich), 324–327
Museum zu Allerheiligen (Schaffhausen), 465
Music, 26–27
Musikalischer Sommer Festival (Baden-Baden), 441
Musikfest Berlin, 34
Mutterland (Hamburg), 681
Mykita (Berlin), 121
MyZeil (Frankfurt), 516

N
Nachtgalerie (Munich), 360
Nagold, 446
Naïv (Frankfurt), 521
Nassauhaus (Nürnberg), 202
Nationaldenkmal Brüder Grimm (Brothers Grimm Memorial; Hanau), 571
Nationaltheater (Munich), 359
Natural History Museum (Naturkundemuseum; Berlin), 94
Naturkundemuseum (Natural History Museum; Berlin), 94
Naturschützpark Lüneburger Heide, 686
Neckar Island (Tübingen), 405
Neckar Valley Cycle Path, 386
Ned Kelly's Australian Bar (Munich), 361
Neef (Nürnberg), 214–215
Neubulach, 446
Neue Nationalgalerie (New National Gallery)/ Hamburger Bahnhof, 74
Neue Pinakothek (New Picture Gallery; Munich), 326
Neue Residenz (New Residence; Bamberg), 219
Neue Sammlung (Craft and Design Collection; Munich), 326
Neues Museum (New Museum)
  Berlin, 88
  Weimar, 151
Neuesmuseum (Nürnberg), 206
Neues Palais (New Palace; Potsdam), 138
Neues Rathaus (New Town Hall; Munich), 310, 320
Neues Schloss (New Palace)
  Bayreuth, 227–228
  Munich, 366–369
  Stuttgart, 390
  Überlingen, 474

Neue Synagogue (New Synagogue; Berlin), 83
Neue Wache (New Guardhouse; Berlin), 79
Neuf-Brisach, 426
Neuleiningen, 580, 583
Neurotitan (Berlin), 122
Neuschwanstein, 291–296
Neustadt-an-der-Weinstrasse, 582
New Green Vault (Dresden), 182
New Year's Ski Jump, 33
Niederwald Monument, 569
Nikolaikirche (Church of St. Nicholas)
  Leipzig, 168–169
  Potsdam, 140
Nikolausbrücke (Calw), 447
Nivea (Hamburg), 681
Nonnenhaus (Tübingen), 408
Nördlingen, 276–278, 281
Null Zwo Elf (Düsseldorf), 557
Nürnberg (Nuremberg), 196–215
  accommodations, 210–211
  arriving in, 200
  exploring, 201–210
  getting around, 200
  guided tours, 201
  restaurants, 212–213
  shopping, 214–215
  visitor information, 200
Nürnberger Herbstvolksfest, 34
NY Club (Munich), 361
Nymphenburg Palace (Schloss Nymphenburg), 364–366

O

Oberammergau, 301–304
Oberammergau Museum, 303
Oberer Schlossgarten (Stuttgart), 390
Oberwesel, 567
Obletter's (Munich), 358
Oevelgönne (Hamburg), 671
Oktoberfest
  Lindau, 467
  Munich, 34, 310, 315, 355
Old Castle and Württemberg Regional Museum (Stuttgart), 392
Old Synagogue (Erfurt), 159–160
Old University (Marburg), 624
Olympia Park (Munich), 334
Olympiaturm (Olympia Tower; Munich), 334
Olympic Ice Stadium (Garmisch-Partenkirchen), 297
Olympic Mountain (Olympischer Berg), 334
Olympischer Berg (Olympic Mountain), 334
Oper der Stadt Bonn, 563
Oper Frankfurt, 520
Oper Köln (Cologne), 542
Oper Leipzig, 175
Orangerie (Potsdam), 139

Original Berliner Trödelmarkt (Berlin), 120
Ornate Chapel (Munich), 323
Ostpaket (Berlin), 122

P

Packhof (Hann. Münden), 632
Palastgarten (Palace Gardens; Trier), 595
Palmengarten (Frankfurt), 506
Pantheon Theater (Bonn), 563
Papa Joe's "Klimperkasten" (Cologne), 542
Paracelsus-Therme und Sauna Pinea (Bad Liebenzell), 463
Pariser Platz (Berlin), 79
Park an der Ilm (Weimar), 148
Parking, 707
Parliament (Reichstag; Berlin), 83, 85
Partnachklam, 298
Passagen (Leipzig), 174
Passau, 235–237
Passiontheater (Passion Theater; Oberammergau), 303
Passports, 713
Peek & Cloppenburg (Frankfurt), 516
Pegnitz Island, 202
Pergamon Museum (Berlin), 88
Perlachturm (Augsburg), 282
Peterskirche (St. Peter's Church; Munich), 321
Petrikirche (St. Peter's Church; Lübeck), 690
Pfahlbauten Museum (Uhldingen-Mühlhofen), 472
Pfänder Mountain, 478
Pfedermarkt (Hameln), 637
Pfingstmesse (Nördlingen), 277
Pforzheim, 443, 444
  accommodations, 459–460
  exploring, 445
Pharmaceutical Museum (Apothekenmuseum; Heidelberg), 377
Pharmacy Museum (Schiltach), 454
Philharmonie Baden-Baden, 441
Philipps University (Marburg), 623
"The Pied Piper of Hameln," 639
Pilatushaus (Oberammergau), 302
Pinakothek der Moderne (Munich), 326–327
Plagwitz, 170
Plank (Frankfurt), 521
Platanenallee (Neckar Island), 405
Police, 713
Porcelain Cabinet (Munich), 323
Porcelain Museum (Meissen), 194
Porsche Museum (Stuttgart), 394–395
Porta Nigra (Black Gate; Trier), 595, 598

Porta Praetoria (Regensburg), 233
Porzellan-Manufaktur-Nymphenburg (Munich), 358
Porzellansammlung (Porcelain Collection; Nymphenburg Palace), 366
Potsdam, 136–141
Prager Strasse (Dresden), 191
Prater Garten (Berlin), 131
Preussenpark (Berlin), 116
Prinoth (Munich), 357
Prinzhorn Collection (Heidelberg), 379
Prinzipal (Berlin), 127
Prinzknecht (Berlin), 135
Prinzregentenstrasse (Munich), 329–330
Propyläen monument (Munich), 327
Protestant Seminary (Tübingen), 406
Pupille (Munich), 357
Puppenbrücke (Lübeck), 690

Q

QF-Passage (Dresden), 191

R

Radhof (Eberbach), 386
Radius Bikes (Munich), 314
Raschi-Haus Museum (Worms), 578
Rathaus (Town Hall)
  Aachen, 545–546
  Augsburg, 282
  Bremen, 646–647
  Hamburg, 663
  Lübeck, 695–696
  Lüneburg, 688–689
  Marburg, 623
  Passau, 236
  Rothenburg, 270
  Stuttgart, 392
  Tübingen, 407
  Ulm, 239–240
  Würzburg, 250
Rathausplatz (Augsburg), 282
Rathausplatz (Nürnberg), 203
Ratssaal (Überlingen), 472
Rattenfängerhaus (Hameln), 637
Rausch (Berlin), 118
R.A.W. Gelände (Berlin), 130
Reeperbahn (Hamburg), 666–667
Regensburg, 230–237
  accommodations, 233–234
  arriving in, 231
  exploring, 231–233
  getting around, 231
  restaurants, 234–235
  side trip to Passau, 235–237
  visitor information, 231
Regions in brief, 37–39
Reichenau Island, 470–471
Reichsburg Cochem, 610
Reichsstadtmuseum (Imperial City Museum; Rothenburg), 270–271

Reichsstrasse
(Donauwörth), 279
Reichstag (Parliament; Berlin),
83, 85
Resident Advisor, 124
Residenz (Palace), Würzburg,
253–255
Residenz (Royal Palace;
Munich), 322–323
Residenz (Würzburg), 250
Residenz Museum (Munich), 322
Residenzschloss (Dresden),
182–183
The Rheingau, 567, 568–570
Rheingauer Weinmuseum
(Rüdesheim), 569
Rheinisches Landesmuseum
(Trier), 598
Rhein-Neckar-Fahrgastschiffahrt
GmbH, 386
Rhine Falls, 465
The Rhineland, 563–587
arriving in, 564
getting around, 564–565
Rhine River, 584
cruises, 530
ferries, 568
Middle, 565–567
Richard-Wagner-Museum
and Haus Wahnfried
(Bayreuth), 228
Riederstor (Donauwörth), 279
Riegel, 427
Riemenschneider, Tilman,
252, 379
Rieskrater-Museum
(Nördlingen), 277
Rigaer Seifenmanufaktur
(Hamburg), 681
Rittersaal (Knights' Hall),
Weikersheim, 262
Road Scholar, 709
Robinson-Crusoe-Haus
(Bremen), 645
Rock Am *See* Festival, 467
Rock climbing, Baden-
Baden, 443
Rödertor (Rothenburg), 269
Roman Bath Ruin (Baden-
Baden), 435
Romanesque churches,
Cologne, 536
Romantic Road
Middle, 274–281
Upper, 261–266
RomantikLabor
(Düsseldorf), 557
Romantische Strasse (Romantic
Road), 245
Romantische Strasse
Touristik, 248
Romantische Strasse Touristik
Arbeitsgemeinschaft
GbR, 248
Römer and Römerberg
(Frankfurt), 504–505
Römerplatz (Frankfurt), 505
Römisch-Germanisches Museum
(Roman-Germanic Museum;
Cologne), 534–535

Rose Weihreter, Puppendoktor
(Nürnberg), 214
Rote Kliff, 700
Rothenburg ob der Tauber,
266–274
accommodations, 272–273
exploring, 268–272
restaurants, 273–274
shopping, 274
visitor information, 268
walking tour, 268
Rüdesheim, 568
Ruhestein, 450
Rüstkammer (Dresden), 182
RVO Bus Company, 304

S

Saar-Huensruck Steig, 593
Sababurg Castle, 634
Sachsenhausen, 141–142
Sachsenhausen (Frankfurt), 518
Sächsische Dampfschiffahrt,
184, 193
Safety, 713
St. Andreas (Cologne), 536
St.-Anna-Kirche (St. Anne's
Church; Augsburg), 285
St. Aposteln (Cologne), 536
St. Cäcilien (Cologne), 534, 536
St. Catherine's Church
(Katharinenkirche;
Nürnberg), 202
St. Georg (Cologne), 536
St. Georgskirche
(Nördlingen), 277
St. Gereon (Cologne), 536
St. Goarshausen, 567
St. Jacobi Kirche
(Hamburg), 663
St-Jakobskirche, 268, 271–272
St. James, Church of (St-
Jakobskirche; Rothenburg),
271–272
St. Johanniskirche
(Lüneburg), 686
St. Kunibert (Cologne), 536
St. Lorenz-Kirche (Church of St.
Lorenz; Nürnberg), 202,
206–207
St. Mangkirche (Füssen), 290
St. Maria im Kapitol
(Cologne), 536
St. Maria Lyskirchen
(Cologne), 536
St. Martin, 582, 583
St. Martiner Castell, 583
St. Martiner Castle, 582
St. Mary's Chapel
(Marienkapelle; Würzburg),
249, 253
St. Mary's Church
(Marienkirche), Lübeck,
693–694
St. Mary's Church (Marienkirche,
Würzburg, 252
St. Michael's Church
(Michaelskirche;
Munich), 320

St. Michael's Fountain
(Bernkastel-Kues), 602
St. Nicholas, Church of
(Nikolaikirche; Leipzig),
168–169
St. Oberholz (Berlin), 134
St. Panteleon (Cologne), 536
St. Pauli (Hamburg), 659, 660
St. Peter's Church (Lindau), 477
St. Petri Kirche (Hamburg),
663–664
St. Sebaldus-Kirche (Nürnberg),
207–208
St. Severi, Church of
(Erfurt), 159
St. Severin (Cologne), 536
St. Stephan's Minster (Breisach),
427–428
St. Stephen's Cathedral (Dom;
Passau), 236
St. Thomas Boys' Choir
(Thomanerchor;
Leipzig), 169
St. Thomas Church
(Leipzig), 169
St. Trudpert Abbey
(Münstertal), 431
St. Ursula (Cologne), 536
Salü Saltztherme
(Lüneburg), 689
Salzspeicher (Lübeck), 690
Sammlung Boros (Berlin), 85
Sammlung Frieder Burda
(Baden-Baden), 435–436
Sandeman's (Berlin), 89
Sankt Blasien, 452, 456–457
Sansoucci+ (Potsdam), 136
Sanssouci Park (Potsdam), 136
S. A. Prüm Winery (Bernkastel-
Wehlen), 605
Sarcletti (Munich), 336
Sausalitos (Munich), 361
Saxon Switzerland, 184
Schack-Galerie (Munich), 330
Schaezlerpalais (Augsburg), 285
Schatzkammer (Munich), 322
Schatzkammer (Treasury;
Munich), 323–324
Schaubühne Lindenfels
(Plagwitz), 171
Schauinsland, 421
Schauinsland-Bahn, 421
Scheuring's Tabakladen
(Heidelberg), 385
Schillerplatz (Stuttgart), 392
Schillerstrasse (Frankfurt), 517
Schillers Wohnhaus (Schiller's
Residence; Weimar), 151
Schiltach, 451, 454
Schirn Kunsthalle
(Frankfurt), 505
Schladerer Distillery
(Staufen), 431
Schleswig-Holstein Music
Festival, 34
Schleswig-Holstein Music
Festival (Lübeck), 690
Schliffkopf, 450
Schloss Belvedere (Berlin), 75

Schloss Cecilienhof (Cecilienhof Palace; Potsdam), 139
Schloss Charlottenburg (Charlottenburg Palace; Berlin), 75
Schloss Hambach, 582
Schloss Hohentübingen (Tübingen), 407
Schloss Homburg (Bad Homburg), 523
Schlosskirche (Castle Church)
Bayreuth, 228
Friedrichshafen, 475
Lutherstadt Wittenberg, 176
Schloss Landesberg, 612
Schloss Linderhof, 296, 301
Schloss (Castle) Linderhof (Oberammergau), 303–304
Schlossmuseum (Castle Museum; Weimar), 151
Schloss Nymphenburg (Nymphenburg Palace), 364–366
Schlosspark (Nymphenburg Palace), 366
Schlossplatz (Stuttgart), 390
Schloss Sanssouci (Potsdam), 136, 137–138
Schloss Steinau, 620
Schloss Thum und Taxis (Regensburg), 233
Schloss- und Stiftskirche St Michael (Pforzheim), 445
Schloss Weikersheim, 262–264
Schluchsee, 452
Schmeiden, Heino, Martin-Gropius-Bau (Berlin), 74
Schmuckmuseum (Museum of Jewelry; Pforzheim), 445
Schnatterloch (Miltenberg), 258
Schniederlihof (Oberried), 421
Schnookleloch (Heidelberg), 385
Schnoor (Bremen), 643
Schokoladen Museum (Chocolate Museum; Cologne), 535
Scholl, Hans and Sophie, 237
Schonach, 453
Schöner Brunnen (Beautiful Fountain; Nürnberg), 209
Schötting (Bremen), 642
Schulmuseum (Friedrichshafen), 475
Schumann's Bar am Hofgarten (Munich), 361
Schüttemühle museum (Schiltach), 454
Schwabinger Podium (Munich), 360
Schwarzes Café (Berlin), 134
Schwarzviertel (Black Quarter; Miltenberg), 258
Schwarzwald (Black Forest), 414–416, 443–465
accommodations and restaurants, 457–462
arriving in, 443–444
getting around, 444

hiking and walking, 464
regional specialties, 424
Schwarzwald Card, 416
spa culture, 433
spas, 462–463
visitor information, 444
Schwarzwald Card, 416
Schwarzwaldhochstrasse (Black Forest High Road), 443–444, 449–457
Schwarzwaldhochstrasse Information Center, 450
Schwarzwald-Museum Triberg (Triberg), 454–455
Schwarzwald Panoramastrasse (Black Forest Panorama Road), 444, 465
Schwebebahn (Dresden), 181
Schweigen-Rechtenbach, 583
Schweinehirt und seine Herde (Pig Herder Statue; Bremen), 642
Schwimmbad Titisee, 464
Schwörwoche (Ulm), 238
SchwuZ (Berlin), 135
Seasons, 33
Seebuck, 452
Seehaus (Munich), 355
Seepromenade (Friedrichshafen), 474
Semperoper (Semper Opera House; Dresden), 192
Senckenberg Naturmuseum (Frankfurt), 506–507
Sendlingertor (Munich), 315
Senger (Bamberg), 222
Siebenbirge (Seven Mountains), 558, 559
Siegfried Wagner House, 228
Sieggessäule (Victory Column; Berlin), 92
Sightseeing Gray Line (Munich), 336
Silberturm (Silver Tower; Frankfurt), 499
Silent Green (Berlin), 128
Ski Stadium (Garmisch-Partenkirchen), 297
Skyper (Frankfurt), 499
Smoker's Lounge (Freiburg), 425
Smoking, 713
SO36 (Berlin), 128
Sögestrasse (Sow's Street; Bremen), 642
Solar (Berlin), 134
Solymar Therme, 263
Sommernächte festival, 467
Sowieso (Berlin), 127
Space Hall (Berlin), 122
Special events and festivals, 33–34
Speer, Albert, 203, 205
Speicherstadt (Hamburg), 668
Speyer, 583–587
Spielbank (casino)
Baden-Baden, 442
Hamburg, 685
Lindau, 486

Spielzeugmuseum (Toy Museum)
Munich, 337
Nürnberg, 208
Spinnerei (Lindenau), 170
Spitaltor (Rothenburg), 269
Spreepark (Berlin), 90
Spree River (Berlin), 93
Spreewald, 142–143
Spy Museum (Berlin), 94
Staatliche Kunsthalle (Baden-Baden), 436
Staatsgalerie (State Gallery of Stuttgart), 395
Staatsgalerie moderner Kunst (Gallery of Modern Art; Munich), 326
Staatsoper (Berlin), 125
Staatsoper (State Opera), Stuttgart, 403
Staatstheater (State Theater), Stuttgart, 403
Städel (Frankfurt), 500–501
Stadtgarten (Town Garden; Lindau), 477
Stadthaus (Ulm), 239
Stadtkirche (Parish Church)
Freudenstadt, 448
Lutherstadt Wittenberg, 176–177
Stadtmuseum, Überlingen, 472–473
Stadtmuseum (Baden-Baden), 437
Stadtmuseum Fembohaus (Nürnberg), 208–210
Stadtrundfahrt (City Tour; Munich), 336
Stadtrundfahrt Dresden, 180
Stadttheater Konstanz, 485
Stadt Verkehrsamt, 568
Standseilbahn (Dresden), 181
Starkbierzeit (Munich), 315, 355
Stasi Museum (Berlin), 84
Stasi Museum (Museum in der Runden Ecke; Leipzig), 168
Staufen, 430
Stefan Fink (Hamburg), 682
Stein am Rhein, 465
Steinau an der Strasse, 618–621
Steinauer Marionettentheater (Steinau), 620
Steinerne Brücke (Stone Bridge; Regensburg), 231
Stephenskirche (Church of St. Stephen; Mainz), 573–574
Stern und Kreisschiffart (Berlin), 89
Stiftskirche
St. George (Oberzell), 471
St. Peter and St. Paul (Niederzell), 471
Stiftskirche (Tübingen), 408
Stilwerk (Berlin), 120
Stolpersteine (Berlin), 81
Strasbourg, 426
Strauss, Richard, 146
Straussenwirtschaften (Straussie), 429

Struwwelpeter Museum (Frankfurt), 507
Studentenkarzer (Student Jail; Heidelberg), 379–380
Studienzentrum Karl-Marx-Haus (Trier), 597
Stuttgart, 388–403
  accommodations, 397–398
  arriving in, 389
  exploring, 390–396
  getting around, 389
  guided tours, 389–390
  performing arts, 403
  restaurants, 398–401
  shopping, 402
  visitor information, 389
Stuttgart Art Museum (Kunstmuseum Stuttgart), 393
Stuttgart Ballet, 403
Stuttgart Beer Festival, 374
Stuttgarter Weindorf (Wine Festival), 34
Stuttgart Wine Festival, 374
Südblock (Berlin), 132
Südschwarzwald Radweg, 465
Südwestdeutsche Philharmonie Konstanz, 485
Suicide Circus (Berlin), 130
Swimming, Lake Constance, 487
Switzerland, 465
Sylt, 698–701

T

Tageskarte (Berlin), 67
Tageskarte (Munich), 313
Täubchenthal (Leipzig), 175
Taunus Therme (Bad Homburg), 523
Taxes, 713
Taxis, Munich, 314
Technik-Museum (Museum of Technology; Speyer), 585
Technisches Museum (Pforzheim), 445
Teddyland (Rothenburg), 274
Telephones, 713
Television Tower (Fernsehturm)
  Berlin, 80–81
  Stuttgart, 396
Tempelhofer Feld (Tempelhof Field; Berlin), 91–92
Teufelsberg (Berlin), 90–91
Theater Aachen, 543
Theater am Goetheplatz (Baden-Baden), 441
Theater-Kasse (Bonn), 563
Theatinerkirche (Munich), 321
Thimble Museum (Fingerhutmuseum; Creglingen), 264
Thomanerchor (St. Thomas Boys' Choir; Leipzig), 169
Thomaskirche (Church of St. Thomas; Leipzig), 169
Thüringer Wald, 157
Thuringian High Road, 157
Tiergarten (Berlin), 92

Tierpark Hagenbeck (Hamburg), 670–671
Tierpark Hellabrunn (Munich), 335, 337
Tierpark Sababurg, 634
Tigerpalast (Frankfurt), 520
Tilman Riemenschneider Room (Munich), 330
Tipping, 713–714
Titisee, 452
Tom's Saloon (Hamburg), 684
Tonhalle (Düsseldorf), 557
Toni Baur (Oberammergau), 302
Topography of Terror (Berlin), 86
Tours, 709
Toy Museum (Spielzeugmuseum; Nürnberg), 208
Traben-Trarbach, 606–608
Track 17 (Berlin), 81
Train travel, 703, 704–706
Transportation Museum (Deutsches Museum Verkehrszentrum; Munich), 332
Treasury (Schatzkammer; Munich), 323–324
Treptower Park/Soviet Memorial (Berlin), 92–93
Tresor (Berlin), 130
Triberg, 451–452
Trier, 592–602
  accommodations, 598–600
  arriving in, 593
  exploring, 595–598
  getting around, 594
  nightlife and entertainment, 601–602
  restaurants, 600–601
  visitor information, 594
  walking tours, 594–595
Trier Cathedral (Der Trierer Dom), 596–597
Trinkhalle (Pump Room; Baden-Baden), 437
Triumph des Willens (Triumph of the Will; film), 198
True & 12 (Munich), 336
Tübingen, 403–412
  accommodations, 410–411
  arriving in, 404
  outlying sights, 409–410
  restaurants, 411–412
  visitor information, 404
  walking tour, 405–408
Turkish Market (Berlin), 116

U

Überlingen, 471–473
Uferstudios (Berlin), 125–126
Uhrenstrasse (Clock Road), 444
Ulm, 237–243
Ulmer Museum (Ulm), 240
Ulm Münster, 239, 241
University Library (Heidelberg), 378
University Museum (Heidelberg), 378

Unter den Linden (Berlin), 79
Unteruhldingen, 472
Upper Romantic Road, 261–266
Urban Spree (Berlin), 130

V

Valentino (Frankfurt), 519
Vereinigte Hospitien (Trier), 595
Verkehrsbüro Endingen, 429
Verkehrszentrum (Munich), 332
Vetter's Alt Heidelberger Brauhaus (Heidelberg), 385
Victoria Bar (Berlin), 134–135
Viking River Cruises, 565
Viktualienmarkt (Munich), 319
Visitor information, 714
Vita Classica Therme (Bad Krozingen), 431–432
Vogtsbauernhof (Gutach), 451
Vogtsbauernhof (Gutach im Schwaarzwald), 455–456
Volksbühne (Berlin), 126
Von Mespelbrunn, Julius Echter, 255

W

Waahnsinn (Berlin), 123
Wagner, Richard, 146, 162, 294, 304
  Richard-Wagner-Museum and Haus Wahnfried (Bayreuth), 228
Walderdorffs (Trier), 602
Wald Königsberger Marzipan (Berlin), 118
Waldshut-Tiengen, 457
Walking and hiking, 709
  Baden-Baden, 443
  Black Forest, 464
  Kaiserstuhl, 429
  Konigshaus Am Schachen, 299
  Moselle Valley, 593
  Traben-Trarbach and Bernkastel-Kues, 606
Wallfahrtskirche Maria in der Tanne (Church of Our Lady in the Fir Tree; Triberg), 456
Wallraf-Richartz Museum (Cologne), 535
Wallringpark (Hamburg), 672
Wannsee (Berlin), 93
Wartburg (Eisenach), 162
Wasscherschloss (Hamburg), 681
Wasserfälle Gutach (Gutach Falls), 452
Watergate (Berlin), 130–131
Wattwanderungen, 700
Weather, 33
Wedding House (Alsfeld), 622
Weihnachtsland am Zwinger (Dresden), 192
Weihnachtsmarkt (Dresden), 191–192
Weihnachtswerkstatt (Christmas Workshop; Rothenburg), 274
Weikersheim, 262–264

Weimar, 145–164
   accommodations, 153–155
   arriving in, 146
   day trips from, 157–164
   exploring, 146–152
   nightlife and entertainment,
      156–157
   restaurants, 155–156
   visitor information, 146
Weimarer Fürstengruft (Ducal
   Vault; Weimar), 152
Wein Museum (Wine Museum;
   Speyer), 585
Weinzentrale (Dresden), 192
Weishaupt Gallery (Ulm),
   239, 242
Weissenhofmuseum
   (Stuttgart), 396
Weissenhofsiedlung
   (Weissenhof Estate;
   Stuttgart), 395–396
Wenningstedt-Braderup
   (Sylt), 699
Weser River, 631–632
Westerland, 699
White Trash Fast Food
   (Berlin), 130

Wieskirche (Wies), 287
Willkomm-Höft (Welcome Point;
   Hamburg), 669
Wine House (Alsfeld), 622
Wines, 31–32
   Moselle, 610
   suggested itinerary, 56–58
Winterfeldplatz (Berlin), 116
Wintergarten Varieté
   (Berlin), 127
Winzerfest wine festival, 467
Wolfach, 451, 456
Wolfsschlucht pass, 443
Woodcarvings,
   Oberammergau, 302
World War II Art Bunker
   (Nürnberg), 209–210
Worms, 577–580
Wurm and Köck, 235
Wurst, 31
Würzburg, 245–261
   accommodations, 255–256
   arriving in, 246
   exploring, 249–255
   getting around, 248
   restaurants, 256–257
   side trip from, 257–261

   special events, 249
   visitor information, 248–249
Würzburgtor (Würzburg Gate;
   Miltenberg), 258

Z
Zapfanstalt (Dresden), 192
Zeitgeschichtliches Forum
   Leipzig (Leipzig Forum of
   Contemporary History),
   169–170
Zell an der Mosel, 608
Zeltmusik festival
   (Freiburg), 425
Zeppelin, 476
Zeppelin-Museum
   (Friedrichshafen), 476
Zeughaus (Armory; Berlin), 79
Zitty, 124
Zoologischer Garten (Berlin
   Zoo), 92
Zugspitzbahn, 299
Zugspitze, 298–299
Zum Köbes (Cologne), 542
Zum Sepp'l (Heidelberg), 385
Zwinger (Dresden), 183–184